Aspects of the
Botswana Economy
Selected Papers

Edited by
J.S. Salkin
D. Mpabanga
D. Cowan
J. Selwe
M. Wright

Lentswe La Lesedi

Lentswe La Lesedi
Publishers
Gaborone

James Currey
Publishers
Oxford

Aspects of the Botswana Economy: Selected Papers

Published by
Lentswe La Lesedi (Pty) Ltd
PO Box 2365, Gaborone, Botswana.

ISBN 99912–71–04–1

Published in the United Kingdom and elsewhere by
James Currey Ltd
73 Botley Road, Oxford OX2 0BS, United Kingdom.

ISBN 0–85255–159–2

First published 1997

Distributed in Botswana by
The Research Department, Bank of Botswana
P/Bag 154, Gaborone, Botswana.

Distributed elsewhere in Southern Africa by
David Philip Publishers (Pty) Ltd
PO Box 23408, Claremont 7735, Cape, South Africa.

Trade orders to
Plymbridge Distributors Ltd.
Estover, Plymouth PL6 7PZ, United Kingdom.

Typeset, Illustrated and Designed by
Lentswe La Lesedi (Pty) Ltd
Tel 303994, Fax 314017, e-mail Lightbooks@info.bw

Cover artwork by
Helena Schüssel

Printed and bound by
Printing and Publishing Botswana (Pty) Ltd

Contents

CHAPTER 4
Industrial Development Policies and Strategies

CHAPTER 5
Employment and Living Standards

CHAPTER 6
International Trade, and Botswana in the Regional Economy

ACKNOWLEDGEMENTS

Many people contributed in various ways to the production of this book, all of whom deserve our thanks. That they willingly gave their support, despite often severely competing demands on their time, is a reflection both of the strength of the Bank of Botswana as an institution and the abiding affection for Botswana held by so many.

First of all, the Executive Committee and the Board of the Bank of Botswana agreed to the project and its funding as part of the work programme of the Research Department. Without this crucial support, the project would not have started.

In bringing together the various papers, the Editors received valuable assistance from those who kindly agreed to review drafts as requested and to act as referees. The Editors gratefully acknowledge those reviewers and and referees listed below. Various Research Department staff provided logistical support; in particular, Hilda Nozwane and others from the National Economics Unit, who kept track of the various drafts and related correspondence. We are also especially grateful to the early contribution of K.S. Masalila, who unfortunately had to leave the editorial team when he departed for long-term study leave.

Charles Bewlay and his staff at Lentswe La Lesedi carried out the task of publishing the book with a combination of diligence and cheerfulness, and justified fully the decision the Bank made to work with a Botswana-based publisher. The support provided by James Currey Publishers in publishing the book outside Botswana is also much appreciated.

Finally, of course, thanks must go to the authors. Here, our appreciation must be extended not only to those whose papers are included in the book, but also to those who expressed interest in producing papers, but, for one reason or another, were not able to have their work included in the final publication.

The Editors

Reviewers and Referees
In addition to the Editors, the following kindly agreed to review and referee papers:

S. Chakrabati	–	Ministry of Finance and Development Planning
T. Duncan	–	Maendeleo Botswana
M. Faber	–	Ministry of Finance and Development Planning and Institute of Development Studies, United Kingdom
N.H. Fidzani	–	University of Botswana
P. Freeman	–	Ministry of Mineral Resources and Water Affairs
C. Harvey	–	BIDPA and Institute of Development Studies, United Kingdom
D.J. Hudson	–	Phaleng Consultancies
J.C. Leith	–	Bank of Botswana and University of Western Ontario, Canada
J. Isaksen	–	BIDPA and Christian Michelsen Institute, Norway
K. Jefferis	–	Bank of Botswana
T. Nyamadzabo	–	Ministry of Finance and Development Planning
L. O. Ndzinge	–	Investec Botswana

Notes on Contributors

All authors are grateful for the comments they received on various drafts of their papers. The opinions expressed in the published papers are those of the authors and should not be taken to represent the views of institutions with which they are or have been associated.

Dr D. Cowan

Principal Research Officer (Statistics and Information Services) in the Research Department, Bank of Botswana. Prior to joining the Bank of Botswana, he worked for the Ministry of Foreign Affairs of the Kingdom of Saudi Arabia.

B. Gaolathe

Governor of the Bank of Botswana since July 1997. Mr Gaolathe joined the public service in 1968 as Assistant Secretary and later became Under Secretary in the Ministry of Commerce, Industry and Water Affairs. In 1973 was appointed as the first Permanent Secretary in the Ministry of Mineral Resources and Water Affairs, and for the Ministry of Finance and Development Planning as Permanent Secretary from 1976 to 1992. He was Managing Director of Debswana Diamond Company (Pty) Limited from January 1992 to June 1997. He has also served as Chairman of Barclays Bank of Botswana Limited, Sefalana Holdings Limited and the Botswana Institute for Development Policy Analysis. In addition to serving on various committees within the Government, Mr Gaolathe has served on the boards of the Debswana Group of Companies, the Bank of Botswana, the Botswana Development Corporation Limited and various other parastatal bodies and public companies. He is presently Convenor of the Presidential Task Group on a long term vision for Botswana.

N. Gaolathe

Assistant Research Fellow at the Botswana Institute for Development Policy Analysis (BIDPA). He worked for a short time as a Consultant for the Namibian Government on the establishment of an Export Processing Zone before joining BIDPA at the end of 1995. He also served as a research assistant in the Bank of Botswana in 1992 and 1993.

Professor M.L.O. Faber

Resident Consultant, Public Enterprises Monitoring Unit, Ministry of Finance and Development Planning. He is former Director of the Institute of Development Studies at the Universtiy of Sussex, and for nine years (1988–1997) was a Main Board Member of the Commonwealth Development Corporation. He serves on the Bank of Botswana – Ministry of Finance and Development Planning Working Group.

Professor C. Harvey

Professional Fellow of the Institute of Development Studies (IDS) at the University of Sussex. He has also taught at the Universities of York, Zambia and Botswana, and at Williams College, Massachusetts. He worked for the Bank of England from 1960 to 1964, the Bank of Botswana from 1976 to 1979 (and for short assignments subsequently), and is currently on leave of absence from IDS as a Senior Research Fellow at the Botswana Institute for Development Policy Analysis. Since 1981, he has acted regularly as Economic Consultant to the Ministry of Finance and Development Planning in Botswana. He is author, co-author or editor of a number of books, including *Macroeconomics in Africa, Analysis of Project Finance in Developing Countries, Public Choice and Development Performance in Botswana* (with Steven R. Lewis Jr.), and, most recently, *Constraints on the Success of Structural Adjustment Programmes in Africa*. His new book on banking will be published soon.

H.C.L. Hermans

The first Governor (1975-1977) and fifth Governor (1987-1997) of the Bank of Botswana. Mr Hermans first served as Assistant Secretary (Development), Bechuanaland Protectorate Administration from 1961 to 1965. He has worked as Senior Executive Officer (1965-1967), Ministry of Finance, and Permanent Secretary (1967-1975), Ministry of Finance and Development Planning. Between 1977 and 1987, Mr Hermans was employed in various posts by the World Bank, Washington D.C. He has served as Senior Planning Advisory Officer, Loans Officer (East Asia and Pacific Programs Department) and as Chief (Thailand/Indochina Programs Division). Mr Hermans has served as founder member, chairman, president and board member of various clubs, institutions, commissions and parastatal organisations in Botswana.

Dr D.J. Hudson

Managing Director, Phaleng Consultancies (Pty) Ltd. Dr Hudson came to Botswana to work in the Central Statistics Office (CSO), where he played a leading role in the preparation of the 1974/75 Rural Income Distribution Survey (RIDS). He joined the Bank of Botswana when it was established in 1976 as Director of Research, and later became Deputy Governor before retiring to join the private sector in 1990. He continues to serve on the boards of prominent Botswana companies.

Dr K. Jefferis

Deputy Director in the Research Department, Bank of Botswana. Prior to coming to Botswana he taught economics at Kingston University in London, and had also worked in Swaziland for the National Industrial Development Corporation. He also worked as Lecturer and Senior Lecturer in the Department of Economics at the University of Botswana from 1989 to 1996. Besides working as a teacher, researcher and policy analyst, he has also taken part in a number of consultancy projects in Botswana, for clients such as the Government of Botswana, UNICEF, UNDP, and the Botswana Confederation of Commerce, Industry and Manpower (BOCCIM).

A. Kahuti

Research Officer (National Economics), in the Research Department, Bank of Botswana.

Dr Z. Kone

Senior Research Officer (Money and Financial Markets), in the Research Department, Bank of Botswana. He taught introductory and intermediate economics courses at Colorado State University in the USA from 1991 to 1994.

Professor J.C. Leith

Senior Policy Advisor, Bank of Botswana, and Professor of Economics at the University of Western Ontario, Canada. Professor Leith is the author of a number of books and articles concerning international economics and developing countries. He has served previously as Economic Consultant in the Ministry of Finance and Development Planning, and Director of Research Department, Bank of Botswana. At the University of Western Ontario, he has been Chairman of the Department of Economics, and Vice-President (Academic). He has also held visiting teaching and research positions at the University of Ghana, the Catholic University of Peru, the University of Stockholm, and the Harvard Institute for International Development. Prior to his academic career, Professor Leith was a Canadian Foreign Service officer.

W. Mandlebe

Chief Economist (Macroeconomics) in the Ministry of Finance and Development Planning responsible for, among others, macroeconomic planning. Prior to joining the Ministry in October 1992, he had worked as a Research Officer in the Bank of Botswana.

K.S. Masalila
Principal Research Officer, in the Research Department, Bank of Botswana, currently on long term study leave for a Ph.D at the University of Manchester. He has also worked in the Bank's Financial Institutions Department. Prior to joining the Bank, he worked as an Assistant Commercial Officer in the Department of Commerce and Consumer Affairs, Ministry of Commerce and Industry from 1984 to 1985.

L.K. Mohohlo
Deputy Governor, Bank of Botswana. Mrs Mohohlo joined the Bank shortly after its establishment in 1976 as Secretary, and has served in various capacities, including Board Secretary, Deputy Director of Administration, Deputy Director of Research and Director of the International Department. In the latter capacity, she was responsible for the management of Botswana's foreign exchange reserves. Mrs Mohohlo has also worked for the International Monetary Fund, under its Special Appointee programme, in the African Department, and in the Monetary and Exchange Affairs Department, serving as a member of official missions abroad. She was appointed to the Presidential Commission of Inquiry into the affairs of the Botswana Housing Corporation, and she is a member of the task force for the development of a national policy on small, medium and micro enterprises. She serves on the boards of major corporations in Botswana.

A. Motsomi
Principal Research Officer (Money and Financial Markets) in the Research Department, Bank of Botswana. He has, also, during the past 13 years of service in the Bank, worked in the Banking, Exchange Control and International Departments.

D. Mpabanga
Research Officer (National Economics) in the Research Department, Bank of Botswana. She has also worked as an Industrial Officer and Head of the Project Research Unit in the Department of Industrial Affairs, Ministry of Commerce and Industry, from 1984 to 1995.

A. Ncube
Executive Director, BARD Investments (Pvt) Limited, Harare, Zimbabwe. He joined the Economics and Policy Department of the Reserve Bank of Zimbabwe in 1980 where he worked until 1989 when he joined the Research Department of the Bank of Botswana as Principal Research Officer. While in the two Banks, he worked mainly in areas of money and financial markets, public finance and the balance of payments. Mr Ncube left the Bank of Botswana in 1996.

Professor J. Peat
Chief Economist at the Royal Bank of Scotland (since early 1993) and Honorary Professor of Economics at Herriot-Watt University in Edinburgh. Previously he served as an Economic Adviser to the British and other governments. He worked in Thailand from 1972 to 1974, and was Employment Coordinator in the Ministry of Finance and Development Planning in Botswana from 1980 to 1983, at the time the Financial Assistance Policy (FAP) was conceived and introduced. Professor Peat was a member of the 3rd FAP Evaluation Team in 1994. He served on the Bank of Botswana – Ministry of Finance and Development Planning Working Group.

J. Reinke
Senior Research Officer (International Finance and Trade) in the Research Department, Bank of Botswana. Mr Reinke has also worked at the University of Cape Town, where he was involved in research on trade and exchange rate issues, and has taught at the London School of Economics, where he is enrolled in the economics doctoral programme.

Professor J.S. Salkin

Director of the Research Department, Bank of Botswana. He has formerly served as Principal Research Officer and Acting Deputy Director in the Research Department. Professor Salkin has taught economics at various universities in the USA, and at Thammasat University in Thailand. He first came to Botswana in 1981 to work as a Senior Planning Officer in the Employment Policy Unit of the Ministry of Finance and Development Planning where he worked until 1985. Professor Salkin returned to the Ministry of Finance and Development Planning in 1987 as Principal Planning Officer in the Division of Economic Affairs, and later as Director and Chief Economist of the Macro-economic Planning Section until 1993, when he left the Ministry to join the University of Botswana as Associate Professor of Economics. He has also served as an applied economist and policy analyst for the Government of Indonesia, the Government of Nepal, and the United States Agency for Interntional Development.

P. Siwawa-Ndai

Senior Research Officer (National Economics) in the Research Department, Bank of Botswana. She also worked for nearly a year in the International Department at the Bank before being seconded to the Botswana Confederation of Commerce, Industry and Manpower (BOCCIM) from 1993 to 1996, as Chief Economist/Policy Analyst and Head of the Economic Policy Unit.

M. Wright

Principal Research Officer (National Economics), Research Department, Bank of Botswana. Mr Wright first came to Botswana on leaving college in 1985, working in the Macro Unit of the Ministry of Finance and Development Planning. Before returning in 1994 to work in the Bank of Botswana, he held posts in the British Foreign Office, as an Economic Advisor to the Government of Lesotho, and as Government Economist in the Turks and Caicos Islands, a British territory in the West Indies.

FOREWORD

Despite Botswana's remarkable economic success over the past thirty years, the country still faces difficult development challenges if it is to achieve its goals and objectives of sustained development and adequate standards of living for its people. The accomplishments of the past have been ascribed both to the good fortune Botswana had in discovering and exploiting minerals after Independence and to the sound economic management, based upon solid policy research and analysis, that was pursued by Government. Just as success in the past can be ascribed to our ability to confront hard policy choices and make good decisions based on reliable information and credible analysis, so too will future success depend on our abilities to investigate and evaluate critical issues.

This book presents a collection of papers on various aspects of the Botswana economy. The topics included relate in some way to the operations, functions and roles of the Bank of Botswana in the economy. The book is intended to fill gaps on research and analyses of the Botswana economy, and what has happened, especially, over the past ten years, since *Selected Papers on the Botswana Economy* was prepared by the Bank of Botswana. The papers in this book, spanning a wide range of topics, should contribute to improved understanding of the structure of the economy, of many of the changes and transformations that have occurred, of the major issues that have challenged policy makers over the years, and continue to do so, and of the directions that various scholars see the economy taking in the future. Not only do these papers help to expand our knowledge of how things work in the economy, they also provide us with many valuable lessons that the policy makers have learned, which, if we are careful, will enable us to avoid repeating mistakes of the past.

The book has given a select group of researchers and policy analysts, who have had intimate experience with the Bank of Botswana, and/or the Ministry of Finance and Development Planning, an opportunity to comment on economic developments in Botswana, and has allowed opportunities for policy analysis on current issues to find timely expression. The researchers and policy analysts who have contributed to this book have had opportunities to raise the level of policy debate about such issues, as well as to clarify or correct current misconceptions and erroneous 'facts' about Botswana.

As might be expected from a preponderance of economists with backgrounds in the Central Bank and/or the Ministry of Finance and Development Planning, this book gives much emphasis to issues of economic growth, macroeconomic stability, monetary policy, public finance, central banking, industrial development, wages and productivity and international trade and investment. Other topics, such as income inequality and poverty, are also investigated; but, one can think of many other areas of serious concern that are not addressed in depth, including, *inter alia*, employment and unemployment, human resources development, the environment and women in development. There are critical policy issues that Botswana must face in all those other areas; and that might set a theme for the next volume of papers on the Botswana economy, that might be prepared under the auspices of the Bank or other institutions, such as the University of Botswana or the Botswana Institute for Development Policy Analysis.

It is hoped this book will find a receptive audience in the academic and professional community in Botswana, and may serve as a useful resource for students at the University and other institutions of higher learning. We also think that officials in Government, policy makers, members of the various political parties and the media can benefit substantially from the papers presented. This book should also be of value to regional and international research and academic institutions, bilateral and multilateral external funding agencies, as well as to researchers and consultants interested in more up-to-date analyses on Botswana.

It is for the above reasons that we are pleased to recommend this book to all those interested in the economy of Botswana and its development. It is our particular pleasure to be associated with this project as the current and recently-departed Governors of the Bank of Botswana. We are pleased to see that the Bank has developed its research capacity over the years to the extent that it can bring together a group of authors to produce such a book. We wish to thank the authors and the editors for the contributions they have made to expanding our knowledge and understanding about Botswana and the challenges it faces.

<table>
<tr><td>H. C. L. Hermans</td><td>B. Gaolathe</td></tr>
<tr><td>Governor, Bank of Botswana</td><td>Governor, Bank of Botswana</td></tr>
<tr><td>until 30 June 1997</td><td>from 1 July 1997</td></tr>
</table>

Introduction

Jay S. Salkin

The economy of Botswana is young and dynamic; it is full of adventure and challenge. It has been that way for over thirty years. Like many exciting adventures, Botswana's development has had its ups and downs, its pluses and minuses. To some, that leaves the cup of Botswana's record half full; to others, it makes the cup half empty.

This book of papers on the Botswana economy tries to capture some of the various economic and financial facets of that adventure, from some of the earliest episodes of establishing a monetary system with a central bank and introducing a new currency, the Pula, to some of the more recent advancements in financial sector development, industrial development, public sector reform and exchange control liberalization.

The book also reflects upon many of the current critical policy issues and development challenges facing Botswana as the nation prepares to enter the new millennium in a rapidly evolving global economy. Many of the challenges examined in this book, such as economic diversification, regional economic integration, savings mobilization, eradicating poverty, and so on, will test the will and capabilities of policy makers, as well as those who will be called upon to implement needed policies.

This book was conceived as a project to prepare a collection of new and up-to-date papers on the economy of Botswana, with a special focus on topics that relate to the role of the Bank of Botswana in the economy. It has been ten years since the last such volume of *Selected Papers on the Botswana Economy* was prepared by the Research Department of the Bank of Botswana; and there have been many developments in the Bank, and many developments in the financial sector and in the economy in which the Bank has played a major role, which have not been adequately reviewed, analysed and reported.

The purpose of the book is to fill some of the gaps in research and analyses of the Botswana economy; to give researchers and policy analysts an opportunity to comment on economic developments in Botswana since the last books on the Botswana economy were written in the mid to late 1980s. It is also an opportunity for policy analysis on current issues to find timely expression and distribution; to allow new economic topics, models and hypotheses, as well as new techniques, to be applied to Botswana; and to give researchers and policy analysts opportunities to clarify or correct current misconceptions and/or erroneous 'facts' about Botswana, or just to raise the level of policy debate about such issues.

All of the authors of papers in this book were selected on the basis of having a present or a past relationship with the Bank, either as a Board member, a staff member, an attached researcher or a member of the joint Bank of Botswana – Ministry of Finance and Development Planning Working Group. They were invited to make their contributions on topics of their interest; but there was a bias towards topics which focus on the operations, functions and roles of the Bank of Botswana in the economy. However, because the Bank is directly and indirectly involved operationally and on an advisory basis in many areas of the economy, it provided a very broad mandate.

Chapter 1 of the book looks at Botswana's record of economic growth. While Botswana has grown extremely rapidly over the past thirty years, that growth has occurred in fits and starts, as major mineral expansions and the intermittent introduction of large, lumpy Government projects and programmes ratcheted the economy sporadically up a series of development stairs to higher plateaus, while intermittent droughts and other adversities caused periodic contractions in agriculture, construction and other sectors. Over that period, the economy was transformed from a predominantly low productivity agriculture-based system to an increasingly more productive industrial (including mining) and service sector oriented system.

In *Growth and Structural Transformation in Botswana*, J.C. Leith examines what happened to both inputs and outputs, as well as the relationships amongst them over the period from 1974 to 1994. With respect to inputs, Leith investigates the changes to both the quantity and quality of primary inputs used in production, describing how the capital stock increased in real terms more than four-fold, growing about 7.15% p.a., while the labour force growing at a rate of 2.76% p.a. increased about 70% over the period. However, the author notes the qualitative change in the labour force as skilled labour, due to rapid expansion of education and training, increased even faster that the capital stock. Leith also shows how the structure of the economy was changed from a heavy dependence on agriculture, which was intensive in its use of land and unskilled labour, to orientation towards mining and Government, with the former relatively mineral (and skilled labour) intensive and the latter labour intensive. While both capital and labour inputs grew rapidly over the period, output expanded even more rapidly, reflecting the growth in total factor productivity (output per unit of input) over the period. In analysing this, Leith discovers that total factor productivity growth averaged 2.2% p.a. over the twenty year period. However, when disaggregated into the periods from 1974 to 1984 and from 1984 to 1994, the author finds that most of the productivity growth occurred in the first period (4.0% p.a.), with very little productivity growth in the latter period (0.5% p.a.). Leith goes on to examine what may have caused both the rapid total factor productivity growth in the first period and its deterioration in the second period. He argues that policies, which may have contributed to Botswana's success in the period from 1974 to 1984, such as those which affected the supply of primary inputs, both their quantity and quality, or those which affected the relationship between inputs and output, may have lost their influence as the structure of the economy changed. In light of this, Leith warns that future development will depend on how well policy makers adapt the policies of the past to meet the changing circumstances.

In *Botswana's Boom and Recession: A Discussion*, N. Gaolathe reviews the economic ups and downs Botswana went through, with a special focus on the recent boom in the late 1980s and early 1990s, and the subsequent contraction that was felt especially hard in the private sector. He chronicles some of the more salient features of that business cycle, identifying the major causes of the boom in the changing levels and composition of public expenditures, rapid credit expansion and overoptimistic expectations, especially regarding housing prices and rentals. N. Gaolathe notes that when the bubble burst, and the recession set in, it was not just one factor that was responsible. Some exogenous factors came into play, such as drought, the imposition of sales quotas on diamond exports and the substantial devaluation of the Zimbabwe Dollar, while other domestic factors were also at work, such as the suspension of the BHC construction programme, completion of some major mining and Government projects, the collapse in housing prices and rentals as supply caught up with demand, rising interest rates to positive real levels and the return of the economy to more 'normal' rates of growth.

In *The Real Costs of Inflation in Botswana*, A. Kahuti and M. Wright investigate whether there have been significant real costs to the economy over the past two decades since the introduction of the Pula due to inflation; and whether efforts to reduce inflation from its current level of nearly ten percent would be worth the costs. The paper reviews both the theory and evidence on the costs of inflation, in terms of its adverse effects on resource allocation, on distribution and on growth. In Botswana's case, the authors argue that because the dominant and rapidly expanding sectors of the economy, diamonds and Government, are not very sensitive to inflation, aggregate economic growth has not been significantly affected. They note that while price stability should be a long-term objective of the authorities, at present levels the rate of inflation is not generating such excessive real costs as would warrant new anti-inflation measures that would entail other real costs to the economy and to employment. However, the authors emphasise the point that there is no room for complacency. Although much of the development success in the past may have been impervious to inflation, future growth in a more diversified economy will be increasing dependent upon sectors more sensitive to inflation when business decisions are being made, while the greater monetization of the economy will increase the welfare costs associated with high inflation.

Chapter 2 presents a collection of papers by staff of the Research Department of the Bank looking at macroeconomic policies and strategies, both those that have been pursued in the recent past, and those that will become increasingly important for the future. Long-term development of Botswana will require high levels of capital formation, which will require increasing the mobilization of savings from households, a topic covered in the two papers by Motsomi and Reinke. The mechanism of open market operations through which monetary policy is effected in Botswana is the subject of A. Kone's paper. Public sector issues, involving privatization of public enterprises and the public finances are dealt with in the papers by Ncube and Wright, respectively.

A. Motsomi, in *Policy Options for Savings Mobilization in Botswana*, takes a look at the policy and institutional developments that can enhance the mobilization of savings, especially medium and long-term savings by the private sector. Such mobilization is crucial for Botswana's development, since Government, which has been the major source of national savings in the past on account of rising mineral revenues, cannot be counted on indefinitely to run budget surpluses and channel resources to maintain the growth momentum in the economy. The author also focuses on the role that macroeconomic policies, such as keeping inflation low and stable, holding deficits within sustainable limits and maintaining positive real rates of interest, can play in stimulating private and public savings. As regards institutional development, Motsomi notes that expanding Batswana savers' access to financial instruments (through wider branch networks), as well as increasing the diversity of the instruments available (e.g., stocks and bonds) to them, could go a long way in generating additional savings. Unfortunately, in terms of liquidity and its capacity to mobilise capital from savings, the author finds Botswana's capital market deficient. To improve on the current situation, Motsomi argues that the real return on savings accounts at commercial banks and other non-bank financial institutions should be positive, while efforts should be made to establish a bond market through parastatal bond issues and increase the number of shares on the Botswana Stock Exchange by privatising some parastatals through a public floatation of shares. He also recommends the introduction of additional tax incentives to encourage the development of the contractual savings industry.

In *Savings Mobilization in the Household Sector: The Case of Botswana*, J. Reinke puts the case more starkly: Botswana's high growth has been due to 'windfall gains', not hard toil and frugal spending habits. But, mineral rents will inevitably decline in importance as the economy grows and the non-replenishable resource becomes exhausted; and Government's ability to generate savings from mineral revenues will subside. Thus, if Botswana is to continue on a long-term, high growth path, private sector savings will be crucial. In his analysis, Reinke shows that Botswana, while avoiding many of the pitfalls associated with mineral booms, has allowed the growth in mineral rents, which was transmitted into excess liquidity in the economy, to undermine the incentive of households to be thrifty. Instead, he argues that a credit-driven consumer culture has emerged in Botswana, based on cheap credit. Reinke believes that inculcating a savings habit in Botswana is hampered by the unattractiveness of the formal savings instruments available: their low yield, the inconvenience of accessing such instruments, and the lack of alternative choices of savings instruments. He notes that savings accounts, the most convenient saving instrument in the financial system available to savers, all offer negative real rates of interest. But, while Reinke argues for making positive real rates of interest available to savers through Bank of Botswana Certificates (BoBCs) or other instruments, he comes down hard on the easy access to cheap consumer credit, contending that households should be 'compelled to use savings as opposed to credit for intertemporal decision making.' He concludes there is a need for policy makers in Botswana to become more proactive in encouraging savings mobilization, both in terms of dissuading the pervasive credit culture that has been spawned, and in terms of developing the financial system's ability to attract savings and intermediate them into productive investments.

Botswana's financial system took a big step forward in May 1991, with the introduction of BoBCs, which are short-term money market instruments of the Bank of Botswana sold through auctions at a discount. Z. Kone, in *The Transmission Mechanism of Monetary Policy in Botswana: Through Bank of Botswana Certificates*, reviews the way monetary policy operates through the auctioning of BoBCs to affect the level of the monetary base, domestic credit and interest rates. Kone explores, both theoretically and practically, some of the various ways in which the effects of open market operations are transmitted throughout the economy: selling BoBCs raises interest rates, reduces asset prices, decreases commercial banks' lending abilities, discourages spending, lowers stock prices, reduces firms' and households' ability to borrow on the basis of collateral, and so on. For Botswana, the introduction of BoBCs provided a handy and effective tool for the authorities to use to neutralise the potential expansionary effects on the money supply that diamond export sales and current account surpluses would have. In so doing, BoBCs have assisted the Bank to achieve its objective of maintaining monetary stability.

Public sector reform has gained increasing prominence as governments strive to improve their performances, both in terms of the quality of goods and services delivered to the public, and the cost-effectiveness of their delivery. In *Privatization of Public Enterprises through the Stock Exchange,* A. Ncube takes a look at one area of public sector reform that can improve economic efficiency, several of the various means by which it can be achieved and Botswana's experience of privatising enterprises in which Government has a shareholding interest. Botswana, while espousing free market principles and emphasising private sector development, has evolved a relatively large public sector in most areas of the economy through establishing statutory parastatals (such as BPC, WUC and BHC), indirectly investing in enterprises through the Botswana Development Corporation, and by setting up departments (such as the CTO), which perform tasks that can also be done by private sector firms. Government has also invested directly in several large mining ventures. While various types and methods of privatization are considered, such as deregulation and contracting out provision of Government services, Ncube concentrates on the conventional privatization of selling of state-owned assets to the public or other investors through the stock market. The author reviews the case to be made for using the stock market to effect privatization, highlighting how such an approach can economise on search costs, promote tradeability of assets, facilitate attracting foreign capital and help deal with lumpy assets. Ncube also notes that privatization through the stock exchange encourages policy transparency, and can foster capital market development. The author reviews Botswana's experience of using the stockmarket to transfer ownership of several enterprises in which Government, mainly through BDC, had interests, including Sechaba Investment Trust, Financial Services Corporation and Botswana Insurance Holdings – all successful divestments. However, Ncube raises the concern that privatization, in order to have wide public support, must provide opportunities for a large portion of the population to acquire shares. This leads the author to consider funding schemes, such as 'partly paid shares' or an 'Investment Trust Fund' or a 'Credit Scheme', through which Batswana can acquire ownership of shares. Ncube also considers the needs of privatised firms to have access to some form of Government financing and support to assist it with the transition from public to private ownership. These aspects of the paper may be the most contentious, in that they would leave Government involved with the enterprises and exposed to various risks and hazards. In considering some of the parastatals that could be privatised, the author identifies the National Development Bank, Botswana Telecommunications Corporation, Botswana Power Corporation, Botswana Meat Commission, Air Botswana and the Botswana Vaccine Institute as potential candidates, subject to various restructurings and legal changes. Ncube further suggests that Government could divest from a substantial portion of its shareholding in Debswana, which would really boost the Botswana Stock Exchange, and perhaps provide an opportunity for a local company to be listed on some major international stock exchanges. Developments, such as those suggested in the paper, could go a long way in broadening the size and scope of the Botswana Stock Exchange, and the opportunities Batswana could have to save and invest in productive ventures in Botswana.

Botswana's fiscal circumstances have changed dramatically over the past thirty years as Government moved from a position of deficits and dependence on donor assistance, mainly from the UK, to finance both its development and recurrent budgets, to one of sustained surpluses over an extended period and sizeable accumulated savings. In *Fiscal Policy in Botswana: Challenges for Public Sector Finance in the Mid-*

1990s, M. Wright reviews the budgetary developments of the past, paying special attention to National Development Plan 7 (NDP 7), in order to identify strategic opportunities for the public sector that could promote future prosperity, as well as constraints that could frustrate such progress. Wright notes the large and dominant role Government has played in the economy, not only as a direct producer and provider of goods and services, but also as an investor and a source of transfers. Such dominance poses problems for private sector development, and is not likely to be sustainable in the longer term. But, the record of past budget surpluses and the accumulated savings give rise to pressures for increases in public expenditure, which may not have positive long-term payoffs to society, and for relaxation of the disciplined approach to fiscal management that has been practised in the past. Facing and overcoming this challenge to sound public finance will be crucial if Government is to be able to contribute to future sustained increases in real income levels.

In **Chapter 3**, an assortment of papers relating to financial sector development are presented. The development of the Central Bank, and its roles as promoter of monetary stability, protector of the nation's wealth, source of Government revenues and supervisor of the financial system are dealt with in four of the papers, while the fifth paper in this chapter reviews a unique financial institution set up by Government in 1973 – the Public Debt Service Fund (PDSF).

Mr H.C.L. Hermans, who served as both the first and fifth Governor of the Bank of Botswana, reviews the background that in 1974 led Government to opt for monetary independence, and many of the salient developments that occurred since 1975, when Parliament approved the Bank of Botswana Act, which established the Central Bank and provided for the introduction of Botswana's currency, comprising Pula notes and Thebe coins. *Bank of Botswana: The First 21 Years* is rich with historical details regarding developments about physical infrastructure, institutional arrangements, staff matters, operations, the Bank's financial performance, monetary policy, exchange rate policy, exchange controls, financial sector development and management of the nation's foreign exchange reserves. The Governor's chronicle is testimony both to the adventure that Government embarked upon in creating a monetary system for Botswana, and to the strength and wisdom of those policy makers and staff who served to make the Bank a sound and reputable institution which could effectively conduct monetary policy that has ensured monetary stability and a strong, credible currency. With that background, the Bank is well-positioned to be able to evolve into an even stronger institution in the future that can better fulfil its statutory obligations and contribute to financial sector development.

C. Harvey, in *Monetary Independence: The Contrasting Strategies of Botswana and Swaziland*, reviews the different approaches that two High Commission Territories, that were members of the Rand Monetary Area, took after achieving independence in 1966 and 1968, respectively. Both countries at independence, and for some years thereafter, used the Rand as their currency and held all their foreign exchange reserves with the South African Reserve Bank. They had, in essence, given to the South African authorities the power to determine interest rates, exchange rates and exchange controls in their countries, with no voice in decisions over such policy matters, and no compensation either for the interest free loan given to South Africa for the Rand currency which circulated in their countries, or for the loss of discretion over monetary policy. There were advantages, of course, to being in a monetary union, such as the absence of exchange controls within the union, the absence of exchange rate risk in the monetary area, the absence of transactions costs of changing from one currency to another within the union, the ability to invest in more developed South African financial markets and access to the foreign exchange reserves held by the South African Reserve Bank. Harvey argues that the crucial advantage, however, of belonging to a common monetary area turned out to be that it prevented the governments from financing a budget deficit by money creation (i.e., borrowing from the central bank). Botswana chose to leave the Rand Monetary Area in 1976 and introduced the Pula. But, because of mineral developments and rapid growth in Government revenues, along with prudent macroeconomic policies, Government never resorted to borrowing from the Central Bank. Swaziland chose to remain in the Rand Monetary Area and negotiated improved compensation from South Africa for Rand in circulation, along with some additional concessions that gave it discretion over some aspects of monetary and financial sector policy. While there were differences in the experiences of Botswana and Swaziland, Harvey finds that their approaches to monetary policy have tended to converge; and very crucially in both cases, the Central Banks have not been used to finance unsustainable government deficits through money creation. He concludes by noting that the increased international financial integration that is occurring in Southern Africa will impose additional fiscal discipline on governments, and leave the monetary authorities better able to pursue policies aimed at monetary stability.

Botswana has acquired a good reputation for sound economic management, as reflected in the healthy balance of payments and Government budget surpluses that have been recorded since the early 1980s, and in the sizeable foreign exchange reserves that have been accumulated. L.K. Mohohlo, in *Central Banks as Protectors of National Wealth: Botswana's Case*, explains the general principles and practices that have been applied to manage those reserves. While most countries hold modest levels of foreign exchange reserves to enable them to pay their international obligations for imports of goods and services, as well as debt service, in a timely manner, Botswana, with foreign exchange sufficient to pay for about 28 months of imports of goods and services, has reserves in excess of that needed for normal transactions and precautionary purposes. Mohohlo explains the institutional framework that has been developed in the International Department of the Bank of Botswana to watch after and manage those reserves in a prudent and conservative manner. The Bank has adopted a broad investment policy that takes into account the importance of safeguarding and maintaining the of value of the reserves, ensuring their liquidity if needed, and earning the best return possible within acceptable limits of risk. The author further describes how the Bank has also established operational guidelines to manage the various types of risks involved in investing the foreign exchange reserves: *viz.* the risk associated with being in different foreign currencies, whose exchange value might fluctuate; the risks associated with being in different financial instruments whose values might fluctuate with changes in interest rates; the credit risks associated with lending money to someone who might not be able to repay the money; and the liquidity risks associated with not being able to get your money when you want without having to bear an excessive cost. As international reserves began to accumulate rapidly in the 1980s, as a result of the rapid growth of mineral exports, it was recognised that Botswana had more reserves than were necessary for normal transactions purposes. Mohohlo explains why the authorities then decided to split the reserves up into three tranches or portfolios: one for normal transactions and precautionary purposes, the Liquidity Portfolio; one to ensure that the country would always be able to service its external debt obligations, the Matched Asset-Liability Portfolio; and one to ensure that Botswana's national savings would be able to make the greatest contribution to sustained national economic development, the Pula Fund. The justification for the Pula Fund is well explained in terms of ensuring that national savings are used productively and yield the highest return possible to Botswana. The author further describes some of the more recent institutional arrangements for reserve management, including the use of fund managers, mainly for the equity investments of the Pula Fund, and a global custodian to better protect the Bank's assets and provide various other prudent investment services. While Mohohlo gives a good account of the various steps the Bank has taken to protect the nation's wealth held in foreign exchange reserves, she stresses that the Bank will need to become even more sophisticated and competent in the future in managing the reserves so that when resources are required to finance projects that will contribute to sustainable development, to the greatest extent possible, those resources are there. She is confident the Bank will be up to that challenge and will evolve the needed capabilities to protect and promote the nation's wealth in the future.

One of the primary reasons that Botswana left the Rand Monetary Area and introduced the Pula was to enable Government to accumulate foreign exchange reserves, the earnings on which could be a source of additional revenues. Little did they anticipate that foreign exchange reserves would accumulate to over P13 billion by the end of 1995. Nor did they expect that earnings on the foreign exchange reserves would become the second largest source of Government revenue, after minerals. J. Salkin, in *Measures of Central Bank Performance in Botswana: Returns on Foreign Exchange Reserves and Revenue Paid to Government*, reviews those developments over the past twenty years, comparing the actual recorded returns and revenues to Government, against a currency benchmark, the SDR, and the IMF's rate of remuneration (i.e., rate of interest), taking into account exchange rate changes that have occurred over the period. Salkin shows that for the period 1980 to 1995, the actual gross returns of the Bank, mainly the earnings on the foreign exchange reserves, in SDR terms were 35% higher than that which would have been achieved if the foreign exchange reserves had been invested at the SDR rate of remuneration. Analogously, Salkin estimates that the total gross operating profit of the Bank plus the revaluation gains or losses recorded averaged 17% of the level of the international reserves. On the basis of the Bank's net income and revaluation gains or losses, Government, the sole stockholder in the Bank, received over P6 billion in revenues from the Bank, and earned the equivalent of a 19.5% return on the funds it had invested or deposited in the Bank. Even after adjusting for inflation, Government's investment yielded a 7.4% real return, which compares favourably to 1.3% real rate of return that would have been earned if the international reserves in SDR terms had been invested at the SDR rate of remuneration. Salkin also discusses the issue of the variability of the Bank's revenues to Government, and the proposal to stabilise them and make them more predictable, while preserving the Bank's ability to conduct monetary policy in a more liberalised exchange control environment.

K.S. Masalila, in *Banking Supervision and Regulations: The Case of Botswana*, provides an instructive review of the regulatory framework for financial institutions, the various stages and processes involved in banking supervision and their links with the effectiveness of monetary policy. Botswana's regulatory framework, which covers internal governance of banks, market discipline and official supervision, dates back to the Financial Institutions Action of 1975, which was subsequently replaced with the Banking Act of 1995. Masalila takes us through the various elements of the regulatory framework for financial institutions, including licensing and regulation of entry, management or liquidation of banks in distress, prudential requirements for capital adequacy, risk exposures, liquidity and quality of management, and provision of information. He stresses that bank supervision, by helping to ensure that banks remain commercially sound, makes for an effective and responsive banking system; one in which monetary policy initiatives can be efficiently transmitted to influence credit, interest rates and monetary stability. Inefficient, unsound or insolvent financial institutions, which can put the entire financial system under stress and cause monetary instability, make formulating and implementing monetary policy more difficult. Masalila, thus, highlights that monetary policy should work in tandem with effective banking supervision. He also provides an interesting review of the performance of the commercial banks over the period from 1980 to 1995, reporting on profitability, competition, efficiency-productivity, service to the public, structure of deposits and lending, as well as their capital, advances and assets. In discussing the increasing scope of bank supervision, Masalila covers three areas which will pose new challenges to banking supervision, *viz.* financial sector liberalization, which will increase the banks' potential exposure to various risks, such as credit, market, foreign exchange and interest rate risks; globalization and cross-border operations, which may create opportunities for regulatory arbitrage and avoiding adequate prudential supervision; and technological developments, especially information technology, which will require the banking supervisors to become increasingly conversant with electronic banking, and the adequacy and appropriateness of the systems and controls being used.

In the early 1970s, when Botswana's economic and fiscal prospects were expected to improve dramatically as a result of the mineral developments at Selebi-Phikwe and Orapa (as well as the renegotiation of the Southern African Customs Union Agreement), Government established the PDSF and the Revenue Stabilization Fund (RSF) as mechanisms that would, respectively, enable the country to service its debt obligations and cope with temporary revenue shortfalls that might arise from fluctuations in international mineral markets, drought or other contingencies. M. Faber, in *Botswana's Somnolent Giant: The Public Debt Service Fund – Its Past, Present and a Possible Future*, reviews the record of the PDSF, which became the largest lending institution in Botswana, lending primarily to state-owned enterprises, public institutions and local authorities. By 1996, the loans and advances of the PDSF, at P2156 million, were larger than those of all the commercial banks combined. In his article, Faber provides the legal and operational background of the PDSF, which came to be a major source of subsidised credit to the economy. He identifies not only how such credit helped to promote infrastructure development and low tariffs for public utilities, but also how it served to disguise management deficiencies, such as slack work discipline and extensive over-staffing, led to over-investment with low rates of return and retarded the development of the private domestic capital market. The PDSF has grown to comprise assets far greater than total public debt, and thus could quickly pay off the entire Government debt if it were advantageous to do so. However, Faber argues that because of the concessionality associated with much of the debt, and because the parastatals are servicing that part of the public debt that was contracted on their behalf, it would not be advantageous for Government to do so. The author notes the need for reform in this area of public sector financing, arguing that the PDSF should become more commercially minded. This is buttressed by Faber's observation that because of the subsidised interest rates charged, the PDSF is only worth about sixty percent of its book value; and that does not take into account the inherent riskiness of the underlying assets; i.e., some of the public enterprises and institutions are not very sound and cannot service their PDSF obligations without Government subventions. While according to an unwritten Government convention, any debt service shortfalls of the parastatals are met by Government equity injections and/or recurrent budget subventions, such bailing out does not make for a healthy loan portfolio. In considering future options for this somnolent giant of a financial institution, Faber argues strongly against the continuation of the *status quo*. Rather he suggests that consideration be given to turning the PDSF into an investment bank, with staff capable of effectively appraising and monitoring loans, that could become actively involved in the management and decision making processes of the state-owned enterprises it lends to, and that could enable the fund to become an underwriter of parastatal bond issues. Such an investment fund would also pay dividends to its stockholders, and even raise funds through issuing bonds and other instruments to enable it to finance future expansions of the nation's infrastructure. A successful investment fund, however, need not be a Government enterprise; and Faber suggests that over time Government could divest its shares in such an institution, and give more Batswana a direct stake in the efficient and profitable operation of the PDSF.

The authorities in Botswana, since the earliest days when plans were being made for the development and exploitation of the mineral deposits at Selebi-Phikwe and Orapa, recognised that successful development would require that they find some way to channel the returns expected from the mineral developments into projects and programmes that could contribute to sustained development of other sectors throughout the country that could provide jobs and incomes for Batswana. **Chapter 4** takes a look at some of the various industrial development policies and strategies that have been pursued, the constraints that have been encountered and some of the new directions that will likely be taken to achieve the NDP 8 objective of sustainable economic diversification.

In *Industrialization in Botswana: Evolution, Performance and Prospects*, P. Siwawa-Ndai reviews the alternative strategies that developing countries have been advised to pursue in order to foster industrial development. In Botswana's case, Siwawa-Ndai argues that the orientation of industrial development policy has been directed towards laissez faire solutions, with minimal direct Government interventions, usually in the form of short-term subsidies, such as the Financial Assistance Policy (FAP), rather than through tariffs, protection or direct ownership. In her paper, she reviews the various policies, programmes, regulations, trade policy instruments and arrangements that have been adopted and used by Government to influence industrial development. Siwawa-Ndai finds that Botswana's legal and regulatory environment has not been a constraint to company formation, and, indeed, the environment has been especially conducive to the formation of small and medium-scale enterprises. She also reviews the trends in industrial growth, noting that the manufacturing sector grew very fast from the early 1970s up to the most recent period; but, this growth was swamped by the even more rapid growth of the mining sector. Unfortunately, the employment creating potential of the mining sector is very limited, due to its capital intensive nature, while the manufacturing sector has the potential to create substantial employment opportunities. To foster employment growth, the author notes how the Government at first sought to encourage import substitution. It was only in the late 1980s that non-traditional exports were promoted. Siwawa-Ndai recognises that the biggest challenge facing Botswana remains how to foster sustainable industrial activity, noting the major constraints to such development arising from insufficient private domestic capital, a small domestic market, the absence of a critical mass of citizen entrepreneurs, a limited raw material base, inadequate skilled manpower, infrastructure and supporting services, along with an unfavourable wage–productivity relationship. The answer lies in export development, but this, too, is constrained by the lack of trade financing and the ready availability of appropriate trade information. Siwawa-Ndai reviews many of the trade policy issues relating to the Southern African Customs Union and the multilateral liberalization of trade, as they relate to Botswana's industrialization, noting the potential difficulties they pose for Botswana. Under certain circumstances, as world trade becomes liberalised and more competitive, Botswana could stand to lose international markets, export earnings and revenues. To meet these challenges, Botswana must vigorously promote production for export markets; and for this to be successful, it is crucial that productivity be raised and that production costs be minimised.

In her paper, *Constraints to Industrial Development*, D. Mpabanga reviews Botswana's progress in industrialization, noting the rapid growth achieved from 1982/83 to 1988/89, and the subsequent slower growth from 1989/90 to 1994/95, which included contractions in 1992/93 and 1993/94. While noting the favourable political and macroeconomic environment Botswana has had, which should have served to promote industrial development, she also examines the various constraints that have impeded expansion and diversification of industry. These commonly cited constraints to industrial development include, *inter alia*, shortage of serviced land, smallness of the domestic market, lack of an industrial culture, Government regulations, Immigration Department delays in processing work permits for expatriate staff, high interest rates, and the fact that Botswana is a land-locked country. Mpabanga also considers some of the specific problems faced by small and medium-scale enterprises, *viz.* lack of access to capital, poor quality of products, high transport costs, shortage of raw materials and fierce competition from imports. Further, Mpabanga finds that there are several existing policies and programmes that are in conflict with the Industrial Development Policy and its objectives, including: the Citizen Reservation Policy, which restricts entrepreneurship, acquisition of technical and management skills, innovation and the ability of locals to form joint ventures with foreigners who have the necessary capital and know-how to ensure long-term sustainability; the previous National Policy on Education, which did not give adequate attention to developing human resources with the skills and knowledge needed for a modern industrial society; and the Incomes Policy, under which wages were allowed to get too high relative to productivity. She covers many of the various policy initiatives Government has adopted to overcome the constraints to industrial development, including the Industrial Development Policy, the Financial Assistance Policy, the Local Preference Scheme, the Selebi-Phikwe Regional Development Project, participation in trade fairs, developing a science and technology policy, promotion of non-traditional exports, promotion of import substitution production and reduction in the company income tax for manufacturing. Mpabanga draws a few lessons from the experiences of other countries, such as Mauritius and the Eastern Asian success stories, highlighting the potential benefits of having a more effective trade and investment promotion agency, further exchange control liberalization, financial sector development, encouragement of domestic savings and targeting of specific industries for development.

One of the more innovative policy initiatives the Government of Botswana introduced to create additional employment and diversify the economy beyond the traditional beef and large-scale mineral industries was the Financial Assistance Policy (FAP) in 1982. J.A. Peat, one of the architects and subsequent evaluators of that project, assesses the experience of that programme to subsidise the use of unskilled labour in the tradeable goods industries in his *Review of the Initial Objectives and Rationale of FAP*. FAP had other objectives as well, including upgrading citizen skills and promoting active citizen ownership of business ventures. Peat reviews the justification for a market intervention such as FAP, explaining how FAP was intended to correct the market price for labour, which had been distorted by minimum wages, as well as to provide temporary support for infant industries and provide a remedy to a market failure in training Batswana for skills that were transferable to other enterprises. In evaluating the cost-effectiveness of introducing programmes such as FAP, Peat highlights the importance of getting the signals faced by decision makers right, maximising the 'additionality' of the benefits generated, minimising the 'displacement' that the programme might cause, maximising linkages, external benefits and other positive externalities, and maximising the survival rates of the new activities promoted. While designing and getting approved a subsidy programme such as FAP always involves balancing conflicting interests and reaching a compromise, Peat makes a good case that FAP was an appropriate means to achieve stated ends.

No one doubts that the development of the mineral sector has played an extremely important role in Botswana's economic history. But, minerals, to the extent they are exploited, are a wasting asset, which eventually become depleted. For Botswana, this then poses the development challenge of how to use the mineral wealth wisely to foster a diversified and productive economy that can provide adequate incomes to the large majority of the population throughout the country not directly engaged in the mining sector. B. Gaolathe, in *Development of Botswana's Mineral Sector*, presents a wide-ranging and informative overview of the history of mining in Botswana, the various contributions it has made to GDP, Government revenues, exports, employment, and so on, and the sector's potential in the coming years. In covering such a broad topic, the author introduces readers to many insights regarding Botswana's strategies and policies for mineral development, the technical and economic aspects of exploration, negotiation, extraction and marketing, and what and where are the existing and prospective mineral projects. Gaolathe describes how the mining sector, which was virtually non-existent at Independence, grew rapidly from the early 1970s to represent over 50% of GDP by 1988/89, providing 59% of Government revenues and almost 90% of exports. However, the mining sector is relatively capital intensive, with requirements for skilled labour rather than unskilled labour; and direct employment in the mining sector has represented less than 10% of total formal sector employment, with that proportion falling to 5% in recent years. The author provides some analysis of the benefit to Botswana from the major mineral projects at Selebi-Phikwe, where copper-nickel ore is mined, the diamond mines at Orapa, Letlhakane and Jwaneng and the coal mine at Morupule, showing that the retained value to Botswana of the projects has represented some 50%–70% of exports. While Botswana has been the subject of extensive exploration activities over the years, the thick Kalahari sands and geological structures mean much is still not known about Botswana's mineral potential. In considering possible future developments, Gaolathe takes the reader through a linguistic exploration of aeromagnetic and electro-magnetic surveys, investigating the hydrocarbon potential in sedimentary basins, the brine reserves at Sua Pan and copper mineralization of proven and indicated ore reserves in economically exploitable grades among proterozoic mineral provinces and phanerozoic sub-provinces, as well as mineral occurrences of diamondiferous kimberlite ore bodies and crustal studies in search of other minerals. Thus far, only the exploitation of diamonds, which have the potential to be mined at current rates well into the next century, has yielded substantial net benefits to Botswana. Both the copper-nickel project at Selebi-Phikwe and the soda ash project suffered from technical and financial problems, aggravated by depressed mineral prices. This dependence on diamonds is a concern to Gaolathe; and he argues that Botswana should set aside a portion of the diamond revenues for future generations, which could generate a growing stream of income for the day when production declines or markets soften. The author also describes how various other known mineral deposits have not proven themselves to be economically exploitable, such as Botswana's vast coal reserves, because of its low grade and the high transportation costs that would be needed to get the coal to markets. As Gaolathe shows, environmental issues have not been ignored in Botswana's approach to mineral development, with considerable attention being paid to environmental protection in the planning and implementation of mineral projects. He credits Botswana with being in the forefront of legislation and policy commitments, such as the National Conservation Strategy, that serve to promote environmentally friendly mineral development. To be sure, Gaolathe believes there is much more to be hoped for in the development of the mineral sector, in both size and diversity, and in its ability to contribute to future growth.

One of the enduring features of Botswana's strategy for development has been the emphasis given to creating as many productive job opportunities for Batswana as rapidly as possible. Underlying that strategy was the recognition that providing opportunities for productive employment, including self-employment, would be the most effective way to alleviate the widespread poverty in the country, especially in the rural areas, and achieve a more equitable distribution of income. **Chapter 5** presents several papers relating to employment and living standards, both the progress that has been made and the challenges that remain.

With the increasing competition to be expected as world trade liberalises, Botswana producers will need to raise productivity and reduce their costs if they are to be able

maintain their existing markets and even expand into new markets for non-traditional goods and services. In *Trends in Real Wages and Labour Productivity in Botswana,*
W. Mandlebe reviews the data available for the past two decades on wages, productivity and unit labour costs, focusing on various sectors, such as manufacturing, tourism, and financial services, thought to be key for Botswana's NDP 8 strategy of sustainable economic diversification. In theory, in competitive markets, there is a simple
direct relationship between the real wages that firms would be willing and able to pay
workers, and the marginal product of labour; and one would expect to find that movements in real wages would track those of labour productivity. Indeed, Mandlebe finds
such patterns in the data, with, for example, real wages in the manufacturing sector
declining 4.9% p.a., while labour productivity fell 3.5% p.a. over the period from
1974/75 to 1993/94. One common, but partial way of looking at competitiveness is
through measures such as unit labour costs; i.e., the average labour cost per unit of
output. If Botswana's unit labour costs, say for manufacturing, were to be rising,
relative to those of competitors, the country would become less competitive in the
production of such goods. Mandlebe finds, however, that unit labour costs in the
aggregate, as well as for manufacturing, have decreased in Botswana, which, on the
surface, indicates Botswana has not been losing its competitiveness in the international market. With respect to one of the other crucial non-traditional sectors, financial services, the author observes that unit labour costs rose throughout the 1980s,
although they have decreased during the early 1990s. Mandlebe believes that future
success with respect to competitiveness, which will be necessary if Botswana is to
achieve sustainable economic diversification, will depend critically on wage restraint,
coupled with improved productivity. In that regard, he recommends revisiting minimum wages (as they seem inappropriate with high levels of unemployment), additional programmes by the Botswana National Productivity Centre and others to raise
productivity, and reform of FAP to make its grants more tied to productivity improvements.

D.J. Hudson and M. Wright, in *Income Inequality in Botswana – Trends Since Independence,* go a long way in using the best available evidence to set the record straight
on what has happened to the distribution of income. While there are significant disparities in income, and a substantial proportion of the population remain in poverty,
the authors find that contrary to assertions and anecdotal evidence reported in the
media, over the past twenty years, income inequality has decreased, slightly, especially in rural areas, and incomes across all categories of the income distribution have
increased. In addition to providing an interesting review of the early concerns over the
income distribution in Botswana, tracing them through development plans to the
implementation of the Rural Income Distribution Survey (RIDS) in 1974/75, Hudson
and Wright very carefully explain the data sources that they draw upon, the 1974/75
RIDS and the 1985/86 and 1993/94 Household Income and Expenditure Surveys
(HIES), and the limitations inherent in using such data. By carefully disaggregating
the data to comparable categories, the authors show that the conventional income
distribution measure, the Gini coefficient, which ranges from zero for perfect equality
to one for extreme inequality, decreased for rural households from 0.520 in 1974/75
to 0.505 in 1985/86 and to 0.498 in 1993/94. For the urban population, the comparable data on individual incomes for 1985/86 and 1993/94 show the Gini coefficient
going from 0.536 to 0.539, not a significant difference. For the nation as a whole, the

authors find that the income distribution for both households and individuals has become less unequal. With the levels of real household incomes rising by 31% between 1985/86 and 1993/94, and the income distribution becoming less unequal, Hudson and Wright note that income gains are distributed widely to all income groups. Among the many other interesting findings is the result – not perhaps surprising – that excluding non-citizens' incomes increases equality. The authors also provide some insight into some of the many factors that affect the income distribution, including the drought cycle, the structure of economic growth, investment in human resources development and various Government policies, not all of which are found consistent with improving income equality.

Poverty represents a failure of development; it remains a major challenge for Botswana. In *Poverty in Botswana,* K.R. Jefferis provides both a conceptual framework to analyse the manifestation of poverty and its causes, as well as a comprehensive review of how poverty in Botswana has changed over the period 1985/86 to 1993/94 on the basis of the HIES in those two years. He argues that poverty is more than just lack of money; it takes on many forms, including lack of adequate shelter and clothing, high mortality and morbidity, malnutrition, dependency, child vulnerability and lack of economic and social mobility. In analysing the causes of poverty in Botswana, the author examines failures with respect to economic opportunities (lack of jobs and incomes), social provision (inadequate social safety nets, health care, education) and individual-family decisions (unequal distribution within households, dependency syndromes and large family sizes). For Botswana, the traditional view has been that poverty is due to drought, which reduces incomes and income generating assets; and if drought were to go away, people would no longer be poor. Jefferis challenges that view, arguing that unlike many other Sub-Saharan African countries, Botswana's agricultural potential, given climatic and soil conditions, is too weak to provide adequate incomes for all the population. In analysing the extent of poverty in Botswana, Jefferis uses both the conventional income-based measures of poverty datum lines and capability measures that attempt to reflect important aspects of the quality of life. His findings indicate that there has been a significant decline in the extent of poverty in Botswana, with the percentage of households falling below the poverty datum line decreasing from 49% in 1985/86 to 37% in 1993/94. He also shows that most of the reduction in poverty has occurred amongst the very poor in rural areas – those whose incomes were inadequate to pay for basic food necessities. This is interpreted as suggesting that policies to alleviate poverty have had some beneficial effects, and have been reasonably well targeted. Despite the progress in reducing poverty, Jefferis observes that 23% of the households remain very poor, which warrants additional and more effective approaches to poverty alleviation. Amongst the many results reported, Jefferis notes that female-headed households suffer a higher rate of poverty than male-headed households, and that poverty rates are higher for older household heads, for those with lack of education, for larger households, for those with fewer members employed and for those living in rural areas. To further reduce poverty, programmes have to be designed to target the poor effectively, in their various categories. While special care must be directed at those who are destitute, the disabled and the elderly, the main way to eliminate poverty on a sustained basis is to ensure there is sufficient job creation in economically viable businesses.

Botswana is a very open economy, with both exports and imports representing high proportions of GDP. In many respects, that openness is increasing as Botswana strives to diversify its economic base and produce additional non-traditional goods for export, as well as develop and expand sectors such as tourism and financial services. In **Chapter 6**, various authors review policies relating to international trade, finance and investment promotion, both how they have influenced Botswana's development in the past, and how changes that are emerging with respect to such policies may affect Botswana's prospects in the future – for better or for worse.

In *Exchange Control Liberalization*, K.R. Jefferis reviews the origins of exchange controls in Botswana, the costs of maintaining such controls and the case for and against complete abolition of exchange control in one 'Big Bang'. While Botswana has operated one of the most liberal exchange control regimes in Africa, and has progressively liberalised such controls over the years, especially since 1990, the author finds that Botswana's system of exchange controls is costly to administer, an impediment to inward investment, a tax on savers and a source of inefficiency in resource allocation, which reduces growth and incomes. He also notes that Government may have been able to extract greater revenues in the past from residents in Botswana as a result of exchange controls, but that with the current monetary policy stance of targeting positive real rates of interest, that benefit to Government has largely fallen away. More importantly, however, the author makes a compelling case that Botswana no longer needs such controls, and that complete abolition of exchange controls would provide benefits, not only in terms of resource savings and increased efficiency, but also in terms of attracting additional investment and diversifying the economy, especially with respect to the financial sector.

Jefferis comprehensively addresses the various concerns that authorities often raise about capital flight, monetary instability, control over interest rate and exchange rate policies, loss of Government revenue and the potential use of Botswana as a conduit for capital flight from neighbouring countries and illegal 'money laundering' transactions. For each issue, the author clearly shows that the concerns are misplaced. Botswana does not have to worry about capital flight, as Botswana has ample reserves, the great proportion of which belong to Government and thus cannot flow out of the country unless Government (completely apart from any exchange controls) chooses to dispose of them some way. Capital inflow may be more of an issue, as it may be a source of monetary instability, but the authorities can deal with this through suitable monetary policy tools at their disposal. The authorities will continue to have the ability to manage both interest rates and exchange rates, as long as they do not try to peg them at unsound and unsustainable levels. Loss of tax revenue, which would tend to be modest in any event, can be better addressed through changing to a source based system of taxation, improving tax administration and making double taxation agreements with other countries. Capital flight from other countries, trying to use Botswana as a conduit, should be left to those authorities to deal with and should not be used as an excuse for delaying reform in Botswana. Banking regulations and other criminal legislation, not exchange controls, are the appropriate instruments for dealing with money laundering.

In the light of these arguments, Jefferis' paper poses a serious challenge for those authorities who are reluctant to complete the process of exchange control liberalization. Their reluctance reflects poorly on their confidence in the economy and their ability to manage the economy properly. Eventually, they may come to recognise the strengths of the Botswana economy and their ability to manage the economy in a more liberalised environment. In the interim, the prospects and the potential of the economy will be that much diminished.

J.C. Leith, in his paper on *Botswana's International Trade Policies*, gives an interesting account of the multi-faceted trading arrangements Botswana has evolved up to the present, and provides an insightful analysis of many of the current trade policy issues facing Botswana. Leith explains Botswana's relationship in De Beers' diamond cartel, and how, because of Botswana's position as a major low cost producer of high quality gem diamonds, it is in both parties' interest that they work together to maintain the stability and profitability of the industry. He also describes the trading arrangements that pertain to Botswana's other, albeit smaller, exports, including copper-nickel matte (which is sold at world prices), textiles (which have benefited from the Botswana-Zimbabwe Trade Agreement, the SACU Agreement and the Multi-Fibre Agreement), motor vehicles (which sell mainly in SACU) and beef (which receives preferential European Union treatment under the Lomé Convention). The SACU Agreement is, of course, of special importance to Botswana, not only because most of the country's imports are sourced from South Africa, but also because much of Botswana's potential for developing additional non-traditional exports that can help to diversify the economy and create the substantial number of new job opportunities needed are most likely to be found in the Southern African region. Leith explains many of the important features of the SACU Agreement, the costs and the benefits to Botswana, and the key areas of concern in the current renegotiations of the Agreement. The author also touches on Botswana's exchange rate policy, and how that has been directed at avoiding the 'Dutch Disease' of having too strong a currency that deters production of exports and tradeable goods. Finally, Leith discusses the new preferential trading arrangements on the horizon, including the proposed Southern African Development Community (SADC) Free Trade Area and South Africa's (and hence SACU's) negotiations with the European Union for a preferential trading arrangement. Both of these developments can have potentially significant implications, for better or for worse, for Botswana and the other members of SACU.

The construction of the BCL mine at Selebi-Phikwe was one of the major development projects in Botswana's history. It was massive in relation to the rest of the economy, it had very significant direct effects on employment and indirect effects on Government revenues, and it was expected to be a substantial source of foreign exchange and income to the nation, which could then be reinvested in the development of other sectors and regions in Botswana. In the event, the financial viability of BCL came into question early in the mining venture's life, and Government eventually came to realise that the region around Selebi-Phikwe would need to develop other sustainable economic activities, if the town were to survive and the communities around it to prosper. D. Cowan, in *The Selebi-Phikwe Regional Development Project – A Case Study of the Costs and Benefits of Foreign Direct Investment*, reviews the history that eventually led to the formation of the Selebi-Phikwe Continuation Study Group, the formulation of the Regional Development Strategy for Selebi-Phikwe, and the establishment and operation of the Selebi-Phikwe Regional Development Promotion Unit, which was intended to implement the strategy. As part of the strategy to diversify the economic base of Selebi-Phikwe and the region, the Unit undertook to attract investors, mainly foreign manufacturing enterprises, to Selebi-Phikwe, as well as introduce an irrigated agricultural programme in the vicinity of Selebi-Phikwe. Cowan describes the Special Incentive Programme that was developed to attract foreign investors to Selebi-Phikwe, which was more generous than the Financial Assistance Policy. The author then considers, both theoretically and empirically, whether the efforts and incentives to attract foreign direct investment to a location, such as Selebi-Phikwe, are worth the costs. The basic proposition being that while additional investment can raise local incomes, both directly and indirectly, if too much in the way of incentives and grants are given to the foreign investors, the net benefit to the host country could be negative. Cowan reviews the earlier efforts to evaluate the costs and benefits of the Selebi-Phikwe Regional Development Project, and develops in some detail his methodology, based on that of evaluating export processing zones, to assess the project. He recognises the data and conceptual limitations in such an exercise, especially the inherent difficulty in assessing the external and dynamic benefits from stimulating new activities, giving previously unskilled rural labour experience and training, developing additional public and private infrastructure in the region and providing opportunities for downstream and related local industries; but he is unable to incorporate them directly in his analysis. In the end, Cowan finds he cannot answer unambiguously the question of whether the project does or does not represent a net benefit to Botswana. If the past and current business ventures are just taken into account, with continued attrition of existing firms, the author estimates a net loss to Botswana from the project of P31.8 million. In contrast, if the project can maintain the current levels of employment in the businesses that were attracted to Selebi-Phikwe for at least five years, the project could start to generate a net benefit to Botswana. Researchers will have another opportunity in the future to assess the net benefit to Botswana from such programmes; and this paper will provide some background and tools for such an exercise.

Finally, **Chapter 7** concludes with an epilogue on the policy choices and the economic prospects facing Botswana. Botswana has not yet achieved all its development aspirations; and those aspirations are being revised in a long-term vision for the year 2016. There is a wide range of possible future outcomes for Botswana, depending upon the policy choices made and how they are implemented. The report of the past, as described and analysed in many of the papers, with both the successes and the failures in attempting to achieve development objectives, provides many lessons and insights for how those future policy decisions should be made and implemented. With luck, this book will contribute to ensuring that some of the lessons of the past have been learnt, that some mistakes of the past will not be repeated and that better decisions can be made in the future to deal with new challenges to the continued development of the Botswana economy.

Chapter 1

Economic Growth and Performance

Growth and Structural Transformation in Botswana

J. Clark Leith

1. INTRODUCTION

In the three decades since Independence, Botswana's economy has grown rapidly, increasing GDP per capita many times over. This did not happen simply with all inputs and outputs growing at the same rates. Rather, the mix of inputs and outputs, and the output per unit of input, also changed dramatically. At Independence, economic activities were predominantly unskilled labour and land-intensive, with little capital employed. The goods produced were mostly agricultural. In the intervening decades, the economy has become a much more intensive user of skilled labour, capital, and mineral resources. A major share of output now comes from the mineral sector, but in addition there are substantial sectors which are capital and/or skill intensive.

The rapid growth and the structural transformation are not unrelated: changing stocks of factor inputs have changed the production possibilities of the economy. This result has not been simply accidental. In the process, key policy choices have had major influences on the outcomes.

This paper is concerned about Botswana's growth, structural transformation, and the connection between the two. First, the growth of inputs is reviewed, followed by consideration of the growth of outputs. Then, the changing shares of output are considered relative to the factor intensity of the sectors, to see how the changing structure of production relates to the factor intensity of production. This leads to a consideration of the relationship between inputs and outputs, namely productivity. Finally, some of the key policy choices which have influenced the results are reviewed.

Much of the data cited below only cover the national accounts years from 1974/75 through 1994/95.[1] This is because some key data sources do not provide the detail necessary to go back further. Nevertheless, the growth and structural transformation which it has been possible to document in this shorter period of two decades are sufficiently dramatic to point towards conclusions which cover the full three decades of independence.

2. GROWTH OF FACTOR INPUTS

There are several possible classifications which might be used to describe the factor inputs employed in any economy. By far the most common is the simple distinction between capital and labour. This is a useful start, but as will become evident, some

---

[1] The national income accounts use the year 1 July to 30 June.

further distinctions are critical in understanding the transformation of the Botswana economy.

Looking first of all at the growth of the labour force and the capital stock, the increase has been substantial. These two series for the period 1974/75 through 1993/94 are shown in Figure 1 – see the Appendix for details of construction of the series. Note especially that the capital stock has grown much faster than the labour force. While, the latter grew at an average rate of 2.76% per annum, which is rapid by most standards, the real capital stock was growing at 7.15% per annum. As a result, the capital intensity of production has increased dramatically.[2]

FIGURE 1. LABOUR FORCE AND CAPITAL STOCK, 1975 – 1995

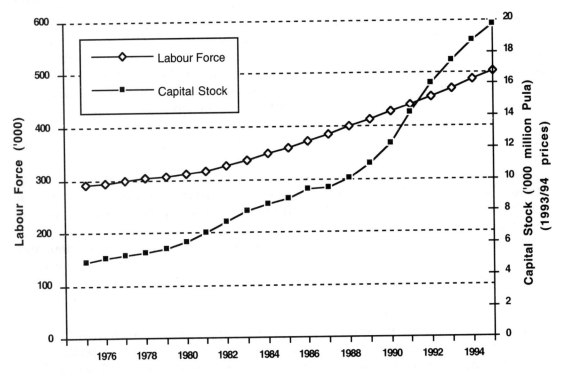

The change in the quality of the labour force over the period is also important. Precise measures are not easily constructed. However, Government spent heavily on improving access to education and health. This included heavy capital expenditure in the education and health sectors (which is incorporated in the capital stock data). Government recurrent spending on health and education (in constant prices) also grew rapidly, with health growing at 13% per annum and education at 16% per annum (see Figure 2).

The result of these expenditures may be seen in a variety of indicators. A useful

---

2   Although the capital intensity of production increased most dramatically over the past decade, the share of income going to capital has *not increased* (see Table 2). A forty percent factor share to capital is quite close to those found in many other economies around the world.

Figure 2. Health and Education: Recurrent Expenditure, 1974/75 to 1994/95, 1994/95 Prices

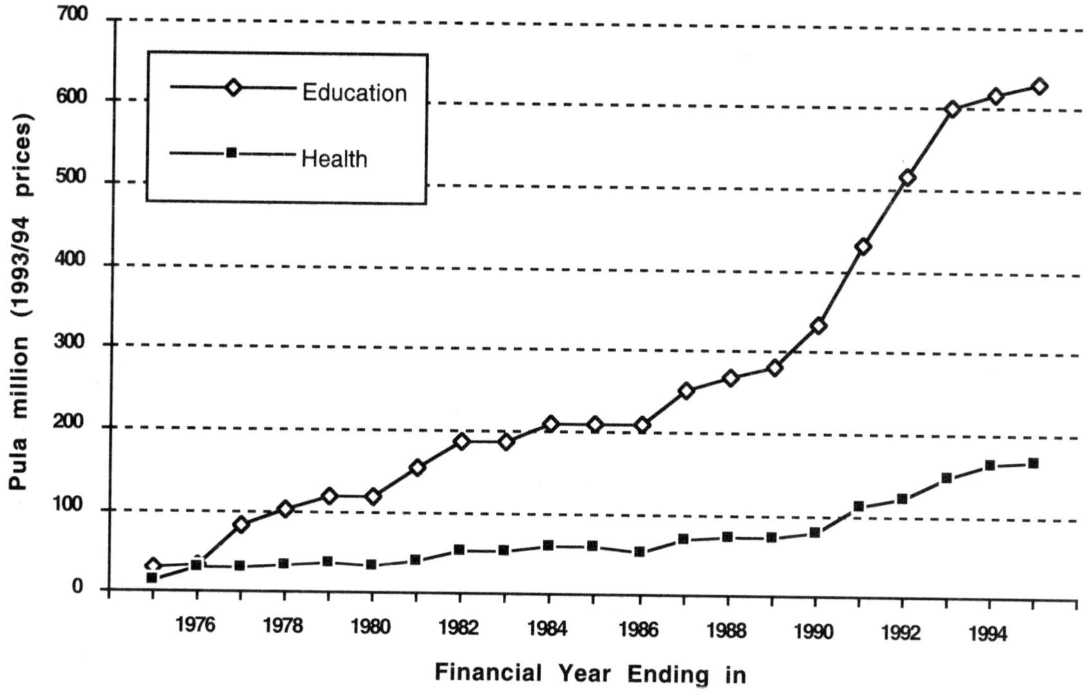

Table 1. Years of Educational Attainment, 1964–1991

Census Year	Years of Schooling
1964	1.46
1971	2.45
1981	3.11
1991	4.82

Source: author's calculations from *Population Censuses,* CSO.

summary indicator of the change in health status is life expectancy at birth, which has risen to 65 years, from 50 years in 1970. The education status of the population is measured every census year. From these data it is possible to construct an average years of education of the population aged 15 to 64. The results, in Table 1, show a substantial increase, with a more than tripling from 1964 to 1991. This is all the more dramatic when it is recognised that the improvements in the averages of health and education status were occurring while the working age population (aged 15 to 64) was also growing at 2.76% per annum.

3. Growth of Output

A rapid increase in both the quantity and quality of inputs, in the absence of significant declines in productivity, would yield very rapid growth of outputs. For much of the post-Independence period, growth of output was indeed very rapid. This is illustrated in terms of aggregate output in Figure 3, where real GDP over the two decades 1974/75 through 1994/95 is shown.[3]

However, not all sectors of the economy shared in the rapid growth. Looking first of

---

[3] The three year moving average growth rate is also shown, indicating a decline in recent years. We shall turn to this when we take up productivity issues below.

FIGURE 3. REAL GDP AND REAL GDP LESS MINERAL RENTS (1993/94 PRICES, PULA MILLION)

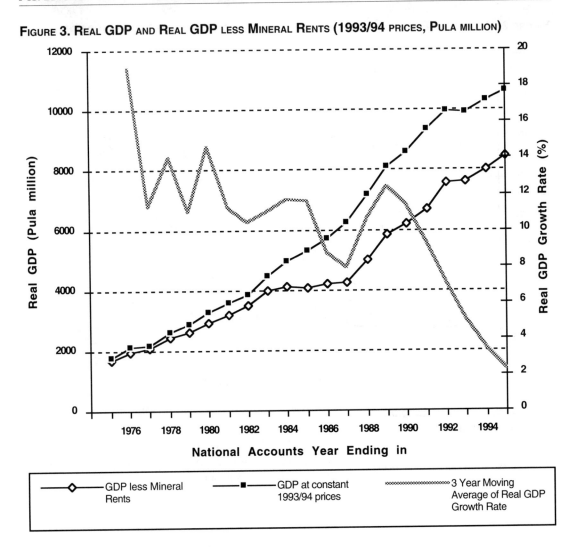

all at four critical sectors – agriculture, mining, manufacturing, and government – it is evident in Figure 4 that there was a dramatic shift in sectoral shares of GDP. Agriculture and mining effectively swapped places. Agriculture shrank from 32% of GDP in 1974/75 to just over 4% in 1994/95; while mining expanded from 8% to a peak of 53% in 1988/89 before shrinking to 33%. The share of manufacturing fluctuated, reflecting to a considerable extent the impact of drought on the rate of slaughter of cattle.[4] In the meantime, other manufacturing increased its share of sectoral output. Government, for its part, had taken an increasingly large role in the economy in recent years.

In addition to sectoral shares of output, the shares of the primary factors, labour and capital, may be calculated. However, part of the output of the mineral sector, as conventionally measured, includes mineral rents – the difference between the opportunity costs of the inputs and the value of the output. The rents are thus not attributable

---

4   To a certain extent at least, systems of indexation (such as variable interest rates) may be able to lead to the amelioration of some of the effects of inflation, most effectively when such inflation is properly anticipated.

FIGURE 4. SHARES OF GDP BY TYPE OF ECONOMIC ACTIVITY, SELECTED YEARS 1974/75 TO 1994/95

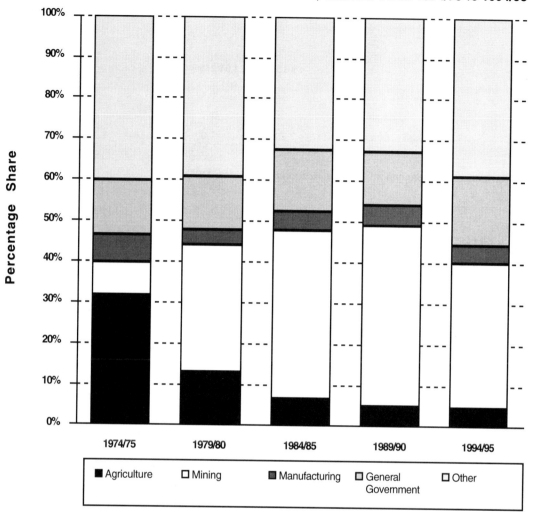

to labour or capital inputs. Hence, to look at primary input factor shares, the measure of output should exclude the mineral rents. Mineral revenues to Government have been used as an approximation of the mineral rents, and thus have been deducted from real GDP before calculating real output.[5] From the mid-1980s onwards, the difference between the measure of real output including and excluding mineral rents was significant (see Figure 3).

Having separated out the mineral rents, it is possible to compute the shares of primary factor payments. In doing so, it is useful to distinguish between shares going to skilled and unskilled labour as well as to capital. These are recorded in Table 2 for 1985/86 and 1992/93. What is notable is the increase in the share going to skilled labour, and the corresponding decline in the share of capital, while the share of unskilled labour remained virtually the same.

---

[5]   These are not in themselves arguments against inflation. The costs of reducing inflation would need to be compared to those of introducing 'inflation proof' tax systems.

TABLE 2. SHARES OF FACTOR PAYMENTS TO CAPITAL, SKILLED LABOUR, AND UNSKILLED LABOUR, 1985/86 AND 1992/93 (PERCENTAGE)

	1985/86	1992/93
CAPITAL	42.7	38.1
SKILLED LABOUR	36.5	41.7
UNSKILLED LABOUR	20.8	20.3

Source: Author's calculations from *Social Accounting Matrices,* CSO.

4. STRUCTURAL CHANGE AND FACTOR INTENSITIES

The various sectors of the Botswana economy differ sharply in the intensity of their use of the available primary factor inputs of capital, labour, land, and minerals. If we consider intensity of input use, in the sense that a sector uses relatively more of that input per unit of output than the average of all sectors, then we can rank the sectors by degree of input intensity. Obviously, mining is most intensive in the minerals factor, while agriculture is the most intensive in the land input. Government is by far the most labour intensive activity in the economy, with the share of compensation of employees running at about 65% of value added. Manufacturing has from one third to one half of its value added in compensation of employees. The public utilities are generally the most capital intensive.

Putting the changing share of output together with the factor intensity of the sectors, it is possible to see how the changing structure of production relates to the factor intensity of production. This is seen by considering the 'diamond' in Figures 5a and 5b, for which the four axes are shares of GDP in the activities which are capital

FIGURE 5A. 1974/75 PERCENTAGE SHARE OF GDP BY FACTOR INTENSITY

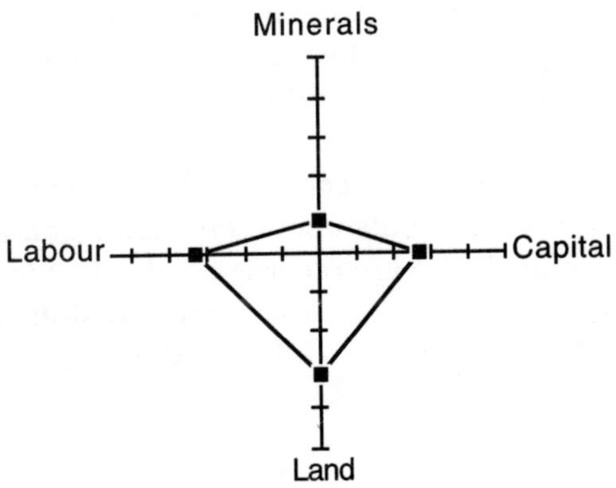

FIGURE 5B. 1994/95 PERCENTAGE SHARE OF GDP BY FACTOR INTENSITY

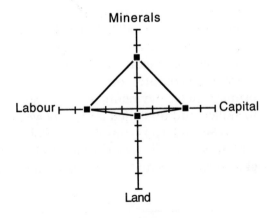

Note: the dimensions of each axis are 100% of GDP along both the vertical and horizontal axes.

intensive, labour intensive, land intensive, and minerals intensive.[6] The diamond for 1974/75 is shown in Figure 5a, while the diamond for 1993/94 is shown in Figure 5b. There has been a dramatic shift from land intensive to mineral intensive production. The Botswana economy has thus become relatively less concentrated on land intensive activities and much more concentrated on mineral resource intensive activities. There has been virtually no change between capital-intensive versus labour-intensive activities. The growing share of Government in the economy offsets the declining share of the construction and manufacturing sectors, all of which are labour intensive.

Total Factor Productivity

Having traced what has been happening to both inputs and outputs in recent decades, we now consider what has been happening to the relationship between inputs and outputs – i.e., productivity. The best overall measure of this is 'total factor productivity' (TFP) growth, which takes into account the fact that part of the increased output is attributable to increases in the various inputs. The TFP measure does this by calculating the gap between the rate of growth of output and the weighted average rate of growth of the inputs. Other measures, such as the incremental capital output ratio, do not take into account the effect of changes in other inputs. At the same time it should be recognised that the total factor productivity approach does not measure productivity directly, but rather as a residual.[7]

One issue encountered in measuring TFP growth in Botswana is that there is no measure of capacity utilization of the capital stock, or, until recently, no annual measure of unemployment. Thus, the measures reported here should be thought of as comparing actual output growth with growth of potential inputs. If we were able to adjust for underutilised inputs, such as unemployment of labour or underutilised capital, as long as these influences do not display a secular trend, there would be some year to year variation in the total factor productivity recorded below, but the overall trend of total factor productivity would remain much the same.

Inputs of labour, and similarly capital, are often treated as uniform or undifferentiated, implicitly assuming that each additional input is identical to all previous inputs of that factor. If, however, the composition of the labour force, or of the capital stock, is changing substantially over time, it is important to distinguish sub-categories of inputs. In the Botswana context, a significant part of the increased productivity recorded over the period to 1993/94 is due to improved quality of the labour force. One approach to sorting out the influence of the sub-categories of inputs is to divide the labour force between skilled and unskilled on the basis of whether or not the individuals had completed more than primary school. The factor shares of skilled versus unskilled labour reported in Table 2 permit a differentiation between the growth of the educated/skilled labour force and growth of the lesser educated/unskilled labour

---

6   The GDP share data are from the CSO, *National Income Accounts,* while the relative factor intensity data are from the CSO, *Social Accounting Matrices* for 1985/86 and 1992/93. There are no changes in relative factor intensity of sectors between the two years. The labour-intensive sectors are manufacturing, construction, trade hotels and restaurants, government, and social and personal services.

7   One consequence of this approach is that the measure of total factor productivity growth contains the errors of measurement of both the output and the inputs, which may be either compensating or offsetting.

force. Unfortunately, it has not been possible to carry out a similar exercise to incorporate the improved health status of the labour force or to differentiate different categories of capital. (For details of the calculations, see Appendix.)

The results of the TFP growth calculations are reported in Table 3. The picture over the two decades, 1974/75 to 1994/95, is reported in the final column. The real growth of GDP less mineral rents was 8.5% per annum. The average annual growth rates of the inputs of capital, skilled labour, and unskilled labour were 7.3%, 7.7% and 1.2%, respectively. The input shares (Table 2) can be used to calculate the weighted average growth rate of inputs of 6.3% per annum. This leaves a TFP growth rate of 2.2% per annum.

TABLE 3. TOTAL FACTOR PRODUCTIVITY GROWTH, 1974/5 TO 1993/4

	SHARE	GROWTH RATE 1974/75 TO 1984/85	GROWTH RATE 1984/85 TO 1994/95	GROWTH RATE 1974/75 TO 1994/95
REAL OUTPUT	1.000	9.4	7.6	8.5
CAPITAL STOCK	0.404	6.2	8.5	7.3
LABOUR FORCE	0.596	2.2	3.4	2.8
Skilled	0.391	6.9	8.5	7.7
Unskilled	0.205	0.9	1.6	1.2
TOTAL FACTOR PRODUCTIVITY GROWTH				
Undifferentiated Labour Force		5.6	2.6	3.8
Differentiated Labour Force		4.0	0.5	2.2

Source: Appendix.

The TFP growth rate for the two decades is similar to the rates sustained by very fast growing Asian countries over somewhat longer periods: Hong Kong (2.3% per annum, 1961–1991) and Taiwan (2.1% per annum, 1966–1990). Botswana's TFP growth of 2.2% per annum for the past two decades is thus certainly high by international standards.[8]

To see the importance of taking into account the differentiated labour force growth, the calculations can be redone simply using the rate of growth of the labour force as a whole in Table 3 of 2.8% per annum. This yields a TFP growth rate of 3.8% per annum. The difference between the two calculations may be interpreted as showing that the improved educational status of the labour force contributed on average 1.6% per annum to Botswana's growth rate.

Looking at the past two decades as a whole hides some significant variation over time. The yearly evolution of TFP growth (taking into account the differentiation of the

---

[8] The total factor productivity growth for Hong Kong and Taiwan are taken from A. Young (1995). 'The Tyranny of Numbers: Confronting the Statistical Realities of the East Asian Growth Experience', *Quarterly Journal of Economics* Vol.110 (August), pp641–680.

labour force between skilled and unskilled) is traced in Figure 6. Because of erratic annual swings in the series, the chart also shows a three year moving average. What is particularly notable is the decline of total factor productivity growth in the 1980s, followed by some recovery[9], and then a decline again in the 1990s. The decline in the 1980s reflects the fact that considerable infrastructure was being put in place without a corresponding immediate increase in real output.

Taking the period 1974/75 to 1984/85 (Table 3, column 2) as a whole reveals a remarkably rapid growth of total output of 9.4% per annum; all the more so when it is recalled that the measure of output excludes mineral rents. During this period, the capital stock grew at 6.2% per annum while the skilled labour force grew at 6.9% per annum, and the unskilled labour force at only 0.9% per annum. The resulting TFP growth rate for that decade was an exceptional 5.3% per annum.

The TFP growth data for the most recent decade (Table 3, column 3) show quite a different story. While the output growth rate, on average, was very rapid by international standards at 7.6% per annum, over 90% of that growth was brought about by increases in factor inputs of skilled labour, capital, and unskilled labour. Less than

FIGURE 6. TOTAL FACTOR PRODUCTIVITY GROWTH, 1975/76 TO 1994/95

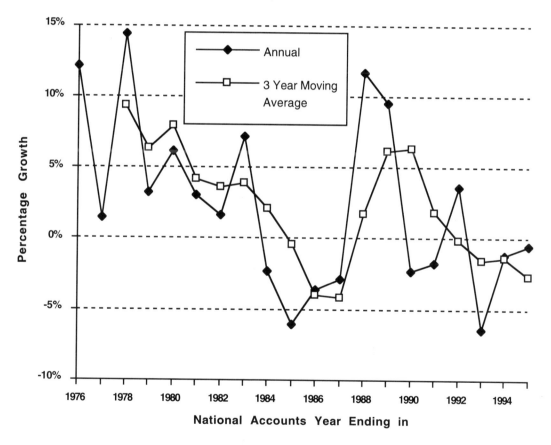

---

[9]   The sharp upward spike in 1987/88 is in part the result of the sale in July 1987 of the diamond stockpile which had been accumulated from 1982 to 1986 during which time production exceeded the sales quota. In addition, some subsequent discontinuities in diamond sales resulted in unusually large sales in 1988/89.

10% of the growth in output was attributable to increases in productivity.

5. INTER-RELATIONSHIPS AMONG GROWTH AND STRUCTURAL TRANSFORMATION

The foregoing analysis has shown that inputs of skilled labour and capital have grown very rapidly, yielding even more rapid growth of output. However, the contrast between the latest decade and the preceding decade is striking: from 1974/75 to 1984/85 productivity was growing very rapidly, while from 1984/85 to 1994/95 on average the rate of growth of productivity was much slower.

A careful look at the major shifts in share of GDP (Figure 4) reveals that the major change in the structure of the economy occurred in the earlier period (from 1974/75 to 1984/85), when the agricultural and the mineral sectors switched places in terms of shares of output. This had important implications for productivity growth. The economy was able to reduce sharply the share of output of a sector which is widely acknowledged as exhibiting, on average, very low productivity, namely agriculture. At the same time, there was a sharp increase in the share of output in the minerals sector which generally has high productivity (even after deducting the mineral rents).[10] This switch in itself contributed in a major way to the rapid growth of total factor productivity over the 1974/75 to 1984/85 decade.

The sectoral shift worked in the other direction however, in the decade from 1984/85 to 1994/95. The share of the economy attributable to the minerals sector actually *fell* from 1984/85 to 1994/95. Furthermore, during this decade, the share of Government in GDP rose. Since the calculation of Government in GDP involves measuring output by the value of the inputs, there is by definition *no* change in productivity in this sector. For both these reasons, the productivity gain arising from changes in sectoral composition which had contributed to the spectacular productivity growth of the earlier decade was not present in the later decade.

Another unique feature of the structural transformation was that it did not place undue pressure on scarce factor inputs. The big change, as shown in Figure 5, was from activities intensive in land to activities intensive in minerals. This reduced the share of land rents and increased the share of mineral rents, but it did very little to create pressures on the returns to other factors.

The major shortage associated with this exceptionally rapid growth was of some highly skilled workers which the economy was not able to produce fast enough. To meet the needs of the economy, reliance was placed on expatriate workers. Even into the 1990s, this was an important safety valve for the economy as non-Batswana accounted for 5.8% of formal sector employment in September 1995.[11]

---

[10] One measure of the absolute differences in productivity is sectoral GDP per employee. This can be calculated at census years, using sectoral employment from the census, and GDP per sector from the national income accounts. Such a comparison, reported in Bank of Botswana, *Annual Report, 1995*, Chart V.4, shows a dramatic difference between GDP per employee in agriculture and industry, with the latter approximately four times the former in 1991.

[11] CSO (1996).

6. POLICIES

Various policies contributed to the outcomes described above. It is convenient to think in terms of three different types of policies: (1) those which affected the supply of inputs; (2) those which affected the quality of inputs; and (3) those which affected the relationship between inputs and outputs, namely productivity.

7. SUPPLY OF INPUTS

The supply of inputs includes both primary factors, and various purchased goods and services. As shown in Figure 1, the most spectacular increase occurred in the capital stock. This was made possible through several related policies.

The openness of the Botswana economy was a major contributing factor in the rapid growth of the capital stock. The policy of remaining in SACU after Independence meant that Botswana was restrained from pursuing the extreme forms of import substituting industrialization which many other African countries followed in their post-Independence periods. In addition, the exchange rate policy pursued after the Pula was established as an separate currency in 1976, avoided the common pitfall of an overvalued currency and the associated shortage of imports. Together these policies meant that Botswana had an ample supply of imported investment goods available.

The rapid capital stock accumulation was financed initially by a combination of foreign direct investment and donor financing of major infrastructure projects, and later, to a substantial degree, by Government's own savings. Each of these sources required an appropriate policy thrust. The private foreign direct investment, mostly in the mineral sector, required policies which provided reasonable returns to both the foreign investor and the nation. Donor financing required careful cost-benefit analysis of major development projects, a willingness to commit to sound macroeconomic policies, and often required covenants which limited distortions, such as under-pricing of public utilities. Government's own savings were accumulated largely due to the continuation of disciplined spending, strongly guided by clear national development plans, in the face of exceptionally rapid growth of revenues, particularly mineral revenues.

The growth of the labour force was also affected by policy over the long run in various ways. Policies which improved health status, such as reduced infant mortality and increased life expectancy, directly increased the growth of the economically active population. Meanwhile, the lack of an aggressive population policy meant that the demographic transition to a lower birth rate, in light of the lower death rate, was slow in coming.

Policies concerning outflows and inflows of labour had a bearing on the size of the labour force at the margin. In the early post-Independence period, continuation of the policy of facilitating employment of Batswana in South African mines meant that the excess supply of labour was reduced. Later, as the mining sector developed in Botswana, some of these experienced miners returned home.

The policy of easing shortages of skilled labour by employing expatriates served to alleviate bottlenecks, and obviated the dissipation of mineral rents into quasi-rents for particular skills in short supply. In the short run this clearly worked. However, it also meant that the labour market was not putting out signals to bring about an alleviation of those shortages.

Government also acted in the early post-Independence period to facilitate the provision of essential services, such as housing, telephones, water, electricity and transportation, by setting up Government departments and/or parastatals. Such provisions were indeed indispensable to the rapid early growth of the economy. However, as the years passed, the lack of market discipline in the provision of some (but not all) of these services has imposed significant excess costs on the rest of the economy. Not only are their charges higher than necessary, but some have become bottlenecks due to delays in providing services or in the introduction of modern technologies.

8. QUALITY OF INPUTS

The major effect of policy on the quality of inputs has been the heavy investment in education and health which has yielded a substantial improvement in the health status and educational attainment of the labour force. As noted above, both recurrent and capital expenditures in these areas have been considerable.

In addition to the effect of policy on the quality of the labour force, somewhat more subtly, the lack of import restrictions and associated regulations has enabled Botswana to acquire the latest technology when purchasing imported capital equipment, and when attracting foreign investment. This benefit of an open economy policy has been offset to some extent by Botswana's membership in SACU. The restrictive tariff policy pursued by South Africa, particularly during the sanctions era, has meant that many of the durable goods available in Botswana have not been the most up to date technology.

9. PRODUCTIVITY

Productivity has been favourably affected in many parts of the Botswana economy by the policy of openness to foreign competition. Many sectors have had to face the discipline of foreign competition, either because they must compete by selling in international markets, or because their production must contend with foreign competition in the domestic market. As a consequence, they have had to achieve improvements in productivity in line with that occurring elsewhere in the world.

Other sectors of the economy, however, have not had to face such discipline, and as a consequence their productivity has lagged. This has been particularly true in those sectors which, for one reason or another, have been sheltered from foreign competition, including Government. In the latter case, as Government became less dependent on foreign donor financing for its development projects, the discipline of careful ex-ante cost benefit analysis of projects was muted. Marginal projects were approved, and when costs escalated, turning once high return projects into low or even negative return projects, the original approval was seldom re-evaluated.

Low productivity was not confined to the public sector. Marginal private sector projects were made feasible by the policy of negative real interest rates pursued from the mid-1980s through to the early 1990s. Overall then, the falling productivity of investment in protected sectors of the Botswana economy has been a major contributing factor to the decline in total factor productivity.

10. Conclusion

This review of Botswana's experience – of rapid economic growth over the first twenty-five years of Independence, followed by the somewhat slower growth in the 1990s – reveals a complex combination of influences at work. While the discovery and exploitation of mineral deposits was the initiating force, there were many other influences at work individually, and in combination with each other.

The opening up of major rich mineral deposits began the process. In turn, the capital stock and labour force grew very rapidly in both quantity and quality. These factor supply increases did not flow uniformly into all sectors of the economy. Following the increase in mineral output, the Government and service sectors were the major growth nodes, while in relative terms the agricultural sector declined. This combination meant that the major change in the factor intensity of the economy was simply the switch from one natural resource type of input, land, to another, mineral deposits. Readily available capital and labour did not constrain output growth either sectorally or in aggregate. Given the significant differences in absolute levels of productivity between sectors, (and substantial differences in productivity growth across sectors) the changes in composition of output had a dramatic effect on the total factor productivity growth.

Many of these changes were profoundly shaped by a wide-ranging set of policies which impacted on the economy. Policies contributed to the rapid growth by bearing on the quantity and quality of primary factors, the composition of output, the factor intensity of output, and the rate of growth of productivity in various sectors.

With the changing circumstances, however, the influence of a given set of policies is altered. Policies which are initially growth inducing, gradually became less effective in stimulating further growth. This occurred in several ways. For example, in the early years after Independence an expanding role for Government and its parastatal enterprises was undoubtedly growth-inducing, whereas in the present circumstances the opposite is almost certainly true. Similarly, in the early years high rates of investment in physical capital generated rapid economic growth because of the high productivity of those investments, whereas today such investment rates are yielding far less growth because of the low productivity of many of those investments. The future growth of the Botswana economy will thus depend critically on how the policies pursued in the past are altered to meet the changing circumstances.

Appendix: Factor Inputs and Output: Data Sources and Methods

1. Consider the inputs of capital, skilled labour, and unskilled labour, and output of GDP less mineral rents.

2. The capital stock series was derived employing a perpetual inventory approach, with additions via gross fixed capital formation and deductions from depreciation. Since there was not any benchmark capital stock measure, an initial capital to output ratio for 1974/75 of 2.72, equal to South Africa's for 1975, was assumed. Gross fixed capital formation and depreciation in current prices were drawn from the Central Statistics Office, national income accounts, and deflated using the GDP deflator, as a consistent deflator for the components was not available for the entire period.

TABLE A1. FACTOR INPUTS AND OUTPUT, 1974/75 TO 1994/95 (1985/86 PRICES)

NATIONAL ACCOUNTS YEAR ENDING IN	GDP (PULA MILLION)	GDP LESS MINERAL RENTS (PULA MILLION)	CAPITAL STOCK (PULA MILLION)	LABOUR FORCE (PERSONS)	SKILLED LABOUR (PERSONS)	UNSKILLED LABOUR (PERSONS)
1975	746	706	2 029	290 844	46 906	242 568
1976	888	823	2 134	294 812	49 690	243 657
1977	919	870	2 229	298 833	52 640	244 752
1978	1 098	1 024	2 283	302 909	55 765	245 851
1979	1 207	1 104	2 405	307 041	59 075	246 955
1980	1 380	1 232	2 579	311 230	62 581	248 065
1981	1 511	1 347	2 831	315 475	66 296	249 179
1982	1 624	1 475	3 126	326 236	71 904	253 151
1983	1 884	1 683	3 386	337 365	77 986	257 186
1984	2 101	1 739	3 558	348 873	84 583	261 286
1985	2 252	1 725	3 700	360 773	91 738	265 451
1986	2 421	1 774	3 954	373 080	99 499	269 683
1987	2 636	1 799	4 016	385 806	107 915	273 981
1988	3 039	2 116	4 238	398 966	117 044	278 349
1989	3 437	2 476	4 644	412 576	126 945	282 786
1990	3 634	2 627	5 192	426 649	137 683	287 294
1991	3 955	2 837	5 978	441 203	149 330	291 873
1992	4 210	3 195	6 775	456 253	161 962	296 526
1993	4 196	3 223	7 389	471 817	175 662	301 253
1994	4 366	3 395	7 913	487 911	190 521	306 055
1995	4 502	3 578	8 353	504 554	206 638	310 934

3. The labour inputs were derived using the labour force from the population census of 1964, 1981, and 1991. The intervening years were interpolated, using the annual growth rate. For the years 1992 to 1995, the growth rate of the decade to 1991 was assumed to continue. The 1971 census data were not used because of significant under-enumeration.

4. The unskilled proportion of the population at each census was taken as a proxy for the proportion of the labour force. Those who never attended school, and who did not complete primary school were classed as unskilled, and the remainder treated as skilled.

5. The output series was GDP less Government's mineral revenues, deflated using the GDP deflator. GDP and its deflator were from the CSO, national income accounts, and while mineral revenues were from MFDP, *Financial Statements, Tables and Estimates of Consolidated and Development Fund Revenues.*

6. The factor shares were from the CSO, *Social Accounting Matrix*, 1985/86 and 1992/93. In calculating the factor shares, the mineral revenues noted in paragraph 5 above were deducted from the net operating surplus of the mining sector.

REFERENCES

Bank of Botswana. *Annual Report, 1995.*
Central Statistics Office. December 1996. *Employment 1995.*
Central Statistics Office. *National Income Accounts*, various years.
Central Statistics Office. *Social Accounting Matrix, 1985/86*, and *1992/93.*
Young, A. 1995. The Tyranny of Numbers: Confronting the Statistical Realities of the East Asian Growth Experience', *Quarterly Journal of Economics*, Vol.110 (August), pp641–680.

Botswana's Boom and Recession Experience: A Discussion

N. Gaolathe

1. INTRODUCTION

Many authors attest to Botswana's rapid economic expansion since 1966. There were, in particular, waves of mining and construction booms during the periods 1965–69, 1969–74 and 1978–81. The first boom owed its character to Government's construction of offices and residential houses when Botswana's capital was established in Gaborone in 1965. Later, the development of the Selebi-Phikwe mine and town and the Orapa diamond mine and town during 1969–74 helped induce an average annual GDP growth of 22%. The building of Jwaneng mine and town followed, and between 1978 and 1981 GDP grew by an annual average of 11% (Harvey and Lewis, 1990).

There were, during this process of vast economic transformation, episodes of more modest growth. 1974–78 was one such period: GDP grew by an average of 8% while non-mineral GDP grew by 2%. Later, the 1981 recession came as a surprise, prompting the Government to effect austerity measures so as to cope with declining diamond exports. The accumulation of diamond stock piles between 1981 and 1986 meant that the 11.6% growth rate during that period exaggerated the modest economic conditions (Harvey and Lewis, 1990).

Despite the numerous episodes of prosperity, for many people 1987–1991 stands out as a true boom period, as non-mining per capita incomes expanded at consistently rapid rates. Although many factors contributed to the boom, its origins are clearly traceable to the robust Government capital expenditures, resulting mainly from the high diamond revenues. The boom, therefore, owed part of its bubble character to the unsustainable growth patterns of capital expenditures during 1987, 1988 and 1989.

The sluggish demand for diamonds, Botswana's most valuable commodity, due to economic recession among industrialised nations, worked in concert with other less discussed factors in depressing Botswana's economy during 1992–94. Among other factors contributing to the recession were: slower growth in Government expenditure; the depressed high cost property market, the effects of which are likely to have depressed aggregate demand; and the erosion of Botswana's textile market in Zimbabwe.

It is the intention of this paper, in the second section, to provide a general background of experiences in, and ideas on, economic fluctuations. Section 3 makes a claim that there was a boom and a recession during the latter part of the 1980s and the early 1990s respectively; it provides common sense arguments based on the unusual GDP growth rates, exceptional unemployment rates and actual versus potential

GDP trends. The section also summarises some of the main features of this boom and recession period and incorporates other analyses of the period.

The fourth section chronicles some of the major economic currents of modern day Botswana, and so provides a basis for speculating on what the origins of the boom and the recession were. The boom and the recession seem have been attributable to numerous factors. The fifth section discusses several potential causes of the boom and identifies Government's expansionary fiscal policy during the period as a key element in the fluctuation. The conclusion generalises some lessons to be learned from this experience.

2. THEORETICAL CONCEPTS

As an explanation of economic fluctuations, Hatrew and others proposed that it is low interest rates and credit expansions that spark general booms (Medio, 1987). They argued that cheap money prompts producers, dealers and consumers to increase expenditures. As incomes rise, an 'excitement' erupts, dealers accumulate inventories with the hope of increased sales, and this encourages producers to produce more. For Hatrew, as inventories accumulate and production rises, money demand grows slower than incomes and for that reason the credit expansion continues. However, as soon as the demand for money catches up with increasing incomes and the resultant fall in bank liquidity bids up interest rates, credit falls and sparks a downward process that in turn cuts incomes. This in turn leads to a rise in liquidity and hence a repetition of the boom – bust process.

Keynes (1987) observed that there are different types of booms. He believed that excessive foreign investments and credit booms were by their nature temporary and may, under certain circumstances, lead to a slump. Although he advocated public spending during slumps, he realised that, alone, such spending could not be a cure. The debate on how to mitigate recessions has since escalated, with some economists advocating expansionary policies and others cautioning against any intervention.

For other economists, an explanation of the business cycle lies with the activity of entrepreneurs. Wicksell and Schumpeter argued that growth occurred in lumps rather than smoothly (Medio, 1987). Popular innovations come about haphazardly, and when they do come they spark boom periods.

Lucas (1977) provides another definition of the business cycle when he talks of 'repeated fluctuations in employment, output, and the composition of output, associated with a certain typical pattern of co-movements in prices and other variables'. Their qualitative features are manifested in the co-movement of output, prices and employment, showing a positive movement during booms and a negative one during recessions. According to him, technology and tastes underlie changes in relative prices which in turn are the driving forces of sectoral fluctuations. He concluded that money supply changes, which induce general price changes, are the root cause of general economic fluctuations.

In his review of the debate that surrounds the depression in the United States in the 1930s, Calomiris (1993) brings a new dimension to the business cycle debate when he discusses allocative effects of capital market imperfections and links between financial disruptions and economic activity. He echoes Friedman's sentiments that the Federal Reserve and its contractionary monetary policy may have precipitated the Great Depression.

Unlike in industrialised countries, discussion of cyclical episodes among developing countries is more commonly related to commodity booms and busts. A commodity boom refers to exceptional performance of a particular commodity usually in the export sector. In some cases, this sector may be a large component of total national output so that the commodity boom automatically translates into significantly greater output for the economy as a whole. If all the proceeds from the sector were saved abroad and not spent locally and other sectors not affected, then this would not really be an economic boom in the cycle sense. It turns out, however, that such exceptional performance in any sector usually affects positively consumer and producer expectations of future incomes and hence expenditure and consumption patterns. Through other linkages, a commodity boom usually leads to an economic boom – a state where actual output exceeds potential output.

The 1960s and 1970s were particularly turbulent periods characterised by cyclical episodes across many countries. The *1991 World Development Report* refers to two distinct but related types of booms, one with internal origins and the other with external origins. The first type came about due to high but unsustainable government expenditures. The effects of the boom depended on whether the additional expenditures were mostly directed towards consumption or investment goods. The usual reason for unsustainable expenditure by a government is its inability to distinguish between temporary windfalls and permanent increases in export earnings. Permanent increases in earnings imply that a government can sustain higher expenditures, so that there was no real danger of economic collapse except, perhaps, in isolated markets that need readjustment in accordance with demand and supply pressures.

The boom with external origins is not much different from the first type, except that it may occur without government involvement. The booming (export) sector expands in accordance with exogenously determined fortunes. The local currency appreciates with increasing exports and induces higher relative prices in favour of non-tradeables. Foreign goods become cheaper and the incentive to manufacture tradeables, domestically, is eroded. This is commonly referred to as the 'Dutch Disease'.

If there was a single reason and a single cure for recessions, they would hardly persist as they do. However, economies are different, and so are factors that produce fluctuations in them. It is interesting to attempt to relate Botswana to some of the alternative ideas expressed in the previous paragraphs.

3. WAS THERE A BOOM AND A RECESSION?

It is the opinion of the author that the periods 1987 to 1991 and 1992 to 1994 were, respectively, periods of unusually rapid and slow economic growth in Botswana. There is evidence that, between 1987 and 1991, for GDP, non-mineral GDP and formal employment, swings in growth rates surpassed those experienced earlier in the decade. Moreover, there were signs that actual output exceeded potential output and that literally, every sector was buoyant. This was a particularly prosperous period for the household sector.

During the late 1980s, complaints of economic stagnation or lack of opportunities were hard to come by in the local newspapers. This changed in the early 1990s when Government was often kept on the defensive about its policies by a population plagued by economic uncertainty. The strong showing of opposition parties at the 1994 elections was no surprise. Real GDP, GDP per capita and the level of formal sector employment were all estimated to have fallen during 1992/93. The decline in GDP was mostly due to the low diamond sales.

Actual output and employment

Total GDP and non-mineral GDP grew during 1987 and 1988 by 15.3% and 26.1%, respectively; the related per capita growth figures were 11.2% and 21.6% (see Figure 1). The growth in non-mineral GDP was the highest ever in Botswana. While at times aggregate growth was similarly high, the first half of the 1980s did not constitute a boom. Such growth as did occur was driven mainly by the fortunes of the mineral sector: for example, in 1982/83 when growth overall was 16%, non-mining GDP actually contracted by 3.1%. It was during this time that the depressed aggregate demand was recovering from the 1981 recession and when the drought impeded much agricultural activity and, due to water shortages, slowed down construction work.

FIGURE 1. GDP GROWTH, 1982/83 TO 1994/95

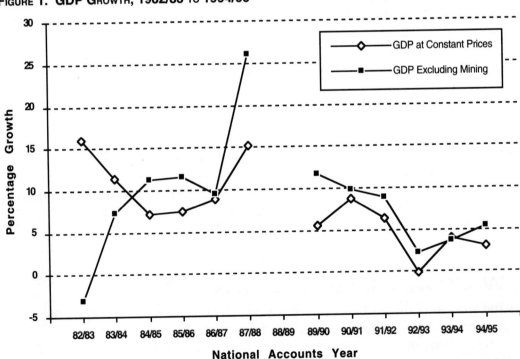

Note: 1988/89 growth rates not available due to re-basing of national accounts data starting that year.

Source: Ministry of Finance and Development Planning, *Annual Economic Report 1996.*

Figure 2. Formal Sector Employment, 1980 to 1995

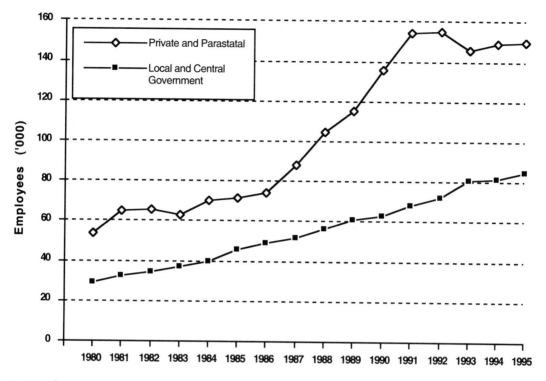

Actual output versus potential output

Potential output is that output realised at normal rates of capacity utilization and employment. The level of employment during 1987–91 significantly surpassed that experienced earlier during the 1980s (see Figure 2). There was no evidence of idle capacity in any sectors during the 1987–91 period. The existence of demand pressures were evident: for example, there were long order waiting lists in the vehicle and building sub-sectors. This may serve as an indirect indication of an associated high capacity utilization. The output of the economy probably exceeded the output that would have been realised under normal employment and capacity utilization conditions.

But in 1992/93 real GDP declined by 0.1%; imports declined in real terms during 1991/992; private sector employment fell by about 6% from 155 300 employees in 1992 to 145 500 employees in 1993. The suspension of building projects by the Botswana Housing Corporation resulted in a relatively idle construction sector. Textile exports to Zimbabwe fell dramatically. Waiting lists in car purchase were hard to come by. Although there is no data on potential output, the early 1990s carried the characteristics of an economy whose actual output was below its potential.

Household credit

Another manifestation of the boom was the consumer credit explosion during 1988–92. The household sector commanded a progressively higher percentage of all loans during the late 1980s. Households accounted for 39% of all loans during 1990 versus 16% in 1982 and 18% in 1986. Average credit growth exceeded 50% during 1988,

1989 and 1990. Expenditure was mainly on consumer durables – vehicles and household luxuries. The retail business flourished.

The property market

Speculation in, and development of, high cost property became a major preoccupation for the well off, particularly local senior employees of Government and major corporations. Rentals and property values rose rapidly between the mid-1980s and 1990: 'rentals of P2000 per month were not uncommon for an ordinary three bedroomed house, which could cost P100 000 to buy or build in 1986. By 1990, the same house could easily fetch P4000 per month in rent, or be valued at P250 000' (Nteta, 1996). But, by 1993, cases of default on loans and repossessions emerged and became more serious in 1994 and 1995. House prices and rentals plummeted.

Some reasons given for boom and recession

It is the opinion of Government that the boom 'was overwhelmingly due to the revenues from diamond exports, in large measure a windfall gain' (Government of Botswana, 1991); and that Government expenditure and lending were the avenues via which windfall gains were transmitted to the rest of the economy. In his 1993 Budget Speech, the Vice President and Minister of Finance and Development Planning attributed the subsequent recession to the depressed diamond market and the prevailing drought conditions in the region.

Leith (1994) identifies the economic slow down in industrial countries and the subsequent fall in prices of minerals as a contributor to the recession in Botswana. According to Leith, the high Government expenditures of the late 1980s were unsustainable and other factors, such as declining productivity growth and high public sector wages, acted as catalysts to the 1992/93 recession.

4. SOME MAJOR ECONOMIC EVENTS OF THE 1980s

This section is composed of two parts which chronicle some of the main economic currents from the early 1980s to the early 1990s. The first part suggests: firstly, that Botswana's leaders, unlike many of their neighbours, were inclined towards a free market economy, and that both Government and household priorities are different from those of the past; and, secondly, that there were several problem areas during the first part of the 1980s, some of which authorities were concerned about. The second part traces several features of fiscal and monetary policy measures during the period under discussion, and summarises some sectoral developments and international economic trends.

The general picture

The changing Botswana

There are several matters worth noting about the 1980s. One of them is that policy makers, notably those who served on the several Presidential Commissions appointed throughout the 1980s to address the problems of the day, were inclined towards free market solutions. Such an inclination supported the views of leading politicians in Government.

Another feature of the 1980s was Government's departure from past priorities of the 'basics', i.e., water, shelter, food and primary health. Vague references to industrialization became more practical and within reach, as were Government's attempts to encourage the private sector, particularly manufacturing.

Thus monetary policy was initially tailored to render imports affordable, especially for the less well-off, by keeping the Pula exchange rate strong. By the mid-1980s, however, policy-makers talked much about the need for a competitive non-traditional sector; this led to discussions about the use of the exchange rate to foster a competitive non-traditional sector although this sentiment seems not to have been pursued aggressively. However, during the early 1990s, authorities devalued the Pula several times, despite the increasing inflation at the time; the resolve to encourage the non-traditional sector was growing.

The early 1980s

Botswana's rapid growth of the late 1970s and early 1980s, induced mainly by mineral sales and investment on the development of infrastructure towards the new Jwaneng diamond mine, came to an end in 1981, at the outset of the world recession. GDP per capita, exports, imports and several sectors declined during 1981 and 1982. Government's response to the world economic climate was immediate and entailed real cuts in expenditure, mandatory credit ceilings on commercial bank lending, devaluation of the local currency by 10% and an increase in the prime lending rates.

Despite the overall annual economic growth of 5% during 1981–86, the economy was beset by difficulties. These included drought, lack of serviced land, increased interest rates (until 1986) and relatively modest household and business expectations after the 1981 experience. As regards drought, according to National Development Plan 7 (NDP 7), 'The six consecutive years of drought from 1981 to 1987 were the worst sequence since the early 1920s (Government of Botswana, 1991). Garden watering and car washing were, occasionally, prohibited; and water shortages hampered construction activity. The performance of agriculture, a preoccupation for the majority of the population, was dismal, and output declined in 1982, 1983 and 1984.

In the 1980s, the population of Gaborone and incomes were growing at a faster pace than the Government was able to provide serviced land for housing and business requirements. Government admitted on numerous occasions that lack of serviced land was a major constraint to development. This contributed to the skyrocketing of rentals. Government's conduct in the provision of serviced land reflected little or no sense of urgency whatever, and however legitimate the reason was for the Government's complacency, it would end with a rushed land servicing programme during the late 1980s.

A notably restrictive policy in the provision of housing was a clause in the Building Societies Act that limited the Botswana Building Society's lending activities to urban centres only. It was not until April 1986 that the Parliament amended the law to accommodate lending facilities to rural areas. This would later contribute towards the construction boom, especially of residential property in the villages around Gaborone.

As from 1982, excess liquid funds in the banking system posed a major headache for the authorities. The reason for the excess liquidity was that diamond revenues by far exceeded the absorptive capacity of households and non-mineral business sectors. Also, capital account restrictions limited the flow of capital towards investment opportunities outside Botswana, while the largest borrowers, the parastatals, sourced capital from the Government's Public Debt Service Fund.

Some monetary developments

Interest rates and the banking system

Real interest rates for lending in Botswana hovered at about zero percent during the first half of the 1980s, but became increasingly negative as from 1986 until 1991. They returned to positive levels in 1991, and have been close to zero percent throughout the 1990s.

The increase in interest rates in 1982 was meant to curb the demand for imports. Interest rates were progressively decreased from 1984 to 1988 in an attempt to stimulate the economy, although in 1984 and 1985 this was largely offset by declines in the rate of inflation.

In 1986, the Bank of Botswana introduced a set of measures intended to ease credit and hence jump-start the economy. Although maximum lending rates could not exceed 15%, commercial banks could now, in consultation with the Bank of Botswana, set their own interest rates. The Bank of Botswana reduced the Bank Rate from 9.0% to 8.5%, while the call rate for commercial banks remained 3.5%. Foreign-owned companies were better placed to source funds locally. Most other interest rates were also reduced. The Government increased its guarantee on citizen housing loans in 1986, and coverage was expanded in February 1990 when a guarantee scheme on commercial loans was also introduced.

In response to the 1986 policy measures, excess liquidity fell initially, but surged again in 1987. This was mainly a result of the vibrant world diamond market which enabled the sale of accumulated diamond stocks. At the same time, low interest rates, predictably, started to encourage spending on unproductive investments.

By 1989, interest rates were on the rise as there was a resolve to return to positive real rates to encourage a more efficient allocation of resources between consumption and investment. The subsequent introduction of Bank of Botswana Certificates in 1991, hindered first by the accelerating inflation in 1991 and 1992, 'has proved to be an effective instrument for absorbing the excess liquidity' (Leith, 1994). Indeed, interest rates on the Certificates attained positive levels of between one and two percent from 1993 and onwards.

Exchange Rate management

Botswana's real exchange rate with the South African Rand was kept 'very stable' during the 1980s (Harvey, 1995). However, the rapid depreciation of the Rand against world currencies during the period caused the Botswana Pula also to depreciate against those currencies. The Pula did, however, appreciate, in nominal terms, against regional currencies, including the South African Rand.

Most authors on Botswana's economic experience agree that Botswana circumvented the 'Dutch Disease', but Love (1994) and Mogotsi (1996) question this conclusion. Love argues that the decline of the arable sub-sector was the result of the Pula's appreciation against the South African Rand; Mogotsi suggests that without Government's Financial Assistance Policy (FAP), Botswana may have felt the effects of the 'Dutch Disease', especially in the manufacturing sector which is the primary benefi-ciary of FAP assistance.

Inflation in Botswana is believed to be imported from South Africa where Botswana derives most of its manufactured goods and food. Botswana's openness as an economy has rendered the exchange rate policy an important policy tool in controlling inflation.

When, in 1976, Botswana attained monetary independence from the South African dominated Common Monetary Area, the local currency was pegged, like the South African Rand, to the US Dollar. South Africa's decision to de-link the Rand from the Dollar in 1979 caused instability between the Rand and the Pula. This prompted authorities to peg the Pula against a basket of currencies.

The Pula was revalued in April 1977, September 1979 and in November 1979. Botswana's almost total dependence on South Africa for food means that its poorest citizens are the ones most reliant on imports because of the high food content in their consumption basket. The revaluations were, therefore, intended to favour the less well off. It is believed that the first revaluation was a major success; inflation in Botswana declined to be significantly lower than that of South Africa. The other two revaluations had only a modest impact (Harvey, 1995).

The first devaluation came about in 1982 as part of the austerity measures geared at slashing imports in accordance with the reduced export revenues. There is a possi-bility, as Mogotsi (1996) suggests, that the devaluation was overdue given the Pula's consistent appreciation against the Rand since 1980. The Pula was devalued again, by 15%, in 1985.

The Pula was revalued by 5% in 1989 and again in 1990. The Pula continued to appreciate rapidly against the Zimbabwe Dollar as that currency was devalued as part of Zimbabwe's structural adjustment programme, prompting a further 5% de-valuation of the Pula in September 1991. Inflation surged following the latter devaluation reaching nearly 18% in 1992 from levels of around 10% in 1989. Leith (1994) argues that the devaluation contributed to the high inflation.

Fiscal Policy (the late 1980s)

Time series data between 1973 and 1995 (see Table 1) reveal that the Government experienced budget deficits up to 1979 as well as during 1981 and 1982 at the time of a recession. The rest of the period was characterised by budget surpluses and, in-deed, while nations world wide sought ways to raise their revenues, Botswana did not spend a good share of its annual revenues. Government spending continued to be an important policy instrument for economic management in the Botswana economy. This was both at the aggregate level and through the way Government expenditure patterns in the 1980s differed with that of earlier periods.

Soon after 1982, the phenomenal rise in diamond revenues, most of which accrued to Government, meant that revenues persistently grew faster than Government ex-penditure. The overall budget surplus, for instance, grew by 83.6% and by 120.1% during 1983/84 and 1984/85, respectively. Revenue was never such a constraint to additional expenditure during the 1980s as was the Ministry of Finance and Develop-ment Planning's commitment to sustainable budgeting and manpower capacity considerations.

Harvey (1992) applauds Botswana's history of fiscal discipline, but raises fears that Government development expenditures may have been 'out of control' during the 1987–90 period. Government expenditure grew exceptionally during 1986/87, 1987/88 and 1988/89 by an annual growth of more than 40% during each of the three years. Harvey points out that actual expenditures, for the first time, exceeded planned expenditures during this period. He suggests that the Ministry of Finance and Development Planning was unable to contain expenditures in accordance with capacity considerations. Leith (1996) refers to Government's budget experience during 1987–90 as a 'huge development expenditure programme'.

Prior to the 1980s, the largest share of Government development funds were channelled towards roads. Although education had always been a major component of Government expenditure, this became more prominent in the late 1980s. During some of the years in the late 1980s, however, the largest share of development expenditures went towards the Accelerated Land Servicing Programme. This stands in contrast with the meagre amounts devoted to land servicing during the first half of the 1980s.

Of the 1986–90 budget experience, Hudson (1991) expresses an opinion that budget ceilings of NDP 6 (1985–91) were based on incorrect variables that were fed into Botswana's macroeconomic model. Of particular importance for Hudson was the sale of diamond stockpiles in 1987: 'the failure in 1985 of the mining economists to predict that the stockpile would be sold during the plan period means that mineral revenue was badly under-forecast. This led to a host of errors.'

TABLE 1. GOVERNMENT EXPENDITURE AND BUDGET BALANCE, 1974–1995 (PULA MILLION)

FISCAL YEAR	TOTAL SPENDING AND NET LENDING	BUDGET SURPLUS	DE (TS AND NL) (%)
1973/74	61.40	−13.40	49.3
1974/75	73.24	−5.48	44.8
1975/76	89.26	−2.20	39.0
1976/77	108.09	−20.73	34.8
1977/78	123.02	−5.44	36.1
1978/79	172.20	−5.69	46.0
1979/80	228.04	21.07	43.1
1980/81	308.36	−1.73	39.4
1981/82	341.36	−18.74	33.0
1982/83	414.76	−21.03	38.7
1983/84	460.12	102.93	30.6
1984/85	614.71	188.21	34.0
1985/86	719.18	414.70	34.4
1986/87	1 008.21	539.32	40.1
1987/88	1 312.01	513.02	42.5
1988/89	1 787.52	768.50	44.6
1989/90	2 214.69	536.46	37.4
1990/91	2 942.69	798.02	37.0
1991/92	3 372.20	697.23	32.6
1992/93	3 770.95	881.30	32.0
1993/94	4 481.16	878.30	34.8
1994/95	4 276.84	195.65	32.2

Note: DE (TS and NL) (%) = Development expenditure as a proportion of total spending and net lending (%).

It may be, however, that the Ministry of Finance and Development Planning deliberately augmented expenditures, especially development expenditures, in the light of the diamond windfall in 1986. Also, the growing complexity of the economy may have warranted a departure from manpower planning considerations in favour of a more liberal budget system increasingly determined only by revenue considerations.

Another notable feature in Government expenditure during the late 1980s was the changed share of current and development expenditure in total Government expenditure. Development expenditure's share in total Government expenditure and net lending oscillated between 30% and 50% (see table 1) during the 1973–1995 period: it was particularly pronounced during 1973/74, 1978–80 and 1986–89, all of which were periods of high GDP growth.

Sectoral developments

The expansion of sectors in Botswana has not been uniform over the years – more so during the earlier periods of development than the later periods. This is not surprising given that the base from which the economy grew during the 1960s and 1970s was low. The rapid expansion of Botswana's economy during the 1970s and early 1980s was attributable to several major projects, related mainly to mining. There were also a handful of projects in the provision of basic amenities and services, as well as trading in goods imported mainly from South Africa.

The manufacturing sector provides an interesting case of evolution. Meat processing's share of manufacturing (dominated by the operations of the Botswana Meat Commission) declined from 90% in the 1960s, to 40% during 1970s, 17% in 1987/88, and to less that 13% in 1992/93 according to the Social Accounting Matrix (SAM) produced for that year.

Initially, this decline resulted largely from the setting up of a brewery in 1975, and then from the establishment of a textile industry in the early 1980s.[1] By 1987, chemicals, dairy, agro-processing industries and metal industries had become important. The latter supplied material to the then booming construction industry. Subsequently, a rejuvenated textiles sub-sector and vehicle assembly plants have developed.

FAP, started in 1982, boosted local effort in manufacturing through, among other things, its subsidies towards the hiring of unskilled labour. Mogotsi (1996) emphasises FAP's role in manufacturing during the 1980s and suggests that without the policy, manufacturing may not have fared as well. Formal manufacturing firms were about 209 in 1984 (Harvey and Lewis, 1990), and the number of firms increased by 475 between 1985 and 1990 (Government of Botswana, 1991). By 1994 textiles had replaced meat processing as the most important employer in manufacturing.

After major growth in activity during the late 1970s and early 1980s due to the development of mining and other infrastructure, construction was suppressed by drought conditions during the early to mid-1980s. Even then, smaller local firms came into being to act as sub-contractors for the larger foreign owned firms and to engage in smaller scale construction work. Construction costs grew at exorbitant rates during the late 1980s; and it was during this time that numerous construction companies emerged. Costs were checked during the early 1990s when Government liberalised conditions for contract-bidding. The result was an influx of 'Chinese' firms.

The international scene

Economic growth in industrial countries slowed, from 3.3% in 1989 to 2.5% in 1990 and to 0.8% in 1991 (World Bank, 1991). Prospects of recovery came in 1992 when

---

[1]   During the early 1980s manufacturers based in Zimbabwe relocated to Botswana for export to Zimbabwe. More than 74% of textile exports at that time were destined for the Zimbabwean market.

growth in industrial economies rebounded to about 1.5% per annum. It seems, therefore, that Botswana's diamond revenues, which are closely linked to the world economy, were threatened as early as 1990.

South Africa's economy experienced difficulties as early as 1987. The economic sanctions against South Africa in protest against the apartheid regime contributed to the economic decline. In Zimbabwe, the Government resorted to IMF prescribed structural adjustments in an effort to revive the country's economy. The Zimbabwe Dollar was devalued dramatically, effectively making Botswana's exports uncompetitive in that market.

5. What Were the Causes of the Boom?

The boom

The common and, indeed, plausible explanation of the origins of the boom is that it was fuelled by the rapid, and somewhat unexpected, rise in diamond revenues. The subsequent economic decline was identified with the world recession in 1992.

Why then is it that the boom only materialised after some four to five years (since 1982) of persistently rapid growth in diamond revenues? Maybe that was just the right amount of time required for investors and consumers to regain confidence in the economy – maybe there were many other important factors involved in fuelling the boom.

The boom was a result of the convergence of stimulative factors in the economy. First, was the rapidly growing Government expenditure, especially on development projects during 1987–89; second, were monetary policy developments with falling interest rates and appreciation of the Pula *vis-à-vis* the South African Rand; third, was the ending of a drought period, providing scope for a previously suppressed construction sector; fourth, were the effects of other Government policies such as FAP and credit guarantees; and fifth, were the confidence and expectations of prosperity among businesses and households.

Government expenditure

The origins of the boom can be levelled at Government expenditure patterns of the 1980s. First, the magnitude and the annual growth rate of the Government budget were especially high during the latter half of the 1980s. Secondly, expenditures were increased abruptly in favour of development spending. This happened against a background of an economy fully recovered from the 1981 recession.

It has been convincingly argued by other authors that Government expenditure is pivotal in Botswana's economy. Government expenditure and net lending exceeded 30% of GDP throughout the 1980s. It is also accepted that the diamond windfalls of 1986 occasioned significant rises in both recurrent and development spending during 1986/1987, 1987/88 and 1988/89. This augmented aggregate demand in the economy.

The composition of expenditure changed significantly in 1986. Development expenditure, as a percentage of total expenditure and net lending, increased from 34.4% in 1985/86 to 40.2% in 1986/87 (see Table 1 on page 46) and to 44.6% in 1988/89, its highest level in ten years. This implied a bias of economic activity in favour of construction as development expenditures are geared mainly towards physical infrastructure development. Also, the multiplier effects of construction tended to be high due to the industry's direct impact on the purchase of durables.

The change in expenditure composition was abrupt, and therefore occasioned adjustments in the relative importance of sectors. This implied vast opportunities in almost all sectors except the agricultural sector. Botswana's entire history of economic fluctuations has entailed abrupt changes in the composition of Government expenditure: for instance, the abrupt increase in development expenditure as a proportion of total spending and net lending in 1978/79 coincided with the then boom; the abrupt fall in development expenditure as a proportion of total spending and net lending during 1981/82 coincided with the recession then. Of course, such changes largely depended on Government mineral revenue. The point is, it was Government's timing, and avenues of expenditure, rather than revenues *per se*, that dictated economic trends.

It is evident that by 1986, the economy had already recovered from the depressing effects of the 1981/82 recession. In particular, there were no obvious signs of idle capacity as had been the case during the first half of the 1980s when construction activity was low. The response of an economy to an injection at full capacity differs with its response in cases of idle capacity. Government's liberal spending during the late 1980s came at a time when the economy could only cope by adding to its capacity. This required more time than the escalating demand pressures allowed. The result was inflationary pressures especially in the construction sector.

Unlike the case with development expenditure, Government seems to have had little control over its recurrent expenditures. All measures suggest that this expenditure grew more or less automatically for most of the 1980s and early 1990s. This is a normal experience for any government not forced to take drastic actions, for instance by retrenching its civil servants.

In conclusion, an important feature of Botswana's fiscal policy has been the role played by development expenditure. Government has had much control over these expenditures, decreasing and increasing their overall level at will, in reaction to the fortunes of the diamond sector. This direct control of the pattern and level of development expenditure played a pivotal part in the recent experience of economic fluctuation in Botswana.

Monetary policy

Something to note is that real interest rates were significantly lower in the late 1980s than they were during the first half of the decade and the early 1990s. The low interest rates of the latter part of the 1980s catalysed the already stimulative effects of fiscal policy including Government's loan guarantee schemes. There may have been much justification for expansionary monetary policy before 1987, but there was no need to influence interest rates to lower levels during the period 1987–90.

Leith (1996) suggests that by 1990 the Bank of Botswana realised that it could not control excess liquidity via passive absorption of liquidity into its call account. This raised concerns that the monetary instruments at the Bank's disposal were insufficient to steer the economy. It consequently introduced open market operations in 1991. These have proven effective in absorbing excess liquidity. However, these measures were introduced too late, at a time when they were no longer urgently needed. Monetary policy was allowed to fuel the boom, but did not cause it.

Credit

It appears that Government's car loan and other loan guarantee schemes, also adhered to by the private sector, played a significant role. Increasingly negative real interest rates, a vibrant economy and an optimistic banking sector fuelled the credit explosion. The high borrowing and lending propensity put further impetus to the economy.

Even so, a credit explosion commencing in 1988 in itself did not cause the boom. Consider, for instance, the high credit growth episodes of 18% and 40% in 1983 and 1984. Far from sparking a boom, they were followed by slower credit growth over 1985, 1986 and part of 1987. Moreover, construction, trade, manufacturing and transport showed signs of exceptional growth in 1987 before the credit explosion.

The role of expectations

Optimism was a major component of the factors contributing to the boom. Banks would not have loaned out funds if they had no confidence in borrowers' ability to repay. Households borrowed heavily – in belief that repayment would be possible. Firms expanded rapidly in anticipation of bright prospects.

Optimism stemmed from various currents within the economy. Housing shortages in urban centres drove up rentals and hence fuelled optimism among property developers. Government projects were perceived to be 'here to stay', and retailers were encouraged by long order lists.

Some notes about the recession

It was during the early 1990s that declining capital expenditures, increasing interest rates, erosion of the Zimbabwe manufacturing goods market and the depressed diamond market converged. The short-term effects of each of these had depressing effects on the Botswana economy. The Botswana Housing Corporation's suspension of housing projects added to the difficulties.

Declines in the share of capital expenditures in total spending and net lending were abrupt and persistently so more than at any time during the 1980s. They came about shortly after the appointment of a new Finance and Development Planning Minister in 1989, whose sentiments about fiscal discipline have been a source of much discussion among local newspapers. The real development expenditure cuts, coupled with the suspension of building projects by the Botswana Housing Corporation, caused a mismatch between the construction industry's capacity and the level of available construction work. The result was the laying off of workers from the industry.

Another reason for idle construction capacity was that previously excluded potential contractors were now permitted to vie for Government contracts. This attracted relatively large 'Chinese' firms, many of which came with much of their labour force requirements. In many ways, the new construction capability was enhanced beyond the intermediate term building requirements.

High cost property development was a major preoccupation for many individuals during the late 1980s and early 1990s. Rents fell significantly after mid-1992, and this had significant consequences on the economy. According to Mishkin's household

balance sheet hypothesis, household expenditure on durable goods is largely dependent on a household's current wealth and indebtedness. Households are insensitive to
the 'net' between debt and wealth and sensitive to the two independently (Mishkin,
1977). By early 1993, and into 1994, house prices had fallen; and the empty houses
without tenants accumulated debt. The consequences of the accumulating debts seem
to match Mishkin's predictions of a fall in the demand of durables (and aggregate
demand in general).

Government's high expenditures during the late 1980s were financed by exceptional diamond revenues. It was obvious that the 1987 diamond revenue increases
were exceptional and that they would be temporary. Why did Government not realise
this? One could argue that it did, and actually believed that, given the large surpluses, it was not being particularly expansionary.

The economy was therefore bound to return to normal growth rates. For this to
happen, the economy needed to adjust by shedding off 'unrequired' capacities. During the boom, the economy had 'over-responded' by establishing capabilities that
were only required temporarily. The return to normal conditions dictated the shed-
ding-off of these capabilities – unfortunately this included employed members of the
labour force. In many ways the recession was a 'mild' one.

6. CONCLUSION

Several conclusions and lessons emerge from the period under discussion. One of
them is that Government is able to cause major fluctuations in the economy, not only
via the volume of its overall expenditures, but also in terms of major shifts in its
expenditure patterns. These shifts reflect corresponding changes in priorities. An
example of a change in priorities occurred when, during 1987–93, Government embarked on a major land servicing programme after years of complacency.

Another notable conclusion is that the economy of Botswana has increasingly become deregulated and wealthier, so that decisions by the businesses and households
continue to have an increasing impact on the economy. It is the decisions of players in
the high cost property market that stirred the property market to 'crash' in 1992 and
1993. The economy remains a relatively small one so that any major injection (by the
private sector or Government) may cause a noticeable fluctuation.

There were two components of the 1990s experience. Modest growth came about as
the economy slowed down in accordance to long-term factors of labour, capital and
technical progress. Other components were the falls in export markets, the high cost
property crash and decline in relative importance of capital expenditures. All these
exacerbated the symptoms of an economy that was already toning down.

REFERENCES

Atta, J., Jefferis, K., and Mannathoko, I. 1996. 'Small Country Experiences with Ex-
    change Rates and Inflation: The Case of Botswana', *Journal of African Economies*.
    Vol.5, No.2.
Bank of Botswana. Annual Reports, various issues, 1980–95. Bank of Botswana,
    Gaborone.

Calomiris, C.W. 1993. 'Financial Factors in the Great Depression', *Journal of Economic Perspectives*, Vol.7 No.2, Spring 1993, pp61–85.

Eisner, R. 1989. 'Budget Deficits: Rhetoric and Reality', *Journal of Economic Perspectives*, Vol.3 No.2, pp73–93.

Government of Botswana. 1985 and 1991b. National Development Plans 6 and 7. Government of Botswana.

Government of Botswana. 1991a – 1996a. Budget Speeches. Government of Botswana.

Government of Botswana. 1996. *1996 Annual Economic Report*. Government of Botswana.

Harvey, C. and Lewis, S.R. 1990. *Policy Choice and Development Performance in Botswana*. Macmillan Press, London.

Harvey, C. 1992. 'Botswana: Is the Economic Miracle Over?' *Journal of African Economies*, Vol.1, No.3.

Harvey, C. 1995. 'The Use of Monetary Policy in Botswana in Good Times and Bad'. Discussion Paper No.DP204, Institute of Development Studies, University of Sussex.

Hope, K.R. 1996. 'Growth, Unemployment and Poverty in Botswana', *Journal of Contemporary Studies*, 14.

Hudson, D. 1991. 'Booms and Busts in Botswana', *Botswana Notes and Records* Vol.23, 1991, pp46–67.

Jefferis, K.R. 1997. 'The Characteristics of Successful Manufacturing Exports: Botswana's Experience', *The Research Bulletin*, Vol.15, No.1. Bank of Botswana, Gaborone.

Keynes, J.M. 1987. *Collected Writings of J.M. Keynes*, Volume 13, reprinted 1987. Macmillan Press, London. pp22–24.

Leith, J.C. 1996. 'Interest Rates in Botswana', *The Research Bulletin*, Vol.14, No.1. Bank of Botswana, Gaborone.

Love, R. 1994. 'Drought, Dutch Disease and Controlled Transition in Botswana Agriculture', *Journal of Southern African Studies*, Vol.20, No.1.

Lucas, R. 1977. 'Understanding Business Cycles', *Journal of Monetary Economics*, Vol.5, No.0, pp7–21.

Medio, A. 1987. 'Trade Cycle'. In: *The New Palgrave: A Dictionary of Economics*, Volume 4, pp666–671. Macmillan Press, London.

Mishkin, F. 1977. 'What Depressed the Consumer? Household Balance Sheet and the 1973–75 Recession', *Brookings Papers on Economic Activity*. Vol.1, No.0, pp123–64.

Mogotsi, I. 1996. 'The Diamond Boom and the Dutch Disease in Botswana'. Unpublished Ph.D. dissertation, University of Sussex, 1996.

Nteta, P. 1996. 'Housing Market, Boom and Bust.' Unpublished.

Watson, M. W. 1994. 'Business Cycle Durations and Post-war Stabilization of the US Economy', *American Economic Review*, Vol.84, No.1, pp24–96.

World Bank. 1991. *World Development Report*. Oxford University Press, Oxford.

World Bank. 1993 and 1994. *World Economic Outlook*. World Bank, Washington.

The Real Costs of Inflation in Botswana

A. Kahuti and M. Wright

1. INTRODUCTION

Compared to other developing countries both in Southern Africa and, indeed, over the world, inflation in Botswana has been modest: it has consistently remained below levels that elsewhere have been labelled 'moderate' (Dornbusch and Fischer, 1993). It has also been highly stable. But compared to the advanced industrial countries, inflation in Botswana remains at levels that would be regarded as unacceptable.

This paper investigates if there have been significant real costs to the economy of Botswana over the past two decades resulting from inflation, and whether there is much to be gained from seeking to reduce inflation further from its current levels.

This is a question that is central to the activities of an institution such as the Bank of Botswana. Pursuing policies that promote price stability is a key function of monetary authorities, and the Bank of Botswana is no exception. To quote from the Bank's Mission Statement: 'Central to its mission is the maintenance of public confidence in the national currency' (Bank of Botswana, 1996). However, whether this means a relentless pursuit of zero inflation or a targeting of inflation rates that are low and stable is less clear. While many central banks continue to use the zealous language of the former goal, their actions are in many cases a reflection of a more pragmatic pursuit of the latter (Krugman, 1996).

There is overwhelming evidence that economic growth underpins the creation of employment opportunities and, as such, is a basic precondition for increasing economic welfare. There is also little doubt that high levels of inflation may have both a negative impact on growth and, in addition, distinct adverse welfare effects as the basic functions of money are undermined. However, these undesirable consequences are most obviously apparent only at higher levels of inflation. Some have argued, further, that very *low* inflation can be harmful in that it reduces the scope for real price adjustments in the face of psychological resistance to nominal price reductions, especially for wages.

Conversely, studies have typically shown the immediate costs of reducing inflation to be high at all levels.

In this context, Botswana presents a very relevant case study. In the years immediately following Independence inflation is estimated to have been around three percent per annum. Since then, while never having been held at rates close to zero, a conservative macroeconomic policy has generally resulted in inflation that is both stable and at levels below those where the falling worth of the currency becomes an everyday and pressing concern. At the same time, sustained growth has been achieved at rates near to world record levels.

Can it be concluded that Botswana is an example of how inflation, if kept to modest, but clearly non-negative levels, can reap most of the benefits of actual price stability while avoiding the final costs of achieving it? Perhaps, but such a conclusion would be premature without proper consideration of the structure of both previous and projected growth. Unless a constant marginal sensitivity of national income to inflation can be presumed, the past performance may say little about the future. In addition, the increased monetization of the economy may make other inflation connected welfare effects assume a greater significance.

The literature on inflation is frequently complex to the point of being obscure. In contrast, this paper employs a simple framework based on the standard optimising conditions of equalising marginal utility and cost. This is used to characterise an Optimal Rate of Inflation (ORI) for Botswana which serves to illustrate the basic point that the optimal rate can differ from zero or, more generally, the ideal rate of inflation, even when the associated costs of reducing inflation are very low. This framework is used further to isolate factors that may influence this rate, and also to point to trends that may make continued pursuit of lower inflation in Botswana a desirable path to follow, if not one that is an immediate priority.

The paper is organised as follows. The next section reviews the economic consequences of inflation, both theory and evidence. From this, Section 3 develops the analytical structure. Section 4 examines the historical experience of inflation and growth in Botswana in the period since 1976 – the year when the country obtained some degree of monetary autonomy – and discusses possible future trends. Section 5 looks at the conduct of anti-inflationary policy in Botswana. Section 6 concludes.

2. THE EFFECTS OF INFLATION AND ANTI-INFLATIONARY POLICY: THEORY AND EVIDENCE

Inflation is the rate of increase in the general price level or, equivalently, the rate of decline of the value of money. Statistically this is measured through price indices, but it should be recognised from the start that these measures can only approximate the 'true' rate of inflation. They are based on sample baskets of goods, the composition of which is only changed periodically. As such, in the short term they do not adjust to shifts in consumption patterns due either to changes in tastes or, importantly, in reaction to relative price changes. Also, they take no account of quality improvements which may accompany price rises. For these reasons, such indices are commonly thought to overstate actual inflation.

As a simple proposition, the belief that inflation is unambiguously harmful has become a frequent assertion in modern economics. Previously, while the welfare costs of inflation were recognised, there was a belief that there could be a trade-off where these costs were accepted in order to achieve other objectives. In particular, the famous 'Phillips curve' suggested that lower rates of unemployment could be achieved if higher inflation was also permitted. However, the alleged empirical relationship broke down with the 'stagflation' (low growth with high inflation) experiences of industrial countries in the 1970s and 1980s.

At the theoretical level, the rationale for the trade-off was also undermined, due principally to incorporating inflationary expectations into the model. The resulting expectations-augmented-Philips-curve predicted a 'natural' or

'Non-Accelerating Inflation Rate of Unemployment' (NAIRU) below which inflation would continue to accelerate. In the simple model, the NAIRU is not itself affected by the rate of inflation: that is, there is no link between unemployment and inflation in the long run.[1] Under these conditions all a government will achieve by attempting to trade higher inflation for lower unemployment is a short-term reduction in unemployment and a *permanently* higher rate of inflation (Stevenson *et al.*, 1988, chapter 3).

The NAIRU hypothesis has become a commonly accepted wisdom.[2] It points to the role of macroeconomic policy as tackling inflation, while structural or supply side policies are used to reduce the NAIRU itself.

Importantly, however, the basic NAIRU model did not rule out all trade-offs between inflation and output. In order to reduce inflation, unemployment would, under most assumptions, have to increase temporarily, and growth in output would slow.[3] The loss associated with increasing unemployment and lower output would need to be compared to the costs of continuing inflation. In principle, this comparison is amenable to the basic net present value calculations of cost-benefit analysis.

The costs of inflation

The objections to inflation are a mixture of philosophy, abstract theory and empirical analysis. The practical manifestation of any harmful effects will differ according to circumstance. But, despite the often involved arguments, the basic case that inflation has negative effects is simply put.

Take first the possible pure welfare effects: that is, assuming that the effect of inflation on real economic activity is insignificant. Money has certain well-established characteristics: its roles as a unit of account, a store of value and a medium of exchange. Quite clearly, all these functions are impeded, even if only to a small degree, by a continuing fall in the value of money, which is the definition of inflation. This is even more so if the rate of this decline is not predictable, i.e., the rate of inflation is uncertain.

This is the core of the key welfare argument against inflation. Essentially, inflation is a tax on holding money.

Distributional considerations suggest further adverse effects. Some people may be relatively well placed to avoid the worst of the welfare effects. This may be through access to close substitutes that fulfil some if not all of the functions of money, or, more bluntly, through wielding economic power which is sufficient to maintain the real value of incomes and financial assets. Others, usually the poor and other groups without these opportunities, will not be able to take such defensive actions and so suffer relatively more. The end result is one of 'transferring national income from the uncomplaining to the militant' (Economist, 1996b).

---

[1] Graphically, the long-run Phillips curve, drawn with axes showing inflation and unemployment rates, is vertical, rather than backward sloping as in the original model.

[2] Although this acceptance is not universal. For example, Galbraith (1996, Chapter 6) argues that the original Phillips curve trade-off between inflation and unemployment is still relevant. However, this polemic does not face head on the challenges to this model raised by the NAIRU hypothesis.

[3] The exception to this is under conditions of fully free markets and 'rational expectations' where the adjustment process would be instantaneous.

Independent of the pure welfare argument is the suggestion that inflation has a negative impact on activity in the real economy, as measured by output or employment. This is easy to see, at least in principle. The very process of making the monetary system inefficient is unlikely to leave unaffected the economic activity which it supports, as resources are diverted into finding ways to protect the value of existing assets rather than generating additional wealth. These real effects are likely to be particularly pernicious when inflation is unpredictable, as economic agents – both consumers and investors – have increased difficulty in distinguishing between nominal and real price changes.[4] In the face of such uncertainly, people tend to factor greater risk premia into their economic decisions. A particular concern is that both saving and productive investment will be adversely affected in favour of consumption and acquiring physical assets.

The problems are aggravated when there is interaction with taxation systems that do not allow for the effects of inflation. Personal income taxes are famously subject to 'bracket creep' as the real value of the width of tax bands and allowances is eroded by inflation. Also, returns on investments can be reduced if it is the nominal return, whether in the form of interest or capital gains, that is subject to tax.[5]

In short, disintermediation occurs and resources are misallocated. Assuming that these costs increase as inflation rises, this points to a higher NAIRU at higher rates of inflation. In this case, the correlation between inflation and unemployment becomes positive and the long-run Phillips curve slopes forward rather than backwards as in the original hypothesis.

At the level of abstract principle, these concerns seem legitimate. But this says nothing about the practical size of such costs. Quite clearly very high inflation can debilitate an economy. For example, the abiding national fear of inflation in Germany, as reflected in the anti-inflationary zeal of the Bundesbank, is commonly attributed to the hyperinflationary experience in that country in the 1920s. But most countries are not in situations of hyperinflation.

In that it is more amenable to statistical investigation, the literature has concentrated on quantifying the effects on economic growth and employment rather than the pure welfare effect. But even here the analysis is problematic. The raw data for both inflation and growth needs to be filtered to allow for cyclical factors that may suggest a positive correlation between the two series: indeed, the very logic of the NAIRU hypothesis is that in the short term higher inflation will be associated with higher output growth. The data need to take into account the many factors other than inflation that may retard or enhance growth. Also, all aspects of the inflationary process, including its harmful effects, are notoriously subject to long and variable lags.

In addition, it should not be assumed that observed pairings of inflation and growth are points on the production possibility frontier: i.e., that growth is being maximised given the rate of inflation. Low inflation by itself is not a guarantee of higher growth. Other policies may also be required – to deregulate markets for example. If these are not in place, a country's growth potential may not be realised, however favourable the

---

4   To a certain extent at least, systems of indexation (such as variable interest rates) may be able to lead to the amelioration of some of the effects of inflation, most effectively when such inflation is properly anticipated.

5   These are not in themselves arguments against inflation. The costs of reducing inflation would need to be compared to those of introducing 'inflation proof' tax systems.

inflationary climate. Conversely, it is also true that higher rates of inflation may be associated with lower output growth precisely because of the accompanying anti-inflationary policies which depress growth in the short term.

Overall, the results of empirical studies into the relationship between inflation and real variables – primarily the rates of output growth and unemployment – have been mixed. There is certainly no unambiguous statistical support for those who wish to emphasise the harmful effects of inflation (Briault, 1995). Recent studies have produced estimates of between 8% and 40% for the threshold above which the harmful effects of inflation on growth become significant (Tanzi and Zee, 1996). A wider study by Bleaney (1996), where inflation is only one aspect of macroeconomic instability, does not find *any* significant correlation between inflation and growth in a sample of developing countries.[6]

A recent, much publicised, study is that by Barro (1995). This examines data from 1960 to 1990 for over one hundred countries, both rich and poor. Divided into three decadal blocks, the data were able to show periods, rather than specific instances, of high/low inflation and growth of output. The data also showed quite clearly the strong correlation between the level of inflation and its variability.

The basic conclusion of this research was that a 1% increase in inflation reduces the rate of economic growth by between 0.02% and 0.03% per annum. While this result may be significantly different from zero in the statistical sense, '...nor is it exactly earth-shattering.' (Economist, 1995). For example, while an economy with 100% inflation is sacrificing growth at between two and three percentage points per annum, a rate of sacrifice which is clearly undesirable, the output loss for inflation between zero and 10% inflation may not seem very large at all.

This type of conclusion is supported further by analysis which seems to suggest a non-linear cost of inflation where the most disruptive effects occur only at rates which are high and variable. Barro himself concludes that the clearest evidence for adverse effects of inflation on growth and investment is from countries where inflation is greater than about 15%, and below this rate the effects may not be significant. Bruno and Easterly (1995), while arguing for the further benefits of holding inflation below the 5% level, also suggest the negative effects are reduced once it falls below about 25%.

Some researchers have suggested an even stronger conclusion than that reached by Barro: that, at very low levels of inflation, a further reduction may in fact be harmful to growth (Akerloff et al., 1996). The argument here is that due to an aversion by workers to nominal cuts, real wage reductions that may be necessary to promote employment will be difficult to achieve if there is not some upward movement in the general price level.

This argument, which alleges a rudimentary form of money illusion, is a modern restatement of the traditional 'Keynesian' view that there is downward rigidity in nominal wages. In this case the authors appeal to a sense of fairness which allows real but not nominal wage cuts. While there may be some evidence for its continuing psychological importance, this denies certain precepts of rationality to which many economists

---

[6] To explain this, he suggests that studies which do show such a link may be picking up a negative effect on growth of real exchange rate volatility which, in his data sample, is positively correlated with inflation and is not usually included as a separate variable when studying the inflation–growth relationship. It should be noted that the data set used here was based on only 41 countries in the 1980s. This is much smaller than an inflation-specific studies such as Barro (1995).

are these days very attached. These would suggest that such resistance is likely to be a symptom of lingering worries of future inflation rather than a genuine obstacle during conditions of true price stability, pointing out that the 'defeat' of inflation in some countries is at best a recent phenomenon (Prowse, 1996). To this others would reply that people are simply not rational, at least not in the narrow sense that economists would like them to be.[7]

A final point is that price stability is not to be equated with zero inflation as statistically measured. As already noted, price indices are both imperfect and may systematically tend to overstate 'true' inflation: so a policy which pursued the objective of zero inflation might be too repressive. Studies have suggested that, for the USA, the Consumer Price Index (CPI) may overstate inflation by between 1% and 2.5% per annum (Economist, 1996a).[8] However, this effect will be less the more the CPI basket is made up of goods where quality improvement is less likely to be a significant factor. It might be plausible to suppose that this is the case for many developing countries where consumption in poor, rural communities, is based on staple foods, cheap clothing and simple housing.

A separate problem with current measures of inflation is that they reveal little about inflationary expectations. The harmful effects of previously high inflation may linger if the new, lower, rates are not expected to last. The costs of constantly checking the inflation rate will be the same whatever that rate is: they will only be reduced if the need for such checks is also reduced. This requires stable expectations. Much of the literature emphasises the importance of establishing an anti-inflationary culture where price stability in the general sense is taken for granted, rather than zealous pursuit of a particular measure (Brittan, 1995). This said, it is likely that a sustained reputation for zealous anti-inflationary policy may be the most effective way of establishing firmly such a culture.

While most recent research may suggest relatively weak links between inflation and growth, especially at low levels, this remains one set of claims in an ambiguous area. Estimates, such as those of Barro, are at the lower end of the effects that have been estimated in reputable studies, and, as Barro is keen to emphasise, the cumulative consequences of small annual restrictions on growth may be substantial over many years. This last point is well-taken. But it is likely that in any well-structured cost-benefit equation, the chosen social discount rate will limit the impact of these longer term effects, giving a greater weight to the immediate, even if only temporary, negative consequences in terms of a loss of output and jobs of policies that reduce inflation. It is to these costs that this discussion now turns.

The costs of reducing inflation

The costs of reducing inflation will vary very much according to the context. However, outside the special situations where the free lunch of a costless reduction of inflation may be possible, these costs are likely to be significant.

---

7   It seems well-established, for example, that pure rationality does not solely govern decisions regarding risk taking (Bernstein, 1996).

8   For example, a report in late 1996 by the Congressional Advisory Commission on the CPI, estimated that in recent years the real rate of inflation in the United States has been overstated by an average of 1.1 percent.

The major factors which affect the cost include, *inter alia*: the institutional conditions of the country concerned, the particular anti-inflationary policy that is adopted and the past track record of the authorities in dealing with inflation. Governments with strong anti-inflation credentials and which operate in an environment of flexible markets that can easily adjust to new price levels and expectations of future inflation are likely to help minimise these costs.[9]

Among these factors, the structure of the labour market is likely to be key (Agenor, 1996), with greater flexibility allowing for less costly adjustment. One obvious, but important point, is that increased labour market rigidities may be one of the serious consequences of inflation, as employees seek to find ways to preserve the real value their wages in the face of rising prices.[10]

More generally, it should be clear that the neat dividing line in the original NAIRU models, with macroeconomic policy being concerned mainly with price stability and micro policy with reducing the NAIRU, does not hold in practice. An economic environment that promotes a low NAIRU is likely to be one where the costs of disinflation are also relatively low.

In addition to the overall level of costs, how they are spread over time is also important: the trade off between a short, sharp shock and a more gentle, but lingering one must be compared.

The literature on the comparative costs of various inflation-reducing policy packages is large and growing. One general message is that the cost of fighting inflation is not to be underestimated, especially during the final stages. While situations of high inflation may be relatively easy to ameliorate, once both the political will and the framework to impose tight monetary and fiscal policies are in place, the next move to actual price stability may be more costly. A variety of reasons for this have been advanced (Briault, 1995). For instance, Lucas (1973) suggests that at low levels of inflation, with accompanying low variability, movements in prices are more likely to be interpreted as changes in relative prices rather than the general price level; in turn this will lead to larger adjustments in employment and output.

Empirical studies seem to confirm that the costs of inflation reduction are significant. For example, Dornbusch and Fischer (1993) studied countries that have experienced 'moderate' inflation: moderate here being defined as inflation of between 15% and 30% for at least three years. They conclude that there is '...unfortunately little encouragement...' for the view that inflation can be reduced to very low levels at little cost. Successful anti-inflation policies are based on tight fiscal and monetary controls and, often, taking advantage of favourable supply side conditions – lower prices in key goods – to ratchet inflation downwards.

---

[9] Here, the special topic of central bank independence has attracted considerable interest. The idea is that such independence can work against any inflationary bias which might result from discretionary policy making by government. While there is as yet little evidence that legal arrangements for independence are by themselves sufficient to promote price stability, other factors, such as the stability of a central bank's leadership, which may affect the *de facto* independence, do seem to be significant (Barro, 1995). The accountability and transparency of central bank operations may also be important (Briault *et al.*, 1996).

[10] A related policy issue is the question of whether employment contracts that include elements of wage indexation are a help or a hindrance in reducing inflation (Jadresic, 1996). This is likely to depend on the type of indexation, whether it reflects past, actual, inflation or signals of future inflation. The former will both tend to preserve inflation and make it easier to live with; the latter may speed the adjustment to lower inflation

In a study of recent experience of anti-inflationary policy in Poland, Pujol and Griffiths (1996) concluded that structural problems in the real economy can undermine seriously the anti-inflationary efficiency of monetary and fiscal policies when inflation is at low levels. Such supply side constraints emphasise further the possible importance of favourable supply side shocks in reducing inflation to very low levels.

Even when low rates of inflation have been achieved, establishing low expectations of future inflation may be a longer process (Bank of England, 1996). To the extent that this requires policies that are excessively tight for a long period, this adds to the total costs of inflation reduction.

3. A CONCEPTUAL FRAMEWORK

Taking into account the main points made in the previous section concerning the theory and evidence on the costs of inflation and of its reduction, a simple analytical framework suitable for analysis of the situation in Botswana has been adopted. This is illustrated in Figure 1.

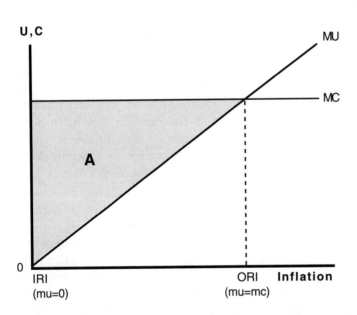

It is assumed that curves showing the marginal cost (MC) and marginal utility (MU) of reducing inflation can be drawn corresponding to different levels of inflation, with the units of utility (U) and cost (C) being some present value measure of output. The key assumptions are that, while the marginal utility of further reductions of inflation is diminishing, the marginal cost of reducing inflation is largely invariant to the level. Both curves are shown as straight lines, and the MC curve is horizontal. This is for simplicity: for the argument that follows the crucial condition is that MC is positive when MU equals zero. From what has been said in the previous section this seems reasonable; there may even be good reasons to suppose that, at least for low rates of inflation, the MC of further reductions might actually be rising.

An important distinction is made between the *ideal* rate of inflation (IRI) and the *optimal* rate of inflation (ORI). The former is where the marginal utility is zero, and is ideal in the sense that it is the rate which would be chosen if moving to it were costless. This is shown as zero in the diagram, but could be at a positive rate if the considerations of money illusion discussed above are important.[11] ORI on the other

---

[11] The unlikely theoretical cases that conclude that ideal inflation should be negative to allow holdings of currency to earn a return are ignored here.

hand is optimal in the normal economic sense of equating marginal cost and marginal benefits.

Except in the special situations where either the MU curve is discontinuous and drops to zero exactly at the ideal rate or the MC curve itself is at zero, ORI will be higher than IRI. Unless IRI is less than zero (see footnote 10), ORI will be greater than zero. Any move beyond ORI to IRI will result in a welfare loss. The area A in the diagram is the total welfare loss of the move between ORI and IRI.

Clearly any upward movement of the MU curve, or downward movement of the MC curve, will lower ORI. Assuming that the IRI is anchored at the same rate, the former will take the form of a rotation of the MU curve to the left. This will happen if additional costs to inflation are identified. A reduction of the marginal cost will occur if less costly anti-inflation policy 'technology' is developed. Such technological development may be seen as a goal of policy formulation.

What then can be said about the ORI for Botswana?

4. TRENDS IN INFLATION IN BOTSWANA

This study reviews the inflation trends beginning in 1976. This is the year that Botswana introduced its own currency independent of the South African Rand and thus achieved a degree of monetary autonomy (see papers by Harvey and Hermans in this volume). Inflation since 1976 is charted in Figure 2, which shows the annual average inflation rate as measured by the Botswana CPI. From 1976 to 1995, the rate of inflation averaged about 11.5%, and has been relatively stable with a standard deviation of 2.3%.

FIGURE 2. INFLATION IN BOTSWANA 1976–1995

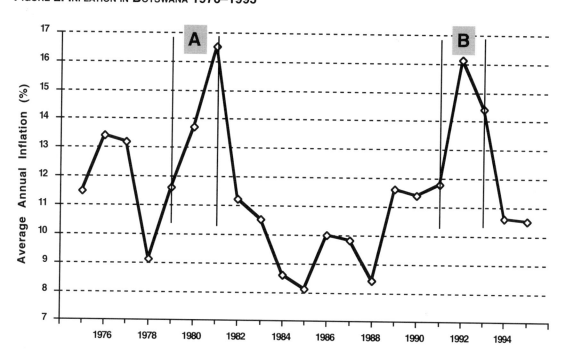

This stability itself immediately hampers investigation of any effects on growth. Individual annual observations are unlikely to reveal much in a process that will typically be subject to variable lags. And it is difficult to identify any period of sustained high inflation in Botswana. Such periods have formed the basis for other case studies.

If a period of high inflation is defined as being at least three successive years where inflation was above the mean for the whole period then for Botswana only the periods 1979–81 and 1991–1993 (marked 'A' and 'B' in Figure 2) meet this criterion. In only two years (1981 and 1992) has the average inflation rate exceeded 15%. This is the rate at which other studies have suggested that the negative effects of inflation on growth will start to bite more severely, and the bottom of the range elsewhere labelled as moderate inflation.

Table 1 shows inflation in Botswana compared to some other developing countries in the period 1970 to 1995. Among the African economies shown, inflation in Botswana has been significantly lower than Uganda and Nigeria and Sub-Saharan Africa as a whole, and similar to those of its regional neighbours, South Africa and Mauritius. Compared to Latin American countries, such as Brazil and Bolivia, Botswana stands out as a low inflation economy.

TABLE 1. AVERAGE INFLATION, SELECTED COUNTRIES, 1970–1995

	1970–1980	1980–1990	1990–1995
SUB-SAHARAN	13.8	15.7	26.4
BOTSWANA	11.6	10.9	12.5
SOUTH AFRICA	9.0	14.6	11.8
MAURITIUS	13.8	11.4	8.2
NIGERIA	15.4	21.5	35.8[a]
UGANDA	27.8	94.0	23.0
SOUTH KOREA	16.4	8.4	6.6
SINGAPORE	6.7	2.9	2.7
BRAZIL	35.3	557.7	1548.1
BOLIVIA	18.8	1259.0	12.9
INDUSTRIAL	8.4	5.7	3.4

Note: [a]Does not include figure for 1995.
Source: IMF, International Financial Statistics.

But compared to an economy such as Singapore, which since 1980 has held average annual inflation below 3%, inflation in Botswana is quite high. Also, the typical rate of inflation in Botswana is far above what is thought to be acceptable in the main industrial economies, where inflation in excess of 3% is now viewed as too high. Overall it is probably appropriate to describe inflation rates in Botswana as 'modest', that is somewhere between moderate and low.

The structure of inflation in Botswana is dominated by the movements in prices of tradeable goods. These constitute 75.3% of the CPI basket, nearly two-thirds of which are imported tradeables, sourced mainly in South Africa. In this situation, it comes as little surprise that it is well established that inflation imported from South Africa is a major component of the inflationary process in Botswana (Atta *et al.*, 1996).

The dominance of autonomous growth

Figure 3 shows clearly the lack of any obvious correlation between inflation and growth in aggregate economic activity in Botswana.[12] As noted already, this is not surprising and cannot be taken as evidence that inflation has not been detrimental to growth: the counterfactual of the growth that would have taken place in the absence of inflation is, of course, not shown.

FIGURE 3. PRIVATE SECTOR GDP GROWTH RATES, 1977 TO 1995

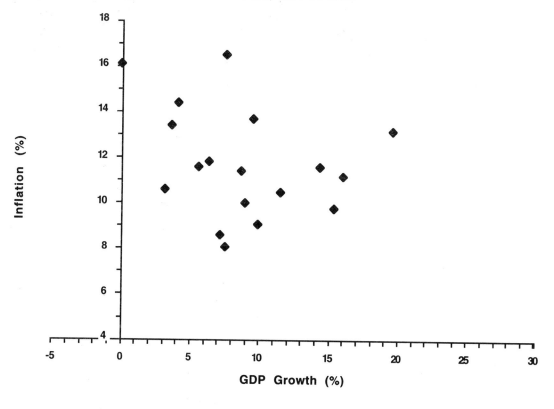

This said, it can be asserted with a fair degree of certainty that at the level of aggregate economic growth, the development of the Botswana economy has not been affected significantly by the presence of persistent but modest and generally stable inflation. This is for the simple reason that much of the growth has come from sectors whose inflation elasticities of production are likely to be low. Conditions for this can occur when the return on an investment is not directly financial or it is so large in nominal terms as to make concerns about inflation of secondary importance. In Botswana, the former condition has applied to the Government and the latter to diamond mining.[13] Together these two sectors have dominated the development of the economy.

Agricultural growth will also have been largely unaffected by inflation, although for somewhat different reasons. Subsistence agriculture is conducted largely on a non-

---

[12] In this diagram the annual average inflation rate is matched against the growth of GDP in the national accounts year beginning in July. This implicitly allows a half year lag for inflation to affect real economic performance. This is not based on any assumption that the lags involved in such a process do in fact approximate to six months in Botswana.

monetary basis and the dominant influence on output in any year are the prevailing climatic conditions.

Figure 4 shows the inflation-growth scatter diagram for GDP excluding the minerals and general government sectors. The same qualifications apply as before about the danger of spurious correlations. But, for this data set the years of high inflation have in general corresponded to lower growth rates, although the reverse of low inflation and high growth does not seem so apparent. This correlation includes instances when the slow growth was itself a product of the anti-inflationary measures: most obviously perhaps in 1992/93 when the collapse of the construction sector, caused in part by the tightening of monetary policy (see below), was the main cause of negative growth for the non-mineral private sector.

FIGURE 4. NON-MINING PRIVATE SECTOR GDP GROWTH RATES, 1977 TO 1995

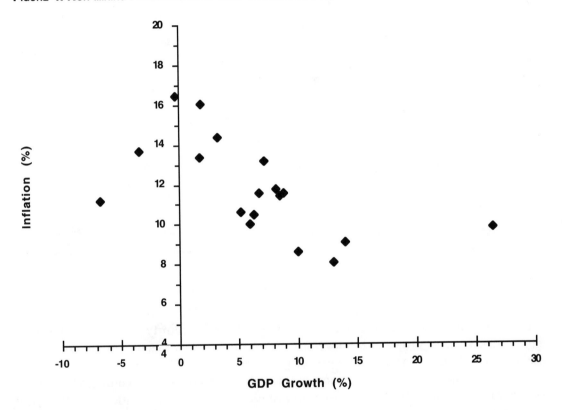

Despite this analysis of the past, it must be recognised that this trend of growth that has been largely impervious to trends in inflation cannot be relied upon for the future. The declared goal is diversification away from established sectors. In turn this

---

13 This is not claiming that inflation has not affected diamond mining in Botswana. First, global inflation in the 1970s and 1980s would have been an important influence on international diamond market conditions, with potential feedbacks for the mining operations. Second, if a reputation for low inflation had been in place at the time of the original agreements between De Beers and the Botswana Government, the share of returns to the latter might have been even more favourable. However, neither of these points affects the argument here that growth of the diamond sector, as measured by the sectoral GDP, has not been affected adversely by domestic inflation

means a greater emphasis on industries which are likely to be more sensitive to inflation. Even if further mining development were to emerge, this could well be in projects
more marginal and, therefore, also more sensitive to variables such as the rate of
inflation.

This consideration has become more important recently. As other countries within
the region have continued to normalise their socio-political conditions, it will be increasingly difficult for Botswana to trade on its reputation for general stability. The
specifics of this stability will come more to the fore.

In other words, structural change which is seen as desirable for the macro economy
is rotating the marginal utility curve leftwards and hence lowering the ORI in Botswana.

High inflation, 1991–1993

It might be hoped that close examination of the 1991–1993 period would provide
some more clear indication of how a sharp and sustained acceleration of inflation
impacted on the economy. This is especially the case since at first sight the simple
correlation might seem clear cut: one of the only periods of 'high' inflation in the past
twenty years was followed with only a short lag by the only 'recession', as shown by
negative real GDP growth in 1992/93.

FIGURE 5. MONTHLY INFLATION RATES, 1991–1995

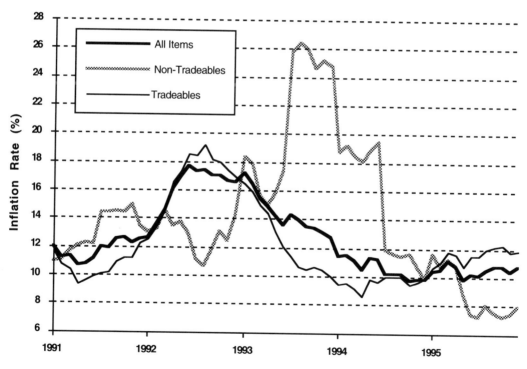

Figure 5 shows the inflation from 1991 to 1995 on a monthly basis. This is both in
aggregate and in its tradeable and non-tradeable components. While overall inflation
was high (for Botswana) for a sustained period, its composition changed considerably.

In 1991 the inflationary leader was non-tradeable goods and services, although inflation due to tradeables also moved onto an upward trend. This latter effect reflected devaluations of the exchange rate in both August 1990 and 1991, aimed at improving the competitive position of non-traditional industries (Bank of Botswana, 1995).

This continued through 1992 with tradeable inflation pushing the overall rate above 16% for the last nine months of the year. During this time, non-tradeable inflation was much lower, although highly variable. In 1993, however, tradeable inflation subsided rapidly as the effects of the earlier devaluations had run their course; it was purely inflation of non-tradeables that was keeping the price level rising fast overall. This domestically generated inflation was the culmination of a long period of fairly loose monetary policy with an emphasis on low interest rates to stimulate bank lending and, subsequently, the acceleration of Government spending between 1987 and 1991 (Harvey, 1992 and N. Gaolathe in this volume).

It is clear that inflation had some major distortionary effects during this period. The huge increases in construction costs at that time were a major cost to the economy. The return on both public and private sector investments was reduced. This is to an extent that has caused considerable subsequent distress, most notably perhaps for residential property owners.

Also consider, as a simple, but not unimportant, example, the fifteen percent nominal increase of Botswana Housing Corporation (BHC) rents that had been applied for many years. This formula was aimed at gradually increasing the real level of rents. As the rate of inflation moved above more normal levels, this purpose started to be thwarted and, in 1992, it was negated altogether as the nominal increase was below the rate of inflation. Also, in the face of rapid increases in other prices, which both reduced living standards and necessitated action to reduce inflation (see below), the resolve to continue to raise this administered and highly sensitive price may have been put under pressure.

More generally, the inflation of this period was both fuelled by and resulted in real interest rates that were significantly negative. These promoted spending patterns that were not conducive to high and sustainable growth in the long run as resources were drawn into unproductive investments and consumption. Moreover, it is very possible that left unchecked the inflation could have moved to higher levels that would more clearly have been dysfunctional for the operation of the economy. This is especially so if demand had continued to be fuelled by wage increases – led by the annual adjustment to wages and salaries of Government employees – that compensated for past inflation.

But this does not mean that the major concerns about current and future growth in the economy that were being frequently expressed, were due to inflation. The slowdown in growth in the early 1990s was clearly influenced by other factors. The world diamond markets were depressed. Manufacturing was hit by being cut off from the major outlet in Zimbabwe: indeed the devaluations of 1990 and 1991, which brought about the period of high tradeable goods inflation, were themselves a direct response to the depreciation of the Zimbabwe Dollar.

Not surprisingly, since it was escalating building costs that had fuelled domestic inflation, construction was the major casualty of the anti-inflationary policy. This contributed to a shake out in that sector which accounts for much of the slowdown in growth seen at the aggregate level (Bank of Botswana, 1995). But there were also other causes for the sectoral slowdown. Most obviously, much of BHC's investment programme was suspended as a consequence of a corruption scandal.[14] It also seems that the boom and bust in the private housing market was fuelled not just by loose monetary policy; the 'inexperience' of urban Batswana households in the property market may have aggravated the situation (see paper by N. Gaolathe in this volume).[15]

Costs of low inflation?

What about the money illusion arguments in favour of a modest degree of inflation? It seems clear that this psychological consideration has been exploited by Government in recent years. Since 1993 when civil service salaries were adjusted sharply upwards, the annual increases to both these salaries and minimum wages have been below the rate of inflation, and thus their levels have fallen in real terms. Given the importance of these as benchmarks and legal minima, it is likely that this trend has spread through the economy. This was quite clearly the Government's intention: the freeze on civil servants salaries during 1994/95 was intended to 'send a strong signal ... on Government's policy of encouraging wage restraint, designed to enhance our competitiveness.' (Government of Botswana, 1994, p153).

This may have been beneficial in terms of improving the competitive position of the Botswana labour force. However, the existence of such administered prices in an inflationary situation may work in less desirable directions. It might be tempting to allow the real price of other items to fall. The example of BHC has already been mentioned. The same applies to utilities more generally, although the legal requirement that the utility companies set prices that earn a reasonable return on capital may act as a buttress against any such populist tendency. The point is that the constant revision of administered prices purely to allow for inflation places some cost on the economy. This is especially so when the price concerned is public and sensitive, which are usually the very reasons why these prices are administered in the first place. In such a situation the costs of such revisions are potentially high. In particular, governments face being continually put in a position where difficult choices have to be made; and the more often this occurs the greater the risk that concerns for popularity will have a damaging influence on appropriateness of the final decision.

Another area of concern is the prevalence of negative real interest rates, especially for savers. Except for those with incomes high enough to access Bank of Botswana Certificates (BoBCs), it is nearly impossible to get a positive real return for domestic savings.[16] This clear disincentive helps cause the problem of chronically low personal saving – or at least financial saving – and high levels of borrowing in Botswana (see paper by Reinke in this volume). Since it is commonly supposed that nominal interest rates cannot be negative it might be argued that lower inflation would at least reduce

---

[14]   However, it could be argued here that this scandal was itself a product of the inflationary construction boom: that corruption was a likely consequence of large amounts of money being pumped into the Corporation.

[15]   It should be recognised of course that many other countries' property markets also continue to be afflicted by similar 'inexperience'.

[16]   For example, in October 1996 the highest interest rate on savings published by Barclays Bank was 9.5%. This was for savings greater than P10 000. This compares to a national inflation rate in September 1996 of 9.6%, although it was somewhat lower in the urban areas (CSO, 1996b). Even this marginally positive real interest rate can become significantly negative if income tax is payable, as it is on interest payments above P1000 per annum.

the extent to which real rates could be negative.

However, such an approach would be simplistic and problematic. In such a situation it is likely that the deposit takers – mainly the commercial banks – would look for other ways to restore their rates of return. Charges for bank services might be increased further and/or operations could be rationalised. These effects may already have been seen as, following the rapid fall in inflation in 1993, some commercial banks began to discourage small-scale savings deposits through zero interest rates and handling charges on low balances. Also banks could charge higher lending rates in an attempt to maintain the spread.

A switch away from a wide interest rate spread to higher charges for specific services can sometimes be considered appropriate from the point of view of allocative efficiency. But this should be the result of structural changes that improve further the competitive environment in the financial sector, rather than relying on the indirect and uncertain consequences of a further reduction in inflation. Higher lending rates to maintain the spread would dilute any gains made from lower risk premia being attached to lending as inflation fell. Finally, any reduction in the coverage of services would impede the objective of extending further the reach of the banking system in the economy.

Monetization of the economy

From a welfare point of view the degree of monetization in the economy will be important. Obviously, while non-monetary systems have a variety of inefficiencies (the very ones that lead to the development of money) they have the advantage of being secure from the effects of inflation.[17] This is to the extent that policies that resist further monetization have been used on occasion in other countries to protect vulnerable groups from inflation (Selwe, 1994).

In Botswana, monetization has proceeded with the development of the economy. One indicator of this is the use of money as a means of transaction. Looking at the Household Income and Expenditure Survey (HIES) for 1985/86, the ratio of cash income to total income was 0.76 (CSO, 1988). The HIES for 1993/94 estimates that this had increased to 0.82 (CSO, 1996a). The non-monetization was mainly in the rural areas. For urban households the ratio was around 0.9 in both surveys. Poorer households also use money less: the Gini coefficient for total disposable income is lower than that for cash income only (see paper by Hudson and Wright in this volume). Thus, to a certain extent, in the past this part of the population have been protected from the inequities of high inflation.

But the process of monetization continues. The lesser monetization in the rural economy in large part reflects the importance of subsistence farming to those communities, especially the poorer households. Between 1985/86 and 1993/94 the consumption of own produce by rural households as a proportion of total income fell from 23% to 14% (Bank of Botswana, 1996). As consumption increasingly becomes based on goods produced by others, monetization follows.

This process has been helped by the extension of Government services where payments and benefits are in the form of cash. As a recent example, the introduction, in

---

[17] Although this security will start to be reduced as soon as any good(s) start to acquire some of the functions of money.

October 1996, of the P100/month old age pension will have such an effect in that it will add to or replace private transfers that, in part at least, would have been in goods rather than cash.

Moreover, monetization does not only involve an increased use of money for transactions. A greater use in its other functions – notably as a store of value – is another facet of the process. As real incomes grow and the financial sector deepens, financial assets become increasingly important.

In light of this anticipated trend towards further monetization, it can be judged that in the future the welfare costs associated with high inflation in Botswana will be higher than previously. This, too, will rotate the MU curve to the left and reduce the ORI.

The foregoing suggests, even before looking at the costs of inflation reduction, that there are trends in the economy that point to a reduction in the ORI in Botswana. This is from the point of view of both welfare and productive efficiency. From Figure 1 it is clear that this conclusion is valid even if the marginal costs of reducing inflation are rising.

5. Anti-inflation Policy in Botswana

In recent years there have been three components of anti-inflation policy in Botswana. These can be matched to the principal causes of inflation.

Most constantly used has been the exchange rate. This is hardly surprising given the importance of imported inflation in Botswana. Since gaining monetary independence in 1976, the appreciation of the Pula against the South African Rand is a reflection of the generally lower inflation rates in Botswana. Indeed, the stability of inflation in Botswana is in large part due to an exchange rate policy that has often sought to counter inflationary disturbances arising from Botswana's high dependence on imported goods. Managed carefully, such a policy, based on small movements that maintained the real exchange rate with the Rand within a small band, was able to ameliorate inflation without imposing any apparent costs on the domestic economy in terms of undermining the competitiveness of non-traditional exporters. By the same token, when the exchange rate has been used for other purposes, notably to maintain the competitiveness of domestic industry against falls in the value of other currencies, the inflationary feedback has, as already noted when looking at the inflation of the early 1990s, been rapid.

Such a policy of frequent small revaluations has been effective in the case of Botswana, in the sense that the costs of keeping down imported inflation from South Africa were negligible. Therefore, the benefits of the resulting lower inflation can be seen as a pure welfare gain (see paper by Harvey in this volume). However, the policy clearly has its limits since, if applied more aggressively, at some stage the size and/or the frequency of the revaluations required to effect a wider inflation differential with South Africa would become sufficient to risk affecting significantly the competitiveness of local producers.

Second, the use of domestic monetary policy through interest rates. This has been used less extensively. Interest rates were not needed to support the exchange rate during much of the period when exchange controls were in place. In addition, for many years the focus was on the problem of excess liquidity and the perceived need to encourage lending by the commercial banks. In this environment the tendency was to cut interest rates. Only in recent years has the principle of positive real interest rates been established, and even then only somewhat tenuously, with the policy coming under repeated criticism. But the potential effectiveness of monetary policy in reducing the component of inflation that was domestically generated was made clear by the recent inflationary experience.

The third component is the use of pay restraint and other incomes policy measures both to reduce aggregate demand in the economy and to break vicious inflationary circles. This has been particularly important for Botswana given the Government's leadership in setting wages in the economy. This is due both to a long established policy of intervention in what has always been regarded as a crucial area for the balanced development of the economy – hence the introduction of an explicit Incomes Policy in 1972 – and to Government's dominant role as an employer.

Government has used this pivotal position to pursue a variety of objectives, and in recent years interventions in the setting of wages have been less direct (Bank of Botswana, 1996). But, it seems clear that the unambiguous policy of wage restraint since 1994 – a pay freeze followed by two years of increase noticeably below the prevailing inflation rate – has been effective in quickly reorienting the climate in the labour market regarding wage expectations. In turn, it is likely that knock-on effects in the form of lower inflationary expectations in general have followed. This is seen in Figure 6 which shows the annual growth rate in Central Government and private and parastatal sector citizen wages since September 1991 (CSO, 1996c).

In current circumstances, if Government were to seek actively to reduce inflation further, the exchange rate would be the most potent policy instrument, although with

FIGURE 6. NOMINAL WAGES INCREASES FOR CITIZEN EMPLOYEES, 1991–1995

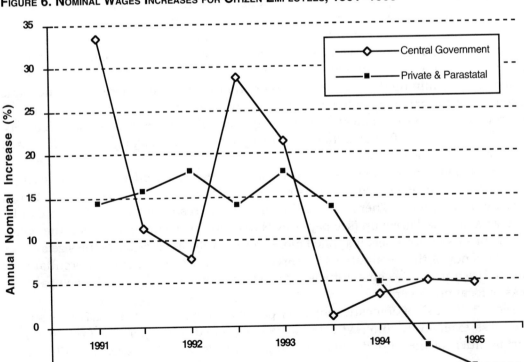

the gradual loosening of exchange controls, domestic monetary policy would also be affected. The domestic component of inflation has already been squeezed to a level considerably below the overall rate and, in addition, tradeables continue to make up nearly three quarters of the current CPI basket. In these circumstances, the effects on overall inflation of a further tightening of monetary policy or dampening of domestic demand will be limited.

This represents a clear policy dilemma given the other roles of the exchange rate, principally that of promoting competitiveness of locally produced tradeable goods. To preserve the manufacturing base that it has already established, an aggressive anti-inflation policy could be harmful. As explained above, the short-term marginal costs could be high. But at the same time, as already argued, in the longer run to further develop this sector a climate of low inflation will be highly desirable.

In reaction to the fall of the Rand against major currencies during much of 1996, the Pula was allowed to fall also. In doing so, the authorities clearly showed a preference for maintaining competitiveness over taking a proactive approach to stamping out inflationary pressures that might be anticipated as a result of the falling Rand. But, at the time of writing, these pressures have yet to emerge. Inflation in South Africa has not risen significantly as an immediate response to the currency fall, and in the second half of 1996 inflation in Botswana moved marginally below the ten percent level.

There is an argument that the final inflationary response to the fall of the Rand will also be muted, reflecting the counter effects of cost reductions in a more competitive economy. Indeed, this may be the main impetus for a further fall in inflation as the Southern African economy faces greater competitive pressures due to its continuing reintegration into the world economy, falling tariff barriers under the World Trade Organization framework and increasingly sophisticated consumers. The hoped for economic diversification will itself prove helpful in this respect. Such positive effects could together make up the positive supply side shock that, as noted earlier, is often required to reduce inflation to very low levels.

6. Conclusions

In Botswana, a more aggressive anti-inflationary policy is not at present high on the agenda. This is in large part understandable. Inflation is at levels which are tolerable in the everyday sense that protecting the value of income and assets is not a day-to-day concern in Botswana. In contrast, the task of generating employment opportunities for a growing labour force with an unemployment rate that has grown rapidly to exceed twenty percent is a major challenge that must be the highest priority. Botswana has established a good reputation for not allowing inflation to get out of hand, but not yet one for driving it out, and the Government is not being pushed to take a firmer stance on inflation by the electorate.

The purpose of this paper was to see whether the issue should be being taken more seriously.

The analysis has not tried to deny the twin propositions that inflation is costly and that where possible should be avoided. The former is true for a variety of fundamental reasons and, accepting this, the latter follows as a matter of logic. However, it has been argued that the possibility that an economy's optimal rate of inflation, properly defined to include the costs of reducing inflation, may be significantly different from the ideal rate, should be taken seriously. This should not be surprising since in general what is ideal and what is most desirable given the circumstances coincide only rarely.

In the case of Botswana it has been argued that there is little evidence that past inflation has impeded the growth of the economy to any serious extent. This is partly due to the absence of relevant data, since in Botswana sustained periods of high inflation have not occurred frequently, if at all. Also, the evidence on the negative consequences of inflation from elsewhere, while not conclusive from any standpoint, does not seem to suggest that inflation in Botswana has been at levels at which the negative effects start to be felt seriously.

Moreover, it was suggested that the structure of the Botswana economy has been based mainly on sectors that have been relatively impervious to inflation.

On the other hand, current trends suggest fairly strongly that the negative consequences of inflation for Botswana are likely to increase. The necessary diversification away from minerals and Government-led growth may be impeded in that this needs to be based on investment decisions in areas more likely to be sensitive to the inflationary climate. This consideration will gain in importance as other countries become increasingly competitive. In addition, the continuing process of monetization in the economy will inevitably increase the welfare costs of inflation, especially among the poorer households.

For these reasons it seems desirable that looking for further opportunities to permanently reduce inflation should be a serious concern to the Government and, in particular, the Bank of Botswana. Saying this, however, is not to ignore the problems of reconciling this objective with other goals, especially in the short term.

This conclusion is reinforced by looking to the even longer term. It has been emphasised in a variety of fora that Botswana must look to compete on standards that are fully international in outlook and comparison. In the long run, reliance on performance levels that are only relatively good will not count for much. This consideration must also, presumably, apply to matters of macroeconomic policy. In this regard, it is quite clear that the established international standard for inflation is to target rates that may be regarded as constituting price stability. Monetary policy in Botswana should clearly have this as a long-term objective.

References

Agenor, P. 1996. 'The Labour Market and Economic Adjustment', *IMF Staff Papers* Vol.43, No.2. IMF, Washington.

Akerlof, G., Dickens, W., and Perry, G. 1996. 'The Macroeconomics of Low Inflation', *Brookings Papers on Economic Activity*, 1996, No.1.

Atta, J., Jefferis, K. and Mannathoko, I. 1996. 'Small Country Experiences with Exchange Rates and Inflation: The Case of Botswana', *Journal of African Economies*. Vol.5, No.3, pp22–43. Oxford University Press, Oxford.

Bank of Botswana. 1994. *Annual Report 1993*. Bank of Botswana, Gaborone.

Bank of Botswana. 1995. *Annual Report 1994*. Bank of Botswana, Gaborone.

Bank of Botswana. 1996. *Annual Report 1995*. Bank of Botswana, Gaborone.

Bank of England 1996. 'Economic Growth and Employment Through Stability', *Bank of England Quarterly Bulletin*, Vol.36, No.3, pp323–328.

Barro, R. J. 1995. 'Inflation and Economic Growth', *Bank of England Quarterly Bulletin*, Vol.32, No.2, pp166–175.

Bernstein P. L. 1996. *Against the Gods, the Remarkable Story of Risk*, John Wiley and Sons.

Bleany, M.F. 1996. 'Macroeconomic Stability, Investment and Growth in Developing Countries', *Journal of Development Economics*, Vol,48, No,2pp461–477.

Briault, C. 1995. 'The Costs of Inflation', *Bank of England Quarterly Bulletin*, Vol.32, No.1, pp33–45.

Briault, C., Haldane, A., and King, M. 1996. 'Central Bank Independence and Accountability: Theory and Evidence', *Bank of England Quarterly Bulletin*, Vol.33, No.1, pp63–68.

Brittan, S. 1995. *Capitalism with a Human Face*. Edward Elgar, Aldershot.

Bruno, M. and Easterly, W. 1995. 'Does Inflation Lower Growth?' *Finance and Development*. IMF/World Bank, Washington.

Central Statistics Office. 1988. *Household Income and Expenditure Survey 1985/86*. Central Statistics Office, Gaborone.

Central Statistics Office. 1996a. *Household Income and Expenditure Survey 1993/94*. Central Statistics Office, Gaborone.

Central Statistics Office. 1996b. *Consumer Price Statistics, September 1996*. Central Statistics Office, Gaborone.

Central Statistics Office. 1996c. *Employment 1995*. Central Statistics Office, Gaborone.

Dornbusch, R. and Fischer, S. 1993. 'Moderate Inflation', *The World Bank Economic Review*, Vol.7, No.1, pp1–44.

The Economist. 1995. 'The Cost of Inflation',13 May, p90.

The Economist. 1996a. 'Shoot to Kill?', 7 September, p84.

The Economist. 1996b. 'Colchester's Crunchiness', 5 October, p16.

Galbraith, J.K. 1996. *The Good Society: The Humane Agenda*, Sinclair-Stevenson, London.

Government of Botswana. 1994. *1994 Budget Speech*, Ministry of Finance and Development Planning, Gaborone.

Harvey, C. 1992. 'Botswana: Is the Economic Miracle Over?', *Journal of African Economies*, Vol.1, No.3, Oxford University Press, Oxford.

Krugman, P. 1996. 'Stable Prices and Fast Growth: Just Say No', *The Economist*, 31 August 1996.

Jadresic, E. 1996. 'Wage Indexation and the Cost of Disinflation', *IMF Staff Papers* Vol.43, No.4. IMF, Washington.

Lucas, R. E. 1973. 'Some International Evidence on Output – Inflation Trade-offs', *American Economic Review*, No.63, pp526–534.

Prowse, M. 1996. 'Inflation Apologists', *Financial Times*, 30 September 1996, p16.

Pujol, T. and Griffiths, M., 1996. *Moderate Inflation in Poland: A Real Story*, IMF Working Paper WP/96/57. IMF, Washington.

Selwe, J. 1994. 'Monetization and Evidence for Botswana', *The Research Bulletin*, Vol.12, No.1, pp33–47. Bank of Botswana, Gaborone.

Stevenson, A., Muscatelli, V., and Gregory, M. 1988. *Macroeconomic Theory and Stabilisation Policy*. Philip Allan, Hemel Hempstead.

Tanzi, V. and Zee, H. 1996. *Fiscal Policy and Long Run Growth*, IMF Working Paper WP/96/119. IMF, Washington.

Chapter 2

Macroeconomic Policies and Strategies

Policy Options for Savings Mobilization in Botswana

A. Motsomi[1]

1. INTRODUCTION

From the 1960s through to the 1980s, governments in developing countries intervened both in the design and operation of the financial system. The nature of their intervention in the financial system was largely through the establishment of Government owned financial institutions and directed lending at concessional interest rates. As a result of this heavy intervention, savers were largely discouraged from holding domestic financial assets due to the prevalence of negative real interest rates. As a result, by the second half of the 1970s, governments in developing countries often depended heavily on external borrowing to finance budget deficits. When the inflow of foreign capital diminished in the 1980s, many of these countries were faced with a difficult dilemma of how to reduce their deficits owing to the difficult social and political implications of effecting drastic expenditure cuts in the face of tightening borrowing constraints.

Consequently, most governments resorted to central bank borrowing as their financial markets were too shallow to cater for their substantial financing requirements. In cases where such financing entailed issuing money, the result was an acceleration in inflation, which had an adverse impact on the pace of financial sector development. The acceleration in inflation aggravated the situation of negative deposit rates, which then induced investors to make portfolio adjustments from financial savings to real assets, as well as foreign denominated assets. Other alternative measures adopted to curtail the inflationary financing of the deficits were also tantamount to a tax on the financial system and further retarded its development. For instance, requiring banks, insurance companies and other financial institutions to hold part of their investment in low-yielding government securities.

Compared to other developing countries, Botswana's financial system during the post-Independence era has not been repressed for the purposes of financing government budget deficits as the Government has generally been operating budget surpluses. However, the Government's role as a major lender in the financial system has had a pervasive impact on the development of the financial sector by stifling private sector financing initiatives. However, prior to the liberalization of the financial sector in the 1990s, real interest rates were negative, which did not augur well for domestic savings mobilization.

On an international comparative basis, the period from the 1960s to the early 1990s saw gross domestic savings in East Asia increasing more than two-fold relative

---

[1] I wish to thank Dr D. Cowan, Dr Z. Kone and Dr J.S. Salkin for their comments and A. Kganetsano for the preparation of the tables and graphs.

to Gross Domestic Product (GDP), or from 14% in the 1960s to more than 35% in the 1990s. In contrast, over the same period, Latin American savings rates were stagnant, and Sub-Saharan African gross savings rates declined from 12% of GDP in the 1960s to 6% in the 1990s. These regional savings trends were also reflected in the regional growth performances during this period. In the last twenty years, per capita growth in GDP averaged close to 5% in East Asia, 1% in Latin America and 0.5% in Sub-Saharan Africa. The policy implication of the apparent close correlation between savings rates and per capita growth of GDP is that increasing domestic saving should be accorded priority if high per capita income growth is to be attained.

Botswana's savings rate which averaged 15.5% in 1992/93 has been much higher than the 6% average for Sub-Saharan Africa recorded in the 1990s primarily on account of Government budget surpluses, which derived from the diamond export earnings and were accumulated as foreign exchange reserves held by the Central Bank. However, if forecast budget deficits emerge in the 1990s, the contribution of Government savings to overall national savings will decline, and policies for mobilising savings from the private sector will become of critical importance in order to maintain the growth momentum in the economy.

Financial intermediation is an important channel for mobilising domestic savings and funding investment; hence, a successful strategy for savings mobilization requires institutional development, that is, the establishment and promulgation of policies that will facilitate financial intermediation. Whilst commercial banks are currently the key intermediaries, and are likely to remain so for some time to come, non-bank financial intermediaries, such as finance companies, investment trusts and insurance companies, stock exchanges and organised bond markets, play a key role in more developed financial systems and will hopefully do so in Botswana.

This paper discusses policy and institutional developments that can enhance the mobilization of savings with a special emphasis on medium and long-term savings. The second part of the paper focuses on macroeconomic policies that can stimulate private and public savings, and the third section of the paper discusses the role of money and capital markets in savings mobilization. The fourth section summarises the main conclusions and recommendations.

2. POLICIES FOR SAVINGS MOBILISATION

The maintenance of macroeconomic stability[2] is important for providing signals to the private sector regarding the overall direction of economic policies and the credibility of the authorities' commitment to the efficient management of the economy. A stable macroeconomic environment encourages savings and capital accumulation, as well as facilitating long-term planning and investment decisions. A low and predictable rate of inflation is important in the sense that if the private sector anticipates higher inflation, this results in lower expected returns, which in turn induce portfolio reallocations away from real money balances. If such a situation prevails in an economy such as Botswana, which is characterised by underdeveloped capital markets, the

---

[2] That is, an environment of low and predictable inflation, an exchange rate which does not deviate significantly from its equilibrium level, a well managed budget and a reasonable budget deficit relative to national output.

resultant portfolio adjustments would generally be from real money balances to real assets, such as property and cattle.

It is, therefore, important for the Government, especially since it has committed itself to further capital account liberalizations, to avoid being trapped in a situation whereby the ratio of external debt to exports is high. This may signal a 'debt overhang' and as firms and households anticipate higher tax liabilities that will be necessary to service the debt, this may induce them to externalise funds and hence deplete national domestic savings. The role of Government should largely be confined to regulatory functions and its intervention must be geared towards strengthening financial markets and assisting in the promotion of financial development. In this connection, the establishment of a Capital Market Authority to regulate and supervise the activities of the stock exchange, stockbrokers, securities dealing and underwriting, pension and insurance fund managers, unit trusts, and so on, will be a major step in encouraging the further development and deepening of the financial sector. The Government's regulatory and supervisory function should also be geared at ensuring the soundness and solvency of the financial system.

If Government finances were to progressively change to deficits, it should be noted that experience from other developing countries, which have run large deficits, has demonstrated that the reduction in public deficits, which usually entails reforming quasi-public enterprises, the finances of local authorities and the Central Government, have contributed significantly to raising national savings. Since reductions in public recurrent expenditures are often difficult to effect in the short-run, improving tax compliance is another strategy that can help raise public savings. It is, therefore, important to note that smaller budget deficits in addition to their direct impact on savings, also lead to lower inflation and a stable macroeconomic and financial environment. In turn, the lower inflation, through higher real tax revenue, increases public saving levels.

As noted earlier, the Government sector has contributed substantially to national savings in Botswana, which suggests that increasing public savings is an effective means of raising national saving. However, this situation is expected to change in due course, if budget deficits emerge. In order to keep the deficits at sustainable levels, wastage in Government will have to be curtailed and recent efforts to hive off some activities to the private sector will have to be pursued further. In financing its deficits, the Government will have to refrain from borrowing from the insurance and pension systems, as it will crowd out long-term savings that could be invested in private sector assets, but should instead establish a government bill market which will encourage the emergence of a broader market for corporate bonds. The Government should, further, get the financing mix right in that it should not overly or extensively rely on domestic debt to fund the deficits as this can lead to high domestic real interest rates and may in turn result in the deterioration of the deficit. The thrust or centrepiece of an interest policy aimed at promoting savings mobilization is maintaining a positive real interest rate environment. Such rates should not deviate substantially or by wide magnitudes from those prevailing in international capital markets, especially as capital account barriers are dismantled.

Governments have, across the world, embarked on measures such as interest liberalization and raising nominal interest rates to levels above the inflation rate to make the return on savings positive in real terms. However, the empirical investigation of the effect of real interest rates in raising the level of savings yields mixed results. For instance, according to Schmidt-Hebbel *et al.* (1996), country and cross-country studies which have been carried out to test for the impact of interest rates on savings by Giovannini (1983), Corbo and Schmidt-Hebbel (1991), Deaton, (1992) and Edwards (1995) have yielded results which do not show much impact on savings. They further indicate that, studies done by Gupta (1987) and Fry (1988) only showed a small positive response of savings to the real interest rate. The two policy implications of the general insensitivity to the real interest rates are that the reduction in real interest rate would not necessarily curtail private savings and financial liberalization that *inter-alia* raises the real interest rate would not lead to an automatic increase in private savings.

Although empirical studies, which investigated the efficacy of interest rate policies, suggest that they have a negligible impact on savings rates, negative real interest rates if maintained for prolonged periods could induce capital flights out of financial savings. The advantage of such a policy is that positive real returns on financial savings encourage economic agents to save; and with the progressive liberalization of controls in Botswana and its integration into the global economy, positive returns reduce the incentive for capital outflows.

Following the adoption of the Financial Sector Development Strategy in 1990, the Bank of Botswana adopted the maintenance of positive real interest rates as the key intermediate target or objective of monetary policy. Since the adoption of this policy stance, the ninety day Bank of Botswana Certificate (BoBC) rate and the lending rates of commercial banks and other financial institutions have generally been positive in real terms except during times of high inflation, whilst on the other hand, deposit rates of commercial banks and other non-bank financial institutions have largely remained negative in real terms. For instance, deposit rates offered by commercial

FIGURE 1. ULC INTEREST RATES ON DEPOSITS

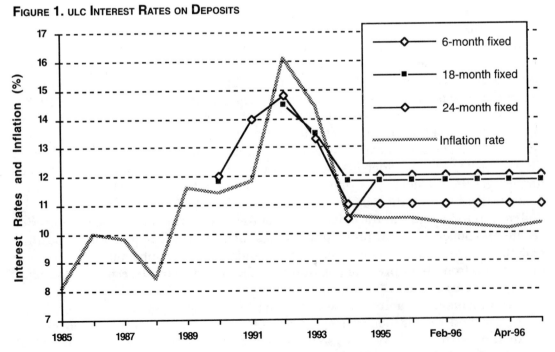

Note: Botswana Financial Statistics are the source of all figures on interest rates on deposits.

FIGURE 2. BSB INTEREST RATES ON DEPOSITS

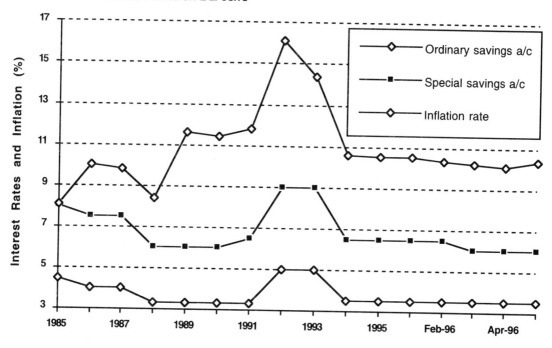

banks on savings accounts, ordinary savings accounts and special savings accounts at the Botswana Building Society (BBS) and the Botswana Savings Bank (BSB) have consistently remained negative in real terms since 1990. The leasing company ulc stands out as the exception to the foregoing observation, as the deposit rates it offers have been positive in real terms since 1994. The persistence of negative real interest

FIGURE 3. BBS INTEREST RATES ON DEPOSITS

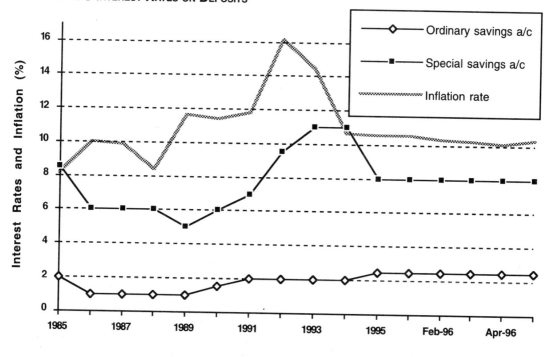

on deposit accounts alluded to above does not accord or augur well for savings mobilization, as savers are not adequately rewarded. Moreover it undermines Government's fiscal incentives to small savers, such as exempting from tax the first P1000 of interest accrued on time and savings deposits.

FIGURE 4. COMMERCIAL BANKS' INTEREST RATES ON DEPOSITS

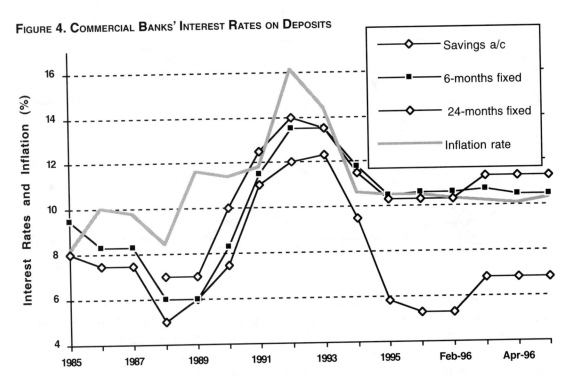

As can be noted from the graphs, interest rates on term deposits (6 and 12 months fixed deposits) offered by commercial banks have only been positive since March 1996. The graphs above depict the trend in selected deposit rates offered by commercial banks, ulc, the BSB and the BBS compared with the annual inflation rate since 1985.

3. POLICIES AIMED AT INSTITUTIONAL DEVELOPMENT TO PROMOTE SAVINGS MOBILIZATION

Introductory notes

The importance of a capital market stems from its critical function of mobilising savings and channelling those savings into productive investments. The capital market can be divided into roughly two distinct segments: the non-securities segment comprising financial intermediaries, typically banks and non-bank financial institutions providing term loans and mortgages; and the securities segment in which negotiable securities, such as bonds and shares, are used to mobilise long-term savings. The financial system in Botswana is characterised by a fairly well developed banking sector, a money market, the absence of a bond market, and a small, but growing, stock market.

Institutional development *per se* cannot guarantee an increase in savings for a developing country like Botswana where a considerable amount of savings is held in non-monetary assets such as cattle. But the development of bond and equity markets may, in the long run, not just bring about portfolio shifts from non-monetary assets, but may eventually increase the annual flows of savings into financial assets.

One of the key institutional prerequisites for the mobilization of savings is the extent or degree of accessibility to banking and other non-bank institutions. The East Asian experience is instructive in this regard as James *et al.* (1987), rightly note that:

'The growing reach of the financial systems in Asian countries during the 1970s and 1980s led to the substitution of financial for non-financial instruments over the past two decades, have been a powerful stimulus for increased saving.'

The extension of branch banking to make depository institutions readily accessible, as well as increasing the volume and diversity of financial assets, has been found to have provided the necessary momentum to the efforts to mobilise savings in the East Asian countries. The ongoing closure of rural branches by commercial banks in Botswana, whilst it is a reflection of the freedom enjoyed by the banks under a liberalised financial environment to close unprofitable branches, nevertheless does not augur well for efforts to mobilise savings as this reduces the accessibility of the banking services to the savers in the areas affected. The provision of new types of savings instruments other than bank deposits to cater for the sophisticated urban savers with higher incomes, who are generally responsive to yield and liquidity differentials and are often prepared to take a risk in order to gain higher than expected returns, has equally been found to be a major stimulant to savings mobilization in East Asian countries. In general, if Botswana were to increase the supply and diversity of financial instruments which can readily be traded in well organised markets, this could go a long way in generating additional savings.

The money market

The introduction of the BoBCs in May 1991 ushered in the establishment of the money market in Botswana. The Certificates were primarily introduced to mop up excess liquidity in the financial system and to promote the development of a bond market. The P50 000 minimum value of the certificates implies that small savers who are currently earning negative real returns on their savings accounts at the commercial banks and other non-bank financial institutions are effectively precluded from earning the higher positive real return on the certificates enjoyed by the commercial banks and other large depositors. In the light of this, it has been argued that in order to encourage small-scale savers, access to the certificates should be relaxed to not only to diversify the menu of savings instruments at the disposal of savers, but also to enable access to higher positive real returns, and thus assist efforts to mobilise savings.

The need to develop a bond market

Issues relating to the establishment of a bond market in Botswana have been on the agenda since the adoption of the Financial Sector Development Strategy in NDP 7. This section briefly discusses how the development of a bond market can contribute towards efforts to mobilise medium and long-term savings.

The Government's role as the major lender of long-term finance to parastatal bodies through the Public debt Service Fund (PDSF)/Revenue Stabilization Fund (RSF) at submarket interest rates over the years has been recognised as an impediment to the development of a bond market in Botswana. However, some progress has been made in this regard, the escalation of PDSF interest rates closer to market rates, (i.e., to 12.1% and 14.6% for financial and non-financial parastatals, respectively) is a positive development in addressing concessionary funding to these organizations. Secondly, Government announced in the 1996 Budget Speech that the PDSF will be managed like a revolving fund, and, in particular, the explicit pronouncement was given that:

> 'The implications of this change for the parastatals is that if they require new funds to expand or improve their services, they will have to depend, to an increasing extent, upon surpluses which they can generate themselves or upon funds which they can raise from the domestic capital market. Such a change should be welcomed because not only will it oblige the parastatals to become more commercial in their conduct, but it will also constitute an important factor in the development of the domestic financial sector'[3].

This announcement raised hopes that the Government is now ready to move forward with parastatal bond issues. The two major issues that would require resolution prior to the bond issues are the need for some form of guarantee and the establishment of a rediscounting facility. A rediscounting facility will enable investors to discount the bonds if they require liquidity prior to maturity. Listing the bonds would also enhance the liquidity of the bonds concerned.

The development of a bond market in Botswana would diversify the menu of financial instruments at the disposal of investors, and would provide especially for institutional investors, such as pension funds and insurance companies, an additional outlet into which to diversify their portfolios. The non-cash portfolios of these investors is currently spread between real estate, shares and offshore investments. The emergence of a bond market may induce these investors to allocate a higher share of their investments to bonds, a development which would make a substantial contribution towards the mobilization of long-term savings.

Although institutional investors will continue to invest part of their assets in offshore markets as a means of risk diversification and return enhancement, if the emerging domestic bond market offers sufficiently attractive returns comparable to those prevailing in external markets, this may induce these investors to allocate a higher proportion of their investments to the local bond market, a development which will increase the level of funds available for domestic investments.

The excess liquidity that is currently absorbed by BoBCs is not necessarily all short-term money, as part of it is invested in the certificates for lack of alternative medium to longer term instruments. The emergence of a bond market would in future result in the absorption of such medium and long-term funds in bonds, thus enhancing the level of medium to longer term savings in the economy.

---

3   1996 Budget Speech, p9.

The development of the Botswana Stock Exchange

Generally, equity markets are important for their role in attracting or tapping foreign savings and in this regard, can assist countries in avoiding excessive dependence on foreign debt which can expose them to higher debt servicing obligations during times when global interest rates rise. Apart from acting as a conduit for channelling foreign savings, stock markets contribute to the mobilization of domestic savings by enhancing the menu of financial instruments to investors to diversify their portfolio.

The Botswana Stock Exchange (BSE) has grown from a market capitalization of P255 million in December 1989, to P1202 million in November 1996. In order to assess the state of development of the BSE, three indicators of stock market development have been computed, and international comparisons made with selected stock markets in Africa, Latin America, East Asia and Industrialised Countries. These are summarised in Table 1. The three ratios computed are the market capitalization ratio, and two measures of stock market liquidity, the total value traded to GDP ratio and the turnover ratio. The market capitalization ratio is defined as the value of listed shares divided by GDP. The economic importance of this ratio is that it is assumed that market size has a positive correlation with the market's ability to mobilise capital and risk diversification. Liquidity ratios capture the ease with which shares are bought and sold. Total value traded/GDP is equal to the total shares traded on the market divided by GDP. The ratio '...measures the organized trading of equities as a share of national output, and should therefore positively reflect liquidity on an economy wide basis' (Demirgüç-Kunt and Levine, 1986, p295). The second liquidity measure is the turnover ratio which is the value of total shares traded divided by market capitalization. A high turnover ratio is regarded as an indicator of low transactions costs.

Inspection of Table 1 shows that the BSE capitalization ratio is 0.16 which indicates that although the BSE has grown since its establishment in 1989, it still has limited capacity to mobilise capital. Compared to a selected number of African countries, its market capitalization ratio is higher than that of Nigeria, but lower than those of Zimbabwe and South Africa. Compared to the Latin American countries, the ratio for Botswana is higher than that of Brazil, but below those of Mexico and Chile. Compared to the East Asian countries, Botswana's market capitalization is lower than all of them except Indonesia and is equal to that of India. The two measures of liquidity indicate a market whose liquidity is very low which reflects that there is relatively little activity in the market. The BSE's turnover ratio compares favourably with other selected African markets, exceeding that of Nigeria and Zimbabwe, but lower than that of South Africa. The BSE's ratios come no way near the more liquid markets of East Asia. The BSE's low liquidity is due largely to the fact that at the end of 1996, with only twelve companies listed on the market, there is a limited supply of shares, and in the absence of alternative long dated instruments, investors tend to hold on to their shares.

It is worth noting that for Botswana, non-mining GDP has been used in order to remove the pervasive effect of the dominant mining sector.

Two inferences can, therefore, be drawn regarding the level of development of the BSE based on the ratios in Table 1. Despite progress that has been made on the number of companies that have been listed and the resultant increase in market capitalization, the equity market in Botswana is still deficient in terms of its capacity to mobilise capital and the market's liquidity still remains very low.

TABLE 1. INDICATORS OF STOCK MARKET DEVELOPMENT, 1986–1993[a] (ANNUAL AVERAGE)

ECONOMY	MARKET CAPITALIZATION [b]	TOTAL VALUE TRADED/GDP[c]	TURNOVER [d]
INDUSTRIALISED			
France	0.27	0.09	0.35
Germany	0.24	0.35	1.47
Japan	1.08	0.62	0.54
UK	0.92	0.41	0.44
USA	0.64	0.41	0.65
EAST ASIA			
Hong Kong	1.36	0.59	0.44
India	0.16	0.06	0.5
Indonesia	0.06	0.02	0.23
Israel	0.21	0.11	0.72
Malaysia	1.28	0.46	0.24
Philippines	0.24	0.04	0.23
Singapore	1.04	0.35	0.34
Thailand	0.36	0.22	0.7
LATIN AMERICA			
Mexico	0.22	0.09	0.56
Brazil	0.11	0.05	0.48
Chile	0.52	0.04	0.08
AFRICA			
Botswana	0.16	0.01[e]	0.04
Nigeria	0.04	0	0.01
South Africa	1.54	0.08	0.05
Zimbabwe	0.18	0.01	0.03

Notes:
[a] 1989–1993 for Botswana (author's calculations).
[b] Market capitalization ratio is the value of stocks divided by GDP.
[c] Total value traded/GDP is the total value of shares divided by GDP.
[d] Turnover is given by total value traded divided by market capitalization.
[e] For Botswana, non-mining GDP is used in the computations.

Source: Demirgüç-Kunt and Levine (1996).

Other than life insurance and pension funds, shares on the BSE are the only other financial instruments available in the financial sector for the mobilization of long-term savings, hence the need for appropriate incentives and legislative reforms to raise the volume of savings channelled through to equities, as well as to increase the supply of equities in the market. The Government has provided fiscal incentives to help increase the supply of equities by encouraging companies to list on the BSE, as well as providing demand incentives to increase the attractiveness of equities as an alternative savings instrument.

An announcement was made in the 1991 Budget Speech to the effect that companies which sell 25% of their share capital to the public will receive a deduction from taxable income, which would effectively reduce their rate of tax by one-eighth to 35% at that time over five years. The Government also abolished the double taxation of dividends by stipulating that they be taxed once only as corporate income, and be distributed to shareholders as net dividends. Furthermore, the enactment of the Botswana Stock Exchange Act in July 1994 strengthened the legality and transparency of the business and conduct of the exchange, thus providing the much needed confidence to investors that improprieties and market manipulation will be guarded against. Other countries, such as Mexico, Brazil and Egypt, have used demand incentives in the form of either special tax credits or deductions from taxable income to individuals investing in shares of public companies.

However, notwithstanding the above measures, the BSE, as noted earlier, still has a low capitalization ratio and low liquidity, which implies that its potential to mobilise long-term savings can still be improved. One of the legislative reforms that is necessary to enhance the BSE's capacity to tap the global savings market is in place. The next step is to consider the abolition of the current exchange control restriction that foreign portfolio investors should not own more than 49% of the free stock of the company unless prior permission has been granted by the Bank of Botswana. Although the rationale for this regulation was well intentioned to ensure that foreign portfolio investors do not crowd out citizen investors, recent experience, whereby the Botswana Development Corporation's exclusive offer of 46 million of Kgolo Ya Sechaba and Sechaba shares to citizen and resident entities resulted in only 34% of the offer being taken up, puts into question the justification of this provision. The abolition of this regulation will remove an administrative bottleneck, which can unleash portfolio investment on the exchange, thus boosting long-term savings.

In addition, structural reforms, such as partial or complete privatization of public enterprises, has helped in some countries to enhance market capitalization and the general activity in the stock market through an expansion of the supply of equities which are attractive even to foreign investors. The Government's undertaking in the 1995 Budget Speech to privatise Air Botswana once it is profitable, might, if it materialises, provide the much needed impetus to the BSE's market capitalization, as well as general activity, which might increase the liquidity of the market in the long run. This, however, is dependent on whether this and other parastatals are privatised through public issue.

Contractual savings institutions

Contractual savings institutions encompass national provident funds and life insurance companies, as well as pension schemes. Given the long-term nature of their liabilities, coupled with their relatively stable cash flows, these institutions are an ideal source of long-term savings as they generally cater for the longer-term requirements of savers.

As savers acquire more financial assets and become more sophisticated, they demand longer-term investments yielding higher returns as compared to those offered by the banking sector. Contractual savings institutions offer savers an alternative to banking sector products, hence, they provide an opportunity to diversify national savings, as well as to assist with the development of capital markets.

With the exception of Malaysia, Singapore and a handful of others, most developing countries only have small contractual savings industries with their financial systems dominated by large commercial banks. Based on a sample of 13 developing countries with fairly advanced financial systems, the World Bank (1989) estimated that in 1985 commercial banks accounted for more that 50% of total financial sector assets against the contractual savings institutions' share of a mere 5%.

TABLE 2. ASSETS OF FINANCIAL INSTITUTIONS IN BOTSWANA (PULA MILLION)

	1990	PERCENTAGE SHARE
Commercial Banks	1353.9	61.6
Development Finance Institutions	623.8	28.4
Life Insurance	101.5	4.6
Pension/Provident Funds	120.0	5.4
TOTAL	2199.2	100.0

Source: NDP 7.

The data in Table 2 show that Botswana is no exception in this regard, as the country's financial system is also dominated by commercial banks whose assets in 1990 accounted for 62% of those in the financial sector, whilst the assets of contractual savings institutions accounted for only 10%.

Whilst life insurance is generally motivated by the necessity to provide financial protection to the insured person's dependants, governments often encourage the savings component of life insurance through the provision of fiscal incentives. Botswana is no exception in this connection, as the income earned from the investment of life premiums is exempt from tax. Furthermore, life policy holders benefit from a consolidated tax allowance in respect of life insurance premiums, medical and educational costs. Fiscal incentives in the form of an allowance equal to P9000 per annum or 15% of salary, whichever is lower, is in place for the encouragement of pension schemes.

There are a number of reasons why the life insurance industry in Botswana is not well developed as shown by the size of its assets in relation to the financial system. These include income and wealth constraints, and possibly a lack of financial sophistication on the part of savers. In addition to the Government tax incentives outlined above, the following are some of the measures that can be embarked upon to encourage the further development of the contractual savings industry in Botswana in order that the industry may contribute significantly to the mobilization of long-term savings.

With respect to life insurance, Botswana Life Insurance effectively has a monopoly in this industry and the encouragement of new players will stimulate competition and bring about product diversification and competitive premiums to stimulate demand for life policies. The Government may also consider appropriate incentives to promote group based business, as this has been a major contributory factor to the growth of life insurance and pension schemes in developed countries. The distribution of income and wealth has an impact on the demand for life insurance; hence if the industry is to make a bigger contribution to mobilization of national savings, it is important for the Government to strive for a more equitable distribution of income and wealth. As mentioned earlier in this paper, a low and stable rate of inflation is also important in encouraging savings in general; but it is also essential for stimulating the demand for life insurance as high inflation results in low investment returns on the insurance companies' reserves invested in financial assets. The maintenance of an effective regulatory and supervisory system for insurance companies and pension funds is necessary to protect consumers, and ensure that they maintain sufficient reserves to enable them to meet future claims, as well as ensuring that reserves are not invested in speculative assets.

Evidence from other developing countries, especially the East Asian countries of Singapore and Malaysia, shows that if they are well structured and properly managed, national provident funds can make a substantial contribution to the mobilization of long-term financial savings. For instance, the reserves of the Central Provident Fund of Singapore were equivalent to 65% of GDP in 1989; while the Employee Provident Fund of Malaysia, had reserves equal to 41% of GDP in 1987. Given the success of these schemes in mobilising long-term savings, the question is whether a similar scheme may be introduced in Botswana. In view of the fact that there are several employer based pension schemes, the introduction of a National Provident Fund (which by nature is a forced savings scheme, which entails state set employer and employee contributions) may adversely impact on employment creation. Corporations may be inclined to curtail employment levels in order to minimise the impact of National Provident Fund (NPF) contributions on their cost structure and hence reduce the effect on their profits. The authorities may equally find it difficult to force an NPF on corporations that already have well established employer based pension schemes. To encourage long-term savings through contractual savings institutions, the Government may have to explore additional preferential tax treatment to these institutions.

4. CONCLUSIONS AND RECOMMENDATIONS

The mobilization of savings from the private sector will become increasingly important if the economy is to maintain growth rates similar to those in the past, especially in view of the projected emergence of Government budget deficits and the consequent decline in the level of public sector savings. To stimulate private sector savings, the authorities will have to maintain a stable macroeconomic environment, that is, a low and predictable rate of inflation, sustainable budget deficits and a stable real exchange rate. To run sustainable deficits, the Government will have to reduce wastage in the public sector, reform parastatal enterprises and increase tax compliance.

On the monetary front, positive real interest rates that are in line with those prevailing in international capital markets will be necessary to prevent capital flight, especially as capital account controls are progressively abolished. The real return on savings accounts at commercial banks and other non-bank financial institutions has to be positive in order to adequately reward savers and pre-empt portfolio adjustments from financial to non-financial assets. Access to the attractive returns earned on BoBCs will have to be widened to accommodate small savers.

In order to diversify the menu of savings instruments and to tap long-term funds, especially of contractual savings institutions, the authorities have to expedite efforts to establish a bond market through parastatal bond issues and embark on measures to increase the supply of shares on the Botswana Stock Exchange by privatising some parastatals through a public floatation of the shares. The current exchange control restrictions on foreign investors on the exchange will have to be abolished to enhance its capacity to mobilise external savings.

Whilst national provident funds have led to substantial accumulation of long-term savings in countries such as Singapore and Malaysia, it is the contention of this paper that such a scheme, if established in Botswana, may impose an additional financial burden on corporations and can induce corporations to reduce employment in order to curtail contributions to the National Provident Fund. It is, therefore, recommended that additional tax incentives be considered to encourage the contractual savings industry. Regulatory and supervisory structures for the stock exchange, stock-brokers, pension and insurance fund managers will have to be strengthened by establishing a capital market authority.

REFERENCES

Corbo, V. and Schmidt-Hebbel, K. 1991. 'Public Policies and Saving in Developing Countries', *Journal of Development Economics*, Vol.36, No.1, pp89–114.

Deaton A. 1992. *Understanding Consumption*. Oxford University Press, New York.

Demirgüç-Kunt, A. and Levine, R. 1996. 'Stock Market Development and Financial intermediaries: Stylized Facts', *The World Bank Economic Review*. A Symposium Issue on Stock Markets and Economic Development. World Bank, Washington..

Edwards, S. 1995. 'Why are Saving Rates so Different Across Countries? An International Comparative Analysis. NBER Working Paper 5097'. National Bureau of Economic Research, Cambridge, Mass.

Fischer, B. 1989. 'Savings Mobilization in Developing Countries: Bottlenecks and Reform Proposals', *Savings and Development*, Vol.78.

Fry, M. 1988. *Money, Interest and Banking in Economic Development*. The John Hopkins University Press, Baltimore.

Giovannini, A. 1983. 'The Interest Elasticity of Savings in Developing Countries: The Existing Evidence', *World Development*, Vol.11, No.7, pp601–07.

Government Budget Speech. Various Issues, Government Printer, Gaborone.

Government Gazette, Botswana. 1995. Vol.33, No.29.

Gupta, K.L. 1987. 'Aggregate savings, Financial Intermediation and Interest Rate', *Review of Economic Statistics*, Vol.69, No.2, pp303–11.

Holst, J. 1990. *Savings and Development, Personal Savings and Financial Development: Policies and Prospects*. Department of International Economic and Social Affairs, United Nations.

James, W.E., Naya, S. and Meier, G.M. 1987. *Asian Development: Economic Success and Policy Lessons*. University of Wisconsin Press, Wisconsin.

Ministry of Finance and Development Planning. 1991. *National Development Plan 7, 1991–1997*. Government Printer, Gaborone.

Naya, S. and McCleery, R. 1994. *Relevance of Asian Development Experiences to African Problems.* ICS Press, San Francisco.

Schmidt-Hebbel, K., Servén, L. and Solimano, A. 1996. 'Savings and Investment: Paradigms, Puzzles and Policies', *The World Bank Research Observer*, Vol.11, No.1 pp87–117.

Vittas, D. and M. Skully. 1991. *Overview of Contractual Savings Institutions.* The World Bank Working Papers.

World Bank. 1989. *Financial Systems and Development.* World Bank, Washington.

Savings Mobilization in the Household Sector: The Case of Botswana

Jens Reinke[1]

1. INTRODUCTION

Since Independence, Botswana has developed from one of the poorest countries in the world to one of the wealthiest in Africa. Its experience of high growth rates over long periods of time has invited comparisons with the 'miracle' economies in Asia. Unlike other high growth countries during that time, Botswana's success is not associated with sweat shop labour and the frugal life, but with 'windfall gains', the discovery and efficient exploitation of its mineral reserves. In most high growth countries, households generally make a large contribution to gross national savings and thus to investable capital. Next to efficient policy makers and innovative entrepreneurs, thrifty households constitute the third pillar of high growth economies. In Botswana, households are large borrowers from the banking system while savings are mostly generated by Government. Before long, this situation will prove untenable. As the economy grows, mineral rents decline in importance and Government savings dwindle, private sector savings will, therefore, be the key to keeping Botswana on a high, long-term growth path. A savings policy, therefore, should be an integral part of long-term growth strategies and should receive adequate policy support although Botswana does not presently suffer a capital shortage.[2]

While Botswana avoided the most typical phenomenon of commodity booms, the Dutch Disease, income rose much quicker than productive capabilities during the diamond boom. Excess liquidity, it is argued, has undermined the remunerative nature of thrift and created a credit-driven consumer culture. As mineral rents have spoilt Government, so has cheap credit spoilt many households. On the other hand, countries with very high savings rates, mainly East Asian economies, are poorly endowed with natural resources, but richly with thrifty households.

This paper seeks to clarify issues relating to household savings and present a critique of the present policy which sets the framework for savings decisions by private

---

[1]   I wish to thank the editorial committee and an anonymous referee for helpful comments. Further valuable suggestions were made by Charles Harvey and Johanna Boestel, who also supported my efforts with data and insights on Asian countries.

[2]   Gross domestic savings in Botswana are sufficiently high, although they have declined from 47.6% in 1988/89 to 29.9% in 1993/94. Yet, Government contributed 79.9% to total savings in 1993/94. Private households' outstanding loans from commercial banks stood at 121.9% of households' deposits with commercial banks. The net indebtedness stands at 118.0% if deposits and loans from the Botswana Savings Bank are included (Bank of Botswana, 1996a).

households in Botswana. It will stress the need for a micro-economic understanding of savings behaviour and will scrutinise the economic environment in Botswana. In recent policy debates, often dominated by the Financial Liberalization Hypothesis, it is argued that interest rates – stable and positive real interest rates – are the single most important anchor for a savings policy.[3] However, economic theory remains ambiguous about the role of interest rates, and this paper will argue that there are other, equally important determinants of savings behaviour, notably the policy framework and institutional development. Policy makers are thus called upon not only to remove interest rate ceilings, but also to reorganise the credit markets, to remove subsidies from markets that serve as substitute savings, to review legislation that regulates deposit-taking financial institutions and to consider taxation as a further variable that influences household savings decisions.

Section 2 clarifies the concept of savings for this study, Section 3 considers factors that influence the attractiveness of holding financial assets in formal markets, while Section 4 explores households' dependence on holding such assets. Section 5 evaluates key micro-economic variables in Botswana with regard to the incentives to save. Section 6 overviews the issue of forced savings, and Section 7 maps out possible policy directions for Botswana, while Section 8 concludes.

2. CONCEPTUALISING SAVINGS BEHAVIOUR

Economists define savings as the difference between income and consumption during some specific time period. However, in the context of policy debates, the concept of savings has assumed multiple meanings. Contributors to debates about financial sector development in developing countries argue about the proper understanding of savings and the relative significance and desirability of savings in various forms.

Defining savings

In simplistic statistical data, savings are usually equated with deposits at formal financial institutions, that is, those that are licensed to accept deposits, such as banks and building societies. However, in many countries formal financial institutions are not well developed and the functioning of financial markets is impaired. Under such conditions, deposits with informal financial intermediaries often play an important role. Some economists have argued that informal intermediaries are at least as efficient as formal ones, and thus savings held in the 'curb market' are as desirable, from a policy maker's point of view, as are those of formal institutions (van Wijnbergen, 1985). In the long run, most economists acknowledge financial development is meant to enable formal financial institutions to absorb the bulk of, if not all, financial savings.

---

3   It should be noted, however, that the role assigned to interest rates has only evolved over time as theory was adapted to policy. The Financial Liberalisation Hypothesis, as established by McKinnon (1973) and Shaw (1973), emphasised interest rates and institutional aspects in even measure. Later, in the policy debates of the 1980s and 1990s, the Financial Liberalisation Hypothesis became more associated with Fry through his writings (1980, 1987) and in advisory roles. Unfortunately, some of the complexity of the original was lost in application of economic theory to policy and political debate, as has been the tendency with many other 'great theories' before.

However, Batswana save much more than either of these approaches acknowledges. Savings rely on a 'store of wealth' which can be provided by money-based assets. But in underdeveloped countries with fragmented or inefficient financial markets and institutions, other forms of savings – such as property or livestock, but also gold and other valuables – usually play a large role. In Botswana, both private sector housing and cattle appear to be important assets in household savings portfolios, especially for high income groups. It is often argued that savings based on physical assets are induced by the absence of sufficiently attractive financial assets (Gupta, 1984). Thus financial development will encourage savers to hold a larger part of their savings portfolio in the form of financial assets. Savings held as physical assets are sometimes deemed undesirable from a policy point of view, although such an evaluation depends on the assumptions about the efficiency of intermediation and the productivity of various forms of savings.

While the analysis of household savings has to incorporate the issue of non-financial and informally held savings, this paper identifies the objective of a savings policy in Botswana as raising the level of savings deposited in formal financial institutions, including banks, building societies, credit unions and insurance companies. Thus there are two distinct effects through which savings policy can achieve its objective: it can either increase monetary savings by discouraging consumption; or it can induce portfolio shifts towards assets held in the financial system.

Determinants of savings

In standard macroeconomic models, savings depend on either of two variables, interest or income.[4] In Keynesian-type models, income is the determinant of the savings level. The savings function consists of an autonomous savings component that is normally thought to be negative and a coefficient stating the marginal propensity to save in relation to income. Such a simple model, however, does not allow an understanding of determinants of the size of the two parameters. Savings policy may affect either parameter, but Keynesian theory offers little insight into the determinants of that function. Savings, in any case, are not the focus of 'demand side' economics.

In contrast, supply side economics – neo-classical theory and especially the Financial Liberalization Hypothesis – emphasises the importance of savings because they are viewed as the quantitative constraint on investment and growth. In this framework, savings are seen as dependent primarily on the interest rate. This assumption has received scrutiny in the context of the Financial Liberalization Hypothesis and extensive empirical studies have been conducted. The controversy, however, is continuing.[5] While the evidence may, in fact, point to the verification of the importance of interest rates for variations of the savings level over time, it is equally clear that interest rate differentials cannot explain the differences of savings levels across countries.[6]

---

[4]   For presentation purposes, the two standard macroeconomic schools of thought are presented in a rudimentary form. In any case, the point is confirmed that both schools' fundamental arguments do not contribute to the understanding of national savings levels.

[5]   The argument on liberalization is reflected in Fry (1980) and McKinnon (1986), while some neo-structuralist positions are captured by van Wijnbergen (1983) and Diaz Alejandro (1985). Again, it should be remembered that this controversy has, arguably, also led to a distraction from the more important issues as identified by the founders of the Financial Liberalisation Hypothesis, who view institutional development and positive real interest rates as equally important.

Mainstream economists would hold that such variations are determined by the 'autonomous' component, or exogenous factors in a country's savings function, and thus, possibly, beyond the reach of rational economic analysis. The 'autonomous' component could then, according to this argument, only be explained by cultural differences: the Japanese are a thriftier people than the Americans, the Germans will always save more than the British.[7] However, the understanding of long-term trends requires an understanding of the determinants of such 'autonomous' components, of the rationale of individuals' decision-making. Therefore, the interest shifts from macroeconomic aggregation to the analysis of country-specific institutions that impede or support savings at the household level. The micro-economic analysis of the choices that households face will thus be at the centre of this article.

Optimization of the savings rate

When defining the optimal savings rate, economists make implicit assumptions about important policy objectives.[8] From a macroeconomic perspective, the 'Golden Rule' maintains that the optimal savings rate is the one that realises long-term 'steady growth' along the 'maximum path of consumption' (Phelps, 1961 and Robinson, 1962). For practical reasons, this objective is usually simplified to the objective of achieving a 'satisfactory' level of economic growth that provides steadily increasing consumption opportunities while maintaining a stable savings rate. Benchmarks are often sought in the high-growth Asian countries which have savings rates generally in excess of 30% and realised growth rates between 6% and 10% over long periods.[9]

From a micro-economic perspective, macroeconomic performance is seen merely as the outcome of individuals' maximization behaviour. Individuals choose between present and future consumption according to their intertemporal preferences. The sum of all individuals' decisions in a particular economy would thus present the optimal savings rate if there are no distortions or restrictions on individuals' decisions.

---

6   The lack of a generally accepted conclusion cannot be overemphasised. Rather than clarifying the positions, empirical evidence has further fuelled the controversy between Financial Liberalisation Hypothesis proponents and critics. On empirical grounds, disagreement focuses notably at the interpretation of results in face of market 'irregularities' in developing countries, such as the 'curb market', and on the appropriate understanding of aggregate savings in fragmented financial systems.

7   Blundell-Wignall et al. (1991, p13) argue, for example, that macroeconomic results are explained by 'the strongly conservative instincts of German households' and the fact 'that German households are known to have a strong preference for saving'. Similar statements were made concerning Japanese households as Japan maintained a high savings rate despite low interest rates. While such statements illustrate the difficulties to determine savings levels from a macroeconomic perspective, they remain nonetheless unsatisfactory as a guide to savings policy.

8   As a precise optimal savings rate may be problematic to calculate in practice, such attempts encounter a range of conceptual problems (Hahn, 1995). It seems preferable to express the desired level of savings as a range. Almost every government and economic school of thought makes implicit assumptions about the desirability of such a range when discussing the problems of savings being too high, or, more frequently, too low.

9   At times, savings rates in the East Asian tiger economies were well above that level. Singapore has experienced saving raes of over 40% and Korea and Taiwan of close to 40% of GNP (Hahn, 1995; Husain, 1995; Monetary Authority of Singapore, 1991; Republic of China, 1996a). The precise definition of savings measures, especially of those relating to household savings, vary from country to country.

A priori, there is no reason to assume that the ideal savings level of the Golden Rule would coincide with micro-economic maximization. This poses a policy problem as it indicates that private savings have social externalities. Individuals plan their savings and treat growth as exogenous, while in fact growth is determined, *inter alia*, by aggregate savings behaviour.

But in many instances, the two approaches lead to one policy position; in many countries distortions exist that suppress savings. Liberalization – the removal of restrictions leading to a rise of the interest rate or the improvement of other factors – is argued to cause households to increase their planned savings rate and thus their intertemporal welfare. Simultaneously, such a policy would also increase gross national savings, leading the economy onto a higher growth path. In practical application, higher savings are thus seen as improved savings behaviour from both micro and macro economic perspectives, and the question of precise 'optimality' is, for the time being, dispensed with. This view assumes that a savings rate of forty percent is certainly not too high, as it is seen as an important explanation for the successes of East Asian countries. Following this line, in this paper savings policy will refer to any set of policy actions that aims at raising the savings rate above its present level.

Roles of savings for households

Conceptually, savings are thought of, and represented in economic theory, as either an accumulation of wealth, which, if transformed into productive capital, leads to a virtuous cycle of accumulation, or as smoothing out intertemporal consumption in face of uneven needs, emergencies and lumpy expenditure. The first view illustrates the position of Botswana, where savings held as foreign reserves constitute large macroeconomic assets. But, arguably, households save primarily in order to effect intertemporal consumption decisions, to preserve purchasing power for future consumption, and not to change their net wealth independently of intertemporal consumption decisions. Similarly, household credit is normally not related to investment decisions but to 'bringing forward' consumption.[10]

The assumption that household savings in Botswana are significantly below the desirable level, viewed from a long-term, growth-oriented perspective, is in fact quite

TABLE 1. HOUSEHOLD CREDIT AND HOUSEHOLD DEPOSITS WITH COMMERCIAL BANKS AND CREDIT AS A PERCENTAGE OF DEPOSITS IN BOTSWANA (PULA MILLION)

END YEAR	1991	1992	1993	1994	1995
LOANS	328.9	491.1	603.5	646.6	781.8
DEPOSITS	392.0	454.1	558.5	609.5	641.2
LOANS / DEPOSITS (%)	83.9	108.1	108.1	106.1	121.9

Source: Bank of Botswana (1996a).

---

[10] In the case of informal sector entrepreneurs, the problem arises that household and business functions are vested in the same person and are usually not clearly distinguished. This paper proceeds on the assumption that the magnitude of this distortion in Botswana is negligible.

uncontroversial. The household sector is an important 'dissaver' in the Botswana economy, being a net borrower from the banking sector (see Table 1). Also, there are important distortions in the economic environment in Botswana as it presents itself to the household sector. A general overview would suggest that these policies favour consumption over savings and impede important developments of financial markets and the private sector in general, as will be discussed below.

3. PRIVATE COSTS AND PRIVATE RETURNS OF SAVINGS: INTEREST RATES, TRANSACTION COSTS AND PERCEIVED RISK

The attractiveness of specific savings instruments is crucial to households' decisions about the quantity of savings, and the choice of alternative assets. There are various variables that influence the attractiveness of financial savings generally and of specific instruments both on formal and informal financial markets, and of non-financial assets. In the following, three variables will be assessed – interest rates, transaction costs and risk – that influence the attractiveness of financial assets.

Interest rates

Interest rate policy is now generally the first 'port of call' for any savings strategy, following the acceptance of the 'financial repression' view into a mainstream policy critique. This view maintains that household savings are responsive to the return on financial assets, and that insufficient savings are thus founded in low, 'repressed' interest rates, often negative in real terms. The representative individual, or household, is seen maximising total utility over all periods, dependent on the individual's discount rate and the real interest rate for savings, by lowering consumption in response to rising interest rates.[11]

The appeal of the interest rate approach lies in its compatibility with Marshallian models in general and with neo-classical views of micro-economic decision-making in particular. Accordingly, the assertion that interest rates are the dominant

---

[11] A textbook example of this proposition would show a one-asset two-period model where a rational decision maker with 'normal' intertemporal preferences chooses between present and future consumption and unspecified savings. If the individual chooses to consume now, the costs are expressed in foregone consumption in the next period. In the case of an interest rate hike, the costs of present consumption in terms of future consumption are also increased. Therefore, in adjusting to the substitution effect of the interest rate rise, the individual replaces present with future consumption. However, there is also a wealth effect. Higher interest rates make the individual better off in all periods due to income from savings balances. The individual would, in response to increased wealth, tend to consume more. Especially in studies related to the Permanent Income Hypothesis, it has in fact been argued on empirical grounds that interest increases lower the savings rate because of the wealth effect. Additionally, many models incorporate more than one 'store of value'. In this case, interest rates affect only the interest bearing asset while the alternative – such as physical assets or, indeed, informal financial markets – is affected by respective market conditions. Higher interest rates induce a portfolio shift towards bank deposits. In such a case, results could be more mixed. Increased interest rates on formal financial markets would lead to higher savings in the financial system, but may adversely affect savings of the alternative 'store of value'. The level of aggregate savings would thus depend on the linkages between those savings alternatives, but interest rates could exert a 'pull' of saved resources into formal institutions.

determinant of savings has been placed at the centre of the Financial Liberalization Hypothesis. Financial Liberalization has formed part of controversial policy prescription in many countries undergoing Structural Adjustment Programmes and has thus attracted scrutiny itself. A number of studies have tested the hypothesis empirically, concentrating on developing countries (Arrieta and Gonzales, 1988; Giovannini, 1985 and Leite and Makonnen, 1986). While often contradictory and still controversial, the evidence points to the conclusion that 'the real interest rate exhibits a positive, albeit weak correlation with savings rates' in formal financial markets (de Melo and Tybout, 1988, p570).

Various other factors have to be considered which impair a direct and immediate effect of interest rates on the level of savings. A number of studies pointed out that savings react to interest rates only with a considerable time lag, transitory interest movements do not induce changes in the savings behaviour, and savers tend to ignore small changes in interest rates (Balassa, 1989). Turtelboom (1991) argues that interest liberalization is ineffective in the absence of well developed financial institutions and markets. While some studies find statistically significant correlation between interest and saving rates, many do not, although this may be explicable by statistical problems. Most important, while the correlation goes some way to explain intertemporal links between interest rates and savings, it cannot explain the cross-country variations of savings levels. Indeed, people do save under negative real interest rates and even under negative nominal interest rates (Preston-Whyte, 1993). Both observations are not easily reconciled with standard neo-classical assumptions about intertemporal preferences and portfolio choices. Obviously, the assumptions of the maximising decision maker who responds to interest changes in the neo-classical fashion is controversial.

In conclusion, stable and positive real interest rates are certainly a valuable component of a successful savings policy, but interest rates are not in themselves a sufficient criterion. The inability of interest rates to explain fundamental differences between the savings functions of different countries significantly reduces the value of the interest rate-savings link to policy makers. Several other factors may well have a much more important influence on micro-economic decision-making.

Transaction costs and 'consumer surplus'

Interest rates are thought to capture the private return to savings. However, both the costs and the returns on savings depend not only on deferred consumption and monetary returns, but also on the availability of convenient savings institutions and instruments. Transaction costs arising for the user of financial services effectively reduce the private return to savings, while inappropriate instruments reduce their attractiveness.

Proximity and approachability of banking branches have been linked to savings behaviour (Bhatt, 1989). Travelling times to branches, and the queuing and 'hassle' associated with financial institutions create private costs which are a disincentive to using formal financial markets. It has been shown that the costs of dealing with formal financial institutions leads many rural savers to deposit with informal ones or, possibly even more important, to hoard cash and physical assets (Bouman, 1978 and Gupta, 1984). From the savers' perspective, small transaction amounts often do not justify the considerable expense of seeking access to banking services in 'underbanked' areas, while banks find it uneconomic to provide infrastructure, especially to those 'penny economy' customers. However, specialised institutions may be able to bridge this gap on a viable basis.

Similarly, the interest rate approach pays too little attention to the choice of the savings instrument. Besides the interest rate, households are concerned with a range of characteristics of specific savings products that determine their pay-off from a private perspective. The characteristics most important for savers in Botswana and elsewhere are outlined below.

- The choice between contractual or discretionary savings is important. Households with strong income variations may find contractual savings ill suited to their needs, while on the other hand they instil discipline and are easy to administer by financial institutions.
- If minimum balance requirements, minimum transaction amounts, or penalties for low balances and small transactions exist, these will discourage small savers. However, such 'threshold' clauses may be necessary to enable financial institutions to offer savings and transaction services on a commercially viable basis.
- Fixed term structures may be appropriate if a household saves for a specific purpose or event which is predictable in terms of costs and timing. The problems associated with accessing such savings in case of need are, however, often a disincentive for potential savers.
- Access to cash in an emergency without delay is almost always important to savers, especially poorer ones in developing countries where insurance markets are underdeveloped. The route to access may be through a secondary market for bonds or stocks, yet this route involves considerable risk and costs for financial 'laymen'. In several countries, issuers of bonds maintain a buyback guarantee, at a 'penalty interest deduction'.
- Access to loans in emergency is valued as an extension of access to cash. Effectively it requires the lender to accept that regular savings establish a track record for creditworthiness, and to be willing to handle loan requests in an uncomplicated way.

The variety of reasons underlying savings decisions, and the differences in the income and expenditure structure between households suggest that saving rates will be enhanced if a choice of savings products can be offered. If only a limited range is available, or if all products are inadequately 'tailored' to the respective market, households may prefer to save outside formal financial markets or to consume instead.[12] Tailoring financial services to diverse markets is an important aspect of financial innovation. Yet, the mode of operation of major commercial banks often leaves them somewhat behind in reaching out to new markets. But new and innovative institutions can prosper if the regulatory framework makes appropriate provisions. Generally, developing countries with poor savings records often have an uncompetitive banking system that does not offer a wide range of credible savings options and has few innovative savings ideas. This is certainly the case in Botswana.

---

[12] Reports abound that show that informal intermediaries in many developing countries are much more innovative in offering suitably tailored services for poor savers (Vogel, 1981; Bouman, 1990 and Thomas, 1991).

Risk

The attractiveness of savings instruments is essentially subjective, and all factors contributing to it will be perceived differently from various sections of the population. Notably, policy makers are usually better informed than the general public. Especially in countries where formal banking is a historically recent development, informational problems often contribute to the public perception of formal financial institutions. Further, as should be expected with any deposit activity, the credibility of the deposit taking institution is crucial. However, the effects of both objective and subjective credibility – the stability of deposit taking institutions and the trust extended to them by the public – have been omitted from the debate, which instead has focused on interest rates. Trust relates to the value and stability of the national currency, institutional stability of the financial system and promises given by individual institutions. Subjective risk of a 'store of value' affects the attractiveness of this store's perceived return. Perceived risk can thus adequately be seen as one of the cost components for private savers.

Savers who are unfamiliar with financial institutions, and the role of the financial sector as a whole, may well be expected to take a cautious approach to entrusting an impersonal account with their cash and may well prefer physical assets. Instead of interest rates, a subjective measure of security would dominate the portfolio choice. Although Botswana has generally succeeded in providing a stable financial environment, and no saver has lost money in any banking crisis in the country, asymmetric information and cultural unfamiliarity may still cause an unwillingness to deposit money in formal financial institutions. Information – comprising knowledge of and familiarity with institutions and procedures – is a public good that enhances the efficiency of financial markets.

4. Optimization for Savings: Income, Expenditure and Credit over Time

In the previous section the impact of price incentives on private savings decisions was discussed. It was argued that interest rates alone are an incomplete reflection of the true private costs and gains of using the financial system for household savings. The inclusion of transaction costs, the appropriateness of savings instruments and the trust extended to the financial system contribute to a better understanding of the price incentives affecting financial savings decisions. However, in order to gain a fuller picture of private savings decisions it is necessary to assess the motivation for saving and consider whether the policy framework is adequate in prioritising savings over credit and insurance as a means of intertemporal decision making in the household sector. In the following, the three main reasons for savings will be identified – emergency expenditure, lumpy expenditure, and life-time planning – and the substitutability of savings for deficit finance in the light of those motives will be discussed.

Emergency expenditure

In the case of unforeseen emergencies such as illness, crop failure, accidents or any other, most households maintain a savings balance which should be quickly accessible and used at their discretion. Access to insurance will reduce the optimal level of emergency savings. Access to emergency loans, however, will virtually eliminate the need to save for emergencies on an individual basis. In fact, it has been shown that in poor communities informal 'standing' loan agreements are essentially of an insurance character (Platteau and Abraham, 1987). Also, linked credit and financial institutions vested in groups, such as stokvels in South Africa, play an important role as informal insurance providers (Basu, 1984). However, while a standing loan agreement being used as insurance reduces individuals' dependence on savings, other forms of insurance positively contribute to household savings. Like institutional insurance firms, some traditional institutions accumulate savings from which liabilities are paid. Traditional African burial societies, for example, are also a prominent form of group savings in Botswana. Some South African stokvels operate as 'investor clubs' and use relatively sophisticated financial assets (Thomas, 1993).

Lumpy expenditure

A large part of household consumption consists of the use of durable items. Many of these items are too expensive to be purchased from general income and require intertemporal planning in order to accumulate the required purchasing power. Typical products depend on the income level of the household. Poorer households need to plan the purchase of simple household durables in advance, such as cooking equipment or radios, while well-off households would typically plan the purchase of cars, furniture, property and possibly education. In all societies, including Botswana, households typically save to finance social and cultural events such as weddings, funerals and religious holidays, and often also dowries.

Life-time planning

Income and expenditure patterns change during the life-span of individuals. According to the Life Cycle Hypothesis, individuals are net savers during the middle of their lives and dissave in early and late years.[13] In a related argument, the Permanent Income Hypothesis argues that income patterns are much more uneven, over longer periods of time, than expenditure patterns. Thus, individuals need to save or borrow as a regular activity over their lives. In traditional households where several generations share resources, this may not lead to significant variations of household savings as resources can just be passed on from generation to generation. However, where households split, or where extra-household employment becomes important as a sources of income, some external savings mechanism is usually needed to smooth consumption opportunities over an individual's life. Where available, contractual pension schemes are a prominent form of life-time savings, but any other form of asset accumulation may be caused also by life-time considerations.

While these three motives for savings do not constitute a complete list of possible reasons for household savings, they summarise the most important economic events

---

[13] Demography could thus also influence the savings performance. Countries such as Botswana, where the majority of the population is young and thus in the dissaving stage of their lives, would be expected to save less in aggregate than countries with a bell shaped age distribution.

requiring intertemporal income-expenditure gaps.[14] These gaps can be bridged both by credit and savings. Therefore, attractive savings instruments are not, in themselves, sufficient to stimulate aggregate household savings. The need to save stands in a negative relationship to the availability and affordability of credit. Therefore, in the context of a savings policy, creating dependence on savings may in fact be viewed as a more important factor than raising the attractiveness of savings instruments.

5. Voluntary Savings in Context – a Comparison of the Framework in Botswana

In Sections 3 and 4 it was argued that a successful savings performance requires that formal savings instruments are attractive to households, and that households experience dependence on savings for their intertemporal income-expenditure decisions. This chapter will demonstrate that on both counts, Botswana's savings environment is substantially worse than that of high-saving countries.

Financial savings options

The attractiveness of formal savings instruments in Botswana is hampered by their low yield, inconvenience of access and rigidity due to scant choice. The most obvious and convenient savings instruments offered by financial intermediaries, savings accounts, all offer negative real interest rates.[15] Further, interest rates are usually linked to the amounts deposited so that small savers receive real interest rates of around minus ten percent. High income savers are liable for tax on their interest income. Bank of Botswana Certificates (BoBCs) offer positive, if low, real interest rates. Yet the regulation of their issue effectively excludes private individuals from acquiring them. Neither are there agents who offer BoBCs on a competitive and convenient basis to the public, nor is there a secondary market for their premature resale.[16]

At the end of 1995, the public held approximately 267 500 accounts with commercial banks. Just over a third of those were current accounts and the rest savings

---

[14] One might, for example, wish to list social status as a motive in societies where savings are customarily held in visible assets such as cattle. In such a case, the accumulation of wealth is an end in itself, with no reference to future consumption. While such motives are in existence, they are relatively rare. Some researchers associate such patterns to pre-modern social structures.

[15] Only when inflation falls, as in recent months, does the interest rate on large balances become marginally positive. Presently, the real interest rate on balances over P10 000 is positive, but very low. Temporary small moves, without long-term credibility, are unlikely to sway savers' behaviour significantly (Balassa, 1989).

[16] At the end of December 1995, nominal interest rates on savings accounts varied between 2.0% and 6.5%. The highest interest rate commercial banks offered depositors, on 6-month fixed accounts, was 10.53%. BoBCs auctioned on 14 December 1995 attracted 12.67%. Inflation, at that time, stood at 10.8% (Bank of Botswana 1996a). It should be acknowledged, however, that BoBCs can be bought and sold by private individuals through their banks and stockbrokers, and they can also be sold prematurely to the Bank of Botswana. However, these agents are not competing for private savers who would find their procedures complicated and costly. BoBCs have not made a significant impact on household savings decisions.

accounts (Bank of Botswana, 1996a). Further, the public holds around 250 000 savings accounts at the Botswana Savings Bank. Therefore, the density of accounts in the adult population is relatively high. However, considering that many accounts are held by business and Government institutions, and that many households hold several accounts, the distribution of account ownership, and frequent usage of these accounts, is probably highly skewed. For many users, the branch density is insufficient as are the opening times. The commercial banks in Botswana do not seem to be aggressively competing for customers, neither at the high nor the low income end. Specialised institutions which appeal to rural or low income customers do not exist in Botswana, with the notable exception of the Botswana Savings Bank. Such institutions, where they do exist, depend on a high volume of clients for their viability and are therefore actively promoting the expansion of their customer base.

Credit availability

As has been argued in Section 4, the availability and affordability of credit undermines the dependence of households on their own savings for emergency and lumpy expenditures, and for life-time considerations. International experience confirms that credit availability to households reduces the willingness to save. An OECD study of several developed countries shows that financial liberalization eased the liquidity constraint on households and, as consumer credit became more widely available, 'permanent income' decisions were based more on deficit finance than on savings balances (Blundell-Wignall et al., 1991). Many East Asian countries maintained strict limits on consumer credit and realised very high savings rates. In Taiwan, consumer credit was banned until 1986. Following the liberalization of consumer credit in Taiwan, the household savings rate declined rapidly. In 1986 the marginal propensity to save stood at 60%, but within two years it declined to 37% as liberalization led to a national consumption spree due to pent-up demand. Between 1989 and 1995 the marginal propensity to save has averaged 12%. Consumer credit has remained stable at around 25% of household savings (Table 2). The average household savings rate has declined from 29% in 1986 to 18% in 1995 (Republic of China, 1996a).

TABLE 2. HOUSEHOLD SAVINGS, CONSUMER CREDIT, AND CREDIT AS PERCENTAGE OF SAVINGS IN TAIWAN (NT$ MILLION), AT END OF PERIOD

END YEAR	1991	1992	1993	1994	1995
SAVINGS	706 072	714 839	755 936	750 203	895 081
CREDIT	180 024	180 205	180 199	219 588	228 720
RATIO	25.5%	25.2%	23.8%	29.3%	25.5%

Source: Republic of China (1996a, 1996b).

There are three main types of credit available to many Batswana households, namely employee credit schemes in the formal sector, consumer credit extended by banks, and retailer credit extended as part of sales promotion. While different in scope and penetration, all three types combine to undermine the willingness to save and create a credit mentality in Botswana, especially where credit with negative real interest rates is available.

Employee credit schemes

Many formal sector employers in Botswana offer *no mathata* or 'no problem' loans to their staff. These are normally several months' worth of salary as loan advances. Presumably, the original intention was to provide employees with a safety net in case of 'emergency' expenditure. However, *no mathata* loans are administered on a 'no questions asked' basis and are used for many purposes including consumption. In addition to *no mathata* loans, many Government institutions offer car and housing credit to their staff at concessionary interest rates.[17] Other employers, both in the public and in the private sector, offer to guarantee bank credit for those purposes. Therefore, many formal sector employees find it possible to access credit through their employers for both lumpy expenditures and emergency purposes, and some of this credit is subsidised. Thus employees have an incentive to make maximum use of credit, and have little incentive to save.

Bank consumer credit

In a traditional flow of funds model of an economy, the household sector would be presented as a net saver, while the private business sector, and potentially the Government, would be net borrowers. In Botswana, the picture is dramatically different. While Government is the largest saver, households are net borrowers from the banking system. Unlike in the neo-classical critique of interventionism, it is not the Government 'crowding out' private investment, but households must be seen as competing with business for capital.[18]

Since 1992, loans and advances from the commercial banks to households have continuously exceeded household deposits at banks. While households held only 26.0% of deposits at the end of 1995, they accounted for 43.9% of bank loans and advances in that year (Table 3). At the end of March 1996, household deposits had declined to 25.2% while the share of household credit has edged up to 44.2% of total loans and

TABLE 3. HOUSEHOLD SHARE IN TOTAL LOANS AND DEPOSITS OF COMMERCIAL BANKS IN BOTSWANA, AT END OF PERIOD

END YEAR	1991	1992	1993	1994	1995
LOANS (%)	31.6	35.1	38.6	35.0	43.9
DEPOSITS (%)	24.9	25.9	27.8	27.5	27.0

Source: Bank of Botswana (1996a).

---

[17] Government is now taxing the net income accruing from the interest subsidy. This, however, does not raise the costs of borrowing substantially.

[18] Consumer credit for high-value, durable consumer goods, especially cars, is not only available but generally viewed as the 'normal' way of purchasing such goods. In fact, the credit option is further advertised by the fact that one specialised car loan firm – a subsidiary of one major commercial bank – has branches inside car dealerships and works together with sales staff.

advances (Bank of Botswana, 1996b). The credit guarantees offered by employers for staff surely contribute to the continued rapid rise of household credit. Since 1992, credit to private enterprise has actually declined, while household credit continued to expand rapidly.

Finally, however, it should not be forgotten that access to credit can, in fact, be an incentive for savings when the two are linked. In this regard, the experience of many credit unions in Southern Africa have shown that, when credit availability is made conditional on a savings record, the savings performance has improved substantially.[19]

Retail credit

Of all forms of credit in Botswana, retail credit is possibly the one that is available to the largest section of the population. Consumers, even those who are not formally employed and not considered credit worthy by banks, can often purchase goods on credit.[20] Consumer durables with 'intermediate value' are almost always available on credit. For a large share of the population, this purchase-linked credit availability removes the necessity to save for 'lumpy' goods. Further, not only is the strictly pecuniary requirement for savings reduced, but there is no reward for thrift – such credit, and the way in which it is offered, contributes to the 'credit culture'.

The availability of consumer credit – be it from employers, retailers or financial intermediaries – may be viewed as an integral part of a liberal and efficient financial system. However it should also be pointed out that it is not compatible with the goal of achieving very high savings rates. Countries with a good savings record generally have either legal or institutional barriers to consumer spending financed by credit.

Physical assets

One specific feature of the political economy of Botswana, that has been pointed out again and again by researchers as well as policy makers, is the tendency of Batswana, especially among higher income groups, to hold savings in physical assets, notably cattle. While cultural reasons have often been named as the rationale behind this internationally unusual savings behaviour, there are in fact economic incentives favouring such savings decisions. Possibly, not cultural 'irrationalism' but private maximization is driving the seemingly 'semi-feudal' pattern of wealth accumulation and resource allocation.[21] While cattle bestow status on its owner, they also receive implicit and explicit Government subsidies. Government has developed the infrastructure that is necessary to maintain cattle prices in the country – provision of

---

19 The Credit Union League of South Africa argues that, as its lending relies fully on funds generated internally, members now show a solid savings record. Previously, when its lending was subsidised with a donation from American savings unions, members saved far less and default was a more common problem.

20 Many South African retailers have learned, through operation in difficult environments, to maintain good repayment records against all odds (USAID, 1993). The monthly repayment rate is often stated on price lists and in advertisements suggesting 'affordability' of the goods, but also encouraging purchase on credit. Many large retailers in Botswana are South African chain stores. As part of their operation, they have also 'imported' their sales technique of selling goods on credit.

21 It would be desirable to conduct further research on the beef sector in this regard. Neither the motivation nor the economic effects of the bias towards cattle are well understood, (see note 26).

abattoirs, vaccine research and distribution, implicit insurance, and general sensitivity of policy formulation towards the needs and demands of cattle owners. Finally, tax laws are exceptionally generous to cattle owners, and their income and wealth are more easily hidden from the tax department than income from financial assets.

While these measures are, perhaps, justifiable with the view to beef as a strategic export for Botswana, they also raise the value of cattle as an asset and reduce risk. Insofar as one views cattle as an asset for household savings rather than capital in an export sector, Government support for the beef industry is damaging to the effort of savings mobilization. The accumulation of wealth in the form of cattle is indirectly subsidised, and this subsidy reduces the relative attractiveness of financial assets.

The housing boom and bust cycle of the 1980s and early 1990s may also have depressed household financial savings. During the boom years, households were biased towards investing their savings and additional borrowed funds in housing rather than financial assets. When property prices and rental income fell, the wealth effect is likely to have depressed households' willingness and ability to save. However, the data on household savings and credit do not show any discernible patterns during those years (Bank of Botswana, 1996a).

6. FORCED SAVINGS

The previous sections have analysed various variables in the economic environment of households which influence private decisions about the desirable level of savings. In particular, the analysis has focused on two aspects. Firstly, it discussed the possibilities of enhancing the attractiveness of savings by reducing its private transaction costs and by improving the private returns. Secondly, it has looked at measures to raise households' dependence on own savings for intertemporal decisions by making access to credit, and possibly insurance, more restrictive. Both approaches influence households' planned savings level by changing the incentive structure; thus both relate to the voluntary savings of the household sector.

Appropriation of household resources

The concept of forced savings has a long history, but has not generally attracted much theoretical attention recently (Hansson, 1987). Also, in a climate of economic liberalization, forced savings seem to fit in rather awkwardly. However, very high savings rates such as those in the developmental states in East Asia have arguably contributed to high growth over long periods. Some analysts argue that high savings rates are not maintainable without a level of economic coercion (Lee, 1971 and Wade, 1990). Savings rates of around forty percent as experienced by the 'tiger economies' of East Asia are not the result of private intertemporal maximization in a distortion free environment, but of conscious decisions by policy makers to achieve very high rates of savings.[22]

---

[22] Following such an argument, a policy of forced savings may be justified. If we accept a correlation between savings and growth, then private savings decisions would entail positive social externalities. Individuals would free-ride if they saved little, consumed now and wished that others save sufficiently in order to generate growth and raise future expected income. Under this assumption it follows that the optimal savings rate is higher than the one chosen by the representative household in a distortion-free environment.

Forced savings, in the historical, narrow definition, refer to a conscious policy of monetary growth under fixed nominal wage levels. As real wages decline, consumption is repressed. Capital is argued to grow because aggregate savings rise. This understanding is similar to the 'inflation tax' as both work through general price increases. The concept of an inflation tax, however, does not assume that reduced household consumption translates into savings, but resulting Government revenues which could be spent on public consumption.

However, East Asian countries have successfully used forced savings in a low inflation environment. The contemporary, more flexible understanding of forced savings encompasses the manipulation of specific prices rather than the general price level. Such policies are first of all to be seen in the context of taxation policy as they constitute a transfer of resources from the private to the public sector. However, if this 'tax' is consciously imposed because the marginal propensity to consume of the appropriating agency is lower than that of the representative household, and total consumption is thus reduced, then it is also adequate to view this 'tax' as a form of forced savings.

Products to be targeted for price manipulation may fulfil a range of criteria such as low price-demand elasticity, public interest in reduced consumption, or quantity independent utility of consumption. Such goods often have some snob appeal, or they are purchased for religious or symbolic purposes, and the perceived product qualities depend, *inter alia*, on its price. A separate category are compulsory insurance schemes, especially for old-age pensions, which accumulate capital and thus make capital available, through their investment portfolio, to local capital markets or government, depending on regulation. Administratively, price manipulation could be achieved through specific taxes, monopolization of trade of those goods and appropriation of monopoly rents, quantitative restrictions or licensing.

Several Asian countries were rather innovative in identifying goods which lend themselves to surplus extraction from private households, including goods with religious and symbolic value, whose trade was subsequently monopolised. In Taiwan, monopoly revenues made very large contributions to public investment especially at the start of the economic boom. During the period 1961–65, when much of the modern infrastructure was created but income was still low, monopoly revenues constituted 24.1% of total Government tax receipts. In the 1991–95 perios, when Taiwan was already a higher middle income economy and the tax base was much wider, this rate had declined to 6.1% (Republic of China, 1995). Both in Taiwan and Singapore, government funds accumulated compulsory social insurance premiums and made those funds available through the financial sector as investment capital. At the end of 1990, following several years of high real economic growth, the Central Provident Fund in Singapore held assets equivalent to 64.7% of the country's gross domestic product (Monetary Authority of Singapore, 1991). In Taiwan, the household savings rate has never surpassed 30% since 1952 – it peaked at 29% in 1986 – but the national savings rate has generally been around 10% higher. Between 1972 and 1990 it remained above 30% and peaked at 38.5% (Republic of China, 1996a). The difference is to a large part accounted for by assets, accumulated through social insurance premiums, held by the Central Trust of China, and employed in the economy similar to development finance. At the end of the 1994 financial year, total assets held by the Central Trust of China amount to approximately US$60 billion (Central Trust of China, 1994).

Linkages of revenue and investment

In some prominent cases, there is a link between the taxed product and the investment undertaken with appropriated savings. National monopolies often 'overcharge' and use such rent to finance expansion. Many developing telecommunication firms, and other utility corporations, seek to finance their development from revenue. Both Botswana Telecommunications Corporation and Botswana Power Corporation have defended their supposedly high charges with the need to extend their networks, provide more lines, and increase their capacity. Thus, the capital costs of future projects rather than the interest costs of capital employed in the existing infrastructure determines their pricing strategy. Utilities which enjoy such monopoly power can thus avoid seeking capital competitively.

Also widely used are discretionary mechanisms. Revenues accruing from 'overcharging' on alcoholic or symbolic products have been channelled, in many Asian countries, into general government revenue. Without this appropriation of purchasing power, Asian countries could not have financed the large public investment programmes, nor provided targeted credit, on which their phenomenal growth depended. However, many other developing countries have squandered such revenues on wasteful consumption or unproductive 'investment'.

Forced savings in Botswana

The desirability of forced savings is controversial. The main critique aims at the efficiency with which the public sector, or the appropriating agency, invests such savings. Generally, forced savings are collected by the public sector.[23] Forced savings are, therefore, vulnerable to criticism levelled at industrial policy, subsidised credit, and the dominance of public over private investment. The issue here is not merely a quantitative one, relating to the level of savings, but a qualitative one. In contrast to many Asian countries, the public sector is a major saver in Botswana and in no need to be stimulated in this regard. Forced savings and the transfer of resources from the private to the public sector that they entail are thus contrary to the intentions of policy making in Botswana, and to the need to stimulate private sector dynamism. However, the saving ability of the public sector depends on the diamond industry which has only limited revenue potential and whose life span is determined by the availability of exhaustible resources. In the absence of natural wealth, governments wishing to promote rapid growth have to devise mechanisms for raising the aggregate savings rate (Lee, 1971). Therefore, a long-term growth plan needs to incorporate elements of forced savings, although they may have unintended structural effects (Wade, 1990).

---

[23] There are some notable exceptions to the rule, such as the private sector oriented pension scheme in Chile. In many other countries compulsory social insurance companies are regulated in such a way that their capital base is made available to local private markets. However, such schemes do not always appear to contribute to the savings rate as much as do more comprehensive government-orchestrated savings strategies. Further, government's role in designing, popularising and supervising a market-driven compulsory scheme is rather fundamental; hence a 'public sector' image is likely to stick to those schemes.

7. POLICY OPTIONS FOR SAVINGS MOBILISATION

If savings mobilization from the household sector is accepted as an explicit policy goal, and not only as a desirable outcome of liberalization policy, then policy will have to play an active role. Policy measures should aim to improve the private return to investment, to make households more dependent on savings as a means of intertemporal consumption decisions and to apply well tuned forced savings mechanisms where appropriate. This section will contribute a few, sometimes speculative suggestions.

Enhancing attractiveness

In Botswana, institutional interest rates are barely positive, but spreads are large. Private savers have little chance of finding a depository opportunity offering interest above inflation. In the way that government bonds have contributed to a positive attitude to savings in many countries, access to BoBCs should be made available to the general public, having also lower income sections in mind. Providing such access requires that BoBCs should be sold in small denominations at fixed prices, meaning at face value, with a fixed interest yield that could from time to time be revised by the Bank of Botswana. The rules should be simple, and the costs and future returns could be stated and advertised, as there would be no variation after purchase. Either commercial banks should be encouraged, or compelled, to sell BoBCs at a minimal commission, or they could be sold through Government banks and post offices. They should also not bear the buyer's name but be easily bought and sold between private individuals.[24]

Banks are bureaucratic institutions with, from a private individual's point of view, often cumbersome procedures. Especially in Botswana, but also in other African countries, bank procedures and customer services are not 'customer driven', but very conservative (Fry, 1987, p287). As I have pointed out, commercial banks in Botswana do not appear to be actively competing for private household business. Possibly, they do not have the right structures to do so; commercial banks have relatively high unit costs which render transaction relating to savings services unprofitable except for very large savers. Policy should then actively encourage institutions with different production patterns and lower unit costs, and should take specific care to avoid stifling innovative deposit taking institutions by imposing excessively conservative regulation.

Building appropriate institutions

Financial institutions that are created with the specific aim of enhancing the savings record of the household sector and the efficiency of the financial system, by bringing current non-participants into the system, will not succeed if they emulate the working practices of commercial banks. Generally the subsidised provision of banking services in developing countries has failed (Adams et al., 1984 and Von Pischke, 1994).

---

[24] The 'blue books' used for the documentation of car ownership in Botswana could be seen as a model. They are easily understandable, easily transferable and reasonably safe.

The retraction of commercial banks from marginal locations in Botswana illustrates that point. A large part of the population currently is either too poor, or lives in too remote locations, to be considered 'bankable' in the context of current commercial banking production parameters. Innovative institutions that could reach beyond the domain of commercial banks should provide a small number of basic services, have simple and standardised procedures, and very low marginal costs (Adams, 1978). In this category, the Botswana Savings Bank has made good progress. Credit unions have in many countries contributed positively to household savings, and have started to operate in Botswana, apparently with initial success. Credit unions, despite their name, attract more savings from their members than they lend, unless they are subsidised implicitly through donor funding. Their disadvantage is that they usually depend on close physical proximity of their members and tend not to integrate their operation into the wider financial system.

Specialised banks have been established in a few developing countries, focusing on saving services for the 'penny economy' (Chaves and Gonzales-Vega, 1996). Some of these institutions appear to thrive (Boomgard and Angell, 1994; Glosser, 1994 and Robinson, 1994). They operate without the trappings normally associated with banks and rely either on personal contact with customers at convenient locations such as produce markets, like Badan Kredit Kecamatan in Indonesia and BancoSol in Bolivia, or on computerised transaction mechanisms, like People's Bank in South Africa. The third category of low margin savings institutions are financial firms which are not licensed to take deposits from the public, but design and market financial services under their name, while making use of transaction mechanisms and depository facilities of a licensed bank. Especially in South Africa, where electronic transaction systems are highly developed and a relatively dense branch network exists, marginal costs of making individual transactions through automated teller machines are low. These independent institutions concentrate on specialised services and can thus market their products with minimal staffing levels, like the Rural Finance Facility and the Start-Up Fund in South Africa.[25]

The emphasis in the development of such institutions has to be the cost-efficiency in providing financial services to a low-margin market. Botswana's low settlement density and remoteness poses problems as personal contact between bankers and public will remain restricted to higher value business, and to more central locations, including villages serving as market places. However, the development of electronic transaction mechanisms could open the possibility of operating low cost banking schemes similar to those established in South Africa. Also, rapid urbanization – the vast majority of Batswana now live close to the major centres – brings most prospective savers into reasonably close distance to towns and major villages.

While 'distorting' policies in the beef industry may be justified in the context of trade policy, it is important to understand the impact on savings behaviour in the economy. A non-sentimental view towards the beef industry is necessary in order to

---

[25] Despite multiple efforts of creating viable and innovative financial institutions, the savings rate in South Africa is low and falling. This must be ascribed to the credit culture, as entrenched as in Botswana, and the orientation of many new institutions to micro-credit rather than micro-savings.

find a compromise that, while not harming exports unnecessarily, discontinues the practice of siphoning off savings out of the financial domain into cattle ownership.[26] Housing is a fully respectable means of acquiring assets, but it is also desirable that the housing market be sufficiently dull to dissuade individuals from speculative activities. The developments of the housing market have, for the time being, removed much of the attractiveness of property as a means of savings.

Many potential savers in developing countries have seen banks collapse, inflation spiral out of control and whole financial systems become unpredictable. Under such expectations, physical assets provide a better risk-yield compromise. Botswana has generally succeeded in providing a stable economic environment, and has shown the ability to protect the interest of savers even in crisis. However, many potential savers are not always confident with financial institutions, and especially the more advanced instruments – BoBCs and the stock market – have earned little respect with the average saver. Often subjective risk evaluations are dominated by a lack of information and general distrust of the unknown. In this case there is a need for public education and a credible commitment to the safety of deposits from an accepted and trusted authority.[27] Both the convenience and reliability of Botswana Savings Bank accounts should be made central messages in such an education campaign. In several countries, specific 'total safety' saving instruments, often directly linked to the government, have proved a valuable vehicles to overcome the initial distrust by large sections of the population. Low interest but highly trusted and government guaranteed 'savings books' in Germany and Japan – similar to Botswana Savings Bank savings books, but more popular – were influential in creating a savings drive in both countries after the war. Similarly, government issued savings bonds – so called 'letters of treasure' – were prominent in Germany and still play a major role for asset accumulation in more conservative households. A public education campaign in Botswana could explain the virtues of savings in general, but also stress the convenience of BoBCs, if those were made available in small denominations at sales points countrywide, and of the Botswana Savings Bank's facilities provided through post offices.

Enhancing dependency

Probably more important than the attractiveness of saving instruments, it has been argued above, is that households are compelled to use savings as opposed to credit for intertemporal decision making. Regulation and the tax structure should discourage credit for consumption purposes. Banks may be directly discouraged from extending consumer credit, or such credit could be penalised by a 'surcharge'. Also, credit applicants should be required to contribute a large proportion of the purchase price. Additionally, Government and the public sector should take a lead in abolishing subsidised credit schemes for their employees, including credit guarantees. The public

---

[26] Such a compromise should be based on a fuller evaluation of the beef industry than this paper can provide. For example, it has been noted that the bias to the beef industry means that the real exchange rate is not allowed to rise, urban savings do not leave the country, and conspicuous consumption includes little fancy travel.

[27] Therefore, the public education campaign started by the Bank of Botswana should be generally welcome, although it seems lacking in a clear objective and is therefore unlikely to have a desirable effect on savings behaviour.

sector employers are crucial not only because they are 'opinion leaders' and thus set examples for employment conditions elsewhere in the economy, but also because they employ a large proportion of the total labour force and pay a large share of total wages. Together with other private sector employers which offer staff loans – Debswana, the commercial banks, and others – a large number of formal sector employees have access to subsidised credit for emergencies such as no mathata loans and medical aid advances and for lumpy expenditure like car and housing loans.

The availability of easy credit at low interest rates has, in the past, had three effects. Low interest rates reduced the incentive to hold financial assets, housing credit removed the necessity to save in order to build, and generous credit allowances created a temptation to borrow and build speculatively, with low capital endowment. As housing credit will continue to play an important and legitimate role, regulation should limit the amount private individuals can borrow in relation to the value of the property and their income. Countries with good savings records require mortgage applicants to produce 20% to 40% of the purchase price from private savings. Such a requirement raises the incentive for savings and limits the credit amounts. Also, savings records should be used to assess applicants' ability to make repayments.

Finally, major retailers in Botswana offer credit for larger purchases. While their efficiency and marketing abilities are admired, the availability of credit may undermine the household sector's dependence on savings accumulation for lumpy expenditure. Possibly, credit extension could be made illegal for non-financial firms. Alternatively, retailers may lose their privilege of recovering the purchased good as 'collateral', thus making default recovery so difficult that retailers would lose their interest in credit provision. Regulation may also determine the percentage of purchase price required as a deposit as well as the length of credit repayment period.

Finding a role for forced savings

In the context of Botswana, where public savings are relatively high but private household savings need to be encouraged, forced savings may not seem the policy tool of first choice. Notably, price manipulation is likely not only to extract resources from households, but also from private sector firms. However, there are categories of goods which are almost exclusively purchased by private individuals.[28] At the same time, contractual savings for life-time planning as supported by formal sector employers is in its infancy. The principle vehicle – the encouragement of pension funds which accumulate capital on their members behalf – is not yet well developed and appreciated. Although the major employers now operate such schemes, it will be some time before they become important players in Botswana. Policy should accelerate the process and enhance their role perhaps by making them compulsory for all formal sector

---

[28] So-called sin taxes have the world over been imposed on products like alcoholic drinks and tobacco products. Generally, these products are seen as non-essential items, thus raising their price is argued not to endanger the livelihood of poor people, (this is argued in spite of the fact that these goods are in fact consumed by poor people, and raising their price would thus make them worse off). Also, their consumption is generally associated with negative externalities such as alcoholism, health problems and social instability. A decision to extract forced savings from those sources thus needs to balance not only the capital requirements of households and the public sector, but also the adverse effects on the tobacco and brewing industries with reduced health costs and improved productivity of the labour force.

employment.[29] However, compulsory contributions to pension funds must be set at unpopularly high levels if they are to make a decisive impact on aggregate savings. Singapore had contribution rates of up to fifty percent of the nominal wage, shared in equal parts between employer and employee (Husain, 1995).

A specific tax on consumer credit would also lend itself to the extraction of forced savings, having the additional benefit that it would penalise household credit and thus provide an incentive for voluntary household savings.

8. Conclusion

In many countries, people and governments are hoping for 'foreign investors' – and also aid officials – to come to their country, bringing with them capital and creating employment, growth and the prospect of permanent improvement. Much too regularly to ignore, these hopes are disappointed. 'Foreign investors' help those who help themselves. They follow growth, but do not initiate economic miracles. Growth and development remain the responsibility of domestic decision makers. Rapid development is a difficult historical process, and growth requires tough decisions. Policies that limit consumption and favour savings promote long-term growth, but such policies are rarely popular. In Botswana, policy makers acknowledge that saving policy is crucial for maintaining high growth after the mineral boom, but have yet to demonstrate their commitment through appropriate action.

This paper has argued that a successful savings policy in Botswana would require the active involvement of policy makers. Mere reliance on the liberalization of financial markets would be naive. Economic research and advice by international institutions relating to financial regulation and policy is currently informed by the 'Anglo-Saxon view' of efficient and liberal financial markets, and the mainly American and British moves towards liberalised markets. In many respects, those policies may have achieved their aims, but on savings performance those two countries, and others who followed them, stand out as poor performers. High savings countries, on the contrary, have always proclaimed a strong commitment to active promotion of savings, at the expense of the credo of 'free markets'. Especially in a country where the 'credit culture' is deeply entrenched, as in Botswana, policy has an important role to play in dissuading private individuals from viewing credit as the principal vehicle for intertemporal consumption decisions. Non-market oriented policies are thus part of savings policy with the view towards strengthening financial markets in their role of attracting savings, and channelling those to productive investment.

Savings need to be channelled towards the financial sector. Therefore, the second important foundation of savings policy is the encouragement of innovative deposit taking institutions. Policy makers may review the role of credit unions and of other non-bank institutions. Public support should be made available, as the development

---

[29] Compulsory pension schemes have the advantage that they provide for an important social need, old age income, and should therefore be more easily politically acceptable than some other policies. In the long run, such reserves benefit private households, but households would be prevented from consuming those assets during their members' working life. The specific evaluation of social impact and institutional design of pension schemes is not within the scope of this paper.

of credit unions, savings institutions and a popular market for bonds would certainly benefit from enhanced public awareness and education. Subsidies, however, should be used cautiously, as they have often exerted a corrupting influence on financial intermediaries.

REFERENCES

Adams, D.W. 1978. 'Mobilizing Household Savings through Rural Financial Markets', *Economic Development and Cultural Change*, Vol.26, No.3, pp547–60.

Adams, D.W., Graham, D.H. and Von Pischke, J.D. 1984. *Undermining Rural Development with Cheap Credit*. Westview Press, Colorado.

Arrieta, G. and Gonzales, M. 1988. 'Interest Rates, Savings, and Growth in LDCs: An Assessment of Recent Empirical Research', *World Development*, May, pp589–605.

Balassa, B. 1989, *The Effects of Interest Rates on Savings in Developing Countries*. World Bank Working Paper S56.

Bank of Botswana. 1996a. *Annual Report 1995*. Bank of Botswana, Gaborone.

Bank of Botswana. 1996b. *Botswana Financial Statistics – May 1996*. Bank of Botswana, Gaborone.

Basu, K. 1984. *The Less Developed Economy – A Critique of Contemporary Theory*, Oxford.

Bhatt, V.V. 1989 *Financial Innovation and Credit Market Development*. World Bank Working Paper, Washington.

Blundell-Wignall, A., Brown, F. and Cavaglia, S. 1991. *Financial Liberalization and Consumption Behaviour*, Working Paper GD(91)77. OECD, Paris.

Boomgard, J.J. and Angell, K.J. 1994. 'Bank Rakyat Indonesia's Unit Desa System: Achievements and Replicability'. In: Otero, M. and Rhyne, E. (eds.). *The New World of Microenterprise Finance*. Intermediate Technology Publications, London, pp206–228.

Bouman, F.J.A. 1990. 'Informal Rural Finance – An Aladdin's Lamp of Information', *Sociologia Ruralis*, Vol.15, No.2, pp155–73.

Central Trust of China. 1994. *Annual Report Financial Year 1994*. Taipei.

Chaves, R.A. and Gonzales-Vega, C. 1996. 'The Design of Successful Rural Financial Intermediaries: Evidence from Indonesia', *World Development*, Vol.24, No.1, pp65–78.

de Melo, J. and Tybout, J. 1986. 'The Effects of Financial Liberalization on Savings and Investment in Uruguay', *Economic Development and Cultural Change*, Vol.34, pp561–88.

Diaz-Alejandro, C. 1985. 'Good-Bye Financial Repression, Hello Financial Crash', *Journal of Development Economics*, Vol.19, No.1, pp1–24.

Fry, M. 1980. 'Savings, Investment, Growth and the Cost of Financial Repression', *World Development*, Vol.8, pp317–28.

Fry, M. 1987. *Money, Interest, and Banking in Economic Development*. The John Hopkins University Press, Baltimore.

Giovannini, A. 1985. 'Saving and the Real Interest Rate in LDCs', *Journal of Development Economics*, Vol.18, pp197–217.

Glosser, A.J. 1994. 'The Creation of BancoSol in Bolivia', In: Otero, M. and Rhyne, E. (eds.) *The New World of Microenterprise Finance*. Intermediate Technology Publications, London, pp229–250.

Gupta, K.L. 1984. 'Financial Intermediation, Interest Rate and the Structure of Savings: Evidence from Asia', *Journal of Economic Development*, Vol.9, pp7–24.

Hahn, J. 1995. 'Do Koreans Save Optimally?', *Journal of Development Economics*, Vol.47, pp429–42.

Hansson, B. 1987. 'Forced Savings', In: Eatwell, J., Milgate, M. and Newman, P. (eds.), *The New Palgrave: A Dictionary of Economics*. Macmillan Press, London, pp398–99.

Husain, A.M. 1995. 'Determinants of Private Saving in Singapore', In: Bercuson, K. (ed.), *Singapore – A Case Study in Rapid Development*. IMF, Washington.

Lee, Teng-hui. 1971. *Intersectoral Capital Flows in the Economic Development of Taiwan, 1895–1960*. Cornell University Press, London.

Leite, S.P. and Makonnen, D. 1986. 'Savings and Interest Rates in the BCEA Countries: An Empirical Analysis', *Savings and Development*, pp219–31.

McKinnon, R.I. 1973. *Money and Capital in Economic Development*. Brookings Institution, Washington.

McKinnon, R.I. 1986. *Financial Liberalization in Retrospect: Interest Rate Policies in LDCs*. Centre for Economic Policy Research, Publication No.74. Stanford.

Monetary Authority of Singapore. 1991. *Annual Report 1990/1991*. Singapore.

Phelps, E.S. 1961. 'The Golden Rule of Accumulation: A Fable for Growthmen', *American Economic Review*, Vol.51, pp638–43.

Platteau, J.-P. and Abraham, A. 1987. 'An Inquiry into Quasi-Credit Contracts: The Role of Reciprocal Credit and Interlinked Deals in Small-scale Fishing Communities', *The Journal of Development Studies*, No.23, pp461–90.

Preston-Whyte, E. 1993. 'Petty Trading at Umgababa: Mere Survival or the Road to Accumulation?'. In: Preston-Whyte, E. and Rogerson, C. (eds.), *South Africa's Informal Economy*. Cape Town, pp262–279.

Republic of China. 1995. *Yearbook of Financial Statistics of the Republic of China, 1994*. Department of Statistics Ministry of Finance, Taipei.

Republic of China. 1996a. *Taiwan Statistical Data Book*. Council for Economic Planning and Development, Taipei

Republic of China. 1996b. *Financial Statistics Abstract*. Statistics Office, Bureau of Monetary Affairs, Ministry of Finance, Taipei.

Robinson, J. 1962. 'A Neo-classical Theorem', *Review of Economic Studies*, Vol.29, pp219–26.

Robinson, M.S. 1994. 'Savings Mobilization and Microenterprise Finance: The Indonesian Experience', In: M. Otero and E. Rhyne (eds.) *The New World of Microenterprise Finance*. Intermediate Technology Publications, London.

Shaw, E.S. 1973. *Financial Deepening in Economic Development*. Oxford University Press, Oxford.

Thomas, E. 1991. 'Rotating Credit Associations in Cape Town'. In: Preston-Whyte, E. and Rogerson, C. (eds.), *South Africa's Informal Economy*. Cape Town. pp290–304.

Turtelboom, B. 1991. *Interest Rate Liberalization – Some Lessons from Africa*. IMF Working Paper 91/121.

USAID. 1994. *Community Based Credit Study*, (mimeo). Cape Town.

van Wijnbergen, S. 1985. 'Macroeconomic Effects of Changes in Bank Interest Rates: Simulation Results for South Korea', *Journal of Development Economics*, Vol.18, No.2, pp541–54.

Vogel, R.C. 1981. *Savings Mobilization: The Forgotten Half of Rural Finance*, World

Bank Occasional Paper. Washington.

Von Pischke, J.D. 1991. *Finance at the Frontier – Debt Capacity and the Role of Credit in the Private Economy.* The World Bank, Washington.

Wade, R. 1990. *Governing the Market: Economic Theory and the Role of Government in East Asian Industrialization.* Princeton University Press, Oxford.

The Transmission Mechanism of Monetary Policy in Botswana – Through Bank of Botswana Certificates

Z. Kone[1]

1. INTRODUCTION

The Bank of Botswana uses three indirect instruments to manage domestic monetary conditions: the Bank Rate, the primary reserve requirement, and open market operations through sales of the Bank of Botswana Certificates (BoBCs). The objectives of monetary policy in Botswana are to attain positive real rates of interest, which will promote savings and discourage unproductive investment, and to maintain price stability and real interest rate comparability with world financial markets, with variations from that parity depending on economic conditions.

In the mid-1980s mineral revenues started growing, the resulting current account surpluses led to pervasive excess liquidity in the financial system, in the context of exchange controls and a fixed exchange rate (Milne *et al.*, 1994 and Leith, 1996). Attempts by the Bank of Botswana to mop up the excess liquidity through the use of the call account were not successful. The real call rate was negative at the time, and failed to absorb the excess liquidity, which subsequently led commercial banks to lend at a negative real prime rate (Leith, 1996). This, combined with Government loan schemes to the parastatals, led to an explosion of credit in Botswana (Leith, 1996). Since the call account was not successful in absorbing the excess liquidity, the Bank of Botswana introduced the BoBCs to manage the domestic monetary conditions. The BoBC market has grown substantially since its inception in May 1991, from P200 million in May 1991 to P2900 million as at 6 December 1996.

The purpose of this paper is to present a simple and illustrative account of the transmission mechanism of monetary policy through auctions of the BoBCs, i.e., the mechanism or process that links the auctions of the BoBCs to nominal income or total spending in the economy.[2] As a first systematic study of the transmission mechanism of the BoBC auctions, naturally some parts are theoretical with simple illustrative examples. The paper is structured as follows.

Section 2 discusses the capability of the central bank to peg a real interest rate below or above the natural rate. In Section 3, BoBCs are linked to the net foreign

---

[1]   The author would like to thank Jay Salkin, David Cowan, Keith Jefferis, Andrew Motsomi, Christine Moloi, and an anonymous referee for helpful comments and suggestions.
[2]   The BoBCs are sold at market related prices using the uniform price auction (Kone, 1996).

assets, domestic credit, and the Government budget. BoBC auctions can contain the rise in net foreign assets, and at the same time dampen the rise in domestic credit and inflation. To paraphrase Mundell (1968), a growing economy, such as Botswana, should make some provisions for increasing its international reserves over time to provide the extra safety, convenience, and choice of adjustment measures. Section 3 also discusses some short run effects of BoBC auctions on selected economic variables in a simple monetarist model. BoBC auctions raise interest rates, decrease the prices of assets and thus dampen spending. Section 4 covers some of the implications of nominal interest rate targeting, and Section 5 provides some conclusions and suggestions.

2. CAN THE CENTRAL BANK PEG REAL INTEREST RATES?

A key issue in monetary economics is whether a central bank can permanently peg real rates of interest at any arbitrary level it chooses. Economists disagree on this issue. Classical and neoclassical monetary economics literature largely provides strong support for the view that a central bank is powerless to peg real rates of interest above or below a real natural rate[3] of interest (Humphrey, 1993). The powerlessness of the central bank to peg real interest rates above or below the natural rate is found in the work of Friedman (1968). Attempts to do so will merely affect the price level. The deviation of real rates from the natural rate has contractionary effects on the economy, thus making the natural rate a benchmark against which real interest rates are gauged. Real interest rates that are persistently below the natural rate lead to eventual resource bottlenecks and rising inflation, which eventually engender economic contraction. Rates maintained above that natural level tend to be associated with slack, deflation, and economic stagnation (Greenspan, 1993).

Contrariwise, some economists of the Keynesian tradition tend to argue that the rate of interest is itself a monetary phenomenon. Therefore, the central bank interest rate policy cannot be neutral and is an important determinant of economic prosperity (Smithin, 1994). The implication of this view point is that a consistent and sufficiently determined policy by a central bank regarding the real interest rate will eventually achieve its objectives. Therefore, the real economy must adjust to the policy determined real interest rate, rather than vice versa. This is the opposite of the classical and neoclassical view on the powerlessness of the central bank to peg a real rate of interest different from the natural rate.

To paraphrase Friedman (1968), although monetary policy cannot peg real interest rates at predetermined levels, it can have important effects on real interest rates in the short run. Moreover, monetary policy can provide a stable background for the economy. The economic system works best when consumers, producers, employers, and employees can proceed with full confidence that the inflation rate will be low and

---

3   The natural rate is identified as the marginal yield or internal rate of return on newly-created units of physical capital. It is also the rate that equilibrates real savings with intended real investment at the economy's full capacity level of output. Or what amounts to the same thing, it is the rate that equates aggregate demand for real output with the available supply. In other words, if the rate of interest or the market rate of interest were at the natural rate, price stability would prevail (Humphrey, 1993).

stable. In short, though the Bank of Botswana cannot peg real interest rates at predetermined level different from the natural rate, it can influence them in the short run. As it is discussed in Section 3, BoBC auctions raise nominal interest rates, and the latter are translated into real interest rates as the asset markets are assumed to clear first.

3. TRANSMISSION MECHANISM OF MONETARY POLICY THROUGH BoBC AUCTIONS

BoBCs, net foreign assets, domestic credit and the government budget

Changes in the net foreign assets have their counterparts in changes in the level of high-powered money (base money) and the level of domestic credit of Bank of Botswana.[4] For the Bank of Botswana, changes in net foreign assets are the changes in total reserves. Domestic credit includes the Bank of Botswana credit to financial institutions, including commercial banks and Government. High-powered money (base money) refers to currency outside the Bank of Botswana, banks' deposits at the Bank of Botswana, and cash in their vaults.

Net foreign assets include foreign exchange reserves less liabilities to foreign exchange holders. As an illustration, the simplified consolidated balance sheet of Bank of Botswana before the introduction of BoBCs shown here helps unravel the relationship between domestic credit (DC), net foreign assets

TABLE 1. A SIMPLIFIED BANK OF BOTSWANA BALANCE SHEET BEFORE THE INTRODUCTION OF BoBCs

ASSETS	LIABILITIES
Net Foreign Assets	
Domestic Credit	High-powered Money

(NFA), high-powered money (H) and BoBC auctions.[5] The change in net foreign assets excluding revaluation gains and losses equals the current account balance. High-powered money equals the sum of domestic credit and net foreign assets. Therefore, the change in high-powered money equals the sum of the change in the net foreign assets and the change in domestic credit. This is illustrated in Equations 1 and 2. As Botswana records current account surpluses (increase in net foreign assets), the money supply swells. This is discussed below.

$$\Delta H \equiv \Delta DC + \Delta NFA \qquad\qquad (1)$$

$$\Delta NFA \equiv \Delta H - \Delta DC \qquad\qquad (2)$$

The symbol Δ indicates change.

---

[4] This is adapted to Botswana from Dornbusch (1980).

[5] The current Bank of Botswana balance sheet is a reshuffled balance sheet: it already contains the effect of open market operations. The unshuffled balance sheet is illustrated in Table 1. However, it should be emphasised that the current auction schedules are geared to maturing BoBCs and the expected size of diamond receipts based on a schedule. Both of these increase liquidity in the financial system.

Equation 1 indicates that an increase in NFA is matched by an increase in high powered money, all else being equal. The growth in high-powered money can be reduced if the Bank of Botswana offsets increases in NFA by cutting down on domestic credit. This means that the Bank of Botswana will organise contractionary open market operations to frustrate the automatic swelling in the money supply. This is done through the sales of BoBCs. The net effect of the sales of BoBCs in response to an increase in net foreign assets held by Bank of Botswana, is a reduction in high-powered money and domestic credit. High-powered money is reduced or held constant when the increase in net foreign assets is more than or exactly matched by the sales of the BoBCs or the decrease in domestic credit. Although the BoBC auctions affect the monetary base, a proactive stance by the Bank of Botswana will be to set a domestic credit target and consequently conduct open market sales of BoBCs.

Open market operations are the exchange of money for the BoBCs. They lead to a decrease of commercial banks' deposits at the Bank of Botswana or vault cash, thus reducing the monetary base. This is illustrated in Table 2, where CB is commercial banks deposits at the Bank of Botswana or their vault cash.

TABLE 2. THE EFFECT OF BoBC AUCTIONS ON BANK OF BOTSWANA BALANCE SHEET

BANK OF BOTSWANA		COMMERCIAL BANK	
Net Foreign Assets	↑ BoBCs	↑ BoBCs	
↓ Domestic Credit	↓ Commercial bank deposits	↓ Commercial bank deposits	
↓ High Powered Money	↓ High Powered Money		

Suppose there is an increase in net foreign assets, i.e., a current account surplus. High-powered money increases. The increase in high-powered money can be frustrated by selling BoBCs. This decreases domestic credit (DC), and increases BoBCs held by the primary counterparts, including commercial banks. The monetary base (or high-powered money) falls by the amount of the auctioned BoBCs. This is illustrated in the equation below.

$$\Delta BoBC \equiv -\Delta CB = -\Delta H$$

Extension to the broader money supply, M3

Domestic credit can be further divided into credit to Government and the non-bank public sector, to trace the implications of a budget surplus or deficit. This is done below by including the changes in the net foreign assets of the banking system, domestic credit of the banking system to the economy, and the money supply $M3$ in equation 3. The superscript B indicates the banking system including the Bank of Botswana. The money supply $M3$ equals the sum of net foreign assets and domestic credit. In other words, the money supply $M3$ equals (in reality, an identity) the sum of domestic credit of the banking system to the economy and net foreign assets of the banking system. Therefore, the change in the money supply $M3$ equals the sum of the change in the domestic credit and the change in the net foreign assets:

$$\Delta NFA^B \equiv \Delta M3 - \Delta DC^B \qquad (3)$$

Equation 3 indicates that there is a one to one relationship between increase in the net foreign assets of the banking system and the money supply $M3$. The change in domestic credit from the banking system (DC^B) can be divided into change in domestic credit to Government (DC^G) and change in credit to the non-bank public (DC^{NB}), i.e.:

$$\Delta NFA^B \equiv \Delta M3 - \left(\Delta DC^{NB} + \Delta DC^G\right) \qquad (3a)$$

A Government budget deficit may be financed by Government borrowing from the banking system or abroad. More precisely:

$$G - T \equiv \Delta DC^G - \Delta NFA^G \qquad (4)$$

where G is Government spending and T is tax receipts. The two terms on the right side of the equation indicate credit to Government and Government borrowing from abroad, respectively. The change in domestic credit to Government equals the differential between Government deficit less Government borrowing from abroad to finance this deficit:

$$\Delta DC^G \equiv G - T + \Delta NFA^G \qquad (5)$$

Substituting equation 5 for DC^G in equation 3a yields equation 6.

$$\Delta NFA^B \equiv \left(\Delta M3 - \Delta DC^{NB}\right) + \left(T - G - \Delta NFA^G\right) \qquad (6)$$

The superscript NB indicates that the credit is to the non-bank public (private) sector.

Carefully interpreted, Equation 6 shows that an increase in the Government budget surplus[6] is matched by a corresponding fall in the domestic money supply. As the Bank of Botswana is the banker to the Government, the excess of taxes over spending deposited at the Bank of Botswana depresses the money supply, i.e., tightens monetary conditions. This could have been obtained by expanding equation (2) in both Government budget and credit to the banking sector by exploiting the characteristics of the balance sheet. In the presence of a budget surplus and maintenance of a current account surplus, the growth in the money supply can be controlled by reducing the banking system credit to the non-bank public (NB). Furthermore, BoBCs bought by the banking system for their own account (as they decrease the monetary base) have a depressing effect on the money supply and aggregates $M1$, $M2$, and $M3$ as each of the monetary aggregates is the product of the monetary base and a money supply multiplier.

Illustration of the effect of BoBC auctions on asset markets[7]

Open market sales of the BoBCs change the stock of money relative to the stocks of

---

6   G-T is negative.   7   This draws heavily on Meltzer (1995) and is adapted to Botswana.

other domestic and foreign assets, and change the marginal utility (marginal product) of money relative to the marginal utility (marginal product) of these other assets and the marginal utility of consumption. Money holders attempt to restore equilibrium by equating the ratios of the marginal utilities to the relative prices of all assets and current production and consumption. This involves changes in many relative prices, in spending and in asset portfolios (Meltzer, 1995 and Pigou, 1917/18).

To capture some of the short run effects of the BoBC auctions on relative prices, a monetary model[8] is introduced that has at least three assets; the base money that provides real services as a medium of exchange; bonds and securities that yield a nominal return, the rate of interest, R; and the stock of real capital, or claims to real capital, that yields a real return. A unit of real capital that has a price P, is introduced. P reflects the prices of houses, land, and more generally non-tradeable goods as Botswana is mostly a price-taker on the international market. It is assumed that the different assets are substitutes, but not perfect substitutes.

With these three assets, and the definition of wealth, the model must determine two relative prices to achieve portfolio balance for the economy. The asset market equilibrium in the economy is determined by the intersection of the base money market equilibrium, and the bonds and securities market equilibrium. In Figure 1, the base money equilibrium is indicated by the BM curve and the securities and bond market equilibrium by the SB curve. The positions of the SB and BM curves are defined for given asset stocks and for given output, commodity prices and expectations. Changes in these underlying values shift the BM and SB curves.

The BM curve shows the combination of the interest rate (R) and the asset price level (P) at which existing money balances are willingly held. Its slope is positive. As the interest rate rises, wealth owners reduce their desired money balances; a rise in P restores equilibrium by lowering desired holdings of existing real capital and increasing desired holdings of money (and bonds). The slope of the SB curve is negative. A higher interest rate increases desired bond holdings. A fall in P restores equilibrium by inducing asset owners to shift into real capital.

The auctions of the BoBCs are the exchange of money for BoBCs, i.e., securities. BoBC auctions reduce the base money and increase the stock of securities or Bank of Botswana debt held by the commercial banks or the public. As a result of the sales of the BoBCs, starting at equilibrium E_0, the BM line shifts to the left. Thus, less base money must be willingly held. As the demand for money is negatively related to the interest rate and positively to the asset price, the rise in the interest rate and the decline of the asset price continue until the additional base money is withdrawn.

The auctions of BoBCs increase commercial banks and the public holdings of securities or the Bank of Botswana Certificates. In other words, more Bank of Botswana

---

8   This framework of analysis is chosen because it is simple and comprehensive: it takes into account marketable assets and different interest rates and can apply to countries with both sophisticated or undeveloped financial markets. In other words, the choice is motivated by the desire not to force the transmission mechanism of BOBCs to go through a given channel. This does not mean, however, that the particular pattern of relative price change will not vary from cycle to cycle and from country to country. For example, Botswana's export-led expansion (growth), in the presence of exchanges controls, changes relative prices by depressing interest rates and bidding up the prices of assets, whilst an expansion led by Government spending financed by bond issues may raise interest rates (see Friedman, 1971 and Meltzer, 1995).

debt must be willingly held. The SB line shifts to the right. Open market sales increase interest rates to R_1, but their effects on the price of assets (P_1) depend on the magnitude of the shifts in the SB and BM lines (see Figure 1). The portfolio balance is restored at the new equilibrium E_1 with higher interest rates. By the same token, an expansionary monetary policy decreases the interest rate and may bid up the prices of assets, *ceteris paribus*. This describes amply the situation of Botswana, as an increase in net foreign assets swells the money supply, interest rates fall and asset prices rise. Starting at E_0 in

FIGURE 1. TRANSMISSION OF BoBC AUCTIONS TO ASSET MARKETS

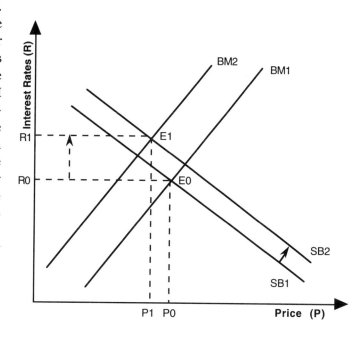

Figure 1, an increase in net foreign assets increases the base money which will push interest rates downward and bid up the price of assets, all else being equal.[9] Sales of BoBCs help alleviate this liquidity problem by decreasing the base money.

Some predicted routes of how BoBC auctions lead to changes in spending

Having completed the exercise on the potential effects of BoBC auctions on asset prices and interest rates in a simple yet powerful model, the following routes to spending are straightforward. The auctions of the BoBCs affect short-term interest rates as represented by the yield on the BoBCs themselves. As it is shown above, the transmission mechanism of the BoBC auctions to the economy may not be confined to the small corner of the BoBC market.

- Open market sales of the BoBCs may reduce the price of assets, such as houses, shares, consumer durables, producer's capital and claims to capital. This decline in wealth discourages individuals from spending their current income as consumption is positively related to wealth.
- They can lead to higher interest rates which reduce the attractiveness for individuals and companies of spending now rather than later. Domestic credit, the quantity of money and real demand all decrease.
- One route which has received extended coverage in the monetary policy literature is the interest rate channel (Mishkin, 1995), the traditional Keynesian view of how monetary policy is transmitted to the economy. As it is shown above, this channel is part of a broad transmission mechanism in this

---

9   As individuals expect inflation to rise they may incorporate this in nominal interest rates.

monetarist framework. The interest rate channel indicates that a rise in the real interest rate raises the cost of capital, thereby causing a decline in investment, thereby leading to a decline in aggregate demand. This channel equally applies to consumer spending on residential housing and consumer durable expenditure.

- As the auctions of BoBCs raise real interest rates, they may lower the prices of stocks, thus weakening companies' balance sheets through lower net worth. This has implications for their borrowing capabilities from commercial banks.

A simple reality check: total credit responsiveness to interest rates

Having predicted some routes of BoBC auctions to nominal spending, the following attempts a simple estimation of financial institutions credit in relation to the BoBC rate. Growth in Botswana has been mainly led by the export sector – diamond exports – which contributed to the creation of liquidity with its depressing effect on domestic interest rates (these two concepts tend to be inseparable in the Botswana context of exchange controls), all else being equal. A channel through which BoBCs might have helped to alleviate this liquidity problem and help financial institutions adjust their portfolio is explained below.

A simple loglinear regression model of the total outstanding credit as the dependent variable and the nominal three-month BoBC mid-rate as the independent variable indicates an inverse relationship between these two variables from January 1993 to the end of February 1996. The logic behind the use of this simple model is two-fold: the log form gives the elasticity of total credit with respect to the BoBC mid-rate, and the choice of the mid-rate of the three-month BoBC as a proxy for the lending rate is based on a main theoretical conclusion of the capital asset pricing model applied to financial institutions. The equilibrium conditions in an asset market is that risk adjusted returns have to be the same (Simonds, 1987 and Varian, 1994). This conclusion allows for an ample use of the BoBC mid-rate assuming that financial institutions are holding their equilibrium portfolio. The results of the regression based on 38 monthly observations are as follows:

$$c_t = 9.62 - 0.84 r_t$$

$$(10.97)$$

$$R^2 = 0.77$$

The model has a good fit, for it says that 77% of the movements in the total credit in the sample can be explained by the movement in the three month BoBC rate. The total credit is somewhat interest inelastic; a one percentage point rise in the three-month BoBC rate leads to 0.84 percentage point fall in the total credit. However, the model has some limitations. First, the model uses the market equilibrium level of total credit. It is possible to have a positive as well as a negative relationship between the total credit and the BoBC mid-rate. One reason for this is that both the demand for, and the supply of, loans could be shifting. Second, some relevant variables must have been omitted. For example, variables such as risk and household wealth could also be explanatory variables. The omission of these variables may lead to serial correlation, thus weakening the model. It is hoped that more investigation and empirical studies will be forthcoming on the effect of BoBCs on total credit.

Achievement of positive real rates of interest

The Bank of Botswana has generally succeeded in keeping the real money market rates as indicated by the three-month BoBC rate and measured with respect to the twelve month inflation rate and the three-month moving average of the three month inflation rate positive (see Figure 2). This is an achievement in line with the objectives of monetary policy in Botswana set out in the introduction of this paper. Figure 2 indicates that the nominal three-month BoBC rate was above the twelve month inflation rate and the three-month moving average of the three-month annualized inflation rate most of the time since 1993. The two measures of the inflation rate have been generally below the three-month BoBC rate from January 1993 to October 1996, an indication that real interest rates have been positive in these periods.

FIGURE 2. THE THREE-MONTH BoBC RATE, THREE-MONTH MOVING AVERAGE OF THE THREE-MONTH ANNUALISED INFLATION RATE (3MMA), AND THE TWELVE-MONTH INFLATION RATE

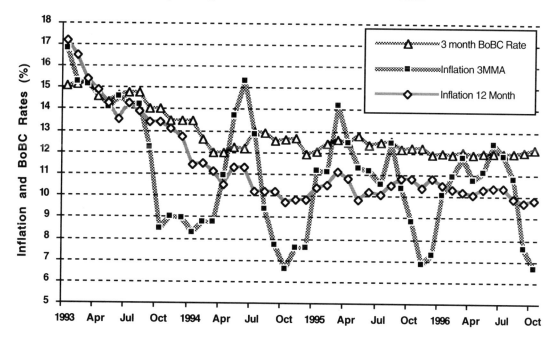

4. SOME IMPLICATIONS AND DISCUSSIONS

Nominal lending rate regulation

I n the following, some implications are discussed under the assumptions that Botswana allows nominal interest rate ceilings and targeting in the asset market model outlined above. An interest rate ceiling on lending rate (upper limit imposed on the lending rate) may not be necessary to encourage borrowing (binding on lending institutions, i.e., commercial banks) when acquisitions of net foreign assets lead lending rates to fall below it. For example, assume that the base money rises following the export of diamonds by Debswana. Furthermore, assume that the ceiling on the lending rate of commercial banks is set at R_1 in Figure 1. The increase in the monetary base following the export will shift the BM curve to BM_1, from BM_2. The interest rate falls and the relative prices of assets increase, thus the interest rate ceiling is not constraining commercial banks' lending. The increase in the relative prices of assets and the low interest rates boost spending. In short, in a country with increasing net foreign assets, an interest rate ceiling may not be binding to the loan market, all else being equal. The market determined interest rate may fall below the interest rate ceiling anyway.

Nominal interest rate target and inflationary pressures

A nominal interest rate target in the Botswana context may lead the Bank of Botswana to sell the BoBCs to achieve the target level. Figure 1 can be used to illustrate this point. Assume that R_0 is the nominal interest rate target, with equilibrium in the asset market E_0. As the base money increases from the current account surplus, the BM curve shifts to the right, thus putting a downward pressure on interest rates. To frustrate the fall in the interest rates, the Bank of Botswana will have to sell BoBCs, shifting back the BM curve. The SB curve also shifts up from SB_1 as more BoBCs are willingly held by the public including commercial banks. The net effect is an increase in the price of assets, and an unchanged nominal interest rate (equilibrium not shown in Figure 1, but is to the right of E_0). However, spending is being encouraged as the price of assets rises.

5. CONCLUDING REMARKS AND SUGGESTIONS

The main conclusion of this paper can be stated succinctly. In a country such as Botswana, acquisitions of net foreign assets through diamond exports and current account surpluses have an automatic expansionary effect on the money supply. The auctions of the BoBCs work to neutralize this expansion, and may even reduce the money supply when sales of the BoBCs exceed the increase in net foreign assets.

An excess of tax receipts over spending by the Government, deposited at the Bank of Botswana tightens up monetary conditions, and thus helps passively the process of mopping up excess liquidity.

Sales of the BoBCs work to contain the increase in the net foreign assets, and affect the prices of real assets such as housing, consumer durables and capital. In other words, the sales of the BoBCs work to offset the effect of the increase in net foreign assets on the monetary base.

In a context of nominal interest rate targeting, the Bank of Botswana may still have to sell the BoBCs to maintain the targeted nominal interest rate if ever the Bank adopts such a policy. This, however, may encourage spending as the prices of assets rise and this may stimulate the production of these assets such as housing if the economy has not reached full employment.

The evidence presented in the paper must be supplemented with further empirical evidence and more elaborate models. It is hoped that more empirical evidence on the effects of BoBCs on domestic credit, and the structure of real interest rates in Botswana will be pursued in other studies.

REFERENCES

Bernanke, B.S. and Gertler, M. 1995. 'Inside the Black Box: The Credit Channel of Monetary Policy Transmission', *Journal of Economic Perspectives*, Vol.9, No.4, pp27–48.

Chiang, A.C. 1984. *Fundamental Methods of Mathematical Economics, 3rd edition.* McGraw Hill, New York.

Dornbusch, R. 1980. *Open Economy Macroeconomics.* Basic Books, New York.

Friedman, M. 1956. 'The Quantity Theory of Money: A Restatement'. In: Friedman, M. (ed.), *Studies in the Quantity Theory of Money.* University of Chicago Press, Chicago, pp3–24.

Friedman, M. 1968. 'The Role of Monetary Policy', *American Economic Review*, pp1–17.

Friedman, M. 1971. *A Theoretical Framework for Monetary Policy Analysis.* National Bureau of Economic Research, New York.

Greenspan, A. 1993. 'Testimony of Alan Greenspan, Chairman, Federal Reserve Board', *Monetary Policy Objectives*, Federal Reserve Board, Washington, July 20, pp3–13.

Hicks, J.R. 1935. 'A Suggestion for Simplifying the Theory of Money', *Economica*, pp61–82.

Hogarth, G. 1996. *Introduction to Monetary Policy.* Centre for Central Banking Studies, Bank of England, London.

Humphrey, T. 1993. *Money, Banking and Inflation.* Edward Elgar, England.

Kone, Z. 1996. 'A Brief Overview of Monetary Management in Botswana and the Case for the Dutch Auction', *The Research Bulletin*, Vol.14, No.2, pp74–81. Bank of Botswana, Gaborone.

Krugman, P. and Obstfeld, M. 1988. *International Economics.* Scott, Foresman and Company, USA.

Leith, J.C. 1996. 'Interest Rates in Botswana', *The Research Bulletin.* Vol.14, No.1, pp1–12. Bank of Botswana, Gaborone.

Meltzer, A. 1995. 'Money, Credit and Other Transmission Processes: A Monetarist Perspective', *Journal of Economic Perspectives*, Vol.9, No.4, pp49–72.

Milne, E., Marston, D. and Skafte, B. 1994. *Issues Related to Money Market Development and Monetary Management in Botswana*, Vol.1. IMF, Washington.

Mishkin, F.S. 1995. 'Symposium on the Monetary Transmission Mechanism', *Journal of Economic Perspectives*, Vol.9, No.4, pp3–10.

Mundell, R. 1968. 'International Economics', Macmillan Company, New York.

Pigou, A. 'The Value of Money', *Quarterly Journal of Economics*, Vol.32, 1917/1918, pp38–65.

Simonds, R.R. 1987. 'Modern Financial Theory', In: Wilcox, J.A. (ed.), *Current Readings on Money, Banking, and Financial Markets.* Little Brown, USA.

Smithin, J. 1994. *Controversies in Monetary Economics.* Edward Elgar, England.

Taylor, J.B. 1995. 'The Monetary Transmission Mechanism: An Empirical Framework', *Journal of Economic Perspectives*, Vol.9, No.4, pp11–26.

Tobin, J. 1969. 'A General Equilibrium Approach to Monetary Theory', *Journal of Money, Credit, and Banking*, pp13–29.

Wicksell, K. 1935. *Lectures on Political Economy, Volume 2, Money.* George Routledge and Sons, London.

Privatization of Public Enterprises through the Stock Exchange

Alphious M. Ncube

1. INTRODUCTION

Since Independence in 1966, Botswana developed a relatively large public sector covering activities in most areas of the economy. The investment programme was implemented through three methods: (i) setting up a parastatal by an Act of Parliament; or (ii) indirectly through Government's investment arm, the Botswana Development Corporation (BDC), which was established in 1970 mainly as agent for commercial and industrial development; and finally (iii) by forming departments which performed tasks that in more developed economies are predominantly performed by the private sector, such as the Central Transport Organization (CTO) (this supplies, maintains and manages the Government vehicle fleet). Thus, over the years, Government investment expanded to hotels, tourism, transport, financial institutions (banking and insurance), agriculture and estates management. However, it is important to note from the outset that, except for parastatals, the relationship between the Government and the companies it invested in was principally one of arms length dealings with each other.

The main reason for Government's involvement in the private sector in Botswana was due to the realization of the poor state of the economy at Independence and the reluctance of the private sector, both local and external, to venture into any significant projects outside the mining sector. One way in which Government strove to overcome this reluctance was through the establishment of the BDC. Through the BDC, Government could help encourage private sector development with financial involvement in a new project, but keep such involvement to a minority interest, thus helping to foster private sector led initiatives.

By the 1990s, this rationale had been overtaken by events, and the potential for wider participation by the private sector in the economy had increased. Government activities focused on complementing activities of the private sector, rather than establishing its own industrial and commercial enterprises. In this regard, privatization in Botswana is seen as an integral part of a shift towards greater market orientation of economic policy, rather than as a principal solution to an immediate financial crisis. In other words, the main catalyst for change is the desire of Government for more dynamic and efficient management and provision of services.

While the rationale behind a country's privatization strategy is an important subject area in itself, the main concern of this paper is how privatization of public enterprises is conducted once the decision to privatise is made. The paper will put forward the viewpoint that privatization through the stock market can help to stimulate both primary and secondary market activity, thereby widening and deepening the financial sector. Second, this method of privatization can also be used to promote a fair distribution of national assets and the development of the financial sector, particularly at a time when the country is seeking to establish itself as an international financial centre.

2. TYPES AND METHODS OF PRIVATIZATION

Types

There are many types of privatization, but this paper will only briefly describe three of the more important mainstream approaches. *Deregulation* is the introduction of competition into statutory monopolies by removing restrictive statutes. These changes are usually introduced in non-competitive markets. In Botswana, deregulation would be possible in the cases of the Botswana Power Corporation, the Botswana Telecommunications Corporation, the Water Utilities Corporation, and others. Another type of privatization frequently used is contracting out where Government invites competitive tenders from private firms to provide goods and services to, and on behalf of, the public sector. Examples include: refuse collection, vehicle maintenance and servicing, land surveying, cleaning provision, and other such services. Finally, there is the distribution of various publicly owned assets to the general public and international investors. If done on the basis of a non-financial basis this is usually called *mass privatization*, and the criteria for receiving assets range from citizenship of a country to the fact that one is an employee of the firm being removed from state ownership. Meanwhile, the selling of state owned assets to the public, or other investors, is called *conventional privatization*.

While there is scope to discuss the first two types of privatization in Botswana, with the Government having already announced the intention to contract out some of its services, this paper is concerned with the conventional type of privatization. It would appear that in the short run, contracting out is going to assume a more important role in the privatization process in Botswana than other types of privatization, notwithstanding the fact that in the 1996 Budget Speech the Minister of Finance and Development Planning mentioned the need for 'rationalization and commercialization' of public enterprises. The Minister defined rationalization as 'asking ourselves which activities really need to be undertaken by the state, and which are best left to private sector enterprise' (p39); but also noted that it can take the form of ensuring that those enterprises which remain in public ownership conduct their affairs along efficient commercial and cost effective lines. Commercialization involves the appropriate pricing of the goods and services produced by state owned enterprises.

While no firm commitment was made in the 1996 Budget Speech about the privatization of parastatals[1], some important steps have since been taken. The first is the formulation of the National Development Plan (NDP 8), which will give a clearer indication of the policy framework for any future divestment programme. Government is

---

[1] Although the 1995 Budget Speech had stated that Air Botswana would be privatised once it had become profitable.

committed to undertaking a review of the size and structure of the public sector, including parastatals, early in NDP 8 which will, *inter alia*, establish a privatization programme with targets for activities currently carried out by Government, as well as parastatals. The second important development was that the Botswana Confederation of Commerce, Industry and Manpower (BOCCIM) commissioned a privatization study in June 1996. The main focus of the study was to provide a detailed policy and procedural framework to help provide impetus to the Government's programme.

Methods

This paper presents a short review of various methods of privatization. In this regard, the paper will also look at the issue of lack of savings to purchase firms being sold, the lack of entrepreneurial skills to ensure effective management of private firms, and problems associated with making adequate estimates of firms' market value, and so on, as some of the constraints facing Government in following one single method of privatization.

The self-management system or management buy out

This approach to privatization involves transferring ownership rights directly to the workers of each particular enterprise. The main problems with this approach are the issues of equity and fairness, as the system benefits only those who hold jobs in the company being privatised. Further, issues of efficiency also come up as self-managed enterprises may not always become more efficient simply due to the change in ownership.

Financial intermediaries

Under this system, several methods of sale could be employed, *viz.*: (1) the public offer for sale of shares through the Botswana Stock Exchange[2]; (2), the private placement of shares in cases where Government holdings are small, and the enterprise already fulfils the listing requirements of the Stock Exchange; (3) the sale of assets where the enterprises concerned have poor track records and future outlook is considered bleak; and finally, (4) a deferred public offer, where a willing buyer/willing seller price can be negotiated based on valuations of the underlying assets of the enterprise; and, if following a flotation the stock market valuation of the company is markedly out of line with the agreed sale price, an additional compensation/reimbursement payment can be made.

While the establishment of financial intermediaries that hold shares in the individual enterprises, with the public in turn owning the equity of the intermediaries, is an interesting idea, this paper will only examine the possible establishment of an 'Investment Trust Fund' through which shares can be transferred from the Government to individual shareholders.

Voucher schemes

This involves the distribution of vouchers to each citizen of a country (or by any other agreed criteria) which represents an entitlement to some amount of equity shares in a

---

[2]   When established, the Botswana Stock Exchange was initially called the Botswana Share Market. Its name was changed in 1995.

particular enterprise. These could be made to have no monetary value, or be trade-able between individuals, and could only be used to bid for shares in state supervised auctions of individual enterprises. A major problem with this approach is that an unsophisticated public may not bid rationally at the auctions of enterprises because they cannot assess the value of companies. The numerous stages involved in the auctions can also pose a serious problem.

3. The Case for Privatising through the Stock Market

Private ownership usually leads to more efficient use of resources in that owners are more concerned about minimizing costs of production, as well as monitoring, assessing and controlling managers' performance.[3] On the other hand, public enterprises tend to distort market forces by underpricing their services, thereby causing mis-allocation of resources. One of the best ways of measuring the competency of management is through the demand of the company's shares on the stock market. At the most basic level, the absence of a capital market limits the Government in its choice of privatization method to direct sales. The existence of a weak capital market pushes the Government in the same direction, with the capacity of the market determining the number and size of sales that can be absorbed. If Government is forced to sell an enterprise directly because of the non-existence of a capital market, or the presence of a thin one, this imposes potentially significant costs on the Government.

Resource Mobilization

Search costs

The essence of a capital market is to provide a mechanism through which the aggregate demand of a large number of small buyers can be channelled into the supply of entitlements to a small number of large assets. In the absence of such a market, sellers (i.e., government in the case of privatization), can incur extensive search costs in identifying individual buyers with sufficient resources and capacity to acquire the assets.[4]

Wealth distribution

In cases of highly skewed wealth distribution, direct sales of assets to only those agents that have accumulated resources can exacerbate the adverse welfare effects of concentration of asset ownership. Ownership concentration can, without appropriate regulation, lead to situations where dominant firms/agents act to limit the economic effects of privatization in terms of pricing and production.

Tradeability

Privatization programmes often aim to broaden the economic participation of a wider range of people. In the absence of a capital market, significant barriers can be con-

---

[3]   Although this also depends on the competitive nature of the market in which they operate.

[4]   Although this does depend on the nature of the enterprise for sale. In some cases, interested parties have been known to approach governments rather than governments having to actively seek buyers.

fronted in trying to involve as many people as possible. If it is an important requirement that if shares are distributed widely, they must also have a tradeable market to allow for smooth transfers of such shares. This is where the existence of a capital market is useful. In addition, capital markets can assist in eliminating one of the major barriers to fixed capital accumulation by reducing the minimum size of investment in financial assets for any individual agent.

Tapping foreign capital

It may be the case that foreign investors are the only source of capital sufficiently large for privatization. In addition, foreign participation in the domestic economy may bring in technical and management expertise. But, foreign ownership is still viewed as a disadvantage in many developing countries. Blending and tapping both the domestic capital base and, significantly, offering a market through which foreign investors' equity stakes can be liquidated in future, facilitates foreign participation in the privatization programmes.

Dealing with lumpy assets

Finally, capital markets permit governments to deal with the 'lumpiness' of assets sales, especially through the use of multiple tranches in the divestiture of the same enterprise (the case of the sale of Sechaba in 1995 is a good example in Botswana). This reduces the demand on domestic resources by any single tranche (thereby avoiding dramatic relative price changes and subsequent crowding out) and smoothes the flow of government revenues, and establishes more accurate pricing of assets.

Tradeability and efficiency

The previous section dealt primarily with the role capital markets can play in facilitating the primary sale of assets, but secondary trading capacity is also essential. Secondary trading of shares enhances the perceived liquidity of equity, and in economies where investment uncertainty is high, will increase the purchaser's valuation of the asset. In addition, a listed company, because of the listing disclosure requirements, is viewed more positively by the banking sector, thereby enhancing the company's access to credit. More importantly, share trading in a company provides a direct valuation of the net worth of an enterprise, and movements in the share price (relative to appropriate indices) can generate information to shareholders on management performance. Hence, capital markets can provide appropriate incentives and monitoring environments for continued efficiency improvements after sale. In the absence of efficient capital markets, the costs of performance monitoring and the creation of appropriate incentive structures tends to be higher.

Policy transparency

In general, public share issues impose the legal conditions of clarity, transparency and consistency on the vendor. Public share issues normally require independent statements of valuation of the firm to be sold, full dissemination of information, a declaration of actual and contingent liabilities, clear statements of corporate policy, and future disclosure obligations. The government is also compelled to specify clearly its intended future policy towards the firm. Such conditions are not so likely to characterise direct sales, which provide opportunities for less clarity and transparency in the sale of publicly owned companies.

The above arguments, however, are not meant to suggest that there is no role for direct sales. On the contrary, they help to assert some of the advantages of public share sales.

Capital market development

The ability and capacity of a capital market to intermediate and allocate commercial risk develops over time depending upon the nature of the asset flows through the market. Although the effects of privatization on nascent capital markets are not unique to privatization *per se*, the fact that most privatization issues are often large in relation to other equity shares, and to the market itself, is of particular importance. There are other aspects too. For example, these enterprises may be concentrated in certain sectors of the economy, such as transport and communications, be of similar vintage, and be of larger than average size. Privatization programmes can be used to stimulate other market developments: for example, the launching of new instruments, development of market regulations, and so on. Issues of public enterprises tend to have a high profile compared to other issues, and often involve a greater number of players (many of whom may be new to equity trading). Hence, the impact of privatization on capital markets development is not neutral. Privatization affects the capital market in four main ways: (i) it increases the volume of equity listed on the market; (ii) it alters the number and type of players on the market; (iii) it imposes demands on the technological, regulatory, and operational capacity of the market; and, (iv) it constitutes a significant (if only short to medium-term) intervention by the Government in the capital market.

4. THE EXPERIENCE OF BOTSWANA

The first question to be confronted is whether or not the Botswana Stock Exchange is sufficiently large for a programme of domestic share sales of public companies to be a

TABLE 1. CAPITALIZATION AS A PERCENTAGE OF GROSS DOMESTIC PRODUCT

	1989	1990	1991	1992	1993	1994
BOTSWANA	4.4	6.0	7.5	8.0	7.2	8.6
MALAYSIA	106.2	113.7	124.4	162.0	342.0	274.5
THAILAND	37.0	29.7	39.0	56.4	108.5	91.6
INDONESIA	2.4	7.6	6.0	9.4	22.7	27.4
CHILE	36.6	44.3	82.3	72.0	102.2	124.8
KENYA	6.0	5.3	7.9	7.6	25.5	35.0
ZIMBABWE	3.8	17.0	20.7	12.4	13.3	23.6

Source: Botswana Stock Exchange, *IFS Emerging Stock Markets Factbook 1995.*

viable option? In this respect, it is clear that compared with other emerging markets where share issues have been frequently used, the Botswana Stock Exchange is young and relatively small. The Botswana Share Market was launched in June 1989 and at that time Barclays, BGI (later Engen), Sechaba, Sefalana and Standard Chartered were already public companies. The listing of these companies was a significant boost to the launch of the stock market. In addition, the short period under which the Botswana Stock Exchange has been operating makes it difficult to compare with other emerging markets.

The Botswana Stock Exchange is not, however, insignificant compared to markets where successful flotations have been made: its capitalization between 1989 and 1994 averaged 7.0% of GDP as against 14.6% for Kenya and 15.2% for Zimbabwe for the same period. In contrast the capitalization ratio of the more dynamic emerging markets of Indonesia, Malaysia, Chile, and Thailand averaged 12.6%, 187.1%, 77.0%, and 60.4%, respectively.

The Botswana Stock Exchange and some examples of privatization

The nascent Botswana Stock Market witnessed substantial growth between 1989 and 1995, as its index rose from 149.3 at the end of 1989 to 332.8 by the end of 1995 (see Figure 1). In terms of market capitalization, the ratio of market capitalization to gross domestic product rose from 4.2% in 1989 to 8.8% in 1995 (see Figure 2). There were several factors behind that growth, but the two most important were the sales of BDC equity onto the market by the Government (or the privatization of the companies concerned); and the booming economy of the late 1980s.

To date, the Government has not engaged in any large-scale sale of parastatal equity on the Botswana Stock Exchange. However, it has sold some of its equity holdings in BDC on the Stock Exchange. This gives a useful indication as to how

FIGURE 1. THE STOCK MARKET INDEX, 1989 TO 1995

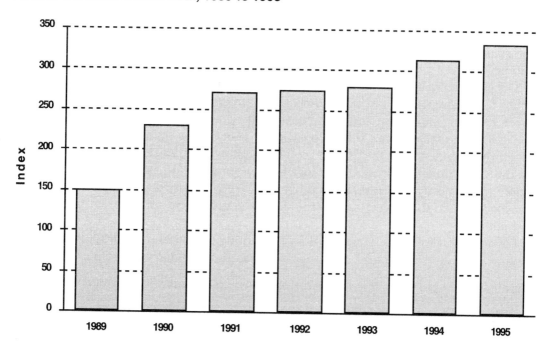

FIGURE 2. CAPITALIZATION AS PERCENTAGE OF GDP

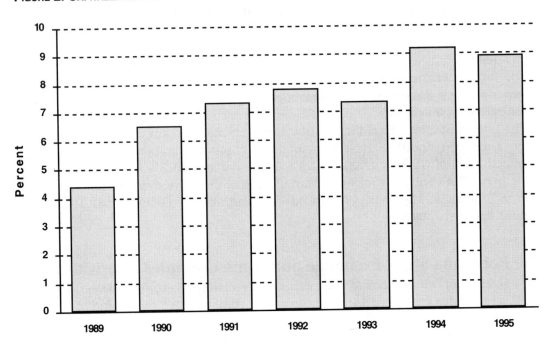

privatization through a stock exchange can work in Botswana and the potential benefits of this approach. The first step in the sale of equity by this route was in 1984, when shares in nine of BDC's more successful subsidiaries were transferred to the newly established Sechaba Investment Trust Company. The company was the first Botswana investment trust company, and represented an important step in both the development of the capital market and in attracting public interest in equity investments and also to enable investors to invest in a diversified portfolio of equities in a variety of companies. Upon formation, Sechaba Investment Trust Company's paid-up share capital was P7 450 950 and the single shareholder was the BDC, but shares in the Trust were offered to the public[5] for the first time in December 1984 at a price of P50 per share.

The successful approach used in disposing of shares in the Sechaba Investment Trust Company (SIT) case was a necessary precursor to the use of the Botswana Stock Exchange for privatization purposes. The Government was not forced by financial circumstances to sell these companies, but did so mainly to promote private sector development and the distribution of share ownership. The method of sale used by the Government represented a logical step forward to privatization in a country where the majority of the state holdings are large, and involve unique management knowledge such that direct sale to the domestic private sector may not be an attractive option.

Following on from the successful sale of equity in the SIT, in 1990 shares in the Financial Services Company, a finance and leasing subsidiary of two parastatals (the

---

5   Only Batswana and certain qualified entities (BDC, insurance companies, pension funds, trade unions, cooperative societies) were eligible to hold SIT shares.

TABLE 2. SOME CHARACTERISTICS OF THE BOTSWANA STOCK EXCHANGE

KEY RATIOS	1989	1990	1991	1992	1993	1994	1995
MARKET CAPITALIZATION (PULA MILLION)	255.1	423.6	545.4	657.2	668.8	1024.3	1120.3
MARKET TURNOVER (PULA MILLION)	0.2	1.1	1.2	2.7	4.0	6.9	7.3
VALUE OF COMPANIES PRIVATISED (PULA MILLION)	3.0	16.8	3.2	2.4	1.4	29.0	278.2
VALUE SOLD VIA STOCK MARKET (PULA MILLION)	2.9	4.9	3.0	2.3	0	21.2	269.6
AMOUNT RAISED ON STOCK MARKET (PULA MILLION)	11.8	11.25	24.7	28.0	0	13.7	68.0
NO. OF COMPANIES LISTED	6	7	9	11	10	11	12
NO. OF COMPANIES PRIVATISED	4	5	5	5	4	7	11
NO. OF COMPANIES SOLD THROUGH STOCK MARKET	1	1	4[a]	3[b]	0	1[c]	0
SHARE INDEX (JAN 1989 = 100)	149.3	230.5	271.7	273.9	278.7	312.9	332.8

Notes:
[a] Includes Standard Chartered Bank and Barclays Bank rights issues.
[b] Includes IGI rights issue.
[c] BIHL rights issue.

Source: Botswana Stock Exchange, Botswana Development Corporation.

BDC and the National Development Bank), were sold in the second flotation on the Botswana Share Market.[6] In 1991, shares in another BDC subsidiary, Botswana Insurance Holdings, were sold in the fourth Botswana Stock Exchange flotation. The total amount raised on the stock market was P11.25 million.

The final, and perhaps most significant privatization exercises in the period covered by this paper was the phased disposal by BDC of its brewery interests. The exercise was started in late 1994 with the restructuring of SIT so as to own only shares in Kgalagadi Breweries and Botswana Breweries. Non-brewery interests were being disposed of into a separate company. Shares in SIT were then offered in stages, initially to residents of Botswana, and then more widely. By March 1996, BDC's holding in SIT had been reduced to approximately 25%.

Apart from its size, this process was important because of the care taken to balance various interests. Allowing small, local investors initial access to the shares,

---

6   Although the Financial Services Company was eventually merged with First National Bank of Botswana in 1993.

which subsequently rose rapidly in price when the market was opened to other traders, reflected a concern that share ownership should be spread beyond a few institutional holders. At the same time, the objective of ensuring that efficient management of the breweries was achieved by allowing the 40% holding in each brewery by South African Breweries (SAB) to have double voting rights. In other words, majority control rests with SAB, but majority dividends are dispersed to the shareholders of SIT.

TABLE 3. VALUE OF SHARES AND NUMBER OF COMPANIES DISPOSED OF BY BDC

	1989	1990	1991	1992	1993	1994	1995	CUMULATIVE TOTAL
VALUE SOLD (PULA MILLION)	3.0	5.0	3.2	2.4	1.4	29.0	278.3	322.2
VALUE SOLD ON SM (PULA MILLION)	2.9	4.9	3.0	2.3	0	21.2	269.6	303.9
COMPANIES SOLD	4	4	5	5	4	7	11	40
COMPANIES SOLD ON SM	1	2	2	3	0	3	4	15
VALUE SOLD ON SM AS % OF TOTAL VALUE SOLD	97.8	98.7	91.6	96.3	0	73.1	96.9	94.3
NO SOLD ON SM AS % OF TOTAL NUMBER SOLD	25.0	50.0	40.0	60.0	0	42.9	36.4	37.4

Note: SM = Stock Market. The number of companies sold each year refers to sales (as BDC can actually dispose of shares from a single company in tranches over a number of years). Similarly, the number of companies sold through the stock market refers to privatization transactions as opposed to single sale of companies.

Source: Botswana Stock Exchange, Botswana Development Corporation.

In value terms, sales by the BDC through the stock market have accounted for approximately 94% of the total value of privatization over the seven year period under review. However, in terms of the number of companies privatised, flotations on average have accounted for about 38% of the total number of privatised companies. As already mentioned, the main reason for the low number of companies sold through the stock market was either because the company concerned did not meet the minimum listing requirements, or because it was under 'private treaty' which restricted the sale to initial partner shareholders.

The developments listed above had significant implications on the growth of the Botswana Stock Exchange: its market capitalization rose from 4.4% of GDP at the end of 1989 to 8.9% in 1995. At the same time, ownership distribution widened considerably as the companies were floated. For example, ownership rose from two in 1984 for the Financial Services Company, to about fifteen after flotation in 1992; and from one to eight major shareholders for SIT (with 18.4% shares owned by the public) by August 1993. As at March 1996 total shareholders in SIT numbered 2352, the large majority of whom had only very small holdings (SIT, 1996).

The flotation of shares in public enterprises on the Botswana Stock Exchange increased the value of turnover from P0.2 million in 1989 to P7.3 million by the end of 1995. These expansionary developments imposed some demands on the technological, regulatory and operational capacity of the nascent market. Initially, the absence of a secondary market made it difficult to determine the true market values of shares. As a result, shares such as SIT were substantially undervalued resulting in large wealth transfer from the Government to individuals and corporations which were able to purchase the shares. This phenomenon is partly demonstrated in Figure 3, which shows very low proportions of the actual amount raised relative to the market capitalization, reflecting substantial increases in share prices after flotation.[6]

FIGURE 3. ACTUAL AMOUNT RAISED AS A PERCENTAGE OF CAPITALIZATION

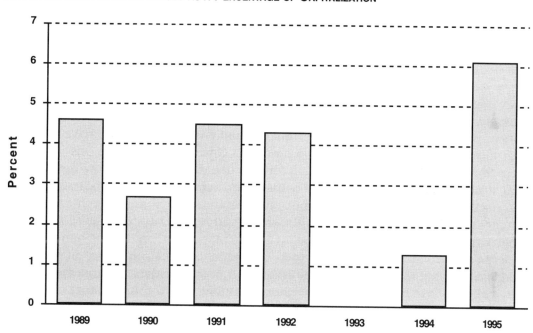

Despite these positive developments, it is important to note that most companies owned by the BDC do not meet the stock market listing requirements. In cases where the company does not meet the minimum listing requirements, there are two ways by which shares can be disposed of. The first method involves joint venture companies under what is termed a 'private treaty' where the treaty specifies how the BDC would divest its shares. These 'private treaties' contain pre-emptive clauses normally giving first preference of buy to joint partners. In the second method, an advertisement is placed in the print media, which only indicates that the BDC would be selling a company in a specified sector of the economy and inviting only serious investors to bid. At this stage no further detailed information is provided, but once BDC is satisfied that the potential investors are serious, detailed financial information is divulged to them.

---

[6] However, the low ratio may have nothing to do with share prices, *per se*, but the fact that the amount raised was small compared to the size of the market.

5. FINANCING OF PRIVATIZATION

The attempt to use the Stock Market to sell Government shares in companies in Botswana, particularly the ground breaking Sechaba Investment Trust case, overlooked one important aspect that has to be considered when adopting this route for privatization: the provision of finance. To date, interested investors were left to organise their own financing for the acquisition of shares. While the matter of who buys state assets is of less concern in developed economies, it is of overwhelming importance in developing economies like Botswana, where, in many cases, the sale of a major state owned asset to private interests is usually a highly charged political event. Given the prevailing perception in Botswana, regarding lack of access to credit finance by the majority of the people, this author considers a deliberate move to provide such a facility is a necessity when selling state assets. In other words, to encourage massive support for the programme of privatising through the Stock Exchange, a large body of interested persons have to have access to some sort of funding scheme.

The financing of privatization through a stock exchange can be structured in two phases: first, the accessibility of the privatised shares by the majority of local investors; and second, facilitating the smooth transfer of the privatised entity from sovereign risk category to that of commercial risk. The first step is to support the transfer of ownership of shares in public entities to as many people as possible. This means, that in its privatization strategy, the Government must ensure that people have access to some form of finance. The question is how does Government achieve this objective? There are several ways, but the option chosen depends largely on how the Government structures the sale of an entity. Furthermore, in most privatizations, governments rarely sell a company at one time, but often retain some shares which are sold in tranches in the years following the initial sale. Furthermore, a certain level of international investment in the entity may be invited by placement, on the one hand, and by tender to select a strong alliance partner to provide technical expertise, on the other. Therefore, it is only the balance of the shares left over after these arrangements have been made that can be sold to local investors by public offer through a stock exchange.

To encourage as many people as possible, including first time small participants, to purchase shares, one strategy is split them into various categories. First, there could be groups of small 'partly paid' shares, specifically reserved for small investors. These would require a fifty percent initial payment and the balance to be paid over a period of twelve months. Of course, partly paid shares would not be traded on the secondary market until they are fully paid. Then, the rest of the shares can be floated under a normal full payment basis for whatever amount one is allotted, but the financing of share acquisition by both small and large local investors can be facilitated by the establishment of a trust fund discussed below.

Another way of financing privatization is for the Government to set up an 'Investment Trust Fund' where shares from public enterprises are transferred, and later sold to locals in small tranches over a designated period. The establishment of such a trust fund also has the advantage of preserving Government investment for future generations by not converting them into current revenue. The administrator of the trust would manage the loan on behalf of the financing party (which could be the Government selling the shares, or a financial institution, or both) and would ensure that the buyers meet all their obligations prior to the transfer of shares upon full payment of the loan.

A third alternative is the setting up of a 'credit scheme', which is funded from either budgetary appropriation, a loan, or from proceeds of sale of public enterprises. Such a scheme could be a joint venture between Government and the banking system targeted at facilitating the transfer of share ownership by providing finance to the majority or unsophisticated investors at cost recovery levels. However, the existence of a separate credit scheme to facilitate the purchase of shares by the public should not erode the long-term objectives of the Investment Trust Fund, i.e., preserving national assets rather than consuming them.

Following on from a share transfer, the privatised public entity moves from the credit category of sovereign risk to that of commercial risk. This transition to private ownership can prove to be a difficult period for the enterprise, and thus may require financial provisions to be made to cushion such enterprises from loss of Government funds, subsidies, guaranteed loans and lines of credit. Several internal and external factors affect the financing requirements of the privatised enterprise. The availability and organization of the country's capital markets and the banking system affect financing, as does Government's willingness to permit foreign private capital shareholders. Once privatised, the entity would require a combination of long-term capital for modernization of equipment and technology and short-term revolving lines of credit to finance operations of the enterprise. The fact that sale proceeds of public enterprises accrue to Government, means that the enterprise itself remains with little finance to modernise and expand its markets.[7]

There are several factors that affect the method of privatization and thus financing requirements. Some of the factors are the quality and size of the business to be privatised. For most of the companies disposed of by BDC, this has been an overriding factor as most of them are small in size. As mentioned earlier, the availability and organization of the capital market and the banking system, and the willingness of the Government to permit foreign private capital shareholders, as well as the availability of private domestic capital, and, of course, the willingness of locals to take risk and invest in equity in sufficient amounts, are crucial determinants. Almost all these factors were not present in the Botswana case, thus limiting the use of this important tool in the privatization process.

6. IDENTIFYING CANDIDATES FOR PRIVATIZATION

Botswana is a small economy with only fifteen parastatals, of which nine are non-financial and six financial. In addition, industrial and commercial entities in which the BDC owns an equity share on behalf of Government numbered about ninety in 1995. Hence, in discussing the privatization issue in Botswana we must not lose sight of the fact that we are dealing with a comparatively small number of enterprises. It also means that, once the criteria for selection have been put in place, identifying candidates for privatization should be relatively easy for Government. Nonetheless, it is imperative to stress that once the decision to privatise is made, a systematic, step by step procedure has to be followed.

---

[7] Although in many privatisations, the enterprise will have been restructured, and had a fresh capital injection, prior to its sale.

An example of this type of approach used in other countries is the establishment of a special committee made up of key officials from the Government and the entity concerned, and dedicated solely to the privatization of that entity. This has worked well because it has created a clear line of command and avoids future problems on who should be consulted when certain pertinent issues arise. Each step in the process must also be conducted in the best interest of the nationals, in this case Batswana. After this first step has been taken, many countries have then established an advisory team composed of independent consultants who work closely with the special committee, and adhere to the principle of strict transparency at every juncture. Finally, the experiences of other countries also shows that the privatization process is made easier if a structure is created that enables the advisory team to produce business analyses of important matters (after consultation with interested parties in Government, trade unions, and among the prospective investors), which can be presented to the highest levels of authority in the country.

In two recent cases of privatization in Kenya and Zimbabwe, the advantages of following the steps mentioned above were clearly demonstrated. Kenya strictly adhered to these principles in divesting from Kenya Airways, and enjoyed a smooth transfer of shares through both placement to the international investors and public offer to local investors (over 113 000 local investors were able to participate in a total of 22% of the shares). In contrast, lack of proper planning and transparency in the sale of Hwange Thermal Power Station in Zimbabwe led to widespread condemnation of the deal. The Government was accused of employing unorthodox tactics by both prospective local and external investors; and the Board of the enterprise dissociated itself from the deal and in the end was fired. This is clearly one of the ways of not doing things properly.

Since identifying public enterprises for privatization is not a primary objective of this paper, we will discuss some of the parastatals considered suitable for privatization through public offers only in passing. To prepare parastatals for privatization in Botswana, a number of which are either making losses or performing poorly, would require the Government to restructure these enterprises for sale to the public by the selling of some of the assets to down-size the enterprises. Further, the Government may have to infuse more funds to improve the capital base of these companies. Alternatively, Government can commercialise the parastatals and hire management from the private sector to improve operating efficiency and bring in a market-driven philosophy.

Before the enterprise is sold to the public, certain important considerations regarding the process of selling need to be made. The first step would be to undertake the capital restructuring and evaluation of the enterprise. Second, the Government may try to identify a strategic investor, usually a technical partner, as the next step. Once the strategic investor has been identified, negotiations on the price (which usually includes sale of shares at a discount to compensate for his technical and management know-how) and the size of his share are initiated and agreed. Further, it may be critical for Government to retain a residual stake in the enterprise and also to clearly state ownership restrictions, e.g., the maximum percentage that foreign investors can hold.

Purchase incentives for staff and local investors are also very critical if the privatization programme is to enjoy citizen support. These incentives can take various forms, such as share options for employees, discounts and staged payments for local investors to overcome the problem of high entry costs which the small investors would find unaffordable.

However, there are few parastatals and public enterprises which can be considered as good candidates for privatization through the stock market. For example, the recently restructured National Development Bank could be privatised through the stock market, but a more appropriate method is likely to be a negotiated sale. Conversely, the Botswana Telecommunications Corporation appears to be a good candidate for privatization through the stock market, and is even likely to attract foreign investors by virtue of its area of operation (the information industry is a growth area worldwide, and attracting investors would not be a major problem). However, before the Botswana Telecommunications Corporation can be privatised there is need to transfer regulation to an independent authority, liberalise the market and establish a regulatory policy. In the case of other companies the decisions are less clear. For example, the Botswana Power Corporation and the Botswana Vaccine Institute: in these cases, the choice of a negotiated sale, or sale via the stock market would have to be examined closely.

The Botswana Meat Commission and Air Botswana also are two of the parastatals that can be privatised through the stock market. But, as in the case of the Botswana Telecommunications Corporation, certain things would have to be done first. In the case of both Air Botswana and the Botswana Meat Commission, there would be need to establish them as companies under the Companies Act, restructure them where necessary, and then establish a financial track record before listing (the Botswana Meat Commission probably has a stronger financial track record than Air Botswana, and would need less restructuring).

There is a school of thought that argues that if privatization through the stock exchange is to be meaningful, then Debswana is the most attractive candidate. Debswana is by far the largest corporate entity registered in Botswana, and Government owns 50% of this giant mining company. A release of, say, 30% of Government shares to the general public would stimulate activity on the Botswana Stock Exchange. Such a move could also boost substantial foreign participation on the local bourse, and probably open a way for a Botswana company to be listed on some major international stock exchanges.

7. CONCLUDING REMARKS

Privatization of state owned enterprises increased the value of equity traded on the Botswana Stock Exchange. The nature of privatised equity 'blue chip' stocks and the demonstration effect of the initial issues, were significant factors in injecting dynamism in the market. Capitalization of the market grew, but was no longer concentrated on a limited number of companies. The broadening of both capitalization and trading was an important development, as it transformed the market from an underdeveloped and under used one, to one where risks are being genuinely intermediated. But, is the economy benefiting from this growth? It can be argued that by improving the efficiency with which money is channelled from savers to investors, the stock market brought some economic benefits.

The number of players on the stock market has not been quantified in this paper, but it can be said that through the launch of public offers such as Sechaba, a substantial number of players were introduced to the market. However, the entry of these new investors did not bring aggressive market players which could have raised the efficiency of risk intermediation through the Botswana Stock Exchange. Secondary trading is still predominantly conducted by institutional investors, with little participation from the new individual investors. At the launch of the SIT shares, the ownership and transfer restrictions which specified Batswana as the only legitimate participants expressly worked to limit the development of the market. This restricted the Botswana Stock Exchange's function as an efficiency-inducing weapon, and retarded its development as a risk intermediator. Significantly, these ownership and transfer restrictions have now been phased out.

If the majority of the people have no access to funds for the purchase of privatised shares, privatization through the stock market will not succeed in one of its main objective, i.e., a wider ownership of shares. This could undermine the integrity of the privatization process as it would be interpreted as a ploy to transfer state owned assets to the rich few. To overcome this problem, there is need for the Government, in collaboration with the private sector, to set up a credit scheme to facilitate the purchase of shares by the general public.

Since the sale of state assets in Botswana is not prompted by financial constraints, the proceeds of sales of public enterprises must not be used for current expenditure. Rather, such proceeds should be channelled into a trust fund and invested for future use (including funding of the credit scheme proposed above).

To facilitate the development of the stock market, the Government must accommodate institutional and foreign investors by allowing them reasonable proportions of investment in privatised entities (through portfolio investment).

There are several issues the Government must address in order to facilitate the sale of public enterprises and to ensure a smooth transitional operation of the company after sale. In cases where the balance sheet of the privatised entity is weak, the Government must assist in down sizing the operations of the entity to improve its asset quality by providing transitional funding to cushion the company from loss of Government funds, subsidies, guaranteed loans and lines of credit. Even prior to flotation, Government may be required to assist in the improvement of the creditworthiness of the enterprise to encourage finance through investment bank underwriting, bond issues, loans, and other means.

REFERENCES

Adam, C., Cavendish, W. and Mistry, P. 1992. *Adjusting Privatization*, James Currey, London.

'Economic Reform Today', No.2. 1996. *The CIPE Magazine of Change and Public Policy.*

Hanke, S. (ed.). 1986. *Privatization and Development.* International Centre for Economic Growth, ICS Press, San Francisco.

IFC Review, Summer 1996.

Sechaba Investment Trust Company Limited. 1996. *Sechaba Investment Trust Company Limited, 1996 Annual Report.*

Fiscal Policy in Botswana: Challenges for Public Sector Finance in the Mid-1990s

M. Wright

1. INTRODUCTION

Following political independence in 1966, the goal of financial independence for Botswana was a priority objective for the then impoverished nation. The specific aim was to eliminate, in the shortest possible time, the reliance on grant-in-aid funds from the UK Government to cover recurrent budget expenditures (Government of Botswana, 1966, p45). This important, but clearly limited goal was attained in the financial year 1972/73. In a recent biography of Sir Seretse Khama, this achievement is described as one of the 'proudest moments' of the late President's life (Parsons *et al.*, 1995, p294).

The current situation regarding public finances is a far cry from those early years of Independence. From 1983/84 to 1995/96, the Government ran a continuous series of budget surpluses, covering both recurrent and development spending. As a result, the nation as a whole has been a net saver, and large levels of financial reserves have been built up, in both domestic and foreign currencies. At the end of 1995, accumulated foreign exchange reserves were P13.2 billion, equivalent to US$4.7 billion, which were among the largest in the world on a per capita basis; and at the end of financial year 1995/96 Government cash balances stood at P7.7 billion, or 149% of total Government expenditure during the year.

Since Independence, the Government has, by and large, continued to both preach and practice the virtues of careful planning and fiscal restraint. 'Planning is choosing', as the foreword to the second National Development Plan (NDP 2) succinctly put it (Government of Botswana, 1970). Through successive Development Plans Government has stuck to this credo, both recognising the importance of other constraints – the availability of skilled manpower for example – and setting spending ceilings despite the growing abundance of financial resources. This is not to say, however, that there have not been times when the view that 'money is not an obstacle' has prevailed.

But, in the second half of the 1990s, management of public finance in Botswana may be entering a new phase. This is for two reasons. First, the long period of sustained accumulation of financial resources appears to be over, even if it remains less clear the extent to which current trends are pushing the budget towards large, persistent and increasing deficits. The reserves may appear to provide a comfortable cushion, but their availability as general resources, while commonly supposed and demanded by Batswana, remains highly problematic.

Second, even if this were not so – and Government's previous forecasts of deficits have been contradicted in practice to the extent that such forecasts have developed a 'crying wolf' character – it has also been argued that scaling down the importance of Government in the economy is a structural necessity regardless of the state of the budget bottom line. Government once played a pivotal role in undertaking certain crucial tasks in the absence of a significant modern private sector, and in providing basic public infrastructure. As a result of this development pattern, today the Government dominates the economy in terms of, for example, its contribution to national output, numbers employed, and its control over the nation's financial resources.

But there may now be a danger of this role moving away from that of facilitator of economic development, as Government's appetite for resources restricts the wealth creating potential of the private sector. Concern has been expressed in recent years that the productivity of public sector investments has been falling overall (Bank of Botswana, 1994, 1996), and it is clear that the present dominant role played by Government is far removed from the 'small government' models that are commonly advocated.

Is the Government prepared to meet these challenges? This paper looks at two broad issues in relation to this general question.

First, while the move away from surpluses may affect the 'climate' of budgeting, can old mechanisms continue to be relied upon or does Government require new disciplines? Many years of surpluses that have been achieved seemingly effortlessly – sometimes, even, unintentionally – may have made Government somewhat 'flabby' in its financial management. In particular, the dominance and ease of collection of a few major revenue sources could serve to stunt efficiency in both the development of other revenue sources and rigorous control of expenditure. Also, some of the mechanisms put in place to ensure fiscal discipline, such as the establishment of the special funds for budget deficit and debt management, may now be dwarfed by the current scale of Government's financial activities.

Second, while many economists see a need to reduce the role of government in the economy, there remain considerable pressures for further public expenditure. At the same time, constraining Government expenditure would, in the short to medium term at least, reduce measured GDP growth to an extent that might be difficult to accept. What can Government do, if anything, to reconcile these apparently conflicting demands?

An underlying theme of this paper is that, while facing these pressures, Government is not in a position that calls for crisis management, of being driven to raise revenues and cut expenditures simply to balance the books. Expenditure programmes and the structure of revenues can be adopted and rejected on their merits, without continual reference to the current bottom line. Can Government use this time productively to overhaul thoroughly the efficiency and character of its operations? Or is this ready availability of funds a curse rather than a virtue, encouraging complacency? In particular, just because Government can *afford* to do something does not necessarily answer the more fundamental question of whether it *should*.

The paper examines these issues in the overall context of the sustained period of budget surpluses, but with special reference to the annual budgets during NDP 7, i.e., since 1991. In doing this, the aim is not to propose specific policy measures. Rather, the emphasis is on identifying both strategic opportunities that could contribute to future prosperity in Botswana, and constraints that may hamper the rational future development of the Government sector.

2. THE DOMINANCE OF GOVERNMENT

Botswana is frequently lauded as an example of how an open, market economy has worked in Africa. However, this description has been made relative to other African economies where historically the emphasis has been on inward looking development and a strong role for Government in many aspects of economic life. It should not be imagined that Botswana conforms to all the characteristics of a market economy as perceived more widely.

Most obviously, the leading role played by Government has been a central feature of the country's development. This has been both in ensuring essential services in the absence of other alternative providers and, more generally, acting as a conduit through which the huge surpluses created by the mining sector could be channelled into the development of the general economy.

Table 1 shows some indicators of the current dominance of Government based on statistics for 1994/95.[1] The direct contribution of Government to GDP in 1994/95 is estimated at 17.2% in both current and constant prices. This is second only in importance to the minerals sector, and reflects growth in Government over the previous decade somewhat higher than that of the economy as a whole. In 1984/85 general government GDP was 15.2% of the total. Development expenditure, including net lending, was nearly 11% of GDP in 1994/95. At P1375 million, this was 45% of total gross fixed capital formation, demonstrating clearly the importance of Government as an investor in the economy.

Employment by Central Government in March 1995 was 29.6% of the estimated total of paid employees. This

TABLE 1. INDICATORS OF GOVERNMENT'S IMPORTANCE, 1994/95

	PERCENTAGE OF GDP[a]	PERCENTAGE OF TOTAL
GENERAL GOVERNMENT GDP	17.2	n.a.
TOTAL REVENUES	34.1	n.a.
TOTAL EXPENDITURE	35.7	n.a.
OF WHICH, DEVELOPMENT SPENDING AND NET LENDING	11.0	45.0[b]
EMPLOYMENT	n.a.	29.6[c]

Notes:
[a] The National Accounts year is July-June while the Financial year of Government is April to March. The figures have not been adjusted for this slight difference.
[b] Against total gross fixed capital formation.
[c] Against total estimated paid employees.

Source: Bank of Botswana, *1995 Annual Report.*

is slightly lower than ten years previously when the share exceeded 30%. But, after a fall in the late 1980s, the share has been rising in recent years with an average growth since 1990 of 6.1% per annum, compared to 1.9% per annum in the private sector. This growth was boosted, in particular, by the rapid expansion of employment in Government schools which grew by 11.2% per annum. Also, the figures somewhat understate

---

[1] This year is used because at the time of writing it is the most recent for which national accounts estimates are available.

the true situation since they do not include those employed in the Botswana Defence Force (BDF). This number is kept secret for reasons of national security, but, on the basis of defence-related recurrent expenditures in the Government budget, it is safe to conclude that recent employment growth in the BDF has been rapid.

The current picture hardly resembles the standard parameters of 'small' Government that is commonly advocated as an essential ingredient for encouraging dynamic economic development. A recent example is the programme put forward by J. Sachs, an economist well-known for his efforts in promoting structural adjustment. Writing in *The Economist* in June 1996 on growth prospects for African economies, he advised that governments should function with expenditures less than 20% of GDP, and also that government investment spending be held at 5% of GDP or less, with private investors being encouraged to take on many of the traditional roles of public investment (Sachs, 1996).

Government expenditures and revenues as a proportion of GDP are a common basis for making international comparisons. Figure 1 charts these ratios in Botswana since 1984/85, shown as three year moving averages. For the period since 1987, two variants are shown for each measure. This is to show the significance of the effect arising from recent upward revisions to the GDP estimates since 1988/89 (Central Statistics Office, 1996a). For the affected years, this revision averaged 7.1%. An unfortunate consequence of the way this revision was carried out has been to make comparisons of income levels with earlier years very difficult.[2]

FIGURE 1. GOVERNMENT REVENUE AND EXPENDITURE AS A PROPORTION OF GDP, 1984/85 TO 1993/94

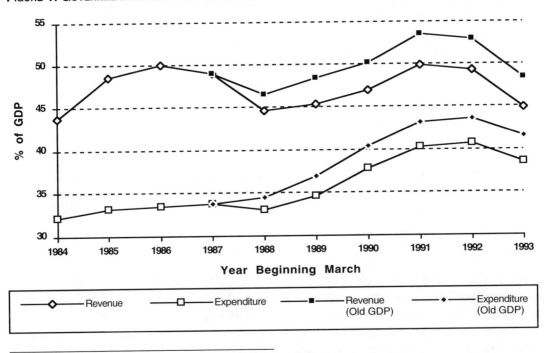

---

2   The basis of the revision was the preparation of final accounts for 1992/93, which in turn incorporated the results of a Social Accounting Matrix (SAM) based on that year (CSO, 1996b). The SAM pointed to underestimation of output in certain sectors. Surrounding years were then rebased using the already estimated growth rates. While this method of revision is a standard statistical procedure it has the effect of causing a break in the national accounts time series, since the years up to 1987/88, based on an earlier SAM, were not adjusted.

The overall effect of using the new figures has been to reduce the importance of Government, as measured by these ratios, in the period covered by the revision. This is of some significance, in that these indicators have been used to support the suggestion that Government currently dominates the Botswana economy to an extent that is unhealthy for future growth and development (Bank of Botswana, 1994). This said, despite the revisions, these ratios remain high when compared to other developing countries.

Looking first at revenues, which are an important indicator of Government's direct control of financial resources; here, on the basis of the old figures it could be argued that Government revenue as a proportion of GDP was among the highest in the world (Shome, 1995, Tables 7–12).[3]

The current estimates (which also avoid the measurement problem highlighted in footnote 3) bring Botswana further back into the pack. For the period 1986–1992 the average of revenue/GDP was 48.4% compared to 50.8% using the old estimates. But over the same period the figure for the whole of Africa was about 20%, and only rarely exceeded 30% in individual cases (ibid., Table 11). The figure for Botswana is more comparable with the advanced economies of north-western Europe, and even then is higher in almost every case (ibid., Table 6).

Similarly for expenditure. Despite the downward revision, Botswana remains at or close to the top of the list of African countries. Of the countries reporting to the IMF, only Lesotho has a higher government expenditure/GDP ratio; and this is a special case, distorted by the severe imbalance between GNP and GDP, the former being much higher as a result of the importance of migrant workers' remittances to that country's national income. More generally, recently published research from the World Bank estimates that the 'normal' size of government in a market economy with a per capita GDP similar to that of Botswana (about US$2900 in 1992/93) is an expenditure to GDP ratio of 25% to 30% (World Bank, 1996, Figure 7.2).[4]

Again, spending proportions as high as in Botswana are more akin to those seen in Europe[5], where a figure in the range 35% to 50% of GDP is not unusual. However, in these cases, current transfers typically account for 60% or more of total expenditure. A major component of these transfers is welfare payments to households; in the United Kingdom in 1993, for example, such payments were the largest single item in the expenditure budget (IMF, 1996). This item has yet to feature in the Botswana budget; while total transfers are a significant part of the budget – 23% in 1992/93 – these were mainly subsidy payments to non-financial public enterprises and payments to local authorities (ibid.). Transfers to households made up less than 5% of total expenditure.

This said, it would be right to point out that, from a different perspective, the Government of Botswana has been heavily involved in transfers. This is in the sense that a major role of Government spending since Independence has been to act as a

---

[3]   Although the raw data presented in these tables itself produces an exaggerated measure for Botswana by combining a national accounts year ending in June with a Government financial year beginning the previous April and, therefore, overlapping by only three months.

[4]   There should, of course, be no inference from this that the 'normal' size of Government is also the 'correct' size.

[5]   The emphasis is on Europe because the North American economies are based on federal structures and, consequently, the influence of the central government is much less.

conduit by which the rents earned from the extraction of diamonds are transferred from the minerals sector to benefit the population at large. The difference is that these transfers have taken the form of capital spending on public infrastructure rather than cash payments to households.

Figure 2 shows the spending in the 1992/93 Botswana budget by basic economic classifications as defined by the IMF. These are shown in relation to GDP. A comparison is made with two stylized examples, a 'typical' economy from each of Europe and Africa.[6]

In addition to the greater extent of transfers, the European case is characterised by smaller shares – both of expenditure and GDP – spent on wages and salaries, intermediate consumption and capital expenditures. As well as almost negligible spending on debt interest payments, Botswana differs from the general African case by a smaller share of total spending, although not of GDP, going on wages and salaries and more on intermediate consumption of goods and services and spending on capital goods. This pattern reflects financial constraints which, elsewhere in Africa, have resulted in a squeeze on investment and spending on goods and services, but less so on labour costs.

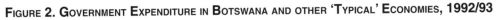

FIGURE 2. GOVERNMENT EXPENDITURE IN BOTSWANA AND OTHER 'TYPICAL' ECONOMIES, 1992/93

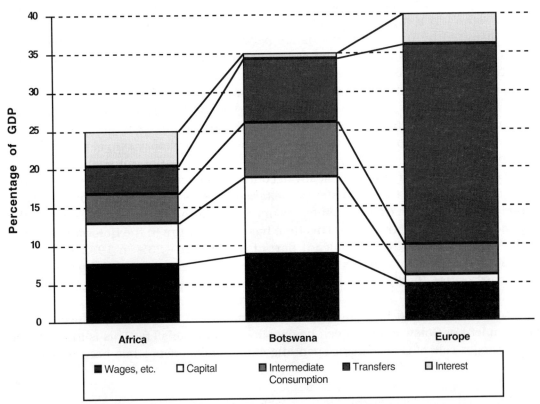

---

6   The figures included in these examples were chosen on a judgemental basis rather than through any precise averaging process. The source data is from IMF, 1996. The aim is to identify characteristics that are reasonably common within the two groups of countries. It should not be expected that any individual economy matches its 'typical' representative in every respect.

From Figure 2 it should also be clear that the atypical structure of Government expenditure in Botswana leads to an exceptional impact on GDP. The sectoral GDP of general government comprises mainly wages and salaries and the consumption of capital. Both of these are relatively high in Botswana compared to the stylised examples. This has two important implications.

First, national income figures for Botswana must be interpreted carefully. The construction of general government GDP, as directed by the System of National Accounts (SNA) does not include any measure of operating surplus: a government's 'output' is valued at cost, with intermediate consumption being subtracted to obtain value added. Therefore, expanding the cost of government activities and, in particular, the cost of employment, will show up uncritically as increased output in the national accounts, regardless of whether this output is of any real value.

Second, this problem of measurement may serve to reinforce any tendency to rely on government as a source of growth. Such reliance is likely to be greater, the larger the government's existing contribution to measured GDP. This has clear potential for producing a situation that is viciously circular in character.

This problem is seen clearly in the production of realistic medium-term growth scenarios for Botswana. The Government, understandably, wishes to be seen to be rapidly returning the economy to high growth rates. However, this will be difficult to achieve immediately if, simultaneously, restraint in the growth of the Government sector is also targeted, as the Government also claims, or if the balance of public spending is to be adjusted away from those elements that contribute to measured GDP. Such a tendency will be a likely consequence of any pressures to move to a more 'European' government model that concentrates on its role as a manager of transfers rather than as a producer. Since such transfers may in general be considered to be 'luxury' goods, the demand for which rises as real income levels increase, the emergence of such pressures in Botswana must be considered likely. The recent decision to introduce a state-funded old age pension scheme from October 1996 is a clear illustration of this.[7]

As an illustrative calculation, if real GDP growth is to average 5% in the eight years from 1994/95 (the last two years of NDP 7 plus the full NDP 8 period), while at the same time Government output is held constant, the rest of the economy will need to grow by an average of 5.8% per annum. If average growth in the mining sector is also restricted to, for instance, 2.5% per annum, the burden of growth on the rest of the private sector increases further to 7.6% per annum. These figures contrast with the recent growth experience. In the three years since 1991/92, real growth in the non-mining private sector has averaged only 3.4% per annum.[8]

Furthermore, restraining the growth of Government may itself have a negative

---

[7] Further evidence of such pressures was seen at the symposium *The Quality of Life in Botswana* in October 1996, organised by the Botswana Society. This featured repeated calls both from presenters and from the floor for Botswana to move towards the establishment of a welfare state. Similar calls were made at the subsequent seminar on the development of a national social security policy organised by the Ministry of Labour and Home Affairs.

[8] While the realism of this calculation has been reduced by the announcement in 1996 of a significant expansion of the Orapa mine that will increase mineral output signficantly over the NDP 8 period, it remains relevant. The impact of the non-mineral private sector on overall GDP growth continues to be limited due to the dominance of the mineral and Government sectors. Also, the mining expansion will not do much directly to create additional long-term employment opportunities.

impact on the development of other sectors, where sales to Government are often a major source of business revenue. Most obvious, perhaps, is the construction sector, given the Government's role as the dominant investor in the economy, but also affected are the suppliers of the wide range of goods and services consumed by Government. As resources are reallocated these negative effects should be reversed. But this progress towards a new general equilibrium is longer term in nature and less clear in direction. As such, it is likely to be discounted heavily by those immediately affected.

The Government is also among the most labour intensive of producers (Bank of Botswana, 1996, and Leith, in this volume).[9] As a consequence, similar problems arise when trying to produce an optimistic scenario regarding the generation of employment opportunities which simultaneously tries to rein in the growth of Government employment.

Indeed, the difficulty here may prove more intractable. For an abstract measure such as GDP to be credible, or even improved, alternatives may be found. For instance, growth projections could be published with a headline rate based on the non-mineral private sector. But jobs represent a crucial determinant of access to income opportunities. As such, measures of employment that exclude certain categories may well be viewed with suspicion.[10]

In this context, a ready availability of financial resources that can support the further growth in the Government sector in the short to medium term could prove to be a danger rather than a blessing. The general strategic need for growth that does not rely on further expansion of the Government may be generally accepted. But, in particular instances, the immediate effects of taking steps that actually move in this direction may be unpalatable in terms of the short-term impact on employment and measured output.

The underlying problem is a divergence of discount rates. The political discount rate, dominated by the short-term horizons of the electoral cycle, is almost inevitably higher than that suggested by the imperatives of economic efficiency. As a result, cost-benefit analyses using the former will give a greater weight to the costs of any transition period, and will favour policies that minimise these costs regardless of whether this also reduces the longer-term benefits.

3. GOVERNMENT FINANCES: THE CURRENT SITUATION

As already stated, the Botswana Government budget has been in continual surplus since 1983/84. This is shown in Figure 3, both in constant 1995 prices and as a proportion of GDP, a figure which has averaged 10.6%.[11]

---

9 Note, however, that compared to many other countries the Government in Botswana is fairly capital intensive. This results from the high levels of public investment which, through depreciation, show up as consumption of capital in sectoral output. In 1992/93 this accounted for about 35% of general government GDP (Central Statistics Office, 1996b).

10 For example, the many redefinitions of unemployment that have taken place in recent years in the UK have put into doubt the credibility of the official statistics. This is especially since the changes tended to reduce the reported levels of unemployment.

11 There is no GDP proportion for 1995/96 since GDP estimates have yet to be produced for that year.

The combined total of these surpluses in nominal terms is P6.9 billion, which has been largely reflected in a build up in Government cash balances. At the end of 1995/96 these cash balances totalled P7.7 billion, or 149% of total Government expenditure in that year. Overall, it may seem safe to conclude that Government's financial position is one of robust good health. This assessment is, however, subject to important qualifications.

FIGURE 3. BUDGET BALANCE, 1982/83 TO 1995/96

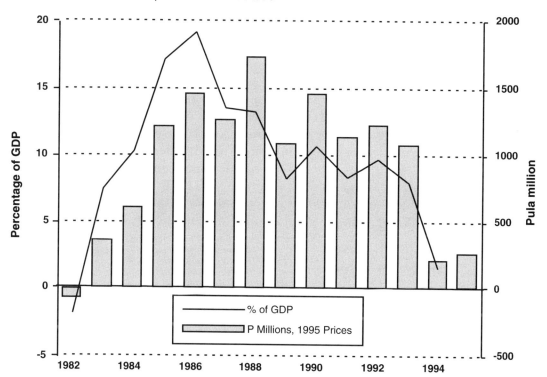

Surpluses in decline

While the aggregate figures represent a substantial accumulation of financial resources, it is clear from Figure 3 that the annual surpluses have declined for several years. By both measures, the surplus peaked in the first half of the period. This was somewhat earlier for the surplus as a share of GDP, a measure which has also shown a sharper and more consistent decline. This is a reflection of the generally positive growth trend of the economy. For both measures the fall was particularly sharp after 1993/94.

It may be pointed out of course that while this decline is clear, it is far less severe than has frequently been forecast by the Government. Official forecasts have been projecting an imminent emergence of budget deficits since the mid-1980s (see Section 4 below).

A virtuous circle of returns

The build up in reserves has generated a virtuous circle of returns. The Government's Pula cash balances are mainly held at the Bank of Botswana and do not earn any interest. However, substantial returns are made as the Government receives significant revenues from the Bank.[12] Since 1991/92, with the exception of 1992/93, these revenues to Government have been greater than the overall budget surplus. In the period since 1983/84, the total revenues to Government under this item amount to 89% of the cumulative budget surplus. Looked at this way, the underlying budget, (i.e., before taking into account interest related payments and receipts) in Botswana, has been in deficit for most of the current decade, and in only modest surplus for the period as a whole.

These revenues channelled through the Central Bank[13] have been based on the returns from investing the accumulated foreign exchange reserves. The reserves are, in turn, the counterpart of balance of payments surpluses and, as such, are linked only indirectly to the Government budget. However, it is clear that the country's position as a net saver – the implication of a balance of payments surplus – has been due largely, if not totally, to savings by Government. Overall, the private sector has been a net borrower; most importantly, perhaps, the net savings of households have been negative (Bank of Botswana, 1994). So, unless there were a matching increase in private sector savings, any move by Government toward dissaving would result in a fall in the foreign exchange reserves and hence negative feedback on Government revenues. Any expectation that this will happen automatically, as the private sector compensates for Government's reduced savings rates, is likely to be optimistic.[14] There is serious concern that the propensity to save in the private sector remains chronically low in Botswana (see papers by Reinke and Motsomi in this volume).

Revenues from asset sales

A further concern is raised when looking beyond the standard measure of aggregate surplus or deficit on an annual basis by decomposing the Government financial surpluses and accumulated reserves. This can be done in a variety of ways, but particularly instructive for Botswana is to concentrate on the use of mineral revenues. These represent the sale of assets, a transformation of stocks which cannot simply be regarded as part of Government income.[15] The crucial question is whether the assets have been transformed into productive *sources* of income for the country as a whole, including future generations, or treated *as* income and consumed by Government and the current generation.

---

[12] This revenue is currently provided on the basis of a formula set out in the Bank of Botswana (Amendment) Act, 1987. For more details see paper by Salkin in this volume.

[13] Commonly referred to as Bank of Botswana 'profits'. This is somewhat erroneous given the interest-free status of deposits from Government. Also a significant proportion of the payments arise from the Revaluation Reserve, which is an accumulation of past exchange rate gains and losses, rather than just from the annual net income.

[14] Through so-called 'Ricardian equivalence' mechanisms whereby the private sector adjusts savings patterns to compensate for the effect that Government's net borrowing position has on future consumption levels.

[15] In economics, income is commonly defined as the level of consumption that is possible without reducing the value of assets. Regarding the proceeds of asset sales as income runs contrary to this. In Botswana, this mainly applies at present to minerals. Elsewhere it takes other forms, a particularly topical one being the appropriate use of revenues from the sale – privatization – of Government owned enterprises, where there is a frequent concern that the proceeds from such sales are being used to finance consumption expenditure or tax cuts.

The Government of Botswana has accepted the importance of this concern. In 1994 it adopted publicly the principle that all mineral revenues should be reserved for productive investment (Government of Botswana, 1994a). Two aggregate measures have been developed which can be used to monitor this commitment: the Sustainable Budget Index (SBI) and the Accumulated Investment Surplus (AIS). The detailed derivation of these measures is presented in the appendix.[16]

The SBI is the ratio of non-investment spending to recurrent revenues.[17] The logic is that should this exceed unity then the Government, during that budget period, is either borrowing or using proceeds from asset sales to finance consumption, neither of which is generally seen as being desirable. The Government itself has used a version of this measure since the Mid-Term Review (MTR) of NDP 7, (Government of Botswana, 1994b).[18]

The SBI is to be interpreted as an indicative ceiling rather than as a target. Recurrent spending levels are determined by requirements, derived largely from previous development spending, which the Government in Botswana has gone to considerable lengths to gauge accurately (Salkin, 1995). It is not necessarily the case that this will match the recurrent revenues that are raised in the same budget period. The purpose of the SBI in this context is to back-stop this process by acting as an alarm. Treating it as a target would be to apply a much sterner criterion; that of requiring a balance on the recurrent budget. Such a rule has not been actively considered.

The SBI deals with flows within a budget period. The AIS extends the logic to the stock of financial reserves, arguing that asset revenues that remain un-spent on productive investments – the Investment Surplus – cannot be used subsequently to finance consumption spending.

This approach to decomposing the Government's finances has attracted the criticism that it is too inflexible. In this view, it ignores the intangible returns on public spending that produce social cohesion which, as a public good, raises the general return on all investments. As such, it is sub-optimal to apply rules that restrict the scope of such spending.

Possibly so, but the frailty of this ideal should also be obvious. On this basis, almost any spending could be justified as productive simply through the process of democratic approval. The whole point of adopting rules, such as the SBI, is not that they lead to the optimal outcome in all circumstances but that discretion is restricted in areas where the down-side risk is judged to be especially large. In the circumstances in Botswana, where the process of diversifying away from minerals still has a long and uncertain way to go, it seems prudent to place a heavy emphasis on preserving the value of current assets for posterity.

A more relevant criticism perhaps is related to issues of equity. The purpose of the SBI/AIS approach is to preserve the value of assets to avoid the impoverishment of future generations. But, as Professor Solow has recently written, 'Those who are so urgent about not inflicting poverty on the future have to explain why they do not

---

[16] This is based on Wright (1995).

[17] Note that for this measure the definition of recurrent revenue does not match that used in the IMF Government Finance Statistics (GFS) manual and which is also used in calculating the 'recurrent budget surplus' as published in the Botswana Financial Statements. This includes the revenues from mineral sales that are paid in the form of company income tax.

[18] Although it has not adopted the SBI label. This originates in Salkin (1994).

attach even higher priority to reducing poverty today' (UNDP, 1996, p16). However, again the particular circumstances must be considered. In the case of Botswana this may be answered relatively easily in that the assumption that future generations will be at least as well off as at present is one that is extremely risky in the absence of rules that preserve the value of the current wealth. This said, it is recognised fully that the SBI/AIS approach is not designed to deal comprehensively with issues of intergenerational distribution.[19]

Practical use of these measures requires a definition of what constitutes investment spending. In the standard accounting conventions for government finances, the distinction between current and capital spending tends to ignore both the productive effects of spending on non-physical assets, and the non-productive nature of some capital spending. It is '...not an indication of the resources devoted to growth....' (IMF, 1986, p98).

In Botswana, the Government has chosen to also include a significant proportion – thirty percent – of the recurrent budget as investment spending. This is on the basis that recurrent spending in areas, such as health and education, represent investment in human capital (Government of Botswana, 1994b, Table 3.5). This may be a valid argument, at least qualitatively. However, to include all spending in these categories may be taking it to an extreme. In particular, it is questionable whether pursuing policies that maximise educational opportunities and health care coverage is also optimal from the point of view of developing human capital.[20]

Also, this approach ignores the question whether all capital expenditures can properly be counted as productive investments. There are a variety to reasons to expect that this is not so. At the most basic level, some projects do not succeed, and, especially given the admission by Government that monitoring and evaluation of projects remains very weak (*ibid.*, p8), it cannot be presumed that this is not the case in Botswana. Some capital expenditures may be for 'monuments' rather than investments, and whole areas such as military spending are highly problematic.[21] Finally, some items may be classified as capital expenditure for other reasons, for example to attract more support from aid donors who may be restricted from assisting with recurrent spending. This is the case with drought relief assistance in Botswana.

These issues are important, since the definition of investment spending influences critically how the current financial position in Botswana is characterised. Wright (1995) models the SBI and AIS using a variety of possible assumptions concerning the investment components of recurrent and capital spending. These suggest that under the assumptions used by Government non-recurrent revenues have been invested productively and the cash balances represent un-spent recurrent revenues. However, this assessment quickly changes if the definition of investment is made more restrictive. This is especially if the productive investment component of recurrent spending is reduced.

Table 2, which updates these calculations, shows this clearly. The SBI and AIS for

---

19 Wright (1995) deals more extensively with this subject in the context of Botswana.

20 This is not to assert that such policies should not be pursued, but to make the point that the non-productive or purely social component in such spending must be allowed for.

21 The guidelines from the IMF do not include any military spending as part of capital expenditure (IMF, 1986, p183), on the grounds that it plays no direct role in a productive process. In the Botswana budget, however, such expenditures are treated as investments.

TABLE 2. SBI AND AIS, 1995/96

	SBI[a]	AIS[b]
		(PULA MILLION)
BASE	0.85	422
BUDGET	1.21	11 504
NON-PRO	0.97	6 122

Notes:

[a] The SBI is calculated as a three-year moving average centred on 1994/95.

[b] The AIS is measured in 1995/96 prices.

Source: Author's calculations using Government data.

the end of 1995/96, are shown under three sets of assumptions:

BASE – as in the Government's calculations, 30% of recurrent spending is included as investment;

BUDGET – investment includes only the capital expenditure as recorded in the budget documents;[22]

NON-PRO – while 30% of recurrent expenditure is again assumed to be investment, 20% of capital spending is non-productive.

The position with the SBI ranges from a healthy margin of safety under the BASE assumptions to a significant breach of the ceiling in BUDGET. Figure 4 plots the path over time of the SBI in this scenario, showing that the current high value is part of a sharp upward trend in the last two years. This is in line with the more general decline in the budget balance. But, whereas the overall budget is in surplus, using these assumptions a significant danger point has already been passed according to the SBI measure. Less damaging is allowing a large degree of non-productive capital expenditure in NON-PRO, reflecting the relative size of the recurrent and capital budgets.

Even more dramatic is the difference in the AIS in the three cases. For BASE, over the years almost all asset revenues have been spent productively. Hence, the AIS is very close to zero and, in consequence, very little of the Government cash balances are reserved for investment spending. In NON-PRO, the AIS of P6.1 billion is nearly 80% of the total Government cash balances at the end of 1996; and, for BUDGET, the AIS is much larger than the cash balances. Again, the removal of the 30% of recurrent spending in BUDGET has a greater impact than the exclusion of 20% of capital spending in NON-PRO, because the recurrent budget is much larger.

These results may be seen as indicative at best. In practice, the productive investment component of the budget is only crudely described by the summary coefficients; it will depend on the detailed breakdown of spending during the period in question.[23] The extent of *bad* (non-productive) spending will vary from year to year. For example, it might be argued that recently the productive component of recurrent spending has increased in line with the greater emphasis in the budget on health and education. Allowing for this has the effect of dampening the recent growth of the SBI and AIS (Bank of Botswana, 1996, Chart II.2).

Also, the degree to which expenditure is employed productively may well be nega-

---

[22] Which here is assumed to include Financial Assistance Policy (FAP) grants, on the basis that these are intended to support the development of sustainable, productive activities. This is slightly at odds with Government's presentation of its finances which tends to treat such grants as a recurrent item.

[23] These coefficients could be broken down further to allow for the distinction between capital spending that is in fact consumed and genuine investment that is *ex post* unproductive, by sector and over time.

tively correlated with the overall level of spending, particularly that on the development programme. As implementation capacity is stretched, the likelihood of 'bad' projects being approved will increase. Also, a greater demand for investment may lead to shortages and price increases in inputs.[24] The result is reduced and delayed returns from all projects, and, possibly, previously good projects becoming unproductive. It seems plausible that this problem has affected the productivity of the Government's investment programme, particularly in the late 1980s and early 1990s when the level of capital spending rose rapidly (see Harvey, 1992, and N. Gaolathe in this volume).

How can the AIS be larger than actual cash balances? Four mechanisms are potentially important.

First, the draw-down can happen at source, as funds from the investment surplus are used to support consumption expenditure. This would be reflected in an SBI greater than unity. However, as Figure 4 shows, even on the BUDGET assumptions this has not happened to any great degree. The only period for which the SBI has been consistently greater than unity was in the first five years following Independence when the recurrent budget was supported by grant-in-aid payments. The SBI as calculated here includes all grant payments as non-recurrent. This is generally correct, but the immediate post-Independence period represents a special case, in that these grants were provided precisely in order to support a recurrent budget that could not be sustained domestically. Also, the amounts involved are small relative to the total

FIGURE 4. SBI SINCE 1966, BUDGET ASSUMPTIONS

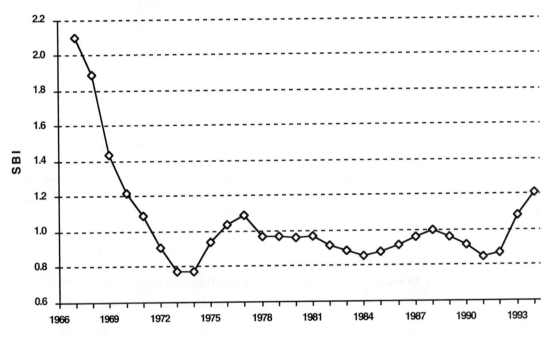

---

24 These shortages can affect both capital and recurrent expenditures. Consider, for example, a programme of school building. The costs of construction can rise; then, later, any shortage of trained teachers will mean either that schools operate below capacity or that more has to be spent on recruitment and training. All these effects will lead to a lowering of the return on the investment.

sums now involved.[25] Since then, it is only very recently that any significant erosion of the AIS has taken place as a result of an excessive SBI. In the two most recent financial years this has totalled P1663 million under the BUDGET assumptions. But even then, this is less than the AIS for the same period of P2152 million, so the cash balances have continued to be supplemented by unspent investment funds.

Second, cash balances could be used to finance budget deficits. Again, clearly this has not happened to any significant extent. In the period prior to 1983/84 where budget deficits were a common feature, cash balances continued to be built up in most years as the deficits were frequently matched by external borrowing, often on very concessional terms, to finance development projects.

Third, the AIS could be held in non-cash form.[26] But, in Botswana, the predominant form of financial assets held by Government outside of cash balances is the lending through the Public Debt Service Fund (PDSF). At the end of 1995/96, the outstanding balance of such lending was approximately P2.1 billion. This lending, and subsequent repayment, is recorded in the budget as capital expenditure, and so has already been taken into account when calculating the size of the AIS.

Lastly, all the revenues to Government from the Bank of Botswana are counted as recurrent. As such, under the SBI framework they are available for non-investment purposes. However, this revenue is based on the nominal net return on the Bank's investments. But under the standard definition of income it is only the *real* return on assets which can be consumed. The portion that is due to inflation should not be consumed, since it is needed to preserve the value of the asset. Therefore, this current institutional arrangement provides for a route which allows consumption of funds which should be used to maintain the value of the assets. Acceptance of the logic of the AIS suggests the need for some reform of this mechanism.

Therefore, Government would do well to establish a convention that distinguishes between the real and inflation-related components of revenues from the Central Bank. But saying this is not to suggest a particular form that such reform should take. The breakdown of Bank of Botswana revenues is undoubtedly more complicated than is captured in the framework used here. In particular, there is a significant portion which is not associated with the return on the Government cash balances (see paper by Salkin in this volume). The intention here is to point to a possibility of serious erosion of the AIS through the current method of calculating revenues to be paid by the Bank to Government. The new Bank of Botswana legislation, which at the time of writing was being considered by Parliament, contains provision for establishing a long-term investment fund into which some of the revenues will be paid. This may, to some extent at least, address this problem.

Unplanned surpluses

The fourth major qualification is that the recent 'success' in prolonging the period of budget surpluses is not just attributable to Government's careful management but also to the combination of circumstances. Looking at the annual budgets since the

---

[25] Although they were, as is evident from the very high values of the SBI for those years shown in Figure 4, large relative to the size of the the budget at the time.

[26] Not, however, in the repayment of borrowing made to finance earlier investment. This borrowing will already have shown up as a negative IS.

start of NDP 7 in 1991/92, the original budget estimates projected an aggregate deficit of P824 million.[27] A surplus was only forecast for one year, P109.3 million in 1992/93. This compares to the actual outcome of an aggregate surplus of P2921 million, with surpluses recorded in all years.

FIGURE 5. VARIATION BETWEEN ANNUAL BUDGET FORECAST AND FINAL RESULT, 1991/92 TO 1995/96

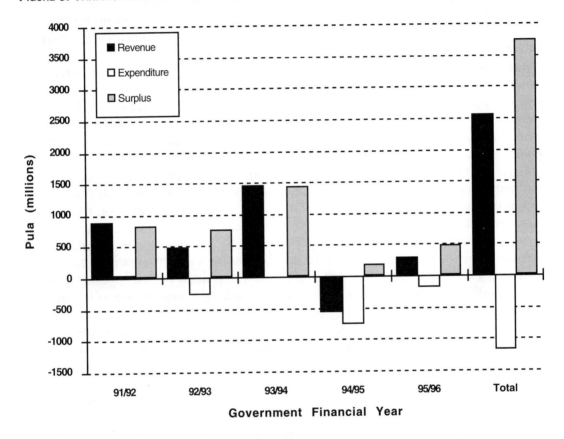

There is a total variance between the initial budget forecasts and actual results of P3745 million. The breakdown by year and between revenue and expenditure is shown in Figure 5. Of this total, P2564 million, or 68%, came from higher than forecast revenues. This is equivalent to 11.9% of total budgeted revenues during the period. The principal factor that caused this was higher than anticipated minerals receipts. Bank of Botswana revenues were also a major source of variability – indeed, over the years this item has seen the greatest overall divergence between budget forecast and final result[28] – but the net contribution from this source to the additional revenue

---

27 The original estimates referred to here are those presented annually, before the start of the financial year, at the time of the Budget Speech. These should not be confused with the even earlier projections contained in NDP 7 itself, which contained projections for much higher deficits.

28 This is not surprising. Many of the Bank's investments, while chosen for their long-term yields, show great variability in the short term, something which is very difficult to allow for in preparing annual budget forecasts.

during this five year period was relatively small, because 1994/95 saw a large short-fall from the budget forecast.

P1180 million, or 32%, of the variation between budget and actuals was due to under-expenditure. This was 5.3% of total budgeted expenditures. While smaller in both absolute and proportionate terms than the revenue effects, this under-expenditure is significant. In aggregate it was large enough by itself to cancel out the forecast deficits even if revenue collection had been in line with the initial projections. Also, for management of public finances, it covers areas where Government has more direct control than with revenues. This is especially the case if, as in Botswana, the extent of endogenous expenditures in the budget is limited.[29]

Underspending can easily be pinned down to a consistent shortfall in capital expenditures, defined here to include net-lending and FAP grants. Over the five year period, capital spending below the annual budgets totalled P1337 million, whereas recurrent expenditure was marginally *over*spent.[30] This is equivalent to 14.5% of the total capital budget, a proportion that rises further if the value of subsequent supplementary estimates is also included when calculating total underspending.

This said, the aggregate figures may also overstate the extent of the problem. The totals are dominated by 1994/95 where capital spending was 33% below the original budget, which accounted for 49% of the total underspending. This was to the extent that, for only the second time in the history of independent Botswana, total nominal Government spending fell from one year to the next; and a surplus rather than a deficit resulted even though revenues were also significantly below forecast. In other years the shortfall in capital spending has been much smaller, as low as 2.2% in 1993/94.[31] Nonetheless, it does seem that currently there is a systematic tendency to overestimate the development expenditure budget.

Underspending the development budget has been attributed by Government to problems of 'implementation capacity'. This is a generic term used to describe a variety of constraints within Government, including operational inefficiencies and manpower shortages, combined with '...the overly ambitious development programme, due largely to promises which are more than Government can deliver...' (Government of Botswana, 1994b, p52). It has become recognised as such a problem that the 1996 Budget Speech accepted explicitly that the spending levels estimated in the 1996/97 budget are once again unlikely to be achieved (Government of Botswana, 1996, p86).

The extent to which surpluses have been built up because of Government inefficiencies cannot be desirable. If the spending is indeed needed, then the underspending

---

[29] Indeed, in Botswana the major endogenous expenditure, that related to drought relief, is not included in the initial Budget estimates. Given that, for much of the period covered, funds were subsequently appropriated for drought relief as supplementaries to the budget, the levels of spending of the originally budgeted funds is even lower than the figures quoted may imply.

[30] This means that recurrent budget spending was higher than the original estimates. This happened in three of the five years reviewed here, although there was also some underspending in the last two years caused, it seems, by high vacancy rates in the public service.

[31] Given that the development programme is made up of a whole range of individual projects, any summary statistics will lose a lot of information. This points to the difficulty in improving the procedures for forecasting items such as the development programme through seasonal adjustment of part year figures, a process that requires the assumption that yearly spending follow 'typical' and stable paths.

is sub-optimal. This is especially so since the spending which does take place will be due to ease of implementation rather than in line with the hierarchy of expected benefits. Conversely, for those who wish to see levels of Government spending held back, relying on these constraints to continue to hold is inefficient and non-robust as a control mechanism.

Also, the continued surpluses, even when deficits are forecast, may have negative consequences in terms of public perception. Almost certainly this will engender a degree of complacency towards calls for the belt of public sector finance to be tightened. Some critics have gone further, even as far as to suggest a conspiracy theory that deficits are forecast as a deliberate ploy to deprive Batswana of their rightful access to Government's financial resources.[32] Such a charge is a variant on the common suspicion that governments use creative accounting and forecasting techniques to misrepresent their budgetary positions, although this applies more usually to situations where a government wishes to spend more.

4. EMERGING PROBLEMS

Stagnation of revenues and increased demands for public spending

Almost since the beginning of the period of surpluses the Government has worried that it would soon come to an end, believing it likely that revenues would quickly reach a plateau while demands for spending, including the recurrent implications of past development expenditures, would continue to increase. The base case macroeconomic forecast for NDP 6 placed this 'crossover problem', after which budget deficits would become the norm, in 1989/90 (Government of Botswana, 1985, Figure 2.16), and argued that more favourable scenarios would only postpone the problem, not eliminate it (ibid., para. 2.68).

The main factor driving these forecasts was an unwillingness to project continued rapid growth in the diamond industry and in the resulting revenues to Government. While with hindsight this has proved to be unduly pessimistic, at the same time the prudential value of such caution should be recognised. Many of the uncertainties that were perceived in those earlier years remain relevant today; and, as Figure 1 above showed, the trend for a decline in the budget balance has still been evident.

In these circumstances, lacking perfect foresight, it is understandable that Government should continue to be cautious. The Keynote Policy Paper for NDP 8, produced in August 1995, included real growth rates for the diamond sector of less than one percent per annum for the plan period (Government of Botswana, 1995). Subsequent developments, indicating a general improvement in the international market conditions culminating in an announced significant expansion of the Orapa mine during NDP 8, will have raised this significantly. But it is likely that Government will stick to

---

[32] For example, in *The Botswana Guardian* of 23 February 1996 (p6), a columnist argued that '...a projected deficit enables the government of the day to plead bankruptcy whenever the voting public raises questions about why the government is not delivering...'.

the basic thrust of its policy of caution[33], and continue to warn that growth from this source will not continue forever.

But while the Government must act on the logic of its assumptions that future revenue growth is not assured, the ability to restrain Government spending is likely to be placed under severe pressures. Sources of such pressures have already been mentioned. One is the difficulty in weaning the economy off a heavy reliance on expansion of Government as a source of economic growth, while at the same time continuing to target ambitious objectives for output and employment growth.

More fundamentally, perhaps, even if such targets were of little concern, it is likely that pressures for more public spending would continue to exist, for two distinct reasons. First, there is considerable momentum in the development programme that cannot simply be switched off. This is not only due to actual projects that are in the pipeline, but also the considerable expectations that exist regarding the continued extension of Government services on a equitable basis through the country. Second, new demands on Government spending will emerge as real incomes grow. There will be expectations that the quality of services, such as education, health and police protection, will rise. Also, it was argued earlier that concern for issues of income distribution and associated demands for transfers will also increase.

An erosion of central control?

As already noted, the Government has recognised that underspending has been, in part, a consequence of development plans that promise more than its administrative machinery can currently deliver. This acknowledgement raises two important points.

First is that the expenditure figures in the budget that is presented to the National Assembly at the time of the annual Budget Speech are requests for the *authority* to spend funds during the budget period. This is not the same as a forecast of the level of spending that will actually take place. It seems likely that in an ideal situation the two figures should coincide. What is the point of authorising spending levels which are significantly more or less than are likely to be achieved? However, in practice such a situation can easily occur, as it clearly has in recent years in Botswana.

Looking at potential causes, it seems plausible that this is especially likely to develop if the budget process is decentralised, building up spending requests as a series of uncoordinated wish-lists from ministries and departments rather than a rational assessment of what is both feasible and desirable at the macro level.

A related problem is that there are typically strong tendencies in a budget process that funds specific spending programmes from a common pool of revenues for the total levels of Government spending to be higher than is desirable in terms of maximising the net social benefits from that spending (von Hagen and Harden, 1996). In some countries this shows up in excessive deficits. In Botswana, such a tendency may be reflected in 'hidden deficits', or deficits which do not materialise because the funds, while approved, are not spent because of other constraints rather than the rigorous application of fiscal prudence.

---

[33] And rightly so. The future trends in the international diamond market remain far from settled. This was shown clearly in 1996 by the withdrawal of the Argyle mine in Australia from the Central Selling Organisation and, of greater importance to Botswana, the continuing failure to reach agreement on participation in the cartel by Russian diamond producers.

Again, this weakness is likely to make itself felt most strongly in situations where the budget process is decentralised, so that those who shape spending programmes have little direct concern for the associated costs. Some empirical studies have concluded that there exists a strong correlation between indicators of fiscal laxity and the degree of centralization of the budget process. Increasing the power of the treasury or ministry of finance in intra-government negotiations and reducing that of parliaments to amend budget proposals are examples of how such centralization might be increased (*ibid.*). Alesina and Perotti (1996, piii) make similar points, arguing also for the use of independent agencies, truly separate from Government 'to check the accuracy and transparency of public budgets'.

The implication that increased centralization in decision-making is desirable is clearly vulnerable to the charge of being anti-democratic. Nevertheless, in terms of the economic imperative of preventing excesses in expenditure it may well be a powerful tool for increasing the role in spending decisions of those who have a fuller appreciation of the associated costs at the macro level.[34]

In the light of these considerations, it is certainly reasonable to enquire whether the budget process in Botswana has become more decentralised in recent years. This will not necessarily be a result of any explicit institutional reform. Indeed, this has clearly not occurred in Botswana. But such decentralization could also be a consequence of factors which serve to alter the balance of practical influence exerted by the various branches of Government. More widely, this can include other factors, such as the consequences of changes in the political balance: something which clearly *has* happened in Botswana as the once unchallenged hegemony of the Botswana Democratic Party has been eroded in recent years.[35]

The central question is whether there has been any loosening of the authority exercised by the Ministry of Finance and Development Planning (MFDP) in coordinating the budget process. While this is too broad a topic to be pursued fully here, it certainly seems fair to observe that certain factors will not have helped MFDP maintain its strategic dominance. Again the existence of substantial financial reserves is a mixed blessing. Identifying a hard budget constraint is a key tool for a finance ministry. But doing so convincingly in Botswana has become increasingly difficult.

That MFDP did lose control is certainly the conclusion drawn in Harvey (1992). Harvey looks at the explosion in Government spending in NDP 6 when in the last years of the 1980s actual development spending consistently exceeded the original estimates by significant amounts (*ibid.*, Table 9). From this perspective, while subsequently other constraints on the ability to spend intervened, resulting in the hidden deficits of the 1990s, this is a continuation of an already existing erosion of control.

In countering such suggestions the Government can rightly point to an array of

---

[34] Saying this is not to suggest that a centralised system is all that is needed for a well-coordinated budget. Clearly, a central finance ministry is not likely to have such a good appreciation for local and sectoral constraints that may have a separate impact on the capacity to spend budgetary allocations efficiently. These are better evaluated at the local and sectoral levels. However, it is unlikely that a line ministry would use knowledge of such constraints to argue for lower spending authorisations.

[35] This is seen most obviously in the electoral progress made by the opposition Botswana National Front, but also in the persistent reports of serious internal divisions within the ruling party.

tools that have helped promote a disciplined approach to budgetary management. These are integral to the whole process of putting together the National Development Plans and their subsequent breakdown into component annual budgets. These structures are still in place, as evidenced by the care being taken, at the time of writing, over the preparation of NDP 8. It can further point to the foresight with which the PDSF and the Revenue Stabilization Fund (RSF) were created, precisely in order to provide a structured framework to handle Government borrowing and short-term budget deficits.

The existence of these planning tools points to a demonstrable and substantive concern with sound financial management. But the effectiveness of budget management tools must be seen in the context of the budgetary process viewed at a strategic level. It is here that the issue of centralization becomes important. There is no necessary contradiction in both suggesting that control has been eroded in terms of the levels of spending that are authorised and accepting that systems of control – only funds authorised by Parliament can be spent, for example – remain in place. Nonetheless, the current situation suggests several potential problems that may undermine the effectiveness of their practical use.

A further symptom of an erosion of centralised control is the Government's treatment of the SBI. Already it seems that when put under pressure the status of this measure has quickly become ambiguous. In its original official formulation it was a *ceiling* which must not be breached (Government of Botswana, 1994b, p24). Now, as all future projections point clearly to such a breach in the near future, its status has been changed to that of a *measure* that needs to be monitored closely.

The PDSF/RSF structures needs to be examined in the light of current circumstances. Here it is far from clear that they provide a relevant framework to guide public finances if the period of surpluses ends. Over the years the PDSF has become principally a vehicle for the lending of public funds, mainly to parastatal organizations. This may be contrasted with the original purpose which was to '...receive and safeguard moneys ... which are to be utilized to meet ... future payments of debt charges to be made by the Government' (Government of Botswana, 1973a, p4). While Government has maintained the integrity of the fund in the face of loans that could not be repaid[36], it does not seem that the amounts assigned to the Fund have been driven by a strategy for future debt management but rather by the demands of the borrowers.

As for the RSF, this fund was established to cover temporary shortfalls of revenue. This was in order to '...ensure the maintenance and orderly expansion of public services...' (Government of Botswana, 1973b, p4). While the development of this fund has been driven by lending requirements far less than the PDSF, it is not clear that it has been based on its role as a buffer stock either.

In this context, what should also be emphasised is the large amount of Government cash balances that are not assigned to these funds. At the end of 1995/96 about P3.2 billion, or just over forty percent of the total could be assigned to funds the use of which is prescribed. Therefore, a series of substantial budget deficits could be supported simply through the discretionary drawing down of cash balances, which

---

[36] Typically through injections of 'equity' into parastatals which are then used to reduce the outstanding borrowing from the PDSF.

would avoid being subjected to the discipline envisaged by the establishment of such funds.[37]

An alternative to re-centralization of the budget process is to consider matching revenue sources with particular uses. A good example is that of a Road Fund, paid for by road users to cover the costs of supporting the national road network. This is an idea which is currently being examined, with some enthusiasm, in the context of Botswana.[38]

Such hypothecation of revenue has typically been viewed with suspicion by finance ministries. This is largely, it seems, because it represents a different form of threat to their control (Brittan, 1996). However, in principle at least, it would seem to provide an alternative route to meeting the problems caused by the common pool of revenues. As well as working against any tendency towards over-expenditure, such systems might also allow for the fuller funding of popular spending programmes, with contributors being less concerned that the funds are being siphoned off for other purposes. More generally, it might be seen as establishing stronger, more rational, links between the users and providers of services. Such links can serve the goals of both efficiency and equity.

This said, over-enthusiasm for this approach would be a mistake. If the source of revenue is not closely matched to the recipients of benefits, issues of equity and fairness quickly emerge; as will also happen if the users' 'social' requirements are considered to be important. Such specific revenue items add to the list of sensitive prices which governments have to administer with the consequent risk that they will depart from sound principles of cost recovery. Finally, experience elsewhere suggests that the discipline of such earmarked revenues can easily disappear over time as either the funds prove insufficient and are topped-up from elsewhere in the budget, or are 'raided' to support other spending programmes.

A fiscal 'Dutch Disease'?

The final concern that is examined here is the extent to which the dominance of certain revenue sources may have retarded the development of others, currently less important, but which might be expected to be significant sources of future revenue growth. In the 1995/96 budget, mineral revenues made up 47% of the total. Together with the revenues from the Bank of Botswana and the Southern African Customs Union (SACU) the contribution was 82%. In contrast, non-mineral income tax and the sales tax accounted for 6% and 4% of total revenues, respectively.

Such a tendency can be characterised usefully in the same terms as the so-called 'Dutch Disease' problem of exchange rates. This is where the rapid development of one sector, in this case the mineral sector with its substantial revenues to Government,

---

[37] This point can be taken further. The Government has substantial liabilities, most importantly perhaps the obligations for future civil service pensions. Even if these are not taken care of through any explicit funding mechanism, the future cost implications should be factored into any calculation of the sustainability of the budget.

[38] This was a major item for discussion at the National Roads Conference held in November 1996. It is understood that, as a first stage, such a fund would aim at cost recovery measures to meet the costs of maintenance. The further development of additional road infrastructure would continue to be met from the general development budget.

has knock-on effects that serve to retard development elsewhere, possibly on a permanent basis.

In examining this possibility, it must be acknowledged immediately that the Government in Botswana has not ignored the development of alternative revenue sources. Most significantly, perhaps, it has gradually extended the scope of the sales tax since its introduction in 1982. This has been in terms of both the coverage and the introduction of higher rates for sales of alcohol and tobacco. Such decisions have usually been unpopular, including, most recently, the extension of the tax to many basic foodstuffs in the 1995/96 budget and to additional classes of business in 1996/97.[39] At the same time, the overall contribution to revenue has remained small. Since its introduction to the end of 1995/96 a total of only P0.9 billion in total had been collected, and in no year would its non-collection have turned the budget surplus into a deficit. In this context of risking discontent, while hardly being of immediate importance for the health of the budget, Government's resolve to push through these changes is impressive.

Also, with the budget bottom line exerting less pressure on the development of revenue policies, the Government has been able to take a wider view of taxes, not just as sources of revenue, but as they affect the overall development of the economy. Most notably, perhaps, it has embarked on a radical revision of the structure of income taxation, based on the supply-side incentive of low taxes to stimulate additional growth in the economy. Since 1994 the top marginal rate of personal income taxation has been reduced from 40% to 25% as has the standard rate of company tax. For these businesses which successfully apply to Government for the status of 'manufacturing' operations, the rate of company tax is only 15%.

The Government has been able to do this secure in the knowledge that the hoped-for benefits of these policies can be given time to materialise without running the risk of causing immediate budgetary difficulties. This is a luxury not commonly available, and has certainly given Botswana a clear advantage within the Southern African region in having the potential for establishing itself as a low tax jurisdiction.[40]

On the other hand, the existence of a degree of complacency would hardly be surprising. This is especially true as regards income tax collection, where the mineral contribution is not only overwhelmingly important, but, particularly easy to collect in that it centres around one company, Debswana, which is half owned by Government. Over the whole recent period of surpluses, complete non-collection of non-mineral income tax would not have been sufficient to move the budget into deficit, neither directly nor indirectly.[41] In these circumstances a lack of enthusiasm for tackling

---

[39] The extensions were to newspapers and the service industries of hotels, dry cleaners and hairdressers. The last was particularly unpopular, as hairdressing is an important source of small-scale employment. The Government could argue, however, that all these categories of business produce luxury goods, and that the main substantive problem was the practicalities of effective collection rather than a matter of principle.

[40] However, the emphasis on *potential* is of some importance. The implementation of the new low taxes has not been unproblematic. In particular, the manufacturing concession, while announced in early 1995, was not brought into effect until the middle of 1996, and then only with surrounding bureaucracy and a restricted definition of manufacturing that could together reduce its attractiveness. Some commentators have argued that a simple tax system based on a single low rate for both companies and top income tax payers would be a better option (Bank of Botswana, 1995, Chapter II).

other problematic areas to boost collection further would be easily understandable.[42] For example, *The Botswana Gazette* of 31 July 1996, in one of a series of articles on the subject, reported that the Tax Department has a policy of not investigating the cattle industry.[43]

5. CONCLUDING OBSERVATIONS

The Botswana Government has continued to build up financial resources over a long period. While this may normally be thought of as an unambiguous blessing, it has potential drawbacks also. Most significantly, perhaps, it is all too easy to view the budget constraints faced by the Government as being extremely soft. This perception is enhanced as the frequent forecasts of imminent budget deficits have failed to materialise. One consequence is that the centralised control exerted by MFDP over the budget formulation process as a key element of discipline in previous years may have been weakened. Other socio-political factors have contributed to this also.

The clear, stated intention of Government is to hold back further growth in its expenditure. This is in recognition of both the longer term revenue constraints and that the role of Government as a producer should also be limited.

However, while this commitment may be strong at the general level, a variety of circumstances may be conspire to thwart practical movement in this direction in particular instances. On the one hand, the currently soft budget constraint means that Government has yet to be forced into a position where it has to evaluate spending plans critically in terms of their long-term pay-off to society, rather than affordability within the shorter term of the electoral cycle. The latter criterion tends to ignore the interests of future generations of Batswana.

On the other, the incentives to do so are limited. To move away from growth that is dependent on Government may prove difficult, especially when the other sources of growth are yet to be firmly established. Moreover, people's expectations regarding public spending are likely to remain high due to both the momentum of the current development programme and rising aspirations, the latter a reflection of sustained increases in real income levels.

What is the extent of these problems; are they emerging or well-entrenched? The Government of Botswana maintains, on balance, an enviable record of sound financial management including a commitment to anticipate and adjust to difficulties before they become too serious. However, the problems arising from the continuous 'success'

---

41 Over the whole period total non-mineral income tax was P3.1 billion, the equivalent of 44.8% of the total surplus. Even reducing Bank of Botswana revenues by a similar proportion, as a crude indication of the indirect consequences, would not be sufficient to result in an overall deficit.

42 An actual manifestation of this effect may be the low degree of priority which is reportedly given to examining the validity of tax returns made by farmers.

43 This issue is something which has recently received a degree of critical reporting in the local media, largely on the grounds that it is effectively inequitable to ignore the taxation of one group – already well-off in terms of support from other policies – while at the same time extending the taxation system, through the sales tax, elsewhere (see, for example, *The Botswana Gazette* of 31 July 1996).

of accumulating budget surpluses have been developing for several years now, to the extent that there has been a loss of centralised fiscal control. This first occurred in the mid-1980s.

To act decisively against this potential malaise is the next major challenge for the Botswana Government in managing its financial affairs.

APPENDIX: CALCULATING THE SBI AND THE AIS

Algebraically, the SBI is defined as:

$$SBI = \frac{X_n}{R_n}$$

where X and R are, respectively, expenditures and revenues, and the subscript n stands for non-investment (expenditures) or recurring (revenues). There are parallel components, X_i and R_i, for investment expenditures and non-recurring revenues.

For numerical calculations presented in this paper the following formulation was used:

$$SBI = \frac{REC(1-a)+bDEV}{R-(GRA+MIN+OTH)}$$

where:
   REC is the recurrent budget and a its productive component.
   DEV is the development budget and b its non-productive proportion.
   GRA are grants.
   MIN are all mineral related revenues.
   OTH are other asset sales.

While single values of a and b are used here, separate coefficients could be employed for the various components of expenditure broken down by economic sector, functional classification, or by year. For example, the value of 0.3 for a used by the Government of Botswana is an approximation for setting the value at 1.0 for health and education and 0.0 for other sectors. An important disaggregation of b would be to distinguish between non-investment and, *ex post*, unproductive investment, components of development expenditure.

While clearly a useful indicator, the SBI provides only limited information on the productive use or otherwise of funds. Most importantly, perhaps, it is a measure based on the balance of recurrent revenue and non-investment expenditure *flows* within the budget period. It is, therefore, silent on the breakdown of non-recurrent revenues between investment and savings, and the changing composition and level of the *stock* of financial assets that will result from any imbalance in these flows, both overall or within sub-categories.

The logic of the SBI can be extended to cover these areas. The basic case to consider is when, in any time period, there is an imbalance between productive non-financial investments and available funds. Such imbalances are likely since there is no automatic matching of the rate of mineral extraction and sales, which is determined by conditions in the international markets, with domestic investment opportunities. In such circumstances, for that budget period there will be an *Investment Surplus (IS)* which will have a matching counterpart in an increase in the stock of financial assets.

The discipline of the SBI can and should be applied to the use of the accumulated portion of financial assets that is due to investment surpluses. Simply because they are not used immediately to acquire productive physical assets does not mean that these funds then become available for any form of expenditure in the future. Their value, in real terms, must be preserved for future productive investment. This leads directly to the concept of the *Accumulated Investment Surplus (AIS)*.

$$IS = (GRA + MIN + OTH) - [DEV(1-b) + aREC]$$

$$AIS = \sum_{t=k}^{0} z_t IS_t$$

$$NRB = B - AIS$$

where z_t is an index converting prices at time t to the time *(t=0)* when the measurement of the AIS is taking place, and B is the chosen measure of financial assets. The NRB, or *non-reserved balance*, measures the funds that are not reserved for investment purposes, and is simply the difference between B and the AIS.

REFERENCES

Alesina, A. and Perotti, R. 1996. 'Budget Deficits and Budget Institutions', *IMF Working Paper WP/96/52*. IMF, Washington.

Bank of Botswana. 1994. *Annual Report 1993*. Bank of Botswana, Gaborone.

Bank of Botswana. 1995. *Annual Report 1994*. Bank of Botswana, Gaborone.

Bank of Botswana. 1996. *Annual Report 1995*. Bank of Botswana, Gaborone.

Brittan, S. 1996. 'Appeal of Earmarked Taxes', *Financial Times* 15 January 1996. London.

Central Statistics Office. 1996a. 'National Accounts Statistics', *Stats Brief 96/1*, Central Statistics Office, Gaborone.

Central Statistics Office. 1996b. *Social Accounting Matrix – 1992/93*. Central Statistics Office, Gaborone.

Government of Botswana. 1966. *Transitional Plan for Social and Economic Development*. Government of Botswana, Gaborone.

Government of Botswana. 1970. *National Development Plan 1970–1975*. Government of Botswana, Gaborone.

Government of Botswana. 1973a. *Public Debt Service Fund Order*, Cap 54:25. Government of Botswana, Gaborone.

Government of Botswana. 1973b. *Revenue Stabilization Fund Order*, Cap 54:27. Government of Botswana, Gaborone.

Government of Botswana. 1985. *National Development Plan 1985–1991*. Government of Botswana, Gaborone.

Government of Botswana. 1994a. *1994 Budget Speech*. Government of Botswana, Gaborone.

Government of Botswana. 1994b. *Mid-Term Review of NDP 7*. Ministry of Finance and Development Planning, Gaborone.

Government of Botswana. 1995. *Keynote Policy Paper for National Development Plan 8*. Ministry of Finance and Development Planning, Gaborone.

Harvey, C. 1992. 'Botswana: Is the Economic Miracle Over?', *Journal of African Economies*, Vol.3, No.1. Oxford University Press, Oxford.

International Monetary Fund. 1986. *A Manual on Government Finance Statistics*. IMF, Washington.

International Monetary Fund. 1996. *Government Financial Statistics Yearbook 1995*. IMF, Washington.

Parsons, N., Henderson, W. and Tlou, T. 1995. *Seretse Khama 1921–1980*. The Botswana Society, Gaborone, and Macmillan Boleswa, Braamfontein.

Sachs, J. 1996. 'Growth in Africa', *The Economist*, June 29th 1996.

Salkin, J.S. 1994. 'A Brief Review of the Central Government Budget', *Barclays Botswana Economic Review* 2/94.

Salkin, J.S. 1995. 'The Recurrent Budget Implications of Development Budget Expenditures', *The Research Bulletin*, Vol.14, No.1, pp34–63. Bank of Botswana, Gaborone.

Shome, P. (ed.). 1995. *Tax Policy Handbook*. International Monetary Fund, Washington.

UNDP. 1996. *Human Development Report 1996*. Oxford University Press, New York.

von Harden, J. and Harden, I. 1996. 'Budget Processes and Commitment to Fiscal Discipline', *IMF Working Paper* WP/96/78. IMF, Washington.

World Bank. 1996. *World Development Report 1996*. World Bank, Washington.

Wright, M. 1995. 'The Reservation Principle in Sustainable Budgeting: The Case of Botswana', *The Research Bulletin*, Vol.13, No.1, pp1–21. Bank of Botswana, Gaborone.

Chapter 3

Financial Sector Development

Bank of Botswana:
The First 21 Years[1]

H.C.L. Hermans

1. INTRODUCTION

The first part of the paper outlines the situation which prevailed before the Bank was established and provides background information on the events leading up to the decision to introduce a national currency and to create a central bank. The second part of the paper traces the institutional development of the Bank over the past 21 years. The third part examines the Bank's performance in the conduct of monetary policy; its agency roles with regard to the administration of exchange controls and the supervision of the financial sector; and its management of Botswana's foreign exchange reserves.

2. BACKGROUND

The colonial period

Since the introduction into Southern Africa of metallic coins and bank notes from Europe, various foreign currencies had circulated informally in what is now Botswana. Following the proclamation of Bechuanaland as a British Protectorate in 1895, foreign currencies were unilaterally accorded official legal tender status in Botswana. In the absence of any formal monetary agreement, for example, Proclamation No.5 of 1895 bestowed legal tender status on the currency of the Cape Colony, and Proclamation No.73 of 1960 recognised the Rand as legal tender after South Africa withdrew from the British Commonwealth.

The monetization of Botswana's subsistence economy proceeded very slowly, and barter was used as the principal means of effecting payment well into the 20th Century. Even as late as the 1960s, 'good-fors' were widely used as a medium of exchange. These were credit notes, issued by rural trading stores to acknowledge payment for livestock and agricultural products sold to them. They were valid only for purchases

---

[1] This is an abbreviated account of the first 21 years of the Bank of Botswana, the full version of which originally appeared in a Special Edition of the Bank's *The Research Bulletin* to commemorate the 20th Anniversary of the Pula and was prepared to coincide with the 21st Anniversary of the establishment of the Bank and the opening of the Francistown Branch on 14 September 1996. Although I have relied heavily on my personal papers and recollection of events, I wish to acknowledge and record my appreciation of the research undertaken by the Special Assistant to the Governors, Sarah Masale. In addition, the comments of Derek Hudson, a former Deputy Governor and Member of the Board of the Bank, have been invaluable.

of goods from the same stores, giving rural traders both monopoly and monopsony powers.

Although both Barclays Bank and Standard Bank, operated from Mafeking, provided rudimentary banking services for many years in Lobatse on a regular weekly basis, it was not until 1953 that permanent branches of commercial banks were established in the Bechuanaland Protectorate, at Lobatse and Francistown. South African currency entered local circulation mainly through the remittances of mineworkers via the South African Post Office Savings Bank (whose operations in Botswana were administered by the Bechuanaland Post Office until January 1963 when the Botswana Savings Bank was created).

Withdrawal from the Rand Monetary Area (RMA) was not regarded as a viable policy option before Independence. The 1963-68 Development Plan made no mention of the monetary arrangements, nor did the manifestos of the political parties contending the first national elections in 1965. In contrast to the situation prevailing in Namibia and South Africa, and increasingly in other countries, Botswana's Constitution neither entrenched, nor made any reference to a national currency or a central bank. The first official indication that the Botswana Government was dissatisfied with the monetary *status quo*, and wished to negotiate 'a more favourable arrangement', appeared in 1966.[2]

TABLE 1. BOTSWANA'S NATIONAL DEVELOPMENT PLANS (NDP)

PLAN NAME	YEARS COVERED	TYPE OF PLAN
Bechuanaland Protectorate Plan	1963–68	Five Year Development Plan
Transitional Plan for Economic and Social Development	1966–68	Two Year Transitional Plan*
NDP 1	1968–73	Five Year Rolling Plan
NDP 2	1970–75	Five Year Rolling Plan
NDP 3	1973–78	Five Year Rolling Plan
NDP 4	1975–81	Five Year Rolling Plan
NDP 5	1979–85	Six Year Plan and Mid-Term Review
NDP 6	1985–91	Six Year Plan and Mid-Term Review
NDP 7	1991–97	Six Year Plan and Mid-Term Review

Note: * This provided time to prepare the first NDP.

Quadripartite monetary negotiations

It was only after the completion, in 1969, of the renegotiation of the 1910 Southern African Customs Union Agreement that the monetary relationships within the common customs area came under more active scrutiny. As in the case of the Customs Union negotiations, the Botswana Government took the lead in seeking to have the

---

2   The Transitional Plan for Social and Economic Development, paragraph 72.

issue discussed. Based on preparatory research undertaken by the Botswana Ministry of Finance and Development Planning in 1971 and 1972, the Governments of Botswana, Lesotho and Swaziland (BLS) sought to negotiate a monetary agreement with the Government of the Republic of South Africa.

The expectations of the three former Protectorates were initially quite modest. They sought merely to clarify and codify the mutual rights and obligations of the countries in which Rand currency was legal tender, there having been no previous agreement in this regard. The quadripartite negotiations started slowly in 1973, preceded by a series of tripartite meetings through which the BLS Governments developed a common negotiating position.

The main issues raised by the three smaller countries were fourfold: the lack of consultation on matters of monetary policy; the need for coordination in the application of South African exchange controls; the right of access to the foreign exchange reserves of the RMA; and the sharing of the profits made by the South African Reserve Bank on the fiduciary issue and from the investment of the foreign exchange reserves. Also raised was the issue of access to South Africa's money and capital markets. The South African representatives saw little reason to change the informal *status quo* and discouraged the BLS Governments from pressing for a formal agreement. The concept of 'profit-sharing' was particularly strongly opposed.

The position of the BLS Governments in this latter regard was not unreasonable. The existing legislation in force in South Africa provided that the profits of the Reserve Bank could be distributed to any other state using South African currency as its legal tender, in proportion to the currency in circulation in each state. The Southern Rhodesian Government had actually received seigniorage for its use of South African coins between 1926 and 1931.[3] Citing this precedent, the BLS Governments sought to include provision in the proposed monetary agreement for the sharing of the Reserve Bank's annual profits. This proved difficult for the South African negotiators to accept. In the first place, the South African Reserve Bank, established in 1921 (making it the third oldest central bank in the world), is privately owned, with its shares quoted on the Johannesburg Stock Exchange. It is fiercely jealous of its independence from the South African Government and was a reluctant participant in the negotiations for this reason. In the second place, for historical reasons, gold comprised a significant part of South Africa's foreign exchange reserves, earning no income. The private shareholders were thus unlikely to agree to any dilution of their share of the profits made by the Reserve Bank, however insignificant. The position of the BLS Governments was that these were domestic matters which did not affect the general principle of profit-sharing.

The negotiations stalled on this issue in 1974, despite the fact that the Reserve Bank had already started to consult the BLS Ministries of Finance informally on some monetary policy matters without waiting for the finalization of a quadripartite monetary agreement. The unilateral decision of the Government of Swaziland, in the middle of the negotiations, to introduce a national currency, the Lilangeni (plural Emalangeni), and to establish a monetary authority, further complicated, but did not disrupt the negotiations.

---

[3]   Basil C. Muzorewa, 'Botswana's Share of Revenue from the Use of Rand Currency: A Note', *Botswana Notes and Records*, Vol.6 (1974).

The Monetary Preparatory Commission

As it had done in many other areas of economic policy, the Botswana Government had anticipated the problems which might be encountered and had started to make contingency plans in the event that the negotiations were not successful. A Monetary Preparatory Commission was appointed by the President in 1973, chaired by Mr H.C. L. Hermans, the Permanent Secretary of the Ministry of Finance and Development Planning (MFDP)[4], to consider Botswana's options. In addition to senior Ministry officials (including Mr P.H.K. Kedikilwe, then the Director for Financial Affairs, currently Minister for Presidential Affairs), the Committee included technical advisers from the International Monetary Fund (IMF) and Professor A.N. McLeod of York University, Canada, whose services were made available under the Commonwealth Technical Assistance Programme.

The Monetary Preparatory Commission and the Government were strongly influenced by a paper produced by Professor McLeod which examined the advantages and disadvantages of different kinds of currency boards, monetary authorities and central banks, and concluded that Botswana's interests would be best served by establishing a fully-fledged central bank. Interestingly, Professor McLeod placed greater emphasis on the potential benefits which monetary independence could confer in relation to the development of domestic financial institutions and money markets, than he did on the possibility of generating income from reserve investments.

> 'The most significant benefit from a national currency system is the opportunity it offers to expand the range of domestic financial institutions and thereby give access to non-inflationary sources of domestic credit that should eventually far exceed the fiduciary element in the note issue, and benefit the economy of Botswana to the extent of many times the earnings from the investment of the reserves behind that issue.'[5]

Although the Monetary Preparatory Commission was coming to the conclusion that monetary independence offered Botswana more policy options than remaining within the RMA, it was concerned about the risks Botswana would run if it tried to manage its own currency. Views were sought from as many interested parties as possible. Without exception, the advice received was overwhelmingly against withdrawal from the RMA. The IMF advised strongly against it on technical grounds, arguing that the extreme openness of Botswana's economy, and likely fluctuations in the balance of trade and payments, would require Botswana to hold exceptionally large reserves, at levels higher than the Botswana authorities could afford to maintain, given the country's 'poor long-term economic prospects'. Concerns about Botswana's ability to manage a national currency and its own reserves efficiently were also expressed in several quarters, while the business community was equally strongly opposed to Botswana's withdrawal from the RMA on the grounds that any locally issued currency, in contrast to the 'strong and stable Rand', would be inherently weak and volatile, discouraging foreign investment. The South African authorities, while sharing these views, were also concerned about the exchange control implications of any move in Botswana towards greater monetary independence.

---

4   The Ministries of Development Planning and of Finance were merged to form the Ministry of Finance and Development Planning with effect from 1 April 1970.

5   Professor Alex N. McLeod, 'Preliminary Report on Alternative Monetary Arrangements for the Government of Botswana', Unpublished report, 8 November 1973, p.7.

Withdrawal from the Rand Monetary Area

The decision to withdraw from the RMA, and to establish a national currency and central bank, was not taken lightly. It was not influenced, as some observers assumed at the time, by political considerations, nor was it motivated by the Botswana Government's impatience over the slow progress of the quadripartite negotiations. In the final analysis, the decision was taken, after prolonged deliberations in Cabinet, on the premise that, as a member of the Southern African Customs Union, heavily dependent on concessional aid, Botswana would have virtually no ability to pursue independent economic strategies if it had to comply, passively, with the monetary policies adopted by the South African authorities in their own national self-interest. This view was stated in the 1973-78 National Development Plan, and reiterated in the 1974 Budget Speech.

The announcement that the Botswana Government had decided to withdraw from the RMA was made by the President, Sir Seretse Khama, in Molepolole on 6 September 1974. He outlined plans to introduce a national currency, and to establish a central bank responsible for the currency issue, as well as for monetary policy formulation and implementation, at the earliest possible date.

With Botswana no longer participating, negotiations between Lesotho, South Africa and Swaziland were quickly concluded and a tripartite[6] Rand Monetary Agreement was signed on 15 December 1974. Ironically, it officially recognised the profit-sharing principle, opposed earlier by the South African authorities, although the actual distribution of profits was based on a formula as the exact amount of Rand currency in circulation in Lesotho and Swaziland was not known.

Preparations for the new central bank

Having announced its intention to withdraw from the RMA, the Botswana Government lost no time in making the necessary preparations for the change. The Chairman of the Monetary Preparatory Commission, Mr H.C.L. Hermans, was relieved of his responsibilities as Permanent Secretary of the Ministry of Finance and Development Planning (MFDP) with effect from 1 January 1975, to work full time on the planning of the new monetary arrangements. Mr F.G. Mogae, then Director of Economic Affairs in the MFDP, (now Vice President and Minister of Finance and Development Planning), was appointed to succeed him in the Ministry.

There was much to be done. Speed was of the essence since a long period of uncertainty about future monetary policy was clearly undesirable. The decision to leave the RMA and to establish a fully-fledged central bank, rather than a currency board, implied that Rand currency would be withdrawn from circulation in exchange for a new independent national currency.

In this regard, the circumstances in Botswana were quite unusual. In every other case of an African country withdrawing from a regional monetary area having a common monetary unit, the currency being withdrawn from circulation was either to be demonetised on a specified date, making it valueless as a medium of exchange thereafter, or it was the currency of a distant metropolitan power and therefore unlikely to remain in circulation long. The withdrawal from circulation of the East African Shil-

---

6   The Government of Namibia became the fourth signatory to the agreement after that country's achievement of Independence in 1990.

ling in 1966, to be replaced by three separate national currencies, was the most recent example. In the case of Botswana, the currency to be withdrawn was not only a 'live' currency, which would retain its legal tender status across Botswana's borders, and elsewhere in the Southern African Customs Union, but it was a currency in which Batswana, in general, and the business and farming communities, in particular, had confidence. Currency hoarding and the externalization of banking accounts were considered to be risks which were likely to grow, the longer the introduction of the new Botswana currency was delayed.

The legislative and policy framework

One of the first tasks to be performed by the Monetary Preparatory Commission after the announcement was to prepare the enabling legislation and the details of the policy framework for the new monetary system. The President, Sir Seretse Khama, had explained, in broad terms in his Molepolole speech, the reasons for his Government's decision to withdraw from the RMA, and the Vice President and Minister and Finance and Development Planning, Dr Q.K.J. Masire, had subsequently addressed many of the questions about the implications of the decision. However, there were numerous details which remained to be worked out before the new system could be introduced. It was a busy time for the Monetary Preparatory Commission and its small complement of staff.

Three separate pieces of legislation had to be enacted: the Bank of Botswana Act; a Financial Institutions Act; and an Exchange Control Act. The first of these was necessary in order to bring the new central bank into existence, to describe its objectives, powers and responsibilities, and to define its relationship with the Government. Having no prior experience with central banking, the citizen members of the Commission sought and relied heavily on the advice and assistance of the IMF and other central banks. A highly experienced former United States Federal Reserve Board employee, Mr J. Nettles, was assigned by the IMF to assist with the drafting of the Bank of Botswana Bill. He, in turn, drew on the expertise of the IMF's lawyers and its central banking experts. Valuable practical advice was also obtained from six Commonwealth central banks, namely those of Kenya, Tanzania, and Uganda in Africa, and Barbados, Jamaica, and Trinidad and Tobago in the Caribbean. The services of Dr S.A. Untermann were provided by the Deutsche Bundesbank as Monetary Adviser to the Ministry and then to the Bank, until March 1976.

It was also necessary to enact legislation governing the conduct of commercial banks and other institutions performing banking business in Botswana, as no local banking legislation existed. The local operations of both banks were governed by the monetary policies, and prudential and other statutory requirements, prevailing in the countries where their head offices were located. By 1975, control of commercial banking operations in Botswana had been transferred to Barclays Bank International Limited and Standard Bank Limited, in London. It was clearly inconsistent with the decision to withdraw from the RMA to allow this situation to continue to prevail. Control over the domestic banking system was a prerequisite if monetary independence from the RMA was to have any significance.

It is of interest to note that the Financial Institutions Bill, which was also drafted with IMF assistance during the first half of 1975, did not prescribe the local incorporation of financial institutions. Indeed, it was envisaged that Barclays Bank

International Limited and Standard Bank Limited would continue to operate in Botswana, after the establishment of the new central bank and the introduction of the new national currency, as branches of their parent banks in the United Kingdom. Without the insistence or encouragement of the Botswana Government, both banks decided voluntarily to incorporate locally as wholly-owned subsidiaries. Special legislation was required to facilitate the cession of the assets and liabilities of the former branches of the parent banks to the new locally incorporated banks.[7]

Also of interest is the fact that the branch of the United Building Society of South Africa, which had opened a branch in Gaborone in 1970, could no longer operate in the country after Botswana's withdrawal from the Rand Monetary Area as South African legislation prohibited building societies from assuming foreign currency exposures. The local assets and liabilities of the United Building Society were taken over at the end of 1976 by the Botswana Building Society, with the assistance of the Botswana Government which subscribed P1.6 million. The United Building Society continued to serve as an adviser to the Botswana Building Society until June 1978.

The third major piece of legislation prepared by the Monetary Preparatory Commission was the Exchange Control Bill. Locally administered exchange controls were considered necessary to enable the Botswana Government to protect, and preserve, Botswana's foreign currency reserves after the introduction of the new currency. The dire warnings of the many institutions, advisers and investors about the inherent weakness of Botswana's new currency had caused the Government to become concerned about possible capital flight and the adequacy of future foreign exchange reserves. The Exchange Control Act, 1976, and the Regulations made under it, closely patterned on those in force in the RMA, imposed a somewhat restrictive regime. Botswana had been accorded IMF Article XIV status at Independence, allowing it to place restrictions on current, as well as capital transactions, although, in practice, the restrictions imposed on international current account transactions were never particularly onerous.

To help Members of Parliament, as well as the public, to understand the full implications of the decision to create Botswana's own central bank and to introduce a national currency, a comprehensive explanatory background paper was presented to Parliament in March 1975 and widely circulated. It spelled out all the currency and monetary system options, analysing the implications of each.[8] The National Assembly debated and duly passed the Bank of Botswana Bill[9]; and the other pieces of legislation passed without incident in April 1975.

The acquisition of premises

The legislative and policy framework having been established, the attention of the Monetary Preparatory Commission turned to practical matters. A development project was prepared and approved in the Government's 1975/76 Development Budget. It

---

[7] The Barclays Bank of Botswana Vesting Act, 1975, and the Standard Bank of Botswana Vesting Act, 1975.

[8] 'A Monetary System for Botswana', Government Paper No.1 of 1975.

[9] The Bank of Botswana Act (1975), with its subsequent amendments, was in force until the end of 1996 when it was replaced by a new Act. Unless stated otherwise, any reference in this paper is to the original Act.

provided funding for the construction and equipping of the Bank's headquarters on a 2.8 hectare undeveloped plot of land situated in the Government Enclave on Khama Crescent, as well as for the acquisition of stocks of the new currency. The land and completed buildings were later transferred to the Bank as the Government's in-kind subscription of the Bank's paid up capital.[10]

The contract for the construction of the new Bank headquarters on Khama Crescent was awarded in an amount of R1.8 million through a competitive tender process, and building commenced in June 1975. In the meantime, as recruitment commenced, Bank Staff occupied temporary offices at several locations in Gaborone.

The high security complex, comprising the main currency vault, currency delivery yard, and note and coin counting offices, was completed, on an extremely tight schedule, by the end of May 1976, just in time to receive the first shipments of the new currency which arrived on 7 June 1976. The initial phase of construction was finished in March 1977, and the Bank was officially opened by Sir Seretse Khama, on 16 March 1978.

The new national currency

Early decisions also had to be made in 1975 about the characteristics of the national currency so that the new notes and coins could be designed and manufactured. First, the name of the currency notes and coins had to be determined. A public opinion poll was conducted which revealed a strong consensus: eighty percent of the respondents proposed that the basic monetary unit should be called the Pula (meaning 'rain' or 'blessings'), and an overwhelming majority recommended that the coin should be called Thebe (meaning 'shield').

Another difficult decision concerned the quantities of the different denominations of notes and coins to be ordered. There were no statistics available to guide the Government since Botswana was essentially a monetary province of South Africa, and the banks did not keep reliable records of the Rand currency issued or withdrawn in Botswana. Estimates prepared by the Monetary Preparatory Commission, based on the 1974/75 Rural Income Distribution Study, had indicated that currency with a face value of between R10 million and R20 million might be circulating in Botswana. A sample survey suggested a figure of R110 as the average holding of cash per household for all households nation-wide, while rural households, due to the greater inaccessibility of banking services, probably held slightly more cash.

These estimates were supported by data on average household currency holdings in other countries of a similar income levels and economic characteristics. Accordingly, a figure of P15 million was used as the estimate of currency in circulation in Botswana at the time. Orders were placed for the initial stocks of notes and coins having a face value of P80 million. Although the demand for some denominations of notes and coins turned out to be considerably higher than anticipated, the estimates of currency in circulation proved to be reasonably accurate, ensuring that the Bank had adequate stocks of all denominations during, and for several years after the currency conversion period.

---

[10] The value of the land, buildings and equipment, transferred to the Bank in tranches, together with the cost of the initial currency stocks, amounted to P3.56 million by 1979. At the time of writing this remains the total paid-up capital of the Bank, although with a new Bank of Botswana Act coming into force in 1997, this is to be increased to P25 million.

With regard to the currency denominations and the note-coin frontier, it was considered advisable, to facilitate the conversion process, not to depart from the denominations of Rand notes and coins to any significant extent. Only in the coin denominations, where a 25 Thebe coin was introduced in lieu of the South African 20 Cent coin, and the metallic content (and therefore the colour of the coins), were changes made.

An interesting aspect of the choice of the name and denominations of the currency units was that, long before the views of the Botswana public had been sought and the final decision on the name of the currency units had been taken by the Cabinet, the British bank note printing firm, Thomas De La Rue and Company, Ltd., had produced sample Pula bank notes which correctly predicted the name of the currency, and the sizes, colours and themes ultimately chosen by the Cabinet. So impressed was the Botswana Government that it awarded the contract for the design and initial supply of bank notes to De La Rue. The contract to design, mint and supply the new coins was awarded to the British Royal Mint.

3. THE FIRST TWENTY-ONE YEARS

The commencement of operations

The Bank of Botswana came into existence on 1 July 1975, when the Bank of Botswana Act was brought into force. The Governor-Designate, Mr H.C.L. Hermans, was appointed as the Bank's first Governor with effect from the same date. The position of Deputy Governor was filled shortly thereafter by Mr G.P. Lambie, a retired Bank of England employee who had worked for the previous ten years in the central banks of Liberia, Nigeria and Uganda under the auspices of the IMF's central banking service programme. Mr S. W. Fryer was seconded from the Ministry of Finance and Development Planning to serve in the dual capacity of Board Secretary and Administrative Manager. A nucleus of essential service staff was recruited locally.

There remained much to be done before the new national currency could be introduced and banking operations could commence, as planned, in 1976. First, the necessary Board appointments were made. In addition to the Governor and the Permanent Secretary of the Ministry of Finance and Development Planning, Mr F. G. Mogae, both *ex officio* members in terms of the Bank of Botswana Act, the Board comprised Mr A.J.L. Clark of Johannesburg, a businessman and chartered accountant who had been associated with the establishment of the Botswana Development Corporation; Mr T.S. Madisa, the Permanent Secretary of the Ministry of Agriculture; and Mr A.J. Woodcock, the General Manager of the National Development Bank.

The inaugural meeting of the Board was held on 11 December 1975. The Vice President and Minister of Finance and Development Planning, Mr Q.K.J. Masire, opened proceedings, exhorting the Board and officers of the Bank to serve the nation with diligence, integrity and professional competence, and to ensure that the public were kept informed about monetary and banking developments.

The following two years were a period of intensive institution-building. The first act of the Board was to approve a basic organization plan for the Bank, as outlined in Figure 1. The Board then considered and approved the Bank's Bye-Laws; salary and grade structures; schemes of service; general conditions of service; service staff regulations; the initial authorised staff establishment; and the budget and operational work programme for 1976. It also authorised the opening of accounts with and for local commercial and overseas correspondent banks, and approved the submission of the Bank's application for membership in the Association of African Central Banks. The plans for the introduction of the currency exchange were agreed.

FIGURE 1. BANK OF BOTSWANA ORGANIZATION CHART, 1976

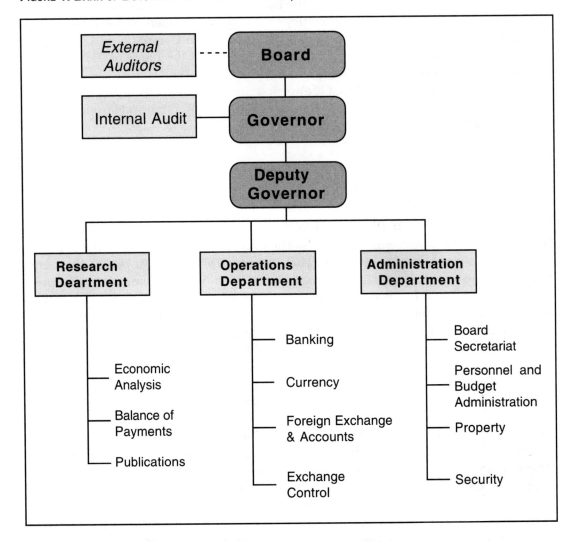

During 1976, a further five Board meetings were held. Resolutions were passed relating, *inter alia*, to the appointment of the Bank's external auditors and legal counsel; the establishment of a contributory staff pension fund, and group life and medical insurance schemes; the Bank's seal and logo; policies concerning interest rates, the external value of the Pula, establishment and maintenance of international reserves, the opening of accounts with other central banks, the appointment of foreign correspondents; primary reserve and liquid asset requirements; accounting standards; and foreign exchange dealing procedures. Regulations and other statutory instruments were drafted, for the approval of the Minister of Finance, under the Bank of Botswana Act, the Financial Institutions Act and the Exchange Control Act.

The Bank's Management was heavily preoccupied at this time with the preparations for the introduction of the new national currency and the associated commencement of banking and foreign currency operations. The target date for the launch of the Pula was set as 23 August 1976.

In view of the doubts which had been expressed about a possible adverse public reaction to the new currency, an extensive nation-wide information programme was planned by the Bank to familiarise the public with the national currency and to explain the currency conversion process. Pamphlets, posters and explanatory brochures were prepared and widely distributed.[11] Ministers, senior Bank staff and Government information teams travelled the country, addressing meetings at District Councils, *kgotlas* and schools; Radio Botswana broadcast a steady stream of information about the impending change; a bumper sticker was produced, proclaiming 23 August 1976, as Pula Day; and a special series of postage stamps was released featuring the new bank notes.

At the same time, contingency plans were quietly formulated to guard against the eventuality that the new currency would not be well received or that the currency conversion would take longer than anticipated, resulting in a shortage of foreign exchange reserves during the initial 100-day currency conversion period, during which time the parity between the Pula and the Rand was guaranteed. It must be remembered that Botswana had no official reserves prior to Pula Day. Lines of credit were therefore secured from Morgan Guarantee Trust Company (US$10 million) and the Reserve Bank of South Africa (R10 million) to enable the Bank to have access to foreign exchange, if the need arose, to supplement the Rand currency withdrawn from circulation and deposited with the Reserve Bank of South Africa. IMF facilities could also have been used. In the event, it was not necessary to use these standby arrangements, and they were soon cancelled.

As the designated currency exchange offices opened all over the country on 23 August 1976, doubts about the acceptance of the new national currency were quickly dispelled. Pula notes and Thebe coins were received with jubilation by the public throughout Botswana.

A large proportion of the estimated amount of Rand currency in circulation was exchanged for Pula and Thebe within a few weeks of Pula Day. In terms of an agreement which had been struck with the South African Reserve Bank, the Rand currency withdrawn from circulation in Botswana and deposited at the Reserve Bank or at other designated banks in South Africa was credited to special Rand and foreign currency accounts opened for the Bank of Botswana at the Reserve Bank. The amount credited to the Rand and non-Rand accounts was determined by the ratio of Rand currency in circulation in the RMA to the assets of the Reserve Bank. With the currency exchange proceeding well, Botswana's official foreign exchange reserves – largely made up of its deposits with the Reserve Bank of South Africa – rose steadily, reaching the equivalent of P21 million by the end of August, 1976.[12] By 31 December 1976,

---

[11] Principal among these were *A Popular Guide to Exchange Controls and Foreign Exchange Transactions,* and *Some Questions and Answers about Money and Banking in Botswana.*

[12] For detailed information on the currency exchange, see Dr D.J. Hudson, 'The Establishment of Botswana's Central Bank and the Introduction of the New Currency', *Botswana Notes and Records,* Vol.10, 1978.

the end of the Bank's first full financial year, Botswana's official foreign exchange reserves had grown to P65 million, representing the equivalent of about four months of imports of goods and services.

Many changes to the domestic banking system were made necessary by the introduction of a national currency and establishment of a central bank. The two commercial banks, Barclays and Standard, having become locally incorporated, had to be licensed under the new Financial Institutions Act. They were designated as Authorised Dealers under the new Exchange Control Act, which the Bank of Botswana was appointed to administer on behalf of the Botswana Government. Henceforth, commercial banks' holdings of foreign exchange, in excess of their authorised open foreign currency positions, had to be sold to the Bank of Botswana by the end of each business day, rather than transferred to their correspondent banks in South Africa or elsewhere.

In addition, the local banks were required to comply with the primary reserve and liquid asset requirements prescribed under the Bank of Botswana Act, maintaining the necessary balances in their newly opened accounts at the Bank. Interbank clearing also took place through the Bank of Botswana's clearing house for the first time, against the commercial banks' accounts with the Bank. Standard Bank, which had been the Government's banker even before it had opened its first branch in the Bechuanaland Protectorate in the 1950s, had to adjust to the transfer of the Government's banking accounts to the Bank of Botswana. This transfer was phased in over a period of two years in order to reduce the financial impact on Standard Bank but the loss of the Government's banking business nevertheless resulted in a considerable reduction in Standard Bank's balance sheet footings. As a result, Barclays overtook Standard as the largest commercial bank in Botswana in terms of total assets and liabilities at that time.

The transfer to the Bank of the Botswana Government's banking business, commencing in 1976, brought the new banking hall into operation. The necessary accounts were established for the Government, and Bank of Botswana chequebooks were issued for the first time. By 31 December 1976, the Government balances with the Bank of Botswana amounted to P28.8 million. Soon all the Government's foreign currency dealings were also conducted through the Bank of Botswana, and accounts were opened for international organizations and foreign lenders dealing with the Government. In turn, as Botswana's foreign exchange reserves started to accumulate, the Bank made increasing use of its relationships with foreign commercial banks and other central banks to make foreign deposits.

By the beginning of 1977, the initial intensive institution-building phase was coming to an end. The necessary legislative, regulatory, policy and procedural framework was in place, and the Bank was performing all of the functions of a conventional central bank. The next twenty years of the life of the Bank have seen many changes, as described below, but Botswana's transition from being a passive member of the RMA to having its own currency and central bank, with the capacity to pursue independent monetary policies, had been successfully accomplished.

The objectives of the Bank of Botswana

The principal objectives of the Bank of Botswana are prescribed in Section 4 of the original Bank of Botswana Act. The overriding requirement is for the Bank to 'promote and maintain monetary stability, an efficient payments mechanism, and the liquidity, solvency and proper functioning of a soundly based monetary, credit and financial system'. In addition, it is the duty of the Bank to ' foster monetary, credit and financial conditions conducive to the orderly, balanced and sustained economic development of Botswana'.

Although the Bank's statutory objectives have remained constant since 1975, changes in the global and local economic and public policy environment over the years brought shifts in the emphasis placed on different aspects of the Bank's functions and operations. Since the mid-1980s, the investment of Botswana's rapidly escalating foreign exchange reserves, the supervision of domestic financial institutions and more active management of monetary policies have come to assume an increasingly important role in the work of the Bank. An account of how the Bank executed these responsibilities is given later in this paper.

The Board of the Bank

A number of changes have been made over the past 21 years in the structure and composition of the Board of the Bank, and in its functions.

The Board itself was enlarged in 1987 from five to seven members to reflect the increasing complexity of the Bank's operations, to provide for greater diversity of experience among Board members, and to enable a quorum to be achieved more easily. The criteria for Board appointments and the statutory quorum requirements were changed to provide a larger role on the Board for representatives of the private sector. Where originally only two of the five Board members could not be 'public officers or persons serving as consultants or advisers to the Government', and only three Board members constituted a quorum, the 1987 amendments[13] increased these numbers to three and four, respectively. To comply with the minimum quorum requirements, at least one private sector representative had to be present. At the time of writing only two of the members of the Board are public officers.

Although the Bank of Botswana Act prescribes that Board meetings must be held at least once each calendar quarter, the number of statutory and policy issues requiring Board consideration or approval soon became so great that it was necessary to schedule at least six Board meetings each year. In some years, seven or eight regular meetings of the Board have been held. Special Board meetings have been convened from time to time to deal with urgent issues or to permit more extensive discussion of matters of particular importance.

From the outset, it was decided to adopt the custom of many other central banks and to use Board lunches as an opportunity to solicit the views of, and to brief, senior representatives from Government, and the business, banking and parastatal sectors, in an informal setting. This tradition survived, and was much appreciated, until 1994 when the length of agendas and the duration of Board meetings made it impossible to accommodate invited guests at Board lunches. To compensate, separate informal briefings have been held each year for the benefit of selected interest groups, including Cabinet Ministers, Members of Parliament, Permanent Secretaries, parastatal chief executives, business leaders, members of the diplomatic corps, and bank executives. In addition, two special press briefings are held each year.

---

[13]   Bank of Botswana (Amendment) Act, (No.12 of 1987).

Over the years, Board members have played a wider role in the affairs of the Bank than merely attending Board meetings. From time to time, they have participated in the selection of external fund managers, interviewed and evaluated candidates for senior management positions, and assisted the Bank in many other ways.[14]

An Audit Committee of the Board was established in May 1986. It is chaired by a non-executive Board member, elected by the Board, and meets twice a year to consider and approve the audit plan, the annual audited accounts, and the External Auditors' management letter. The Internal Auditor serves as the secretary of the Audit Committee.

The organization of the Bank

The organization of the Bank has evolved in stages since 1975, largely in response to changes in the Bank's operational priorities and the external demands placed on it. Many of the early changes involved the graduation of sub-departmental units, formerly part of the Operations Department, into full Departments, directly responsible to the Governor.

A minor reorganization occurred in 1981, concerning the administration of the Financial Institutions Act. It had been the original intention to delegate responsibility for the supervision of banks to the Bank's Internal Auditor. But when the powers under the Financial Institutions Act for the licensing, examination and supervision of banks and other financial institutions were formally delegated to the Bank in 1980, it became apparent that the Internal Auditor was neither qualified nor equipped to undertake this responsibility. A separate Bank Supervision Department was therefore created in 1981, with assistance from the IMF, to monitor the soundness of the commercial banks and to conduct periodic examinations of financial institutions, including some but not all parastatal financial institutions.

The next change occurred in September 1985 when, on the advice of the IMF, the Exchange Control Office in the Operations Department was elevated to full departmental status. The rapid expansion of the economy in the mid-1980s had resulted in a substantial increase in the volume of foreign currency transactions and the number of exchange applications submitted to the Bank, through the commercial banks, for approval. Despite the fact that the growth of Botswana's reserves had surpassed expectations, reaching the equivalent of almost 18 months' worth of imports of goods and services by 1985, and were, by this time, well in excess of the levels anticipated when the Exchange Control Act and Regulations were introduced, the Government was unwilling to contemplate the relaxation of exchange controls. The capacity of the Bank to cope with the ever increasing number of applications therefore had to be strengthened. The restructured Operations Department retained responsibility for the banking, currency, accounting and foreign exchange functions.

Responsibility for the management of Botswana's foreign exchange reserves had remained fragmented for many years, well after the level of reserves started rising so rapidly from 1984 onwards. Investment decisions were made by the Deputy Governor,

---

14 The composition of the Board has changed considerably over the years, although one Board Member, Mr A.J.L. Clark, served continuously since the very first Board meeting until his resignation at the end of 1996. During this time he provided invaluable continuity of advice and institutional knowledge.

within the framework of broad investment strategies approved by the Board, relying on the advice of the Research Department and information from external sources. The decisions were then implemented by the Foreign Exchange Unit of the Operations Department.

More formal arrangements were put in place in 1988 when an internal Investment Committee was established, chaired by the Deputy Governor, and a Portfolio Analysis Unit was created in the Research Department to track international currency, capital and money market developments. However, problems continued to be experienced with the coordination of different aspects of reserve management responsibilities. A more fundamental change was required. In August 1989, the Foreign Exchange Unit of the Operations Department and the Portfolio Analysis Unit of the Research Department were split away to form the nucleus of a new Foreign Department. The Foreign Department was subsequently strengthened by means of an internal reorganization in 1991 and the acquisition of the services of technical advisers. It was renamed the Treasury Department. The Research Department, although still represented on the Investment Committee, thereafter became less directly involved with the management of Botswana's foreign exchange reserves.

In addition to these changes, the Banking Supervision Department was reorganised and expanded in 1992; the Board Secretariat was converted into the Corporate Services Unit, with additional responsibilities for legal services, staff pensions and public relations; and an Estates Unit and Information Technology Unit were established, also in the Governor's Office. The Research Department was also restructured in 1993. The resulting organization of the Bank at the end of 1993 is shown in Figure 2 overleaf.

However, the distribution of responsibilities among the existing Departments continued to display some dysfunctional characteristics, which blurred accountability and generated unnecessary interdepartmental conflict. A major investment in computer networking and systems development had also started to change the traditional relationships between, and the performance of Departments. To resolve these , a major reorganization, approved by the Board, was implemented in April 1994. The main objectives of the 1994 reorganization were to enhance operational synergies and to centralise responsibility for the accounting aspects of financial and investment management in one Department. A new Finance Department was therefore created, to which the functions previously performed by the Accounts Division of the Operations Department, the Budget Unit of the Administration Department and the Accounts Unit of the Treasury Department were transferred. The Administration Department, having relinquished responsibility for the management of the annual budget, as well as for the provision of security services, was renamed the Administrative Services Department to reflect more accurately its service orientation. The Treasury Department, relieved of responsibility for the accounting aspects of reserve management, became the International Department; and the Banking Supervision and Exchange Control Departments were merged to form the Financial Institutions Department, to prepare for the shift in operational focus away from exchange control administration to banking supervision. The former Operations Department, now no longer performing accounting and foreign exchange functions, was converted into a more narrowly specialised Banking Department, to which responsibility for security matters was transferred. The 1994 reorganization also recognised the need to strengthen the ca-

FIGURE 2. BANK OF BOTSWANA ORGANIZATION CHART, DECEMBER 1993

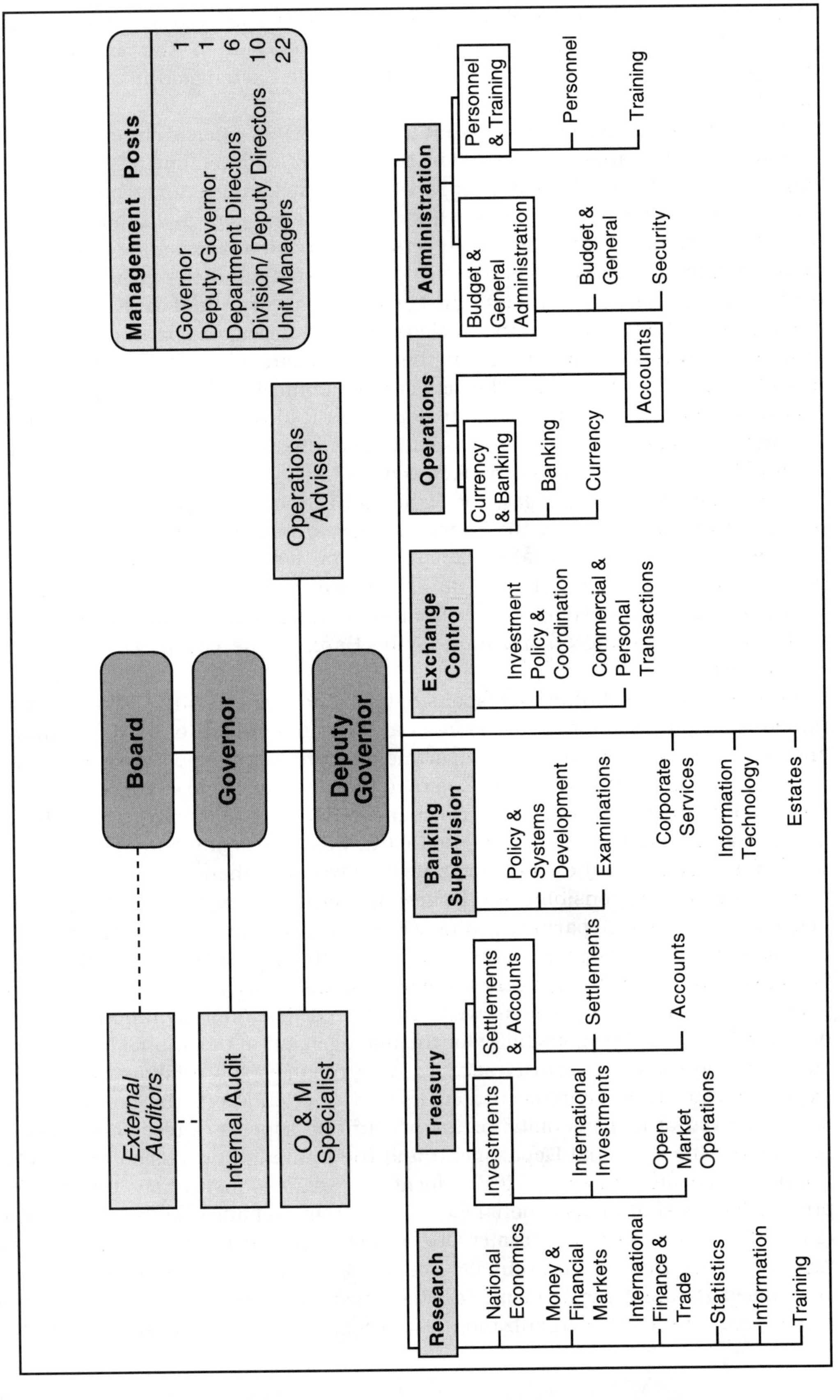

Management Posts	
Governor	1
Deputy Governor	1
Department Directors	6
Division/ Deputy Directors	10
Unit Managers	22

pacity of the Governor's Office to perform a central coordinating role. In addition to creating a post of General Manager, the Information Technology Unit was upgraded to become the Management Systems Division, to coordinate the planning and maintenance of computer applications and to improve the flow of management information throughout the Bank. These changes are reflected in Figure 3.

FIGURE 3. BANK OF BOTSWANA ORGANIZATION CHART, 1994 TO 1996

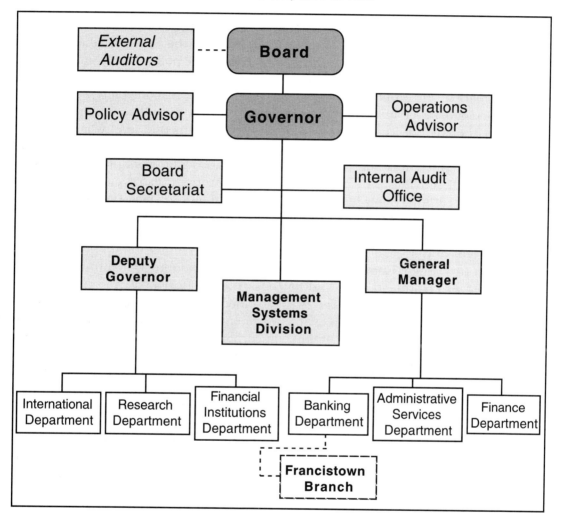

The structure of the Bank, its internal consultative machinery and staff development

In terms of the Bank of Botswana Act, the Governor is the Chairman of the Board, as well as the chief executive officer of the Bank. This arrangement is common to most central banks. Both the Governor and the Deputy Governor are appointed by the President. The Directors and Deputy Directors of Departments (and equivalent) are appointed by the Board in accordance with the Bank's Bye-Laws. The Governor has

---

15   The position of General Manager was removed in 1997 after the enactment of the Bank of Botswana Act 1996, which enabled the post of a second Deputy Governor to be created.

the authority to make staff appointments to posts below the Deputy Director level, but delegates this responsibility to the Director of Administrative Services, except in respect of the appointment of expatriate employees and staff at the Assistant Manager and Manager levels.

As the Bank evolved and the complexity of its operations increased, the need for greater consultation within the organization escalated. In the early years, when the Bank was still quite small, the Executive Committee constituted the main vehicle for consultation, as well as coordination. Comprising the Heads of all Departments and the Deputy Governor, and chaired by the Governor, the Executive Committee, although nominally advisory to the Governor, proved, over the years, to be an effective vehicle for exchanging views on, and resolving Bank-wide policy issues, and keeping all members of the Senior Management Team fully apprised of developments occurring elsewhere in the Bank or impinging on their areas of responsibility.

This mechanism for institutional consultation at the Executive Committee level has, since the late 1980s, been replicated at the departmental level where Departmental Management Teams hold weekly meetings to receive feedback from the Executive Committee meetings, and to discuss departmental work programmes and coordinate staff activities. Full departmental staff meetings also occur regularly but less frequently, at intervals which differ from Department to Department.

Responsibility for the planning, coordination or execution of various other aspects of the Bank's operations has been increasingly delegated to standing interdepartmental committees and special task forces, such as the Accounts Committee, Training Committee, Investment Committee, Open Market Coordinating Committee, Information Technology Planning Group, and Note Destruction Board.

Another important initiative taken in this connection was the organization of management seminars and retreats to enable members of the senior Management of the Bank to keep abreast of current thinking on corporate governance and management issues, to heighten the level of awareness of the national, regional and global developments which impact on the Bank, and to build a stronger team spirit and corporate identity among members of the Senior Management Team. Regular management seminars have been held each year since 1991, on Saturdays in Gaborone, attended by members of the Management Team. Management retreats have been convened each year since July 1992 at locations outside Gaborone to avoid unnecessary interruptions or distractions. All senior staff from the Deputy Director level and above attend all retreats. The entire Management Team participates in the retreats every other year. Members of the Bank's Board have attended some retreats.

To provide a more effective bridge between the senior management and more junior staff, a Middle Management Advisory Group (MMAG) was established in 1994, in response to proposals made at the 1993 Management Retreat. MMAG comprises elected representatives of the middle management personnel in each Department. This Group formulates proposals on internal administrative and management issues for consideration by the Executive Committee, and reviews draft policies and procedures referred to it by the Executive Committee or individual Heads of Departments.[16]

The Central Bank Union (CBU) has also come to play an important advisory and consultative role in the Bank. Registered as a trade union in 1978, the CBU, through

---

[16] Within the Bank, senior management refers to members of staff of deputy director level and above, while the middle management are managers and assistant managers.

its annually elected Executive Committee, represents the interests and concerns of its members on issues affecting their welfare. The original Recognition Agreement between the Bank Management and the Central Bank Union was entered into on 17 January 1980. Although the designation of the Bank as an 'essential service' under the Schedule to the Trade Disputes Act (Cap. 48:02) prevents Bank employees from striking, and the Government's incomes policy leaves little room for the negotiation of salary levels and fringe benefits, the Union has, in most years, made a positive contribution to the efficient functioning of the Bank. It has been consulted regularly about any changes proposed in personnel and compensation policies, and is represented on several management committees, including the Housing Allocation Committee, the Staff Cafeteria Liaison Committee, and the Board of Trustees of the Staff Pension Fund. Relations between the CBU and the Bank Management have generally been amicable and productive over the past 19 years.

The total authorised staff establishment grew slowly but steadily from 86 at the end of 1975 to 558 twenty years later. This included a few quite large increases occurring in years when the Bank assumed additional responsibilities or expanded its operations, such as in 1977 and 1978 when the Government's bank accounts were transferred to the Bank from Standard Bank, or in 1994 and 1995 following a major reorganization of the Bank and in preparation for the opening of the Francistown Branch.

As most of the citizen staff were employed initially mainly in clerical and security positions, or as note counters, the early training was primarily of an induction or on-the-job nature. A full-time expatriate Training Officer was therefore recruited in 1978 to organise the Bank's training programme. Advantage was taken of secretarial, accounts, administrative and tellers' training courses run by the Government, the Institute of Development Management and the commercial banks in Botswana, to enable staff to undergo basic training or to upgrade existing skills in these areas.

However, the training available in Botswana at the time, both arranged in the Bank and at training institutions, was not relevant to all the functions performed by the Bank. Accordingly, a number of Bank staff were sent abroad in 1977 and 1978 on short training courses and seminars run by the Federal Reserve Bank of New York, the Morgan Guarantee Trust Company and the Bank of England. Other staff were attached to other central banks in Africa or participated in seminars organised by the African Centre for Monetary Studies. In-service training was stepped up, and staff were encouraged to register for extra-mural studies with the South African Institute of Bankers and the Chartered Institute of Secretaries. Selected staff also received scholarships from the Bank to study for university degrees at the University of Botswana and Swaziland, or overseas. The first staff member to benefit from this policy was sponsored in 1978 for a Masters Degree in Economics, which she completed in 1980.

The Bank's training programme gained momentum in the 1980s, with numerous staff pursuing a wide variety of qualifications from full time post-graduate qualifications and part time certificates or diplomas in banking related subjects. However, it was also becoming apparent that the Bank's liberal and somewhat unstructured approach to staff training was resulting in some staff obtaining inappropriate qualifications, while the training needs of other staff were overlooked. Accordingly, assistance was requested from the IMF in 1984 to review the Bank's training policies. This led to an IMF-sponsored Training Adviser being attached to the Bank for two years to assess training needs and prepare career development plans for staff members who showed potential for advancement in the Bank.

For the next ten years, an average of 18 citizen staff were absent from the Bank per year on long-term training, while as many as 60 or 70 staff were nominated by the Bank to attend short training courses or job-related seminars. A very high proportion of all citizen staff have received some formal training funded by the Bank, more than one hundred having been sponsored for long-term training. In recent years, training costs have averaged P1.45 million a year. Total expenditures on staff training of all kinds over the past 21 years have exceeded P17 million. Some individual staff members, who joined the Bank straight from school, now hold advanced degrees, having been sponsored by the Bank at each level of their training and at each stage of their careers. The Bank's investment in the training received by a few staff members during the course of their employment by the Bank has already exceeded P250 000 per staff member.

This massive investment in staff development has enabled a large number of employees to acquire academic qualifications and professional skills relevant to the Bank's staffing requirements and enhanced their career prospects, but it has not yielded the results which the Bank had hoped for. Reliance on expatriates to fill many of the more senior positions, particularly in the Research Department, has increased, rather than diminished, over the years. The main causes of the relatively slow pace of localization have been twofold: the general shortage of high level skills in the citizen labour market, particularly of skills needed by the Bank; and the high rate of staff turnover. Many staff members who were trained or acquired advanced degrees at the Bank's expense subsequently left to take up employment elsewhere in Botswana or abroad.

The Bank has been greatly hampered in its efforts to fill vacant posts and to retain trained staff by its inability to offer salaries and fringe benefits comparable to those enjoyed by citizen employees of the commercial bank and other private sector employees in Botswana. In recent years, when the availability of suitably qualified citizen applicants has increased, either from the University of Botswana or in the labour market, this has become a major constraint. A high percentage of former Bank staff who resigned, after benefiting from the training provided by the Bank, cited inadequate compensation as the main reason for leaving the Bank. Limited career advancement opportunities in a relatively small and highly specialised institution, like the Bank, was another factor. Thus, despite the massive outlays on staff training over the years, the vacancy rate in the Bank has risen to almost 20% of the total staff establishment in some years and has exceeded 10% in most years.

The high and continuing vacancy rate, and the acute shortage of citizens in core occupational categories, has forced the Bank to rely heavily on expatriates over the past 21 years. The two principal sources of recruitment of expatriate staff have been the IMF, which has provided the services of up to three senior executive or advisory staff in some years, and the Bank of England, particularly in the early years. Other expatriates, employed on short-term contracts, have either been made available from other central banks, or have been recruited internationally on the open market. To keep total staff costs to a minimum, most expatriates employed by the Bank have been nationals of low income countries, particularly other African countries, for whom the cost of inducement has not been as high as would have been the case if expatriates from high income countries had been recruited.

Following major reviews of the training policies in the 1990s, the Bank's approach to staff training has changed in several respects. First, priority areas were identified in which the Bank's needs were greatest and recruitment on the local market was unlikely to fill vacancies. Economics, accountancy, computer science and finance were assigned the highest priority. Second, cost-effectiveness considerations have caused the Bank to become much more selective in its sponsorship of staff for long-term training. Eligible staff are selected on the basis of internal examinations, as well as interviews and superior performance. Third, the schemes of service were modified after the Botswana Institute of Bankers was established in 1991, to give greater recognition to professional banking qualifications. This encouraged many staff to enrol in the Institute's courses. Fourth, Bank-funded scholarships for postgraduate studies leading to the award of doctoral degrees were introduced for the first time, with the first award being made in 1995.

The Bank's staff pension scheme has always been contributory. In 1976, for reasons of administrative convenience, the Bank joined the Statutory Corporations Pension Scheme (StatCorp) which had been established in 1972 by the Botswana Insurance Corporation, in which the Botswana Development Corporation had a significant shareholding. As the years passed, the Bank became increasingly disillusioned with StatCorp's poor disclosure and accounting of investment returns. The Bank withdrew from the StatCorp Scheme in 1991 and established its own independent staff pension scheme. The contribution levels remained the same as before, namely 16% of basic staff salaries paid by the Bank, and 4% contributed by staff, by way of salary deductions. A Board of Trustees was appointed, including representatives of the Bank's pensioners and the Central Bank Union. Withdrawal from the StatCorp Scheme was effected over five years ending in April 1996. By the end of June 1996, the assets of the pension fund amounted to P12.2 million. There were 430 members and eight pensioners.

Relations with the Botswana Government

From the outset, the Bank has enjoyed close and harmonious relations, at both the policy and operational levels, with the Botswana Government in general, and the Ministry of Finance and Development Planning in particular. In many areas, the relationship is dictated by statute. The Bank of Botswana Act itself, or the Exchange Control Act and the Banking Act (formerly the Financial Institutions Act), reserve certain powers to be exercised by the President or by the Minister of Finance. For example, the Bank of Botswana Act provided that it was the prerogative of the President to determine the *par value* of the Pula, on the advice of the Minister of Finance. However, on each occasion over the past 21 years when the Pula has been revalued or devalued against other currencies, the President has acted on the advice of the Bank, submitted through the Minister of Finance. In matters concerning the design, denominations and other characteristics of the national currency, for example, where the final decision must be taken by the Minister of Finance, the Bank's advice has always been sought.

As banker and financial adviser to, and fiscal agent of the Government, the Bank has performed a number of statutory functions over the years. Since 1976, it has been the official depository of Government funds, operating the main accounts into which Government revenues are deposited and from which payments are made, both locally and abroad. Apart from a very short transitional period in 1976 and 1977, the

Bank has paid no interest on the Government's accumulated balances.

In its statutory role as the Government's principal financial adviser, the Bank has submitted recommendations to the Ministry of Finance and Development Planning each year prior to the preparation of the Government's annual budget, and has rendered advice on different aspects of fiscal policy. The Bank of Botswana has always been represented on the Taxation Review Committee and, since 1994, on the Loans Committee of the Ministry of Finance and Development Planning. In terms of Section 47 of the Bank of Botswana Act, the Bank is required to render advice to the Government and to statutory corporations on the timing, terms and conditions of any proposed borrowings. It has complied whenever financing proposals have been referred to it for appraisal.

In its capacity as the Government's fiscal agent, the Bank is the custodian of the Government's shares in such international organizations as the African Development Bank, the African Export-Import Bank, and International Monetary Fund. The Governor of the Bank of Botswana has served as Botswana's Governor on the Board of Governors of the IMF since the establishment of the Bank, and exercises the Government's voting rights on its behalf. Since the enactment of the Exchange Control Act and Financial Institutions Act in 1975, the Bank has also acted as the Government's agent for the administration of exchange controls, and for the licensing, regulation and supervision of financial institutions, although certain powers under both of these Acts are reserved by the Ministry of Finance and Development Planning. The advice of the Bank has invariably been sought, and usually heeded, on these matters, too.

Under Section 44 of the Bank of Botswana Act, the Bank was entrusted with the responsibility for issuing and managing of Government securities. Due to the Government's healthy financial position, it has never had to raise funds through the sale of public securities to augment its annual revenues. The responsibilities of the Bank in this area have therefore been restricted to managing a small trial Treasury Bill issue for the Government between 1976 until 1981, and assisting the Government to redeem an equally insignificant development bond issue in 1989, before its maturity.

Treasury Bills were introduced on 22 October 1976, with the Bank managing the issue on behalf of the Government. This first issue of treasury bills was worth P1 million and offered a 91-day maturity and a 7.5% yield. The intention was not to raise funds for the Government but rather to promote the creation of a domestic money market. Treasury Bills were discontinued in March 1982, when it became clear that the commercial banks preferred to hold their excess funds in an easily accessible overnight call account facility at the Bank of Botswana. The need for the Government to raise funds domestically for development purposes, by way of longer term debt instruments, was also soon obviated, as budget surpluses accumulated and funding became readily available from international banks and bilateral aid programmes, on highly concessional terms, to finance Government and parastatal development projects.

The Bank has, happily, not been called upon, in the 21 years of its existence, to make any advances to the Government as provided for under Section 48 of the Bank of Botswana Act. Prudent fiscal and economic policies, and buoyant Government revenues, have rendered such borrowing by the Government unnecessary. This has enabled Botswana to avoid the excessively high rates of inflation which prevailed in many other African countries in which government deficits were financed either through the issuance of government debt instruments, typically treasury bills, or simply by overdrawing their central bank accounts.

The relationship between the Bank and the Government has also been marked, equally happily, by the absence of any serious confrontation or disagreement on broad policy issues. Although Section 53 of the Bank of Botswana Act provides that the President may, on the advice of the Minister of Finance and after consultation with the Bank, issue policy directives to the Bank, no such directive has been issued during the life of the Bank.

The inclusion on the Board of the Permanent Secretary of the Ministry of Finance and Development Planning, as an *ex officio* member, was designed to ensure that the policies and activities of the Bank were consistent with, and support the Government's economic strategies and programmes. For many years, it was the policy of the Government to have an equal number of Government and non-Government Board members, although this policy has been relaxed in recent years.

While the strong representation of public officers on the Board has not resulted in any direct political pressure being asserted on the Bank – indeed, no vote has been taken on any Board resolution since the inception of the Bank – the sensitivity of the Board to political concerns has exerted a strong influence over the policies of the Bank. This was particularly the case with regard to interest rate policies, resulting in a long period of negative real interest rates.

At the operational level and in other areas of public policy, the Bank and the Ministry of Finance and Development Planning have maintained a constructive working relationship. A permanent working party of officials from the Bank and the Ministry was established soon after the Bank was established. It has become the principal institutional mechanism for consultation and policy coordination.

Senior Bank staff have been appointed to serve on various Presidential and Government commissions and committees, including the 1989 Presidential Commission for the Review of the Incomes Policy, the Pensions Industry Consultative Committee, the 1991 Salaries Review Commission, and the 1992 Presidential Commission of Enquiry into the Operations of the Botswana Housing Corporation. The Bank is represented by the Governor on the Economic Committee of Cabinet, the National Employment, Manpower and Incomes Council (NEMIC), and the High Level Consultative Committee (established in 1995 as the principal institutional vehicle for consultation between business leaders and Cabinet Ministers). The Bank also has a permanent member on the two sub-committees of NEMIC, the Productive Employment Technical Committee and the Taxation Review Committee, as well as on the Board of the Botswana Stock Exchange. Bank staff have also served on the boards of the Botswana Housing Corporation, the Water Utilities Corporation, and Air Botswana. In addition, the Bank has played a prominent role in, or has advised, official delegations of one kind and other, including investment promotion missions, and has assisted in the renegotiation of the Southern African Customs Union Agreement.

The Bank's finances

The calculations made by the Monetary Preparatory Commission had indicated that the income received by the Bank should be sufficient to cover its costs, and allow it to make a modest profit, one year taken with another. The original Bank of Botswana Act provided that 50% of the Bank's annual net income should be transferred to the Botswana Government. The remaining 50% was to be credited to the Bank's General Reserve until such time as the General Reserve exceeded the size of the Bank's authorised capital of P5 million. If the Bank sustained losses on its operations in any year, the losses could be set off against the General Reserve. If the Bank's liabilities exceeded its assets (or if the General Reserve were inadequate to cover operating losses), the Act provided that the Government would issue non-interest bearing promissory notes to the Bank to rectify the position. These notes would be redeemed from future operating surpluses.

The Act also established a Special Reserve, which was renamed in 1987 as the Revaluation Reserve, to which any capital gains or losses, arising in any financial year purely from changes in the rate of exchange between the Pula and foreign currencies, were to be credited or debited. An amount equal to ten percent of the year-end balance standing to the credit of the Special Reserve was to be transferred to the Botswana Government. This provision was intended to avoid a situation in which the Government would enjoy windfall profits from any large devaluation of the Pula, resulting in a significant nominal increase in Botswana's foreign exchange reserves. The Special Reserve was also established as the first line of defence if losses were incurred arising out of revaluations or other appreciations of the Pula. Since the Pula was expected to depreciate against the United States Dollar and other hard currencies in which Botswana's reserves were likely to be invested, causing the Special Reserve to keep increasing, it was considered that the annual transfer to the Government of ten percent of the Special Reserve would smooth out the flow of these payments to the Government, spreading the impact on Government revenues over a period long enough to discourage devaluation of the Pula for fiscal purposes, while leaving a cushion to absorb possible future revaluation losses.

In the event, the Bank has never experienced an operating loss. Contrary to expectations, Botswana's reserves, thanks largely to the popularity of the new currency and the successful conversion from Rand to Pula, rose quickly to quite comfortable levels. By the end of 1976, the reserves stood at P65 million, equal to about four months' worth of imports of goods and services. The Bank recorded an operating surplus of P215 900 in its first full year of operations, while incurring recurrent expenditures of P292 325, and paid P107 950 to the Government, the balance being credited to the General Reserve.

After that propitious start, the Bank made steady financial progress, despite rapidly increasing costs as interest on Treasury Bills and on commercial banks' call account deposits rose sharply. Botswana's reserves continued to grow at a modest, but satisfactory rate from 1976 onwards, notwithstanding a 5% revaluation of the Pula against the United States Dollar in April 1977. By the end of 1979, the General Reserve, having benefited from the receipt of 50% of the Bank's annual operating surpluses since 1975, had grown to P8.6 million, exceeding the Bank's authorised capital of P5 million for the first time.

Thereafter the Government's share of the Bank's operating profit should have increased to 80%, in accordance with Section 7 of the Act. However, the revaluation of the Pula by five percent against the United States Dollar on 13 September 1979, resulted in an immediate revaluation loss of P11.7 million. This loss exceeded the accumulated balance of P9.7 million, standing to the credit of the Special Reserve at the end of 1978, and made it necessary for the Government to issue non-interest bearing notes to the Bank for the first time, to cover the shortfall. Revaluation gains in the months following the 1979 devaluation enabled the Bank to redeem the notes and to end that financial year with a small positive balance of P41 196 on the Special Reserve.

Another revaluation of the Pula on 6 November 1980, had more serious financial repercussions for the Bank and the Botswana Government. While a large operating surplus of almost P22 million was recorded that year – 77% higher than in the previous year – a revaluation loss of P26.5 million occurred. The loss was far greater than the balance brought forward on the Special Reserve, and also exceeded the share of the operating surplus for the year to which the Government was entitled, now 80%. In accordance with Section 34 of the Act, the Government had to forego receipt of its share of the Bank's operating profits that year, the proceeds being applied to the reduction of the deficit on the Special Reserve account. Non-interest bearing Government promissory notes had to be issued again, in an amount of P6.7 million, to cover the remaining loss on the Special Reserve. It was only in 1981 that the remaining promissory notes were redeemed and the financial relationship with the Government returned to normal.

Valuable lessons were learned from the Bank's experiences in these two early years about the impact of domestic monetary policy decisions on the Bank's balance sheet. Revaluation losses occurred again in 1986 (P9.9 million), 1989 (P284 million) and in 1993 (P7 million), but by then the Special (or Revaluation) Reserve was more than adequate to absorb the losses. It stood at P330 million at the end of 1986. Renamed the Revaluation Reserve, it rose to P415 million by the end of 1989. From 1990 to 1991, it nearly doubled, exceeding P1 billion for the first time.

Botswana's foreign exchange reserves continued to rise in 1979 and 1980 to levels equivalent to almost six months' worth of imports of goods and services, before falling back slightly in 1981, when Botswana experienced its first mini-recession since Independence. But the new Jwaneng diamond mine was about to come into full production, and the economic boom started in earnest in 1984. By then, the Bank's operating surplus had reached P30 million on reserves of P457 million, equal to almost seven months' worth of imports of goods and services. In 1984, the reserves climbed to P737 million, generating profits of almost P54 million for the Bank. The position in 1985 was even more spectacular. Foreign exchange reserves more than doubled to P1.6 billion in that year, representing more than 17 months' worth of imports of goods and services, and the Bank's profits exceeded P100 million for the first time.

By 1985 the Bank's General Reserve, having continued to receive 10% of the operating surplus each year, had risen to almost P35 million, the Special Reserve to P422 million. Within ten years, thanks to Botswana's superlative economic performance, the Bank had achieved a strong financial position, and no longer needed to transfer as much as 10% of its operating surpluses to the General Reserve to cover possible operating losses in the future. Accordingly, the Bank of Botswana Act was amended in 1987 to increase the proportion of the Bank's net income accruing to the Botswana Government to 95%. The opportunity was also taken to make a number of other changes to the Act.[17]

The Bank's operating profits, and its contribution to Government revenues, rose substantially each year from 1984 until 1994, when international capital markets experienced an exceptionally turbulent and bad year. Both equity and bond markets

---

[17] The Bank of Botswana (Amendment) Act, 1987 (No.12 of 1987).

performed poorly that year. This resulted in a major decline in the Bank's net investment income, from P940 million in 1993 to P161 million in 1994, the lowest level in a decade. Due to its entitlement to 10% of the Revaluation Reserve, as well as to 95% of the net income, the Government received P451 million in 1994, thanks largely to a transfer of P298 million from the Revaluation Reserve. The balance of P153 million represented the Government's share of the much diminished operating surplus.

Although the Bank's fortunes rebounded in 1995, when profits of P750 million were realised and the Bank's contribution to Government exceeded P1 billion once more, two more salutary lessons had been learnt. It was apparent, first, that income from the investment of Botswana's foreign exchange reserves was much more volatile than previously recognised and that operating losses could actually occur, despite high reserve levels. The Bank's annual payments to the Government, by then a significant share of total Government revenues, were therefore not a stable and predictable source of revenues. Transfers from the Revaluation Reserve served a valuable purpose for the Government, supplementing its share of operating income in years when net income fell, or operating losses were sustained. Secondly, the Bank's General Reserve needed to be sufficiently large to absorb possible operating losses. Operating income was not closely correlated with reserve levels every year.

The Bank's annual budget has lagged behind the growth of foreign exchange reserves by a significant margin. The principal reason for the relatively modest increase in annual expenditures has been the impact on the Bank of the Government's incomes policy. Introduced in 1972 and modified in 1990, it not only constrained the escalation of salaries and wages throughout the country, but it also required parastatals, among them the Bank of Botswana, to align their pay scales with those applicable to the Public Service, rather than with the salaries and wages paid by private firms in the relevant comparable industry or sector. Since staff costs have comprised a significant part of the Bank's recurrent expenditures, and increases in salary and wage levels have not been allowed to rise in real terms, the increase in the Bank's annual budgeted expenditures has not been commensurate with the expansion of its assets or liabilities, or with the operational demands placed upon it over the years. A high vacancy rate, to which the uncompetitiveness of the Bank's staff compensation levels has contributed, has also affected expenditure performance.

The introduction, in 1991, of Bank of Botswana Certificates and the termination of the Bank's overnight call account facility had a significant impact on the Bank's financial position. Whereas the cost to the Bank of maintaining the call accounts for the banks had been restrained by the artificially low interest rate paid (i.e., 3.5% from 1978 to 1988) and the lower level of excess liquidity in the banking sector for most of that period, the interest paid on Bank of Botswana Certificates was appreciably higher, reflecting market conditions. While the average annual interest payments by the Bank on overnight call accounts averaged less than P25 million before 1991, the interest paid on Bank of Botswana Certificates soared to P126.0 million in 1992, P142.0 million in 1993, P162.5 million in 1994, and P198.5 million in 1995.

In accordance with Section 55 (2) of the Bank of Botswana Act, the Bank's accounts are audited not by the Auditor General, but by auditors appointed annually by the Board, with the approval of the Minister of Finance. A prominent firm of regional chartered auditors, Pim Whitely and Close, was appointed as the Bank's auditors in 1976. By 1982, the name of the firm had changed to Pim Goldby. It was decided in 1985 to use the services of two firms of auditors to ensure that the Bank would have access to the necessary specialist expertise to review all aspects of its accounts and increasingly complex financial operations, and that, by rotating audit assignments every two years, there would be greater continuity and depth of understanding of the Bank's systems and activities. Price Waterhouse was selected as the second external auditor firm by virtue of its extensive international experience in auditing banks and other financial institutions. The 1986 audit was the first to be undertaken jointly. In 1991, Pim Goldby merged with the international firm of certified public auditors, Deloitte, Haskins and Sells, to become Deloitte Pim Goldby, which in turn became Deloitte and Touche in 1992, following another merger of accounting firms.

Notwithstanding the complexity of the Bank's finances, and the fact that most parastatals have four months in which to submit their annual report and audited accounts to the Government, the Bank has succeeded, in every year of its existence, in complying with the stringent financial requirements of the Act. These stipulate that the Bank's accounts must be audited and submitted to the Minister of Finance and Development Planning within three months of the end of each financial year. The Bank has never received a qualified audit, nor has the Minister found it necessary to request the Auditor General of the Botswana Government to examine and report on any aspect of the Bank's accounts.

Currency management

As indicated in the description of the events leading up to Pula Day, the introduction of the national currency in 1976 was remarkably successful. For the first two weeks, the currency exchange was restricted to bank notes in order to reduce the delays and congestion at designated currency exchange centres. The denominations available were the P1, P2, P5 and P10 notes. The introduction of the P20 notes was delayed until March 1978. Coins were issued to the banks on 6 September 1976, initially the 1t, 2t, 5t, 10t and 25t coins only, followed shortly by the 50t and P1 coins. The shipment of Rand notes and coins to the Reserve Bank of South Africa was undertaken by the commercial banks, on the Bank's behalf. The Rand ceased to enjoy legal tender status in Botswana on 23 August 1976, but Rand notes and coins continued to be exchanged without commission until 30 November 1976.

No major changes occurred with respect to the management of the national currency until 1980 when the President, Sir Seretse Khama, died. A minor controversy then arose about the notes. Although the Bank of Botswana Act is silent on this point, many people considered that Sir Seretse Khama's image should feature permanently on Botswana's bank notes, symbolising his role as 'the founder and first President of the nation'. However, the Government resolved that bank notes should always feature a portrait of the current President. Thereafter, a new series of notes was produced, bearing the portrait of the new President.

Ten years passed without any changes being made to the national currency, but by the mid-1980s inflation had greatly reduced the purchasing power of the currency, necessitating the introduction of a higher denomination note. Ever since a local currency had been introduced, Thomas De La Rue and Company Ltd., and the British Royal Mint had produced Botswana's notes and coins, respectively. The need to issue a P50 note prompted the Bank to test market conditions. It invited reputable security printers from around the world to submit designs for the note and quotations for its manufacture and supply. The lowest tender was submitted by Fidelity Printers of

Zimbabwe, a subsidiary of the Reserve Bank of Zimbabwe. The order for the initial stock of P50 notes was placed with that firm at a cost per note significantly lower than that previously charged by De La Rue for the smaller denomination notes, despite the inclusion of additional security features.

Thereafter, the Bank not only invited competitive proposals for the design and manufacture of new and replacement bank notes, but it also retained ownership of the plates used for the printing of bank notes in order to eliminate the duplication of origination costs every time a new firm of security printers was awarded a contract. Although Thomas De La Rue and Company, Ltd., did subsequently succeed in winning back some business with the Bank, including the design and supply of the P100 note, orders have also been placed over the past ten years for the supply of replacements notes with Harrison and Sons of the United Kingdom and the American Bank note Company, all through a competitive tendering process.

Competitive tendering was also used to select suppliers of new or replacement coins. In 1991, the Royal Mint of Canada was awarded a contract for the supply of 1t coins, after bids had been received from many mints, but, apart from this one contract, the British Royal Mint has succeeded in winning all the orders for Botswana's circulation coins since 1975.

The gradual depreciation in the value of the currency resulted not only in the introduction of higher denomination notes, but also shifted the economic note/coin frontier. In recognition of this development, the Bank submitted proposals to the Minister of Finance and Development Planning in 1991 for other changes in the national currency. These were approved, with one exception. The Bank had recommended the demonetization of the 1t coin which, by then, had virtually no value, and cost appreciably more to produce and deliver than its face value. Due to the insignificant value and unpopularity of this coin with the public, the Bank's stocks of 1t coins tended to be quickly depleted after each replenishment as nobody bothered to return surplus holdings of these coins to the commercial banks, but rather threw them away. Fearing the possible price-raising effect if the lowest coin denomination were removed, the Minister decided that the 1t coin should be left in circulation and should continue to enjoy legal tender status indefinitely, but he agreed that the Bank should not replenish its holdings of 1t coins after the existing stocks were exhausted.

Among the other changes approved at that time were the introduction of a new seven-sided nickel-brass P1 coin to replace the original scalloped cupro-nickel P1 coin. This was planned as the lowest denomination coin in a new series of higher value coins, which would ultimately include P2 and P5 coins. Also approved by the Minister were the demonetization of 2t coins, and the introduction of P100 notes. The old P1 and 2t coins ceased to be legal tender on 30 November 1991. The new P1 coin entered circulation on the same day. P100 notes were introduced on 23 August 1993; and the new P2 coins were released on 1 August 1994. To the surprise of the Bank, 1t coins started re-appearing in circulation after it was announced that no additional supplies of this coin would be procured by the Bank. The Bank was also surprised by the speed with which the P100 notes displaced the P50 notes, large quantities of which were returned to the Bank through the commercial banks. Planning for a further major recoinage exercise commenced in 1995.

One of the reasons for constructing a branch of the Bank in Francistown was to provide a second vault in which currency stocks could be held, and to reduce the movement of notes and coin between the northern and the southern parts of the country. It would also stand the Bank in good stead if, for any reason, access to the main vault in Gaborone were restricted.

Figure 4 shows how the volume of notes and coins in circulation has expanded over the past 21 years, at a rate slightly lower than the annual rate of inflation. The rate of growth was somewhat lower during the period 1975 to 1985, despite the novelty of having a national currency and the continuing monetization of the economy, but it accelerated from 1985. It would appear that average holding of currency per household has fallen slightly from around P110 in 1975 to P90 in 1995. This may have been due to the escalating incidence of crime, the greater outreach of, and easier access to, commercial banking services, and heightened competition between the commercial banks, resulting in efforts to keep their holdings of cash to a minimum.

FIGURE 4. VALUE OF NOTES AND COINS ISSUED, 1976 TO 1996

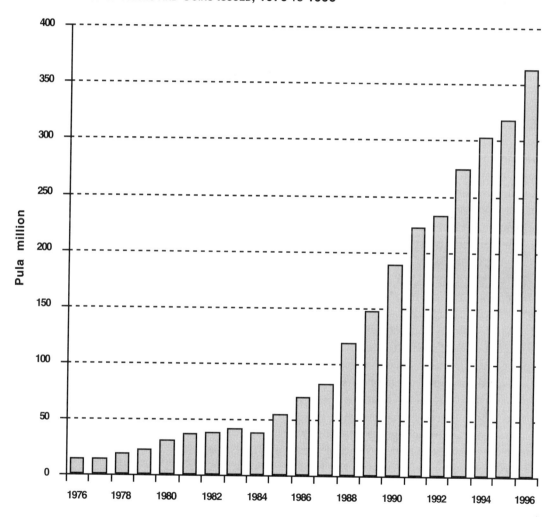

In addition to acquiring and issuing circulation notes and coins, the Bank has also produced proof and commemorative coins from time to time, primarily for commercial sale to coin dealers and numismatists. Although the Government had issued a special 50 Cent coin to celebrate Botswana's Independence in 1966, the first series of

Pula-denominated proof coins was issued by the Bank to commemorate the Tenth Anniversary of Botswana's Independence. Each subsequent commemorative coin, or series of coins, was produced in collaboration with some international sponsor, such as UNICEF or the World Wildlife Fund. However, since 1989 the Bank has declined to commission the production of any more commemorative coins, unless specifically requested to do so by the Botswana Government, as the benefits to Botswana and the Bank are negligible, while the costs, in terms of the distraction of the management of the Bank from other more important duties, are considerable.

Property developments

The cluster of buildings and facilities in Gaborone, constructed between 1975 and 1977, were adequate for the Bank's needs until the early 1980s when staff increases were necessary to enable the Bank to cope with the demands placed on its services by the rapidly expanding economy. A new four-storey office block was constructed in 1984 at a cost of P3.5 million. It was opened by the President on 1 July 1985, commemorating the Bank's tenth anniversary.

Because the additional office space was now in excess of the Bank's immediate needs, the three lower floors of the new office block were leased out to the Government and to two international organizations, the United Nations High Commission for Refugees and the United Nations Special Representative for Namibia. This proved to be a mistake. When the Bank wished to use the floor occupied by the two United Nations organizations, they refused to leave, claiming diplomatic privilege. It was not until 1989 that alternative accommodation could be found for them elsewhere in Gaborone. The Ministry of Mineral Resources and Water Affairs continued to occupy the two lower floors of this building (now referred to as the Research Block) until it relocated to new offices elsewhere in the Government Enclave in mid-1997.

The unavailability of three floors in the Research Block caused considerable congestion in the Bank as staff numbers continued to grow in the late 1980s and early 1990s. The decision was accordingly taken by the Board in 1989 to construct another office block to accommodate Departments whose ability to carry out their responsibilities was being adversely affected by the overcrowding of available offices. The new five-storey block, subsequently named the Governor's Block, was completed in 1992, at a cost of P12 million, inclusive of office furniture and equipment. It was officially opened by the new Vice President and Minister of Finance and Development Planning, and former Governor of the Bank, Mr F.G. Mogae, on 13 February 1993. The opportunity was taken to install a new automated access control system in the new office block, intended to enhance the security of the Bank.

The original buildings, particularly the banking hall, high security area and first office block, were badly in need of renovation by that time. The refurbishment of the original office block, renamed the Finance Block, was completed in 1994. It included the conversion of offices on two floors at the western end of the building into a staff cafeteria, which opened for staff use on 1 July 1995. A bulk store and underground parking facility were also constructed at this time. Work on the renovation of the other facilities was continuing, somewhat unsatisfactorily, at the end of 1996.

Although Bank staff have no entitlement to housing, some institutional housing has been provided over the years. When Mr C.N. Kikonyogo was appointed as Governor in January 1982, a house on a large plot close to the Bank was bought to serve as the official Governor's Residence. Land was also purchased in Gaborone West on which to build institutional accommodation for members of the Security Cadre. Forty-one medium cost housing units were constructed on this site in 1984, and another eighteen units were added in 1994.

The acute shortage of housing in Gaborone in the late 1980s placed the Bank in a difficult predicament. The unavailability or unaffordability of rental accommodation not only affected staff morale, but also led to the resignation of staff if other jobs were offered, with housing provided. Under the circumstances, the Board agreed that the Bank should acquire some institutional housing for staff to rent. A 2.25 hectare plot was allocated to the Bank in Gaborone West on which a mixture of high, medium and low-medium cost housing units was constructed in 1992. Lefika Court, as this estate was named, also provides recreational facilities and enjoys 24-hour security protection. Staff allocated housing units at Lefika Court pay BHC-based rentals for their units.

An institutional house for the Deputy Governor was constructed in 1991, also close to the Bank. A suitable plot had been identified by the end of 1995 on which to construct a second Deputy Governor's residence in anticipation of that post being created following the enactment of the new Bank of Botswana Act.

These property developments in Gaborone were overshadowed by the construction of a branch of the Bank in Francistown to serve the needs of Government agencies and the branches of commercial banks in the northern part of Botswana. The Board's authority had been obtained in 1985 to acquire a suitable plot for this purpose. Many years passed before land was finally allocated to the Bank for the branch in 1989, located at the intersection of the main north-south highway and the road to Maun, opposite the Thapama Lodge Hotel. More time elapsed before the necessary building and town planning approvals were granted, and architects could be appointed. Construction started in March 1993. The Francistown Branch was handed over to the Bank on 24 May 1995, and banking operations commenced on 10 July 1995.

Institutional housing was required for the staff transferred to run the Francistown branch. Construction of a complex of five high cost housing units was completed in February 1993 to be used by the more senior staff and a large plot further out of town was acquired and developed as a high density housing estate, similar to Lefika Court in Gaborone. This housing estate, named Galabgwe Court, was ready for occupation in April 1995. It also provides some recreational facilities for the staff working in the Branch, and a guest house for Board members and staff visiting Francistown. The total cost to the Bank of constructing the Francistown Branch and ancillary housing is likely to amount to P47.4 million.

4. MONETARY POLICY, AGENCY, AND FINANCIAL SECTOR RESPONSIBILITIES

By far the most important of the Bank's statutory responsibilities is to maintain monetary stability. The Bank monitors trends in the domestic, regional and global economies and ensures that the monetary policies implemented by it are conducive to sustained economic growth. The main instruments at the disposal of the Bank for this purpose are the exchange rate, interest rates and control of the money supply.

Exchange rate

As indicated above, the principal reason for withdrawing from the Rand Monetary Area was to enable the Botswana authorities to exercise greater control over the domestic economy. The ability to determine the external value of the Pula is a central aspect of monetary policy. Over the past 21 years the Bank has attempted, with varying degrees of success, to balance the need to maintain the competitiveness of the Botswana economy with the need to constrain the domestic impact of imported inflation.

It did not take long after the establishment of the Bank and the introduction of a national currency for Botswana to exercise its newly acquired monetary independence. The rate of exchange between the Pula and the Rand had been fixed on Pula Day at R1 = P1, and the public had been assured that this rate would not change during the following 100-day currency exchange period. No guarantees had been given regarding the rate of the Pula after 30 November 1976. Indeed, the public was warned that exchange rate changes could occur after the expiry of the initial currency exchange period.

The Pula was, in fact, not directly linked to the Rand at the outset. It was officially pegged to the United States Dollar at a rate (i.e., P1 = US$1.15) which would yield the desired parity with the Rand. This was not difficult to achieve as the Rand was also pegged at that time to the US Dollar, at the same rate of exchange. On 30 April 1977, less than a year after Botswana had left the Rand Monetary Area, the Pula was revalued by 5% against the US Dollar to produce a central rate of P1 = US$1.2075, and a cross-rate with the Rand of P1 = R1.05.

This decision was taken more for strategic and psychological, than for economic reasons. The currency exchange had gone better than anticipated, and the level of Botswana's foreign exchange reserves was continuing to rise, providing an early opportunity to demonstrate that, contrary to the gloomy warnings of international organizations and the business community, the Pula would not necessarily be the weak currency which they had predicted. There were two other objectives. The revaluation was intended to send a message to those people who had transferred their funds to South Africa before Pula Day, and had opened accounts there, in the expectation that the Pula would be a weak and unstable currency. It was also hoped that the small appreciation of the Pula would soften the impact of imported inflation and benefit consumers by making the costs of imported goods and services slightly cheaper in Pula terms.

The revaluation was greeted with disbelief in South Africa. The Governor of the South African Reserve Bank, Dr T. De Jongh, who had advised so strongly against Botswana's withdrawal from the Rand Monetary Area, was speechless when he was informed, as a courtesy, by the Governor of the Bank of Botswana. The IMF also expressed surprise when it was officially notified of the change.

While the first revaluation had the desired effect of instilling some confidence in the Pula and encouraging the transfer back to Botswana of funds previously removed to South Africa, it caused confusion and concern among some groups in Botswana. Batswana working in the mines or on farms in South Africa were upset when their earnings, remitted to Botswana, produced less in local currency than they had expected to receive at the end of their employment contracts.

In 1979, when the Rand was floated, the Pula remained pegged to the US Dollar and therefore experienced some volatility as the Rand fluctuated against the US Dollar. To maintain a more stable relationship with the Rand, the peg with the US Dollar was dropped in June 1980, in favour of pegging to a basket of currencies consisting of Rand and the IMF's composite unit of account, Special Drawing Rights (SDRs). Although the composition of the currencies in the basket, and their relative weights, have been adjusted since then, notably in 1984, 1986 and 1994, the external value of the Pula has been determined in relation to a trade-weighted basket of currencies ever since.

In order to relieve domestic consumers, whose real incomes were being undermined by imported inflation, the Pula was revalued, by a further 5%, on 14 September 1979, and again by 5% on 7 November 1980. This trend had to be reversed abruptly when Botswana faced its first major economic crisis since Independence, resulting from the slump in diamond sales in 1981 and 1982. As part of a package of adjustment measures introduced by the Government and the Bank at that time to rebalance the economy, the Pula was devalued by 10% on 6 May 1982, falling below one US Dollar for the first time since the currency was introduced. Further devaluations, by 5% on 7 July 1984 and 15% on 9 January 1985, were considered necessary to compensate for the continuing appreciation of the Pula against the Rand during a period when the Rand was depreciating rapidly against the US Dollar. The decline in the external value of the Rand exacerbated the domestically induced inflationary pressures in South Africa, resulting in high rates of inflation in Southern Africa throughout the 1980s.

In an effort to mitigate the impact of imported inflation on domestic prices, the Bank turned again to the exchange rate, adjusting the Pula upward by 5% in June 1989. However, in the absence of other supporting macroeconomic measures, the effects of the revaluation were quickly erased, and the experiment was reversed in August 1990 by means of a 5% devaluation. With the Pula continuing to appreciate marginally against the Rand, due to the influence of the stronger non-Rand currencies in the basket, the Pula was devalued again in August 1991 by 5% in an effort to restore Botswana's competitiveness.

Despite the exchange rate adjustments made from time to time by the Bank of Botswana either to maintain Botswana's export competitiveness or to mitigate the impact on domestic prices for imported inflation, the real effective rate of exchange between the Pula and the Rand, the currency of the source of approximately eighty percent of Botswana's imports, has remained remarkably stable since 1986. The Bank learnt from experience that the effects of discrete revaluations or devaluations of the Pula, other than those justified by divergent rates of inflation, tended to be short-lived. In recent years, the policy of the Bank of Botswana has been to maintain a stable real exchange rate with the Rand in the hope that this will lead to the convergence of inflation rates, and encourage investment in non-traditional export industries and economic diversification.

Interest rates

The Bank of Botswana's interest rate policies have also changed over the years. Its initial approach was to try to keep commercial bank and other lending rates low by holding down the central bank call rate, as well as by direct regulation of commercial bank interest rates.

As indicated above, an overnight call account facility had been introduced in 1976 at the request of the two commercial banks to enable them to earn some interest on the excess liquidity in the system, previously easily absorbed by the money market in South Africa. The interest rate for call deposits at the Bank was set, somewhat arbitrarily, at 6.0% in 1976. It was reduced to 4.5% in 1977 and again to 3.5% in 1978. It was to remain at that level for the next ten years. Since the commercial banks continued to experience rising levels of excess liquidity throughout this period, and did not need to borrow from the Bank, the Bank's call rate, rather than the Bank Rate, which was adjusted periodically, assumed greater importance in determining the structure of domestic interest rates.

Not only was the call rate held constant at a level well below the prevailing rate of inflation, but the Bank attempted to control all interest rates by direct intervention. Using the powers conferred on it by the Bank of Botswana Act and the Financial Institutions Act, the Bank imposed ceilings on commercial bank lending rates and floors on deposit rates. The Bank required that all interest rate changes, as well as all bank fees and charges, should be approved by it. This policy reflected the political view then prevailing that a regime of low interest rates was a necessary prerequisite to investment and economic growth, and that exchange controls would be effective in preventing the outflow of domestic savings to money and capital markets offering higher returns.

Both assumptions were false. Botswana's economic boom, which commenced in earnest in 1984, was based on rapidly expanding mineral exports, and the recycling of diamond revenues, through the Government budget, into other economic activities. Low interest rates were not a significant contributory factor. Indeed, the Government itself had become by far the largest source of loan funds through the Public Debt Service Fund and the Revenue Stabilization Fund. It was also an illusion to believe that exchange controls were effective in preventing funds from crossing borders. The balance of payments statistics for that period reveal large balancing items – listed as errors and omissions – which probably represented unauthorised transfers of funds out of Botswana for which exchange control approval had not been obtained. As is commonly found throughout the world, exchange controls were far from fully effective in stemming the outflow of funds at a time when real interest rates in Botswana were below those obtainable elsewhere.

The banks became highly profitable during the 1980s. They reacted to the controls on interest rates by declining to accept large deposits, and they maintained interest rates for deposits which were heavily negative in real terms. This discouraged savings and contributed to the poor savings performance of the household sector, which has continued to this day. It also led to the liberal extension of credit to households and firms, often for unproductive purposes, at a rapidly expanding and ultimately unsustainable rate.

It was not until 1989 that the Bank abandoned the low interest rate policy and allowed market forces to play a greater role in determining the level of interest rates. The Bank then set itself the objective of maintaining moderately positive real interest rates to encourage saving and to ensure that loans were channelled primarily for productive purposes. Interest rate ceilings and floors were scrapped. The commercial banks were allowed to set their own interest rates and bank charges and commissions. The call rate was raised to 6.0% in 1989 and increased to 7.5% in 1990, in preparation for the introduction of Bank of Botswana Certificates in 1991, and the commencement of open market operations.

Since 1991, the level of interest rates has been influenced more by the bids received through the periodic auctions of Bank of Botswana Certificates and through adjustments to the Bank Rate, than through the intervention of the Bank. Although the level of all interest rates rose after 1991, and lending rates became increasingly positive in real terms, most deposit rates remained below the rate of inflation. Under these circumstances, the liberalization and ultimate removal of exchange controls could lead to an outflow of domestic savings, particularly if deposit rates in South Africa remain among the highest in the world in real terms.

Money supply and credit control

The third instrument of monetary policy, namely direct control of the money supply and bank credit, has not been used by the Bank to any great extent. Except for one relatively short period in 1982, when ceilings were imposed by the Bank on the level of credit which the banks could extend, as part of the package of measures introduced to address the balance of payments and budgetary problems occasioned by the downturn in the diamond market, the Bank has not restricted the growth of the money supply, nor has it attempted to curtail credit expansion through changes in the primary reserve or liquid asset requirements. The main argument for pursuing a liberal monetary policy has been that the potential inflationary impact of rapid increases in the money supply is largely neutralised by Botswana's open economy and its membership in the Southern African Customs Union.

With the benefit of hindsight, greater use should probably have been made of the Bank's regulatory powers to curtail the rapid expansion of bank credit which occurred between 1987 and 1992, at annual rates in excess of 30% (including a 55% growth rate in 1990). This unsustainable expansion of credit, particularly to the household sector, not only exacerbated inflationary pressures in the economy, but also created severe problems for both the borrowers and the banks after the boom ended abruptly in 1992.

Administration of exchange controls

It is common practice around the world, where foreign exchange transactions are regulated, for central banks to be charged with responsibility for the administration of exchange controls on behalf of their governments. This approach was also adopted in Botswana following the promulgation of the Exchange Control Act, 1975. Prior to 1975, applications requiring exchange control approval were forwarded by the branches of the banks operating in Botswana to the Reserve Bank of South Africa.

In accordance with the provisions of the Act, the commercial banks were appointed as Authorised Dealers in foreign exchange to whom all residents had to sell any foreign exchange received by them, and from whom foreign exchange could be acquired. One of the first acts of the Bank of Botswana was, therefore, to prepare regulations, for approval by the Minister of Finance and Development Planning under the Act, and a manual of rules for Authorised Dealers.

In terms of the regulations and the manual, commercial banks were free to buy and sell foreign exchange from their customers, without reference to the Bank of Botswana, for all transactions specified as falling within the limits of their delegated powers, provided that the necessary forms were completed. These forms constituted one of the main sources of information, along with data on imports and exports collected by the Customs and Excise Department, for the compilation of balance of payments statistics.

As Botswana had been designated by the IMF as an Article XIV country since Independence, entitling it to impose restrictions of current transactions (i.e., payments for imported goods and services, foreign travel, remittances of one kind and another, dividends, interest payments, etc.), the ambit of Botswana's exchange controls was initially very wide. Virtually every kind of transaction, involving either payments in foreign exchange, or obligations which could result in future claims against Botswana's foreign exchange reserves, covering capital as well as current transactions, was regulated under the exchange control regulations and manual. For many classes of transactions, such as payments for verified imports, and remittance of interest or dividends to foreign lenders or shareholders, authority was delegated to the Authorised Dealers, within specified limits, to approve and process the payments without prior reference to the Bank. For other types of transactions, such as those falling outside the delegated authority of the commercial banks, or involving capital transactions, applications were to be forwarded to the Bank of Botswana. For most of these transactions, the final approval lay with the Bank; for others, the authority of the Ministry of Finance and Development Planning had to be obtained. Nevertheless, by comparison with most other African countries, Botswana's exchange controls were always relatively liberal.

Although exchange controls had become increasingly redundant during the boom years, when Botswana's foreign exchange reserves escalated to levels well in excess of those forecast when Botswana left the RMA, the policy regime was sufficiently liberal that compliance with exchange controls was not perceived as a serious impediment to investment and economic growth. As is so often the case with regulatory controls, exchange controls remained in force in Botswana long after their original rationale had disappeared.

By the early 1990s, when economic growth had started to slow down and unemployment had started to rise, exchange controls became more widely perceived as an obstacle to business efficiency and a disincentive to foreign investment. The administration of exchange controls was, by then, preoccupying a large number of administrators, in the commercial banks as well as in the Bank. Although some minor changes had been made over the years, designed to facilitate foreign exchange transactions, all capital transactions remained tightly regulated and most current transactions were subject to annual allowances or limits. Botswana retained its IMF Article XIV status, even after other African countries had started to remove exchange controls and to accept the obligations of IMF Article VIII, which proscribes restrictions on current transactions.

As early as 1988, the Bank itself had started submitting proposals to the Government, recommending the progressive liberalization and ultimate abolition of exchange controls. However, it was not until the business community began lobbying for the immediate abolition of exchange controls that the Government's stance changed. One of the major recommendations to emanate from the Second Francistown Private Sector Conference, held in Francistown in September 1991, was that exchange controls should be dismantled within a pre-determined time frame. To support this recommendation, the Botswana Confederation of Commerce, Industry and Manpower (BOCCIM) then commissioned a team of consultants to examine the advantages and disadvantages of maintaining exchange controls. The consultant's report, endorsed by BOCCIM and submitted to the Government in October 1993, made a persuasive case for the abolition of exchange controls. In his 1995 Budget Speech, the Vice President announced a package of additional exchange control liberalization, including allowances for outward capital investment, but stopped short of committing the Government to total abolition.

The approval of the Ministry of Finance and Development Planning was secured shortly thereafter in 1995 for a series of amendments to the exchange control manual, making it generally easier for residents to acquire foreign exchange, and introducing annual capital allowances for external investment for the first time, available to both individuals and firms. As anticipated by the Bank, these long overdue reforms, while welcomed by the public, had no perceptible effect on the volume of foreign exchange transactions or the level of Botswana's reserves. However, they did have an immediate impact on the commercial banks and the Bank itself by reducing the burden of exchange control administration. In the expectation that this trend would continue, the Bank combined the Exchange Control Department and the Banking Supervision Department in April 1994, to form the Financial Institutions Department. This change was intended to strengthen the Bank's supervisory capabilities, in anticipation of the expansion and diversification of the financial sector, and to avoid the retrenchment of staff. Exchange control staff were already familiar with the banks and with banking transactions, and could be employed relatively easily on banking supervision duties.

Botswana finally accepted the obligations of Article VIII of the IMF Articles of Agreement with effect from 17 November 1995. Although all foreign exchange transactions remain subject to controls, administered by the Bank, many have in practice been removed and it is expected that remaining exchange controls will be phased out.

Financial sector responsibilities

Another important part of the Bank's agency responsibilities is to license, regulate, and supervise banks and other financial institutions. In this area, too, the Bank's policies have changed over the years.

At the time of the Bank's establishment, the financial sector comprised two privately owned commercial banks, and four other specialist parastatal financial institutions which were owned by, or heavily dependent for funding on the Botswana Government, namely the National Development Bank (NDB), the Botswana Building Society, the Botswana Savings Bank (previously the Post Office Savings Bank), and the Botswana Cooperative Bank. A credit institution, namely Financial Services Company (Botswana) Pty. Ltd., (FSC), jointly owned by the Botswana Development Corporation and the NDB, had been established earlier but was only licensed by the Bank in August 1984.

During the late 1970s and for most of the 1980s, the Bank adopted a highly protective and regulatory stance towards the domestic banking system. Although a new licence was issued in August 1982 to a third private commercial bank, the Bank for Credit and Commerce (Botswana) Limited (BCCB), a wholly owned subsidiary of the now infamous Luxembourg-registered BCCI, the Bank of Botswana continued to restrict competition within the banking sector by discouraging other international banks, as well as local syndicates, from applying for banking licences. It considered that Botswana was already over banked.

The Bank abandoned this restrictive approach in 1987, introducing a new market-oriented licensing policy, predicated on the belief that it was not the proper business of a central bank to determine how much or how little competition should occur in the banking sector. The new policy sought to stimulate competition between financial institutions within a deregulated environment. It provided that banking licences would be issued to any bank or group of investors, foreign or local, which met certain minimum conditions. Among the specified conditions were higher minimum initial capital requirements, the availability of additional capital to be provided immediately if circumstances required, proven managerial capabilities and 'depth', and the provision of retail banking services through a reasonable number of branches or agencies outside Gaborone.

This change in philosophy was endorsed by the World Bank and the International Finance Corporation who had assisted the Bank and the Government to conduct a comprehensive review of Botswana's financial system. The resulting 1989 study recommended, *inter alia*, the progressive curtailment of the Government's provision of loan finance to statutory corporations and other governmental bodies through the Public Debt Service Fund and the Revenue Stabilization Fund; the promotion of the development of money and capital markets; a review of the mandates, operations and viability of development finance institutions, such as the NDB, the Botswana Cooperative Bank and the Botswana Building Society; and the promotion of competition within the banking sector generally. Most of the recommendations of the 1989 study were accepted by the Botswana Government and constituted the framework for subsequent financial sector reforms.

The new policies adopted by the Bank produced early results. Zimbank (Botswana) Limited, a subsidiary of Zimbank Holdings (Zimbabwe) Limited, was granted a banking licence under the Financial Institutions Act in December 1989 and opened for business on 17 May 1990. Another licence was issued in 1989, also to a Zimbabwe-based group, to establish a second credit institution, to be called ulc (Pty) Limited, specialising in the provision of leasing and hire purchase facilities. It commenced operations in March 1990, in competition with the FSC.

This was the beginning of a period of rapid change, restructuring and modernization of the financial sector. First National Bank Botswana Limited (FNBB), a wholly owned subsidiary of First National Bank of South Africa (which had taken over Barclays Bank in South Africa), was the next bank to receive a licence, in 1990. It started operations on 8 September 1991, after acquiring the assets and liabilities of BCCB. Two other banks were licensed during 1991. They were UnionBank Botswana Limited, a subsidiary of Standard Bank of South Africa, and ANZ Grindlays, a subsidiary of an Australian bank of the same name. These two new banks opened in 1992, raising the total number of licensed financial institutions to six commercial banks and two credit institutions.

The need to take over the management of BCCB in 1991 provided the Bank of Botswana with the opportunity to demonstrate its capabilities as a banking supervisor and regulator. After its parent bank, BCCI, had been closed by the Bank of England, the staff of the Banking Supervision Department, augmented by experienced Bank staff from other Departments, effectively ran all of the branches of BCCB from 5 July to 7 September 1991, ensuring that customers had access to their accounts and that the bank remained solvent and functional. This not only facilitated the take-over of BCCB by FNBB, but earned the Bank considerable gratitude and respect, nationally.

The experience gained from this first crisis to have occurred in the banking sector helped the Bank to deal with the subsequent restructuring of the banking system. UnionBank and Grindlays ANZ merged in 1992, with the approval of the Bank, and subsequently became Stanbic (Botswana) Limited, wholly owned by Standard Bank of South Africa. Barclays and Standard Chartered joined Financial Services as companies listed on the inchoate Botswana stock exchange. When FNBB acquired FSC towards the end of 1993, it became the third bank listed on the stock exchange. A further merger occurred in 1994 when FNBB took over the failing Zimbank (Botswana) Limited, whose operations in Botswana had not been a success.

The expansion of the number of privately owned financial institutions, following the deregulation of the banking sector, not only increased the Bank's supervisory responsibilities, but provided greater competition within the banking system. Automated telling machines were introduced to reduce congestion in banking halls; new branches, agencies and encashment points were opened; rapid progress was made in the automation of accounting systems; staff training intensified; and commissions on foreign exchange dealings narrowed. However, competitive pressures also affected the level of profits in the banking sector and drove the older banks to rationalise their branch networks and to introduce other cost-cutting measures.

The experience gained by the Bank during this period enhanced the Bank's reputation as having one of the best banking supervision departments in Africa. At the initiative, and under the leadership of the then Director of Banking Supervision, Mrs Julia Majaha-Järtby, the Eastern and Southern African Supervisors Group was founded in 1993. With enthusiastic support from the IMF, the Bank for International Settlements and the Bank of England, it started organising regional training courses for banking supervisors, and working towards the harmonization of regulatory standards and procedures.

The Bank's involvement in the financial sector has not been limited to private banks and credit institutions. Under the authority conferred on it by the Minister of Finance, it has also conducted limited examinations of FSC, the Botswana Savings Bank, the Botswana Building Society and the Botswana Cooperative Bank (but not the NDB). It worked closely with the consultants engaged to restructure the NDB, and it was instrumental in the closing of the insolvent Botswana Cooperative Bank in 1995. A major project, undertaken by the Bank at the request of the Botswana Government, was the comprehensive review of the Financial Institutions Act, leading to the drafting and promulgation of the new Banking Act, which came into effect on 6 November 1995.

The management of Botswana's foreign exchange reserves

Apart from a slight reduction in reserves in 1981, when the value of diamond exports fell from P237 million in 1980 to P145 million, Botswana's foreign exchange reserves have increased every year over the past 21 years. The reserves accumulated at a satisfactory but unexceptional rate until 1984, when they surged, benefiting from the combined effects of a recovery of diamond markets, and the expansion of diamond exports as production from Jwaneng, the world's largest diamond mine, reached its initial planned capacity. As Figure 5 indicates, the reserves increased almost eighteen-fold from P737 million in 1984 to P13.2 billion in 1995, overtaking South Africa's reserve levels in the process. This growth rate was remarkable both in per capita terms, as well as in terms of months of cover of imports of goods and services. Figure 5 also graphically underscores the close relationship between the growth in the level of Botswana's foreign exchange reserves and the increase in the level of Government balances with the Bank of Botswana.

FIGURE 5. RESERVES AND GOVERNMENT BALANCES, 1976 TO 1996

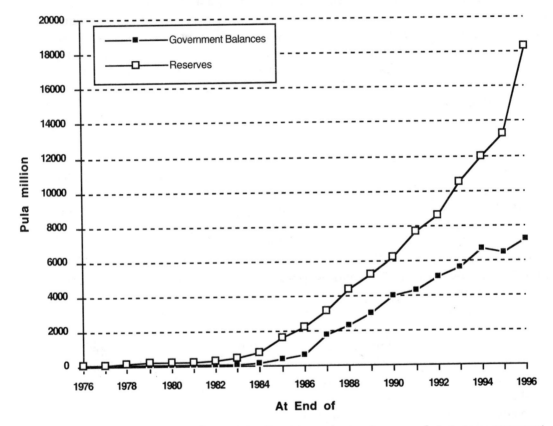

Reserve management, another of the Bank's important areas of statutory responsibility, did not pose any especially difficult problems in the early years. The Bank restricted its investments to highly liquid assets denominated in Rand, US Dollars, Pounds Sterling and Deutsche Marks only. Yen investments were permitted in 1976, and other currencies were added in later years. Although Botswana's foreign exchange reserves soon grew to comfortable levels, when measured in terms of months of imports of goods and services, the vulnerability of the economy to external shocks, as exemplified by the diamond market collapse in 1981, as well as to droughts, outbreaks of cattle diseases, and regional political destabilization, argued for the Bank to pursue conservative reserve management strategies. This entailed holding a relatively large proportion of Botswana's reserves in foreign bank deposits, and investing the balance of the funds in low risk, relatively short duration, fixed interest money market instruments. By maintaining a broad exposure to all major currency blocs, risk concentration in any particular currency was minimised.

This strategy served Botswana and the Bank well until the early 1980s. But as Botswana's foreign exchange reserves started to accumulate, it became clear that the Bank needed professional advice and assistance in managing the investment of the country's reserves. Accordingly, the Board resolved in November 1980 to appoint a discretionary fund manager, and an investment adviser to assist and advise it, respectively, in the execution of its reserve management responsibilities. A small Bank delegation, which included a Board member, visited London in December 1980 to interview short listed firms. Barings Asset Management of London (BAM), a wholly owned subsidiary of Barings Bank, was selected in January 1981 to manage a US$50 million fixed income portfolio on behalf of the Bank. Morgan Grenfell was appointed to serve as the Bank's investment adviser, but the Bank soon transferred funds to its call account facility. The appointment of external fund managers was timely. As the rate of economic growth accelerated, reserve levels escalated rapidly, more than doubling between 1984 and 1985, and again between 1986 and 1988.

In order to spread the risk still further, a third external fund manager was selected in January 1988, with the assistance of Frank Russell Company, an American firm specialising in rating the performance of fund managers. The firm appointed was James Capel, also based in London. At that point, all three external fund managers were entrusted with fixed income mandates with the same benchmark. With their appointment, approximately 20% of Botswana's reserves were externally managed, while 80% remained under the direct administration of the Bank itself. The delegation of greater responsibility to external fund managers was also something of an insurance policy. The Board was concerned that the limitations imposed by the Government's incomes policy increased the likelihood that the Bank would be unable to maintain a critical mass of key trained staff, especially in the esoteric area of reserve management. These fears later proved to be well founded.

The performance of the three fund managers relative to their benchmarks was assessed annually, again with assistance from Frank Russell Company, and compared with the results achieved by the Bank. Bank staff had been sent abroad for many years for training in different aspects of reserve management and had started to build up some competence in dealing and in managing a multi-currency portfolio of relatively short-term money market instruments. However, as the reserves continued to increase, to levels far in excess of those necessary to protect the economy from unforeseen shocks, it became apparent that the long-term return on the investment of Botswana's foreign exchanges could be enhanced by changing the Bank's investment strategy.

The Board agreed in 1993 to divide the reserves into three tranches, each with a different set of objectives, and investment horizon. The liquidity tranche was to continue to serve the purpose of conventional foreign exchange reserves, available as a buffer to accommodate fluctuations in the balance of payments. A matched asset-liability portfolio was created to ensure that part of Botswana's reserves would always be invested in instruments whose currencies and returns matched Botswana's foreign debt service liabilities. The third tranche, the Pula Fund, was conceived as a national investment fund, managed so as to produce longer term returns, within reasonable risk tolerances, for the benefit of future generations of Batswana, after the depletion of Botswana's diamond reserves.

This important shift in investment strategy made a number of other changes necessary. It was intended that investments should be made from the Pula Fund in equities and other longer term securities in which the Bank had not previously invested and which could only be efficiently traded by specialist fund managers close to the different markets concerned. It was therefore necessary to select and appoint additional external fund managers for this purpose. It was also decided to introduce additional mandates, each focused on a particular investment market, in order to obtain the full benefit of the expertise of fund managers specialising in those markets and to limit the risk of failure or underperformance by any single fund manager.

The new strategy also provided for the appointment of a global custodian who would retain possession of the underlying securities and debt instruments that were purchased by the external fund managers. This step was taken to facilitate the maintenance of accurate accounting records relating to foreign investments and to protect the Bank further against the possibility of malfeasance by any of its external fund managers. The Northern Trust Company of Boston was appointed in November 1993 as the global custodian. The wisdom of this decision was soon evident. In February 1995, Barings Bank was placed into liquidation when a rogue trader in Singapore incurred massive losses. Although Barings Asset Management survived and continued operating as a fund manager, the Bank could have been adversely affected by Barings' demise under slightly different circumstances.

In the process of implementing this new policy, the Bank appointed five new fund managers in 1993, retaining the services of Barings Asset Management, but terminating the management contracts of James Capel and Morgan Grenfell. By the end of 1995, the Bank had transferred its custodial business to State Street[18], also of Boston, and had commenced interviewing fund managers for the additional mandates.

Botswana's foreign exchange reserves stood at P13.2 billion (US$4.7 billion) at the end of 1995, more than 200 times higher than the P65 million at the end of 1976.

5. CONCLUDING COMMENTS

The Bank of Botswana has come a long way since July 1975. The foundations for its future institutional development and functional diversification were laid in the 1970s when, with the help of foreign central banking experts, the necessary legislative and policy framework, and organizational structure, were put in place. Since then, the Bank has evolved into a strong and respected national institution, which carries out its core central banking functions in a quiet, but dependable manner. This is, in itself, a commendable accomplishment. The process of monetization of the economy was not yet complete when the Bank was established; the financial system was rudimentary; and there was little understanding in Botswana of the role and functions of a central bank, and even less indigenous expertise in banking.

The introduction of a national currency in 1976 was the first challenge faced by the Bank. Its successful implementation enabled the Bank and its newly recruited staff to tackle the many other formidable tasks which lay ahead with some confidence. But the first ten years were largely devoted to building up the capabilities of citizen staff and to laying the groundwork for an enlargement of the Bank's responsibilities and role in the economy, which was to occur in the second ten years.

This early period was also characterised by a highly interventionist and regulatory approach. The exercise of the Bank's statutory powers was desirable and necessary

---

[18] Although during 1996 the Bank reverted again to The Northern Trust Company after it became necessary to terminate its relationship with State Street.

in some circumstances; for example, when credit controls had to be introduced in 1981 as part of the package of remedial measures introduced by the Botswana authorities to deal with the slump in diamond prices and markets. But the predisposition of the Bank towards the control of economic activity can be seen, with the benefit of hindsight, as having retarded the development and modernization of the banking system, as well as the domestic capital and money markets, and as having reduced the efficiency of the economy by impinging on the healthy interplay of market forces. The Bank's restrictive stance on the licensing of banks and other financial institutions, and its efforts to keep interest rates low, are examples of misguided policy objectives pursued by the Bank during this period. In the early years, the Bank was also more willing to intervene in the foreign exchange market, adjusting the rate of exchange of the Pula in both directions more frequently than necessary, sometimes to no lasting beneficial effect.

To its credit, however, the Bank learnt from its mistakes. As its analytical abilities improved, the Bank was able to review its past performance objectively and critically, and to make the necessary changes in its policies and operations. The second ten years saw the adoption by the Bank of a more market oriented approach to economic management. The reversal in the late 1980s of its restrictive licensing policies, the general deregulation of the domestic financial system, and the removal of controls on interest rates produced immediate and beneficial results. Greater competition in the banking system, coupled with a more flexible monetary policy environment, led to improvements in banking services and to the development of a money market, while the establishment of a small, but efficient stock exchange, with the active support of the Bank, was an important milestone in the development of a capital market in Botswana. The introduction in 1991 of Bank of Botswana Certificates and open market operations represented another important departure from the past reliance on direct controls over interest rates. Market forces thereafter played a much greater role in determining the levels of interest rates, with the Bank exercising its influence through indirect means only.

These changes were driven largely by the transformation of the Botswana economy, and the need to ensure that monetary policies and the financial sector encouraged, and did not restrict, economic modernization, diversification and efficiency. The surge in Botswana's economic development, which occurred from 1984 onwards, placed other demands on the Bank with which it coped reasonably well. The rapid growth in Botswana's foreign exchange reserves over the past ten years forced the Bank to enhance its investment management capabilities and to refine its investment strategies. It is to the credit of all involved that the Bank made the necessary organizational and systemic changes to enable it to manage one of the largest international investment portfolios on the African continent in a competent and controlled manner. The Bank can also rightfully claim credit for its skilful handling of the first banking crisis when BCCB had to be taken over to save it from disaster, and its oversight of the subsequent restructuring of the banking sector.

These high profile accomplishments should not overshadow the Bank's performance over the past 21 years in the less glamorous aspects of its operations. It has managed the national currency efficiently and without incident; it has administered exchange controls with commendable diligence; and it has conducted regular examinations of the commercial banks and other financial institutions in a thorough and professional manner. The quality of the Bank's economic research has improved markedly over the years, enabling it carry out its responsibilities more effectively, and to play a more proactive role in the public policy arena. The Bank's bulletins, reports and annual reports are widely regarded as being among the best and most informative central bank publications in Africa. The Bank has published its monthly statements of accounts in the Government Gazette with regularity, and has generally managed its financial affairs in a sound manner, despite the complexity of its international operations. Indeed, the Bank's greatest accomplishment may have been that it has fulfilled its responsibility to the Government and the nation, without mismanagement, and without any taint of corruption.

Despite having attained the age of twenty-one years, the Bank cannot yet be considered to be a mature institution. The average age of its staff is still below thirty-five years. The high turnover of staff has reduced the average years of experience of its citizen staff, while the Incomes Policy has heightened the Bank's dependence on expatriate staff. As a result, the Bank has had to persist with a much larger training programme than should be required at this juncture in its existence. The Bank has still some way to go before its management systems and capabilities are equal to the onerous national responsibilities with which it is charged. It has also been slow to install and make full use of modern information technologies; and it has not responded effectively to the exhortation of the former Vice President and current President of Botswana, made at the inaugural Board meeting in July 1975, to educate the public in money and banking matters.

Notwithstanding these deficiencies, the Bank can look back on the past 21 years with much pride and satisfaction. Thanks to the commitment and dedicated application of a core of highly competent citizen staff, and to the support and assistance of the Botswana Government, the Board, international organizations such as the IMF, and many outstanding expatriate employees, the Bank has succeeded in fulfilling most of its statutory objectives, without serious mishap. If this momentum is maintained, the Bank can look forward to becoming one of the strongest and best central banks in Africa.

REFERENCES

Government of Botswana Legislation
Exchange Control Regulations, 1975.
Proclamation No.5 of 1895.
Proclamation No.73 of 1960.
Statutory Instrument No.88, 1975. 'Appointed Date – Monetary Unit of Botswana'. June 1976.
Statutory Instrument No.89 of 1975. 'Declaration of Official Rate'. June 1976.
Statutory Instrument No.90 of 1975. 'Appointed Date – Foreign Currency'. June 1976.
Statutory Instrument No.91 of 1975. 'Period of Dual Circulation'. June 1976.
Statutory Instrument No.105 of 1976. 'Maintenance of Primary Reserves'. June 1976.
Statutory Instrument No.112 of 1976. Exemption – Lending to Banks and Building Societies'. August 1976.

Statutory Instrument No.123 of 1976. 'Financial Institutions (Application of Act) Order, 1976'. August 1976.

The Bank of Botswana Act, 1975.

The Bank of Botswana Amendment Act, 1987.

The Banking Act, 1995.

The Barclays Bank of Botswana Vesting Act, 1975.

The Exchange Control Act, 1975.

The Financial Institutions Act, 1975.

The Standard Bank of Botswana Vesting Act, 1975.

The Statute Law (Miscellaneous Amendments) Act, 1977.

National Development Plans

Bechuanaland Protectorate Administration. *Development Plan, 1963–68.*

Government of Botswana: The Transitional Plan for Social and Economic Development, 1966–68.

Government of Botswana. *National Development Plans: No.1, 1968–1973; No.2, 1970–75; No.3, 1973–1978; No.4, 1976–1981; No.5, 1979–85; No.6, 1985–91; No.7, 1991–97.*

Government of Botswana: Speeches and Publications

'A Monetary System for Botswana', Government Paper No.1 of 1975.

'A Popular Guide to Exchange Controls and Foreign Exchange Transactions', 1975.

Khama, Sir Seretse. Speech at Molepolole, 6 September 1974.

Khama, Sir Seretse. Speech at the opening of the Bank of Botswana's new building, 16 March 1978.

Masire, Dr. Quett K.J. Budget Speech 1974, Budget Speech 1976.

Minutes of the Monetary Preparatory Commission: 1973; 1974; 1975. (Unpublished)

'Some Questions and Answers about Money and Banking in South Africa', 1975.

Books

Colclough, C.L. and McCarthy, S.J. 1980. *The Political Economy of Botswana: A Study of Growth and Distribution.* Oxford University Press, Oxford.

Harvey, C. (ed.). 1981. *Papers on the Economy of Botswana.* Heinemann Educational Books, London.

Hermans, H.C.L. 1973. 'Botswana's Options for Economic Existence'. In: Cervenka and Zdenek (eds). *Landlocked Countries of Africa*, Scandinavian Institute of African Studies, Uppsala.

World Bank. 1989. *Botswana: Financial Policies for Diversified Growth.* World Bank, Washington.

Articles

Collings, F.d'A., Donely, G., Petersen, A, Puckahtikom, C. and Wickham, P. 1974. 'The Rand and the Monetary Systems of Botswana, Lesotho and Swaziland', *Journal of Modern African Studies,* Vol.16, No.1.

Hermans, H.C.L. 1974. 'Towards Budgetary Independence: A Review of Botswana's Financial History, 1900 to 1973', *Botswana Notes and Records*, Vol.6,

Hudson, D.J. 1978. 'The Establishment of Botswana's Central Bank and the Introduction of the New Currency', *Botswana Notes and Records*, Vol.10.

Dissertations

Muzorewa, Basil C. 1976. 'The Development of the Monetary Economy and an Analysis of the Monetary and Economic Systems in the Republic of Botswana.' M.Phil. thesis, University of Leeds.

Bank of Botswana Publications and Unpublished Papers

Annual Reports, 1976 to 1995.

Bye-Laws, 1976, revised 1989 (Unpublished).

Minutes of Board Meetings, 1975 to 1995 (Unpublished).

Minutes of Executive Committee, 1975 to 1995 (Unpublished).

Ablo, E.Y. and Hudson, D.J. 1981. 'Monetary Policy in Botswana.' (Unpublished).

Monetary Independence

The Contrasting Strategies of Botswana and Swaziland

Charles Harvey

1. INTRODUCTION – CENTRAL BANK OR MONETARY UNION?

Both Botswana and Swaziland continued to use the Rand after becoming politically independent, in 1966 and 1968 respectively. This differentiated them from most other anglophone African countries which created their own currencies, central banks and monetary systems immediately after their independence. These countries regarded an independent currency and monetary system as a necessary step towards economic independence following the achievement of political independence, but Botswana and Swaziland gave other policies priority.

Later, however, the two countries made different choices. In 1974, the Botswana Government withdrew from the negotiations for the Rand Monetary Area Agreement while they were still in progress, and announced that it would create a central bank and independent monetary system. Swaziland continued with the negotiations, together with Lesotho, and agreement was reached at the end of 1974 (see the paper by Hermans in this volume). As a consequence of these decisions, the Bank of Botswana started operations in 1976 as a fully fledged central bank, while Swaziland remained within the Rand Monetary Area and therefore accepted, so it appeared, continued dependence on South Africa in monetary policy.[1]

The very different policy choices made in 1975 were, however, less divergent in practice than they appeared at first. On the one hand, later negotiations gave Swaziland many of the policy instruments which Botswana obtained by leaving. On the other, it can be argued that nominal monetary independence provided Botswana with relatively little additional room for manoeuvre, because of the country's continuing economic and geographical links with South Africa.[2]

---

[1] The Act of Union, which established the Union of South Africa in 1909, stated that the three 'High Commission Territories' of Basutoland, Bechuanaland and Swaziland would eventually be incorporated into South Africa. Fortunately, the Act also said that this would not occur without the consent of each territory's population. Incorporation was successfully resisted, despite pressure at times from South Africa, including refusal to import Botswana's beef (Hubbard, 1986). In these circumstances, however, there must have seemed little point in disturbing the *de facto* use of South African currency in the three Territories, whose economies were strongly integrated with, and dominated by, that of South Africa.

[2] Lesotho and Namibia also continued to use the Rand. Lesotho did not follow Swaziland in negotiating the use of additional policy instruments, probably because the country remained even more dependent, as regards geography, trade and migrant labour, than either Botswana or Swaziland. Namibia had no choice. Lesotho and Namibia are not discussed in this paper. Most francophone countries became part of the CFA Franc area, with a common currency and a fixed exchange rate against the French Franc (but with some rights to borrow from the Bank of France).

While Botswana and Swaziland continued to use the Rand, money could flow freely between them and South Africa, and residents could keep their bank accounts in South Africa if they wished. This meant that Botswana and Swaziland could not have interest rates significantly different from those in South Africa. Rates below those in South Africa provided an incentive for money to flow out of the smaller countries, and there was nothing to stop those flows from taking place as there were no exchange controls within the monetary area. A major additional disadvantage was that Botswana and Swaziland received no income on the Rand notes circulating in their countries, so that they were in fact making an interest free loan to the South African Government.

South African exchange control regulations were applied on all transactions with countries outside the Rand Monetary Area. This meant that most of Botswana's and Swaziland's foreign reserves were invested in Rand, as the banks, mining companies and other holders of Rand financial assets were not allowed to exchange them for non-Rand financial assets. All foreign exchange was held by the South African Reserve Bank. The South African authorities determined interest rates, exchange controls with the rest of the world, and the exchange rate, without consulting the smaller member countries, taking account only of South African interests. In these circumstances, Botswana and Swaziland were, for all practical purposes, simply part of the South African monetary system, with no independent control over their monetary and exchange rate policies.

It was precisely this type of monetary dependence that induced other African countries to establish their own monetary systems. They wished to acquire the instruments of monetary policy, and to use them in pursuit of national economic interest. Botswana and Swaziland were therefore most untypical, not only in continuing with the existing monetary arrangements, but also in that neither country tried to interfere with the lending policies of the foreign commercial banks that dominated their financial sectors.

For example, Botswana Government statements of economic policy before, during and for some years after Independence, made hardly any reference to credit policy, and none at all to reform of the monetary system. In the Transitional Plan for Social and Economic Development published at Independence in 1966, the only reference to credit was an estimate of the funds that would be required by the National Development Bank for capital projects (mainly the finance of boreholes and the purchase of farms from the Government). These funds had to come from abroad, because at that time, and for six or seven years afterwards, the Government could not finance recurrent spending without grants-in-aid from the British Government; all development projects were also, therefore, dependent on foreign aid (Government of Botswana, 1966).

The 1968 National Development Plan expressed concern that the commercial banks, which were simply branches of British-owned commercial banks in South Africa, were lending less than half of their deposits in Botswana. In the absence of a central bank or local Treasury Bills, the commercial banks simply deposited their spare cash, not lent locally to borrowers in Botswana, with their head offices in Johannesburg.

'Botswana is, therefore, in this respect a creditor nation, a role that she can ill afford to play at this juncture in her development ... At the same time the country is in urgent need of finance for telecommunications, power, water supplies and housing, all of which are sound loanworthy projects. More credit on easier terms also needs to be made available to commerce and industry to stimulate the private sector.' (Government of Botswana, 1968, 80–1)

Despite this strong critique of the existing system, the Government made no proposals at that time to interfere with the direction of commercial bank lending. The Swaziland Government pursued the same policy. In most other African countries, governments intervened in a variety of ways: requiring minimum percentages of lending to go to priority sectors; partly or wholly nationalising foreign-owned commercial banks; requiring commercial banks to lend to priority sectors at sub-market interest rates; setting limits on borrowing from the commercial banks by foreign-owned companies; and, in some cases, creating government-owned commercial banks from scratch.[3]

The advantages and disadvantages, of remaining within the Rand Monetary Area (later the Common Monetary Area), are further discussed in Sections 2 and 3. The experience of Botswana and Swaziland, with the different monetary systems that they chose, are then discussed in Sections 4 and 5 respectively. The main emphasis is on the years immediately following Botswana's decision to have an independent currency. This is for reasons of space and because the immediate effects are more easily identified for that period; other factors increasingly obscure the differences in later years. Section 6 then asks whether, with hindsight, the two Governments chose correctly, and whether they should change their policies in the changed circumstances of the 1990s.

2. ADVANTAGES AND DISADVANTAGES OF MEMBERSHIP OF THE RAND MONETARY AREA (LATER THE COMMON MONETARY AREA)

The apparent advantages of membership in 1976

In the mid-1960s, when Botswana and Swaziland were approaching their independence, and again in the 1970s when the terms of the monetary agreement were being reconsidered, there appeared to be considerable advantages to continuing to use the Rand. These included the following:

- there were no exchange controls within the monetary area;
- all transactions within the monetary area were free of any exchange rate risk;
- there were no costs of exchanging one currency for another (these costs are estimated at 0.5% of GDP in Europe and may be higher in Botswana and Swaziland because they have higher ratios of international trade to GDP);
- residents of Botswana and Swaziland could invest in the well developed financial markets in South Africa; and

---

[3] The underlying objectives of these initiatives were to increase the flow of credit to Africans and African-owned businesses, because it was thought that they had been irrationally discriminated against by the commercial banks during the colonial period. Pressure was also brought on the commercial banks to make longer term loans, to finance development projects. These initiatives were largely unsuccessful, and sometimes had perverse effects (Harvey, 1991).

- residents had access to the foreign exchange reserves held by the South African Reserve Bank.

The first three of these points all reduced the costs and inconvenience of transactions with South Africa, including investment, trade and tourism.

A further advantage of continued membership, or rather the ending of a disadvantage, might have become available if Botswana had chosen to participate in the Rand Monetary Agreement. The Agreement contained a formula for estimating the Rand circulating in each country. The formula would have overestimated the initial note circulation in Botswana (a similar comparison was not possible for Swaziland because Rand continued to circulate there). In addition, the formula for estimating future growth assumed that the local note circulation would increase faster than in the monetary area as a whole. The Agreement provided for interest on the estimated notes circulating in each country, at a rate equal to two thirds of the rate on long-term bonds issued by the South African Government, which was roughly the rate that commercial banks were being paid on their liquid balances at head offices in Johannesburg. These relatively generous terms were presumably agreed to by South Africa because the economies of the smaller member countries combined were less than 2% of the South African economy in 1975, and the South African Government did not anticipate that the smaller economies would grow rapidly (their combined GDP had risen to 5% of South Africa's by 1993).[4]

The apparent disadvantages of membership

On the other hand, being part of a common currency area sharply reduced the policy options available for adjusting to asymmetric economic shocks, that is, shocks which affected members of the currency area differently. For example, if Botswana or Swaziland suffered a negative shock not also affecting South Africa, adjustment to that shock had to be mainly by reducing the government budget deficit, because of the immobility of labour[5] and the impossibility of devaluation. The tightening of fiscal policy would make a recession worse in the short run, without the stimulus to increase tradable output which would be provided by a devaluation.

More generally, a monetary union is optimal if the member countries have wage flexibility, labour mobility between members, and politically acceptable financial transfers from surplus to deficit members when they suffer from asymmetric shocks. Without those attributes, adjustment can be costly. For example, Michigan is part of the United States common currency area. Michigan adjusted to a negative shock by out-migration of labour, together with increased federal transfers. When Belgium suffered a negative shock, it could not adjust significantly by outward labour migration, and intra-European transfers were negligible by comparison with the United States. Bel-

---

[4] Note, however, that there was some uncertainty as to whether South Africa would fulfil this agreement indefinitely; the South African Government had a record of reneging on aspects of the SACU agreement, for example.

[5] South African mines recruited labour from neighbouring countries, but the proportion of foreign labour on the South African mines was sharply reduced, from 90% to 50% approximately, in the early 1970s, and the numbers recruited from Botswana and Swaziland continued to fall. Other migrants working in South Africa were doing so illegally.

gium, however, was able to adjust by devaluing. Belgium also borrowed abroad extensively, and continued, therefore, to have an exceptionally high level of foreign debt. Nevertheless, the argument is that adjustment would have been even more difficult without the option of devaluation (De Grauwe, 1992).

A variation of this disadvantage, not being able to devalue, is where a member of a monetary union has inflation persistently higher than in its main trading partner. This happened in the CFA Franc countries relative to France. Because they could not adjust by devaluing against the French Franc, the CFA Franc countries could only adjust by introducing tight fiscal policy (until, that is, the CFA Franc was devalued by 50% in January 1994, for all of the 14 countries which used it). Tight fiscal policy might have been adequate initially. Where, however, inflation in a member country was higher than in France over a sustained period, fiscal adjustment proved extremely costly while not achieving its objectives.[6] For example, Senegal had zero inflation for five years prior to 1994, but still needed the 50% devaluation in January that year. To illustrate the problem further, if prices in a member country were 30% higher than in France, and inflation in France (and other major trading partners) was 3% a year, it would take nearly nine years of zero inflation to eliminate the competitive disadvantage. Zero inflation can only be achieved with extremely severe fiscal policy, probably with high costs in unemployment, while during eight out of the nine years the currency would continue to be overvalued with all the resulting lack of international competitiveness.

Other disadvantages of monetary union with South Africa included:

- the country's exchange rate against other currencies was determined entirely by fluctuations in the Rand's international exchange rate;
- the country's official foreign exchange reserves were all invested in Rand, losing international buying power if the Rand was weak, and losing the advantage of diversifying risk by investing in a range of currencies; and
- private savings, including those placed with pension funds and other savings institutions, were also invested locally or in South Africa.

A slightly unexpected disadvantage of continued membership was revealed when Botswana left the Rand Monetary Area and established exchange controls on transactions with South Africa. Because importers had to provide import documents in order to buy Rand to pay for imports from South Africa, the statistical coverage of those imports improved, increasing Botswana's claim on the common revenue pool of the Southern African Customs Union (SACU). Swaziland missed out on this windfall gain.[7]

---

[6] It was possible for CFA Franc countries to have higher inflation than in France, because they had some borrowing rights at the Bank of France.

[7] The ratio of recorded imports to GDP was 60% in 1976, the last year before exchange controls became effective on transactions with South Africa; controls were imposed in the last four months of 1976 but most imports were paid for out of accumulated Rand balances in South Africa until the start of 1977. The ratio rose to 68% in 1977, and 75% in 1978; thereafter it fluctuated between 70% and 78%. Other factors were at work, but it would appear that there was a significant reduction in underrecording of imports from South Africa, which comprised 80% of total imports in 1975, the percentage rising to more than 85% in the years 1977 to 1980.

The balance of advantage

Although the above issues were considered important at the time, experience in the rest of Africa suggests that they might have proved relatively unimportant. For most countries, it turns out that the crucial advantage of belonging to a common monetary area, and not therefore having a national central bank, is that it prevents governments from financing a budget deficit by money creation, that is by 'borrowing' from their central banks.[8] This non-solution to the financing of government spending is highly inflationary. Moreover, trying to control that inflation by using monetary policy is only feasible for very short periods. It is possible to reduce the inflation by the government paying very high interest rates. This can induce those with financial assets, including the commercial banks, to lend to the government. However, if the budget deficit is not rapidly reduced, the cost of interest payments rapidly becomes a burden on the budget, while there is a tendency for the commercial banks to prefer holding government paper to lending to the private sector.[9] In addition, producers are normally most unwilling to borrow at high nominal interest, even if inflation is higher, or equally as high, because of the huge risks involved.[10]

With hindsight, the decision of most other African countries to create their own monetary systems and national central banks was extremely costly, overwhelmingly for this reason. There was enormous pressure on governments to spend more than they could raise in non-inflationary ways (that is, through taxation, by borrowing other than from the central bank, and from aid receipts). Resistance to this pressure was weak, causing high and accelerating inflation, and increasingly overvalued exchange rates. IMF and World Bank conditionality concentrated, therefore, heavily on devaluation and the reduction of budget deficits. Unfortunately, devaluation is only successful if budget deficits are indeed sharply reduced. The enormous difficulty of reducing government spending, once spending programmes have become established, has been a major cause of the failure of so many stabilization and structural adjustment policies. In other words, devaluation is a high risk strategy, with an extensive record of failure.

The argument as to whether a country should create an independent monetary system turns, to a considerable extent therefore, on two main questions.

(1) Whether the lack of the additional policy instruments made available by monetary independence is costly.

(2) Whether the opportunity to finance budget deficits through the central bank is abused or not, in other words, whether the Government needs an external constraint on overspending or whether it can be relied on to keep spending within prudent limits.

---

8   This assumes that central banks of currency areas do indeed limit the right of member governments to 'borrow' from them. Of course, if the central bank is unable to control inflation so that the common currency is weak, all the member economies suffer from the resulting costs, as has happened when the Rand was weak.

9   This describes quite accurately what happened in Zambia in the early 1990s.

10 Borrowers are relatively certain that their costs will rise with inflation, because their costs cover a wide range of goods and service; but they are relatively uncertain that the prices of their outputs will rise with inflation because the output of a typical producer is a single product, or a narrow range of (usually closely related) products.

The other advantages and disadvantages are relatively unimportant in most countries, most of the time.

Opinion on the relative importance of independent monetary policy, as against the dangers of excessive money creation, has changed. In the 1960s, when most African countries became independent, the dangers of excessive money creation were largely ignored, and the benefits of additional economic policy instruments were given great weight. In the 1990s, in contrast, some newly independent countries in Eastern Europe and the former Soviet Union (for example, Estonia and Lithuania) have established currency boards and an exchange rate fixed to a major currency, as has Argentina. They have in fact created systems very similar to those in existence in colonial Africa. They made this choice because of the extensive evidence of inflation caused by central bank financing of budget deficits, so that preventing this was more important than the loss of some independent policy instruments. Basically, they believed that governments could not be trusted (indeed that governments could not trust themselves, since it was governments that made the choice to forswear the additional powers provided by independent monetary systems).

The next section examines whether Botswana experienced serious disadvantages from the decision to establish its own monetary system. Delinking from the Rand might have resulted in a downward spiral of accelerating inflation and currency depreciation; it could have had damaging effects on inward investment from abroad, and on tourism; and the increased cost of trading with South Africa might have induced Botswana to trade more with other countries.[11]

3. The Experience of Botswana

Budget deficits and the need for devaluation

On the important question of avoiding irresponsible money creation, Botswana's experience is simply not relevant. The Botswana Government had budget surpluses for virtually all the years after the creation of the Bank of Botswana in 1976, and high levels of financial savings to finance occasional budget deficits. The Government had no domestic debt as a result, and did not ever have any need to choose between tight fiscal policy and borrowing from the Bank of Botswana. There were occasional devaluations. However, mostly these were to correct for Pula appreciation against the Rand, caused by Rand depreciation against the SDR while the Pula was pegged to a currency basket comprising regional and major international currencies. There was one serious financial crisis, in 1981 and 1982, when the demand for large gem diamonds collapsed and it appeared that the foreign exchange reserves would almost disappear within 12 months. The package of measures introduced to stabilise the balance of payments included a Pula devaluation, but even on this occasion it did little more than correct for a Pula appreciation against the Rand during the previous

---

[11] There is an argument that Botswana should import more from other countries anyway. But this argument is premised on Botswana first leaving SACU. So long as Botswana stayed in SACU, shifting to other import sources would have incurred a net cost.

year.[12] The use of exchange rate policy to mitigate inflation imported from South Africa is discussed below.

The Botswana Government has shown that it is aware of the need to restrain Government spending to allow for lower rates of growth of diamond revenue in the 1990s. A number of official statements, in budget speeches and development plans, have made the point very forcefully. Inevitably, though, there is no way of knowing whether the Botswana Government will at some time in the future be able to resist pressure to maintain or even increase its spending, when the only way to do that would be via money creation. The Government did, in fact, yield to pressure to spend faster than the economy could absorb, in the late 1980s; in particular, the development budget multiplied 5.4 times between 1985 and 1990, causing unnecessary increases in construction costs and a deterioration in the implementation of development projects. Because the Government was able to finance this overspending out of rapidly increasing revenues, it could not have been prevented by not having a central bank from which to borrow; but it does show that the Government was vulnerable to pressures to overspend. It could be, therefore, that the extra constraint of membership of a common monetary area could be beneficial in future even though it has not been necessary to date.

Impact on investment

In the 1970s, when Botswana and Swaziland were considering whether to remain in the common monetary area, they were both extremely dependent on investment from South Africa. Clearly, such investment was made much easier because South African investors did not have to obtain exchange control permission to invest, and could freely repatriate any profits. Investment was also made less risky by the absence of any foreign exchange risk, and there were no transaction costs in exchanging one currency for another.

As it happened, gross fixed capital formation in Botswana fell sharply in the year that the decision to delink from South Africa was made (1975), and did not rise above the 1974 level until 1978. In Swaziland, on the other hand, this measure of investment rose steadily throughout the same years, as shown in Table 1.

TABLE 1. GROSS FIXED CAPITAL FORMATION IN BOTSWANA AND SWAZILAND, 1974–78 (1974 PRICES, NOMINAL FIGURES ADJUSTED BY CONSUMER PRICE INDICES)

	1974	1975	1976	1977	1978
BOTSWANA (PULA MILLION)	79.6	51.2	70.8	68.8	100.9
SWAZILAND (PULA MILLION)	21.6	37.1	48.3	56.3	131.8

Source: IMF, International Financial Statistics.

[12] The stabilisation measures taken were effective, so much so that when the Botswana Government decided to make absolutely sure that the policies taken were adequate, and approached IMF for assistance, the measures already taken had reversed the fall in the foreign exchange reserves; in fact they were rising fast, to the point where Botswana was not eligible to borrow under IMF rules.

It is inherently impossible to determine what might have happened to investment in Botswana if the Government had decided to continue to use the Rand. It is equally impossible to know whether some investment, which might otherwise have occurred in Botswana, was diverted to Swaziland. However, there are plausible alternative explanations of the changes in investment in Botswana. 1975 marked the end of a massive mining construction boom resulting from the discovery and development of a copper-nickel mine whose capital costs were greater than GDP, and a diamond mine, which although not quite as large, had capital costs of more than half GDP. These investments were so large in relation to Botswana's economy that it was remarkable that investment did not fall further when the construction boom was over. Equally, the subsequent recovery of investment in Botswana, and its rise to a higher level, is mainly explained by a second mining construction boom following the discovery of another, larger, diamond mine at Jwaneng.

The mining investments were by large international companies with experience of managing exchange controls and foreign exchange risk. It seems unlikely, therefore, that their investment decisions were affected one way or another by whether Botswana remained within the Rand Monetary Area. It is possible that Botswana paid a slightly higher 'price', in that it received a slightly smaller share of the diamond revenues, to compensate foreign investors for the cost of managing the additional risks after 1976. However, Botswana is believed to have negotiated an exceptionally high share of the diamond revenues, so it is difficult to argue that the share might have been even higher.[13]

From 1976, exchange controls on transactions between Botswana and South Africa imposed a considerable additional cost on Debswana, the diamond mining company jointly owned by De Beers and the Botswana Government. Debswana had large holdings of cash between the sale of diamonds and the payment of taxation and dividends out of its profits. It was obliged by Botswana's exchange controls to convert foreign exchange earnings into Pula, to hold these balances at much lower rates of interest in Botswana than could have been obtained in foreign currencies[14], and then to convert that part of them required for foreign payments (notably dividends to the foreign shareholder) back into foreign exchange. However, by the time that this situation developed, diamond mining in Botswana had proved so profitable to De Beers, even after providing a large share of profits to the Botswana Government, that this relatively minor effect on profits apparently had negligible impact on the willingness of De Beers to invest: an investment to increase the output of Jwaneng came on stream in the mid-1990s, and shortly afterwards it was announced that production at the first diamond mine, Orapa, would be doubled.

It remains possible that other less sophisticated investors were put off by the uncertainties created by introducing the new currency. However, if the new currency did reduce investment, this effect was probably only temporary, and unimportant compared to other factors affecting investment. Botswana benefited from a considerable amount of other foreign investment, for example in manufacturing, once a reputation

---

[13] The exact profit split has never been revealed. It was estimated as being something between 72% and 80% in Harvey and Lewis (1990, p126).

[14] Interest rates in Botswana were eventually raised significantly in the 1990s, as part of a programme of financial liberalisation, although deposit rates generally remained below those in South Africa.

for careful management of the new currency had been established. Most notably, when the diamond market collapsed in 1981 and 1982, the stabilization measures introduced by the Botswana Government very pointedly did not include any tightening of exchange control regulations, in sharp contrast to the typical response to foreign exchange crises elsewhere in Africa. Investor confidence may also have been strengthened by the first changes in the exchange rate being positive; the Pula was revalued upwards in 1977 and 1979, and was worth R1.37 by 1990, despite some downward fluctuations.[15]

Impact on tourism

Swaziland was much more dependent in the 1970s than Botswana on tourism in general, and on tourists from South Africa in particular. Swaziland had many more tourist hotels and casinos than Botswana, whose tourist industry consisted mainly of flying people directly from South Africa to the Okavango Delta, which was effectively a tourist enclave where tourists changed little or no money into local currency.[16] Botswana was, therefore, less vulnerable than Swaziland to any negative effect that the new currency may have had on tourism from the region.

TABLE 2. TOURISM IN BOTSWANA 1975–79 ('000s)

	1975	1976	1977	1978	1979
ARRIVALS: HOLIDAY	41.8	43.3	45.3	50.9	62.8
ARRIVALS FROM:					
South Africa	111.1	114.7	123.2	145.0	181.0
Swaziland	1.0	1.4	1.4	1.1	1.6
Lesotho	1.5	1.6	1.6	1.2	1.6

Source: Statistical Abstract, various years; Statistical Bulletin, various issues.

In fact, as far as can be discovered from the available statistics, tourism in general continued to grow in Botswana in the late 1970s. Both the number of visitors stating 'holiday' as the purpose of their visit, and the number of visitors from the countries affected by Botswana leaving the Rand Monetary Area continued to grow (unfortunately, although there are statistics for total tourist arrivals by purpose of visit, and for total arrivals from individual countries in the region, there are no published breakdown of visitors by purpose of entry for individual countries).

---

[15] The Pula has declined against the major international currencies because the Rand has been weak, and there are limits to how far the Pula can delink from the Rand.

[16] It was probably fortunate for Botswana that no major investment was made to attract South African tourists to hotels, or in casinos, because of the subsequent development of Sun City, which is nearer to Johannesburg than tourist destinations in Botswana and retained the convenience of using the Rand. In 1976, Botswana had only one tourist hotel in Gaborone with a casino; Swaziland had a large number of tourist hotels, several with casinos.

Direction of trade

The introduction of exchange controls on transactions with South Africa added to the cost of Botswana's trade with South Africa, which included for the first time the cost of currency exchange, the cost of administering and complying with exchange controls (to the Bank of Botswana, the commercial banks, and the private sector), and the uncertainties created by fluctuations in the bilateral exchange rate. These effects might have been expected to show up in a fall in South Africa's share of Botswana's foreign trade. However, other factors must have offset any effect of these increased costs on South Africa's share of Botswana's imports, because it rose slightly in the years immediately after 1976 (see Table 3). The common external tariff of the Southern African Customs Union, together with the obvious convenience of the more industrialised economy of South Africa being so geographically convenient, had always given Botswana businesses a strong incentive to buy their imports from South Africa. These advantages were not altered by the new rules, however, so they cannot explain the increased share of South Africa in Botswana's imports. Botswana had a trade agreement with Zimbabwe[17], and equally convenient transport, but neither these factors nor exchange control regulations changed after 1976, and cannot therefore explain the fall in Zimbabwe's share of the Botswana market.[18]

TABLE 3. Botswana's direction of trade, 1975–79 (percentages of total imports and total exports)

	1975	1976	1977	1978	1979
Imports from:					
South Africa	79.8	81.4	85.8	84.7	87.6
Zimbabwe	12.8	12.2	9.9	9.9	6.9
Exports to:					
South Africa	23.6	15.1	11.6	13.6	7.0
Zimbabwe	4.5	7.5	8.4	7.4	8.4

Note: the categories in official publications on the direction of trade in the 1970s were 'Common Customs Area', overwhelmingly South Africa, and 'Other Africa', overwhelmingly Zimbabwe.

Source: Statistical Bulletin, various years.

There was, however, quite a marked fall in the proportion of Botswana's exports going to South Africa, and an increase in the proportion going to Zimbabwe. The fall in

---

[17] While referred to as Zimbabwe, for part of the period covered here this country was still, formally, Rhodesia.

[18] Other factors were of course at work, so that it is not possible to be certain that the changes had no effect. It was said that with imports, mainly consumer goods, in which South Africa and Zimbabwe competed for the Botswana market, it was possible to see the changing competitive position of supplies from each country by observing how far up and down the Botswana railway system certain goods could be bought: the more competitive was Zimbabwe, the further south were Zimbabwe products to be found. In other words, the direction of trade was definitely sensitive to the competitive positions of Zimbabwe and South Africa in the Botswana import market. This was despite the escalating state of civil war in Zimbabwe, which might have been expected to interfere with this process.

South Africa's share can be partly explained by the growth of exports of diamonds and copper-nickel matte at that time, neither of which went to South Africa. The increase in the share of Botswana's exports going to Zimbabwe can be partly explained by an increase in textile and other exports, mainly produced by businesses set up by investors from Zimbabwe. They were attracted by Botswana's liberal exchange controls on imported inputs, and by being able to export back to the country they had come from, under the trade agreement already mentioned, while benefiting from an overvalued exchange rate in Zimbabwe. These factors were completely unaffected by Botswana's new currency and monetary system.

South Africa's share of Botswana's imports was still more than 80% in the early 1990s. It then fell below 75% in 1995, mainly because of large imports of semi-knocked down kits for motor vehicle assembly, from South Korea. On the export side, Botswana's trade with Zimbabwe was very badly effected by the sharp fall in the Zimbabwe Dollar from 1990; by 1995 Zimbabwe was buying only about 3% of the Botswana's exports. Some of this export trade, which had formerly gone to Zimbabwe, mainly manufactured goods, shifted to the South African market, whose share of Botswana's total exports rose above 15% by 1995.

Macroeconomic policy instruments, including exchange rate policy

One of Botswana's main objectives, in delinking from South Africa, was to increase the range of economic policy instruments available to the authorities for managing the economy. Prior to 1976, neither an independent interest rate policy nor an independent exchange rate policy was possible. The question arises, therefore, as to whether Botswana derived significant benefits from these newly available policy instruments. This seemed particularly important because Botswana had very little scope for using changes in taxation for macroeconomic management; a large proportion of Government revenue derived from Customs Union receipts and from diamonds, both of which were subject to long-term contractual agreements, and could not therefore be changed in the short term.

Interest rate policy was initially used to maintain interest rates lower than those in South Africa, while capital account exchange control rules prevented surplus liquidity from being invested abroad. The commercial banks had to hold large deposits at the Bank of Botswana. This provided the commercial banks with a strong incentive to lend, because the difference between what they could get on liquid assets surplus to the official requirement, and the rate of return on loans and advances, increased by several percentage points.

Prior to the changeover, the commercial banks were earning 8% on their liquid balances with their head offices in Johannesburg. Apart from a relatively small and temporary issue of Treasury Bills, their surplus liquidity earned much less on call accounts at the Bank of Botswana. The call account rate was 4.5% in 1977, and 3.5% from 1978 to 1988. It was raised to 6.0% in 1989 and 7.5% in 1990, before call accounts were replaced by Bank of Botswana Certificates (BoBCs). The banks also started to refuse to accept large deposits at their advertised rates, forcing the Bank of Botswana to become a deposit taker of last resort, initially to Debswana, but later to other large depositors.[19] This provided the Government, via Bank of Botswana profits, with significant revenue (because earnings from foreign exchange reserves were significantly higher than the rather low cost of call accounts). However, the main objective of interest rate policy after 1976, and throughout the 1980s, was to encourage the commercial banks to lend more of their excess liquidity.

In the 1990s, the authorities changed strategy, and raised short-term interest rates with the objective of making them comparable in real terms to international rates. Meanwhile, exchange control rules were gradually liberalised. Domestic pension and life insurance funds were allowed to invest up to 50% (later increased to 65%) of their assets abroad. Significantly, all their foreign investments were denominated in non-regional currencies because they regarded the Pula as being too closely linked to the Rand to provide significant diversification of their investment portfolios.

Initially, exchange rate policy was used to reduce inflation. The Pula was revalued periodically, in small discrete amounts, or very gradually so has not to disadvantage exporters during the period before the higher rate of exchange fed through into lower domestic inflation and lower wage increases (which were for many years closely linked to the domestic rate of inflation). There were also occasional devaluations, but as already noted above these were mostly to correct for excessive Pula appreciation against the Rand, caused by Rand depreciation against the major international currencies because the Pula was pegged to various combinations of regional and international currencies.[20]

Over an extended period, using the exchange rate to modify inflation was fairly successful. From 1976 to 1990, the Pula appreciated from R1.00 to R1.37, while consumer prices rose 4.3 times in Botswana compared with 6.2 times in South Africa, and 6.4 times in Swaziland. Moreover, this amelioration of inflation was achieved without damaging the competitive position of non-traditional exporters, because the bilateral real exchange rate against the Rand fluctuated by small amounts around a roughly constant trend.[21] This lessening of inflation, without apparently imposing any costs on the economy, was a pure welfare gain for Botswana which would not have been possible without an independent currency.

From about 1990, exchange rate policy became very much more difficult. There is no satisfactory exchange rate policy when foreign currencies important to Botswana fluctuate against each other. Botswana was frequently fortunate, in that Rand depreciation against the SDR (by more than inflation and interest rate differentials) provided the economy with windfall gains. It increased the real purchasing power of export earnings, most of which were in non-regional currencies while most imports were paid for in Rand. It also increased the purchasing power of the foreign exchange reserves because Botswana took full advantage of being able to hold foreign exchange in foreign currencies other than the Rand, and these reserves were mostly destined to be spent eventually on imports from South Africa. However, when the Zimbabwe Dollar collapsed, starting in 1990, manufactured exports were very badly hit. Textile

---

[19] The commercial banks' unwillingness to accept deposits was caused partly by the low return on assets mentioned in the text, partly by the failure (in the early years after 1976) to find new lending opportunities, and partly by capital adequacy requirements being based (at that time) on deposits so that accepting additional deposits which could not be lent forced them to retain a higher proportion of profits each year.

[20] See the 1994 Bank of Botswana Annual Report for a table of the main exchange rate changes.

[21] The real bilateral exchange rate index against South Africa was 94 in 1990, if 1976 is taken as 100. It fluctuated comfortably within the range 90–110 throughout this period (Harvey 1992, p346).

exports, for example, fell by 39% in 1992 compared to 1991. The Pula was devalued by small amounts, but this was wholly inadequate to make exporters to Zimbabwe competitive again, while increasing inflation in Botswana by making the 80% or so of imports from South Africa more expensive. For most of the 1990s, the Pula has been fluctuating against the Rand in nominal terms by very small amounts, so that exchange rate policy has not been very different from a formal peg against the Rand. While this policy continues, Botswana gains little advantage from having an independent currency, while paying for currency exchange, uncertainty and other related costs.

4. THE EXPERIENCE OF SWAZILAND

Swaziland chose to remain in the Rand Monetary Area. There was therefore, by definition, no impact on investment, tourism and the direction of trade from the choice of currency, because nothing changed. Investors and importers continued to take no currency risk, and faced no exchange controls, on transactions between Swaziland and South Africa. Swaziland also received its share of the profits of the Rand note issue, for a number of years. In theory, Swaziland could have enjoyed this increase in Government revenue without spending anything. In fact, the Government chose to establish the Monetary Authority of Swaziland (which later became the Central Bank of Swaziland), and to issue its own currency (the Lilangeni, plural Emalangeni) to circulate in parallel with the Rand within Swaziland. The two currencies were freely exchangeable at par, and Swaziland received income based on estimates of the domestic note circulation, less the circulation of Emalengeni.

Initially, this decision meant that Swaziland continued to suffer from the disadvantages of monetary union, in not being able to have an independent monetary or exchange rate policy. However, the Government subsequently negotiated a number of concessions which gave it a significant proportion of the policy instruments which it had earlier had to do without.

The commercial banks in Swaziland were incorporated locally, with direct ownership from Britain, and therefore ceased to be part of the South Africa branch network. The Central Bank was then able to establish local regulation of the commercial banks, including liquid asset, local asset and capital adequacy rules.

In 1986, Swaziland negotiated the right to alter its exchange rate against the Rand. This right has never been exercised, although the authorities have considered using it, notably at times of large depreciation of the Rand against non-regional currencies. However, at the same time the Rand's status as legal tender in Swaziland was ended. This meant that Swaziland no longer received income from the profits of the Rand note issue, although Rand continued to circulate freely in Swaziland.

Swaziland also negotiated with South Africa the right to diversify the currency denomination of its foreign exchange reserves, although some two thirds continued to be invested in Rand denominated assets. In contrast, Swaziland pension funds continued to invest exclusively in Rand or local currency assets. Given that their liabilities were all in Swaziland, this eliminated all currency risk. However, it also meant that they were exclusively invested in a minor currency in international terms, which depreciated by more than inflation differentials in the 1980s and 1990s. It is a difficult issue whether such funds should eliminate all currency risk, or diversify by investing in assets denominated in a variety of currencies.

Swaziland also negotiated the right to borrow from its own Central Bank, thereby losing one of the principal advantages of membership of the monetary area. However, this right was not exercised on any significant scale; fiscal policy was cautious and responsible. This makes the experience of Swaziland very much more remarkable than that of Botswana, because Swaziland did not enjoy the huge and sustained increases in Government revenue that Botswana had, mainly from diamonds. As in Botswana, however, past fiscal responsibility is not a guarantee of future policy.

Finally, Swaziland has the right to require domestic financial institutions (other than banks) to invest in local assets. Again, this has not produced significant effects. The Government has allowed financial institutions to continue to invest in South Africa, mainly because of a shortage of investment opportunities in Swaziland.

5. Conclusions

Although Botswana and Swaziland chose what were apparently very different strategies in the 1970s, the differences were steadily reduced. On the one hand, Botswana reduced its financial isolation from South Africa and, therefore, reduced its degree of policy independence. The gradual liberalization of exchange controls on the capital account, together with the strategy of having domestic interest rates similar to international rates, removed one area of potential independent policy. Botswana also ended its strategy of using nominal exchange rate appreciation to lower its inflation below that of South Africa.

On the other hand, Swaziland gradually increased its freedom of action despite remaining within the Common Monetary Area. Swaziland acquired many of the independent policy instruments that Botswana acquired in 1976, although Swaziland chose not to use some of the most important ones, notably the right to revalue or devalue against the Rand.

On the most important issue of all, the right to 'borrow' from the central bank, neither country provides conclusive evidence. Botswana has this right, but has had large financial surpluses from diamond mining, so that it has not yet been anywhere near to a position where it might have been tempted to use it. Nevertheless, it is important to note that Botswana's management of Government spending has been cautious through most of the lengthy period of financial surplus, in sharp contrast to the excessive spending of most other mineral boom economies. The Botswana Government is fully aware of the high cost of overspending elsewhere. Swaziland acquired the right to borrow from its Central Bank eventually, but the Government has also had a conservative fiscal policy, to the point that it too did not borrow significantly from its Central Bank. In their different ways, therefore, both countries were most untypical of Sub-Saharan Africa.

Past performance is not necessarily a guide to future policy. Either Government might be tempted to avoid reductions in its spending, higher taxation, or increased interest rates, by financing a budget deficit with money creation, even if such a choice would only postpone painful adjustment and make that adjustment more difficult eventually. The question arises, therefore, as to whether they should remove that possibility, even though it would mean foregoing some degree of policy independence. This would of course be a remarkable reversal of the policy of independence which both countries in their different ways have gone to great trouble (and expense) to establish.[22] They could try to prevent future fiscal mismanagement by replacing them with currency boards, as in Argentina, or by making their central banks more independent.[23]

To some extent, the question is less relevant than it was, for at least two reasons. Firstly, the current trend in Southern Africa, as in the rest of the world, is to reduce barriers to trade and financial flows. This exposes domestic economies to the judgement of international capital markets. Secondly, those markets have become very much less tolerant of unsustainable budget deficits. Many African countries (although not yet Botswana and Swaziland) have also become extremely dependent on aid donors, who have increasingly made their aid conditional on tight macroeconomic policy.

Governments are therefore exposed to large capital outflows if they lose the confidence of international financial markets, and loss of aid if they lose donor confidence. They can continue with irresponsible fiscal policy, therefore, only to the extent that capital outflows can be financed – by their foreign exchange reserves and their ability to borrow internationally on commercial terms without reform of their macroeconomic policy – and to the extent they can do without aid. Small developing countries cannot usually borrow significantly, even at high interest rates, if they pursue what the markets and donors regard as irresponsible policies, and they do not usually have foreign exchange reserves large enough to finance capital flight. The need to lock themselves into low budget deficits by not having a fully fledged central bank is, therefore, much reduced by the existence of an alternative exogenous policy constraint.[24]

As it happens, Botswana currently has exceptionally large foreign exchange reserves; most of these are matched domestically by Government bank deposits, which, therefore, would not leave the country in a crisis of confidence. However, Botswana will eventually move from budget surplus to budget deficit. This was expected to happen in 1996/97 according to the budget estimates, but subsequent events make a deficit unlikely. Several previous forecasts of a shift into budget deficits have proved premature, but it appears unlikely that Botswana will return to the previous situation of consistently large surpluses. So these exceptional circumstances are not

---

[22] Some indication of the cost of establishing and running the Bank of Botswana is given in the published accounts. At end-1995, fixed assets at cost were P114 million (P97 million net of depreciation), and annual administration costs were P50 million, less a notional P25 million which was the proportion of the Bank's annual income attributable to currency in circulation on which Botswana might have expected to receive income had it remained in the Common (formally Rand) Monetary Area (Bank of Botswana Annual Report, 1995, pp12, 16). However, it cannot be assumed that all these expenses would have been saved if Botswana had not established an independent currency. Swaziland established a Monetary Authority (later converted into a central bank). The fixed assets of the Central Bank of Swaziland net of depreciation were the equivalent of P4.2 million, and operating expenses were P16.7 million in 1996 (Central Bank of Swaziland Annual Report, 1995/96). Swaziland received no income from South Africa on the Rand which continued to circulate within the country, as noted in the text.

[23] Note that the independence of central banks cannot necessarily be sufficient to prevent government overspending. African governments have broken other self-imposed rules. Nevertheless, the breaking of rules does provide a warning, and the rules therefore have some use.

permanent. Nevertheless, Botswana has the luxury of having plenty of time before this question might become significant.[25]

However, unless Botswana's increased exposure to international financial markets is reversed, they should impose much of the fiscal discipline which might otherwise require foregoing the potential risks (and benefits) of having a central bank. Much the same arguments apply to Swaziland. They should both, therefore, be able to retain the additional ability to adjust to asymmetric shocks, with rather less concern over the potential for economic mismanagement provided by having a central bank from which to borrow, than would have been the case before the current international constraints became so effective.

References

De Grauwe, P. 1992. *The Economics of Monetary Integration.* Oxford University Press, Oxford.

Government of Botswana. 1966. *Transitional Plan for Social and Economic Development.* Government of Botswana, Gaborone.

Government of Botswana. 1968. *National Development Plan, 1968–73.* Government of Botswana, Gaborone.

Harvey, C. 1991. 'On the Perverse Effects of Financial Sector Reform in Anglophone Africa', *South African Journal of Economics* Vol.59, No.3.

Harvey, C. 1992. 'Botswana: Is the Economic Miracle Over?' *Journal of African Economies*, Vol.1, No.3. Oxford University Press, Oxford.

Harvey, C. and Lewis, S.R. 1990. *Policy Choice and Development Performance in Botswana.* Macmillan Press, London.

Hubbard, M. 1986. *Agricultural Exports and Economic Growth: a Study of Botswana's Beef Industry.* KPI.

---

[24] The risk is not eliminated, however. There are examples in Africa of governments which have ignored both donors and financial markets, even though the penalties are severe. Moreover, governments can get into financial difficulties without being able to borrow from a central bank, as shown for example by Liberia (which used the United States Dollar rather than having its own currency), or indeed by New York City. Both Botswana and Swaziland have low debt service ratios (of foreign debt service to exports) which might allow them to increase their foreign borrowing rapidly for a few years. The newly independent Zimbabwe Government inherited a low debt service ratio in 1980 because of sanctions during the UDI period, found that it could borrow extensively, increased its debt service ratio to excessive levels within two years, and has struggled to cope with the problem that this created ever since.

[25] Having large financial surpluses, both current and accumulated, exposes Botswana to the risk of Government overspending. This happened in the late 1980s with high costs. It could not have been prevented by the international capital market or donor disapproval, nor by inability to borrow from a central bank.

Central Banks as Protectors of National Wealth: Botswana's Case

Linah Kelebogile Mohohlo

1. INTRODUCTION – GENERAL PRINCIPLES OF RESERVE MANAGEMENT

Traditionally, international reserves have been defined as liquid financial assets that a country holds to readily meet obligations arising out of balance of payments transactions. In more recent years, this definition has been broadened to include financial assets readily available for intervention to influence a national currency's exchange rate on the foreign exchange market.

From the definition, we deduce that the primary purpose of holding reserves is to facilitate the timely meeting of payment obligations. However, when absorptive capacity constrains the use of reserves for productive purposes, or large surpluses in the balance of payments, that are transient, arise, a temporary phase of accumulating foreign financial assets in excess of the level required for meeting normal balance of payments obligations cannot be ruled out.

The amount of reserves that should be regarded as appropriate can be classified into two categories: (1) the working balances; and (2) the precautionary balances. Working balances should be held in highly liquid form, either in freely convertible currencies and/or in the currencies of major trading partners. The remainder of the portfolio should follow the investment principles in which the choice of currencies and instruments is based on the principal characteristics of reserve assets, *viz.* safety, liquidity and a competitive rate of return. It hardly needs to be emphasised that reserves, particularly the precautionary balances, should be kept in currency media that are convertible, relatively less susceptible to frequent and sharp exchange rate fluctuations, generally free from restrictions on their use and the products of a well-developed financial market.

In a majority of countries, the responsibility of managing reserves is vested in central banks. Therefore, central banks are indeed protectors of national wealth, as they invest the countries' reserves cautiously, prudently and conservatively.

In the light of the above, this paper addresses the Bank of Botswana's approach to reserve management. Section 1, which serves as the introduction, addresses the general principles of reserve management. Sections 2 to 5 discuss Botswana's case of reserve management, with particular reference to the institutional framework and the practical issues relating to investment policy and guidelines. Section 6 focuses on the tranching of reserves into three portfolios – the Liquidity Portfolio, the Matched Asset/Liability Portfolio and a long-term investment fund, the Pula Fund. Section 7 concludes the paper.

2. BOTSWANA'S CASE

Botswana's economic circumstances cannot be regarded as typical of many developing countries. While its economic base is very narrow, it has the unique advantage of holding one of the highest levels of international reserves in the world, equivalent to approximately 28 months[1] of imports of goods and services. This exceptional level of reserves is a recent phenomenon for Botswana; and, consequently, it is only natural that utilization of these reserves has proceeded slowly, reflecting the fact that formulating and effecting viable development projects that could draw upon the reserves involves time.

FIGURE 1. FOREIGN EXCHANGE RESERVES

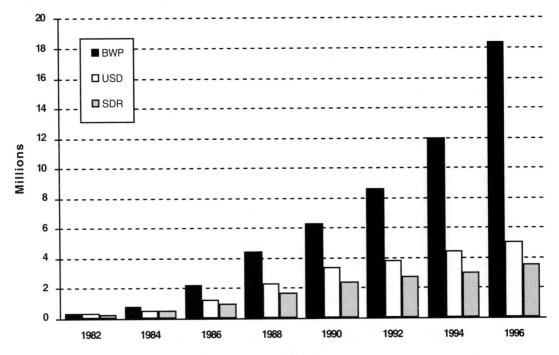

Notes: Gross foreign exchange reserves, including IMF holdings and reserve tranche.
SDR/BWP exchange rate for end of December 1996 = 0.1910.
USD/BWP exchange rate for end of December 1996 = 0.2744.

Botswana is one of the world's leading diamond exporters. The mining sector continues to dominate the economy, contributing approximately 33% of Gross Domestic Product (GDP) and 75% of exports. From 1982/83 until 1988/89, the rising earnings of the diamond sector, most of which accrued to the Government, together with restrained expenditures, resulted in a continued overall balance of payments and Government budget surpluses. Imports partly reflected the purchase of capital goods used in infrastructural development.

Nevertheless, the overall balance of payments situation remains reasonably strong, and gross foreign reserves at the end of 1996 stood at approximately P18.3 billion (approximately USD5 billion or SDR3.5 billion).

The philosophy behind reserve management at the Bank of Botswana, like that at many central banks, is that of conservative asset management. In the early 1980s, the practice was to maintain foreign currency fixed deposits in the international banking system for a large proportion of reserves and to stagger maturities to ensure liquidity. This process necessitated daily meetings of the senior management of the Bank. Over time, the Bank accumulated experience and broadened its investments to include a variety of good quality negotiable instruments, such as negotiable certificates of deposit, repurchase agreements, bankers acceptances, treasury notes and bonds. Because of the increasing complexity of moving from fixed deposits to high-quality bonds and securities, the Bank established a Portfolio Analysis Unit within the Research Department to serve as a 'think tank'.

In view of the growing size of the country's foreign exchange reserves in the second half of the 1980s (Figure 1), the increasing complexities of the international financial markets and the need to streamline the functions of various Departments of the Bank to promote efficiency and better administration, the Bank created the International Department in 1989. This was achieved by merging the Portfolio Analysis Unit of the Research Department and the Foreign Exchange Unit of the then Operations Department (renamed Banking Department since 1994).[2]

3. INSTITUTIONAL FRAMEWORK

The Bank of Botswana Act empowers the Bank to, among other things, establish and maintain an international reserve. It follows, therefore, that these reserves need to be managed, and this responsibility is vested in the International Department.

The International Department: Structure and Mission

Among other responsibilities[3], the International Department advises the Governor on the general strategy of investing Botswana's foreign exchange reserves, and advises the Investment Committee on the day-to-day implementation of that strategy. It also executes any decisions taken by the Investment Committee with regard to changes in the investment portfolio. As at the end of 1997 the Department is divided into the Market Monitoring and Dealing Unit, the Settlement Unit and the Verification Unit.

The Market Monitoring and Dealing Unit obtains views from the Bank's external fund managers[4] and other overseas counterparts[5], observes the Reuters monitor screen

---

[1] As at the end of December 1996.

[2] See the section 'The Organisation of the Bank' in the paper by H.C.L. Hermans in this volume.

[3] The other responsibilities include the implementation of the Bank's exchange rate policy; supplying the authorized dealers with their foreign exchange requirements and buying from them any foreign funds that are surplus to their requirements. The Department also manages the interest rate policy by issuing Bank of Botswana Certificates (central bank paper, akin to treasury bills); and executes foreign currency payments for the Government and other account holders.

[4] The Bank has made a conscious decision to have a portion of the reserves managed by external fund managers for various reasons. For example, the fund managers provide an element of insurance against a possible brain drain from the Bank; they also provide specialist training to Bank staff on a regular basis at their home base; and implicitly provide a benchmark against which the performance of the Bank's staff can be compared.

[5] See note 16 for a description of 'counterpart'.

throughout the day, makes in-depth analysis of markets, and prepares background papers for the Investment Committee.[6] A background paper contains current information on the portfolio's currency distribution, modified duration, the state of the markets and any related recommendations. Charts that indicate, among others, the maturity profiles of the Bank's assets within each investment currency, and yield curves showing for each currency the up-to-date relationship of interest rates, plotted against a number of years to maturity, are also attached to a background paper. The Investment Committee then makes decisions as to changes in the portfolio, if any, in both currency composition and modified duration[7] within each currency, for subsequent implementation.

The Unit is given some working limits as the actual day-to-day positions may deviate by small margins from the decisions of the Investment Committee. Within such limits, the International Department has complete discretion.

The acquisition of advanced computer and software systems helps to enhance market analysis and dealing. These include Bloomberg and advanced Reuters systems, such as Prism Reuters Money 2000 and Dealing 2000. The portfolio management system's (HiPortfolio) front office (dealing and portfolio analysis) techniques are an added advantage.

The Settlement Unit's primary responsibilities are to ensure that the Bank meets its obligations to pay and receive correct value for the transactions with respect to foreign exchange, securities and deposits, as contracted with the counterparts. The Unit also executes foreign currency payments for the Government. The Settlement Unit is organized into two sections, the Back Office and the Transfers sections, which are responsible for the settlement of foreign exchange and securities transactions and for the settlement of foreign exchange payments for the Government and other account holders, respectively. In addition to telex and telephone facilities, the Bank uses the Society for Worldwide Interbank Funds Telecommunications (SWIFT) to enhance the settlement of transactions on due dates. The portfolio management system, which also has back office capabilities that include both the telex and SWIFT interfaces, makes funds transfer easier.

The Verification Unit investigates the movement of funds and follows up on unreconcilable accounting (nostro)[8] ledger items.

---

6   The Investment Committee, which is chaired by the Deputy Governor, meets regularly. All the analysts/dealers from the International Department attend as co-opted members; they are responsible for making presentations on the status of the markets they are responsible for. It also includes the Director of the Research Department and a representative of the Finance Department. On the basis of the presentations, appropriate recommendations (and ultimate decisions) are made regarding currency composition and the duration of the Bank's investments.

7   Modified duration is the percentage price change of a bond (or a portfolio) for a one percent interest rate change. In other words, modified duration can be used to estimate the percentage price volatility of a fixed-income security, thus:

$$\frac{\Delta P}{P} \times 100 = D_{\text{mod}} \times \Delta Y$$

Where: P = Price of a bond (security), Y = Yield (interest rate), D_{mod} = Modified Duration.

8   The Bank's accounts with external entities (e.g., banks).

4. INVESTMENT POLICY

Three considerations guide the Bank's broad investment policy: the maintenance of value (safety), liquidity and return.

Maintenance of Value

At all times, the preservation of the value of the country's foreign exchange reserves should be paramount. The investment strategies pursued should be conservative and diversified to maintain the real value of the assets in terms of a basket of currencies. Safety considerations should include the control of currency, interest rates and credit risk.

Liquidity

This objective ensures the timely availability of adequate resources at a reasonable price to meet all anticipated and unanticipated commitments and, thus, to assure that international payments are fulfilled. Furthermore, liquidity within each currency facilitates currency switches. The Bank achieves the timely availability of adequate resources through the holding of assets in liquid form or assets (instruments) that can be sold without undue sacrifice in value.

Return

Given the first two policy objectives, the foreign exchange reserves must be invested in a manner consistent with maximizing return within a framework of acceptable risks[9], drawing no distinction between current income, capital movements and currency movements.

5. INVESTMENT GUIDELINES

The investment guidelines serve as a strategic set of rules that describe and define the means of achieving the investment policy. They are divided into four categories of risk, *viz.* currency risk, interest rate risk, credit risk and risk with respect to liquidity and instruments.

Currency Risk

In determining the currency composition of the foreign exchange reserves, the Bank has distinguished between investment-grade currencies (in which investments can be made) and currencies with working balances only (to facilitate immediate payment of liabilities as and when they are due for payment). Individual currencies may be moved from one category to another as circumstances change.

---

[9] In an efficient market, reducing the risk level of a portfolio by adding less risky investments implies reducing its expected return. However, the concept of diversification implies no reduction in return; it lowers risk by eliminating non-systematic (non-market) volatility without sacrificing expected return.

In addition, the Bank has determined benchmarks against which the performance of both the Bank and the fund managers are measured. The benchmarks were composed with due regard to the list of priorities contained in the investment policy.

Determination of Currency Benchmark

As indicated above, the main policy objective for the investment of the foreign exchange reserves is the maintenance of value in terms of purchasing power, while the secondary policy objective is to maintain sufficient liquidity in the portfolio. The Bank of Botswana established benchmark currency compositions that are consistent with these policy objectives to allow it to measure whether, and to what degree, the policy objectives have been met. The benchmark is the risk-free policy-consistent position against which the performance of the actual portfolio can be measured.

To find the risk-free currency composition of assets, investors with investment policy objectives similar to those of the Bank of Botswana look to the currency composition of their liabilities. If the two are matched completely, the portfolio of assets and liabilities is immunized against currency movements. In the case of the Bank of Botswana, the liabilities are the anticipated future outflows from the portfolio in the form of payments for imports of goods, services and others.

Earlier, the Bank of Botswana adopted the SDR[10] as a currency benchmark. It was clear, however, that this benchmark was not based on the principles mentioned above because there is a big South African rand value-added component in the Bank's liabilities or potential outflows from the portfolio. The Bank regarded the SDR as a good alternative in terms of diversifying the portfolio's currency risk, and also because of the five component currencies' importance in the world economy and the efficiency of their capital markets. The South African rand holding was made small, partly because it was not expected to perform very well relative to the SDR.

In addressing the question of establishing a more correct currency benchmark, the Bank of Botswana looked only at the immunization of the holdings on the existing stock of reserves, and not at the currency mismatch of the constant flow of payments in and out of the portfolio (because this was beyond the Bank of Botswana's control). Therefore, the current stock of reserves as a store of value against a hypothetically possible abnormal future rundown of the reserves was studied.

In the event of a rundown of reserves, the money would be spent only on those payments for goods and services which are not self-financing in foreign exchange terms. For instance, foreign currency dividends paid by De Beers Botswana Mining Company to De Beers Prospecting Botswana[11] are self-financing in that they are funded by foreign currency diamond sales.

The Bank made a list of only those current account items for which foreign exchange payments would actually be required from the existing stock of reserves. The resulting pattern of payments for non-self-financing current account items was

---

[10] Abbreviation for Special Drawing Rights, which is the unit of account of the International Monetary Fund composed of five currencies with the following weights: US dollar, 39%; Deutsche mark, 21%; Japanese yen, 18%; French franc, 11%; and British pound sterling, 11%. The weights are effective from January, 1996.

[11] De Beers Botswana Mining Company and De Beers Prospecting Company are the Botswana mining and the South African prospecting companies, respectively.

broken down into currencies of origin. The goods paid for in South African rand were separated into South African value-added items, representing genuine rand costs, and those components of Rand invoices which were originally imported into South Africa and then re-exported to Botswana. The re-exports could include (1) an unaltered item (for example, a computer); (2) a component in an assembled item (for example, an imported engine in a South African assembled car); and (3) products such as petrol and diesel that were refined in South Africa from imported crude oil.

To this the Bank added the expected outflow of capital to meet debt repayments. Other more speculative capital movements were not taken into account due to the inability to determine the gross amount on the ultimate currency composition of possible capital flight.

Thus, the resulting purchasing power benchmark is consistent with the main policy objective of maintaining the value of the foreign exchange reserves by maintaining the purchasing power of the foreign exchange reserves.[12]

As the benchmark should also meet the second policy objective of maintaining sufficient liquidity in the portfolio, it became necessary to look at the efficiency of the capital markets involved to determine a purchasing power/liquidity benchmark.

The efficiency of the major currencies' capital markets is excellent, and there are no exchange control problems as far as the Bank's investments are concerned. Conversely, the liquidity of the capital markets of some of the countries with which Botswana trades is not so good; exchange control regulations are very restrictive on the repatriation of investment proceeds.

Against this background, the Bank established a customised benchmark for the measurement of the day-to-day portfolio performance. The main objective is to the performance of the Bank relative to the performance of fund managers against a common benchmark.

Interest Rate (market) Risk

A fundamental feature of fixed-income investments is that the longer the investment's repayment period, the more volatile the asset price; thus, the price of a long-term bond falls more than that of a short-term bond when interest rates go up. Time deposits do not have a variable price, because they are not marketable. The same principle applies to time deposits as that for fixed-income investments, but losses are measured by way of opportunity cost rather than price movement. At the same time, yields are normally higher for longer-term investments than for short-term investments. These principles allow the derivation of an upward sloping, or a positive sloping yield curve. Therefore, there normally is a trade-off between risk and return. In this respect, the guidelines' objective was to define the maximum amount of risk that should be taken, with due regard to the life of the Bank's liabilities, the expected return and the magnitude of risk aversion.

---

[12] This so called 'risk neutral' benchmark should reflect currency weights which would approximate the country's pattern of imports; for example; in the case of Botswana, the weights might be South African rand – 58%; US dollar – 14%; British pound sterling – 10%; Deutche mark – 9%; Zimbabwean dollar – 6%; and Japanese yen – 3%.

Measurement of Interest Rate Risk

In the past, the conventional way of measuring the interest rate risk of a bond or a portfolio has been to calculate the average life to maturity of the asset. As interest rate movements became more volatile and risk control more important, another method was introduced. This method is called duration[13] and is now widely used as a more precise measurement of interest rate risk. Measured by this method, the risk measure, duration, becomes a smaller number than the number of months to maturity (except for zero-coupon bonds). The life-to-maturity method is easier to compute but exaggerates the risk. Furthermore, by using modified duration[14] one gets an even more precise measure for the risk involved.

The Bank has used the weighted average of the three Salomon Brothers' performance indices as the market risk benchmark, for some time. The three indices are as follows:

- a money market index (based on two to three-month Treasury Bills or short-dated time deposits), which has a 50% weight;
- a one to three-year government bond index, with a 25% weight; and
- a three to seven-year government bond index, with a 25% weight.

These indices have a combined average life to maturity of 1.8 years and a combined average modified duration of 1.5 years. A maximum deviation from the benchmark is set in order to ensure that no undue interest rate risk is taken by those managing the portfolio. However, the maximum deviation set should not restrict the ability of the fund managers from exploiting market movements to a reasonable extent.

There is no restriction on the downside; the entire portfolio can be put into cash or short-dated instruments if the Investment Committee deems that choice desirable; for example, if there were a high risk of a widespread rise in interest rates. This strategy ensures that a reasonable amount of cash is always available to meet the near-term outflows and that investments are not concentrated in one maturity area, as interest rate movements tend to be different in one maturity area from another.[15]

The Bank introduced the practice of using forward transactions as a means of hedging currency risk some time ago. There is a small amount of interest rate risk involved in using forwards, depending on the length of the forward transactions entered into.

Credit Risk

Credit risk is the risk to an investor, such as the Bank of Botswana, that a debtor[16]

---

[13] The difference between life to maturity and duration is that maturity only takes into account the repayment of a bond's principal, whereas duration also considers the life-to-maturity of coupon receipts during the life of a bond. Duration is the weighted-average life of all future cash flows of a bond, both interest and capital; it is measured in units of time, either months or years.

[14] See note 7 for an explanation of 'modified duration'.

[15] A change in the shape of the yield curve.

[16] Such as a commercial bank accepting a deposit or a government issuing a bond or a counterpart with whom the Bank has contracted to buy or sell foreign exchange or money and/or capital market instruments.

will be unable to meet its financial obligations on the due date. The Bank of Botswana is mainly involved in three kinds of credit risk: (1) bank risk; (2) sovereign/supranational risk; and (3) counterpart risk. Additional risk arises from the use of fund managers, who are in a position of trust. However, the Bank has appointed a third-party custodian that had to obtain adequate insurance cover against, among others, any failure to account to the Bank for any money resulting from error or omission, wrongful or negligent act, dishonest or fraudulent act of an employee, loss of valuable property on the premises, or electronic and computer crime. There are also a number of safeguards against any potential risk, such as the fund managers' membership of the Investment Management Regulatory Organization (IMRO)[17], and of other regulatory organs in major investment centres.

In general, bank risk is greater than the risk pertaining to good-quality sovereign/ supranational issuers, but the return on bank debt generally is also higher. Because both AA and AAA[18] rated sovereign and supranational risk is of a higher quality than bank risk, there is no restriction on such holdings.

The Bank of Botswana subscribes to the International Bank Credit Analysis (IBCA) rating system, and selects only best-quality banks, where the limits are graduated according to each bank's credit standing. Country limits are set for bank deposits, as well as for sovereign/supranational entities.

Liquidity and Instruments

Liquidity in portfolio management should ensure that outflows can be met without incurring undue costs and should provide flexibility to respond effectively to changing market conditions. The Investment Committee balances the portfolio assets between time deposits and high-quality bonds and securities that are highly marketable. The liquidity of instruments rather than a ladder of maturities of time deposits primarily assures adequate liquidity in the portfolio.

The Bank's assets are invested in a range of money market instruments and bonds, as well as in floating-rate notes. The Bank may not borrow funds.

6. Tranching of Reserves

The role of the Bank of Botswana as a protector of national wealth was given more focus when a decision was made to manage its reserves in three tranches.

The Bank implemented the decision to partition Botswana's foreign exchange reserves into separate segments, or tranches, after extensive consultations with the Government regarding the evaluation of future balance of payments trends. The decision was based on the recommendation of the 1989 World Bank/Government of Botswana report *Financial Policies for Diversified Growth*, which recognised that Botswana needed to maintain somewhat larger reserve balances than most developing countries, because of factors over which it has little or no control. The country is

---

[17] Applicable to the United Kingdom based fund managers only.

[18] The ratings used are by the two major international rating agencies – Moodys and Standard and Poor – in ranking sovereign (government), local government, parastatal and supranational risk or debt.

a relatively undiversified primary commodity exporter; its terms of trade depend to a substantial degree on the real exchange rate between the Rand and the SDR; it is susceptible to periods of sustained drought; and there were geopolitical uncertainties in the region at the time.

The decision to tranche Botswana's foreign exchange reserves also recognized that reserve levels were considerably higher than those required for normal transaction balance purposes, or as insurance against economic adversity. The external sector had been generating an increasing overall surplus for some time. While there had been some slowing in the rate of increase since 1991, the international reserves rose from P311 million at the end of 1982 to P5200 million at the end of 1989. At the equivalent of approximately 18 months of imports of goods and services, Botswana's level of foreign exchange reserve in 1989 had become, in real terms, among the highest in the world.

Consequently, in August 1990, the Bank decided to divide the foreign exchange reserves into three tranches, *viz.* a Liquidity Portfolio, a Matched Asset/Liability Portfolio, and the Pula Fund (a long-term investment fund) to be managed separately to facilitate the meeting of different objectives.

Liquidity Portfolio

In determining the appropriate size of the Liquidity Portfolio, it was felt that the portfolio should be treated as a buffer against short-term trade and capital account fluctuations, as well as a cushion to finance unforeseen developments in the external payments situation. That is, the Liquidity Portfolio was intended to be the conventional central bank transaction balance reserves. Although the equivalent of three months of import cover is generally considered an adequate level of foreign exchange reserves, there is no universally accepted or applicable level that could be taken as a norm, because it depends on a number of exogenous factors, such as international economic developments.

After due consideration of all the factors relevant to Botswana's case, the Bank of Botswana and the Government agreed on a target level of reserves in the Liquidity Portfolio of six months of import cover. Should the holdings in the Liquidity Portfolio fall below that level, the first line of defence to improve the balance of payments would be macroeconomic policy adjustments affecting interest rates, the exchange rate and Government revenues and expenditures, among others. In case such measures prove insufficient to stabilise the reserve level in the Liquidity Portfolio, a trigger point for starting to draw on the Pula Fund was agreed upon. It was agreed that the target level of reserves in the Liquidity Portfolio will be reviewed during the preparation of each (six-year) National Development Plan, as well as the preparation of each Mid-Term Review of such plans.

The Liquidity Portfolio's investment policy and guidelines are the same as those outlined in sections 4 and 5 of this paper, barring potential minor changes of, among others, performance indices.

Matched Asset/Liability Portfolio[19]

The purpose of creating a Matched Asset/Liability Portfolio (MALP) was to set aside foreign currency investments to match the liability side of the country's official balance sheet, i.e., the country's total external debt. Combined asset/liability management leads to better risk management than when asset management and liability management are looked at separately. One of the major reasons for creating the MALP was to signal to the nation that the country has borrowed funds from abroad and has debt service obligations to foreigners; therefore, extra care should be exercised before utilising the reserves.

There may be an adverse impact from having reserves set aside in the MALP in that foreign lenders (governments and development institutions) may get the impression that concessional lending to Botswana is not needed, and, therefore, this source of funding could dry up. However, the lenders must already be aware of Botswana's foreign reserve position, and of the development strategy that has given rise to the accumulation of reserves.

The Bank of Botswana is pursuing a cautious policy and strategy to invest its foreign exchange reserves. If, however, there is a mismatch between the Bank's assets and liabilities of the Government and the parastatals, then the Bank's investments to some extent become leveraged and more risky. At the end of 1996, the public and publicly guaranteed external debt amounted to approximately P2000 million (approximately USD550 million).[20] Committed, but undisbursed loan balances amounted to approximately P1160 million (approximately USD320 million).

Because the main objective for MALP was to minimise the inherent risk between public and publicly guaranteed external assets and liabilities, to account for currency risk, all currencies in which the liabilities were denominated had to be eligible for investment. For practical reasons, however, it became necessary to invest the assets in currencies other than those in which the liabilities were denominated. In such a case, the correlation between the currencies in question had to be as high as possible.

In terms of the interest rate risk, the Bank of Botswana chose the cash-matching[21] approach to minimise the maturity mismatch. In Botswana's case, foreign public and publicly guaranteed liabilities can only be redeemed at par. There is no secondary market where the issuer (Botswana) can buy back its own debt instruments for redemption purposes. Therefore, the liabilities have no interest rate sensitivity; the price of a loan remains at par whether interest rates go up or down. In such a case, a cash-matching approach is preferable. However, in view of the inherent interest rate risk of such an approach, the Bank adopted a duration-matching[22] approach as well, beyond a five to six-year period.

The Liquidity Portfolio's guidelines for the control of credit risk were adopted for the MALP.

---

[19] In a bid to streamline the portfolio structure of the foreign exchange reserves in a manner which delineates the Government's portion and that which belongs to the rest of the economy, the MALP was discontinued at the end of 1996. It is now implicitly part of the Government's portion of the Pula Fund.

[20] This is 14% and 11% of GDP (current prices) and total foreign exchange reserves, respectively.

[21] Cash-matching is a strategy that uses asset receipts to fund liability payments. The objective is to find the lowest cost asset portfolio that provides cash in the form of principal, coupon and reinvestment income on or before the date it is needed to meet each liability payment.

[22] Instead of matching each individual cash flow, one can match the interest rate sensitivity of assets and liabilities by ensuring that they have the same duration. The objective is to find the highest yielding portfolio whose market value and interest rate sensitivity match those of the liabilities.

The investment policy of the MALP stressed low risk, the maintenance of sufficient liquid assets to meet debt service payments and a fractionally higher rate of return for the assets than that paid for the liabilities. The objective was to ensure that Botswana is certain to benefit from the subsidy element of loans granted by governments and international institutions, and to ensure the honouring of debt obligations at all times.

Consequently, the Government established a Loans Committee, comprising senior staff of the Bank of Botswana and the Government with responsibility to, *inter alia*, identify broad criteria for approval of new borrowing and consider the early repayment of existing loans.

Pula Fund[23]

The primary objective of establishing a long-term investment fund was to ensure that Botswana's national savings, broadly defined, are deployed in a way so as to optimise their contribution to sustained national economic development. To the extent that the economy cannot absorb such resources for productive purposes without distorting domestic prices or merely changing the ownership of assets (for example, full or partial nationalization of private companies), long-term offshore investments needed to be considered. A secondary objective for establishing the Pula Fund was to 'depoliticize' the investment of financial resources, and to mitigate or deflect demands for their immediate use for unproductive or unsustainable public purposes.

Another objective was to take advantage of the high foreign exchange reserve level and invest part of the reserves in longer-term assets, such as longer-term bonds and equities, with the expectation of earning a higher return in the long term than could be achieved on conventionally managed foreign exchange reserves. It was considered that this practice could develop a long-term earner of foreign exchange for the country. Such earnings would allow sustained long-term development, even if export earnings were to be adversely affected by factors over which Botswana has no control. Based on historical data over a long period, longer-term bonds and equities are normally expected to outperform short-term assets, such as cash and short-term bonds, which comprise the bulk of investments in the Liquidity Portfolio. Returns on longer-term assets are, however, more volatile than returns on short-term assets; it is, therefore, necessary to have a longer investment horizon to forecast the expected higher return with some degree of confidence.

It was recognized that the Pula Fund may be accessed to meet certain contingencies, such as to finance additional viable domestic development projects not already catered for in the National Development Plans. The Government and the Bank of Botswana noted that the National Development Plan strategy attached greater priority to using the foreign exchange reserves, above those needed for liquidity and contingency purposes, as well as those needed for enabling Botswana to service its debt, in order to invest productively and develop Botswana to the extent such opportunities were available and could be implemented effectively, rather than on establishing a long-term investment fund. The Fund is only viewed as a prudent and yield-maximizing alternative to investing productively in Botswana, until opportunities to do so

---

23 Pula is also the name of the national currency of Botswana. The word means 'rain' and is used as, *inter alia*, a blessing, a toast and a slogan of hope (partly because the country is prone to persistent drought).

arise and can be programmed into National Development Plans. Hence, the investment policies for the Pula Fund were rearranged and prioritised slightly differently from those of the Liquidity Portfolio, as follows: safety (maintenance of value or purchasing power), return and liquidity.

The Pula Fund was formally launched in November 1993 on completion of the legal requirements, first between the Bank and the fund managers, and then between the Bank and the global custodian.

As far as the size of the Pula Fund is concerned, the Bank and the Government agreed that appropriate levels will be determined from time to time after allowing for an agreed target in the Liquidity Portfolio.

The fund managers have managed a smaller portion of the foreign exchange reserves on the Bank's behalf since 1988. The tranching of the foreign exchange reserves and the resulting implementation of the Pula Fund brought about a new approach to external fund management mainly because of the reduction in the size of the Liquidity Portfolio and entry into equity investments.

The Pula Fund was then divided into various mandates to reflect the specialist approach of individual fund managers and to benefit from the expected higher returns inherent in diversified investment portfolios.

After extensive consultation with specialists in external fund management, the Bank reviewed past relationships, evaluated the performance of the most successful fund managers and interviewed leading short-listed firms for each mandate. At the conclusion of this process, the Bank appointed several external fund managers to manage a portion of the Pula Fund under various mandates. In the evaluation exercise, emphasis was placed on investment experience and stability, investment style, decision making process, past performance, willingness to train Bank staff and fees.

The Bank has developed specialised investment guidelines for each mandate, which contain, *inter alia,* the benchmarks against which the performance of the respective portfolios and the individual fund managers are measured. The benchmarks reflect an element of discretion in terms of permissible deviations from the established market parameters. Furthermore, the benchmarks reflect the longer-term duration of the investment instruments of the Pula Fund.

Through discussions with the fund managers and the Bank's portfolio consultants, it became clear that the funds are better protected if they are held with a third-party custodian instead of either the fund managers or their own agents/subsidiaries. Global custody offers advantages through centralised reporting on, among others, portfolio valuation and performance measurement, providing an audit trail of transactions generated by all the fund managers, facilitating and monitoring fund managers' adherence to investment guidelines, and providing the necessary third-party 'checks and balances', to ensure that the fund managers execute their investment activities according to the respective investment mandates and guidelines.

A global custodian was, therefore, appointed for the first time in 1993 for the custody of all the foreign exchange reserves.[26]

---

[26] Excluding SDR holdings and the reserve position at the International Monetary Fund.

7. CONCLUSION

Admittedly, in the majority of countries, central banks enjoy a monopoly as far as the management of foreign exchange reserves are concerned. However, there is no room for complacency in undertaking this major responsibility of protecting national wealth, as demonstrated by the caution exercised by the Bank of Botswana in, *inter alia,* the determination of investment policy and guidelines, the selection of external fund managers and the selection of appropriate investment instruments or asset classes, while not sacrificing the utilization, by the Government, of the reserves in sustainable development and/or infrastructural projects.

In Botswana's case, the foreign exchange reserves are substantial, and the Bank of Botswana will continue to manage them in the best national interest. In particular, the purchasing power that the reserves command from one period to another should at least be maintained in real terms, while the reserves continue to be invested to yield the best returns possible within permissible risk parameters. As the reserves grow, increasingly sophisticated arrangements will continue to evolve to facilitate accomplishing these objectives.

As indicated above, the Bank recognises the need to respond to changes in Botswana's economic circumstances when they affect reserve levels, and will endeavour to reflect these changes in its reserve management activities.

REFERENCES

Alder, M. and Dumas, B. 1983. 'International Portfolio Choice and Corporation Finance: A Synthesis', *Journal of Finance*, June 1983.

Bank of Botswana Annual Reports, 1982 – 1996.

Levy, H. and Sarnat, M. 1984. *Portfolio and Investment Selection: Theory and Practice.* Prentice-Hall, Englewood Cliffs, N.J.

Ibbotson, R.G. and Brinson, G.P. 1987. *Investment Markets – Gaining the Performance Advantage.* McGraw-Hill, New York.

Mohohlo, L.K. 1993. 'Tranching of Botswana's Foreign Exchange Reserves', *The Research Bulletin,* Vol.11, No.2. Bank of Botswana, Gaborone.

Roger, S. 1993. *The Management of Foreign Exchange Reserves.* Bank for International Settlements, Basle.

Solnik, B. 1988. *International Investments.* Addison Wesley, New York.

Measures of Central Bank Performance in Botswana

Return on Foreign Exchange Reserves and Revenues Paid to Government

Jay S. Salkin[1]

1. INTRODUCTION

One of the primary reasons Botswana left the Rand Monetary Area and established its own currency and central bank was to enable the authorities to accumulate foreign exchange reserves on which they could earn interest income (Government of Botswana, 1975, p5, and Hermans in this volume, p179). By putting Pula into circulation and exchanging the Rand that had been in circulation for Pula, the Rand which the authorities expected to acquire could be invested in interest earning assets abroad. Such earnings were estimated to be substantially greater than the cost of establishing a central bank and printing and minting the Pula notes and Thebe coins that were to become the legal tender of Botswana. In addition, the authorities believed that there were other developmental benefits that could be achieved by being able to execute an independent monetary policy.

Over the years since the Pula was introduced the international reserves have grown to some P13.25 billion as at the end of December 1995, equivalent to about 25 months of import cover for goods and services (Bank of Botswana, 1995, p39). In addition, over that same period, the Bank of Botswana has been able to give Government revenues totalling over P6.2 billion, approximately 15% of the total revenue and grants received by the Government (Government of Botswana, *Financial statements, Tables and Estimates of Consolidated and Development Revenues* various issues). By fiscal year 1993/94, when the Bank provided P1107 million, the Bank of Botswana had become the second largest source of revenue to Government, after minerals (Salkin, 1994).

The revenues which the Bank has been able to distribute to Government have derived primarily from the income and revaluation gains that have been recorded on the international reserves held by the Bank. The precise arrangements by which the amounts that the Bank distributed to Government are determined have been

---

[1] The author wishes to acknowledge helpful comments from Matthew Wright and Charles Harvey. Felix Phindela assisted with the data collection. The underlying data for the Bank's performance, which come from the Bank's Annual Reports, the Government's Financial Statements, Tables and Estimates of Consolidated and Development Fund Revenues and the IMF's International Financial Statistics, along with the derived results presented, are available from the author upon request.

specified in the Bank of Botswana Act, which has been revised several times (Bank of Botswana Act, 1975, 1987). They are described in more detail in Section 3.

FIGURE 1. IMPORT COVER FOR GOODS AND SERVICES

While a major source of revenue to Government, the amounts distributed have been highly variable and uncertain, which has been a source of concern to the authorities who would have preferred a more predictable and reliable revenue flow to Government. As a result of the high variability and uncertainty associated with the income and revaluation gains and losses of the Bank from the investment of the foreign exchange reserves, the draft Bank of Botswana Bill, 1996 proposes to alter the nature of the distribution formula of revenue to Government.

Institutionally responsible for managing and preserving the international purchasing power of the foreign exchange reserves, the Bank of Botswana has developed investment strategies and procedures that seek to satisfy several primary objectives, which are conventionally summarised in the terms *safety, liquidity* and *return* (Bank of Botswana, 1994, p64). Safety refers to investing the foreign exchange reserves in a manner that protects their international purchasing power, so that they can ensure that Botswana is able to make future payments for imports of goods and services and debt servicing (*ibid.*, p65). The liquidity of the foreign exchange reserves relates to being able to have adequate financial resources when needed to meet all commitments for international payments, whether anticipated or unanticipated, without having to incur too great a transaction cost. While taking into account the issues of safety and liquidity, the Bank invests the foreign exchange reserves so as to maximise returns, including current income, capital gains and currency revaluations.

As a result of the growth in foreign exchange reserves to levels above that felt necessary for purely transactions and prudential contingency purposes, the strategies for investing the foreign exchange reserves have changed over time (World Bank, 1989, pp171–172). This has involved the partitioning of Botswana's foreign exchange reserves into separate tranches, which at present include a Liquidity Portfolio, a

Matched Asset-Liability Portfolio and a Long-term Investment Fund (Pula Fund), (Bank of Botswana, 1994, pp64–65).

The Liquidity Portfolio serves as a buffer against short-term fluctuations in trade and capital account payments. It is the conventional transaction balance reserve held by central banks. The Matched Asset-Liability Portfolio amounts to having foreign currency investments (external assets) that match the liability side (external debt) of the country's official balance sheet. The Matched Asset-Liability Portfolio ensures that Botswana has international assets of the right currency and maturity that can allow it to repay its debt obligations as and when they come due. The Pula Fund is a long-term investment fund for Botswana's national savings. The Pula Fund is intended to optimise the contribution Botswana's savings can make to sustained national economic development. The Pula Fund, because it represents resources that can not be invested productively in the domestic economy right away, involves investments in long-term assets, such as long-term bonds and equities, with the expectation of earning a higher return than that earned on conventionally managed foreign exchange reserves held in the Liquidity Portfolio.

This paper attempts to review how the Bank of Botswana has performed in managing the foreign exchange reserves, taking into account returns in foreign currency terms as well as in Pula. Because the Pula exchange rate has fluctuated since the currency was introduced, there is need to distinguish changes in the level of the foreign exchange reserves due to depreciation or appreciation of the Pula from changes due to market and revaluation gains and or losses in foreign currencies. In order to do this, the Special Drawing Right, the IMF's unit of account, is used as a benchmark currency; and the IMF's rate of remuneration[2] is used a benchmark return against which to evaluate the Bank's record.

This paper also reviews the stream of revenues which the Bank has provided to Government. The revenues paid to Government have taken into account the major costs of the Bank's operations and the revenue distribution formula in force at the time. These revenues represent in part the return which Government (the sole shareholder in the Bank) has received for the funds it deposited and invested in the Bank. But, part of the return is also reflected in the increased net worth of the Bank; the growth in the Bank's Paid-up Capital, the General Reserve and the Revaluation Reserve.

Finally, the paper concludes with a discussion of the nature of the variability of the payments to Government, as well as the new arrangements proposed in the revision to the Bank of Botswana Act under consideration.

2. Bank of Botswana Assets and Liabilities

The Bank of Botswana's assets and liabilities grew almost 200-fold from P67.4 million at the end of December 1976 to P13 369.4 million at the end of December 1995, an average annual increase of 32% (Bank of Botswana, 1995, p11). On the asset side, almost all of the Bank's assets are comprised of international reserves; fixed assets and other assets accounted for 0.07% and 0.02%, respectively, of total assets at the end of 1995.

---

[2]   The IMF's rate of remuneration is the rate of interest paid on holdings of SDRs (*International Monetary Fund Yearbook*, 1995, p xvi).

TABLE 1. BANK OF BOTSWANA BALANCE SHEET, 1995 (PULA MILLION)

CAPITAL AND RESERVES		ASSETS	
PAID-UP CAPITAL	3.56	INTERNATIONAL RESERVES	
GENERAL RESERVE	271.54	LIQUIDITY PORTFOLIO	7 539.83
REVALUATION RESERVE	3 044.63	MALP	1 257.96
BOTSWANA CURRENCY	318.52	PULA FUND	4 247.90
GOVERNMENT DEPOSITS	6 460.43	IMF	203.42
OTHER DEPOSITS	134.62	OTHER ASSETS	23.58
BANK OF BOTSWANA CERTIFICATES	1 963.76	FIXED ASSETS	96.70
OTHER LIABILITIES	1 172.33		
TOTAL LIABILITIES	13 369.39	TOTAL ASSETS	13 369.39

Source: Bank of Botswana Annual Report, 1995.

Since 1976, Botswana, like the rest of Southern Africa, has experienced considerable inflation, which means that much of the growth observed might reflect just higher prices. The Consumer Price Index in Botswana increased over seven-fold from December 1976 to December 1995, an average annual rate of inflation of 11.3% (Bank of Botswana, 1995, p58). Nevertheless, even if the assets and liabilities of the Bank are measured in constant 1995 prices, there has been substantial real growth; from P516.5 million at the end of 1976 to P13 369 million at the end of 1995.

FIGURE 2. BANK OF BOTSWANA LIABILITIES, CAPITAL AND RESERVES

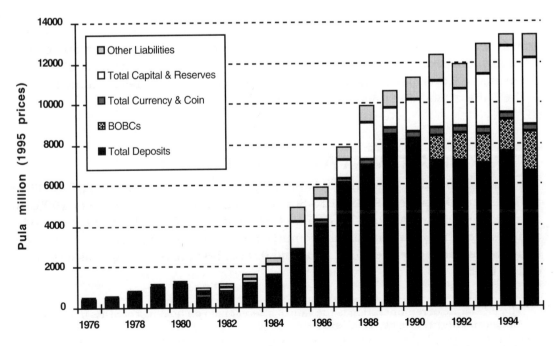

On the liabilities side of the Bank of Botswana's balance sheet, the major categories are deposits (predominantly Government deposits, but also deposits from commercial banks and other financial institutions), Bank of Botswana Certificates (BoBCs, introduced in 1991), currency and coin, capital and reserves, and other liabilities. As the Government's banker, a substantial portion of the Bank's liabilities have always comprised Government's deposits at the Bank. As at December 1995, such deposits were P6460 million, representing 48% of the Bank's total liabilities (*ibid.*, p11). In this respect, Botswana is somewhat unique in having the Government, with no domestic debt, being a substantial net creditor of the banking system.

FIGURE 3. FOREIGN EXCHANGE RESERVES AND THE REVALUATION RESERVE

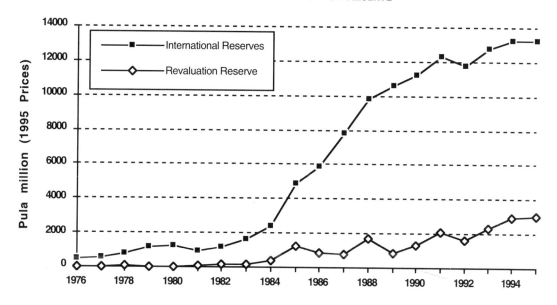

The Bank's capital and reserves at the end of 1995 comprised Paid-up Capital (a rather paltry P3.56 million), the General Reserve (P271.5 million) and the Revaluation Reserve, which amounted to P3045 million. The Revaluation Reserve, formerly the Special Reserve, is used to record any gains or losses to the foreign exchange reserves due to changes in the rate of exchange between the Pula and foreign currencies.[3] Because the Pula has depreciated against most of the major currencies in which the international reserves are invested since 1980, revaluation gains have been generally recorded each year, and the Revaluation Reserve has grown to represent almost 23% of the balance sheet.

---

[3] For example, suppose at the beginning of an accounting period the Bank owned a US Government bond which had a market value of US$10 million. If the US$–Pula exchange rate were US$0.50 per Pula, that asset would be valued at P20 million on the balance sheet of the Bank. If the US$–Pula exchange rate were to change to US$0.40 per Pula at the end of the accounting period, that asset would now be recorded on the balance sheet as being worth P25 million. The additional P5 million would be credited to the Revaluation Reserve at the end of the accounting period.

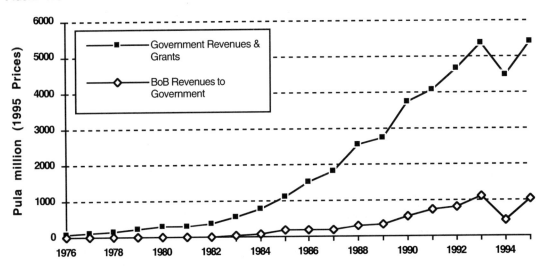

3. REVENUES TO GOVERNMENT

When the Bank was first established, provision was made in the Act for Government to receive 50% of the net income of the Bank, the other 50% was credited to the Bank's General Reserve; at least until that Reserve exceeded the Bank's Paid-up Capital. Beyond that, up to the point where the General Reserve exceeded P5 million, 25% of the Bank's net income was to go to the General Reserve and the remaining 75% to Government. Beyond having P5 million in the General Reserve, the Bank was to give 90% of its net income to the Government each year, leaving 10% to be credited to the General Reserve. It is important to note that the net income of the Bank was exclusive of any valuation gains or losses due to exchange rate fluctuations; valuation changes due to variations in exchange rates were credited to a 'Special Reserve'. In addition to the distribution of the Bank's net income, the Act specified that 20% of any amounts in the 'Special' Revaluation Reserve should be given to Government each year, providing there was at least P50 000 in that Reserve (Bank of Botswana Act, 1975, Section 7). These features of the distribution formula to Government were subsequently revised in 1987, so that 95% of the Bank's annual net income would go to Government along with 10% of any amounts in the Revaluation Reserve (Bank of Botswana Act, 1987).

There were several reasons for altering the revenue distribution formula. In 1979 and 1980, relatively modest revaluations of the Pula exchange rate caused exchange losses which exceeded the amounts in the Revaluation Reserve, as well as the amounts that stood in the General Reserve and the Paid-up Capital, threatening the solvency of the Bank (Hermans, in this volume, pp199–201). As provided in the Act, the Government provided the Bank with non-interest bearing securities, covering the shortfall. As a consequence, the authorities came to believe that the Bank should have a more adequate buffer in the Revaluation Reserve, which could be achieved by reducing the distribution percentage to 10%.[4] With respect to raising the percentage distribution

---

4   It could also be noted that keeping the distribution percentage from the Revaluation Reserve small reduces the incentive for the authorities to depreciate the currency in order to reap additional revenues from revaluation gains.

from the Bank's net income to Government from 90% to 95% in 1987, the authorities believed the Bank was financially strong enough to not need much further growth in the General Reserve (*ibid.*, p201).

The revenues which the Bank has given to Government have grown steadily since 1976, with two notable exceptions. In 1980, because of the revaluation losses recorded, the Bank was unable to give anything to Government, and instead required financial assistance in the form of non-interest bearing notes, which were subsequently retired in 1981 (*ibid.*, p23). In 1994, a sizeable decrease occurred as the Bank experienced a dramatic fall in its revenues from the international reserves, reflecting, in part, extremely adverse bond and currency market developments that year (Bank of Botswana, 1994, pp66–67).

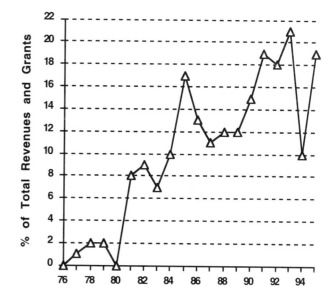

FIGURE 5. BANK OF BOTSWANA REVENUES TO GOVERNMENT IN RELATION TO TOTAL GOVERNMENT REVENUES

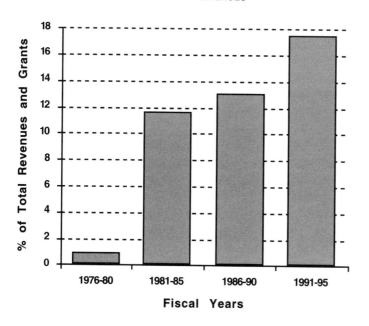

FIGURE 6. BANK OF BOTSWANA REVENUES TO GOVERNNMENT IN RELATION TO TOTAL GOVERNMENT REVENUES

As shown in Figures 5 and 6, the contribution of the Bank to the total revenue and grants of Government has grown substantially over the years, albeit with sizeable fluctuations. In the first five years of the Bank's history, the share that the Bank's revenues comprised of total Government revenues and grants was less than 1%. In the last five year period, the Bank's revenues to Government have represented 17.5% of the total.

TABLE 2. BANK OF BOTSWANA INCOME AND
EXPENDITURE, 1995

INCOME	
Interest	678.7
Market Gains/Losses	63.3
Fund Manager Income	239.1
Commissions	11.5
Other Income	2.3
Total	994.90
EXPENSES	
Administration Costs	49.6
Interest on BoBCs	198.5
Depreciation	4.1
Special Provision	-7.0
Total	245.2
NET INCOME	749.7
Government's Share	712.2
To General Reserve	37.5

Source: Bank of Botswana. Annual Report 1995.

4. THE BANK'S NET INCOME AND REVALUATION GAINS/LOSSES

The Bank's income, for accounting purposes, derives from interest earned on deposits and income from other assets held abroad[5], (plus interest earned in Botswana in its capacity as the 'lender of last resort'), market gains/losses on disposal of securities, (whose prices have increased-decreased from the time they were bought to the time they were sold or matured), commissions earned, (mainly on foreign exchange transactions) and other sundry income.

The Bank's expenses basically comprise administrative costs, (such as salaries and operating expenses), and interest on Bank of Botswana Certificates and depreciation.

In 1995, for example, as shown in Table 2, the Bank recorded P995 million in income as against P245 million in expenses. The net income of P750 million was distributed 95% to Government (P712 million) and 5% to the Bank's General Reserve (P38 million).

The revaluation gains and losses that the Bank has recorded over the years have been highly variable. Since 1976, revaluation gains have exceeded revaluation losses by a total of P4634 million. On average, there were P257 million in net revaluation gains per annum; but, the standard deviation of such gains and losses was P377 million. As can be seen in Figure 7, the magnitude of revaluation gains and losses has increased from the mid-1980s as the level of foreign exchange reserves grew. Over the first ten year period, revaluation gains/losses had a standard deviation of P133 million, while in the second ten year period it was P437 million.

Turning to the distribution of the Revaluation Reserve to Government, by the beginning of 1995 the Revaluation Reserve had grown to P2685 million, to which the revaluation gain of P698 million registered in 1995 was added, yielding a balance before distribution of P3383 million. Of that amount, 10% or P338.3 million was transferred to Government. Thus, along with the P712.2 million, representing 95% of the net income of the Bank, the total amount distributed to Government for the 1995 operations amounted to P1050.5 million.

The amount distributed to Government during 1995 represented 15% of the aver-

---

5   This includes 'Fund Manager Income' (see Table 2), which derives from assets held abroad that are managed by specialist fund managers on Botswana's behalf.

FIGURE 7. REPORTED REVALUATION GAINS/LOSSES ON THE
FOREIGN EXCHANGE RESERVES

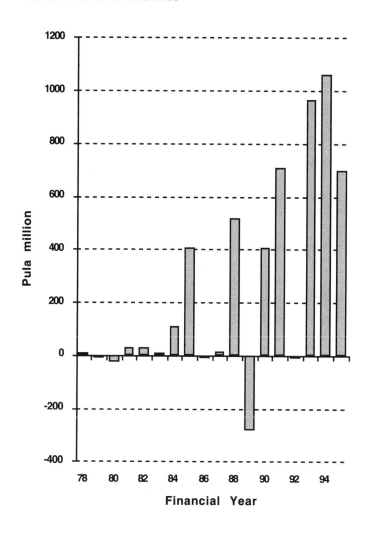

age level of Government deposits (P6995 million) at the Bank of Botswana during that year. The Government investment in the Bank, in terms of Paid-up Capital and Reserves amounted to P2923 million at the start of the year, and increased to P3320 million, a gain to the shareholder of P397 million. Thus, the total return[6] to the Government in 1995 on its funds deposited and invested in the Bank (P9918 million) amounted to nearly P1448 million, a nominal rate of return on the funds employed (deposits plus capital) of approximately 14.6%.

Looked at in this way, the nominal rate of return to Government on funds employed has averaged 19.5% p.a. since 1976, with some notable degree of variability. Recalling that the average annual rate of inflation over the period was 11.3%, the real rate of return to Government on its deposits and funds invested in the Bank has averaged 7.4% p.a.[7] In 1985, the Government received a 53.8% total return on funds employed, mainly due to a P312 million increase in reserves, when a P407 million revaluation gain was recorded. In

---

6   There are other returns to Government being omitted here, such as the 'free' banking services the Bank provides and the other benefits the Government receives from having an institution able to carry out its monetary policy objectives, as well as serve as Government's agent in implementing exchange controls and banking supervision. There is also the cost to the fiscus of being able to implement some policies; e.g., there was nearly P200 million in interest costs on BoBCs in 1995.

7   The real rate of return, r, is

$$r = \frac{1+n}{1+p} - 1 = \frac{1.195}{1.113} - 1 = 0.0737$$

where n is average nominal rate of return and p is the average rate of inflation.

contrast, a total return to Government of 0.8% was registered in 1989 as revaluation losses served to reduce the net worth of the Bank. The revenues distributed to Government relative to funds employed have averaged 12% p.a. over the period, with the 5% return in 1994 being a notable deviation.

5. MEASURING THE RETURNS ON THE INTERNATIONAL RESERVES

Measuring the returns the Bank has achieved in Pula is complicated by the revaluation gains and losses that arise from exchange rate fluctuations. There are two types of fluctuations which complicate measuring the returns on the international reserves; foreign currencies fluctuate against each other, and the Pula fluctuates against other currencies. This latter variability arises mostly as a result of the operation of the Pula Basket, in which the currencies of major regional and international trading partners serve to determine the value of the Pula exchange rate.

Part of the complication arises from cross exchange rate fluctuations amongst other currencies, which, if the currencies are near perfect substitutes, in efficient capital markets get reflected in interest rate differentials. That is, if investors are willing to accept a lower return in one currency, say Deutsche Marks, compared to another currency, say US Dollars, for otherwise equivalent investments, it reflects an expectation that the Deutsche Mark will appreciate against the US Dollar by the interest rate differential. These expectations are not, of course, always correct.

One pragmatic way to deal with measuring the returns on the foreign exchange reserves is to evaluate each investment in each currency in terms of units of SDR (a good benchmark currency).[8] As a composite currency comprised of the major international currencies, the SDR can serve as a reasonable measure of international purchasing power in the major international markets.[9] Underlying Botswana's investment strategy for the international reserves has been the objective of safeguarding and maintaining the purchasing power of the reserves in SDR terms. By using the SDR as the benchmark, one is, in essence, diversifying the risks that fluctuations in the cross exchange rates between, say the US Dollar and the Deutsche Mark or the South African Rand, would seriously reduce Botswana's ability to use reserves held in US Dollars to purchase goods and services denominated in Deutsche Marks or Rands.[10] If all returns are calculated in terms of SDRs, they can be converted back to Pula at the Pula–SDR exchange rate; and a Pula rate of return on the initial investment can be calculated, as well as any further revaluation gains/losses due to movements of the Pula against the SDR.

As a practical matter, however, because there is a continuous flow of international transactions in many different foreign currencies, which causes fluctuations in the

---

8 For an example and some discussion, see the Appendix.

9 The SDR is a weighted average of the five major currencies: the US Dollar (39%), the German Deutsche Mark (21%), the Japanese Yen (18%), the British Pound Sterling (11%), and the French Franc (11%).

10 If the interest rate differentials do indeed reflect the expected exchange rate changes, it does not matter which currency is chosen to be the benchmark. But, since some currency has to be chosen in order to make comparisons, the SDR represents a handy approximation that generalises the choice. This choice is likely to be less controversial than that for any other individual currency.

level of international reserves, it is difficult to accurately measure and distinguish the returns of the reserves from the exchange rate valuation gains/losses. The simple approach used here to estimate the revaluation gains starts with the initial values of the portfolios in SDRs, converts them to Pula at the beginning period and end period exchange rates, and calculates the difference. In addition, any revaluation gains on the changes in the portfolios are taken into account by assuming they arrive in the portfolios midway through the period under consideration.[11] This involves:

$$V_{t+1}^{S} = V_{t}^{S} + \Delta V_{t}^{S} \tag{1}$$

where V^S is the value of the portfolio in SDR terms in period t and $t+1$, and ΔV^S is the change in the SDR value of the portfolio over the period.

The Pula value of the portfolios in period t, V_{t}^{P}, equals the SDR value of the portfolio divided by the SDR-Pula exchange rate, e_t.

$$V_{t}^{P} = \frac{V_{t}^{S}}{e_t} \tag{2}$$

The revaluation gain on the initial portfolio, RG_{0t}, can be expressed as:

$$RG_{0_t} = \frac{V_{t}^{S}}{e_{t+1}} - \frac{V_{t}^{S}}{e_t} = V_{t}^{S}\frac{[e_t - e_{t+1}]}{e_{t+1}e_t} = \left[\frac{V_{t}^{S}}{e_{t+1}}\right]\left[\frac{e_t - e_{t+1}}{e_t}\right] \tag{3}$$

which equals the Pula value of the portfolio valued at the end period exchange rate times the proportionate change in the exchange rate.[12]

The revaluation gain on the change in the SD R value of the portfolio, $RG_{\Delta t}$, similarly can be expressed as:

$$RG_{0_t} = \frac{\Delta V_{t}^{S}}{\Delta e_{t+1}} - \frac{\Delta V_{t}^{S}}{\bar{e}} = \Delta V_{t}^{S}\frac{[\bar{e} - e_{t+1}]}{e_{t+1}\bar{e}} = \left[\frac{\Delta V_{t}^{S}}{e_{t+1}}\right]\left[\frac{\bar{e} - e_{t+1}}{\bar{e}}\right] \tag{4}$$

where $\bar{e} = \frac{e_t + e_{t+1}}{2}$ is the average or mid-period SDR-Pula exchange rate.

The revaluation gain on the change in the SDR value of the portfolio equals the Pula value of the change in the value of the portfolio valued at the end period exchange rate times the percentage change in the exchange rate from the midpoint in the period to the end of the period.

Approached this way, the estimated revaluation gains/losses on the international reserves are similar, but not identical to those recorded using the standard accounting procedures and shown in Figure 8. Part of the reason for the difference involves the accounting practice of not recording revaluation gains or losses until they are

---

[11] In the absence of the detailed arrival and withdrawal dates for any changes to the portfolio, one could alternatively assume that half the change occurred on the first day and half the change occurred on the last day. The difference between this approach and that used in the text is relatively minor if the exchange rates do not change too drastically.

[12] Note that if the SDR–Pula exchange rate depreciates, the result is a positive number.

FIGURE 8. ESTIMATED GAINS/LOSSES ON THE FOREIGN EXCHANGE RESERVES

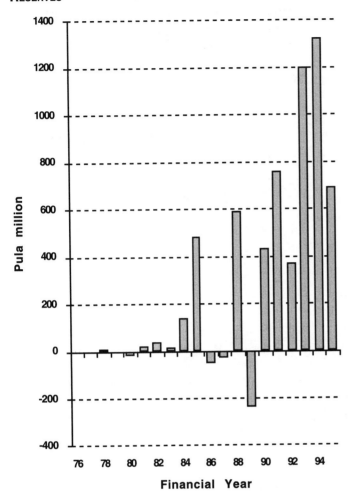

Financial Year

realised by the sales or disposal of the securities invested in. This difference can also be compounded by the practice of not 'marking to market'; i.e., the practice of recording securities at their purchase price, not the latest market value.

6. COMPARING THE BANK'S ACTUAL PERFORMANCE TO A BENCHMARK

There are many alternative benchmarks that could be applied to see how the actual gross return the Bank achieved compares to that which might have been achieved. If the international reserves measured in SDR terms had been invested prudently in nearly riskless SDR-based invest-

FIGURE 9. BANK OF BOTSWANA INCOME: ACTUAL GROSS INCOME VERSUS SDR RATE OF REMUNERATION

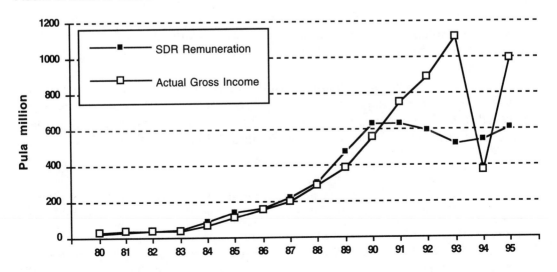

ments, such as those which earn the SDR rate of remuneration, the Bank would have been able to earn an average rate of return of 6.32% per annum, in SDR terms. For the period from 1976 to 1995, multiplying the SDR rate of remuneration times the average level of international reserves, the Bank would have earned a return of SDR1593 million. Converting those SDR returns to Pula at the midyear SDR-Pula exchange rate, a total of P4442 million would have been earned.

As shown in Figure 9, over the period from 1980 to 1988, the gross return (profit) achieved by the Bank closely mirrored what it could have earned by investing the SDR value of the international reserves at the SDR rate of remuneration. But, from 1990 to 1993, the actual gross profit of the Bank increasingly exceeded that which would have been earned if the international reserves had been invested at the remuneration rate. While the gross return achieved by the Bank in 1994 fell below that which would have been earned using the SDR rate of remuneration, the out-turn for 1995 was again better than just investing the international reserves in assets earning the remuneration rate. For the period from 1980 to 1995, total gross returns of the Bank amounted to P6006 million, 35% higher than that which was estimated using the SDR rate of remuneration.

FIGURE 10. Returns and Revaluation Gains/Losses: Actual versus Estimated SDR Remuneration

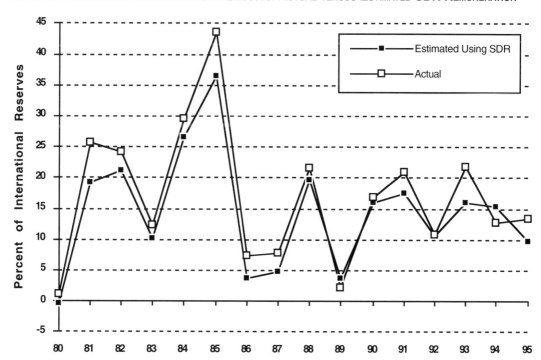

The estimates of the gross returns and revaluation gains/losses using the international reserves valued in SDR and the SDR rate of remuneration converted to Pula can be combined and compared to the actual gross profits and revaluation gains/losses recorded by the Bank over the period 1980 to 1995. As shown in Figure 10, as a percentage of the level of the international reserves, there is a close correspondence between that estimated to have been achievable and that actually obtained. Both series exhibit quite dramatic fluctuations over the period, a notable peak in 1985 and low points in 1980 and 1989. For the period as a whole, the total gross operating profit of the Bank plus the revaluation gains/losses recorded averaged 17% of the level of the international reserves. In contrast, the estimated returns using the SDR rate of remuneration plus the estimated revaluation gains/losses averaged 12% of the level of the international reserves.[13]

7. STABILISING THE FLOW OF REVENUE TO GOVERNMENT

The variability and the uncertainty of the flows of revenues from the Bank of Botswana to the Government have increasingly been a cause for concern. The fluctuations have created problems for planning purposes; and the uncertainty as to the final annual out-turn itself, with generally better out-turns at the end of the year than was estimated at the time of the budget, has on occasion been a source of embarrassment to the Government, eroding the credibility of the Ministry of Finance and Development Planning and the budget restraint it has tried to enforce. The better than originally estimated Bank revenues have contributed to Government budget surpluses, when in some instances the Government was announcing that it expected budget deficits.

The existing formula for determining the revenues from the Bank each year to Government has some stabilising features. Only 10% of any fluctuations in revaluation gains/losses are passed through to Government in the year they occur; the remainder is put into the Revaluation Reserve, from which 10% is allocated in each subsequent year. However, by distributing to Government 95% of the net income, which includes interest income and market valuation gains/losses from the Bank's operations each year, there is a 95% pass through of fluctuations in the market-related returns that get recorded as income on investing the international reserves.

By and large, there were smaller fluctuations in the rate of return on international reserves than in exchange rates over the period. The SDR rate of remuneration, for example, averaged 6.32% p.a. over the period, with a standard deviation of 2.45%. In contrast, the average absolute change in the SDR–Pula exchange rate was 9.29%, with a standard deviation of 7.76%.

But, up to 1993, the international reserves were being invested with a view towards safety and liquidity, mainly in shorter term, interest earning assets. With the build up in the levels of reserves and the decision to establish the Pula Fund, investing part of the international reserves in longer term securities and equities, with a view to earning higher average returns, the risk of fluctuations in returns has increased. Thus, under the existing formula, increasing variability and uncertainty would be expected with respect to the flow of revenues to Government in any one year.

A variety of methods could be used to smooth the flow of Bank revenues to Government, to approximate that which on average might be expected from the investment

---

[13] Figure 9 shows that up to 1988 the SDR rate of remuneration would have provided slightly higher returns than that actually reported according to standard accounting convention. Figure 10 shows that the reported returns plus revaluation gains/losses for those same years exceeded that estimated using the SDR rate of remuneration and the estimated revaluation gains/losses on the international reserves. The difference obviously reflects that reported revaluation gains/losses exceeded those estimated using equations 3 and 4 in those years.

of part of the international reserves in long-term securities. One proposal that has been mooted is to use a moving average of the returns earned on the international reserves, along with the existing formula for distributing ten percent of the accumulated Revaluation Reserve. A second proposal is to give the Government a fraction (less than one) of the Bank's total distributable reserves. A third proposal, which is included in the draft Bank of Botswana Act for 1996, is to establish a special fund, which would be invested in long-term securities, out of which Government could specify the flows of revenues it wants every year. In adopting any such method, care would need to be taken that the actual flows to Government did not impair the soundness of the Bank, and its ability to conduct monetary policy and maintain a liberal exchange control regime.

8. Conclusion

The profits of the Bank of Botswana have been a major and growing source of revenue to Government over the years since the Bank was established. Those profits have derived mainly from the returns earned on the growing levels of international reserves which the Bank is responsible for investing and managing. Those reserves and the income they provide to Botswana may decline as deficits in the Government budget emerge and as domestic interest rates become more aligned with those in major international capital markets as a result of further liberalization of the economy and exchange controls.

Taking into account the revenues distributed to the shareholder and the increase in the shareholders' wealth, the Bank of Botswana has provided an average nominal yield of 19.5% for the funds invested in it by Government. In real terms, after adjusting for the average 11.3% rate of inflation that has been recorded since 1976, the Bank has yielded the shareholder an average real rate of return of 7.4% p.a. That might be compared to the average rate of return that might have been earned if the stockholder's wealth had been invested safely in international assets earning the SDR rate of remuneration. In that case, the nominal rate of return would have averaged 6.32% p.a. After adjusting for the 4.95% average annual rate of inflation in the countries that comprise the SDR[14], the real rate of return would have been 1.31% p.a.

Since 1980, the Bank has recorded gross income totalling P6006 million. If the Bank had merely invested the international reserves in assets earning the SDR rate of remuneration, a total of P4442 million would have been generated. By comparison, the Bank generated about 35% more gross income than what investing the international reserves at the remuneration rate on SDRs would have yielded. That may have been due, in part, to the shift to investing in longer maturity instruments at a time that generally coincided with a long upswing in major stock markets.

The income earned by the Bank of Botswana has been highly variable in recent years, and may become even more so, as a result of exchange rate fluctuations, which can give rise to sizeable revaluation gains and/or losses, and as a result of investing

---

[14] The average annual rates of inflation over the period 1976 to 1995 in the USA, Germany, Japan, the UK and France were 5.50%, 3.08%, 2.68%, 7.20% and 6.12%, respectively. Weighting those rates of inflation by the proportions of the SDR that the currencies of those countries comprise, the average annual SDR rate of inflation is estimated at 4.95%.

larger portions of the international reserves into longer term, more risky, but higher yielding investments.

To cater for this, it is proposed to revise the Bank of Botswana Act and institute new investment and revenue distribution procedures designed to help stabilise and make more predictable the annual flow of revenues the Bank can give to Government, while still allowing the Bank to carry out its other central banking functions. Underlying this proposal is the establishment of a Long-term Investment Fund out of which a steady level of dividends, estimated on an actuarially sound basis, could be paid as income to Government. In addition, the Bank's General Reserve would be augmented to increase its ability to conduct monetary policy and support a liberalised exchange control regime.

APPENDIX: COMPARING RETURNS IN DIFFERENT CURRENCIES – AN EXAMPLE

Suppose the Government saves P600 million in a deposit account at the Bank of Botswana when the Pula equals US$0.40 and the SDR equals US$1.50 (hence, the SDR equals P3.75). That saving equates to US$240 million and SDR160 million. Suppose further that the SDR rate of interest is 5% and the US rate of interest is 12%, for reasons explained below. Assume the Government commissions the Bank to invest the savings prudently to preserve the international purchasing power of the savings. Assume the Bank can either invest those savings in an SDR investment paying 5% p.a. or in a US$ investment paying 12%.

In SDR terms, after one year, the total value of the SDR investment would be SDR 168 million (=1.05x160 million). In US$ terms, the total value of the investment would be US$ 268.8 million (1.12x240 million). The net return on the US$ investment in US$ at US$ 26.8 million looks much more attractive than the SDR return on the SDR investment of SDR 8 million.

But, that obviously ignores what the interest rate differential implied was going to happen to the US$–SDR exchange rate. Logically, the capital markets that established that interest rate differential expected the US$ to depreciate against the SDR to SDR equal US$1.60 by the end of the period. At that end of period US$–SDR exchange rate, the value of the US$ investment at the end of the period of US$ 268.8 million in terms of SDR would be SDR 168 million [US$268.8 million/(US$1.60/SDR)].

For equivalent investments, valuing them and their returns in terms of SDR (the benchmark currency) shows them to have equivalent returns.

Similar analyses for currencies expected to appreciate and thus showing lower interest rates and/or rates of return on assets valued in those currencies would yield the same result that looking at things in SDR terms would show the equivalent investments to indeed be equivalent.

Bringing the SDR 8 million back into Pula at whatever is the prevailing Pula–SDR exchange rate would provide the appropriate measure of the resources available from the investment that would leave the SDR value intact. Suppose the Pula had depreciated to one Pula equals US$ 0.32, (hence, if the SDR equals US$1.60, the SDR would equal P5.00). The SDR investment return or yield of SDR 8 million would provide P40 million of return to the Government, a rate of return of approximately 6.3% on the

P600 million saved. But the value of the SDR investment, excluding the SDR 8 million return, would now be P800 million [= (P5/SDR) x SDR 160 million]. The P40 million of return would represent a 5% rate of return on the revalued SDR investment of P800 million. There would be a revaluation gain in this case of P200 million, which rightly should belong to the saver-investor. Allocating that revaluation gain to Government would not jeopardise the functions of the Bank, and would preserve the SDR purchasing power of the original saving-investment.

While the above is clear for a depreciation, the situation becomes problematic for an appreciation of the Pula. Would Government or any other saver accept a revaluation loss applied to their savings account? If that is understood as one of the conditions attached to managing-investing the Government savings, there is no problem either way. But if there is, it obviously provides a basis for having a Revaluation Reserve, and distributing only a portion of the accumulated balance to Government each year.

REFERENCES

Bank of Botswana. *Annual Report*, various issues.

Bank of Botswana. *Botswana Financial Statistics*, various issues. Bank of Botswana, Gaborone.

Bank of Botswana. 1986. 'Guidelines for the Management of Botswana's International Reserves', (mimeo). Bank of Botswana, Gaborone.

Bank of Botswana. 1987. 'The Management of International Reserves: Some Basic Considerations and Global Experience', In: Bhuiyan, M.N. (ed.). *Selected Papers on the Botswana Economy*. Printing and Publishing Company (Botswana), Gaborone.

Government of Botswana. *Bank of Botswana Act, 1975*. Government of Botswana, Gaborone.

Government of Botswana. *Bank of Botswana Act, 1987*. Government of Botswana, Gaborone.

Government of Botswana. *Financial Statements, Tables and Estimates of Consolidated and Development Fund Revenues*, various issues. Government of Botswana, Gaborone.

Government of Botswana. 1975. *A Monetary System for Botswana*, Government Paper No.1 of 1975. Government Printer, Gaborone.

Government of Botswana. 1991. *National Development Plan 7*. Government of Botswana, Gaborone.

International Monetary Fund. *International Financial Statistics*, various issues.

Salkin, J.S. 1994. 'A Brief Review of the Central Government Budget: 1966/67 – 1994/95', (mimeo), University of Botswana, Gaborone.

World Bank. 1989. *Botswana: Financial Policies for Diversified Growth*. World Bank, Washington.

Banking Supervision and Regulation: The Case of Botswana

K S Masalila

1. INTRODUCTION

In terms of business principles and investment decisions of their owners, banks are like any other business operation: they are primarily driven by the profit motive. Thus, business success is measured in terms of the amount and value of income, in real terms, generated: added value to the shareholders' funds; effective and efficient utilization of assets; and how the real returns thereof compare with other alternative investments. The need for supervision and regulation arises from what may be called the incidental derivatives of banks' operations, which relate to both the nature of their operations and the nature of their relationship with other sectors of the economy. It is in the nature of their operations that banks use only a small proportion of their own funds (capital), in relation to total assets, in the business. Instead, they use depositors' funds in inherently risky ventures in the form of lending for general business activity, innovation and development. With respect to the nature of their relationship with the rest of the economy banks intermediate between savers and borrowers/investors, providing an opportunity to increase the income of both the saver and the borrower; they evaluate alternative investments and monitor performance of borrowers, thus increasing the efficiency of resource use; they transform size and maturity of funds, helping to ensure optimal returns and allocation of funds; and they operate and maintain the payments system, thus facilitating trade and economic activity.

Given the nature of their operations and the nature of their relationship with the rest of the economy, banks lend themselves to being a potent monetary policy tool. This engenders the link between the supervision/regulatory process and the effectiveness of monetary policy. The basic goal of banking supervision is to promote a safe, sound, stable and efficient banking system, as well as payment mechanism. Monetary policy is, in addition to ensuring price stability, about influencing the level of interest rates. Monetary authorities use their direct relationship with the banks to apply monetary policy tools to influence the ultimate interest rates paid or charged by banks. In this respect, it is only a safe, sound and stable financial system that will be effective and efficient in transmitting monetary policy to the real sector or wider economy. The supervisory role is important in the development of a conducive regulatory framework, which, among others, ensures that banks operate within prescribed prudential limits and operational standards, ensures that banks uphold principles of good public policy in their operations and in their relationships with the real economy, and ensures continuing confidence in the banking system.

In Botswana, the Bank of Botswana has responsibility for both monetary policy and banking supervision as provided for in Section 4 of the Bank of Botswana Act. This lists the objectives of the Bank as:

(a) to promote and maintain internal and external monetary stability, an efficient payments mechanism, liquidity, solvency and proper functioning of a soundly based monetary, credit and financial system;

(b) to foster monetary and credit and financial conditions conducive to the orderly, balanced and sustained economic development; and

(c) to assist, as far as not inconsistent with the above two objectives in the attainment of national economic goals.

FIGURE 1. BANKING SUPERVISION OBJECTIVES

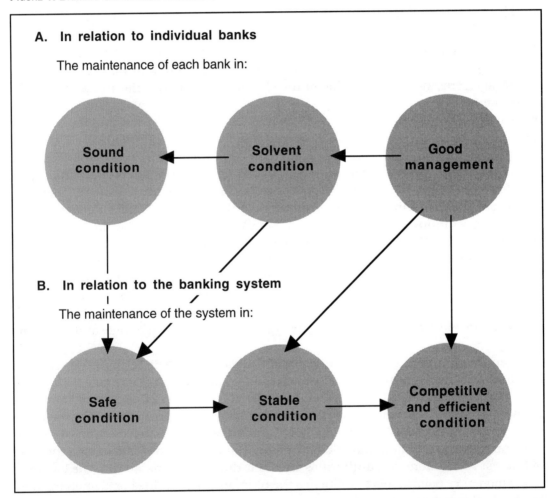

This paper discusses the role of the supervisory process and how it ensures effectiveness of monetary policy in Botswana, and is arranged as follows. Section 2 discusses the regulatory framework as encapsulated in the relevant legislation and prudential requirements, the rationalization for these, how they have evolved over time, as well as the link to, and conformity with, international standards and collaboration. Section 3 discusses the process of banking supervision and the monitoring of performance of banks in Botswana, covering what is involved in on-site examinations, off-site monitoring and discussions with banks. Section 4 highlights the links that exist between monetary policy and banking supervision, noting potential areas of conflict and complementarity. Section 5 highlights the scope for banks in Botswana to be effective in transmitting monetary policy, as reflected in their past performance, in terms of mobilising deposits, credit allocation, adherence to prudential measures, therefore being safe and sound, and the impact of developments within the financial system. In concluding, the paper will highlight emerging trends in the world of banking, namely, globalization, liberalization and infusion of technology, and how these change the operations of banks and challenge the supervisory process.

2. REGULATORY FRAMEWORK – BANKING LEGISLATION AND PRUDENTIAL REQUIREMENTS

The banking supervision regulatory framework, including the legislation and prudential requirements is premised on the basic objectives of banking supervision as illustrated above.

In general, it is considered that to be effective, a regulatory framework or authority must have sufficient authority, established by law; a degree of independence; and adequate human and financial resources. In Botswana, the primary legislation covering the supervision and regulation of licensed financial institutions is the Banking Act. 1995. This legislation has gone through various phases of development since it was first promulgated as the Financial Institutions Act, 1975. Important elements of this legislation are its coverage of:

(i)   the licensing process and qualification as a bank and regulation of market entry;
(ii)   the management and/or liquidation of the banks in distress;
(iii)   prudential requirements with respect to:
    (a) capital adequacy;
    (b) restrictions on exposures;
    (c) liquidity;
    (d) quality of management; and
(iv)   provision of information to the regulatory authority.

The regulatory framework, in essence, covers matters to do with internal governance within individual banks, market discipline within the banking system, and official supervision of the banking system. The core responsibility for bank soundness lies with owners and managers, who, because of the capital risked, have incentives to operate banks prudently. Market discipline provides further pressure and incentives for good internal governance and imposes sanctions for failures. Official supervision is essential to compensate for failures or inadequacies in governance and market discipline. These three aspects are subsumed within the legislation and prudential requirements. Thus, the continuing stability and soundness of the banking system and the extent to which it is effective in facilitating the payments system and intermediating between savers and borrowers is a reflection of efficiency in all the three areas. Table 1 highlights some issues relevant to these three aspects.

TABLE 1. THE COMMERCIAL BANKS' REGULATORY FRAMEWORK

LEGAL AND PRUDENTIAL ISSUES	INTERNAL GOVERNANCE	MARKET DISCIPLINE	OFFICIAL SUPERVISION
LICENSING	Market development	Competition	Licensing policy, need for intermediation, diversity of products and efficient service
CAPITAL REQUIREMENTS	Solvency, growth potential, competition	Growth potential, competition	Enforcement, ensuring solvency, protection of depositors
LIQUID ASSETS REQUIREMENTS	Liquidity management	Money market access, market rating	Enforcement, maintenance of confidence, lender of last resort
LIMITATIONS ON SPECIFIED OPERATIONS	Lending and investment policies	Competition	Control of exposure risk, limit operations to banking activity, restrict insider lending
CALL FOR INFORMATION	Management information	Strategic control and use of information	Supervisory information, analysis of performance, determination of compliance
ACCOUNTING AND DISCLOSURE REQUIREMENTS		Competitive position, user information	Ensure integrity of user information, comparison to past and peer group performance
CONDUCT OF EXAMINATIONS			Insight into banks operations, determination of asset quality and adequacy or accuracy of accounting for capital, assets and provisions
LIQUIDATION	Management capability	Competition	Supervisory management, maintenance of confidence and stability

The following discussion looks at the more significant elements of the legal provisions and prudential requirements, and how they relate to the efficiency of intermediation and efficacy of financial sector policies/monetary policy.

Licensing and definition of banking business

The specific definition of banking business is provided for in Section 2 of the Banking Act:

(i) the business of accepting deposits of money repayable on demand or after fixed periods after notice, as the case may be, by cheque or otherwise; and/or

(ii) the employment of deposits in the making or giving of loans, of investments or engagement in other operations authorised by law or under customary banking practice, for the account of, and at the risk of, the person or persons accepting such deposits, and includes the discounting of commercial paper, securities and other negotiable instruments, for the purpose of extending loans or other credit facilities.

The definition of banking is essentially about intermediation between savers and borrowers. For authorities engaged in the regulation and supervision of banks and operating monetary policy, there is a need, firstly, for this activity to be; formalised, secondly, for the protection of those who place deposits in banks; and, thirdly, to ensure credibility of the system and to have scope for control or influence. Hence the need for statutory provisions and a regulatory framework. In this respect, the thrust of the legislation and the licensing policy is derived from the banking supervision objective of ensuring a stable, safe and sound financial system. The banking system has also to deliver service to the economy, especially in the form of an efficient payment system, provide efficient intermediation between savers and borrowers, and be effective in transmitting policy to the real sector. To ensure formality and scope for control, the statute does not only deal with the definition of banking business, but also provides for prohibition and investigation of unlicensed activities, restrictions on the use of certain words and names likely to imply the carrying on of banking activity, the need for financial institutions to be incorporated under the Companies Act, control of the opening and closing of places of business, and supervision and regulation with respect to mergers and acquisitions.

While the above represent a standard definition of banking business, over the years the scope of banking has been significantly extended. The categories of banking business, licensed under the Banking Act, include commercial banks, merchant banks, discount houses, credit institutions and representative offices.

Some of the major elements of the licensing policy are:

(i)   local incorporation;
(ii) the Bank of Botswana only considers for licensing applicants from companies incorporated or intending to be incorporated under the Companies Act; and
(iii) management strength and supervision by the parent bank.

In accordance with Sections 8 and 29 of the Banking Act the Bank of Botswana has to be satisfied that those applying for a banking licence pass the fit and proper test in terms of qualification, experience and integrity. For foreign bank applications, the Bank of Botswana follows the internationally recommended procedure of ensuring that the parent bank is adequately supervised and that the parent bank's supervisory authority can comment favourably about the applicant. These procedures have been formalised by the Basle Committee of International Banking Supervisors and are outlined below.

(i)   *Adequate capital and back-up*
      Differs for the different types of banking business.
(ii) *Branch Network*
      Applicants for commercial banking are required to submit proposals, including timetables, for the establishment of a branch network. Branch expansion into rural areas is expected.

(iii) *Promotion of competition*

Any new financial institution should be committed to being competitive and be able to provide effective competition in the banking sector. The Bank of Botswana attaches particular importance to the ability of the applicant to provide effective competition to existing licensed financial institutions.

(iv) *Encouragement of local shareholding*

A degree of local ownership in each financial institution is encouraged; hence consideration will be given to applications providing prospects for such participation.

Capitalization – capital adequacy

One of the more important elements in banking legislation is the prescription as to capital. Capital represents owners' commitment to support the level of risk to be undertaken by the bank. Capital adequacy, which is a measure of solvency, refers to the ability of a bank to provide services to the public, while maintaining the legally required ratio of capital to assets. For banking supervision purposes, important characteristics of capital follow below.

(i) It must be permanently available, as this should provide a cushion against losses or risks on an on-going basis, but not on a short-term basis.

(ii) Capacity to absorb losses and asset write-offs.

(iii) It should have some correlation with the degree of risk in the business; hence, it is analogous to an internal insurance fund to cover various non-insurable risks not covered in the bank's pricing.

Thus, the capital adequacy prescription is important for the following reasons.

(i) *Absorption of fluctuations in income*

An adequately capitalised bank should be capable of absorbing fluctuations in income so as to enable the bank to continue to operate in periods of loss or negligible earnings without eroding its capital below the required minimum.

(ii) *Assurance or confidence in individual banks and the banking system*

An adequately capitalised bank provides an assurance that it would continue to provide financial services, hence maintain confidence by the public and depositors in itself and the banking system in general. If, because of capital limitations, the bank fails to carry out its basic and primary functions of, deposit taking, conversion and meeting credit demands, loss of confidence in the bank is likely to arise.

(iii) *Provision of protection to depositors funds*

Through its capital, a bank should provide protection to depositors in the event of threatened insolvency, because it represents the amount of loss a bank can sustain before its ability to honour deposit claims is impaired. Some type of internal insurance is needed, by way of adequate capital, to cover eventualities where a bank faces a liquidity crisis, and is therefore not able to honour its obligations. Where capital is considerably lower in relation to assets, there is a risk of a bank failing completely to meet depositors' claims in case of threatened insolvency.

(iv) *Reasonable growth of banking business*

An adequately capitalised bank should be capable of expanding its business without recourse to injection of more capital or seek external funding. The greater part of a bank's income is derived from interest on lending. A bank can only increase its assets or lending if it has adequate capital. Expansion of lending activities should result in increased profits, whose retained component adds to capital, hence increased potential to expand its assets. The more capital a bank has, the more capacity it has to compete with the other banks in the financial system.

The current prescriptions on capital adequacy in the Banking Act and Regulations derive from international convergence of definition of capital promulgated by the Bank for International Settlements (BIS), Basle Committee of Bank Supervisors, indicated below.

The capital adequacy framework

(a) Core capital

The key element of capital on which emphasis is placed is equity capital (issued and fully paid ordinary shares and non-cumulative preference shares) and disclosed reserves. This element is the most visible in the published accounts of banks, and is the basis on which market judgements on capital adequacy are made. It also has a crucial bearing on profit margins and the ability of a bank to compete.

(b) Capital defined in two tiers

This requires that at least fifty percent of a bank's capital base should consist of the core elements (equity and published reserves), known as tier 1. Other elements of capital, i.e., supplementary capital is admitted into tier 2 capital up to an amount equal to that of core capital.

(c) Elements of supplementary capital

Revaluation reserves – some assets may be revalued to reflect their current value as against their historic cost, and the resultant revaluation reserves included in the capital base. Such reserves may be included within supplementary capital provided they are prudently valued, and fully reflect the possibility of price fluctuations and forced sale.

General provisions – these are created against the possibility of future losses. Where they are not ascribed to particular assets, these reserves qualify for inclusion in supplementary capital. However, where provisions have been created against identified losses or in respect of demonstrable deterioration in the value of particular assets, they are not freely available to meet unidentified losses and do not possess an essential characteristic of capital. Such reserves are not be included in the capital base.

Hybrid debt instruments – in this category fall a number of capital instruments which combine the characteristics of equity and certain characteristics of debt. Each of these has particular features which affect its quality as capital. Where these instruments have close similarities to equity, and, in particular, when they are able to support losses on an on-going basis without triggering liquidation, they may be included in supplementary capital. These may include, perpetual preference shares carrying a cumulative fixed charge, long-term preferred shares, mandatory convertible debt instruments, and others.

Subordinated term debt – these have significant deficiencies as constituents of capital in view of their fixed maturity and inability to absorb losses except in liquidation. Subordinated term debt instruments with a minimum original term to maturity of over five years may be included within the supplementary capital elements, but only to a maximum of fifty percent of the core capital element, and subject to adequate amortization arrangements.

Undisclosed reserves – these include only reserves which, though unpublished, have been passed through the profit and loss account and are accepted by the supervisory authority. The reason for excluding them from core capital is their lack of transparency and the fact, that in many instances, these are not recognized, either as an accounting concept or as a legitimate element of capital.

(d) Deductions from capital

The following deductions are made for the purposes of calculating the risk-weighted ratio (the concept of risk weighting is described below).

(i) Goodwill, as a deduction from tier 1 capital elements.
(ii) Investments in subsidiaries engaged in banking and financial activities which are not consolidated. Where these are not consolidated, deduction is essential to prevent multiple use of the same capital resources in different parts of the group. The deduction is made against the total capital base.

(e) Risk weights

Previously, capital adequacy was determined by a simple gearing ratio of capital to assets, such as a minimum 4% of core capital to total assets or 8% of total capital to total assets. Effective 1988, the supervisory authorities preferred method for determining capital adequacy is a weighted risk ratio in which capital is related to different categories of asset or off-balance sheet exposure, weighted according to broad categories of relative riskiness. The risk ratio has the following advantages over the simpler gearing ratio approach:

(i)   it provides a fairer basis for making international comparisons between banking systems whose structures may differ;
(ii) it allows off-balance sheet exposures to be incorporated more easily into the measure;
(iii) it does not deter banks from holding liquid or other assets which carry low risk.

The Bank of Botswana has adopted a similar approach to capital adequacy measurement. Thus, in terms of the legislation, Section 13 of the Banking Act lists the following categories of capital:

(i) issued and paid-up ordinary shares of the bank;

(ii) issued and paid-up non-redeemable, non-cumulative preference shares of the bank;

(iii) such other issued and paid-up preference shares of the bank or debentures which the central bank may approve in accordance with specific conditions;

(iv) undivided profits, retained income and other reserves which are disclosed in the bank's annual accounts and which are freely available for the purpose of meeting losses;

(v) undivided profits, retained income and other reserves which are freely available for meeting losses, but which are not disclosed in the bank's financial statements;

(vi) such percentage of reserves of the bank resulting from the revaluation of certain fixed assets as may be prescribed; and

(vii) general provisions held against unidentified and unforeseen losses which may arise from the bank's assets.

In terms of the Banking Regulations, 1995, the required ratio of capital (unimpaired) to risk weighted assets is 8%. However, different Pula amounts are prescribed for the different categories of banks. The minimum capital required in the case of commercial banks and investment banks is the greater of P5 or 8% of the risk weighted assets and other risk weighted exposures. In the case of credit institutions and discount houses, the minimum capital required is the greater of P2.5 million and 8% of the risk weighted assets and other risk weighted exposures. Risk weights for the different categories of assets are detailed in Appendix 1.

Asset quality

The quality of a bank's assets is essential to its continued existence. In a banking context, the bulk of a bank's assets are its lendings or advances. To the extent that a bank has adequate and prudent loan administration policies, controls and procedures and succeeds in appraising loan proposals, gathers adequate information on its customers, monitors the performance of the loan and the project, enforces adherence to the terms of the loan contracts and maintains sufficient records of the loan and performance of the project, it is likely to have better quality assets. In terms of the legislation, the quality of a bank's assets and reporting requirements thereto are addressed in Section 17 of the Banking Act, and legislated in the form of limitations on specified operations. These include the following issues.

(a) Large exposures or asset concentrations

There is a restriction on banks' exposure (in the form of all types of advances and off-balance sheet items as reflected in the risk-weights schedule) to individual entities or a group of related entities. Banks are permitted to be exposed only up to an equivalent of thirty percent of their unimpaired capital to a single borrower or group of related borrowers. Any exposure beyond this limit has to be approved by the Bank of Botswana. Past experience and evidence has shown that a significant number of bank failures have been due to credit risk concentration. Large exposures or asset concentrations make the bank unduly dependent on the fortunes of a single or very limited number of counterparties or sectors. It is a general principle of asset or portfolio management that investments should be structured such that the returns converge to a stable acceptable average. This can only be achieved with adequate diversification, which recognises the varying performances of individual assets or investments. The differences in performance, on the other hand, reflect the varying efficiencies and conditions of individual entities and sectors, which may be due to seasonal and cyclical influences. Diversification is intended to stabilise the effects of these diametric performances and periodic fluctuations. Stable returns contribute to the stability of the financial system, which is essential for continuing public confidence and efficiency of the payments system. In turn, this ensures the continuing flow of funds and the efficient allocation of such funds to worthy borrowers and projects.

(b) Group companies and related borrowers

Section 17(5) of the Banking Act provides that where the Bank of Botswana determines that the interest of a group of two or more related persons are so inter-related such that they should be considered a single unit, the total indebtedness of the group is combined and deemed to be in respect of a single person. This has the effect of invoking the prudential asset concentration limit of thirty percent of total assets exposure to a group of related entities. Related persons or entities covers connection through common ownership, control or management and cross guarantees. This applies where two or more persons hold exposures from the same bank or any of its subsidiaries, whether on a joint or separate basis in that:

(i)   one of them holds directly or indirectly power of control over the other;
(ii) their cumulated exposures represent to the bank a single risk, insomuch as they are so interconnected with the likelihood that if one of them experiences financial problems the other or all of them are likely to experience payment difficulties.

(c) Provisions for bad and doubtful debts

Adequate provisioning is essential to reflect the correct amount of a bank's earning assets as well as the true earnings. There are two aspects to this. One is to recognize those assets, or part thereof, that are likely to be bad and, therefore, recognize potential loss in value. The other aspect is to recognize the loss of interest earning potential from these assets and therefore not accrue interest, which could otherwise lead to inflated (unearned) profits. As a general rule, banks are required to maintain a general provision in recognition of the potential for loss in any lending activity. In addition, banks assess each exposure, and where it is determined that repayments are not likely to be forthcoming, specific provisions should be raised. These are not only matters to do with prudence, but also acceptable accounting practice. Section 14 of the Banking Act deals with this in relation to a bank's capital. This provides that, in determining the adequacy of capital, account should be taken of general and specific provisions.

(d) Lending to insiders (directors and employees of the bank)

Exposure to directors of a bank is limited in three respects. Firstly, banks are restricted from extending unsecured facilities to their own directors in excess of 10% of the bank's unimpaired capital without prior approval of the Bank of Botswana. Secondly, exposure in excess of one percent of the bank's unimpaired capital has to be approved by a majority of the entire board of directors. Thirdly, facilities to directors, secured or unsecured, should not at any time exceed 25% of the bank's unimpaired capital. Unsecured facilities to all other employees or officers of the bank should not exceed one year's emoluments of such officers or employees. These provisions encompass the granting of facilities to entities or partnerships in which a director, employee or officer has interest. The aim is to ensure that the bank's officers and employees do not use their privileged position to risk depositor's funds and/or at the same time crowd out the bank's financing of customers. This is because banks provide their owners and officers with a strong incentive for misjudgements that benefit themselves, and regulators need to control such incentive problems.

(e) Equity participation

The financial system should operate in such a way that risks to depositors' funds are minimised. Equity participation by banks in non-banking ventures may expose depositors' funds to abnormally high risks because as the provider of the funds, the bank becomes 'an entrepreneur' and faces the full extent of risks associated with that business. The limitation in this respect is provided for under Section 17 (10) of the Banking Act. This provides that banks should not, directly or indirectly, hold shares in any financial, commercial, agricultural, industrial or other undertaking, except where the shares are acquired in the course of satisfaction of debts due to it, in which case they should be disposed of at the earliest suitable moment. Exceptions are also indicated in the case of dealings for a trust account, shares in a deposit insurance company or in any other undertakings which do not exceed an amount, in relation to unimpaired capital, prescribed by the Bank of Botswana.

Consideration of acceptable limits and exceptions in this respect takes account of, economic efficiency, conflicts of interest, concentration of power and risk. In limiting the extent of equity participation by banks, account is taken of the following:

(i)   there are no wide investment avenues from which to choose, hence there is greater possibility of cross-shareholding between banks and industry precipitating conflict of interest;

(ii) the banks' market is not so saturated in terms of the scope, variety and quality of banking services for them to seek profit lines outside banking activities; thus, extensive participation in other activities may attenuate efforts aimed at increased financial deepening and widening of banking services;

(iii) in case of bank failure, it may be difficult to liquidate the whole of the bank's activities including shares that may be held in other companies. Further, failures in the financial system would affect other sectors of the economy as well, and vice-versa.

The longer term development of banking and financial services can, however, be enhanced by banks' participation in structures that foster the development of the financial market and innovation in the process of financing industrial or other economic activity. Thus, the limitation to equity does not apply in cases where:

(i)   the equity holding in companies enhances the development of the securities market;

(ii) the participation is for the purpose of insuring deposits;

(iii) it promotes the development of the money market; and

(iv) it would enhance the financial mechanism for financing general economic development.

(g) Acquisition of property

Commercial banks' primary responsibility is to mobilise deposits and to use such funds for real sector financing which generate returns to depositors and banks themselves. Direct or indirect involvement in property ownership has the potential to utilise a large proportion of depositors funds in a business activity, which by its nature is prone to wide fluctuations in fortunes. Thus, diversification and stabilization of returns will not be achieved. Further, there is potential to starve other economic activities of funds and the importance of savings as a source of real sector growth will be diminished. Involvement in property ownership is, thus, not considered prudent, nor serving the wider economic needs. The restriction in this regard is provided for in Section 17(11) of the Banking Act.

(h) Facilities granted against banks' own shares

The use of banks' shares as security raises two considerations. Firstly, is the effect on the bank's capital were the shares called up in case of non-performance of facilities and thereafter proving difficult to sell, or sell at a discount. Secondly, the effect on restriction of ownership/shareholding of banks in case the shares are called up and sold. This may raise questions of fit and proper test with respect to the new owner, effective holding of one bank by another, the acquisition of additional shareholding, beyond acceptable limits or controlling interest by the new holder, and so on. The use of a bank's own shares as security is thus considered imprudent and is prohibited under Section 17 (13) of the Banking Act.

To ensure the quality of their assets and compliance with legislation and regulations, banks at a minimum should have clear written policies and reporting systems with respect to the granting of facilities and acquisition and disposal of security. In addition, banks are required to maintain adequate and sound internal controls and administrative procedures to ensure effective implementation of lending policies.

Liquidity

Liquidity refers to the ability of the bank to continually meet its maturing obligations, including commitments to lend or fund and guarantees called up. The bank's obligations, in the form of deposit withdrawals and loan disbursements are met by cash flow, stocks of liquefiable assets and capacity to borrow, the latter two being influenced by the availability and efficiency of short-term money markets. Not only does a bank have to maintain adequate liquid assets, it must have policies and arrangements, including with other institutions, to fund any liquidity shortfalls.

Liquidity is an essential element of banks' operations and is vital for the continuity and sustainability of such operations. Banks are custodians of public funds and institutions through which payments are effected. In such a relationship, there exist implicit and explicit commitments by banks that they will honour the public demand to convert deposits into cash or payment of third parties. On the other hand, banks trade in finance and generate income for themselves by transforming funds deposited with them into riskier and longer term funding which, conceptually, yield progressively higher returns. Thus, at any one time, banks hold a greater part of the public deposits in non-cash form. Their essential function, therefore, entails risk of failure to pay depositors and, where this transforms into loss of confidence, could adversely affect the payments system and efficiency in the economy. The proper measurement, management and regulation of liquidity is, thus, intended to ensure liquidity of the banks and maintenance of confidence in the banking system.

Regulators, therefore, set rules for banks, that establish appropriate prudential liquidity standards and policies for its management and monitor adherence thereto. These rules include prescribing liquid assets to be held as a percentage of deposit liabilities and other similar funds. While a prudential liquidity ratio is the common regulatory focus, it is important to note that a single ratio does not provide an adequate measure of liquidity for reasons to do with differing sizes of banks and their nature of operations. Broader prudential requirements emphasise good management information systems, central liquidity control, analysis of net funding requirements under alternative scenarios, monitoring of maturity gap between assets and liabilities, diversification of funding sources and contingency planning. A liquidity management framework encompasses three aspects. Firstly, having on a daily basis, committed funds to meet deposit withdrawals and funding agreements; secondly, a sufficient stock of assets that can be liquidated at no or minimal cost to meet commitments and obligations; and thirdly, adequate contingency plans to meet extraordinary demands or circumstances. Table 2 illustrates a liquidity management matrix.

TABLE 2. LIQUIDITY MANAGEMENT MATRIX

	CASH FLOW ANALYSIS	STOCK OF MARKETABLE ASSETS	RELIANCE UPON BORROWING
OBJECTIVE	Measurement of outgoing commitments compared with inflow of funds.	To ensure adequate stock of liquid assets to meet unforeseen demands.	To determine ability to borrow market funds at short notice.
INFORMATION	Residual maturity analysis of assets and liabilities in specific time bands.	Analysis of cash and quality assets for which there is a ready market.	Details of committed standby facilities from major banks.
MEASUREMENT	Construction of a maturity ladder identifying net position or mismatch.	Determine immediate marketable value and relate to short-term liabilities.	Integrated into cash flow analysis as short-term inflow (but with caution).
CONTROL	Determine acceptable mismatch for individual banks.	Ensure minimum level of holdings and/or allow inclusion with mismatch profile.	Ensure facilities are irrevocable with no material adverse change clauses.
PROBLEMS	Assets may not mature according to schedule or there may be an early call on liabilities.	Expensive for banks to maintain large quantity of low yield assets.	Interbank market volatile and sensitive to reputation and standing.

In terms of international convergence, the Basle Committee has noted that a broad assessment of liquidity and liquidity management encompasses three scenarios, namely, the going concern scenario, the specific crisis scenario and the general market crisis scenario. It further highlights the three dimensions to this, i.e., measuring and managing net funding requirements, managing market access and contingency planning.

Going Concern Scenario – This scenario is covered by liquid asset requirements, assuming they have been appropriately set with due consideration to prevailing circumstances. In this instance, the bank can use those liquid assets to meet obligations on a daily basis without recourse to costly operations.

Specific Crisis Scenario – The underlying assumption under this scenario is that many of the bank's liabilities cannot be rolled over or replaced and would have to be paid at maturity, so that the bank would have to wind down its books somewhat. In this instance, the bank needs to have contingency plans to liquefy its assets.

General Market Crisis Scenario – In this case, the liquidity situation is adversely affected at all banks in one or more markets. The key underlying assumption is that severe tiering by perceived credit quality would occur, so that differences in funding access of institutions would widen, benefiting some and harming others. An analysis of a bank's liquidity should take account of its position with respect to this.

The maintenance of adequate liquidity is provided for by legislation under Section 16 of the Banking Act. This provides that banks shall maintain, on a daily basis, prescribed liquid assets as a percentage of deposits and similar liabilities and report to the Bank of Botswana as prescribed. Liquid assets are defined to mean freely transferable assets and unencumbered assets, including treasury bills and other securities issued by the Government or the Central Bank maturing within 370 days and approved negotiable instruments payable within 184 days. Effective 1 October 1996, the prescribed ratio of liquid assets is ten percent of a bank's average deposits. The approved liquid assets are outlined below.

(i) Cash.

(ii) Current account balance at the Bank of Botswana.[1]

(iii) Balance due from domestic banks. The availability of liquid assets to meet payment of local depositors is considered important in addressing the liquidity position of banks. Balances held abroad may be subject to sovereignty and jurisdictional constraints when attempts are made to draw-down or liquidate such assets. It is thus, considered prudent to exclude foreign held assets.

(iv) Treasury bills and other securities issued by Government or the Bank of Botswana maturing within 370 days. It is considered that there is no risk in exposure to Government and that Government and the central bank have an overriding duty to protect the liquidity of the financial system. There is, however, a market risk (capital loss) where an active market exists. Further, quite apart from the prudential aspect, the inclusion of Government securities is a

---

[1] Conceptually, since the primary reserve requirement is met by the current account balance at the Bank of Botswana and represents a policy variable that should not be breached to meet the liquid asset requirement, only the excess over the required primary reserve should count as liquid assets.

way to induce banks, when necessary, to finance Government budget deficits.

(v)   Bills eligible for discount or negotiable instruments approved by the Bank of Botswana having two good signatures and payable within 184 days. These are private sector bills and there is both credit risk and market risk. The acceptability of these as liquid assets hinges on their being discountable at the Bank of Botswana and acceptable as security for borrowing at the Bank of Botswana.

Accounting and reporting requirements

Sections 18 to 20 of the Banking Act, 1995 deal with maintenance of records, financial reporting and submission of information to the supervisory authority. In terms of Section 18, banks are required to maintain records necessary to exhibit accurately the true state of affairs of the bank and an explanation of transactions and the financial position that will allow the supervisory authority to determine if the particular bank has complied with the statutory provisions and prudential requirements. Section 19 of the Act deals with the production of annual accounts which must be prepared in accordance with generally accepted accounting practices, audited and in the format prescribed by the Bank of Botswana. These two sections stress conformity to generally accepted standards in the definition of accounting concepts and principles. It is important in evaluating the financial position of a bank to have an understanding of the principles within which the accounts are prepared. Section 20 deals with the submission of more frequent regular returns to the Bank of Botswana in a format prescribed by the Bank of Botswana. Returns are submitted to the Bank of Botswana on a monthly and quarterly basis. These are used to monitor compliance and enable analysis of the performance of individual banks.

The most important element for the banking supervisor, in this context, is accounting for capital, as it impacts on the determination of solvency and capacity to lend. This is ultimately linked to the quality of assets and procedures for accounting for loan losses. Not adequately accounting for potential losses inflates earnings/income of the bank for the particular period, while continuing to accrue interest on non-performing assets similarly creates illusory earnings. Both these hide potential insolvency, since dividends, allocation to reserves and transfers to the capital account are made out of earnings that do not reflect losses due to non-performing assets.

To further enhance the integrity of accounting information there are strict auditing requirements. These are provided for under Sections 22 and 23 of the Banking Act and include the requirement for the bank's accounts to be audited and a report of the audit submitted to the Bank of Botswana. Additional duties that may be imposed on the auditor by the Bank of Botswana require the auditor to report to the Bank of Botswana any serious breaches of pertinent legislation and regulations, criminal offences and serious irregularities. Finally, it is a requirement for the board of directors of the bank to appoint an audit committee.

Quality of Bank management

The quality of bank management has an important bearing on the performance of the individual bank and the extent to which it complies with statutory provisions, and manages the bank prudently and in line with proper banking practice. The Bank of

Botswana has determined that primary responsibility for prudent management of a bank lies with its board of directors and secondarily with the executive management. To this end, the Bank of Botswana regulates as to fit and proper persons to run banks, circumstances warranting disqualification as an officer of a bank and disclosure of interest, in accordance with Sections 29 to 32 of the Banking Act.

Temporary management and liquidation of a bank

While banking supervision is intended to ensure a stable and sound financial system, it cannot and is not intended to eliminate bank failures, but rather to manage bank failures in line with these objectives. Since the exit of weak banks is critical to the incentive structure of a strong banking system, orderly bank failures should not be interpreted as a failure of supervision. Rather the closure of unsound banks reminds other banks that the market and regulatory systems work. The intention is to establish adequate enforcement and intervention options which include mergers and liquidation. The legislation, therefore, provides for a graduated process of handling problem institutions, in the form of warnings, monetary penalties, removal of bank management, withdrawal of licence, mergers and liquidation.

In accordance with Section 33 of the Banking Act, the process of temporary management is invoked when:

(i)   the bank's core capital does not meet the requirements;
(ii) its business is conducted in an unlawful or imprudent manner, or it is otherwise in an unsound financial condition;
(iii) the continuation of its existence is not in the best interest of its depositors;
(iv) it refuses to permit an examination; or
(v)   it has been served with notice to revoke its licence.

The decision on temporary management is taken in consultation with the Minister of Finance and Development Planning and, once taken, is notified to the public. Temporary management by the Bank of Botswana gives it exclusive powers to manage and control the bank, directly or through an appointed representative. In terms of Section 34 of the Banking Act, duration of temporary management is ninety days, within which:

(i)   the bank is restored to its board or management;
(ii) an arrangement for sale of the bank is made;
(iii) a compromise or arrangement between the bank and its creditors or a reconstruction in accordance with relevant provisions of the Companies Act is proposed; or
(iv) the bank is wound up or placed under judicial management of the Bank of Botswana.

3. The Process of Supervision and Performance Monitoring

To fulfil its mission of ensuring a safe, stable, sound and properly functioning financial system, the Bank of Botswana has a full Department dedicated to the task of formulating and implementing a framework for banking supervision and of monitoring the performance of banks licensed under the Banking Act. The three facets of this are: firstly, determining who should operate as a bank and weeding out unlicensed operators; secondly, continuing monitoring of the licensed banks to ensure that they comply with statutes and prudential requirements; and thirdly, managing the safe exit or rehabilitation of delinquent banks. The fundamental attributes of a good and effective supervision and regulatory framework are:

(i)   a legal framework of regulation and supervision;
(ii) the quality of information provided to the supervisor, in terms of completeness, timeliness and accuracy;
(iii) actual practices of banking supervision, in terms of establishing appropriate and sufficient organization and techniques of supervision; and
(iv) experienced and dedicated personnel.

Section 2 highlighted the legal and regulatory framework, which essentially empowers the supervisory process itself. In terms of the supervisory process, there is, generally, a differentiation between reliance on *on-site examinations* and reliance on *off-site monitoring.* As an example, in the United States of America, banking supervision is dominated by regular on-site examination of banks by staff of the Federal Reserve System (central bank), the Treasury Department, and the Office of the Comptroller of the Currency. Thus, there are three supervisory authorities in the USA, all of them practising on-site supervision. Conversely, in the UK, the Bank of England practices off-site monitoring. There are arguments for and against either method. It is argued, for example, that the advantages of off-site monitoring are that it is less costly and involves a lesser number of staff, and that there is less likelihood of affinity to the banks' staff, hence lesser chances of being compromised. The disadvantages are that there is no insight into the banks' methods and nature of record keeping and there is no feel of a particular bank's culture and staff relations. Conversely, the advantages of on-site examinations are that: examiners are able to view bank's records; they can seek explanations and understand the records and methods of accounting; and contact with bank staff is a fertile source of information. The disadvantages are that on-site examinations may be costly, loathed by banks as disruptive, and, of course, there is the possibility that examiners are compromised or 'persuaded'.

In Botswana, given resource constraints and the above arguments, the Bank of Botswana has adopted a combination of on-site examinations, off-site monitoring and a system of bilateral meetings with licensed banks.

On-site examinations

On-site examinations involve staff of the Bank going to individual banks, their branches and other operating offices to examine their books of accounts and operating policies and procedures. The current policy is that on-site examinations for each licensed bank are carried out at least once every 24 months.

In general, banking supervision is carried out under the context of the CAMEL framework. CAMEL is an acronym which stands for Capital Adequacy, Asset Quality, Management (quality), Earnings and Liquidity. Following the examination of a bank, a report is prepared indicating findings in each of these areas and detailing specific violations of applicable legislation and prudential standards. At the outset it is decided whether to carry out a full-scope examination, encompassing all areas, or a limited-scope examination, encompassing selected areas only. Once this is done the preparation for the examination includes, among other things, determining the specific information to be made available to the examination team by the bank, determination of the sample of advances to be reviewed and the classification procedures.

(a) Capital adequacy

In determining capital adequacy, examiners have to answer specific questions as to the comparison between the actual ratios to the standard or prescribed prudential ratios and the trend of these over the past few years. The analytical objectives in this instance are to determine compliance with statutory prescriptions, the composition of capital and how capital relates to the quality of assets. The on-site examination also gives the examiner opportunity and scope to enquire and review policies on movement of capital items, such as revaluations, transfers to reserves and dividend and retention policies. Thus, following examination, the examiners should be able to make conclusions as to whether the bank is adequately capitalised or undercapitalised.

(b) Asset quality

To a great extent, the determination of asset quality is the *raison d'etre* for on-site examinations. On-site examinations are an opportunity for examiners to review in detail the loan portfolio of a bank and comment on its quality and performance, given the loan administration policies and the performance of the individual loans. At the outset and given the size of a bank, the examination team determines a sample of loans (by deciding on a cut-off point by size) to be extensively reviewed and which ones to be subjected to a rule-of-thumb analysis. It is the case that in a full scope examination of a bank, the entire loan portfolio is subject to an opinion, either on the basis of extensive review or rule-of-thumb categorization. There are at least three objectives for this exercise: the determination of the existence, effectiveness and enforcement of loan administration policies; the performance of the loan portfolio; and the adequacy of provisions for loan losses made by the bank.

Having reviewed the loans (large loans, especially) examiners have to determine the classification of the loans in the categories outlined below.

(i) *Pass* – assets under this category are those that are found to have no material or significant performance problems, or technical and or legal documentation deficiencies.

(ii) *Substandard* – a substandard asset is inadequately protected by the current sound worth and paying capacity of the borrower or of the collateral pledged, if any. Assets so classified have well defined weaknesses that jeopardise the liquidation of the debts. They are characterised by the distinct possibility that the bank will sustain some loss if the deficiencies are not corrected.

(iii) *Doubtful* – assets classified doubtful have all the weaknesses inherent in those classified sub-standard with the added characteristic that the weakness makes collection or liquidation in full, on the basis of currently existing facts, conditions and values, highly questionable and improbable.

(iv) *Loss* – assets classified loss are considered uncollectable and of such little value that their continuance as bankable assets is not warranted.

(v) *Special mention* – assets in this category are currently protected, but are potentially weak. These advances constitute an undue and unwarranted credit risk, but not to the point of justifying a classification of substandard. The credit risk may be relatively minor, yet constitute an unwarranted risk in the light of circumstances surrounding a specific advance.

For loans not subjected to extensive review, the policy is to list loans that are three months in arrears as substandard, those four to six months in arrears as doubtful and those over seven months as a loss. For large loans, a rigorous exercise of reviewing each customer file is undertaken. Among other things, the review consolidates each customer's exposure and notes the aggregate exposure with respect to all facilities, including off-balance sheet exposure; determines the performance of the various facilities; assesses the records with respect to controls and monitoring; assesses security arrangements/registration; notes the reasons for non-performance if that is the case; determines whether the customer's financial accounts are regularly submitted to the bank; and, where necessary, it analyses the accounts of the customer to determine viability. It is at this instance that the examiners determine the related entities as indicated by common ownership/directorship, subsidiary holdings and cross guarantees. This review also indicates and records asset concentrations; that is, aggregate exposures to single entities or a group of related entities in excess of thirty percent of unimpaired capital.

Asset quality assessment in respect of both the small and large loans covers an assessment of the use of overdraft facilities. While problems with respect to term loans are revealed by the arrears status, the assessment of overdraft facilities determines problems in terms of excess or drawings over the authorised limit and non-fluctuating account balances. An overdraft facility is provided as bridging finance, normally to pay suppliers, with subsequent receipts clearing the overdraft. A sticky debit balance (or hard-core element) usually means that the sales receipts are not being deposited in the account.

Assessment of asset quality also determines compliance with respect to lending to directors, as well as officers and employees of the bank. Further, examiners make an extensive review of the loan administration policies covering, among other things, existence of documentation, loan portfolio coverage policy, delineation of responsibilities and limits, collection and work-out procedures for problem credits.

As indicated previously, one reason for asset quality assessment is to determine the adequacy of loan loss provisions. The amount of the general provision is recommended to the bank taking into account its loan administration policies and procedures and, in general, the performance of its loan portfolio. With respect to the specific provisions, examiners recommend an aggregate amount equal to 50% of all amounts classified substandard plus 100% of all amounts classified loss. Where the books of the bank show a level of provisions below that determined by the examiners, the bank is required to make adjustments accordingly. This is important to reflect the true value of the bank's assets and also its impact on the bank's capitalization. Firstly, provisions are deducted from income and, therefore, reduce the level of profits; and to that extent, the amount of retained income that may be capitalised is reduced, slowing growth of capital, while a loss situation will result in erosion of capital. Secondly, general provisions are only allowed as supplementary capital. Therefore, to the extent that the examiners recommendations can impact negatively on capital growth, it reveals that the level of protection of depositors, the potential for future asset creation, and the competitive position is not as hiterto shown by the bank's books.

(c) Management

While the success of a banking venture ultimately hinges on the quality of the bank's management, it is, because it is not quantifiable, one of the more difficult areas to assess. However, over the years bank examiners have developed techniques and skills to assess the quality of management. It can be said, though, that the quality of management is ultimately reflected in the performance and compliance with respect to the C, A, E, and L of the banking supervision framework.

Bank management is evaluated with a view to determine the adequacy of the management structure, management control procedures and the decision making process. To a great extent, assessment of bank management relies on a review of the performance of the board of directors, who are deemed to be the overall overseers of operations and ultimately responsible for formulation of policies and ensuring that they are implemented. The role of the board of directors is to control a bank's direction and to be actively involved in the bank's affairs. Both the board and executive management work together to establish realistic goals for the bank and ensure implementation of policy. The board depends on reports from the executive management to perform its monitoring function.

An important technique for assessing the quality of management during an on-site examination is, therefore, a review of the board minutes to establish the board's involvement in establishing policies and monitoring their implementation, responsiveness to recommendations from auditors and supervisory authorities. The review determines any deficiencies in information flow from management to the board, especially given what is known from reviews of other areas. Such a flow of information may cover a review of a bank's operations, briefings on the general economic environment, banking industry, staffing developments, branch network and administrative issues. From this, an assessment is made as to whether management plans are adequate for future conditions and developments. Further, the assessment has to indicate the extent to which management adheres to policies established by the board and the effect of these policies on the financial condition of the bank. The examiners also assess the quality and experience of management as indicated by its depth of knowledge in banking business and board and management continuity.

(d) Earnings and financial condition

An analysis of earnings is done by determining the levels and trends in profitability ratios such as the returns on assets and capital, as well as the composition, and trends thereof in the composition, of the income and expenses elements. The examination process in this respect also involves on-site preparation of a statement of the financial condition as at the date of examination from the bank's accounting records.

Some of the ratios analysed and commented upon are outlined below.

Net Income to Total Assets (or Average Total Assets) – which measures the net outcome of employing the bank's assets over the reporting period, in terms of a percentage return.

Net Income to Total Capital – which measures the return on equity or shareholders funds.

Net Interest Income to Average Total Assets – which measures the bank's interest earnings, after deducting the cost of funding, out of the assets employed over the reporting period.

Non-interest Income to Average Total Assets – which measures the bank's relative earnings from non-core business, in relation to assets, over the reporting period.

Non-interest Expense to Average Total Assets – which measures costs other than costs of funding relative to assets over the report period, and thus is a measure of comparative efficiency.

(e) Liquidity

The assessment of liquidity is essentially intended to determine whether the bank has maintained adequate liquid assets as prescribed by statute. Other elements of the assessment involve ascertaining the bank's liquidity management policy. Of special interest is whether there are documented procedures for liquidity management, including accessing the market. Specifically, the assessment determines the following:

(i)   the bank's compliance with Section 16 of the Banking Act in terms of maintaining adequate liquid assets in proportion to deposit liabilities and the composition of such assets;

(ii) the frequency, trends and levels of the bank's resort to borrowing from the Bank of Botswana, other financial institutions, shareholders or parent bank;

(iii) the amount of the bank's assets that are readily convertible to cash and the proportion of these to deposit liabilities;

(iv) the ability of the bank to access sources of funds other than the discounting facility at the Bank of Botswana;

(v)   the bank's level of dependence on volatile deposits and/or reliance on interest rate sensitive deposits. One of the principles of liquidity management is a diversified funding base, i.e., many small deposits as opposed to a few (concentrated) large deposits. A concentrated and inordinately large volume of highly mobile deposits, such as call deposits, could signal potential funding problems;

(vi) the effectiveness of the bank's asset/liability management, whether the board has established an asset/liability management committee and the bank's compliance with internal liquidity policies; and

(vii) the coverage of the policy and guidelines on liquidity management, in terms of the reporting structure and procedures, assignment of ultimate responsibility, diversification of funding sources, management of market access and contingency arrangements.

(f) Internal controls

Internal controls are defined as the system within the bank consisting of its plan of organization, assignment of duties and responsibilities. This includes the design of accounts and reports, and all measures and methods employed to protect its assets. Internal controls are intended to encourage accuracy and reliability of accounting and other operating data and reports, promote and judge the operational efficiency of all aspects of the bank's activities, and communicate managerial policies and encourage and measure compliance. The on-site examination objectives with respect to internal controls are:

(i)   to determine if the bank has an internal audit section;

(ii) to assess the independence of the internal audit section from other departments;

(iii) to assess the quality of internal audit section staff;

(iv) to determine if the bank complies with the requirements of the Banking Act with regard to external auditing of its records;

(v)   determine and assess the adequacy of internal controls; and

(vi) to assess adherence to internal control procedures.

Assessment of internal controls involves a review of the structure of the bank, operating manuals and policy documents and inspection reports of the head office, holding company or parent bank. The assessment also entails a review of accounting and security procedures.

(g) Meetings with the bank being examined

The examination process also involves meetings with management of the bank being examined in three categories.

(i)   A preparatory meeting before the start of the examination to notify the bank of the scope of the examination, expectations of the examination team with respect to the information that will be provided and for the bank to designate staff who will be available to assist or answer enquiries from the examination team.

(ii) Apart from on-going enquiries during the examination, the examination team also sets up the wrap-up meeting following examination of each operation, e.g., a branch meeting to notify the management of that branch what the initial findings are, to fill in any gaps in information and for the management to respond to the examination teams initial comments. The examination team should get the complete information and inform management of their views given the information, such that final conclusions cannot be challenged on the basis of lack of complete information or not having sought explanations.

(iii) Following preparation of the draft examination report, a meeting of senior management responsible for banking supervision and senior management of the bank being examined to inform the latter of the contents of the examination report, including major conclusions and recommendations with respect to all areas examined. Following this meeting the report is finalised for transmission to the chairman of the board of directors of the bank.

Off-site monitoring

Off-site monitoring, or supervision, relies on information required to be submitted by banks to the supervisory authorities, and has essentially the same supervisory objective as on-site examinations. However, in this instance, the integrity of the information submitted is not readily established. Off-site monitoring is a long-standing supervisory tool; and over time, banks' supervisors have established analytical frameworks that enable them to make credible conclusions as to the soundness of individual banks and the safety and stability of the financial system. An important element that may be missing from an off-site-monitoring-only regime is a deeper analysis of a bank's assets and internal controls. In the Bank of Botswana, off-site monitoring encompasses analysis of compliance and performance from information submitted by the banks and bilateral meetings with the banks.

To facilitate continuous monitoring of performance, the Bank of Botswana has established a system of monthly and quarterly submissions of confidential returns. The Confidential Monthly Return comprises a comprehensive detail of balance sheet items, a breakdown of deposits by type and holder, a breakdown of advances by user, a breakdown of foreign currency accounts by type and currency and records of deposit rates and the prime lending rate. This is used essentially to monitor compliance with respect to liquid assets requirements and capital adequacy. It is also useful as a ready source of information for any incidental reviews on any of the banks.

The Confidential Quarterly Return requires a larger volume of information, and is composed of detailed schedules on Capital and Reserves, Accounts with Other Banks, Off-balance Sheet Items, Breakdown of Advances by Maturity and Interest Rate Charged, Asset Concentrations, Deposit Concentrations, Maturity Ladder, Statement of Income and Expenses, Arrear Status of Advances and Provisions and Staffing. The data is then used to make a standard analysis comprising a determination and trend analysis of profitability, asset quality, capital adequacy and liquidity ratios. Appendix 2 lists the ratios that are commonly analysed.

The Bank also utilises the audited annual statements of banks, not only to review performance, but to determine compliance as outlined below.

(i)   The level of provisions. The amount of both the general provision and the specific provisions have to comply with those recommended following examination.
(ii) The presentation and detail of the financial statements. These should be in compliance with the prescriptions by the Bank of Botswana with respect to disclosure of certain details and accounting principles applied.
(ii) The determination of the capital of the bank. This audited capital will form the basis on which the capital adequacy ratio will be calculated and the limit with respect to asset concentrations.

Bilateral meetings with banks

The above two methods of banking supervision are supplemented by bilateral meetings with individual banks. These are held with each individual bank several times in a year to discuss bank specific issues and pertinent developments within the industry or in the wider economy. It is also an opportunity for the banks to bring up any issues which they feel the Bank of Botswana should be looking into.

4. THE LINK BETWEEN MONETARY POLICY AND BANKING SUPERVISION

Monetary policy is about influencing economic stability through credit, interest rate and exchange rate policies; and banking supervision contributes to the maintenance of stability through its effect on the internal strength of banks. To the extent that bank supervision helps individual banks under competent management to remain strong, it makes for an effective and responsive banking system. As highlighted elsewhere in this paper, banks are at the centre of financial and economic activity, acting as primary providers of payments services and a conduit for monetary policy implementation. Their key roles in the economy include mobilization of savings, intermediation, maturity transformation, facilitation of payments flows, credit allocation and maintenance of borrower financial discipline. Given these roles, the management of monetary policy depends critically on the condition of domestic financial institutions. The size and structure of the financial and money markets in an economy and the soundness and competitiveness of its banking institutions are important factors. Weaknesses in the banking system, if left unattended, could pose a threat to macroeconomic stability. Monetary policy making, otherwise, becomes much more complex when the authorities are faced with inefficient, unsound or insolvent financial institutions; and by extension, efficiency of intermediation and the payments system are affected.

The role of banking supervision is ultimately to prevent stress in the system as a whole, rather than supporting individual banks, unless they pose systemic risks. To succeed in prevention of stress requires well-balanced institutional structures that create proper incentives for strong internal governance and market discipline of financial institutions, combined with supportive regulatory structures and a macroeconomic policy mix that provides the stability necessary for sound banking. Thus, there should be close coordination between bank supervisors and authorities in charge of monetary and credit policies so that the effects of monetary policy measures on banks will be taken account of at an early stage. What is clear is that there is a two-way relationship between banking supervision and monetary policy formulation. Sound banking supervision impacts on the efficacy with which policies are carried through, while macroeconomic policy and financial sector policies impact on the soundness, stability and efficiency of the banking system.

Financial instability distorts the intended effects of monetary policy and reduces the degree of freedom available to policy makers. Financial instability could be precipitated by inadequacies in either of the supervisory or monetary policy areas. Laxity in banking supervision characterised by allowing entry and continuing operation of delinquent banks, not enforcing compliance with statutes and prudential requirements, and not monitoring the performance of banks' management leads to weaknesses in individual banks and ultimately to the banking system, due to contagion. Macroeconomic or stabilization policies could affect the solvency of banks. For example, an economic downturn leading to defaults by bank customers affects the quality of the banks' assets, profitability and, ultimately, solvency. Further, the extent to which macroeconomic and financial sector policies allow for competition, free markets and variety in financial services on offer impacts on the efficiency of the banking system. In a recent IMF study (IMF, 1996), the following issues were identified as likely to have an impact on bank soundness.

(i) Stabilization policies — While inflation and balance of payments targets are typically pursued with monetary, exchange rate and fiscal policies, concern for soundness of the banking system may occasion trade-offs. Such trade-offs may be in the area of choice of policy objectives or the pace with which macroeconomic objectives are pursued.

(ii) Monetary Instruments – The effectiveness of monetary policy instruments depends on the state of the banking system. Open market operations, for example, rely on a sound banking system for rational market responses and for transmission of policy.

(iii) Fiscal balance – Since addressing the unsoundness of the banking system often entails substantial government spending, the fiscal balance itself becomes a constraint on the type of corrective action that can be taken.

(iv) Foreign capital flows – The financial system has become more integrated internationally in an environment of free capital movement. Banks, therefore, face increased exposure to credit and market risk in the international arena. In this scenario, objectives for banking system soundness need to be considered along with monetary, exchange rate, and fiscal policy in the context of an open capital account.

Monetary policy should, thus, work in tandem with effective banking supervision. To this extent there is complementarity between banking supervision and monetary policy. Some of the specific areas where this complementarity is discernible are outlined below.

(i)   In imperfect financial markets, where aggregate data cannot be used with considerable confidence, monetary authorities have to resort to intuitive techniques in reporting on the financial sector, in which case the banking supervisor is the most fertile source of qualitative data, given insight into the operations of individual banks.

(ii) Further, given their more intimate knowledge of individual bank's operations, supervisors can assist analysts in interpreting financial data.

(iii) Supervisors are better placed to check on the accuracy of financial reporting to the central bank.

(iv) With their intimate knowledge of the workings of the financial system, supervisors can help in judging the faithfulness with which the effects of monetary policy measures are transmitted through the financial system.

(v)   Frequently the bank supervisor can warn of the deleterious side effects of monetary policy on the financial system.

(vi) Where structural changes in the financial system are made, involving new legislation, to improve the functioning of monetary policy, the bank supervisor is best placed to judge the probable consequences of these changes.

As is clear from the principal objectives of the Bank of Botswana alluded to earlier, the Bank has responsibility for ensuring the soundness of the financial institutions, the payments system and carrying out monetary policy. Although within the Bank these functions are carried out separately, the fact that success in all of them represents the ultimate mission of the Bank has tended to balance any tendency to move in opposite directions. Thus, the supervisory legal framework, prudential requirements and policies thereto are normally the outcome of collective input from all the relevant areas of the Bank's operations. Further information and analysis generated in either area are major inputs into the analytical frameworks and policy outcome with respect to either banking supervision or monetary policy.

5. PERFORMANCE OF BOTSWANA BANKS, 1980–1995

In looking at the role of banking supervision in relation to the success of financial sector policies, it is important to consider the performance of the banks themselves in terms of continuing viability, efficiency, effectiveness in intermediating and in serving the broader economic needs. One way of assuring efficiency in the financial system is allowing for competition as alluded to in the Licensing Policy. For a long time, there were very few banks in Botswana, a situation which was considered to be inimical to competition. Not only does competition lead to better quality services at lower costs, but it also provides incentives for firms to discover unserved niches in the market. The returns that can be obtained reflect the values the consumers place on these services. Competition affects credit availability, not so much the total amount of credit (which may be related to macroeconomic considerations) but rather the pattern of allocation. The larger the number of banks, the greater the likelihood that these may be more than willing to lend. It is argued, for example, that 'lack of competition in the banking sector has a deleterious effect on the producing sector that goes beyond the high interest rates its monopoly position confers', (Stiglitz, 1993). The basic argument is, therefore, that a competitive environment is more likely to engender stronger internal governance of individual banks, enhanced market discipline and efficient intermediation. Official supervision ensures this, while the prevalence of these attributes bolsters the efficacy of macroeconomic policies and monetary policy in particular. The following analysis reviews the performance of banks in Botswana over the past fifteen years, with respect to competition in the market, profitability and productivity of banks, and the success in intermediating and serving the needs of the general public.

Profitability

Figure 1 shows the index of the concentration ratio along with an index of profitability. Profitability is calculated as the ratio of total commercial banks pre-tax net income to total year end assets. From the chart it can be seen that there has been a downward trend in banks' profitability as competition increased. A number of factors have affected the collective profitability levels of the banks in recent years. One factor contributing to this is the negative returns in the earlier years of establishment of the newer banks due to start-up costs and the take-over of unprofitable financial institutions. The second reason is associated with the onset of competition in the banking system, which forced the longer established banks to innovate, at considerable cost, in order to retain customers and counter the technological challenges of the newer entrants. The third reason is undoubtedly the macroeconomic conditions. Following a period of boom and sustained credit expansion towards the end of the 1980s up to 1992, fuelled largely by negative real interest rates, but also partly the result of the Accelerated Land Development Programme, the introduction of a new monetary policy regime impacted significantly on the performance of the banks' loan portfolios. Consequently, banks have had to increase their loan loss provisions and actually take losses, resulting in lower profits. As noted in the previous sections, this is a reflection of a case where monetary policy had an impact on the soundness of banks. The role of the supervisor is, therefore, given knowledge of the macroeconomic conditions, to ensure that banks take account of these and make provisions accordingly, make

FIGURE 1. PROFITABILITY AND CONCENTRATION INDEX (1980 = 100)

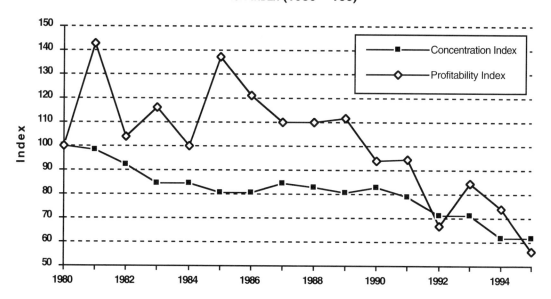

correct judgements on accrual of interest and that their loan policies take account of prevailing conditions. In terms of acceptable levels of profitability, banks in Botswana remain profitable and their returns to both assets and equity compare favourably with both regional and international banks.

Competition

The prevalence of competition is normally contrasted with concentration which presumes lack of competition. Concentration implies that a few firms are dominant in the market and therefore can operate inefficiently. For a discussion of the relevant models of microeconomic theory with respect to multi-product firms such as banks, see Roberts (1994). Drawing from this theoretical framework, an analytical framework for determining concentration is developed. This uses an index of concentration known as the Herfindahl Index, based on the relative sizes of deposits held by individual banks. The index is calculated, for each year, by taking the share of each bank in total deposits of commercial banks and squaring. It is expressed by the formula:

$$Index = \sum_{i=1...n}(D_i \: / \: TD)^2$$

Where TD is total deposits with all commercial banks, and D_i deposits with bank i.

An analysis of this index shows that there have been successive decreases in concentration over the past fifteen years, reflecting the entry of additional banks in the market, especially in the 1990s (see Figure 1). As noted in Roberts (1994), the lowering of the index in the first period from 1981 to 1983 was due to the entry in the market of the Bank of Credit and Commerce Botswana Limited (BCCB). However, since the competitive effect of BCCB was marginal, its market share was largely stagnant, the index did not change much up until the 1990s, when there were significant developments in the local banking industry. This started with the licensing of Zimbank Botswana

Limited in 1990, followed by the takeover of BCCB by First National Bank Botswana Limited (FNBB) in 1991, the licensing of Stanbic Bank Botswana Limited (at the time known as UnionBank Botswana Limited), and ANZ Grindlays Botswana Limited in 1992. Subsequently, FNBB took over Financial Services Company in January 1994, and Zimbank Botswana Limited in September 1994. As a result of these developments, competitiveness within the banking industry improved, at least as signified by the continuing slide in the concentration index since 1990. From this it can be concluded that the supervisory decision to allow more banks into the market and the successful management of reconstruction has bolstered competition in the market, which is presumed to lead to increased efficiency.

As indicated in Roberts (1994), competition arises for two reasons. First, that as the number of firms increase, the new entrants have to develop their own market niches and shares; and second, that the larger the number of banks, the lesser the chance of organised or tacit collusion.

Efficiency and productivity

Productivity is taken to be represented by the relationship of the bank's output to the cost of the inputs. The bank's output is proxied by the total earnings while inputs are represented by non-interest expenses. A higher ratio indicates that higher growth in assets is achieved with relatively lower overheads. Although this is a crude measure, Figure 2 shows that there has been a significant improvement in the productivity of banks since 1986. Productivity has, however, declined from 1992. The apparent huge surge in productivity in 1991, is a reflection of the introduction of Bank of Botswana Certificates (BoBCs), whose attributable overheads are relatively marginal. As indicated in the chart, substituting advances for earning assets reveals a much smaller increase in productivity in 1991. While Roberts (1994) attributed the declines in productivity in 1992 and 1993 to the introduction of new and expensive technology which

FIGURE 2. PRODUCTIVITY

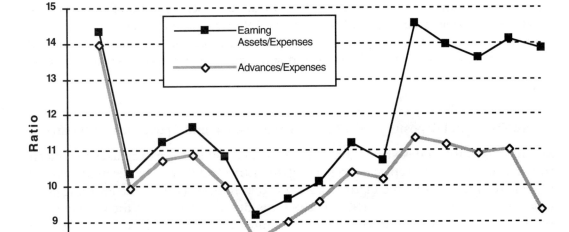

should yield higher returns in future years, the fall in 1995 is due to slower growth in earning assets, without a corresponding decrease in overheads. The bigger fall with respect to advances reflects that, while overheads increased, advances actually decreased. Interestingly this is the period during which some of the banks took exceptional measures to reduce costs and improve productivity by reducing staff numbers and rationalising geographical representation. It may be that the recorded lower productivity reflects these costs of rationalization which, over time, should result in improved productivity. The decrease or slower growth in advances is, on the other hand, attributable to the new monetary policy regime.

Intermediation and service to the public

Roberts (1994) highlights the two distinct operations of banks, that of intermediation and the provision of financial services, such as foreign exchange transactions. Out of the core function of intermediation, banks earn net interest income, which is the difference between what banks earn as interest from lending and what they pay as interest on their funding (deposits). The other financial services earn non-interest income in the form of commissions and fees. The provision of these other financial services is important in that they complement the intermediation role, and also en-

FIGURE 3. NET INTEREST INCOME AS A PERCENTAGE OF ADVANCES BY COMMERCIAL BANKS

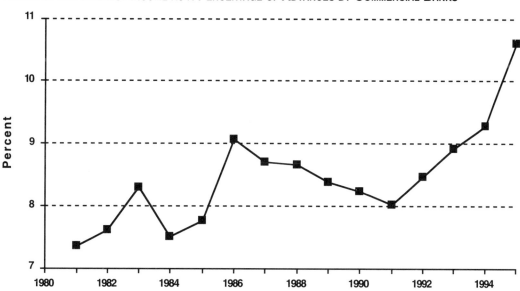

hances the effectiveness and efficiency of the payments system.

Net interest income is the bank's return from intermediation. With less competition and therefore, conceptually, inefficient intermediation, the interest rate on deposits would fall, while that on advances would rise, widening the interest rate spread (the difference between interest on lending and the interest on advances). The nature of deposits and the categories of advances and their maturity structures determines the extent of the interest rate spread. Longer term and large deposits earn relatively high interest rates as does riskier lending. Figure 3 shows the net interest income expressed as a percentage of advances. The conclusion from this is that intermediation was decreasing from 1986, but since 1991 has been rising in line with the lessening of concentration and increased competitiveness in the market.

Figure 4 shows the contribution, over time, of non-interest income to total income. This ratio peaked in 1988 when it was almost 45%, but has since been falling continuously, with a slight rise in 1995. One factor contributing to this decline is the generally higher level of interest rates as compared to 1988, and thus, a higher contribution of interest income to total income. This outcome is in line with the increase in intermediation noted above.

FIGURE 4. NON-INTEREST INCOME, SHARE IN TOTAL INCOME

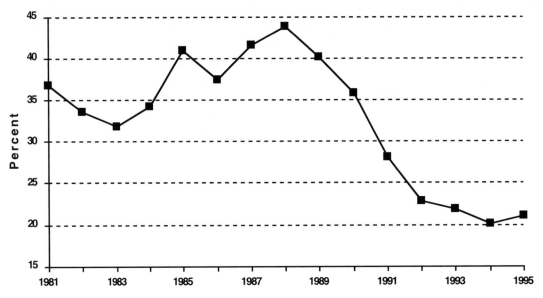

In terms of types of deposits, Figure 4 shows that since 1987 banks have attracted an increasing share of interest earning deposits as against non-interest earning deposits. Botswana has for a long time been saddled with a problem of excess liquidity. This has tended to reduce incentives for banks to actively market themselves to attract deposits. Thus, up to 1990, the greater proportion of deposits was held in non-interest earning current accounts. However, as shown in Figure 4 the combination of monetary policy changes and competition have resulted in an increase in the proportion of interest earning deposits. The introduction of BoBCs in 1991 had the effect of mopping up excess liquidity from the banking system, while increased competition has meant that banks had to compete in the market by offering competitive rates to depositors. This is evidenced by the larger proportion of the lumpy, highly mobile (transitory) call deposits, in total deposits since 1991. For the Bank of Botswana, this represents success in both the supervisory front (licensing policy) and monetary policy. Before 1991, there was inefficient intermediation with the banks sometimes refusing deposits due to lack of competition and because of the excess liquidity.

The success of monetary policy tends to be viewed narrowly in terms of the rate of increase in prices or level of inflation. In broad terms, however, success is viewed in terms of the impact on economic growth. Economic growth is itself a result of increased productive investment. The role of banks as intermediaries is to facilitate

FIGURE 5. CATEGORIES AS A SHARE OF TOTAL DEPOSITS AT COMMERCIAL BANKS

the flow of funds to these productive investments, which normally require longer term funding. Figure 5 shows the trend in the proportions of the various maturities of deposits and Figure 6 the maturity of banks' advances. The latter shows that while the maturity structure continues to be dominated by loans of five years and less and overdrafts, the proportion of loans of over five-year maturity has been steadily increasing.

FIGURE 6. SHARE OF ADVANCES BY MATURITY IN TOTAL ADVANCES

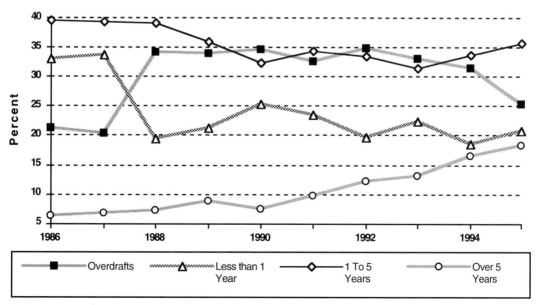

FIGURE 7. CAPITAL, ADVANCES AND ASSETS

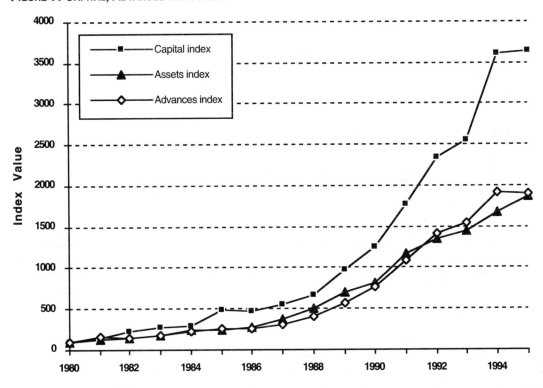

Figure 7 plots the trends in the banks' capital[2], advances and assets. As indicated elsewhere in this paper, the level of the banks' capitalization determines the extent to which they can lend and therefore, increase their assets. Figure 6 shows that while the banks' capital has increased considerably, this has outperformed the trend in advances. Two conclusions can be drawn from this. The asset concentration prudential limit means that while individual (or related) entities may need to borrow more funds, individual banks are limited in the extent to which they can meet this demand. Secondly, this gap indicates significant potential, given the current level of capitalization, for banks to increase their lending, if the demand for lending is from many diversified customers.

From the foregoing analysis, it is shown that banks in Botswana have largely been profitable and solvent, as well as adequately capitalised, such that they can meet the public's demand for productive funding. Further, since around 1991, competitiveness has increased. While there has been a benefit in terms of increased intermediation, productivity had tended to suffer as banks responded to competition.

It is also interesting to note the role of macroeconomic conditions. The cumulative effect of excessive credit growth towards the end of the 1980s and the earlier part of 1990s was increased default rates. This affected the quality of banks' assets, and indeed banks have had to make substantial loan provisions, which impacted nega-

---

2   Total capital was used instead of core or unimpaired capital – which is the basis for calculating the capital adequacy ratio.

tively on their profits. In this instance, the bank supervisor has had to ensure prudence in accounting for these circumstances and that banks' loan policies take cognizance of the monetary policy stance. Further, the bank supervisor has had to manage the safe exit of those financial institutions who were overwhelmed by the changed macroeconomic situation. Although in some instances the exits were not directly linked to the impact of macroeconomic conditions, it is important to note that the management of the exit of BCCB, Zimbank and FSC was such that the integrity, soundness and stability of the banking system was maintained.

6. THE INCREASING SCOPE OF BANKING SUPERVISION

There are at least three areas which pose new challenges to banking supervision.

Financial sector liberalization

Ongoing steps to liberalise, deregulate and widen the scope of the financial sector allow banks to enter unfamiliar areas of business, increasing their potential exposure to credit, market, foreign exchange and interest rate risk. Deregulation also opens the domestic banking system to other financial institutions and to foreign competition. Such changes in the operating environment of banks may increase the turbulence of financial markets and expand banks' opportunities to make mistakes in managing risks. The requirement is that changes be accompanied by prior, or concurrent measures to strengthen the oversight framework. The timely implementation of prudential and bank restructuring policies, in tandem with financial sector liberalization, is essential to avoid major disruptions to stability. For example, of late, bank supervisors have been concerned with, and in the process of, developing a framework for capital adequacy that will adequately insure banks risks in derivative operations.

Globalization and cross-border operations

Related to the diffusion in the scope of banking is the breaking of national boundary barriers, essentially as a result of the increased speed of communications and mobility of finance and capital. One of the major objectives of international convergence of regulatory standards is to eliminate regulatory arbitrage, whereby bankers choose jurisdictions where banking supervision is relatively lax. The allocation of supervisory responsibility for banking groups is important so that banks do not escape regulation. One of the lessons of the collapse of the Bank of Credit and Commerce International was the realization that while it was registered in Luxembourg, and supposedly supervised from there, it had escaped close supervision in areas where it had major operations and there were difficulties in consolidating its operations. In Botswana, the licensing requirement that banks be fully incorporated within the country, as opposed to branches of foreign banks, is intended to ensure full supervision of a relatively independent subsidiary.

Internationally, the Basle Committee of Bank Supervisors has developed two guidelines for supervision of cross-border operations.

(a) Information flows between banking supervisory authorities

This outlines measures to ensure adequate information flows between banking supervision authorities. These are collaboration between head office or parent company supervisor and the host supervisor (where foreign operations would be located) when foreign operations are authorised; an outline of the information needs of both the parent and host supervisors; removal of secrecy constraints; and the need for external audit to gain reassurance from sound international banking standards.

(b) Minimum standards for the supervision of international banking groups and their cross-border establishments

(i)   All international banking groups and international banks are to be supervised by a home-country authority that capably performs consolidated supervision.

(ii) The creation of a cross-border banking establishment should receive prior consent of both the host country supervisory authority and, if different, the banking group's home-country supervisor.

(iii) Supervisory authorities should have the right to gather information from the cross-border establishment of the banks or banking groups for which they are the home country supervisor.

(iv) If a host country determines that any of the above minimum standards is not met to its satisfaction, it can impose restrictive measures necessary to ensure its prudential concerns are consistent with these minimum standards, including the prohibition of the creation of banking establishments.

Technological developments

Technological developments in the banking industry imply that in order to continue to be effective, bank supervisors have to develop skills to supervise areas of electronic banking. Increasingly, banks are using computers to process and record transactions and store information. It is important in this respect for banking supervisors to be knowledgeable with respect to what the computer systems can do and their limits. This is important because supervisors not only form an opinion on the state of affairs of a bank being examined, but also on the adequacy and appropriateness of the systems and internal controls. This is particularly relevant where computer systems are used for recording information and monitoring in areas such as, accounting for advances and liquidity management.

Control over licensing and reconstruction

While the licensing policy for banks confers scope for influencing the number of banks and the diversity of banking services, there are possibilities for undermining competition for which the authorities would have minimal influence. Given that all the local banks are subsidiaries of foreign banking groups, and represent a small investment in terms of their overall size, divestiture decisions with respect to these subsidiaries would have a significant impact on the local banking industry. Similarly, an arrangement to merge operations by any two of the groups would effectively reduce competition within the local banking industry.

7. SUMMARY

The Bank of Botswana is charged with responsibility for both operation of monetary policy and ensuring soundness of the banking system. The foregoing discussion has noted the importance of a sound banking system for transmission of monetary policy. While there are other factors influencing the soundness and effectiveness of the banking system, good banking supervision practice is an important element. Among the essential elements of good banking supervision practice are an enforceable legal and regulatory framework, appropriate systems and processes of supervision, independence and adequate resources. Thus, the extent to which these have been prevalent, and there is good banking supervision in the case of Botswana, can be discerned from the efficiency of financial intermediation and of transmission of monetary policy.

This paper was not intended to test, in elaborate terms, this aspect, but merely to highlight these relationships. It is, however, interesting, that given the elaborate banking supervision framework discussed above, what evidence there is suggests that the banking system remains sound and safe, and has largely been effective in the transmission of monetary policy. The discussion in Section 5 on the performance of banks in Botswana shows them to be solvent, profitable and adequately capitalised and managed to meet the potential demands for financial intermediation in a growing economy. The quest for improvement in intermediation and rationalization of operations, manifested by financial sector liberalization, globalization of operations and technological developments, however, presents new challenges to the banking supervision process. These developments require commensurate improvements in the legal framework, the supervisory process and resources to maintain soundness of a more complex banking system.

APPENDIX 1. RISK WEIGHTS

TYPE	RISK FACTOR
On-Balance Sheet	0%
Cash (Pula notes)	0%
Balance of accounts held at Bank of Botswana	0%
Loans, advances and other credit facilities to the Government of Botswana or fully and unconditionally guaranteed by the Government of Botswana	0%
Assets secured by a lien or pledge over fixed/notice or savings deposits (cash) held by the (same) bank	0%
Central Bank securities (BoBC)	0%
Advances collateralised by BoBC or any securities issued by the Government of Botswana	0%
Foreign notes	20%
Advances to Local Government Authorities	20%

Cash items in the process (course) of collection	20%
Assets secured by cash investments held at other domestic bank/local financial institutions	20%
Due from other banks-demand or maturity under 1 year	20%
Loans and other advances secured by first class bank and guarantees acceptable to the Bank of Botswana	20%
Loans secured by recognized multilateral development financial institutions (e.g., World Bank, African Development Bank, etc.)	20%
Claims to or credit facilities guaranteed by statutory corporations (parastatals)	20%
Claims to or credit facilities guaranteed by Debswana	20%
Other domestic public sector securities	50%
Loans secured by owner occupied residential property	50%
Loans secured by commercial and industrial property	100%
Financial leases, factoring agreements and HP contracts	100%
Due form other banks maturity over 1 year	100%
Credit facilities to subsidiaries of parastatals (claims on commercial companies owned by the public sector entities, e.g., BDC subsidiaries)	100%
Eligible equity investments	100%
All other private sector advances	100%
All other assets	100%
Direct credit substitutes (guarantees, standby Letters of Credit, acceptances)	100%
Asset securitised with recourse	100%
Transaction-related contingent items (performance bonds, bid-bonds, etc.)	50%
Formal commitments, credit lines (original maturity over 1 year) underdrawn commitments, and underwriting and note-issuance facilities	50%
Short-term self liquidating, trade related (documentary credits secured by shipment)	20%
Forward foreign exchange contracts over 1 year	5%
Forward foreign exchange contracts under 1 year	1%
Undrawn commitments, original maturity under 1 year or less or can be cancelled	0%
Currency swaps	0%
BoBCs held on behalf of customers	0%

The framework for risk weights cover five weights, i.e., 0, 10, 20, 50, and 100 percent. Attention is drawn to six aspects of the structure.

(i) *Categories of risk captured in the framework*

For most banks, the major risk is credit risk, i.e., the risk of counterpart failure. There are, however, many other kinds of risk, such as investment risk, interest rate risk, exchange rate risk and concentration risk. The central focus of this framework is credit risk and, as a further aspect of credit risk, country risk.

(ii) *Country transfer risk*

(iii) *Claims on non-central government, public sector entities*

The recommended weights to be ascribed to these are 50%. Commercial companies owned by the public sector attract a uniform weight of 100% in order to avoid competitive inequality *vis-à-vis* similar private sector commercial sector enterprises.

(iv) *Collateral and guarantees*

The framework recognises the importance of collateral, but to a limited extent.

(v) *Loans secured on residential property*

The framework recognises that loans fully secured by mortgage on occupied residential property have a very low record of loss, hence these are assigned a 50% risk weighting. This weighting is specifically not applied to loans to companies engaged in speculative residential building or property development.

(vi) *Off-balance sheet agreements*

All categories of off-balance sheet agreements are converted to credit risk equivalents by multiplying the nominal principal amounts by a credit conversion factor, the resulting amounts then being weighted according to the nature of the counterpart. The five broad categories are outlined below.

(a) Substitutes for loans (e.g., general guarantees of indebtedness, bank acceptance guarantees and standby letters of credit serving as financial guarantees for loans and securities) – these carry a 100% risk conversion factor.

(b) Certain transactions related contingencies (e.g., performance bonds, bid bonds, warranties and standby letters of credit related to particular transactions) – a 50% credit risk conversion factor.

(c) Short-term self liquidating trade-related contingent liabilities arising form the movement of goods (e.g., documentary credits collateralised by the underlying shipments) – a 20% credit risk conversion factor.

(d) Commitments with an original maturity exceeding one year and all Note Issuance Facilities (NIFs) and Revolving Underwriting Facilities (RUFs) – 50% credit risk conversion factor.

(e) Interest and exchange rate related items (e.g., swaps, options, futures). In this instance banks are not exposed to credit risk for the full face value of their contracts, but only to be the potential cost of replacing the cash flow if the counterpart defaults. The credit equivalents will, *inter alia*, depend on the maturity of the contract and the volatility of the rates underlying those types of instrument. The risk weights in this category range from nil for interest rate contracts with less than one-year maturity to five percent for exchange rate contracts with maturity of one year and above.

APPENDIX 2. RATIOS USED FOR REGULAR ANALYSIS OF PERFORMANCE AND COMPLIANCE

PROFITABILITY	ASSET QUALITY	CAPITAL ADEQUACY	LIQUIDITY
Return on average total assets	Concentration[a] to total advances	Total capital to total assets	Advances to deposits liabilities
Net interest income to average total assets	Total concentrations to total assets	Core capital to risk weighted assets	Large deposits[b] to total deposits
Non-interest income to average total assets	Past due to large advances[c]	Core capital to total capital	Liquid assets to total assets
Average return on advances	Bad debts provisions to private sector advances	Unimpaired capital to risk weighted assets	Liquid assets to total deposits
Average costs of deposits	Off balance sheet items to total earning assets		
Net operating margin			
Interest expenses to total funding			
Non-interest expense to average total assets			
Net income before tax to average total assets			
interest income to income			
Return on investment			
Interest income to earning assets			
Net income to after tax to capital			
Staff costs per employee			
Total assets per employee			

Notes:
[a] Excludes off-balance sheet exposure.
[b] Total of individual deposits exceeding 20% of total assets.
[c] Refers to total individual advances in excess of 10% of capital.

References

Committee on Banking Regulations and Supervisory Practices, Various Guidelines and Standards, Bank for International Settlements, Basle.

Erb, R.D. 1989. 'The Role of Central Banks', *Finance and Development,* December issue, pp11–13.

Government of Botswana. *Bank of Botswana Act, 1975.* Government of Botswana, Gaborone.

Government of Botswana. *Banking Act, 1995* and *Banking Regulations (1995).* Government Printer, Gaborone.

IMF. 1996. 'Highlighting the Link Between Bank Soundness and Macroeconomic Policy', *IMF Survey,* May 20, pp165–169.

Roberts, S. 1994. 'Competition in Banking', *The Research Bulletin,* Vol.12, No.1. Bank of Botswana, Gaborone.

Snoek, H. 1989. 'Problems of Banking Supervision in LDCs', *Finance and Development,* December issue, pp14–16.

Stiglitz, J.E. 1993. 'The Role of the State in Financial Markets', *Proceedings of the World Bank Annual Conference on Development Economics,* Supplement to the World Bank Economic Review and the World Bank Research Observer, pp19–61.

World Bank. 1989. *World Development Report.* Oxford University Press, Oxford.

Botswana's Somnolent Giant: The Public Debt Service Fund

Its Past, Present and a Possible Future

Mike Faber

1. INTRODUCTION

The Public Debt Service Fund (PDSF) is the largest source of loan funds in Botswana.[1] On the 31 March 1996 the outstanding loans and advances of the PDSF stood at P2156 million[2] while those of all the commercial banks together totalled P1744 million.[3] Figure 1 shows the growth of credit within Botswana over the ten years from 1985 to 1995, and the PDSF's role within that credit expansion.[4]

FIGURE 1. OUTSTANDING LOANS AND ADVANCES

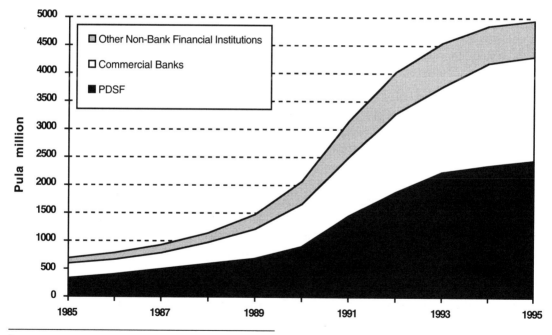

- Other Non-Bank Financial Institutions
- Commercial Banks
- PDSF

---

[1] Does that make the PDSF into a form of bank? Botswana's Banking Act, 1995, defines banking as 'the business of accepting deposits'. However standard dictionaries make no such requirement and, although it accepts no deposits from the public, no one challenges the World Bank's right to call itself a bank.

[2] Source: Accountant General, Ministry of Finance and Development Planning (MFDP), later to be found in the Annual Statement of Accounts.

[3] Source: Bank of Botswana, Botswana Financial Statistics.

[4] The Revenue Stabilization Fund (RSF) and the Development Fund (DF) also lend substantial sums of Government monies.

Yet the PDSF was not founded primarily to be a form of investment bank and in many ways it still does not behave like one. It has no staff of its own, it has no building, it makes loans but demands no collateral, it has revenues but no expenses, it is possessed of very substantial assets but no liabilities. In the twenty-four years of its existence the PDSF has never yet been used for the purpose for which it was overtly founded, but has become instead the main source of loan capital for the country's state owned enterprises (henceforth SOEs[5] or parastatals).[6] The balance of this paper explores this paradox and speculates around some of the ways in which the PDSF might evolve.

2. A BRIEF HISTORY OF THE PDSF

The Public Debt Service Fund Order, 1973, was published as Statutory Instrument No.9 of 1973 in the Government Gazette dated 19 January 1973. In exercise of the powers conferred by Section 23A[7] of the Finance and Audit Act, 1969, the Minister of Finance and Development Planning (at that time Q.K.J. Masire) made an order that 'A Special Fund, to be known as the Public Debt Service Fund (hereinafter referred to as the Fund) is hereby established'.

Paragraph 4 of the Order needs to be quoted in its entirety. It reads:

'The purpose of the Fund is to receive and safeguard moneys made available to it or earned by it which are to be utilized to meet, in whole or in part, future payments of debt charges to be made by the Government pursuant to Section 125 of the Constitution or any other written law, or guarantees given pursuant to Section 21 of the Act, the discharge of which is not the subject of other redemption arrangements.'

Section 123 (1) of the Constitution reads: 'There shall be charged on the Consolidated Fund all debt charges for which Botswana is liable'. Subsection (2) then lists these to include 'interest, sinking fund charges, the repayment or amortization of debt, and all expenditure in connection with the raising of loans on the security of the revenues of the Consolidated Fund of the former Protectorate of Bechuanaland or Botswana, and the service and redemption of debt thereby created'.

Section 21[8] of the Finance and Audit Act simply states that: 'No guarantee involving a financial liability shall be binding upon the Government unless entered into with the written authority of the Minister or in accordance with a written law'. As far as can be ascertained the PDSF has never entered into any guarantee of any other party's loan although, by convention, its own loans to parastatals and local authorities are treated as being guaranteed by the responsible ministries.

The Fund was to derive its resources from two sources. The first source would be 'such moneys as may be appropriated from time to time by Parliament'. The second source would be 'moneys accrued or realised from any investment or deposits made from moneys in the Fund'. Table 1 shows how the Fund has grown from these two

---

5   The annexe lists the SOEs referred to in this paper and their usual abbreviations.
6   It has also become a main source of funding for the capital expenditure of local authorities.
7   Now Section 25 of CAP 54:01.
8   Now Section 22.

different sources in the years between 1973 and 1995. It also shows how the monies have been used.

Table 1 shows both the source of PDSF's financing; and since there are neither expenses nor liabilities to be met, and no provision is made for bad debts, it also cumulatively shows the growth in the book value of the PDSF's assets to a total of

TABLE 1. THE PDSF: ITS GROWTH, USE AND SOURCES OF FUNDS

FINANCIAL YEAR	PUBLIC DEBT	BALANCE IN PDSF	INVESTMENTS	CASH WITH ACCOUNTANT GENERAL	APPROP. FROM CONSOL- IDATED FUND	INTEREST ETC.
1971/72	31.8	-	-	-	-	-
1972/73	49.9	2.6	-	2.6	2.6	0.0
1973/74	74.8	10.6	3.5	7.1	7.9	0.1
1974/75	90.7	15.9	6.8	9.2	5.0	0.3
1975/76	103.7	20.1	13.4	6.6	3.0	1.1
1976/77	129.9	26.0	18.9	7.1	4.5	1.4
1977/78	110.4	33.1	24.2	8.9	5.0	2.1
1978/79	111.3	38.1	24.9	13.2	3.0	2.0
1979/80	88.9	45.3	34.5	10.8	4.0	3.2
1980/81	99.1	78.4	53.1	25.3	30.0	3.1
1981/82	132.8	102.1	74.8	27.3	20.0	3.7
1982/83	199.6	124.3	101.7	22.4	13.0	7.1
1983/84	232.7	197.6	150.2	47.4	66.0	7.4
1984/85	381.0	279.3	216.6	62.7	65.0	16.7
1985/86	411.3	346.4	256.3	90.1	50.0	17.1
1986/87	482.8	440.0	292.8	151.2	70.0	27.6
1987/88	557.8	554.9	358.5	196.3	80.0	30.9
1988/89	737.9	716.4	479.0	237.5	131.0	30.8
1989/90	751.9	1193.2	678.9	514.3	423.4	53.1
1990/91	787.9	1876.9	1079.7	797.2	600.0	83.7
1991/92	965.8	2221.7	1557.9	663.7	304.1	40.7
1992/93	1096.3	3112.5	1919.2	1193.2	693.2	197.6
1993/94	1254.5	3267.9	2154.2	1113.6	-	155.4
1994/95	1377.0	3729.4	2080.5	1648.9	312.3	136.3
1995/96	1438.9	3914.2	2131.7	1782.6	-	184.9

Notes:

ᵃ Figures are in Rand million up to 1975/76 and in Pula million thereafter.

ᵇ The interest figures for 1991/92 and 1992/93 are clearly an aberration. Some P60 million that should have been credited to the earlier year was carried over to the later year.

Source: Annual Statements of Accounts and Office of the Accountant General.

P3914 million as of 31 March 1996. These assets in turn are comprised of two main types. The first are investments, which exclusively take the form of loans to SOEs, local authorities, and other state-administered bodies, such as the University, various training and research centres, and the National Sports Council. The one exception to this generalization consists of the series of loans (totalling P139.4 million) that were made to the Financial Services Company of Botswana (FSC) when that company was a parastatal, but which have remained upon the PDSF's books even though FSC has been absorbed into the private sector through its reverse takeover by First National Bank of Botswana (FNB).[9] The second type of asset held by the PDSF consists simply of money on deposit with the Accountant General. Money on deposit with the Accountant General earns no interest, and in practice becomes part of the Accountant General's balances at the Bank of Botswana. Since such balances are invested by the Bank, the income earned on them contributes to the revenues of the Consolidated Fund, but unlike the interest on PDSF loans, it is not credited to the PDSF.[10]

A later table in this paper (Table 5) displays the PDSF's portfolio of investments in full. At this point, suffice it to notice the way in which the statutory instrument makes provision for investing, apparently on a temporary basis, moneys of the Fund 'not immediately required' for servicing or repaying Government's debt. These monies may be invested by the accounting officer on behalf of the Fund (in effect, by the Permanent Secretary, MFDP) in such investments and on such terms:

(a) 'as shall contribute to the achievement of the objectives of the National Development Plan'; and

(b) as the President, on the advice of the Minister for finance, shall direct, 'provided that such investments or terms shall not in any way prejudice the achievement of the purposes of the Fund'.

The inclusion of the proviso is intriguing. Does it mean that any investment that is unlikely to be recovered in full, or that has little prospect of meeting its interest payments is strictly speaking *ultra vires*?[11]

Looking back, it is relatively easy to see what happened. Earlier Governments of Botswana and of the Bechuanaland Protectorate, say prior to 1966, had little possibility of borrowing, for even the recurrent budget was grant-aided and the capacity to service foreign debt could be seen to be extremely low. Later Governments, post the discovery and exploitation of diamonds, had little need to borrow because post-1970 revenues started to increase more rapidly than the capacity to spend sensibly.[12] The

---

9   FSC was an odd sort of parastatal, being owned by a combination of BDC, NDB and the commercial banks with an increasing amount of PDSF money to supplement public deposits. Later the commercial banks sold their shares, then FSC went public on the stock exchange, then it was absorbed in a reverse take-over by FNBB which thereby obtained a public quotation and some cheap long-term finance to the chagrin of the other banks which claimed that FNBB had been accorded a commercial advantage. (Source: communication from C. Harvey.)

10 Until the end of 1996, PDSF monies held through the Accountant General would have contributed to the Bank of Botswana's profits, 95% of which were paid over to Government. From 1997 such monies will increase Government's investment account at the bank and will result in increased dividends for Government from the Pula Fund.

11 For example the loan to the Botswana National Sports Council for the construction of the sports stadium. But it is easy to be wise after the event and, at the time, this was seen as a potential 'cash cow'.

need (as viewed from the Ministry of Finance and Development Planning) was to protect the budget from the spending departments whose collective claims were likely to
add more to gross expenditure and demand than the real economy could cope with.
This would potentially lead to a combination of inflation, poor project selection, and
declining value-for-money from Government expenditure.[13]

There was also a need rapidly to expand and augment the physical infrastructure –
roads, housing, sanitation, telecommunications, water and power supplies.

Thus in the years following 1973, the PDSF simultaneously became a device for
siphoning Government surpluses away from the recurrent budget and a source of
funding for the capital formation required by the SOEs.

3. TERMS OF PDSF LENDING

Table 2 makes it clear that throughout its existence PDSF has lent on sub-commer-
cial terms and for sixteen years out of twenty-two at negative real interest rates.[14] The
average (unweighted) real rate at which it has lent has been –2.16%. Only for three
years in the middle of the 1980s and then, following a change in policy, since 1994
has the real rate been positive. Even in those years the rates set for the PDSF have not
been high enough to render medium-term lending from the commercial banks competitive with those of the PDSF.

It is worth considering some of the effects of this sub-market rate lending to the
SOEs.

(i)   Unquestionably, low interest rate loans facilitated the development of Botswana's
      infrastructure, which itself both facilitated and helped to cause the country's
      rapid rate of economic growth.

(ii) Given that most parastatals are required to show 'a reasonable return' on a fair
      value of the capital employed, low interest rates loans also helped to keep down
      tariff levels for the services provided. For BHC, BPC, BTC and WUC interest
      charges are a major element in their costs of production so that a subsidised
      interest rate has the effect of reducing the level of rent or tariff necessary to
      realise 'a reasonable return'. Conversely extravagant or inefficient investments
      have the effect, if the relevant law is adhered to, of increasing the required rent
      or tariff.[15]

---

[12] Read literally, this may be misleading. Earlier Governments foresaw the need for the
      parastatals and Central Government itself to borrow and wanted an instrument that would
      absorb the growing revenues in a way that would ensure Government's capacity to service
      future debt obligations. Using the PDSF to fund the investments of the commercially sound
      parastatals was one of the envisaged uses of the Fund. What was not envisaged was (i) the
      unsound nature of many of these investments, and (ii) the growth of the fund to a size well
      in excess of all Government and parastatal debt combined.

[13] For a description of this process at work in the late 1980s, see Harvey, C., 1992.

[14] The question has been raised as to whether this was intentional. If the view was taken that
      inflation and therefore nominal market rates were likely to fall, then the rates being set on
      a long-term basis might have been regarded (wrongly) as commercial. Alternatively, it has
      been claimed that the PDSF rates were deliberately set below commercial market rates
      because of the social benefits that were seen as emanating from the SOEs' investments.

[15] A low interest rate may also encourage capital-intensive investments.

TABLE 2. REPRESENTATIVE PDSF INTEREST RATES – NOMINAL AND REAL

YEAR	BORROWER	SIZE OF LOAN (PULA MILLION)	NOMINAL INTEREST RATE	INFLATION RATE	REAL INTEREST RATE
1974	BHC	0.5	8.0	13.6	−4.3
1975	BHC	3.5	8.0	11.5	−3.1
1976	BDC	2.5	8.0	13.4	−4.8
1977	–	–	–	13.2	–
1978	BPC	0.2	6.0	9.1	−2.8
1979	BHC	5.3	6.0	11.6	−5.0
1980	WUC	0.8	6.0	13.7	−6.8
1981	BHC	9.8	8.0	16.5	−7.3
1982	NDB	8.2	8.0	11.2	−2.9
1983	NDB	13.0	10.0	10.5	−0.5
1984	BPC	21.0	10.0	8.6	1.3
1985	BHC	11.3	10.0	8.1	1.8
1986	BDC	2.5	10.0	10.0	0.0
1987	BHC	28.0	8.5	9.8	−1.2
1988	NDB	7.5	8.5	8.4	0.1
1989	AB	48.5	7.5	11.6	−3.7
1990	WUC	13.0	7.5	11.4	−3.5
1991	BHC	90.0	8.0	11.8	−3.4
1992	BR	24.2	9.5	16.1	−5.7
1993	BHC	57.0	12.0	14.4	−2.1
1994	BHC	136.2	14.6	10.6	3.6
1995	NDB	20.0	12.1	10.6	1.4
	BHC	35.5	14.6	10.6	3.6
1996	BTC	30.0	14.6	10.0	4.2
	BDC	10.4	12.1	10.0	1.8

Note: 'Representative' in this context means that the terms of the loan the interest rates were typical of those granted to parastatals in that particular year. Different terms were normally applied to loans to local authorities, and sometimes a whole variety of different interest rates applied to different loans in the same year – the extreme case being 1993 when AB got loans at 8%; and BCB, BBS and FSC got loans at 9.5%; BHC, AB (again) and BR got loans at 12%; and BDC, WUC, the University of Botswana and Jwaneng Town Council got loans at 14.6%. In 1995, the practice was introduced of lending to financial institutions at a 2.5% lower interest rate than to non-financial parastatals which, it was supposed, would use the funds directly themselves.

Source: The main terms of all PDSF loans are published in the *Annual Statements of Accounts*, most recently in *Statement 8.*

(iii) Low interest rate loans played their part in disguising (and perpetuating) management deficiencies, including instances of slack work discipline and extensive over-staffing.

(iv) The apparently cheap price of capital also encouraged some over-investment, some extravagant investments, and some investments with low rates of return. There is evidence that the productivity of capital has been falling since the mid-1980s.[16] There is also reason to believe that the market value of some parastatals, even some of those in a monopolistic position, is substantially less than what has been spent on them, i.e., their book value.[17]

(v) The ability of the Government to continue supplying the SOEs with all the investment capital required to meet increases in effective demand has stultified the growth of the private domestic capital market.

The overall picture is thus neither wholly good nor wholly bad. There are many worse ways to spend government revenue surpluses than by investing them in a modern infrastructure. But the infrastructure so constructed now needs to be run on more commercial lines. And the infrastructural needs for future development are switching from simple increased physical infrastructure, and more towards the expansion of private sector activities that will make use of the infrastructure which the country already possesses[18] and for that, infrastructure and services must be provided more efficiently and maintained more effectively.

4. A New Direction for the PDSF

New circumstances create the need for new policies. One aspect of such new policies is likely to involve the parastatals moving steadily towards a more commercial mode of operation. As the Minister of Finance and Development Planning indicated in his 1996 Budget Speech:

'The process of rationalization and commercialization of our parastatals will continue. Rationalization involves asking ourselves which activities really need to be undertaken by the state, and which are best left to private enterprise. Rationalization also involves ensuring that those enterprises which remain in public ownership conduct their affairs along efficient commercial and cost effective lines. The public should understand what this involves – for after all, the public are both the owners of these enterprises and the users of their products and services. First, we must insist that management and the boards of the parastatals become more efficient. This means that Government must create a policy environment within

---

[16] This issue is discussed in Chapter III of the Bank of Botswana's Annual Report 1995 and, more fully, in J.C. Leith's paper 'Economic Growth and Structural Transformation in Botswana' in this volume.

[17] This may in part be due to the galloping advance of new technologies, as with telecommunications where old systems can sometimes be replaced by new, providing a better service at half the original cost. The question then arises as to whether the depreciation of the old system at inflation-indexed book value should be treated as a cost of production in determining the tariff needed to produce 'a reasonable return' on a 'fair value' of the assets employed?

[18] These issues, particularly the extent to which low interest rates on PDSF loans amount to a subsidy to the better-off, are extensively discussed in Harvey, C. and Lewis, S.R. (1990)

which management is able to operate efficiently, and has the incentive to do so. It also means that Government, acting on behalf of the public, must be willing to replace poorly performing management and board members just as the shareholders of any major privately owned company would insist on doing. In short, public enterprises must be held accountable for their actions. Commercialization involves the appropriate pricing of the goods and services produced by state-owned enterprises'.[19]

In practice this should mean the following.

(i) The gradual elimination of general or hidden subsidies, such as sub-market interest rates or equity subscriptions that do not require a dividend. In future, any subsidies should be transparent and deliberately targeted towards particular projects or particular consumers.

(ii) A move towards the type of financial structure (in terms of debt-equity gearing, etc.) that would be appropriate for a commercial undertaking operating in that particular sector.

(iii) A more commercially-minded attitude on the part of both the boards and the senior management of the parastatals.

(iv) The incorporation of some SOEs under the Companies Act to facilitate the introduction of private share capital and to regularise accounting and reporting procedures.

(v) The payment of reasonable dividends determined in relation to the value of the shareholder's investment, which may possibly be adjusted in some instances to take account of social or strategic considerations.

The thinking behind this approach is clear. The state has over P3000 million invested in its major parastatals, excluding the reserves of the Bank of Botswana. While Government was enjoying a sequence of budget surpluses, it was thought acceptable to build up the country's infrastructure and, in many instances, to subsidise consumers and to cushion management through the provision of cheap finance and other forms of subsidies. As the budget moves into deficit and reserves begin to be run down, continuous subsidization will become neither a justifiable nor a sustainable policy. On the contrary, the parastatals will be expected to start paying a return on capital commensurate with the value of Government's investment.

Commercial principles should be applied not only to the declaration of dividends, but also to the financing of major new investments. Assuming that the dividend is normally covered by a factor of two or more (in terms of net earnings) a certain amount of routine expansion will be financeable out of retained earnings plus additional borrowings. For major expansions, however, parastatals should expect to be able to call upon additional equity from the shareholders or even, at a later stage, to obtain funds by issuing additional shares on the stock market. As in commercial life, such equity subscriptions will be facilitated and encouraged by an earlier record of profitability and dividend payment. A call for additional equity is also desirable since experience in Botswana and elsewhere teaches that decisions on capital formation to be financed exclusively by loans and retained earnings frequently lead to over-investment (or

---

[19] Source: Budget Speech delivered to the National Assembly on 12 February 1996 by F.G. Mogae, Vice President and Minister of Finance and Development Planning.

extravagant investments) that cannot be fully serviced out of future earnings without a raising of tariffs that would otherwise have been unnecessary.

5. PDSF PROCEDURES

If the parastatals are going to be obliged to become more commercial, it is logical that the PDSF which finances them should be obliged to become more commercially-minded too.

Current PDSF procedures involve an annual circulation of a notice to parastatals and, until recently, local authorities inviting them to submit projects for loan funding by a given date. The submissions are first examined by a Technical Loans Committee which may ask for further justifications on project proposals, or may suggest alternative financing plans, and which – on occasion – summons the officers of the parastatal concerned to explain or justify a particular proposal. Based on these investigations the Technical Loans Committee then makes its recommendations on all PDSF submissions to the Main Loans Committee. In recent years, for the first time, these recommendations have included loan durations of less than the previously standard 25 years, including the initial two years when principal repayments are deferred and interest is capitalised.

The Technical Loans Committee also forwards a recommendation to the Main Loans Committee as to what the interest rate for the year should be. Since interest rates are fixed[20], the rate decided will apply for the whole duration of the loan once it has been drawn down, but will not affect the rates applying to all earlier loans.

The Main Loans Committee considers the recommendations of the Technical Loans Committee on all proposals, and on the interest rate to be applied, and then makes its own recommendations to Cabinet which reaches the final decisions.

This decision-making process has in fact worked better and more harmoniously in recent years than previously. 'Better' in this context means that proposals have been examined more realistically as to their financial viability, and interest rates have been moved closer to the opportunity cost of capital with the result that real rates have become marginally positive. 'More harmoniously' in this context means that officials of the MFDP and of the Bank of Botswana who form the majority of both loans committees have worked more closely together and that at each successive level of decision-making a higher proportion of recommendations have been accepted from the level below.

But, for all that, the PDSF's intensity of examination and the time and expertise applied to individual project appraisals fall below what would be required in a private sector merchant bank, or in one of the more reputable international development banks. And when it comes to monitoring the process of project implementation or evaluating the mid-life and long-term results, the PDSF has no capacity at all because, as has been pointed out, it has no staff. Insofar as lessons are learnt from project successes or project failures, this learning is not institutionalised. It remains

---

[20] Three existing bonds are at floating rate, but this option has not yet been introduced for PDSF borrowers although it has been discussed.

in the heads of individual civil servants or Bank officials, who will, in time, be transferred to other posts or may leave public service.

This raises the question of whether the PDSF can become more commercial without acquiring some permanent staff.[21]

6. THE PDSF AND GOVERNMENT DEBT

As we have seen, the PDSF has two sources of revenue – monies voted to it by the National Assembly and the revenues (mainly in annuity form) from the loans that it makes; and it has two uses for its funds – it makes loans and it leaves cash on deposit with the Accountant General. Table 1 attempted to show how the PDSF has grown and what the sources and the uses of its revenues have been.

How do these funds compare to the quantum of debt that the Government of Botswana will need to service? Table 3 gives an indication of Government external debt at the end of March 1996.

TABLE 3. MEDIUM AND LONG-TERM EXTERNAL GOVERNMENT DEBT AS AT 31 MARCH 1996 (PULA MILLION)

Loans from Governments			**295.0**
of which:	USA	69.1	
	China	5.6	
	Denmark	2.6	
	Kuwait	49.1	
	Saudi Arabia	20.9	
	Sweden	12.0	
	Belgium	5.0	
	Japan	130.7	
Loans from Organizations			**1084.6**
of which:	International Development Association	26.0	
	International Bank of Reconstruction and Development	272.8	
	African Development Fund/Bank	620.9	
	OPEC Special Fund	23.3	
	Commercial Bankers	5.0	
	European Investment Bank	84.9	
	The Arab Bank for Economic Development in Africa	38.8	
	Export Development Corporation	12.9	
	Suppliers Credits and Other	26.5	
Total			**1406.1**

Source: Financial Statements 1996/97.

---

[21] One possible solution would be for the Public Enterprises Monitoring Unit (PEMU) to be professionally staffed, and for that body to become the effective secretariat of the PDSF. However any proposal to do this might well be resisted by some ministries currently responsible for individual parastatals.

The Government has virtually no internal debt, apart from a small bond issue which will be completely repaid by 31 March 1998 and its various unpaid bills.[22] This of course takes no account of the Bank of Botswana's short-term debt, which mainly takes the form of Bank of Botswana Certificates (BoBCs). However, these certificates are issued not to raise funds but to reduce liquidity in the domestic monetary system. The Pula value of the total external public debt (P1406 million) is only 66% of the nominal value of the PDSF's investments, 79% of PDSF's cash deposits with the Accountant General, and barely 36% of the PDSF's nominal total value. Even allowing for the excess of nominal value over realisable value on PDSF investments, it is quite clear that the PDSF could quickly pay off the entire Government debt if it was advantageous to do so, and still be left with a portfolio worth over P1 billion.

In fact it would not be sensible for Government to seek to repay its foreign debt. A lot of it represents loans raised by the parastatals or monies lent to parastatals, which have redemption funds or debt servicing programmes of their own, and want to establish a reputation as reliable borrowers. Much of this debt and of Government's other debt has also been obtained on concessionary terms with the result that the cost of it is less than can be earned on the foreign exchange reserves. This being the case, to repay debt out of forex reserves would actually decrease net forex earnings.

PDSF resources were also held against the possibility of Government being called upon to meet some of its loan guarantees. These are displayed in Table 4. As at 31 March 1995, the Government accounts showed Government had contingent liabilities of P445 million. But these contingent liabilities arose mainly from Government guarantees in respect of various loans (mainly foreign loans) made to the parastatals; and the sum shown is included in, rather than additional to, the figure already quoted for the total public debt.[23]

7. THE VALUE OF THE PDSF

What is the PDSF worth? In other words, what would it be likely to fetch if it were to be sold off in the market? One analyst has suggested that the market value of its portfolio may be no more than fifty percent of the value of its loan book.[24] Is there substance in this appraisal?

We should acknowledge immediately that there is no short-term possibility of selling off the PDSF, either politically or practically. There are simply no investors in the domestic market with resources adequate to contemplate a purchase of that magnitude, and selling the entire Fund off to foreign investors – even if practicable – would be neither politically acceptable nor financially advantageous. Selling off some of the assets of the PDSF, however, could be a different story.[25]

But even if selling off the PDSF as a whole is not a practicable course of action, it

---

[22] The EIU (Economist Intelligence Unit) lowered Botswana's sovereign credit rating below what it would otherwise have been because, although the Government is not short of foreign exchange, several of the ministries have a poor reputation when it comes to the prompt payment of their bills.

[23] Source: Annual Statements of Accounts 1994/95, Statement 17 updated by the office of the Accountant General.

[24] Source: MFDP archives.

TABLE 4. GOVERNMENT'S CONTINGENT LIABILITIES, AS AT 31 MARCH 1996

BORROWERS	SOEs							OTHER		Totals
	BDC	BHC	BMC	BPC	BTC	NDB	WUC	POLS[a]	GoB	
LENDERS:										
European Investment Bank	39.5		5.9	34.0			38.8			118.2
Commonwealth Development Corporation		2.8		20.6	14.6		19.8			57.8
International Bank for Reconstruction and Development				18.5			21.1		1.8	41.4
Nordic Investment Bank				53.0	3.0					56.0
A/S Eksport Finans				14.3	35.8					50.1
Skandinaviska Enskilda Banken					2.2					2.2
African Development Bank						0.1				0.1
Barclays (B)								45.8		45.8
Standard								21.9		21.9
First National Bank								0.0		0.0
Botswana Savings Bank								17.1		17.1
International Development Association									0.1	0.1
International Monetary Fund									33.4	33.4
Multilateral Investment Guarantee Agency									0.1	0.1
TOTAL	**39.5**	**2.8**	**5.9**	**140.4**	**55.6**	**0.1**	**79.7**	**84.8**	**35.4**	**444.2**

Note: [a] Public Officers Loan Scheme.
Source: Annual Statements of Accounts – Statement 17 , pp378–381.

---

[25] Some consideration has been given to the possibility of selling off some PDSF loans to broaden the securities available on the Botswana Stock Exchange and to prepare for the development of a local bond market. However, no such sales have yet taken place. Unlike normal bonds, the typical PDSF loan to a parastatal has been for 25 years with an initial two years' grace period for the payment of both principal and interest, following which the loan is repaid in a sequence of 46 equal semi-annual annuity payments.

may still be instructive to speculate about its market value. The assertion that it is only worth half its loan book can itself be regarded as half true and half misleading. Let us consider first the sense in which that observation may be regarded as true. First, because so many of the loans were given at less than the prevailing market rate of interest – since which time market rates of interest have risen – it must follow that the portfolio as a whole will now have a market value less than its nominal value. This discount to face value will be all the greater because of the long-term maturity of most of the loans and the very limited interest within Botswana for stock as long-dated as most of the PDSF's loans.

Table 2 shows that the very earliest PDSF loans will mature in May 1998, but because the later loans have tended to be larger than the earlier ones the average maturity of the entire portfolio is 13 years.[26] Similarly, from Table 2 it can be calculated that a simple average of the annual interest rates set on the loans – and they are all fixed rates – would be around 9.25%.

The weighted average interest rate, again because of the larger loans being granted in the later years, is of the order of 10.5%. If we look upon the portfolio as having a middle life of 15 to 20 years, and postulate that the market would consider a reasonable yield for that period to be of the order of 16% to 20%, that would in itself suggest a valuation for the invested portion of the PDSF's assets of some 60% of book value.

But that calculation takes no account of the inherent riskiness of the underlying assets. The current distribution of PDSF loans is exhibited in Table 5. It will be seen from there that 85% of the portfolio consists of loans to parastatals (of which almost half are loans to BHC); 7% are loans to local authorities; just under 7% is a loan to a private sector bank; and the remaining 1% consists of loans to educational, training, research or recreational bodies. How secure are these assets? Left to their own devices and deprived of Government funding, some of them (the local authorities and the training and research centres, for instance) would not be very secure at all, as the majority are effectively reliant on Central Government funding to cover their recurrent expenditures, of which debt service to the PDSF is a part.

The situation with regard to the major portion of the portfolio, the loans to parastatals, is rather different. Some of these (the main utilities, for instance) are near-monopolies in their own markets, and left free to provide only services which are profitable and to set their own tariff levels, most would have no difficulty in generating sufficient cash flow to service their PDSF and all other debts. Others (the transport parastatals, for instance), have not been able to avoid losing money and have had to have some portion of their debt converted into equity. The housing corporation (BHC) is a special case. Of all the parastatals, the BHC was the most heavily hit by Government's decision to move to positive real interest rates because its clients (following upon Government's own earlier decisions), had become accustomed to a culture of extensively subsidised rentals.[27] Given the difficulty of adjusting rentals upwards quickly, two consequences ensued. First, the BHC found itself unable to build further housing and to cover the full cost of this construction with rentals at their existing levels. Second, the corporation found itself unable to meet its debt obligations to the

---

[26]   Source: Debt Recording and Management System (DRMS) of the MFDP. The weighted average would be considerably longer, e.g., in the order of 18 years.

[27]   See the Price Waterhouse report, 1995, which found extensive 'overhousing' judged by the ability to pay fully commercial rents out of a normal proportion of wages or salaries.

TABLE 5. BORROWERS FROM THE PDSF, AS AT 31 MARCH 1996 (PULA MILLION)

PARASTATALS	AMOUNT OUTSTANDING
BHC	838.9
BDC	204.2
BTC	182.6
BR	160.2
BBS	128.6
WUC	86.1
BPC	80.4
NDB	52.1
BCB	49.0
AB	48.2
BVI	3.4
BAMB	1.9
BMC	1.1
BLDC	0.5
SUB-TOTAL	1837.2
EDUCATION, TRAINING AND RESEARCH CENTRES	
University of Botswana	12.1
National Sports Council	5.0
Botswana Technology Centre	4.8
SUB-TOTAL	21.9
PRIVATE SECTOR	
Financial Services Company (now FNB)	136.9
SUB-TOTAL	136.9
LOCAL AUTHORITIES	
Gaborone City Council	56.9
Lobatse Town Council	35.6
Francistown Town Council	28.9
Selebi-Phikwe Town Council	28.8
Jwaneng Township	6.2
Sowa Township Authority	3.6
SUB-TOTAL	160.0
Grand Total	**2155.9**

Note: The full titles of the parastatals whose abbreviated names are listed in this table can be found in the Annexe to this paper.

Source: Financial Statements, 1996/97.

PDSF out of cash flow, and therefore was forced to ask for a major capital restructuring.[28]

But under present arrangements, none of the aforementioned worries about the underlying soundness of the assets – not even the insolvency of the BCB[29] – has much effect upon the cash flow or the capital value of the PDSF itself. That is because of the convention that if a parastatal cannot meet its obligations to the PDSF, or it requires a debt to equity conversion, the necessary funds to make good the obligation and to subscribe to the new equity would have to be made good by the sponsoring ministry.[30] The expectation and intention was that such a requirement would make ministers attentive to the borrowing status of their respective parastatals and ensure that only well qualified directors sat on parastatal boards, and that board members in turn would be careful not to approve expenditures which could not pay for themselves. For, after all, if such precautions were not taken, the sponsoring ministry (it was anticipated) would have to pay for the mistake by cutting back expenditures elsewhere in its allocation.

In practice things did not turn out as envisaged. Repeated budget surpluses by Government have induced successive Cabinets to agree that, whenever a parastatal needs bailing out, this should be financed not from the sponsoring ministry's existing vote, but by requesting National Assembly approval for a supplementary budgetary allocation.

In effect, therefore, the required debt-equity conversion is accomplished by the National Assembly voting additional funds to the sponsoring Ministry from the Domestic Development Fund (DDF), which monies are then used to subscribe for additional equity in the SOE. But the SOE itself never has the use of the money, since it is applied immediately to repay an equivalent amount of PDSF debt. Whether this procedure acts as a sufficient deterrent to the boards of the SOEs which have been allowed to drift into such a position is debatable.[31] What is not debatable is that this rather exceptional form of government guarantee has served to preserve the value of the PDSF at a cost to the general exchequer.

Again one can ask: would the Main Loans Committee be more cautious in the loans which it agreed to if this particular form of guarantee was not provided?

We have talked thus far about the value of the Fund's loan portfolio. But that is only part of the total value of the PDSF. The other part consists of the cash which the PDSF retains on deposit with the Accountant General. Table 1 shows how the assets of the PDSF have been divided between the value of loans outstanding and the value of money on deposit with the Accountant General. It will be observed that the sums left on deposit with the Accountant General (and consequently the interest foregone) have on occasion been extremely large.

---

[28] A debt:equity conversion of P250 million in 1996 was preceded by agreement that one recent loan would enjoy a three year grace period rather than the usual two.

[29] The Botswana Co-operative Bank (BCB) was declared insolvent in 1995.

[30] The convention is associated with Mr Baledzi Gaolathe, the MFDP Permanent Secretary at the time of its acceptance by Government. The explanation for its purpose provided in the text derives from an interview with Mr Gaolathe, held on 25 November 1996.

[31] The evidence suggests that it has not. Air Botswana, Botswana Railways, National Development Bank, Botswana Housing Corporation, Botswana Co-operative Bank, and Botswana Agricultural Marketing Board have all required financial rescues, or state funding for the settlement of creditors' claims at the time of insolvency.

8. OPTIONS FOR THE FUTURE

It is assumed for the purpose of this paper that further budgetary transfers into the PDSF will in future be limited. But two other assumptions are also made. First, that when parastatals require a financial restructuring, or have to be liquidated, the Consolidated Fund will continue to be called upon to repay that particular parastatal's PDSF loans. Second, that the funds which are currently on deposit with the Accountant General will remain available for PDSF use.

Even without further budgetary receipts, the PDSF will remain in possession of substantial liquid resources (initially approaching P2 billion, with some of that amount committed, but undisbursed) and in receipt of significant annual revenues (initially approximately P200 million). In the short run, major debt to equity conversions (such as have been agreed for AB, BHC and BR) and liquidations (for example BCB) will have the effect of reducing revenue receipts but increasing liquid reserves.

But, given the changing economic situation of the country and altered financial circumstances for the Government, what should be the Fund's future? Several possibilities suggest themselves, which are briefly canvassed in this concluding section of the paper.

Option A: Carry on as before

This would certainly be both a financial and an administrative possibility for a number of years, but would become increasingly inappropriate and almost certainly, after a time, politically unacceptable. Judged simply on the basis of the efficiency (i.e., profitability) with which it has invested surplus funds on the part of Government, the PDSF would appear to reveal a poor record. Judged on the effectiveness with which it has monitored the performance of the entities in which it has become the leading investor (namely the parastatals), the record would again appear weak – largely because, although it is by far the largest financier of the parastatals, the PDSF has never seen it as a main part of its role to monitor their efficiency or to seek to improve their performance.

But there is another, more profound reason why the *status quo*, or 'carrying on as before' is likely to prove unsustainable. The Government has enabled and allowed the PDSF to accumulate over P3 billion in nominal resources (mainly by appropriations from the budget) upon which resources the PDSF pays no direct return whatever to the Government.[32]

When budget surpluses were the order of the day, and the urgent need was for additional infrastructure and for a source of funding to development finance institutions to channel loans to the private sector, this practice would have appeared not only acceptable, but sensible. But if we are now entering an era when the private sector is highly liquid, much of the infrastructure is adequate (although not always run with satisfactory efficiency), and the crying need is for more recurrent revenue for the budget, then a PDSF that offers no return at all to the Government will be seen as an anachronism.

Instead it is far more likely that, just as the parastatals will increasingly be re-

---

[32] Save to the extent that, as previously explained, sums on deposit with the Accountant General indirectly give rise to increases in the profits at the Central Bank.

quired to show a return on the capital invested in them, the PDSF – Botswana's somnolent giant – will also be required to provide a return on Government's investment in it, and will be increasingly judged by future ministers of finance on the adequacy of that return.[33]

Option B: Become more like an investment bank.

If the forecast offered above turns out to be realistic, this may indeed be the direction in which the PDSF is driven. Many would welcome this. Others would say that Government already owns four financial institutions (it used to be six), all of them heavy borrowers from the PDSF, and does not need another. That is true, and there are indeed grounds for believing that the existing number of financial parastatals could advantageously be reduced by rationalization and mergers. But such an observation misses one crucial point: under current practice the PDSF is the only state-owned facility (other than the DDF and the RSF) that lends extensively to other SOEs.[34]

There are a number of ways in which the PDSF could become more like an investment bank, or, put another way, there are a number of reforms which would have to occur to the PDSF before it became a reputable investment bank, and some are likely to appeal to decision-makers more than others. The list that follows does no more than canvas the main possibilities.

(i)   The PDSF, once it was given the necessary staffing and authority, could start behaving like a major creditor would normally behave in respect of the efficiency and profitability of the enterprises to which it had lent large sums of money. This would involve a far more exacting appraisal of policies and projects, examination of management qualifications, insistence on appropriate gearing, requirements for covenants, warranties, guarantees, and so on.

(ii) The PDSF could itself accept the financial consequences of making future loans which the borrowers proved unable to service. This would relieve the budget of a burden. It would also impose upon the PDSF management a far more onerous responsibility than currently exists to ensure that the SOEs to whom loans were being made would actually be able to service them from the revenue generated by the projects that were being financed. Had this condition existed in the past, a considerable proportion of the existing loans would not have been made. It might also have implications for the interest rates that the PDSF would need to charge to different classes of borrowers in order to cover its costs, make adequate provisions for bad and doubtful debts, and pay an adequate return to its shareholder(s).

(iii) The PDSF could buy from Government its equity stake in the eight or nine major commercial parastatals, whose dividend payments in relation to the equity invested in them are at present negligible. Such a step could have a number of advantages. It would provide the Government budget with a certain amount of additional revenue. It would completely transform the imperatives to which the parastatals would need to respond. It could also lead to a complete

---

[33] The Budget Speech of 1996, quoted in the text, explicitly refers to this new requirement.

[34] As of 31 March 1995 the respective sizes of the three funds were: Development Fund P412 million; Revenue Stabilization Fund P1457 million; Public Debt Service Fund P3729

change in the character, qualifications, degree of commitment and motivation of those serving upon parastatal boards. It would lead to senior management being selected (and remunerated) in line with managerial competence. And it would clarify the respective roles of Government and the board of the company in running utilities and comparable enterprises. It has been shown, almost universally, that while a government's role is best concentrated on regulation and supervision, cost-effective investment decisions and efficient enterprise management are best obtained through private sector disciplines and incentive structures.

(iv) A corollary of this argument is that the shareholders, not a Minister, would elect members to the board based upon their competence and ability to contribute to the success of the enterprise, and the board would select the chief executive officer on the basis of ability to deliver results.

(v) Once the board and management of SOEs were being selected on the basis of their commercial experience and skills, and management decisions were no longer subject to the decisions of a minister, it would be much easier for a parastatal to issue bonds or to float a portion of its equity on the Botswana Stock Exchange.

(vi) The issuance of a parastatal's bonds on the domestic stock exchange and even the flotation of some of its equity could have a number of other advantages. It would raise money for Government. It would diminish the extent to which Government alone would be expected to finance the expansion of a given parastatal. It would increase the number of people who would have a direct interest in the profitability of the parastatals and therefore with the efficiency of management. Finally it would broaden the domestic capital market.

(vii) Consideration could be given to allowing the re-vitalised PDSF to guarantee and to act as co-underwriter of parastatal bond issues. The Government and Central Bank are known to favour the introduction of medium and long-dated bonds, but Government is also known to be adverse to issuing guarantees despite the fact that Government itself makes all the main decisions that determine a SOE's viability. It appoints the chairman, the chief executive and all the board members, decides whether or not the utility will be subject to competition, and sets the prices at which it can sell its products.[35]

(viii) Once its portfolio was currently valued and its management had established a track record of achieving good returns from its investments, the PDSF itself could consider issuing bonds or other instruments should it need further funds for the financing of the expansion of the country's economic infrastructure.

Option C: Eventual privatization

The option discussed above assumes that the PDSF would evolve into a type of investment bank with a proper balance sheet including equity owned by the Government upon which dividends would be paid, and some debt. Its assets would consist of equity in, and loans to, the main commercial parastatals and invested cash balances. Some will argue that once the PDSF has progressed as far as this, the final logical

---

[35] Private companies trying to raise long-term money in such circumstances could expect to be required to provide a guarantee from their one hundred percent controlling shareholder.

step would be for Government to dispose of its shares using the proceeds to repay debt (if that was necessary) or to invest in social infrastructure. Any such divestment would almost certainly have to be phased over time and could be done in a number of different ways. One modality, which might prove appealing in the future programme of some political party, would be to reserve a proportion of the PDSF's shares for equal distribution amongst all adult Batswana. There could be much to be said for giving the users of the country's physical infrastructure a direct stake in the efficiency and profitability with which it is managed.[36]

Annexe: SOEs in Botswana

The following SOEs in Botswana are referred to in this paper:

Organisation	Abbreviation
Air Botswana	AB
Botswana Agricultural Marketing Board	BAMB
Botswana Building Society	BBS
Botswana Co-operative Bank	BCB
Botswana Development Corporation	BDC
Botswana Housing Corporation	BHC
Botswana Livestock Development Corporation	BLDC
Botswana Meat Commission	BMC
Botswana Power Corporation	BPC
Botswana Railways	BR
Botswana Telecommunications Corporation	BTC
Botswana Vaccine Institute	BVI
National Development Bank	NDB
Water Utilities Corporation	WUC

REFERENCES

Bank of Botswana. *Botswana Financial Statistics.* Research Department, Bank of Botswana, Gaborone.

Bank of Botswana. 1995. *Annual Report 1995.* Bank of Botswana, Gaborone.

Bank of Botswana. 1996. *Economic Review, 1996.* Bank of Botswana, Gaborone.

Central Statistics Office. *Statistical Bulletins.* Central Statistics Office, Gaborone.

Government of Botswana. 1973. *Finance and Audit Act,* Chapter 54:01, Laws of Botswana. Government Printer, Gaborone.

Government of Botswana. *Annual Statements of Accounts, 1971/72 to 1995/96.* Office of the Accountant General, Gaborone.

Government of Botswana. *National Development Plan 8, 1997–2002.* Government Printer, Gaborone.

---

[36] The late John Roemer has suggested that any such distribution to citizens should take the form of coupons that would be transferable for shares in other 'coupon firms', but which could not be sold. When a person dies, his or her coupon shares revert to the state treasury and each young person, on reaching adulthood, would receive an endowment of coupons from the treasury.

Harvey, C. and Lewis, S.R. 1990. *Policy Choice and Development Performance in Botswana.* Macmillan Press, London.

Harvey, C. 1992. 'Botswana: is the Miracle Over?', *Journal of African Economies,* Vol.1, No.3.

Mogae, F.G. 1996. Budget Speech, 12 February 1996.

Price Waterhouse, in association with Scott Wilson Kirkpatrick. 1995. 'Strategic Plan and Development Programme for the Botswana Housing Corporation'.

Roemer, J. 1996. 'Coupon Companies Will Ensure Equitable Wealth Redistribution', *Business Day.*

Huda, S.N. 1986. 'A Note on Inflation in Botswana'. In: Bhuiyan, M.N. (ed.). *Selected Papers on the Botswana Economy.* Printing and Publishing Co. (Botswana), Gaborone.

Chapter 4

Industrial Development Policies and Strategies

Industrialization in Botswana

Evolution, Performance and Prospects

Pelani D. Siwawa-Ndai

1. INTRODUCTION

The debate on how best to foster industrialization has revolved around two basic issues: the roles of the state and the market, and the approaches to industrialization, import substitution versus export-orientation. With regard to the role of the state, many economists acknowledge a role for the state in the management of economic activity, but disagree over what constitutes its optimal involvement. Two bodies of theory – structuralist and neo-classical – have influenced the debate on this issue. The structuralist view posits that structural characteristics found in many countries, especially developing ones, ensure that unfettered markets not only do yield sub-optimal outcomes, but also give misleading signals in some instances. Such characteristics take the form of imperfect capital markets, absence of some markets and production externalities (Greenaway and Milner, 1993). Flowing from this, it is suggested that activist policies be pursued by the state to ensure that preferred outcomes are realised. Therefore, structuralist ideas are likely to emphasise state intervention and protection – non-market based restrictions such as import licensing, quantitative restrictions, etc. – that essentially encourage inward-oriented development. The mainstream neo-classical view acknowledges the existence of market imperfections and failures, and suggests that such failures can be selectively addressed by assigning appropriate policy instruments to targets. State failure is considered often to be worse than market failure. State intervention is tolerated only if it is restricted to the provision of public goods (see Greenaway and Milner, 1993; Colclough and Manor, 1991; and Wade, 1990, for a fuller discussion of these points).

The structuralist view sees trade as a source of impoverishment (to the extent that the terms of trade are systematically biased against developing countries), while the neo-classical view sees it as a source of enrichment, the enrichment deriving from both static and dynamic inter-industry and intra-industry exchange. In this regard, neo-classicists are more likely to advocate outward-oriented industrialization and industrial support measures in the form of subsidies and tariffs, in line with the thinking that price signals are better than quantitative controls. The neo-classical view also favours short-term over permanent subsidies.

Although empirical evidence on industrial performance of many economies does not point to an unambiguous superiority of either view over the other, the neo-classical view currently seems to hold sway. Developing countries are constantly receiving advice from both the academic world and international lending institutions to adopt market-led and export-oriented development strategies as opposed to intervention-led and, invariably, inward-looking strategies, because of the perceived success of the former. Oft quoted success stories in support of the market-led approach are the newly industrialising countries (NICs) of Asia, although not all of them followed this exact approach, but sometimes supplemented it with strong direction and state support.

Botswana's industrial policy orientation tended towards the laissez faire solution. The policy emphasis has been more on short-term subsidies (mainly in the form of a grant system known as the Financial Assistance Policy (FAP)) and less on protection through tariffs or import licensing. However, in practice, Government intervened actively, but perhaps not as pervasively as the experience of other countries indicates, by reserving some economic activities for citizens, and investing directly and indirectly in productive activities through state-owned enterprises.

This paper examines the past performance (pattern and pace) of, and the future prospects for industrialization in Botswana. In so doing, particular attention will be paid to the question of how far industrialization has addressed the objectives of industrial development as set out in the Industrial Development Policy (IDP)[1] of 1984. The paper will attempt to address several other pertinent questions, such as: To what extent has industrialization in Botswana relied on import substitution and to what extent on production for export? What direction should industrialization in Botswana take in the future? To what extent do management, finance and investment originate from foreign sources, the public sector or the domestic private sector? How broad-based is the ownership and spatial distribution of industrial activities? What policies have been effective in promoting industrialization in Botswana? Providing answers to these questions will indicate the extent to which the industrial sector has been able to build local capacity to supply the resources it needs, and has stimulated growth of the domestic market for its output, or the extent to which it is still reliant on foreign demand and supplies, and therefore the degree to which it will continue to be vulnerable to exogenous shocks. Furthermore, the responses should make it clear how sustainable the industrial activities are, and therefore, the industrialization process itself. Before delving into the subject matter, however, some definitions are in order.

'Industry' and 'industrialization' – what exactly do they mean? The term industry is seldom defined in economic literature, and where it has been defined, it has taken on alternatively both a narrow and broad meaning. In the first instance it usually refers to the manufacturing sector only, while in the latter instance it includes mining, construction and electricity, water and gas, in addition to manufacturing.[2] But, generally, discussions supposedly about industry have focused exclusively or predominantly on a discussion about the manufacturing sector[3], a bias which reflects not only the apparent limitations of data relating to industrial sectors other than manufacturing, but also that the manufacturing sector is the most dynamic aspect of industry. Perhaps using manufacturing to proxy industry would not matter much if the non-manufacturing component of industry as a proportion of gross do-

---

[1] The IDP is being revised to take into account the changed internal as well as external socio-economic and political circumstances, and to make it a more effective and pro-active instrument for industrial promotion.

[2] The United Nations System of National Account (SNA) Series F. No.2, Revision 3 adopts the broader definition.

[3] Riddell (1990) points out that the United Nations Industrial Development Organisation has similarly applied almost all its energies to analysing aspects of the manufacturing sector as exemplified by the devotion of its Handbook on Industrial Statistics exclusively to manufacturing-related statistics, such as manufacturing value added, production, employment and trade.

mestic product (GDP) were insignificant or followed a path determined by manufacturing. However, as shall be seen in the analysis that follows, in Botswana the share of industry in national output, less that of manufacturing, is not only substantial, but twice (or more) that of manufacturing. Botswana typifies many developing countries in terms of having a significant differential between industry value added (IVA) and manufacturing value added (MVA). In this regard, the major difference between Botswana and other developing countries is that in Botswana the differential is exaggerated by the substantial mineral rents from diamond exports.

What then constitutes industry in Botswana? In this paper industry shall refer to mining, construction, utilities, and manufacturing activities in the formal sector. Due to limited detailed data on industry, save for manufacturing, it is inevitable that the analysis that follows will be biased towards the manufacturing aspect of industry.

Although industrialization has a clear economic definition (the ratios of industrial output and labour force to GDP), it is seldom defined. In this paper, industrialization shall mean the transformation of the economic structure of a country in a way that leads to a shift towards a greater share of industry in macroeconomic variables, such as output and employment. This shift has been observed in many countries the world over. Although industry's contribution to national output in many countries continues to be high, its relative importance has declined as services have taken over as the lead sector. The structural changes that have taken place in Botswana have in no way deviated from this general trend.

The paper is structured as follows. By way of background, Section 2 reviews progress in company formation in Botswana and comments on how the legal and regulatory framework has influenced the profile of company formation. Included in this section is a summary table containing relevant information pertaining to instruments, incentive schemes and policies that have been used to promote industrial development. Section 3 considers some comparative statistical evidence on industrialization and reviews the trends and structure of industry in Botswana. The question of how successful has been the Government's industrial strategy is addressed in Section 4. Section 5 deals with critical issues that are likely to impact, negatively or positively, on the extent of future industrialization in Botswana. Specifically, the role of trade financing and trade information in export development, the renegotiation of the Southern African Customs Union (SACU) Agreement and the implementation of the World Trade Organization (WTO) provisions are considered. The final Section ties together the major strands of arguments that emerge from the discussion.

2. Background

Industrialization comes about as a result of the sustained creation and expansion of firms engaged in the production of industrial products. Industrialization is not an end in itself, but a means to an end. The 'end' could be any number of goals, for example, employment creation or raising incomes. To what extent the firms continue to be viable entities that contribute towards the stated goals depends on supportive strategic industrial policies and the legal and regulatory environment, among other factors. The appropriateness of the legal and regulatory framework to the setting up of companies is the subject of discussion in the rest of this Section, while industrial policies and their impact on the sustainability of companies are taken up in Section 4.

TABLE 1. SUMMARY OF INDUSTRIAL POLICIES; PROGRAMMES; LEGAL, REGULATORY AND TRADE POLICY INSTRUMENTS; CURRENT AND POTENTIAL REGIONAL AND INTERNATIONAL TRADING ARRANGEMENTS ADOPTED AND USED BY GOVERNMENT TO INFLUENCE INDUSTRIAL DEVELOPMENT

TYPE OF POLICY, PROGRAMME, ACT OR TRADE ARRANGEMENT	YEAR OF INTRODUCTION	COMMENT
LEGAL AND REGULATORY INSTRUMENTS		
COMPANIES ACT	1959	Governs company formation.
INDUSTRIAL DEVELOPMENT ACT (IDA)	1968, revised in 1988	Administered by the National Industrial Licensing Authority (located in the Department of Industrial Affairs, Ministry of Commerce and Industry (MCI)), the IDA regulates the establishment of industrial firms through the issuance of manufacturing licenses. Licensing is required for all locally-owned manufacturing firms employing ten or more people and/or using 20kW or more of any form of energy. In the case of non-citizen manufacturers, the licensing requirement applies regardless of the workforce size or the power requirements of their machinery.
TRADE AND LIQUOR ACT (TLA)	1986	The TLA is the counterpart of the IDA and operates on the commercial side of economic activities. It is administered by the National Licensing Authority (NLA) located in the Consumer Affairs Division, MCI. The NLA issues trading and liquor licenses, which restrict participation of foreign investors in 'reserved activities'.
EXCLUSIVE BUSINESS LICENSING	1968	Provides protection by granting businesses, under special circumstances, exclusive licenses for specific periods. Still in place, but Government plans to eliminate this protection.
GENERAL INCENTIVES		
FINANCIAL ASSISTANCE POLICY	1982	Provides capital and labour grants to new or expanding productive activities, and 'linking industries'. Recently it has been extended to selected service sectors.
SELEBI-PHIKWE REGIONAL DEVELOPMENT PROGRAMME (SPRDP)	1988	In addition to incentives that are provided through the FAP, it offered tax breaks and tax rates which, then, were lower than normal corporate taxes. The SPRDP was phased out during 1996 and its investment promotional activities have been merged with those of the Trade and Investment Promotion Agency (TIPA).

LOCAL PREFERENCE SCHEME (LPS)	1978, revised in 1987; replaced by the local procurement programme 1997	Aimed at re-directing General Government and parastatal procurement towards resident manufacturers whose products have a high local content – such products would receive a 40% price advantage on their local content over foreign suppliers.
TRADE POLICY INSTRUMENTS		
SOUTHERN AFRICAN CUSTOMS UNION (SACU) INFANT INDUSTRY PROTECTION CLAUSE	1910, revised 1969	SACU Agreement currently being re-negotiated. A clause provides for protection of domestic infant industries of the customs union countries from competition from each other for a maximum of 8 years. Used in Botswana on two occasions.
IMPORT AND EXPORT LICENSING	1987	Import licences meant to regulate the importation of goods from outside of the SACU area by traders. However, these do not restrict importation of inputs into production by manufacturers who can use their manufacturing licences for this purpose.
REGIONAL AND INTERNATIONAL TRADE ARRANGEMENTS AND AFFILIATION TO INTERNATIONAL ORGANIZATIONS		
BILATERAL TRADE ARRANGEMENTS WITH: ZIMBABWE ZAMBIA MALAWI	1956 rev 1988 1971 1956	Provide for free-trade among the signatories. However, there have been problems with the Botswana/Zimbabwe arrangements when Zimbabwe has sought to restrict the flow of trade from Botswana (for example in 1988).
SOUTHERN AFRICAN CUSTOMS UNION (SACU)	1910, revised 1969	Membership comprises Botswana, Lesotho, Swaziland, Namibia (became a member in 1990 at its independence) and South Africa. Guides trade between the five member states and provides for duty-free movement of goods between them. Being re-negotiated.
SOUTHERN AFRICAN DEVELOPMENT COMMUNITY (SADC) FREE TRADE ARRANGEMENT	To be agreed	A SADC Protocol on Trade is being developed with the intention of creating a free trade area for the SADC states. Being a member of the SADC, Botswana might want to position itself in a way that will allow it to exploit opportunities and take measures to mitigate against risks that might arise from this arrangement.
LOMÉ CONVENTION	1975	Botswana, along with 70 ACP countries, has benefited from preferential access to the EU market – especially in the case of beef, and, to a lesser extent, in the case of textiles and clothing.
WORLD TRADE ORGANIZATION (WTO)	1995	Botswana affiliated to the WTO on 31 May 1995.

INDUSTRY RELATED GOVERNMENT WHITE PAPERS		
NATIONAL POLICY ON ECONOMIC OPPORTUNITIES, GOVERNMENT PAPER NO.2 OF 1982	1982	The White Paper was a reaction to the Presidential Commission on Economic Opportunities whose Terms of Reference were to investigate to what extent policies promoted the participation of Batswana in economic life – in terms of employment and ownership of assets, including enterprises, and recommend ways to enhance their participation.
INDUSTRIAL DEVELOPMENT POLICY: GOVERNMENT PAPER NO.2 OF 1984	1984, being revised	Aimed at promoting industrial development.

The data[4] on company formation appear to indicate that the legal and regulatory environment has not been a major binding constraint on the establishment of companies.[5] Company formation proceeded rapidly between 1985 and 1994 as shown in Figure 1. On average, 1631 new companies were being registered each year between 1985 and 1994, representing an average growth rate of about 28% per annum. New registrations peaked in 1991, thereafter consistently fewer companies were being registered each year. The declining trend in the number of registered companies in the post-1991 period appears to be explained, in part, by the economic downturn that occurred between 1991 and 1992, as well as by other domestic factors that negatively affected the construction sector. In 1994, there were fifty percent fewer registrations of new construction companies than in 1991.

There were more companies registered in the service sector than in industry or agriculture in each year. The share of new firms established in the service sector averaged 69% during the ten-year period, compared with 29% and 2% for industry and agriculture, respectively. Within the service sector, much of the new company formation took place in the distributive trade (commerce) sector, followed by that in the finance, real estate, insurance and business services sector and, to a lesser extent, in profit-making companies in the community and personal services sector. Company formation in industry was dominated by construction and manufacturing

---

4 Data on company survival are not readily available. Therefore, it is not possible to show the life cycle of each of the new companies, nor comment with any degree of certainty about their sustainability. Data on new company registrations are used as a crude indicator of activity in the industrial sector.

5 Although there have been complaints from business people about delays in the processing of applications for business licenses and work and residence permits for expatriate workers. Some deregulation has occurred with regard to the processing of applications for business licenses such that their issuance should, in principle, be automatic, but in practice delays persist due to the requirement that applicants have to satisfy the health, town and regional planning and zoning authorities' requirements. This in itself is a process, but perhaps the requirements are not well publicised for the benefit of potential investors. With respect to work and residence permits, Government has decentralised the adjudication of applications to four localities – Gaborone, Lobatse, Selebi-Phikwe and Francistown. However, the system is still experiencing some teething problems.

In any case, a citizen-owned company intending to employ less than ten workers is not required to obtain a license. Foreign-owned companies are required to obtain a license regardless of their employment level.

Figure 1. New Companies Registered in Each Year

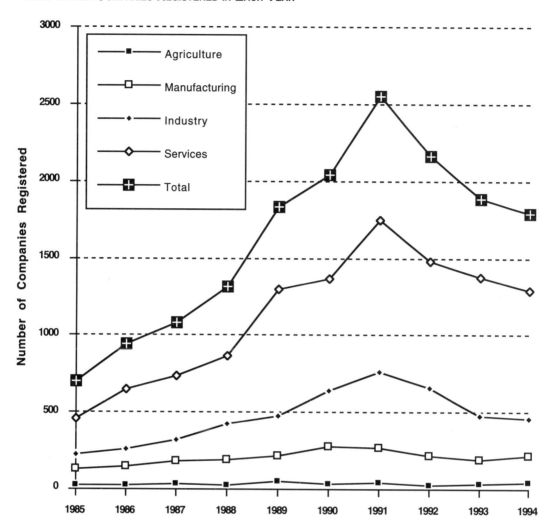

ventures – 259 and 204 companies, respectively – were registered per annum over the ten-year period. This compares with seven mining companies registered in each year.

The majority of companies establishing in Botswana tend to be small[6] (92% were small-scale, while 6% and 2% were medium- and large-scale companies, respectively, in November 1996). Furthermore, these small-scale companies are mainly in the distributive trade, many of them citizen-owned and more evenly spread out across the country. In contrast, large businesses are concentrated in urban areas and many are foreign-owned and/or have some foreign ownership. In terms of export-orientation, a BOCCIM survey of 1994 indicates that small companies are less likely to export than

---

[6] Small-scale companies, as defined by the Central Statistics Office are those that employ less than 29 workers, medium-sized employ between 30 and 99, while large-scale employ 100 and over. The percentage shares of the different company sizes were calculated excluding companies whose size was indicated as 'unknown' in the Central Statistics Office data supplied to the author.

large ones. Therefore, the emphasis placed by the new IDP on export promotion may not be of immediate concern to them, unless steps are taken to ensure that those with export potential are vigorously promoted.

From the above analysis, it does seem that the legislative and regulatory systems have not been a serious bottleneck as far as company formation is concerned. Obviously, this conclusion is based on data on existing companies, but says nothing about those that may have been discouraged from establishing a presence in Botswana by some legal requirement or other regulation, despite the fairly liberal regulatory environment. That there have been concerns about delays in the processing of business licenses and work and residence permits suggests that some companies may have been discouraged from setting up in Botswana because of this. To the extent that this is correct, Botswana may have lost the opportunity to attract firms that could potentially have made a difference in its rate of development.

Having established that there has been substantial registration of new firms, the logical question to ask is how sustainable are these firms? While this question cannot be answered satisfactorily given that there are no published data on the life cycle of firms, an attempt will be made to provide broad indications of the extent of sustainability in Section 4. But next is a review of the industrialization process in Botswana.

3. INDUSTRIALIZATION IN ITS NATIONAL AND INTERNATIONAL CONTEXT

This section places Botswana's industrial performance in an international context in order to highlight trends that are in or out of line with those of other economies and examine the possible implications for Botswana. This is achieved through a comparative analysis of GDP for Botswana and four types of economies: low income (LIEs), lower middle income (LMIEs), upper middle income (UMIEs) and high income economies (HIEs), as well as for selected Sub-Saharan African countries. Secondly, it reviews industrial evolution and performance in Botswana for the years 1974/75 through 1994/95.[7] The review focuses on the sectoral distribution of value added and employment.

Distribution of gross domestic product (GDP)

Table 2 shows the origin of GDP in 1970 and 1993 for Botswana, LIEs, LMIEs, UMIEs, HIEs and Sub-Saharan Africa, while Table 3 shows GDP growth rates for 1970–80 and 1980–93. Changes in the structure of production in the Botswana economy appear to be broadly in line with trends in structural change in many other world economies. GDP originating in industry and services in Botswana increased significantly between 1970 and 1993, resulting in the share of industry in 1993 being well above the average for LIEs and Sub-Saharan Africa, while that of services was at par with the average for Sub-Saharan Africa and some nine percentage points higher

---

[7] Analysis of industrial performance begins in 1974/75 because only crude estimates of real GDP growth figures exist for years prior to 1974. Also, there is a break in the data series in 1988/89 due to data revisions and rebasing from 1989/90 onwards. Growth rates for years prior to and after 1988/89 are not directly comparable and no growth rate for that year is given.

Table 2. Sectoral distribution of gross domestic product-range of sectoral shares for selected groups of countries (averages in parentheses – %)

Region	Agriculture		Industry[a]		Manufacturing		Services[b]	
	1970	1993	1970	1993	1970	1993	1970	1993
Botswana	33	6	28	47	6	4	39	47
Low income economies	11 – 71	10 – 63	9 – 55	9 – 48	3 – 30	4 – 38	19 – 59	2 – 60
	(37)	(28)	(28)	(35)	(19)	(25)	(33)	(38)
Lower middle income economies	7 – 45	7 – 43	19 – 43	19 – 52	10 – 21	4 – 45	36 – 64	18 – 72
	(-)	(-)	(-)	(-)	(-)	(-)	(-)	(-)
Upper middle income economies	3 – 29	5 – 32	22 – 77	28 – 54	0 – 32	4 – 44	7 – 62	29 – 66
	(12)	(-)	(38)	(-)	(25)	(-)	(49)	(-)
High income economies	0 – 12	0 – 8	30 – 67	10 – 57	4 – 38	3 – 28	33 – 68	40 – 82
	(4)	(-)	(38)	(-)	(28)	(-)	(60)	(47)
Sub-Saharan Africa (average)	27	20	28	33	13	16	46	47

Notes:

[a] Industry includes mining, manufacturing, construction, and water, electricity and gas.

[b] Services include all other branches (other than agriculture and industry as defined in note a above) of economic activity, including imputed bank service charges, import duties, and any statistical discrepancies noted by national compilers

(-) indicates that no figure was given in the source.

Source: World Bank. 1995.

than that for LIEs. In 1993 the contribution of agriculture to GDP in Botswana declined more substantially than happened elsewhere. It fell dramatically to just under one-fifth of its 1970 value, contrasting sharply with, say, the situation in Ethiopia where agriculture still constituted sixty percent of GDP. In HIEs, there is a perceptible shift away from industrial and agricultural activities towards services, a process that began at the turn of the century. Production originating from industry and manufacturing declined considerably between 1970 and 1993 for all HIEs (except one) for which data are available. With the exception of three countries, all HIEs had no less than sixty percent of their GDP originating from services. However, with regard to the share of industry and manufacturing in LIEs and LMIEs, the movement was in the opposite direction – both sectors increased their shares in GDP between these two periods. Similarly, a high percentage of these economies witnessed rising shares of value added arising from the service sector.

From Table 3, it is clear that the rate of growth of Botswana's economy was the fastest among economies reported by the World Bank (1995) between 1970 and 1993. However, the growth was not evenly spread across sectors and over time. Economic growth slowed significantly during the 1980–93 period when compared with 1970–80. Although industry and manufacturing recorded the highest growth rates during the 1970–80 period, their rates of growth declined substantially in the next period. The growth rate of services declined much less during 1980–93, indicating their growing

TABLE 3. AVERAGE ANNUAL GROWTH RATE OF GROSS DOMESTIC PRODUCT[a] – RANGE OF SECTORAL GROWTH RATES FOR SELECTED GROUPS OF COUNTRIES (AVERAGES IN PARENTHESES – % PER ANNUM)

REGION	GROSS DOMESTIC PRODUCT		AGRICULTURE		INDUSTRY		MANU-FACTURING		SERVICES	
	1970–80	1980–93	1970–80	1980–93	1970–80	1980–93	1970–80	1980–93	1970–80	1980–93
BOTSWANA	14.5	9.6	8.3	3.5	17.6	9.2	22.9	8.6	14.8	11.6
LOW INCOME ECONOMIES	-5.1 to 9.5 (4.3)	6.1 to 6.0 (5.7)	-1.2 to 6.0 (2.0)	-5.2 to 6.1 (3.4)	-3.2 to 27.8 (6.3)	-4.4 to 11.5 (7.6)	-2.1 to 18.0 (7.3)	-4.2 to 12.2 (8.6)	0.6 to 19.7 (5.5)	-2.3 to 11.1 (6.3)
LOWER MIDDLE INCOME ECONOMIES	-1.3 to 14.5 (5.1)	0.3 to 8.3 (1.6)	0.3 to 8.3 (-)	-5.1 to 4.8 (1.4)	-3.4 to 17.6 (-)	-4.4 to 11.0 (1.8)	-2.1 to 22.9 (-)	-2.4 to 11.8 (-)	1.2 to 14.8 (-)	0.9 to 11.6 (2.9)
UPPER MIDDLE INCOME ECONOMIES	1.8 to 10.1 (5.9)	-3.3 to 5.7 (2.7)	-3.3 to 5.7 (3.2)	-3.0 to 6.9 (1.8)	0.2 to 16.4 (6.1)	-4.1 to 12.1 (2.3)	-0.8 to 17.7 (6.6)	-6.7 to 17.2 (2.5)	2.9 to 10.9 (6.3)	-3.3 to 8.3 (2.9)
HIGH INCOME ECONOMIES	-0.2 to 9.2 (3.2)	-0.2 to 7.5 (2.1)	-0.2 to 7.5 (-)	-6.4 to 9.7 (-)	-2.4 to 8.6 (-)	-1.5 to 6.2 (-)	1.2 to 9.7 (-)	0.3 to 7.2 (-)	2.6 to 8.3 (-)	1.4 to 7.4 (-)
SUB-SAHARAN AFRICA (AVERAGE)	3.8	1.6	1.7	1.7	3.8	0.9	4.3	0.9	4.9	2.2

Note: [a] GDP figures are in constant 1987 US$ prices. A (-) indicates that no figure was given in the source.

Source: World Bank (1995)

contribution to GDP. Growth rates were lowest for agriculture in both periods.

Although the share of manufacturing value added (MVA) in GDP is small in Botswana, MVA growth has been most dynamic when compared with MVA growth rates obtaining in other countries on the sub-continent (Table 4). While the growth rate of MVA in Botswana during 1963–73 was the second lowest, after that of Mauritius, in the next period MVA growth in Botswana was almost at par with that of Kenya's, the highest. During the 1980–93 period, only Lesotho and Mauritius had MVA growth faster than that of Botswana.

As indicated in the introductory section, it would be inappropriate to equate manufacturing with industry in Botswana given the wide differential in their contributions to GDP. Table 5 shows IVA and MVA for Botswana and Sub-Saharan Africa. The differential between IVA and MVA more than doubled between 1970 and 1986 due to the mining boom, which saw the share of mining output in total industry output

Table 4. Trends in Growth Rates of Manufacturing Value Added (MVA) for Botswana and Selected Sub-Saharan African Countries, 1963–1993 (% per annum)

Country	1963–73	1973–79	1980–93
Botswana	6.2	10.3	8.6
Ghana	6.9	-1.9	4.1
Lesotho	34.3	4.0	12.2
Malawi	14.9	5.4	3.6
Mauritius	2.8	4.3	9.8
Kenya	8.6	10.8	4.7
Tanzania	10.2	4.3	0.9
Zambia	12.7	-2.2	4.2
Zimbabwe	10.9	-1.3	2.2

Note: The table from which this table was derived covers 43 Sub-Saharan African economies which were split according to those that had negative growth rates of MVA and those that had growth rates of 0–5% and 5–10% during the first two periods. Botswana was among four countries that had a MVA growth rate of more than 10% during 1973–79. Also, for Botswana, there are no GDP Figures for 1963, so the estimate presented is for the 1966–1973 period, and even then this is a crude estimate.

Source: Riddell (1990) Table 2.3, p18, and World Bank (1995).

rising from zero to 80% over the same period. However, by 1993, this differential had narrowed, but remained substantial at 43%. In the case of Sub-Saharan Africa, the differential was smaller than that for Botswana, but increased slightly from 15% in 1970 to 17% in 1993. The significance of this is that not only has the non-manufacturing component of industry grown faster in the latter period, but in Botswana, mining has an overwhelming influence on the performance of industry and tends to swamp any changes, in either direction, in the other components of industry. Hence, the analysis that follows in the next sections will separate out mining from industry whenever it will shed light on the manufacturing and other industrial developments that occurred.

Table 5. Difference Between Value Added in Industry and Manufacturing, 1970, 1986 and 1993 (%)

Value Added by Sector	1970		1986		1993	
	Botswana	Sub-Saharan Africa	Botswana	Sub-Saharan Africa	Botswana	Sub-Saharan Africa
Industry-total (a)	28.0	28.0	58.3	25.0	47.0	33.0
Manufacturing (b)	6.0	13.0	5.1	10.0	4.0	16.0
Difference c = (a-b)	22.0	15.0	53.2	15.0	43.0	17.0

Source: Riddell (1990) and World Bank (1995).

Trends and structure of industry in Botswana, 1974/75 to 1994/95

As already mentioned above, national output grew very rapidly between 1974/75 and 1994/95, both in nominal and real terms (Figure 2). Real GDP growth averaged 9.3% per annum during this period, growing much faster at 12% per year between 1974/75 and 1984/85, but slowing down to an average rate of 7% per year between 1985/86 and 1994/95. Non-mining GDP grew less rapidly, particularly prior to 1985/86, but gained momentum in the post-1985/86 period. In the earlier period, it grew at an annual average rate of 6%, but rose to 10% per annum in the latter period. The sources of GDP growth and changes in its composition are discussed below.

FIGURE 2. TOTAL AND NON-MINING REAL GDP, 1975–1995 (1985/86 PRICES)

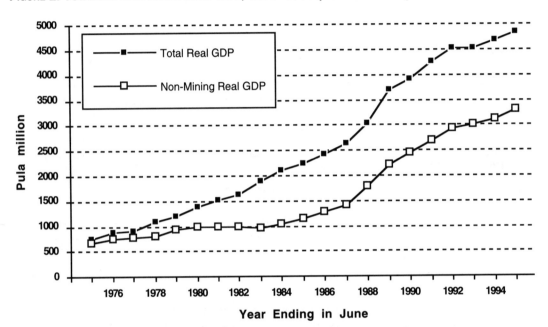

The economy of Botswana has undergone significant structural changes since Independence in 1966. Between 1966 and the early 1970s, Botswana's economic structure was dominated by agricultural activities. These were quickly replaced by industry in the early 1970s, following the discovery and exploitation of diamonds and copper-nickel deposits. Since then, the share of agriculture in GDP has declined gradually (Figure 3). The share of industry in GDP increased rapidly from 36% in 1974/75, to a peak of 63% in 1984, but steadily declined to 46% in 1994/95. The declining ratio of IVA to GDP since 1983/84 is explained largely by four factors. First, the drought of the early to mid-1980s. This curtailed construction, while manufacturing also suffered due to lower BMC throughput and sales as cattle offtake dropped in the face of high mortality rates. BMC's share in manufacturing was 34% in 1983/84, dropped to 30% in the following year and was 11% in 1992/93. Second, manufacturing output was also negatively affected by the trade restrictions (through import surcharges) Zimbabwe imposed on Botswana exports to that country in the mid to late 1980s, as well as the large cumulative devaluations of the Zimbabwe Dollar due to the implementation of the structural adjustment programme (SAP) between 1991

Figure 3. Sectoral Value Added, 1975–1995 (share in total 1985/86 prices)

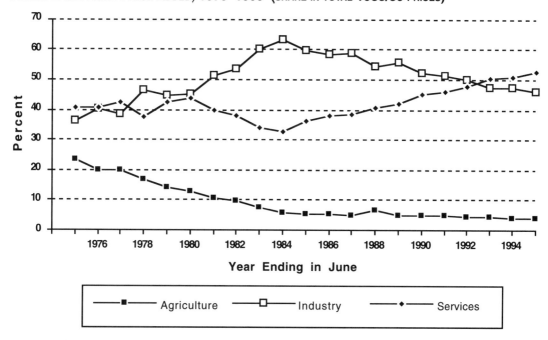

and 1994. Also, the price of the cotton lint that was sourced from Zimbabwe at half the world price hitherto the SAP was raised to the world price, thereby raising domestic input costs and further reducing the international competitiveness of Botswana manufactures. Third, there was the 1992 to 1993 international recession that affected demand for diamonds, and then the quota on diamond sales imposed by the Central Selling Organisation on its suppliers, which in Botswana's case led to a slowdown in production. Fourth, the construction sector contracted mainly on account of the problems that arose from the suspension of some Botswana Housing Corporation projects in 1992, on which the sector was highly dependent.

Within industry itself, mining dominates output. It accounted for 67% per annum, on average, of IVA. Manufacturing had the second highest share (15%) in value added, followed by construction and utilities at 14% and 4%, respectively. While mining GDP increased by 19% per annum on average during the review period, its growth tapered off during the 1986/87 to 1991/92 period and slightly contracted in the last three years. Manufacturing recorded an impressive annual average growth of 10% during the review period, with much of the growth occurring during 1986/87 to 1991/92, a period which coincided with the slowing down of mining economic activity. Like manufacturing, the construction sector grew faster, at 28% per annum on average during 1986/87 to 1991/92. The growth of utilities was roughly consistent through the review period, averaging 12% per year.

The share of services in GDP, which had fluctuated within a narrow band prior to 1984, has since shown an upward trend. Since 1992/93, the service sector has contributed the most to GDP. In the early years commerce was behind the growth of the service sector, while Government has been the driving force since 1983/84.

Although industry has contributed most to output growth, with respect to employment, its contribution has been weak. Accounting for less than a quarter (57 000) of formal sector jobs in 1995, industry is the second largest employer after services (173 000 of which Government accounts for half). Employment in industry grew at 6% per year on average, and was mostly generated by the construction and manufacturing sectors, each of which grew at an annual average rate of 8%. Much of the growth in employment in construction and manufacturing took place between 1986 and 1990. During this period, construction employment growth averaged 22% per annum, while manufacturing growth averaged 20% per annum. The post-1991 period saw an unprecedented loss of jobs in the construction sector – employment declined at the rate of 10% per annum, on average, during the 1991 to 1995 period. Employment in mining is relatively small, and even smaller in the utilities sector.

Commerce has the largest number of companies (44% of all companies in 1994), is the largest private sector employer (34% of all private sector jobs were in commerce in 1995) and is the second largest employer in the entire economy after Government. However, far fewer jobs were created per company in this sector than in the construction or manufacturing sectors. For example, in 1994 a company in the construction or manufacturing sector created 2.4 times as many jobs as did a company in the commerce sector (8.1 versus 3.4 jobs per company). thus the sector's potential to create many of the badly needed jobs is limited.

To conclude, industrialization has occurred at a rapid pace. Both the composition and size of industry have changed. From small beginnings after Independence, industrial output grew enough to end the first half of the 1990s at close to half of GDP; this from a peak of over three-fifths in the mid-1980s. Botswana's economy was the fastest growing in the world between 1970 and 1993, mainly driven by industrial growth, especially mining. The employment potential of the mining sector is, however, limited by the capital intensive nature of its operations. Manufacturing, with episodes of very rapid growth, remains small. Notwithstanding its smallness, it has the potential to create employment. In the 1990s services grew tremendously, while agriculture continued to weaken. But how has this rapid economic growth translated into the Government's social and other objectives? This is the subject of the next section.

4. How Successful Has the Government's Industrialization Strategy Been in Meeting its Social and Other Objectives?

In 1984, Government introduced its second IDP in recognition of the fact that its past efforts at influencing economic and social development had worked best at speeding up economic growth, but had not had enough impact on economic independence, sustained development and social justice. The objectives of the IDP were (a) job creation, (b) better rural/urban distribution of industrial activities, (c) raising the skill levels of Batswana through training to allow them to progress to high productivity occupations, and (d) increasing value added accruing to Botswana and Batswana. These objectives are obviously still relevant, if not more relevant, today than they were in 1984. This is so because the unemployment situation today is worse than it was in the 1980s. Although training has been stepped up over the years resulting in relatively easy availability of people with general purpose skills, new areas of economic activity have arisen which require people with specialised skills. Even for old jobs, retraining is necessary to upgrade skills acquired in the past in order to equip workers with new skills to cope with the new technologies that are introduced from time to time or just to improve productivity. While there is no doubt that value added retained in the country has increased over time, more could be done to improve on this. The spatial distribution of productive activities is still unsatisfactory – after initial signs of spreading out in the mid to late 1980s, the tendency, since the early 1990s, has been towards concentration in urban areas (BOCCIM, 1994), and understandably so. Urban areas offer high incomes, larger markets, better trained and educated workforce, good transport links and infrastructure that is relatively well developed.

The Government's overall policy orientation with respect to industrialization has been that of minimum intervention, at least in so far as direct participation in economic activities is concerned. Government clearly stated in the IDP that its role was limited to that of a service and infrastructure provider and facilitator of industrial development. Excluding major mineral projects, direct participation in economic activity would be the exception, but that it would participate indirectly through the Botswana Development Corporation – and then only to fill a gap where it was perceived that private investment was not forthcoming.

Influenced by the neo-classical view of the functioning of markets, Government adopted an industrial strategy underpinned by a combination of dirigiste and laissez-faire policies. While Government recognised the importance of private ownership and the allocative efficiency of the market mechanism, it was also acutely aware of market failures and therefore adopted a pragmatic approach to industrial development. Government set out to intervene appropriately through, *inter alia*, incentives to correct market prices, as well as the use of protective measures (though these were rarely used). Government was also aware of the need to create a balance in its promotional efforts between import substituting and exporting industries, both as a way of avoiding the vulnerability to external events and to ensuring an adequate and orderly development of the domestic and foreign markets.

The strategy involved, initially, the promotion of import substituting industries that would serve the needs of a few, but relatively large institutions in which purchasing power was concentrated, mainly the parastatals and Government itself, as well as large mining companies (Government of Botswana, 1984). Excluding traditional exports, the export drive did not take off in earnest until the late 1980s (apart from a short-lived notable growth in exports to Zimbabwe in the early 1980s), and even then, the focus was on textiles, mainly to the European Union, South Africa and Zimbabwe, and lately, on vehicles. The new focus on exports should not come as a surprise. Like most countries Botswana has gone through a period of import substitution and, lately, some analysts have argued that import substitution as a strategy for industrialization has reached its limit in Botswana. Whether or not import substitution has fully reached its limits, the domestic market is small and, thus, unlikely to provide economies of scale required for the profitable production of some types of products. Inevitably, Botswana has to promote exports vigorously, to complement any ongoing import substitution efforts.

Evidence on the formation of citizen-owned companies points to a growing participation of citizens in economic activities, but the ownership of major productive capacity in the export and industrial sectors remains in foreign[8] hands. The dominance of foreigners in big business reflects the generally low levels of business skills –

entrepreneurial, managerial and technical – among citizens. Besides filling this skill gap, foreigners bring other valuable ingredients to export success. However, the sourcing of skilled people offshore can be costly. The need to develop the requisite skills cannot be overemphasized, not only to replace costly imported labour, but because the presence of a pool of trained workers is in itself attractive to foreign investors. This points to the need to map out a human resource development plan that is consistent with the nation's vision of the expected future path of industrial development.

Because of the perceived low participation of Batswana in economic activities, Government introduced an assistance programme known as the Citizen Reservation Policy in 1982.[9] Through this policy, Government reserved certain economic activities in the industrial, commercial and service sectors, mainly those requiring simple technological skills and small capital investments, for citizens only. The reservation system, while a good starting point for Batswana to gain an understanding of how to run a business successfully, has tended to channel entrants into activities with low technology, low productivity and low income activities. The combined effects of these factors is to severely limit growth prospects and graduation into medium and large-scale companies. Reserving activities without putting in place effective support programmes and technical assistance that build the internal capacity of entrepreneurs to sniff and seize opportunity, as well as manage and operate properly what has been established, is unlikely to be very helpful.

The biggest challenge facing Botswana in its industrialization efforts has been and continues to be how to foster sustainable industrial activity in the non-mineral sector. Among the major limiting factors are inadequate supplies of domestic financial (private) capital, the absence of a critical mass of citizen entrepreneurs with business acumen, limited raw material base, inadequate skilled personnel, infrastructure, supporting services and an unfavourable wage/productivity mix. These, together with the small domestic market, make industrial investment a risky and costly venture. Possible solutions to these are not discussed here as they are the subject of another paper in this volume. Additionally, export development, which is seen as a way to escape the small domestic market, is constrained by, *inter alia*, the lack of trade financing and ready availability of appropriate trade information. Up until recently, there were no local export credit guarantee and insurance facilities, and local exporting firms were using facilities that were underwritten by a South African company (see Section 5).

Government, being well aware of these limiting factors, has introduced incentive schemes (the centrepiece of which is the FAP) to promote industrialization, as well as achieve other socio-economic objectives. Introduced in May 1982, the FAP gave practical effect to the Government's pronouncements on industrial promotion, although a Local Preference Scheme (LPS) had been in place since 1978.[10] There was also an Industrial Policy of 1974, which together with subsequent national development plans,

---

8   Although it could be argued that Batswana participation in productive activities is significant if Government and the Botswana Development Corporation equity participation in major mineral projects and companies producing non-traditional products/exports are taken into consideration.

9   Government adopted the National Policy on Economic Opportunities following the submission to Government of the Report of the Presidential Commission on Economic Opportunities of 1982. The Commission investigated, among other things, the economic opportunities available to Batswana and how their participation in those activities could be enhanced.

laid out a strategy for industrial development that provided the basis for the IDP of 1984.[11] The FAP has been hailed by the three evaluations conducted to date as having been successful. The major concern has been that the employment created by FAP-assisted firms is largely temporary as firms tend to mechanise once the labour subsidy expires. The latest evaluation goes further to say that failure rates of FAP firms are within acceptable levels, which would seem to indicate that a reasonable number of new companies are sustainable. The LPS has had limited success due to certain design problems and was replaced by a Local Procurement Programme (LPP) in April 1997. While Government is hopeful that this new programme will encourage the development of citizen enterprises, critics are concerned that it is inclined more towards protection than encouraging competition which is so vital to enterprise survival in both domestic and international markets.

Botswana's rapid, albeit uneven, economic growth has been well documented. Equally well documented are the constraints to diversification away from the mining sector, and towards the manufacturing and service sectors. However, what has eluded many analysts is prescribing workable solutions to bring about a sustainable broadening of the industrial base that is accompanied by a sufficient growth in jobs to absorb the rapidly growing labour force. Currently, employment creation has not kept up with the rate of increase in the labour force. This has led to a continuing debate over how best to create employment opportunities. The debate has centred around the question of how much emphasis should be placed on the promotion of big businesses that are capable of creating many jobs per business and how much on small businesses that, generally, create few or no jobs at all (i.e., owner-managed worker-types of businesses) per business. Opinion is divided on this. Some favour a focus on big business, while others think small businesses are a vital part of the industrialization process and cannot be overlooked. Yet other analysts take a middle line, that a balance should be struck in industrial promotional efforts, such that obvious biases in favour of either big or small are eliminated from industrial policies and incentives. To note in passing, the emphasis on export-oriented industrialization espoused in the new IDP has already struck a wrong chord with some industrialists and other interested sections of the population. The concern being that the new IDP almost ignores the interest of small businesses that are unlikely to be major players in this export drive. This concern derives from two interlinked factors, namely, the polarization of firms by size/ownership and ownership/geographic location. Many big businesses are foreign-owned or have some foreign ownership and are concentrated in the urban centres, while small businesses are mainly citizen-owned and are widely distributed. It is this polarization that gives rise to the varied opinion on where the focus of Government industrial promotion efforts should lie.

The position adopted in this paper is that the promotion of both big and small businesses is not incompatible. Small firms almost wholly serve the domestic market, in particular the service sector, while exporting is the domain of medium and large business. The two are complementary and should be encouraged by appropriate meas-

---

[10] The LPS was intended to improve the competitiveness of local manufacturers when tendering for Government supply contracts by giving them a price advantage over foreign manufacturers of 40 percent of their local content.

[11] Republic of Botswana, 1984, Industrial Development Policy, Government Paper No.2 of 1984.

ures. It would be unwise for Government to ignore the concerns of small business (mostly citizen-owned) because the non-development of this section of business could unleash destabilising social, economic and political pressures that could be difficult to deal with. These small firms could also provide the pool from which future large entrepreneurs can be drawn.

5. CRITICAL ISSUES AFFECTING THE PROMOTION OF EXPORT-LED INDUSTRIALIZATION IN THE FUTURE

Given that the expected new Government policy on industrial development (currently being debated and developed) places much emphasis on export-based industrialization, this section initially looks at the role of trade financing and trade information in the promotion of exports. This is an area that has not received adequate attention in the past. This is followed by a discussion on the impact of the new Southern African Customs Union (SACU) Agreement on the development of sustainable and internationally competitive export-oriented business. And finally, the section will evaluate the capability of Botswana firms to produce competitively non-traditional exports in the face of heightened competition in international markets borne out of the global liberalization of trade under the impetus of the Uruguay Round provisions.

The role of trade financing and trade information in the export business

Exporting is a high risk activity, not least because the realization of proceeds from exports is a function of, among other things, events taking place in a foreign country over which the exporter has no control. The fundamental risk with which an exporter is faced is that of non-payment by the foreign buyer, which could mean losing out on an export contract. If substantial, the loss might mean a serious disruption to business as its cash flow is diminished. Non-payment may be occasioned by events that are of a commercial or political nature, resulting in the exporter being exposed to either a commercial or political risk. A commercial risk arises when the buyer fails to meet due obligations to the exporter because of insolvency or other severe deterioration in the buyer's financial position. A political risk arises when the occurrence of some event, for example, civil war or strike, inhibits the buyer from settling obligations towards the exporter. In addition to the risk associated with exporting, exporting manufacturers have to endure long waiting periods before they receive payment for their exports, during which time money is tied up in unsold goods while production has to continue simultaneously. It is not uncommon, therefore, for manufacturers to experience temporary shortages of working capital. Governments, the world over, have recognised these risks and difficulties, and invariably have provided support in one form or another to exporters. But the most common, apart from subsidy programmes, are credit insurance and guarantee facilities.

Export credit insurance, which has existed for over seventy years in Europe, has finally come to Botswana through the establishment of Export Credit Insurance and Guarantee (Botswana) (BECI)[12] in 1996. Currently BECI provides cover for commercial risk only, and insurance for political risk will most likely be in place by the end of

1997. BECI is also looking into the modalities of providing trade finance, perhaps along the lines of pre- and post-shipment credit guarantees. Both provide some sort of bridging finance that helps to smooth fluctuations in production that would otherwise occur when working capital is tied up in export orders. Pre-shipment credit assists the exporter in organising production from the time of signing of an export contract to the time of shipment. Post-shipment credit replenishes working capital that has been invested in exports for which payment has not been received. Export credit insurance is designed to protect exporters against the risk of the buyer's default on an export order due to both commercial and political problems.

Although Botswana has no explicit export incentive programme or package, the establishment of BECI is seen as part of a broader export promotion package. Government has reaffirmed its commitment to an export-oriented development strategy in its yet to be published new industrial policy, but very little has, until recently, been done by way of putting in place effective export financing mechanisms. Trade financing has been noticeably lacking, while credit insurance (for commercial risk) has, hitherto the establishment of BECI, been undertaken on a limited basis by a local insurer, whose policies for commercial risks were, in turn, reinsured one hundred percent by a South African insurer. The credit guarantee and insurance facilities provided by BECI are expected to support industrialization in three major ways. First, by facilitating an increase in production and diversification of exports. Secondly, by attracting new local and foreign investment that is geared to producing for export. Lastly, by easing access to trade finance for new and old exporters, particularly small ones, who are unable to provide collateral in order to secure export finance from the commercial banks. In view of these, the establishment of BECI is seen as a welcome development.

Export financing is not the only input that is critical to export success. Trade information is another, even though it is rarely seen as key, in part because the information requirements of exporting firms may not be well understood. However, trade information is a key competitive asset for any business, but more so for exporting firms. Trade information needs of exporters should not be viewed in terms of export/import data alone, but more broadly to include information on packaging requirements, health and other standards of importing countries, market access conditions, product development and adaptation, and so on. Seen from this perspective, information needs of exporters can more appropriately be described as refined and precise information and market intelligence. The provision of such information should take cognisance of the fact that the information requirements of exporting firms are not homogeneous, but vary depending on the extent of export involvement – starters versus occasional exporters versus regular exporters. But in general, exporters need, in the short term, information that is highly specific, accurate, clear, relevant to the export issue at hand and delivered in a cost-effective way. In the long run exporters require information relating to, among other things, access to, nature and cost of finance for export trade, sourcing and cost of technical assistance, procurement of inputs, development of sub-contracting relationships with larger exporters in the case of small exporters and identification of joint ventures (Cavusgil and Subramanian, 1989). With regard to

---

[12] Licensed on 14 November 1995, BECI started operating on 1 March 1996.

the last point, lessons may be learned from the International Trade Centre programme started in 1987 involving five Asian countries that sought to identify firms with export potential and find appropriate joint venture partners in industrialised countries. The programme was modelled on a successful pilot project implemented in the previous year.

It is possible that the financing and information services recommended here may not be required at all by some exporters, especially well-established and large ones, but it does seem they could make a significant difference in the performance of small exporting enterprises. For small-scale enterprises, while generally acknowledged to have the flexibility, dynamism and capability to respond to sudden changes, their very size tends to be a handicap in terms of resources. This point is clearly demonstrated when it comes to exporting. Their lack of security usually bars them from getting export financing, and credit guarantees turn out to be one of key factors determining how well they perform in the export business.

Promoting exporting requires that agencies that are charged with providing support services to exporters are geared to the job. This means understanding barriers that potential and existing exporters face, understanding how to make occasional exporters regulars, knowing how to help regular exporters expand the frontiers of their existing markets and products, and possessing the techniques for reaching out to non-exporters, identifying export potential and turning that potential into reality, that is, new starts in export business. This is the challenge that the Trade and Investment Promotion Agency and the Botswana Development Corporation, as delegated institutions for promoting investment and trade, have to rise to. Not only should these institutions provide the relevant information, they should interpret that information such that it becomes the basis for decision or action by an exporter. This is especially important in the context of Botswana where there is little tradition of industry and a small pool of experienced entrepreneurs and managers. The current strategy of disseminating information to businesses in passive form is unlikely to achieve much.

SACU and industrial development

The pace, deepening and extensiveness of industrialization in Botswana has largely been circumscribed by strong historical ties with South Africa and the participation of Botswana in the SACU, within which trade is governed by the SACU Agreement of 1910. Last revised in 1969, the Agreement is being renegotiated and as such the future success in industrialization will depend to a certain degree on how favourable to Botswana is the renegotiated SACU Agreement. The basis for renegotiation is that the benefits flowing from, and the costs attributed, the administration, of the SACU Agreement are not equitably distributed. The major issues at stake during the negotiations, from the viewpoint of industrial development, include: the level and form of external protection (SACU Common External Tariff – CET); use of excise taxes; differential industrial promotional schemes; anti-dumping and dispute resolution procedures; and institutional development.

Article 6 of the SACU Agreement is the basic industrial policy instrument in SACU. It permits member countries to levy additional duties to protect infant industries for a maximum of eight years. This protection has been used only infrequently in Botswana, partly reflecting the Government's preference for non-tariff protection and partly because this would have meant that customs duties collected on imports of inputs used by infant industries would have had to be paid into the common revenue pool and shared by all member countries. Also such duties could lead to higher consumer prices! Similarly, excise duties collected on export products from protected industries would be added to the pool, also for the benefit of all. Thus the net benefit of such protection would need to be weighed carefully before it is made available to all deserving industries.

The main issues that relate to Botswana producers in so far as SACU is concerned are five-fold. First, is the high CET whose adjustment in the past mainly reflected the interests of South African producers. The SACU's average MFN tariff on industrial products, currently at 21%, will only be moderately reduced to 14% (some ten percentage points above the average bound[13] tariff in developed countries) in 2000. However, many products will still be highly protected, attracting tariffs in the 20% to 30% range. At this level, the CET provides excessive protection and unduly penalises producers in Botswana, by not giving them much choice but to source inputs from South Africa, whose range and quality are not always comparable to those of inputs that could be sourced internationally and cheaply. Besides, delivery times of supplies to Botswana producers can be highly variable owing to the vertical integration of South African industry which necessitates that suppliers meet local demand first and foreign orders out of excess supplies, resulting in delays in deliveries. Botswana textiles and clothing manufacturers have been at the receiving end of this business practice in recent years. Furthermore, the protection inherently contains an anti-export bias which does not augur well for Botswana's export-oriented industrialization. Overall, Botswana manufacturers would be better served by a low and predictable CET. Specific cases, where a country pronounces a particular industry as being of strategic importance and therefore requiring higher than normal CET could be dealt with on a case by case basis and in joint consultation with other member countries. South African industry is the main beneficiary of this protection and cannot be expected to condemn it, not least because it is partially cushioned against the CET's full impact. Presently, manufacturers in South Africa receive, under the General Export Incentive Scheme (GEIS), export subsidies that could be as high as 20% of export value in order to offset the price-raising effects of the CET. The position of South

---

[13] Binding of tariffs refers to a commitment by a country not to raise further tariff rates that are stipulated in its *schedule of concessions* notified to the WTO. The schedule includes, among other things, both the pre- and post-negotiation (bound rate) tariff rates on a product-by-product basis. The bound tariff rate could, but need not, be the actual rate that is applied on the respective import product. It could be higher. For example, country **A** might have agreed during the GATT negotiations to reduce its tariff on product **B** from, say, 12% to 8%, but stipulated in its schedule of concessions that while the reduced rate (8%) will apply on imports, its bound rate would remain at, say, 10%. In this case, country **A** can raise its tariff rate any time to 10% without infringing any of the GATT obligations. Alternatively, country **A** might have decided to bind its tariff rate at 8%, in which case it would *not* be able to raise its tariff rate above this level unless it enters into another round of negotiations with all interested parties. Although it is possible for a country that has bound its tariffs to secure a release from the binding and increase tariffs above the bound rates, the process for doing so is rather complex. It involves the renegotiation of the tariff with the supplying countries of the product whose tariff needs adjustment, as well as renegotiation with countries with which the tariff concession was initially negotiated. The country in need of the release is expected to make compensatory tariff concessions on other products of export interest to the supplying countries.

African industry may change on this issue if no new export support scheme is introduced as the GEIS is phased out because it contravenes the WTO provisions. Regardless of the South African industry's position, it would be in the interests of Botswana and other SACU members to ensure agreement on lower protection during the negotiations.

Second, is the inclination of South Africa towards the use of non-tariff measures in order to discourage Botswana goods from entering its market and generally frustrating industrial development in the country. The use of such measures have been most notable in the case of motor vehicle exports where South Africa would change and/or interpret differently the very same rules under which the vehicle assembly plants were established in order to ensure that Botswana products do not meet market entry requirements. Third, the discriminatory practice by South Africa of granting its own industrial products appropriate levels of protection, while very little is afforded those from Botswana. Soda ash from Botswana, the main market for which is South Africa, is produced behind a modest CET of 10%, which compares with 20% for caustic soda, a South African product. This, in spite of the well-known threat from foreign producers of soda ash selling in the South African market. Fourth, dumping of products in SACU markets by both member and third countries. Presently there is no established mechanism to deal with dumping issues. There is a need for anti-dumping laws and procedures through which redress could be sought when dumping occurs. Fifth, the local content requirement is set too high for any start-up in Botswana to achieve mainly because of the narrow industrial base that can provide neither the diversity nor quantity of the requisite local raw materials.

South Africa has committed itself to complying with the WTO provisions, which will mean that it has to do a number of things, among them the liberalization of non-tariff measures such as the unfair and restrictive trade and business practices, terminating the excise tax system, the highly protective discriminatory origin rules, as well as the subsidization programmes. A move in this direction will be a step forward in bringing about a new dispensation in the promotion of SACU-wide industrial development. But reforms are also in order in several areas. Adjustments to the CET in the past were effected, invariably, on recommendations of the South African Board of Tariffs and Trade. A SACU-wide institution is necessary here. Also, the CET is not the only protection available. Alternative non-tariff-based protection exists in the form of duty exemption/drawback, temporary admission and bonded manufacturing warehouse, all of which would give manufacturers the chance to source inputs from international markets at world prices. Dispute resolution procedures and the general administration of the SACU are other important areas to be looked at. Allowing for full and equitable participation of all member countries in the SACU governing structures may well be the best starting point in the reform process.

A closely linked issue is the impact of the ongoing South Africa-EU trade negotiations. The negotiations have not been concluded, and, as such, it is pointless to speculate on the type of trade agreement that is likely to emerge, though indications are that the EU may press for a free trade area. Consequently, it is pointless to also speculate on the tariff concessions South Africa is likely to offer to the EU. But whatever those concessions will be, it is safe to assume that they will have some impact (positive or negative) on the extent of Botswana's industrialization if both parties adhere to the principle of reciprocity. Reciprocity would bind South Africa to offer tariff concessions to the EU in return for concessions offered it by the EU. Earlier rounds of negotiations pointed to a situation where the EU was not going to ask South Africa to reciprocate any of the concessions it was offering, but this may change. Botswana needs to follow closely these negotiations and find a way of ensuring that its industrialization objectives are not frustrated by a possible EU-South Africa trade agreement. Botswana may find that South Africa, in fulfilling its obligations to the EU under a trade agreement, is liberalising at a pace that is too fast or too slow in specific areas, which, in either case, may not be appropriate for the development of the affected sectors as seen from a Botswana perspective. Botswana ought to have a say in what is an appropriate level of protection for its industry and whether the CET is the best protection option available.

Multilateral liberalization of trade

One of the major international developments that will affect industrialization in Botswana is the conclusion of the Uruguay Round multilateral negotiations[14], whose main spin off was the establishment of the World Trade Organization (WTO) in 1995. The multilateral trade liberalization that is envisaged to be ushered in by the full implementation of the Uruguay Round Agreements is generally expected to result in some gains for all countries, though in the short term some countries will experience losses. The extent of the estimated gain or loss by individual countries or regions of the world is at best indicative, given that the gain or losse is mainly static, and sensitive to the assumptions made and the methodologies used.[15] The conclusion by some analysts is that the Sub-Saharan African region will most likely gain minimally, if not lose outright in the immediate post-2005 period when all the tariff cuts – which are back-end loaded[16] – are fully implemented. This is based on two arguments. First it is argued that the initial high tariff protection afforded local industries and the subsequent binding of tariffs at high levels have ill-prepared many Sub-Saharan industries for international competition (Table 6 shows the extent of difference in tariffs for developed and developing countries). Secondly, it is also argued that if tariffs are liberalised on a general Most-Favoured-Nation (MFN) basis, Sub-Saharan African countries are likely to suffer because of the erosion of tariff preference margins[17] [where tariff preference margins refer to the difference between the MFN tariff and the tariff applicable to products receiving preferential treatment, i.e., those that have duty-free status or attract tariffs below MFN or Generalised System of Preferences (GSP) rates].

---

[14] The negotiations were formally concluded and a deal signed at a ministerial meeting held in Marrakesh, Morocco on 15 April 1994. The Final Act embodying the Uruguay Round results came into force on 1 January 1995.

[15] Quite apart from the problem of inadequate data, both in terms of quantity and quality, data used in some of these models are not sufficiently disaggregated by product for each of the countries covered in order to permit an in-depth analysis of the impact of the removal of Most Favoured Nation (MFN) tariffs on these countries' exports. Obviously, such an exercise would be unmanageable at the international level, but appears necessary at the national level if a country is to fully appreciate the extent of the impact, and what could be done to best deal with those impacts.

[16] Deeper cuts in tariffs or a significant scaling down of the Multi Fibre Arrangement (MFA) will occur during the last years, if not the final year, of the transition period rather than at the beginning of the period. For tariffs applicable to the agricultural sector, the transition period is six to ten years for developed and developing countries respectively, while in the case of the MFA the transition period is ten years.

Sub-Saharan African countries' exports (of which Botswana's are a part) to the EU, the USA and Japan receive duty-free treatment and/or are subject to tariffs below MFN and GSP rates.

Tables 6 and 7 show pre- and post-Uruguay Round tariffs by country and broad industrial product group, respectively. Three things emerge from these tables. First, from Table 6, tariffs are lower in developed countries (except in South Africa, which is classified as developed in the source) than in developing countries. Being part of the customs union, Botswana's trade is subject to tariff bindings notified by South Africa to the WTO. Therefore, the high South African tariff, which is a common external tariff, could have undesirable effects on Botswana's industrial development. Its net effect, however, is largely an empirical issue. Secondly, developed country tariffs imposed on industrial products imported from developing countries are higher than average tariffs imposed on industrial products imported from all sources, both in the pre- and post-Uruguay Round periods. Thirdly, while reductions in average tariffs for processed products are generally higher than reductions in tariffs for unprocessed products, processed products continue to attract higher average tariffs than unprocessed products. Also, Table A1 in the Appendix indicates that although tariff escalation[18] has been reduced (or eliminated in some instances), particularly at more advanced stages of production, average tariffs for finished goods remain substantial in developed countries. These observations point to the fact that while developed countries may seem the natural export markets for developing countries to aim at given that their overall tariffs are generally low, a disaggregation of tariffs by product lines indicates that finished goods (semi-processed to processed) are still highly protected. Therefore, developing countries aiming to industrialise by producing finished goods destined for developed country markets are likely to face two major problems. One is the relatively high tariffs at product level. The other is stiff competition from low-cost producers, especially those in East and South East Asia. More importantly for Botswana, of all industrial products, textiles are subject to the highest average tariffs in the post-Uruguay Round period. Leather and footwear, another potential export product group for Botswana, attracts the second highest average tariff.

Access to European, the USA and Japanese markets is important to Botswana given that these markets were among the top ten world importers of textiles and clothing in 1992. Within Europe, Germany, France, the UK and Italy shared between them 31% of the world market for textile and clothing imports, while the USA and Japan accounted for 17% and 6% of the market, respectively. Botswana would do well to target these markets given the window of opportunity before MFN tariff cuts

---

17 It is, however, possible that preference margins for some of the developing countries' export products with non-zero preference duties can be maintained at existing levels by reducing both MFN and the preferential tariff. The Uruguay Round focuses on reducing MFN tariffs only, but countries granting preferential treatment to imports from developing countries can, at their discretion, make compensating cuts on non-zero preferential tariffs in line with cuts in the MFN rates, with the result that pre- and post-Uruguay Round margins of preference remain the same. For example, the pre-Uruguay Round average tariff on industrial products entering the USA is 5.4% and the tariff applicable to Botswana's exports to the USA is 3.5%, which gives a preference margin of 1.9 percentage points. The post-Uruguay Round tariff on USA industrial imports is 3.5%, which without adjusting downwards the tariff Botswana exports attract, would wipe out the preference margin. The USA could decide to maintain the pre-Uruguay Round preference margin by reducing the tariff applicable to its imports from Botswana by 1.9%.

TABLE 6. PRE- AND POST-URUGUAY ROUND WEIGHTED AVERAGES OF TARIFFS APPLICABLE TO INDUSTRIAL PRODUCTS[a] IN SELECTED DEVELOPED AND DEVELOPING COUNTRIES (%)

SELECTED COUNTRIES AND REGION	TRADE-WEIGHTED TARIFF AVERAGES	
	PRE-URUGUAY ROUND	POST-URUGUAY
DEVELOPED COUNTRIES	6.3	3.8
European Union	5.7	3.6
Japan	3.9	1.7
Norway	3.6	2.0
South Africa	24.5	17.2
Switzerland	2.2	1.5
United States	5.4	3.5
DEVELOPING COUNTRIES		
Korea, Republic of	18.0	8.3
Malaysia	10.2	9.1
Singapore	12.4	5.1
Thailand	37.3	28.0
Zimbabwe	4.8	4.6
TRANSITIONAL ECONOMIES	8.6	6.0

Note: [a] Excluding petroleum.

Source: International Trade Centre UNCTAD/WTO and Commonwealth Secretariat (1995) Annex Tables 1–3, pp245–247.

are fully implemented. Hong Kong, the third largest importer of textiles and clothing in 1992, is another market to target. Tariffs applicable to Botswana's non-oil exports to the EU and the USA are 0.1% and 3.5%, respectively, while non-oil exports to Japan attract no tariff (Table 9). Given these low tariffs, Botswana exporters would stand a good chance of selling into these markets if it were not for the price raising

---

[18] Tariff escalation refers to a situation where the tariff applied on a product 'chain' rises with the increase in the level of processing of products, that is, import duties are higher on the finished product made of a given raw material than on the raw material in unprocessed form (International Trade Centre, 1995). For example, cotton may be generally freely traded or may be subject to a small duty. However, once it has been processed into yarn, textiles and clothing, duties applicable at each of the successive stages of processing increase. Table A1 shows that the average tariff applied to raw materials under the category 'all industrial products' was 2.1% while that for finished products was 9.1% in the pre-Uruguay Round period, but will be reduced to 0.8% and 6.2%, respectively, in the post-Uruguay Round period. Clearly the 6.2% tariff on finished products is much higher (almost eight times higher) than the 0.8% tariff on materials. Hence, high rates of effective protection are provided to the importing country's processing sector. Consequently, production of processed goods in developed countries increases behind high tariff walls and displaces imports of the same goods from developing countries, thereby inhibiting industrialisation in developing countries. (ITC 8 Commonwealth Secretariat 1995:70.)

TABLE 7. DEVELOPED COUNTRY REDUCTIONS IN BOUND TARIFF RATES BY MAJOR INDUSTRIAL PRODUCT GROUP

PRODUCT CATEGORY	IMPORT VALUE		TARIFF AVERAGES WEIGHTED BY:					
	All Sources (US$bn)	Developing Economies (US$bn)	IMPORTS FROM ALL SOURCES (%)			IMPORTS FROM DEVELOPING ECONOMIES (%)		
			Pre-UR	Post-UR	% Red	Pre-UR	Post-UR	% Red
Industrial Products:	*736.9*	*169.7*	*6.3*	*3.8*	*40*	*6.8*	*4.3*	*37*
Fish and fish products	18.5	10.6	6.1	4.5	26	6.6	4.8	27
Wood, pulp, paper furniture	40.6	11.5	3.5	1.1	69	4.6	1.7	63
Textiles and clothing	66.4	33.2	15.5	12.1	22	14.6	11.3	23
Leather, rubber, footwear	31.7	12.2	8.9	7.3	18	8.1	6.6	19
Metals	69.4	24.4	3.7	1.4	62	2.7	0.9	67
Chemicals and photographic supplies	61.0	8.2	6.7	3.7	45	7.2	3.8	47
Transport equipment	96.3	7.6	7.5	5.8	23	3.8	3.1	18
Non-electric machinery	118.1	9.8	4.8	1.9	60	4.7	1.6	66
Electric machinery	86.0	19.2	6.6	3.5	47	6.3	3.3	48
Mineral products and precious stones	73.0	22.2	2.3	1.1	52	2.6	0.8	69
Manufactured articles n.e.c.	76.1	10.9	5.5	2.4	56	6.5	3.1	52

Note: UR = Uruguay Round; Red = Reduction.

Source: International Trade Centre UNCTAD/GATT (1995), Vol.1, p6.

effect of the CET, which raises domestic production costs via high costs of imported inputs. High prices of imported inputs will feed into export product prices and reduce the latter's attractiveness to consumers in targeted markets.

It has been argued that some developing countries are likely to gain minimally from the multilateral reduction in MFN tariffs because of the erosion of margin of tariff preferences. This appears to hold in the case of Botswana too as Table 8 shows. Virtually all (99%) of Botswana's line item products are zero duty (26%) or preference line (73%) items. This compares with 4% each for Taiwanese and South Korean line items that attract zero duty or a preferential tariff. Only 1% of Botswana's line item products (as against 96% each of Taiwan's and South Korea's) with a non-zero MFN

TABLE 8. BOTSWANA EXPORT PRODUCTS FACING MFN OR PREFERENTIAL DUTIES IN THE EUROPEAN COMMUNITY (NOW EUROPEAN UNION)

	NUMBER OF TARIFF LINES					
	BOTSWANA	(%)	TAIWAN	(%)	SOUTH KOREA	(%)
Tariff lines facing a zero MFN duty (a)	33	(26)	19	(4)	153	(4)
Zero preference rate lines (b)	94	(73)	0	(0)	0	(0)
Total Lines with zero duties c = (a+b)	127	(9)	19	(4)	153	(4)
Non-zero preference rate lines (d)	0	(0)	0	(0)	0	(0)
Zero duty or preference rate lines (e) = (c+d)	127	(9)	19	(4)	153	(4)
Non-zero MFN duty lines (f)	1	(1)	4 080	(96)	3 350	(96)
Total Tariff lines (g) = (e+f)	128	(100)	4 272	(100)	3 503	(100)

Note: Figures in parentheses show the percentage of all tariff lines covered. The EU customs schedule differentiates between 9506 line item products. At 128 line items, Botswana's export products are an insignificant proportion of the EU's schedule of line items that can potentially be exported.

Source: Yeats (1994), adapted from Table 3, p10.

duty stand to gain from a reduction in MFN tariffs. It should not be surprising, therefore, that Botswana may not gain as much as Taiwan, Korea or any other non-preference receiving country. Clearly, the success of some Asian and Eastern European countries at increasing their exports to the EU, notwithstanding that their exports did not receive equally generous preferential treatment, is very revealing. Yeats (1994) estimates that over 95% of all African tariff line products entering the EU receive duty-free treatment, while other suppliers of the same products pay duties up to twenty percentage points higher. If these non-preference receiving countries exporting to the same EU markets as Botswana and other African economies now get MFN and/or duty free access, they will be able to undercut Botswana and other African countries by up to 20%. Logically, prices will fall. This could have the effect of undermining Botswana and other African exporters if the volume of their exports do not rise in response to the expected higher demand in order to mitigate against the resulting fall in export earnings brought about by lower prices.

Table 9 shows the nominal average tariffs applicable to exports from Botswana, Taiwan and Korea to the OECD, EU, Japan and the USA. The column entitled 'preference margin' refers to the average tariff margin of preference, where a negative (positive) figure indicates the number of percentage points each country's average tariff is below (above) the average tariff facing other countries. Clearly, Botswana has lower average tariffs than Taiwan or South Korea in all markets, as well as higher preference margins. As argued previously, the preference margin for Botswana is highest in the EU (where its exports are subject to an average tariff that is 2.9 percentage points lower than the average tariff facing other exporters of the same products) and lowest in the USA, followed by Japan, presumably because of the tighter rules of origin applying in these two countries. The effect of MFN tariff cuts would be to reduce or eliminate these preference margins and lower prices. Lower prices could mean two things: they could translate into lower export earnings if export volumes do not increase due to, say, supply side constraints; or if volumes adjust accordingly the expected increase in world income and demand could translate into higher export earnings. The final outcome depends on a country's circumstances.

TABLE 9. THE INCIDENCE OF OECD TARIFFS ON BOTSWANA, TAIWAN AND KOREA'S NON-OIL EXPORTS (%)

REGION/COUNTRY	BOTSWANA		TAIWAN		KOREA	
	TARIFF	PREFERENCE MARGIN[a]	TARIFF	PREFERENCE MARGIN[a]	TARIFF	PREFERENCE MARGIN[a]
OECD AVERAGE	0.3	-2.8	6.1	0.9	6.0	0.6
EU	0.1	-2.9	7.5	4.0	7.8	4.2
JAPAN	0.0	-2.1	2.5	-2.2	2.7	-2.2
USA	3.5	-1.1	6.8	0.7	7.1	0.7

Note: [a] Negative values show the average preferential tariff margins (in points) that Botswana, Taiwan and Korea have over all other exporters of the same goods. Positive values indicate that the exporter faces a higher than average tariff due to preferences other countries receive. All tariffs shown are the simple average (unweighted) of duties paid on the country's exports.

Source: Yeats (1994), adapted from Table 4, p12.

The precise impact on Botswana exports of the reduction in MFN tariffs arising from the gradual phasing in of the WTO provisions is largely an empirical question. However, it is possible to sketch a few possibilities based on estimates by Yeats (1994) and Davenport et al. (1995), and this is done below for five of Botswana's major exports, diamonds, copper-nickel matte, beef, textiles and vehicles.

Diamonds. It is highly unlikely that diamonds will be affected by the liberalization of MFN tariffs given the manner in which they are marketed, through a cartel. However, the cartel may not continue indefinitely given that some major diamond suppliers (Russia) appear keen to supply the market directly and not through the Central Selling Organisation's marketing channel. For the moment, the chances of this happening have been reduced by the two-year agreement which binds Russia to sell most of their valuable output through the Central Selling Organisation. While no formal agreement has yet been signed, Russian representatives continue to say that leaving the Central Selling Organisation framework is not a viable option. However, if the cartel breaks up, and major suppliers (including Botswana) sell directly to the market, the likely outcome is an over supply in the short-run and the consequent reduction in prices. The level and relative stability of diamond prices could not be guaranteed any more. Individual suppliers may make short-term gains, but in the long run all producers stand to lose. Having said this, there could be modest growth in diamond exports induced by the higher world income expected to arise from freer trade.

Copper-Nickel. The major markets for copper-nickel matte have been Norway and Zimbabwe. Although tariffs in both markets are relatively low and, thus, unlikely to be a major constraint to exporting, a MFN tariff cut is irrelevant in this case for two reasons: the owner of the copper-nickel mining company, BCL, not only does not get tariff preferences but is operating at full capacity, which means that the company could not expand production even if tariffs fell and market opportunities improved. Secondly, BCL is tied to the world price which, apart from occasional increases, has generally remained depressed. Its fortunes are pinned on improved world prices of copper and nickel rather than on tariff cuts.

Beef and the Lomé Convention. Although a tariff cut is also largely irrelevant in this case, the phasing out and tariffication of quotas will have an impact on beef exports. Botswana's beef has benefited from the Beef and Veal Protocol of the Lomé Convention[19] which provides Botswana, along with six Sub-Saharan African countries, a 92.1% reduction (90% prior to the conclusion of the mid-term review of Lomé IV in 1995) in the variable levy. At 18 916 tonnes per year, Botswana's beef quota is the most generous, being 1.8 times higher than the second highest (for Namibia) and 133 times more than Kenya's, which has the smallest quota. Although Botswana has never been able to fill up the quota, its usage of the quota has been increasing – rising from 60% in 1985[20] to 81% in 1992. This indicates the growing importance of the EU market for Botswana beef exports. This market is likely to yield lower prices for Botswana beef exports when Lomé IV expires in 2000.

Following the successful application by the EU and the ACP for a waiver from the MFN principle[21], beef exports from Botswana to the EU will continue to benefit from the variable levy until the expiry of Lomé IV. What happens thereafter is unclear, but Davenport *et al.*, (1995) foresee three scenarios. They suggest that the EU might continue with the Convention, but withdraw the non-reciprocal preferential treatment from countries that have reached a relatively advanced development level. Secondly,

---

[19] The Lomé Convention came into being in 1975 and has provided preferential access to African, Caribbean and Pacific (ACP) countries, a category of countries often referred to as EU's preferred partners, because of the very low duties on, or few non-tariff barriers put up against, their exports to the Union. The preferential access accorded the ACP states has been non-reciprocal, mainly to provide the incentive to these countries to industrialise. Duty-free access is granted for exports of manufactures originating in ACP states, while preferential access for agricultural products is determined by the EU's Common Agricultural Policy. The latter is based on concessions on duties and levies imposed on imports into the EU. Of more relevance to the ACP states is the guaranteed access given to specific quantities of certain commodities under its protocols for sugar, rum, bananas, and beef and veal exports to the EU. Botswana benefits from the protocol on beef and veal.

[20] The author was unable to get the percentage of the quota filled for earlier years from the BMC.

[21] The waiver will remain valid until 29 February 2000.

the Convention might be extended to the least developed countries of the world, and not just be restricted to the ACP region. Third, the EU might set up a Free Trade Area (FTA) with the ACP countries on a regional basis. They note that while this latter option is closer to the EU's thinking on regional integration, it is unlikely that it could materialise given that little regional integration has occurred elsewhere in the ACP besides that which has taken place in Southern Africa and the Caribbean. Whichever option is taken, it is highly unlikely that Botswana will maintain its present market share in the EU beef market in the post-2000 period. The partial loss of this market will have a significant impact on beef revenues given that beef prices in this market have generally been higher than world market prices. Davenport *et al.*(1995) estimate that Botswana will lose US$15 million a year in export earnings from agricultural products (mainly beef) in the post-Uruguay Round period. Furthermore, the tariffication of the beef quota will result in higher beef tariffs, and therefore, less easy access to the market. This analysis obviously ignores the effect of improved efficiency in beef production by both the BMC and cattle producers. Improving efficiency is at the top of the priority lists of the BMC and the Ministry of Agriculture. It remains to be seen the extent to which improvements in efficiency, if any, and hence increases in volume and value, will offset reductions in export earnings that could arise from the partial loss of the EU market and the likely subsequent shift to lower priced beef markets.

Textiles and vehicles. Access has not been a major problem in the EU and South African markets (besides the occasional use by South Africa of non-tariff measures (NTM) in the case of vehicle exports) because of preferential treatment in the former and duty free entry of exports in the latter, and can be expected to remain so for as long as the preferences last. Botswana textile and clothing exports to the EU have not been subject to quantitative restrictions under the Multi-Fibre Agreement (MFA) or other non-tariff measures (e.g., eco-labelling). However, regulations concerning quality, safety, health and the environment may become a barrier to successful exporting, especially to the EU which has, or will soon, issue directives on standards that have to be met in all four areas by products entering the EU. It would be in the interests of Botswana textile manufacturers to familiarise themselves with such standards in order to ensure that they do not lose this market.

The average tariff in the Zimbabwean market, the second largest market for Botswana textiles, has come down slightly, but has been very low compared with that of South Africa. Under these circumstances, market penetration could not have been easier. The problem area has mainly been restrictive business practices and unfavourable factors not related to demand in the Zimbabwean market. Import surcharges occasionally imposed by the Zimbabwe authorities on imports from Botswana, and adverse currency and input price movements – such as the large devaluations of the Zimbabwe dollar in the early 1990s, and the sharp rise in the price of cotton lint (an input in textile manufacturing) – have been more important in determining access to the Zimbabwean market. These may remain the major obstacles to exporting to Zimbabwe than the tariff rates.

The South African market has been an important destination for Botswana textile and motor vehicle exports, especially in recent years. As explained above, tariffs as a barrier to successful exporting to that country are not important, but NTM are. While Botswana textiles and garment manufacturers appear to have found a niche market there, and seem to be tackling competition well, the same could not be said of motor vehicle exports. As discussed in the previous subsection on SACU, the South African authorities have maintained a tight grip on exports of motor vehicles from Botswana by, for example, changing the eligibility criteria for rebates for certain categories of imported vehicle components and, more recently, press reports indicate that certain types of vehicles imported from Botswana were impounded under the pretext that these had entered the country illegally. There is no doubt that these actions have been taken to limit competition to the motor vehicle industry there. Such actions do not augur well for a steady growth of exports to this market.

6. CONCLUSION

This paper has sought to trace the extent of industrialization in Botswana and map out its future. The section on data analysis has shown that industrial development has occurred rapidly in Botswana, but that this has largely been because of the rapid growth of the mining sector. Excluding minerals from the analysis indicates that the manufacturing sector also grew very fast, except in the most recent period. However, the sector remains very small not only in relation to other sectors, but also in comparison with manufacturing sectors in other countries, both on the sub-continent and internationally. What also emerged from the analysis is that, in contrast to manufacturing or construction, mining is not labour intensive. While the FAP has played a crucial role in the economic diversification that has occurred to date, other support services that address non-finance issues, for example, supply of trade information, should be put in place.

Having surveyed several international and domestic developments that have a bearing on industrialization and successful exporting in Botswana, the paper concludes that world markets are rapidly getting more competitive as a result of the multilateral liberalization of trade. Intensifying competition will gather momentum as the Uruguay Round agreements are fully implemented. The paper argues that Botswana has to encourage the development of industries whose products are not dependent on preferential treatment in export or domestic markets, because many of these preferences are likely to be phased out less than a decade from now. In addition, vigorous promotion of production for export markets appears to be the only viable way of escaping the small domestic market. This underlies the importance of raising productivity and minimising costs of production by, *inter alia*, reforming the SACU Agreement.

APPENDIX

TABLE A1: CHANGES IN TARIFF ESCALATION ON INDUSTRIAL PRODUCTS IMPORTED BY DEVELOPED COUNTRIES FROM DEVELOPING ECONOMIES, BASED ON BOUND TARIFF RATES

PRODUCT CATEGORY	IMPORT VALUE US$ (BILLION)	AVERAGE TARIFF (%)	
		PRE-UR	POST-UR
ALL INDUSTRIAL PRODUCTS			
Raw materials	36.7	2.1	0.8
Semi-manufactures	36.5	5.4	2.8
Finished products	96.5	9.1	6.2
ALL TROPICAL INDUSTRIAL PRODUCTS			
Raw materials	5.1	0.1	0.0
Semi-manufactures	4.3	6.3	3.4
Finished products	4.9	6.6	2.4
NATURAL RESOURCE-BASED PRODUCTS			
Raw materials	14.6	3.1	2.0
Semi-manufactures	13.3	3.5	2.0
Finished products	5.5	7.9	5.9

Note: UR = Uruguay Round.
Source: International Trade Centre UNCTAD/GATT (1995) Vol.1, p6.

REFERENCES

Bhuiyan, M.N. (ed.). 1986. *Selected Papers on the Botswana Economy.* Printing and Publishing Co. (Botswana), Gaborone.

Botswana Confederation of Commerce, Industry and Manpower. 1995a. *Industry Survey 1994: Report of Major Findings.* BOCCIM, Gaborone.

Cavusgil, S.T. and Subramanian. 1989. Meeting the Information Needs of SMES for Exports'. In: International Trade Centre, *Exports from Small and Medium Enterprises in Developing Countries: Issues and Perspectives.* Geneva.

Central Statistics Office (various years) *External Trade Statistics.* Government Printer, Gaborone.

Central Statistics Office. 1993. *Trade Statistics Supplement 1990–1992.* Government Printer, Gaborone.

Colclough, C. and McCarthy, S. 1980. *The Political Economy of Botswana: A Study of Growth and Distribution.* Oxford University Press, Oxford.

Davenport, M., Hewitt, A. and Koning, A. 1995. *Europe's Preferred Partners? The Lomé Countries in World Trade.* ODI Special Report. Chameleon Press, London.

Government of Botswana. 1982. *National Policy on Economic Opportunities.* Government Paper No.2 of 1982. Government Printer, Gaborone.

Government of Botswana. 1984. *Industrial Development Policy.* Government Paper No.2 of 1984. Government Printer, Gaborone.

Government of Botswana. 1988. *A Businessman's Guide to the Local Preference Scheme.* Government Printer, Gaborone.

Greenaway, D. and Milner, C. 1993. *Trade and Industrial Policy in Developing Countries: A Manual of Policy Analysis.* Mackays of Chatham, Chatham, Kent.

Harvey, C. and Lewis, S.R. 1990. *Policy Choice and Development Performance in Botswana.* Macmillan Press, London.

Helleiner, G.K. (ed.). 1992. *Trade Policy, Industrialization and Development: New Perspectives.* Oxford University Press, New York.

International Trade Centre. 1989. *Exports from Small and Medium Enterprises in Developing Countries: Issues and Perspectives.* Geneva.

International Trade Centre and Commonwealth Secretariat. 1995. *Business Guide to the Uruguay Round.* Geneva.

Kaplinsky, R. 1991. 'Industrialization in Botswana: How Getting the Prices Right Helped the Wrong People.' In: Colclough, C. and Manor, J. (eds.). *States or Markets? Neo-Liberalism and the Development Policy Debate.* IDS Development Studies Series. Oxford University Press, Oxford.

Lindauer, D.L. and Roemer, M. (eds.). 1994. *Asia and Africa: Legacies and Opportunities in Development.* Braun-Brumfield, Inc., Ann Arbor, Michigan.

Ministry of Finance and Development Planning. 1994. 'An Overview of the SACU from the Botswana Perspective: Implications of the Historical Record and Contemporary Situation for Re-negotiation of the Arrangement', *The Research Bulletin,* Vol.12, No.1. Bank of Botswana, Gaborone.

National Institute of Economic Policy. 1994. *Reconstituting and Democratising the Southern African Customs Union.* Report of the Workshop Held in Gaborone, Botswana. Elite Print cc, Johannesburg.

Riddell, R.C. 1990. *Manufacturing Africa: Performance and Prospects of Seven Countries in Sub-Saharan Africa.* Overseas Development Institute, London

Steel, W.F. and Evans, J.W. 1984. *Industrialization in Sub-Saharan Africa. Strategies and Performance.* World Bank Technical Paper No.25, World Bank, Washington.

The Services Group. 1994. *Botswana Export Incentives Study.* Prepared for the Ministry of Commerce and Industry and the Botswana Development Corporation, Gaborone

Wade, R. 1990. *Governing the Market: Economic Theory and the Role of Government in East Asian Industrialization.* Princeton University Press, Princeton.

World Bank. 1995. *World Development Report 1995: Workers in an Integrating World.* Oxford University Press, Oxford.

Yeats, A.J. 1994. *What are OECD Trade Preferences Worth to Sub-Saharan Africa? World Bank Policy Research Working Paper 1254.* Policy Research Dissemination Centre, World Bank, Washington.

Constraints to Industrial Development

Dorothy Mpabanga[1]

1. INTRODUCTION

The purpose of this paper is to update existing research and analysis on the progress of industrialization in Botswana, with a specific focus on examining the constraints to industrial development, and in particular, the manufacturing sector. Section 2 looks at the overall progress of industrial development in Botswana. Section 3 reviews the progress as measured by macroeconomic indicators, such as the manufacturing sector as a percentage of Gross Domestic Product (GDP), manufacturing employment as a percentage of total formal employment, and the manufacturing share of non-mining GDP. Section 4 examines constraints facing the development of the manufacturing sector, including other conflicting policy objectives. Section 5 discusses some of the policies that Government has introduced in an attempt to overcome these constraints, as well as the successes and failures of these policies. Section 6 explores some lessons Botswana may be able to learn from other countries, particularly Mauritius and South East Asian countries. The last section contains the conclusions of the paper.

2. OVERALL PROGRESS OF INDUSTRIALIZATION IN BOTSWANA

Industrialization has widely been considered as one of the main sources of potential growth and development in many developing countries. This has led to developing countries offering various types of incentives to attract capital, particularly foreign capital. In addition to incentive schemes, developing countries are striving hard to attract investment through the provision of generally stable and conducive economic and political environments, as well as the presence of infrastructure and institutional support systems to facilitate investment. Developing countries have also adopted explicit industrial development policies, specifying major objectives and strategies of industrial development. Botswana has also followed all these approaches and has developed policies and incentives aimed to promote industrial development.

Botswana is a small open economy, and was one of the poorest countries in Africa at Independence. However, in the thirty years since Independence in 1966, the economy has been transformed. Real GDP growth has averaged 13% per annum from 1980 to 1989, led by the rapid development of the mineral sector. Other contributing factors to the rapid growth were the stable democratic political system, cautious fiscal and monetary policy and transparency in the decision making process. Botswana has

---

[1] The Author would like to thank colleagues in the Research Department of the Bank of Botswana who have provided invaluable comments for this paper.

advantages of liberal exchange controls (further liberalization is under way), reliable utility supplies, is a member of Southern African Customs Union (SACU), which allows it free trade with member countries, as well as benefits from access to the European Union (EU) market under the Lomè Convention. The Botswana Government also espouses a free enterprise, market-oriented system, which gives companies freedom to produce, market and finance their products and services. The private sector is viewed as a major contributor in the growth of the non-mineral sector.

The Government has, over the high growth years, reinvested the mineral revenue heavily in social services and economic sectors, such as health, education, infrastructure and the provision of clean water throughout the country. These developments have brought about general improvement in the standard of living of Batswana and the overall improvement in the level of education supporting the development of a more skilled labour force. The rapid economic development and growth since Independence has created employment opportunities for locals in the formal and the informal sectors. By March 1995, a total of 234 500 were estimated to be employed in the formal sector (CSO Statistical Bulletin, 1995), showing a growth rate of about ten percent per annum since 1966 (the figure excludes employment in the Botswana Defence Force).[2]

However, the economy of Botswana is still heavily dependent on the mineral sector, which accounts for over 30% of GDP, 70% of exports and nearly 50% of Government revenue. The Government has realised the disadvantages associated with being dependent on one sector, which is capital intensive, a non-renewable resource, and has only limited direct linkages to the rest of the economy. During the 1960s and early 1970s, Government was more concerned with pressing development issues such as provision of basic social and physical infrastructure. There was an Industrial Development Act of 1968, which had objectives aimed at regulating and licensing of the industrial investment and supporting infant industry under the SACU Agreement. The Government's focus on economic diversification has been a prominent goal since National Development Plan (NDP) 4. The Government has thus adopted the policy of economic diversification through industrial development. The major statement in this respect has been the adoption of an Industrial Development Policy in 1984, which aims at economic diversification, employment creation, promotion of non-traditional exports and the creation of an environment to foster the growth of the private sector. Industrial promotion will be continued through NDP 8. The manufacturing sector was targeted as the alternative source of growth to achieve this objective. The Industrial Development Policy is under review with a view to focus more on the promotion and development of export-oriented manufacturing.

3. OVERALL PROGRESS OF MANUFACTURING AS MEASURED BY MACROECONOMIC INDICATORS

The growth of the manufacturing sector

The manufacturing sector experienced an average growth rate of about 7.6% between

---

[2] For more details of growth of the labour force, see Bank of Botswana Annual Report 1995.

1982/83 and 1988/89. This growth rate declined to about 3.3% per annum between 1989/90 and 1994/95.

Manufacturing share of total GDP

The manufacturing sector's share of GDP has averaged about 5.6% between 1982/83 and 1988/89. The sector's share or contribution to GDP has averaged 6% between 1989/90 and 1994/95. This was a slight increase, but is still less than the contribution of several sectors of the economy. The manufacturing sector has been the fourth largest contributor to total GDP, after mining (37.1%), Government (14.1%), and trade, hotels and restaurants (14.3%). The sector of manufacturing in GDP has, since 1988/89, been overtaken by the development of banks, insurance and business services (7.7% in 1988/89 and 10.5% in 1994/95); manufacturing in 1994/95 was the fifth largest contributor to GDP.

TABLE 1. THE PERFORMANCE OF THE MANUFACTURING SECTOR FOR SELECTED YEARS

MANUFACTURING SECTOR	82/83	84/85	87/88	89/90	90/91	91/92	92/93	93/94	94/95
REAL RATE OF GROWTH (% P.A.)	-8.1	-20.4	29.9	4.8	6.6	6.4	-1.0	-1.3	4.3
SHARE OF GDP (%)	6.1	4.7	5.1	5.0	4.8	4.9	4.9	4.5	4.7

Source: Bank of Botswana, 1995 Annual Report.

Manufacturing employment as a percentage of total employment

As indicated in Table 2, employment growth in the manufacturing sector has been very rapid, increasing by 245.3% between 1986 and 1991. The sector has, since 1995, been the second largest employer in the private sector (after construction). However, between September 1991 and March 1993, employment in manufacturing fell from 26 300 to 22 100, a decrease of 15%.

According to the Bank of Botswana Annual Report, 1995, employment in manufacturing continued to fall by 1.8% in the year to March 1994, to 21 700. However, employment in the manufacturing sector increased by about 7.3% between March 1994 and March 1995, from 21 700 to 23 400 (CSO 1995). By 1995, the manufacturing sector accounted for 17.1 % of total wage employment in the private sector. Much of this improvement was due to the general improvement in the Botswana economy, as well as that of South Africa. Several Botswana firms were reporting increased exports to South Africa and elsewhere in the region and the world. For example, export of non-traditional products increased from P290 million in 1992 to P700 million in 1994.

In 1990, the sector accounted for 11.7% of total formal employment, an increase from 8.5% in 1985. However, the sector accounted for 10.0% of total formal employment in 1995, a slight decrease from 1990.

TABLE 2. SELECTED NON-GOVERNMENT SECTORAL EMPLOYMENT, 1986–1993

SECTOR	1986 (MARCH)	1991 (MARCH)	CHANGE (%)	1993 (MARCH)	CHANGE (%)
Agriculture	4 900	6 700	36.7	5 900	−11.9
Mining and Quarrying	7 500	7 800	4.0	8 400	+7.7
Manufacturing	10 600	26 000	245.3	22 100	−15.0
Construction	12 000	33 000	281.7	28 300	−16.3
Commerce	20 000	41 000	201.0	40 700	−0.7
Finance and Business Services	7 300	16 100	220.5	16 800	+4.3
Community and Personal Services	3 800	8 600	226.3	8 200	−4.7

Source: Central Statistics Office.

4. CONSTRAINTS TO INDUSTRIAL DEVELOPMENT

Commonly cited constraints

Although Botswana has many positive features to its economy, and a range of incentives to attract investment, there are various constraints that continue to hamper the development of industry for employment creation and economic diversification. The major constraints facing the industrial sector include: the smallness of the domestic market, poor quality of products, lack of personnel with relevant managerial and technical skills, high wages in relation to productivity, lack of access to long-term finance (especially to small to medium scale manufacturers) and the high cost of utilities. Despite efforts by Government to accelerate the development of industrial and commercial sites, acute shortage of industrial land presents a constraint to existing and potential investors. Botswana is a land-locked country and is heavily dependent on South Africa for transporting the bulk of its products. Its remoteness from larger markets, such as Europe and the USA, results in high transport costs for trade with these areas. There are also some disadvantages posed by Botswana being a member of the SACU. Other constraints emanate from conflicting policy objectives, such as the Citizen Reservation Policy and the Revised National Policy on Education. These constraints are discussed below.

Smallness of domestic market

Botswana has a small population, estimated at 1.5 million people in 1996, and this acts as a disadvantage to manufacturers because it limits the size of their most immediate market. The economy is still developing, having started from a subsistence agricultural economy with few other income earning opportunities. The majority of the population (around 75%) still live outside formally established urban areas, i.e., towns and cities (although most of the traditional major villages in the rural areas are now semi-urbanised and classified as urban settlements for statistical purposes). The rural income base and the dispersed population reduces the purchasing power of people and hence limits opportunities to enjoy economies of scale.

Lack of serviced land

An acute shortage of serviced industrial plots and factory space has been cited as one of the major problems in slowing down, and inhibiting the establishment of manufacturing industries. The recent breakdown of computer systems set up to maintain a land register and maintain a land bank has left would be manufacturers stranded without land. The Trade and Investment Promotion Agency (TIPA) has not been successful in keeping a 'land bank' on behalf of investors. Due to manpower constraints, TIPA has not been able to channel all applications for land, together with supporting letters, and applications for other permits, licences and industrial incentives for processing by relevant ministries.

Geographical

Being a land-locked country has partially slowed down the development of industry because the cost of accessing distant markets is high. There is no direct access to sea ports, which results in high transportation costs, and a dependency on transit routes through South Africa for the transportation of bulk exports and imports. Road and rail transport is expensive, making some domestic products more expensive in some locations in Botswana than imports from South Africa, where local manufacturers source most of their raw materials and equipment. In short, the other advantages of locating in Botswana must be significant to overcome the geographical disadvantages confronting local producers. This constraint is, however, being eased by technological progress. For example, air transport is becoming increasingly economical; some firms in Selebi-Phikwe export to the USA by air.

Lack of entrepreneurial and technical skills

Industrial activities have not been established in Botswana for long enough to enable the emergence of adequate numbers of experienced citizen entrepreneurs who can run profitable businesses. Entrepreneurship is still developing in Botswana. Although the Government has, in the past, been engaged in the provision of education to Batswana, the education system has not been geared to satisfy the requirements of industry. The system was mainly aimed at educating the population up to the primary and secondary levels. There is, thus, currently a shortage of people equipped with the technical skills required in industry.

Technology

The majority of manufacturing companies in Botswana use simple technology in their production processes. The choice of technology is normally determined by the relative cost of capital and labour. In this sense, the relatively high cost of labour in Botswana has encouraged more capital intensive investment (although FAP has countered this by encouraging labour intensive production through the unskilled labour grant). Know-how and state of the art technology is normally expensive to acquire, especially by small-scale producers.

Limited access to finance impedes the acquisition of improved technology for increased production and improved productivity. Unavailability of funds leads to firms purchasing simple technology which might not necessarily be efficient. The acquisition of high/improved technology in production is also limited by the availability of locals with relevant technical skills and experience required by industry. Companies have to import people with the technical skills to meet their requirements; but this often adds quite a bit to the cost of doing business in Botswana. The maintenance and servicing of technology purchased from overseas is also a problem for most producers. The delays in obtaining spare parts from South Africa and overseas results in production losses, leading to manufacturers not being able to deliver orders according to schedule (although this can be largely be dealt with through proper planning).

There is a lack of a scientific environment and culture, and a lack of assistance and guidance in technology selection and acquisition. The Botswana Technology Centre, with the assistance of line ministries, such as the Ministry of Commerce and Industry (MCI), which were supposed to have taken the lead in this aspect, have not been able to play this role effectively.

Institutional

Investors have complained about the poor performance and effectiveness of some institutions created to facilitate investment. MCI has been criticised for exercising too much regulatory control on the establishment and operation of industries and trade through the Government's Industrial Development Policy. Investors have complained of burdensome regulatory procedures on trade and industry, such as the lengthy licensing process, which discourages productive investment and impedes expansion in exports. TIPA's poor performance in acting as one-stop service to investors and attracting foreign direct investment (FDI) has been noted previously. Investors have also complained of the lack of institutional support with respect to finance and the purchase or acquisition of technology.

High utility costs

Investors have also complained of the high cost of utilities, such as power, water and telecommunications, in Botswana. The high cost renders some of Botswana-produced goods expensive in the domestic, regional and international markets. But it must be accepted that the provision of some services in Botswana will continue to be relatively expensive, due to a small population spread over a wide area. The utility companies have been criticised for poor and slow service in connecting telephones, water and electricity to industry. Lack of a developed infrastructure in rural areas has also been blamed for very few industries being established there.

Once installed, however, the provision of utility services is good, with few (if any) occurrences of non-supply or breakdowns.

Specific problems facing small to medium-scale enterprises

Lack of access to capital

Limited access to long-term finance is one of the major impediments that hamper development of the manufacturing sector in Botswana. The problem is particularly acute for small-scale enterprises, who have not established banking relationships or do not have a business track record with commercial banks. Banks are reluctant to extend loans to projects where the viability is not clearly demonstrated through other supportive market studies and financial backing. Banks normally require borrowers to have collateral when applying for loans. Most local businesses lack the collateral, and this inhibits their access to finance to implement their projects and expansion plans. Enterprises located in rural areas and those owned by women (married women have to seek permission from husbands to apply for loans) are worse off due to limited access to finance and credit.

Many entrepreneurs, particularly small and medium-scale, continue to face financial difficulties. They are not able to finance their projects and implement their investment/expansion plans due to unavailability of finance. Some of the major contributory factors to poor cash flows experienced by companies are high utility costs and high costs of imported raw materials and machinery. Some of the problems peculiar to local investors are caused by the fact that profits accrued by the business are not reinvested into the firm to improve on quality and technology. The profits are instead spent on other projects not related to business, or for personal benefits such as building houses and buying vehicles for private use.

The findings of the several studies of large-scale firms investigated by Jefferis (1996) show that high utility costs or financial problems were not the major difficulties faced by the exporting firms in the sample survey. None of the firms saw this as a major constraint in Botswana. This, however, is not the case with citizen owned small and medium sized firms. Many firms have cited financial problems as the main reason for poor performance and lack of improvement in production and management techniques.

Poor quality of products

Manufactures products in Botswana have access to the SACU, SADC, European Union (EU) and other markets. Access to any of these markets is, however, limited by the sometimes poor quality of products from Botswana. The majority of firms in Botswana are small to medium-scale and are not able to undertake thorough market research and invest in technology improvement. Access to international markets is, therefore, limited by the fact that local companies are not able to meet the quality and specification requirements of international markets.

High cost of transport and lack of foreign exchange in some countries in the region

Manufacturing firms in Botswana have the opportunity to sell in the regional market. Access to international and overseas market is, however, limited by the high cost of transportation, insurance and poor communication systems existing in some countries in the region. The unavailability of foreign exchange in most of the countries in the region (and elsewhere in Africa) has also hindered local producers from selling in those markets. Some manufacturers have, in the past, attempted to export to countries, such as Zambia, Tanzania and Malawi, and have experienced delays in payment or not being paid at all due to shortages of foreign exchange. Some firms have attempted to use the exchange of goods for goods, but typically have not been successful in the long run. The Export Credit Insurance and Guarantee Company (Botswana) (Pty) Ltd was established in 1996 in order to protect exporters against the risk of not being paid for the commodities they have exported.

Shortage of raw materials and other inputs

Due to the unavailability of raw materials locally, the majority of firms are forced to import these, as well as machinery, equipment and other inputs, either from South Africa or the international market. This can render local products more expensive than imports of finished goods, although ultimately this depends upon whether such local production is relatively inefficient to begin with, and/or whether it is cheaper to transport finished products than to transport the inputs.

Fierce competition from imports

The local market is further limited by imports from South Africa, which are usually cheaper and of better quality. South Africa is a large country, with a relatively advanced and diversified industry, producing better quality goods at large economies of scale. Botswana companies have, in the past, attempted to sell to local chain stores such as Jet, Pep, Cash Bazaar, Metro, Cash Build, and others, and they have not been successful in penetrating the market, the reason being that the chain stores in Botswana are supplied from head offices in South Africa. The commodities are purchased from manufacturers in South Africa through contracts to specifically produce for the chain stores. Manufacturers in Botswana have and will be, therefore, always faced with problem of having to compete with imports, particularly imports from South Africa.

Specific problems facing large-scale firms

The three most prominent problems cited by large-scale export manufacturers were high interest rates, problems with immigration department for delays in the processing of applications for expatriate staff work permits, and duties charged on materials imported from outside SACU. Very few of the large-scale firms studied by Dr Jefferis complained about low productivity of unskilled labour in Botswana. Some of the companies in the survey complained that technical training outside the company is expensive. Off-the-job training also carries the risk for the employer that the employee will leave after successful completion of such training. Other firms have complained of a lack of Bureau of Standards for Botswana, although this is now being addressed.

Infant industry protection clause

The SACU has also influenced and affected the industrialization process of member countries. Botswana's Industrial Development Policy is designed to accommodate the customs agreement and its requirements. For example, the SACU Agreement has an infant industry tariff protection clause, which allows member countries to provide temporary protection and an exclusive license for new industries serving the local market. The objective of the tariff protection is to allow new industries to establish and grow without being displaced by imports.

The infant industry protection has rarely been used in Botswana. Under tariff protection, the cost of the protection is borne by the consumer, as opposed to the Financial Assistance Policy (FAP) where costs are more explicit and are borne by the Government. The conditions for protection are that the protected company should be able to sufficiently supply at least 75% of the domestic market. Producers should be able to reach and supply most parts of the country, the quality and price of products should be good and match that of imports. Imports of similar products are restricted for the protection period and any such imports are subject to duty.

The tariff is found to be useful as it changes the habits of consumers and retailers and encourages them to purchase locally produced goods. Botswana has used the protection provision on only two firms: the Kgalagadi Soap Industry (KSI) and the Kgalagadi Breweries Ltd. The two companies are still operating after the protection (although both have changed ownership) and are profitable and performing very well. They have increased the range of products and are competing well with imports of similar goods.

South Africa has served to obstruct industrialization efforts of some smaller SACU member states. For example, in the case of Botswana, a vehicle manufactured by Hyundai, which exports mainly to South Africa, is soon going to be paying duty of about 75% on semi knocked down (SKD) components imported from Korea. The move was mainly meant to discourage the plant from exporting to South Africa and become well established. Mainly because of Hyundai, exports of vehicles were the largest source of export growth (including diamonds) in the most part of 1996. It is aimed at rendering Hyundai vehicles more expensive to sell in South Africa, since the company is giving RSA motor manufacturers a bit of tough competition. Despite the above, the Hyundai plant has managed to meet all the conditions imposed on it by South Africa, including the latest pressure to adjust from a SKD operation to a completely knocked down (CKD) operation by the end of 1997.

Other conflicting policy objectives

There are other policy objectives which tend to conflict with the Industrial Development Policy and other measures established to foster rapid industrialization. These include; the Citizen Reservation Policy, the Incomes Policy and The Revised National Education Policy on Education.

Citizen Reservation Policy

The Citizen Reservation Policy was introduced in 1988 in order to promote active participation of citizens in industrial development. A number of industries that require relatively simple technological skills and low levels of capital were reserved for citizens. These simple activities are the production of ordinary bread, cement and baked bricks, school uniforms, protective clothing, burglar bars, school furniture, and milling of sorghum. Commercial activities reserved for citizens include: bottle stores, boutiques and liquor restaurants. The Citizen Reservation Policy is still under review.

The Reservation Policy prohibits foreign investors from participating in the activities reserved for citizens. The policy restricts partnership with foreign companies and thus conflicts with the aim of promoting entrepreneurship and acquisition of technical and management skills from foreign companies. If foreign companies were allowed to go into joint venture with Batswana, the quality of products would improve because of the capital and technical skills injected into the project. The restriction also limits citizens from having the opportunity to go into business with foreigners who have the necessary capital and know-how to ensure long-term investment and sustainability of business ventures.

The Revised National Policy on Education

The national policy on education has, in the past, concentrated on the education of the population up to the primary and secondary school levels, primarily to supply the general needs of Government, both Central and Local. The needs of the private sector and industry in particular were not a priority during that period. Botswana thus lacks human resources adequately trained with technical, science and business skills, and knowledge of modern industrial technology. The private sector has to import people with such qualifications, which often proves to be too costly for them. The Revised National Policy on Education aims to provide a strong programme in science and technology.

Wages and salaries

Wages in Botswana are said to be high compared to productivity (World Bank, 1993). This discourages firms from investing in Botswana. Instead they opt for other countries in the region where productivity is higher and wages are lower. The labour grant under FAP encourages firms to employ more in order to claim more for unskilled labour. This encourages labour intensive investment without relating it to output. However, recent investigations indicate that worker productivity may not be as bad as reported, and that it is not simply a problem of lack of skills. That productivity is affected by many factors including lack of loyalty to the companies, ineffective management, the choice of product, paying higher wages before productivity could justify them, crowded working conditions in some factories and workers going slow when supplies of raw materials run low to avoid being sent home without pay.

Income distribution

Botswana has been criticised for having experienced rapid economic growth and yet the distribution of income is still highly unequal. However, compared to other African countries in the region, income distribution in Botswana is not obviously highly unequal. Of countries where data is available, only Ghana has an apparently more equal distribution (Bank of Botswana, 1996). One of the aims of the Industrial Development policy is to promote social justice, in order to improve the quality of life and to enable all to share in the fruits of development. This would be achieved by creating income earning opportunities for the population. However, the number of those without jobs has been increasing. The situation has been aggravated by the 1992/93 economic slow-down, where unemployment is estimated to have increased from about 14% in 1991 to 21% in 1994. However, the 1993/94 Household Income and Expenditure study undertaken by the CSO indicate that income inequality has been slightly reduced in Botswana over the period since 1985/86, particularly in rural areas. According to the United Nations Human Development Report of 1996, Botswana has been performing well in terms of the Human Development Index (HDI) measure (a measure developed by the UNDP as an indicator of a country's social progress, incorporating measures additional to income levels). In 1992, the average for Sub-Saharan Africa was 0.389 compared to 0.763 for Botswana, ranking Botswana third in the region after Mauritius and Seychelles, respectively (Bank of Botswana, 1996).

5. GOVERNMENT POLICIES TO OVERCOME CONSTRAINTS

Industrial Development Policy and Act

The Industrial Development Act of 1968 has been the main instrument of controlling industrial development in Botswana since Independence. The Industrial Development Policy was introduced in 1984 to accelerate the industrialization process in Botswana. Its primary objectives included:

- the creation of productive jobs for citizens;
- the training of citizens for jobs with higher productivity;
- the diversification of the productive sectors of the economy and consequent reduction in vulnerability to economic factors beyond Botswana's control;
- the growth of value added, or GDP, accruing in Botswana to Batswana; and
- the dispersion of industrial activities to rural areas.

At the time of writing, the Industrial Development Policy was under review to accommodate several developments which have occurred since it was introduced in 1984. The Policy was last reviewed in 1988. Of the changes which have occurred, one of the most important has been the political changes in the region, mainly the democratization of South Africa, Botswana's main trading partner. As a result, the regional economy has also changed, with increased opportunities for economic cooperation and investment. Botswana is, therefore, reviewing the prevailing Industrial Development Policy and incentive schemes in order to eliminate limitations posed by the existing ones. The revised Industrial Development Policy aims at creating an attractive environment for encouraging foreign direct investment. The Policy is also aimed at accommodating changes which would occur as a result of the review of SACU.

The Industrial Development Act was introduced in 1968, amended in 1988 and revised in 1995 (following the Revised Incomes Policy of 1990). Changes made to the Act in 1995 involved automatic granting of licenses. Licensing authorities are no longer allowed to make commercial judgements on applications. The changes also led to the elimination of objections by competitors.

Various institutions and organizations were established by the Government to formulate and coordinate the Industrial Development Policy and promote industrial development. MCI is the main arm of Government responsible for the formulation and implementation of the Industrial Development Policy and the Act, including the Trade Act and various industrial incentives.

MCI also houses the Integrated Field Services (IFS) section, which is mainly responsible for assisting small-scale entrepreneurs with business advisory services, including training in management and technical skills. Additional support, such as training, marketing and the provision of factory space, is extended to manufacturers. Special assistance is also given to small-scale, informal and rural enterprises in order to balance and direct industrialization to both rural and urban centres

TIPA, under MCI, was created for the dissemination of information to a wider audience and to promoting investment and trade locally and abroad. It has regularly been agreed that this role should be expanded to include facilitation. TIPA is being restructured to better serve investors.

The Government has also amended the Botswana Telecommunications Bill to abolish the Botswana Telecommunications Corporation's monopoly position and to provide for the licensing of others to provide such services in Botswana. It is hoped that this will alleviate the problem of investors and the public having to wait '1–2 years for a telephone' (Bank of Botswana, 1996). More widely, it is a significant step in allowing the private sector to participate in areas previously monopolised by Government and parastatals. Further moves of this sort are likely to be a feature of NDP 8, which commences in 1997.

Financial Assistance Policy

The FAP was introduced in 1982, to assist and support new and expanding projects that create productive employment. Financial assistance comes in the form of capital, unskilled labour and training grants (and a sales augmentation grant in the past) limited to five years. The grants are available to small (restricted to citizens), medium and large-scale businesses. They are principally for manufacturing ventures, although the extension to tourism in 1996 was an important recent development. Evaluations of the FAP programme were undertaken in 1984, 1988 and 1995. The 1995 FAP Evaluation study concluded that the incentive has stimulated investment and employment generation for unskilled citizen employees in a fairly effective manner. The objective of encouraging citizen participation in business seems also to have been achieved, in that most of the companies (mainly small and medium scale) receiving approvals were purely citizen owned. There has also been considerable diversification of economic activity (see Table 6). Locals have also gained some business and technical experience during the process. There have been some spin-off effects in the service and informal sectors. Exports of non-traditional products has increased over the last few years.

Local Preference Scheme

The Local Preference Scheme (LPS) was introduced in 1976 and modified in 1986, in order to direct a substantial share of the purchases of Government, local authorities and parastatals to local manufacturers. The scheme is aimed at increasing production in Botswana and encouraging the use of local raw materials and labour in manufacturing. The firms which qualify for LPS are allowed a price advantage over foreign produced goods when tendering for Government contracts. The price advantage is based on an assessment of the local content in production. The LPS was reviewed in 1994 to assess its impact and effectiveness. The LPS has been replaced by a new policy, the Local Procurement Policy (LPP), effective from 1 April 1997.

Selebi-Phikwe Regional Development Project

The Selebi-Phikwe Regional Development Project (SPRDP) was introduced in 1988 to encourage investment in non-mining economic activity in the Selebi-Phikwe area. This was in order to promote regional diversification and sustainability beyond the life of the copper-nickel mine which supported the growth of the town. Financial assistance is extended to industrial projects locating in Selebi-Phikwe and meeting certain other conditions. However, with the reduction of company tax on manufacturing to 15%, the financial incentives provided under the SPRDP have effectively been extended to the whole country.

The SPRDP was evaluated in 1992, and the results of the review were that the location has several disadvantages which provide a disincentive for investment there. The SPRDP has now been terminated and absorbed into TIPA, as financing from the World Bank loan has been used up.

The performance of the textile and clothing sub-sector has also improved, as evident by the increase in the number of firms established in Selebi-Phikwe, particularly since 1995. The number has increased, with a significant increase in the number of jobs created. 'Between 1988 and 1993, the SPRDP looked as if it would not create a net benefit for Botswana, because the main benefits were insufficient to off-set the cost of attracting investment to Botswana. The situation, however, changed in 1995' (Cowan, in this Volume). In the paper the author concludes that the SPRDP has started to generate significant benefits to Botswana, which may in time outweigh the costs. The project has created about 500 jobs per year between 1988 and 1994. About 4000 were created in 1995 alone. He further notes, however, that there is the problem of companies sustaining jobs beyond the FAP pay-out period.

A very public example is SportsLine (Pty) Ltd, which closed down early in 1996 after receiving FAP. However, more detailed analysis suggests that these cases are the result of problems specific to the companies concerned, rather than the incentives themselves. Apart from SportsLine, some of the above developments are encouraging as they are an indication of the partial success of the efforts by Government to diversify the economy away from the mining and beef sectors. It also shows that the manufacturing sector has some potential to lead to economic growth in the future. As shown in Table 4, there was a significant increase in the number of citizens operating in the reserved activities of textiles, wood and wooden products, metal products and building materials between 1985 and 1991. This indicates the growth of local entrepreneurship in the reserved areas. It is worth mentioning that most of the business in the reserved areas are located in rural areas, thus fulfilling the Industrial Development Policy objective of dispersion of industrial activities to rural areas.

TABLE 3. MEDIUM AND LARGE-SCALE APPROVALS BY CITIZENSHIP

OWNERSHIP OF COMPANY	NO. OF FIRMS	PROJECTED EMPLOYMENT	AVERAGE PROJECTED EMPLOYEES PER COMPANY	TOTAL APPROVED GRANTS (PULA MILLION)	AVERAGE APPROVED GRANTS PER COMPANY (PULA '000)	AVERAGE APPROVED GRANT PER EMPLOYEE (PULA)
CITIZEN	374	12 345	33	101	270	8 200
JOINT VENTURE	130	6 626	51	41	315	6 200
NON-CITIZEN	259	18 950	73	79	305	4 200
TOTAL	773	37 921	147	221	285	5 828

Note: only about 54% of approvals proceed to disbursements. The other 46% fail to take up FAP because they cannot satisfy conditions set for receiving grants or the venture never proceeds to the implementation stage.

Source: 1995 FAP Evaluation Report.

Participation in trade fairs

Other current efforts in assisting local manufacturers to look beyond the domestic market include assistance to participate in local and international trade fairs. Some firms have succeeded in securing local and international orders through the fairs, while others have failed. Some of the local manufacturers, particularly citizen-owned, have failed to supply orders secured during the fair. Customers have complained that consignments sent are sometimes not of similar quality as the items displayed at the fair. This has led to either rejection of orders by the customers or no additional orders placed. The same investors also tend to expect continued financial support from the Government to enable them participate in the fairs. This again reflects the general inexperience of entrepreneurs in Botswana.

TABLE 4. PROFILE OF THE FORMAL MANUFACTURING SECTOR: NEW MANUFACTURING LICENCES ISSUED (1985 TO 1992)

PRODUCT GROUP	CITIZEN OWNED	ESTIMATED EMPLOYMENT	JOINT VENTURES	ESTIMATED EMPLOYMENT	FOREIGN OWNED	ESTIMATED EMPLOYMENT
MEAT	4	218	0	0	2	85
AGRO	42	1 046	27	845	37	1 552
BEVERAGE	0	0	5	591	3	216
TEXTILES	19	602	32	885	44	1 236
LEATHER	2	218	3	100	5	440
CHEMICAL	4	139	23	721	33	1 134
WOOD	12	647	9	238	17	508
PAPER	9	222	6	63	13	323
METAL	43	1 151	21	801	40	1 482
BUILDING	50	2 358	14	576	15	850
PLASTIC	6	178	16	933	8	480
ELECTRICAL	6	282	9	512	11	1 096
H/CRAFT	1	234	3	28	3	1 047
TOTALS	198	7 295	168	6 293	231	11 649

Source: Department of Industrial Affairs, Ministry of Commerce and Industry.

Development of appropriate technology

Institutions established by the Government to assist companies with the selection, acquisition and the development of appropriate technology have had some successes. The Rural Industries Innovation Centre (RIIC) has been successful in the development and adaptation of dehullers for use in the milling of sorghum and baking ovens for use in rural areas. RIIC has recently developed a manually operated washing machine, which is affordable and easy to operate and use. The washing machine was displayed during the 1996 International Trade Fair in Gaborone, for consumers to view and appreciate. The Botswana Technology Centre has been involved in the development and use of solar energy in Botswana.

Development of a science and technology policy for Botswana

Botswana is in the process of developing a Science and Technology Policy, aimed at redressing the some of the shortcomings in technology acquisition and development. The core policy objective is 'to establish and strengthen national capacity to research, evaluate, select, acquire, adapt, develop, generate, apply and disseminate suitable technologies in order to realise national socio-economic objectives'. Government has accepted the importance of the Policy, although the details, especially the financial implications have yet to be concluded.

Promotion of non-traditional exports

The partial fulfilment of the industrial development efforts by the Government can be seen in the improvements in the export of non-traditional products, which constitutes all exports other than diamonds, beef and copper-nickel. Non-traditional exports include principally, textiles and clothing, soda ash, foodstuffs and motor vehicles. They have increased from P290 million in 1992 to P700 million in 1994, increasing their share of total exports from less than 10% in 1992 to about 20% in 1995. As indicated in the 1995 Barclays Botswana Economic Review, most of the increase was

TABLE 5. PERFORMANCE OF NON-TRADITIONAL EXPORTS (PULA MILLION)

YEAR	VEGETABLE PRODUCTS	CHEMICAL PRODUCTS	FOOD AND BEVERAGE PRODUCTS	VEHICLES & OTHER RELATED PRODUCTS	WOOD PRODUCTS	FOOTWEAR PRODUCTS	TEXTILES
1987	2.9	16.9	27.0	39.3	2.3	4.5	71.8
1988	3.7	16.7	9.5	51.7	2.2	7.5	74.9
1989	2.5	19.8	25.4	74.3	3.2	9.9	104.5
1990	12.1	18.5	34.6	60.0	2.5	19.4	155.5
1991	14.0	45.8	46.7	57.1	4.6	12.2	168.5
1992	13.4	72.9	47.8	70.9	5.4	14.7	102.0
1993	13.1	79.6	51.3	128.7	1.8	9.5	1 28.7
1994	14.4	63.0	62.2	406.7	1.5	8.4	234.3

Source: CSO, External Trade Statistics.

accounted for by the rapidly rising exports of motor vehicles. The vehicle industry has contributed greatly to the increase in the export of non-traditional products. Vehicle exports increased from P91 million in 1994 to P300 million in 1995. The growth appears to have sustained itself in the first half of 1996. It has also changed the structure of non-traditional exports for Botswana. These exports are destined for South Africa.

Import substitution production

The production and processing of agro-based products, such as dairy, poultry, horticulture and pig rearing, has also increased. These products are geared for the domestic market (import substitution), which has been dominated by imports mainly from South Africa. Employment in beverage and soap production has also increased since 1985. The beverage and the soap producers benefited from the protection provided under the SACU Agreement, which they enjoyed for eight years. The metal (school furniture), school uniforms and protective clothing industries increased partly because of FAP and the Citizen Reservation Policy. These products are, to a greater extent, produced mostly for the domestic market, although some of the firms also export.

Reduction of income tax for manufacturing

Government has reduced the company tax rate from 40% to 35% and then to 25%, with a lower rate of 15% for manufacturing in order to ameliorate the financial burden of taxes and boost the cash flow position and profitability of firms. The reduction in tax is also expected to enhance Botswana's incentives for domestic and foreign investment and improve the country's competitiveness in the region. It is too early to judge whether this incentive has had the desired effect.

6. LESSONS FROM OTHER COUNTRIES

SADC

Botswana does not have much to learn from the SADC countries due to the countries' differences in macroeconomic outlook and investment promotion policies, with the exception of Mauritius (see below). Most of the SADC countries (e.g., Zimbabwe, Zambia, Mozambique and Lesotho), have investment promotion policies which are geared towards increased foreign exchange earnings, while Botswana aims for economic diversification and employment creation. These countries offer tax deductions and lengthy tax holidays, which are costly, import duty exemptions, subsidised labour and both land and credit at concessionary rates. However, Botswana can learn from the experiences of South Africa and Zimbabwe in the development of the tourism and service sectors.

Mauritius

Mauritius might have more to offer to Botswana, in terms of experience sharing. The country's economy has undergone similar experiences of rapid economic growth and development, but which also entailed substantial economic diversification and employment growth. The Mauritian economy is an open and outward looking economy, and its policies encourage investment by offering various incentive schemes. Mauritius has been successful in establishing Export Processing Zones (EPZs), a success story from which Botswana can learn. However, recent research (Cowan and Phetwe, 1997) indicates that Botswana does not need to establish EPZ. What the country needs is a liberal economic environment country-wide (which partially already exists) to allow investors to choose to locate anywhere in the country. Botswana can also learn from the Mauritius Export Development and Investment Authority, which has been very successful in attracting foreign trade and investment.

East Asia

It was apparent from a seminar recently held in Gaborone on *Southern Africa and East Asia: Experiences and Opportunities in Development*, that Botswana can learn from the East Asian countries' experiences. The East Asian countries have, in the last few decades, adopted outward looking and market oriented development strategies. They have maintained realistic and stable exchange rates, have efficient labour, are politically stable, have favourable investment environments and have been successful in attracting foreign direct investment through innovative schemes.

Botswana has maintained a somewhat similar macroeconomic environment, as well as policies and strategies similar to some of the East Asian countries. Botswana has been successful in some areas of economic growth and development, while it has lagged behind in others. Botswana can learn from the East Asian experience in the areas of: further liberalization of exchange controls; development of the financial sector; inducement of domestic savings; development of local entrepreneurship through joint ventures and on the job training; targeting and encouraging development of specific industries; encouraging commercial education; reducing Government control and regulation; and developing private sector initiatives.

7. Conclusions

The manufacturing sector has, in the period under review, experienced both rapid growth and periods of decline. The growth of the sector has been enhanced by some of the policies aimed at developing the sector. Botswana's political stability and sound macroeconomic policies have also contributed to the growth of the manufacturing sector. The sector has, however, been faced with many constraints which have hampered its further development. Particularly prominent are the problems of a shortage of serviced industrial land, the smallness of the domestic market, a lack of industrial culture, burdensome Government regulations and the fact that Botswana is a landlocked country.

Botswana must build on her existing advantages, which are political stability, liberal exchange controls and generous investment incentive schemes. The revised Industrial Development Policy addresses the prevailing constraints with a view to minimising them. Efforts should be made to address the acute shortage of industrial land in Botswana.

The Government should continue to support and encourage citizen participation in industry and encourage joint ventures with foreign investors for the acquisition of technical and managerial skills, an improvement in the quality of products and services and the termination of reserved activities.

The new developments in the regional and international economy are opening market opportunities for local manufacturers. Botswana exporters of manufactured goods should be encouraged to identify new markets in Europe and the USA, with a view to moving away from dependency on just one market. Lessons from the past have shown that it is economically risky to rely on just one major export market; Zimbabwe in the past, South Africa in the future. The revised Industrial Development Policy should take account of the many existing constraints to further development with a view to relaxing or removing them.

REFERENCES

Bank of Botswana. *Annual Report, 1993, 1994* and *1995*. Bank of Botswana, Gaborone.

Bank of Botswana. *Botswana Financial Statistics*, Various issues. Bank of Botswana, Gaborone.

Botswana Confederation of Commerce, Industry and Manpower. 1995. Industry Survey 1994, BOCCIM, Gaborone.

Harvey, C. and Lewis, S.R. 1990. *Policy Choice and Development Performance in Botswana*. Macmillan Press, London.

Cowan, D. and Phetwe, M. 1997. 'Export Processing Zones: Does the Mauritian Experience Provide Lessons for Botswana's Efforts to Diversify Exports and Boost Employment?' *The Research Bulletin*, Vol.15, No.1. Bank of Botswana, Gaborone.

Government of Botswana. 1991. *National Development Plan 7*. Government of Botswana, Gaborone.

Government of Botswana. October 1984. *Industrial Development Policy*, Government Paper No.2 of 1984. Government Printer, Gaborone.

Government of Botswana. 1988. *Industrial Development Act*, Government Paper No.2 of 1988. Government Printer, Gaborone.

Government of Botswana. September 1990. *The Revised National Policy on Incomes, Employment, Prices and Profits*, Government Paper No of 1990, Government Printer, Gaborone.

Jefferis, K.R. 1995. 'The Economy in 1994', *Barclays Botswana Economic Review*.

Jefferis, K.R. 1997. 'The Characteristics of Successful Manufacturing Exports: Botswana's Experience', *The Research Bulletin*, Vol.15, No.1. Bank of Botswana, Gaborone.

Phaleng Consultancies. 1995. *The Third Evaluation of the Financial Assistance Policy (FAP)*. Prepared for the Government of Botswana, Ministry of Finance and Development Planning. Government Printer, Gaborone.

Riddell, R.C. 1990. *Manufacturing Africa: Performance and Prospects of Seven Countries in Sub-Saharan Africa*. Overseas Development Institute, London.

Salkin, J.S. 1994. 'The Economy in 1993', *Barclays Botswana Economic Review*, Vol.5, No.1.

Shah, S. and Toye, J. 1978. 'Fiscal Incentives for Firms in Some Developing Countries: A Survey and Critique'. In: Toye, J. (ed.), *Taxation and Economic Development*. Frank Cass, London.

Todaro, M. 1992. *Economics for a Developing World*. Longman Group, United Kingdom.

Whiteside, A.W. 1986b. 'A Summary of Incentives Available in the Southern African States'. In: Whiteside (ed.), *Industrialization and Investment Incentives in Southern Africa*. James Currey, London.

World Bank. 1989. *Botswana: Financial Policies for Diversified Growth*. World Bank, Washington.

World Bank. 1993. *Opportunities for Industrial Development in Botswana, An Economy in Transition*. World Bank, Washington.

Review of the Initial Objectives and Rationale of FAP[1]

Jeremy A. Peat

1. INTRODUCTION

The concept of a Financial Assistance Policy was developed at the beginning of the 1980s. Perhaps the true genesis of the idea that some scheme to subsidise productive activities was justified was the report on *Employment and Labour Use in Botswana* by Michael Lipton.[2] Indeed it was as a result of Michael Lipton's work and report that an Employment Policy Unit (EPU) was established, and the author of this paper was recruited to act as the first head of that unit. The head of the EPU was, initially to be Human Resources Monitor, but this was changed to the less prefectorial 'Employment Co-ordinator'.

Lipton's broad conclusion was that high levels of unemployment were likely in Botswana during the 1980s and 1990s, unless a wide variety of major policy adjustments could be introduced to attack demand and supply side problems. Lipton anticipated that the problems of rural unemployment, in part to be caused by population growth and the lack of agricultural employment possibilities, but also due to an anticipated decline in mining employment opportunities outside Botswana, would lead to urban drift on a substantial scale. Thus there would be economic and social problems in both rural and urban areas. Urgent and tough actions were required, across a broad front.

This is not the place to detail the variety of policy initiatives which Lipton proposed, nor indeed to detail the policy initiatives considered and implemented by the Government of Botswana. But a few examples should be noted, as exemplifications of the consideration given to a raft of policies and as they relate to some of the aspects of FAP objectives which will be discussed later.

- In the rural areas attempts were made to promote productive employment and income generating activities in both traditional agriculture (e.g., via the Arable Lands Development Programme – or ALDEP), and non-traditional rural industries (e.g., via the Rural Industrial Officer programme). In rural and urban areas

---

[1] In this paper I have attempted to provide an objective assessment. But I was Secretary to the Subsidies Policy Working Group and heavily involved – with the likes of Ken Matambo and Stephen Lewis – in the FAP design; and also as Employment Coordinator responsible for initial FAP implementation.

[2] Lipton, M. *Employment and Labour Use in Botswana*. For FAP *per se* the huge intellectual influence of Professor Stephen Lewis, Economic Consultant to the Minister of Finance and Development Planning, should also be acknowledged from the outset.

the Ministry of Local Government and Lands attempted via the planning system to provide serviced plots and factory shells for entrepreneurs to utilise.

- The wages policy was retained and in some instances strengthened. Via this policy attempts were made to damp down wage pressures in the high value/high productivity sectors of the economy. The objective of this approach was to avoid demand for labour elsewhere being unduly constrained by a generally high level of wages throughout the formal sector. At the same time efforts were made to constrain the increases in minimum wages in real terms, for similar reasons.

- An active manpower planning system was established, on the clear understanding that an increase in both the broad skills base and the availability of specific skills was required to maximise employment prospects from both domestic and inward investment.

But by 1980 it had been determined that these initiatives on their own were not going to be sufficient to deal with the anticipated unemployment problems. This judgement, coupled with macroeconomic and financial forecasts anticipating some budgetary slack, at least in the short to medium term, resulted in the creation of a high-powered and multi-dimensional[3] group, termed initially the Subsidies Policy Working Group, to bring forward to Cabinet recommendations on the use of financial inducements to generate additional productive activities and hence additional employment opportunities.

2. FAP OBJECTIVES – ENDS AND MEANS

As should be clear from the above, additional employment, via additional productive activities, was the key objective of the search for a subsidy policy. But there were other factors which the group had to bear in mind. First, there was a preference for the maintenance of a solid, viable, rural population. Hence it was determined at an early stage that the incentives for Batswana to remain in rural areas should be greater than the norm in the new policy. Second, diversification away from cattle and minerals was seen as essential for a stable and growing economy in the longer term. This objective was fully consistent with the key productive employment objective. In FAP these sectors (cattle and minerals) were excluded, except small-scale mining.

There were three further related objectives which merit a mention. First, there was a preference for the production of goods for export or import substitution. Second, there was seen to be specific benefit in the upgrading of citizen skill levels through training. Third, priority was to be given to the promotion of active citizen ownership of economic ventures, in particular (at least at the smaller end of the spectrum) females and owner-operators in the rural areas.

It is always difficult to categorise objectives, but I would suggest that the emphasis on employment generation, economic diversification and traded goods combined to give the *key framework of economic ends.* The rural bias, along with priority for citizens,

---

3   The Working Group included policy advisers, practical economists with experience of implementing assistance programmes and academics. Part of the success of the FAP which emerged was due to this composition and that it was realised that there had to be trade-offs between the academically perfect, the politically desirable and the doable.

women[4] and owner-operation can be seen as *socio-political ends* – albeit to achieve these ends the ventures would have to be viable in the post-FAP period. But the Government was prepared to provide a higher degree of assistance for rural, citizen-owned businesses, thus exemplifying the existence of a secondary objective.

The skills emphasis looks to be *more of a means to an end than an end in itself* – albeit that skills enhancement can be seen to bring social as well as economic benefits. From this stage I shall focus on the economic rather than social objectives. I characterise the former as 'efficiency' and the latter as 'equity'. My chosen focus does not imply that efficiency ends are somehow *better* than equity. I accept that both are essential components of a policy framework. However, as an economist – and an expatriate – my expertise applies more on the economic and efficiency front. (To clarify, I should make explicit my view that expatriates may be less well placed to advise on equity based trade-offs than what is desirable on 'technical' efficiency grounds.)

Having clarified the ends, the obvious next question relates to means. There are various strands here which need to be differentiated. Consider first *the economic justification for intervention in the market.* Given appropriate market circumstances, the most efficient economic outcome will arise from the interaction of market forces. However, this is contingent upon the assumption of perfect competition in all markets; that market prices accurately reflect economic costs and benefits; and a non-distorted decision-making context – the all-knowing invisible hand or auctioneer who automatically optimises the allocation of scarce resources. Even in larger and more fully evolved economies these assumptions do not apply fully. Hence the range of intervention policies which remain in such countries.[5] In Botswana in 1980, it was evident that the perfect market assumption was not valid. Therefore, it was agreed that two justifications for intervention, based on efficiency arguments, were as follows.

- *To correct market prices*, where these were out of line with opportunity costs. Without such correction decision makers will be basing their decisions on the 'wrong' prices and decision-making may be rational – given the information available – but incorrect so far as economic optimization is concerned. A classic example in this context is unskilled wages. For various reasons (most obviously because of minimum wages) the going unskilled wage rate may be very much higher than the output foregone from employing an additional unskilled worker. It may be deemed appropriate that the unskilled workers should receive this higher wage; but that economic decision-makers should (by means of a subsidy) base their decisions on a much lower cost of unskilled labour – more akin to the opportunity cost.

- *To capture benefits or compensate for costs*, which may not accrue directly to the individual enterprise, but rather to the economy as a whole. Here the classic example is training. Some training is specific to a company or industry, but a majority is more of a general nature, i.e. of value to the trainee in a variety of

---

[4]   The issue of female ownership is a good example of how an idea, which is good in principle, has proved problematic. There is certainly a concern that 'fronting' by nominal female owners is a problem in such projects.

[5]   The subsidies which remain within the European Union are not perfect examples of this discussion. Thus the Common Agricultural Policy does not follow market prices, and there has not yet been an end to protective subsidies in some other industries. Also there are a range of regional programmes, whose objectives are more equity than efficiency based.

potential jobs within the domestic labour force. If training is left to individual employers they will tend to under-invest in anything other than training specific to their company or plant. There are means by which companies in the same sector can be encouraged to make appropriate training decisions for their industries[6], but for training which has even wider potential uses, the optimal approach tends to be some mixture of payment by government and the individual.[7]

An additional, and conceptually different, economic argument for intervention was that of 'infant industries'. Thus it was suggested that new industries in developing countries, such as Botswana, are exposed to a range of start up problems, which lead to low profitability and vulnerability to cash flow problems. Under this argument there may be nothing wrong with the competitive framework for decision-making, or there may be an inappropriate myopia in that decision-making. The usual instance is that leaving the market alone is deemed to fail to generate the type of new industry that planners wish or see as appropriate for the next stage of an economy's progression. The theoretical argument for infant industry support generally rests upon some imperfection in the capital markets. Due to non-availability of finance, or inappropriate funding structures for such capital as is available, the long-term viability of the project does not translate into an adequate availability of the required type of funds in the short term.[8]

The infant industry argument can be highly dangerous and has in some countries been used as a rationale for support to industries which have little chance of becoming competitive within any reasonable time span. Also it is extremely difficult to make judgements as to which activities have the potential to evolve out of their nappies into 'house-trained', competitive and thriving businesses. The argument needed to be handled with care.

Lying underneath a good deal of the analysis undertaken at the time FAP was developed was concern about the development of a dual economy within Botswana. Thus there was a highly successful diamond industry and a thriving public sector – largely as a result of diamond revenues. There was also a thriving – and well supported – cattle sector. The overall macro economy, balance of payments and public finances were in good health. Two results were a high exchange rate and high wages.

A strong Pula made sense in macro terms, but acted as a distinct impediment to the creation of exporting and import-substituting industries. Another 'problem' was the degree of competition, not always 'fair' in economic terms, from the Republic of

---

[6] One example is the grant/levy system used by Industrial Training Boards in the United Kingdom in the 1970s.

[7] The more that the benefits flow to trainees as enhanced income, and the less constraints there are on individuals financing their own training, the more that they should, conceptually, pay for their own training. Where wage differentials do not fully reflect training-induced efficiency gains and/or the cost of personal credit is markedly higher than the cost of Government borrowing (or availability constrained), then Government finance tends to be appropriate.

[8] One specific infant industry case is where there are learning effects, which might lead to efficient activities being generated, but which are underestimated by the capital markets. Hence, what could be efficient industries are not financed, as 'externalities' are not wholly allowed for. Nevertheless, I still believe that this infant industries argument is conceptually different from other externalities-based arguments for intervention.

South Africa and at times Zimbabwe. A weaker Pula might well have been seen as appropriate for the rest of the economy, traditional agrarian agriculture, new rural businesses and new manufacturing and service sector activities. To some extent the infant industry argument can be seen as having been used in lieu of full admission that a dual exchange rate regime was desirable for the key economic objectives addressed by FAP. The FAP instruments developed on the back of the infant industry argument[9] could equally have been justified on the grounds that the exchange rate was too high.

A tendency to relatively high wages flowed from the success of diamonds and the relative strength of the public finances. Partially in the interests of cross-sector equity, the minimum wage for other sectors was set well above opportunity costs, if not far from the lower end of diamond and Government wage scales. This difficulty was straightforward to deal with via the justification of correcting market prices, and an unskilled labour subsidy.

The Subsidies Policy Working Group grappled with all these issues, and came up with two main elements of the approach to FAP, which were described as follows in the White Paper.[10]

- 'First, Government funds should only be used to support those new ventures (or expansion of existing ventures) where we could reasonably expect the benefits to Botswana, in terms of new incomes and new jobs created, to outweigh the costs of assistance or grants. There are elaborate ways of making the analysis for some projects, but the basic idea is simple and important; we should not simply give away money without having a good chance of creating new and productive jobs.
- Second, the assistance from Government should be temporary, that is, should only last for at most five years. By adopting this approach, there is a better chance of new developments being viable on their own, and even contributing to tax revenues. If we did not have a system to stop the assistance to new ventures after some time, we would quickly come to a point where we did not have enough money to help any more businesses or individuals, and no more new projects could be assisted.'

It would be close to impossible to argue with the first of these two policy tenets. All policies and programmes should pass some cost-effectiveness test – value for money will always be a key requirement. Unfortunately, measuring value for money for FAP or other industrial assistance type schemes is always problematic – as we discovered in the latest FAP evaluation.[11] Cost-effectiveness, or a positive cost-benefit balance can never be proven, it must always in these instances be a matter of judgement.

What of the second tenet? Why should assistance be time-limited? Under the infant industry argument the rational appears clear. Short-term assistance makes sense, generally justified on the capital market imperfection grounds discussed above. Continuing support of uncompetitive industry cannot be expected from the financial

---

[9]   The Sales Augmentation Grant and the Capital Grant are the major examples.

[10] Government Paper No. 1 of 1982.

[11] *The Third Evaluation of the Financial Assistance Policy (FAP).* Phaleng Consultants report to the Ministry of Finance and Development Planning, January 1995.

sector[12], and can only be justified on market failure or market distortion rather than infant industry grounds. But the first two means objectives discussed above were grounded on market distortions. What if unskilled wages after five years were still above opportunity costs? Why should the subsidy – the market correction – end? What if training would be sub-optimal without subsidy? Why not continue to support means of appropriately adding to the skills of the Batswana labour force?

These are difficult and complex arguments, but on balance I come to different conclusions in the two cases. On the wage front, I would first suggest that over a five year period even those at the bottom of the skill profile in different plants should become less than wholly unskilled. Their productivity should have increased markedly over that period. Some will leave and need to be replaced, but with a mature plant there should be means by which basic skills should be rapidly acquired and hence productivity enhanced. In other words the opportunity costs should have increased to at least close to the going market wage – even if that is distorted by minimum wages and high wages in other sectors. I would also argue that if a policy which creates price distortions is maintained for a number of years, despite the knowledge of that distortion, then a decision has *de facto* been made that markets should act as if that distorted price was the true economic price. The grounds for intervention become increasingly tenuous.

For training, however, the issue is not a distortion, but a market imperfection that can only be corrected by price intervention. The standard means of optimising is by government subsidy for specified general skills. This is the economic foundation for free universal secondary education. Certainly the costs should increasingly fall on the trainees where they capture the financial benefits and have access to the means of payment. But some government intervention and subsidy looks essential on a continuing basis. Indeed ideally training assistance would not have been part of FAP, but a specific and broader government scheme. A training grant under FAP was very much second best – but preferable to no training assistance.

One further element of the design of FAP which merits reference at this stage is that the various elements of assistance were provided in grant form. Theoretically loan or equity finance would have been preferable, e.g., if the infant industry argument was used to justify government funds being made available to replace those which 'should' have been made available via the financial sector. The decision to found FAP on grants was based upon practical thinking rather than theoretical niceties. Thus grants were far easier to administer than loans or equity, and it was determined from the outset that administrative costs should be minimised.[13] Furthermore, grants were seen as more appealing to potential investors – citizen and non-citizen – and it was recognised that any loan has a 'grant-equivalent' level, i.e., there is nothing conceptually different between grants and loans. There are conceptual differences between grants and equity, but other bodies, such as the Botswana Development Corporation, already existed to provide equity finance.

---

[12] I accept that there may be instances of the continuing failure of the financial institutions to provide appropriate finance causing this lack of competitiveness, but would argue that the funding problem is more often due to lack of confidence in initiatives at the start up stage.

[13] A decision certainly justified by subsequent experience. The resources devoted to managing FAP – appraisal, record keeping, basic monitoring, evaluation, etc. – were minimal.

3. THE APPROACH TO COST-EFFECTIVENESS

I have indicated above that decisions on the cost-benefit position of programmes such as FAP must always be judgements rather than statistically secure certainties. But there are means by which it is possible *ex ante* to lay down ground rules which make cost-benefit success more likely. In brief these may be summarised in the following terms.

- So far as possible, make adjustments so that financial costs and benefits facing the decision-maker equate to economic costs and benefits, and hence the decision-making process will tend to optimise.
- Maximise the 'additionality', i.e., the extent to which activities supported by FAP would not have happened without FAP, and the support provided approximates to the minimum necessary.
- Minimise 'displacement', i.e., the extent to which FAP supported activities compete with and tend to displace the output of existing – supported or non-supported – activities.
- Maximise *linkages, external benefits,* and other *positive externalities,* i.e., the extent to which there are other economic benefits for Botswana resulting from FAP supported activities.
- Maximise 'survival rates', i.e., minimise company failure during the support period and thereafter.

In the above section I have discussed the extent to which FAP grants tended to be justified on the grounds of differences between financial costs and opportunity costs. Where this was the case the first of the above conditions tended to be satisfied.

So far as additionality is concerned, there are always problems satisfying this condition. Essentially the perfect project is one which is not financially viable without support, but does satisfy economic cost-benefit tests, and is financially viable with FAP, during the support phase – and without thereafter! For the implementation of FAP, software programmes were written on spreadsheets to undertake economic and financial cost-benefit analyses. Thus in the proposals put forward to the decision-making committees a judgement was made on this issue of whether support was required to generate economically viable activities.[14] The FAP appraisers and decision-makers had to both guard against over-optimism in submissions, which would lead to projects which would not be viable even with assistance being approved, and the equally unacceptable outcome of granting scarce FAP funds to projects which would have been viable in their own right and attract suitable funding from the financial sector.

On the minimum necessary, there is never going to be a clear answer. What is the minimum required overall return for different ventures? What is the cost of debt, the appropriate gearing ratio and the required return for equity stake-holders? There are no simple answers; judgement has to be the key.

Displacement is another tricky issue to judge, *ex ante* or *ex post*. But again the conceptual issue was addressed and attempts made to minimise displacement. Thus

---

[14] It would appear that local financial advisers soon learned the rules of the game, and devised their own similar spreadsheets. So, many projects as submitted stacked up appropriately; and the key questions then related to whether the data and assumptions used for such projects were acceptable.

some studies were undertaken, by the Ministry of Commerce and Industry in particular, to examine the extent to which some market segments were already reasonably served by domestic output. This was mainly undertaken for small-scale FAP, with the studies tending to be undertaken for local rather than national markets. These studies were often of limited value to support sensible decision-making and even knowledge that an adequate quantum of supply already exists does not necessarily demonstrate that a further project should not be supported.

Turning next to externalities, it is pleasing to note that yet again the topic was addressed by those planning FAP and its implementation. Whilst service sector activities were initially excluded, it was agreed to include so-called 'linking industries' which worked to the benefit of a range of activities within an area, i.e., brought about a range of external benefits for other local activities. One continuing disappointment has been the failure to accept that a range of service sector activities, primarily traded services, should be treated in the same way as manufacturing in consideration for FAP support. It has recently been accepted that certain tourism activities should be eligible for FAP, but why not all traded services? In the latest FAP evaluation[15] it was concluded that there should be a positive list of service sectors to be eligible (traded and internationally mobile services), a negative list (primarily those selling to the personal sector whose sales tend, at the margin, to be substitutes for other domestic purchases) and a third list of sub-sectors for case by case consideration.

Further on externalities, the training grant is a classic example of a grant aimed at externalities, in this instance acceptance that the benefits of training flow more widely than just to the trainer company or indeed the trainee. To follow through the argument, training should be supported and subsidised at all times (where the skills involved are in short supply) rather than just for FAP projects. This has been discussed, for example in FAP evaluation reports.

Finally let us consider survival rates. For any grant scheme of this type, survival is likely to be nowhere near one hundred percent. That is especially true for assistance schemes aimed at small-scale projects, where survival rates can be very low and the schemes still justified. This is because survival rates for new small-scale businesses are generally very low and any improvement can be treated as yielding benefits. At the small-scale level in particular, great efforts were made to provide support and guidance in the early months of new ventures and expansions. For industrial schemes this was through the Rural Industrial Officers.[16] For agricultural projects, the advice came via the local Ministry of Agriculture staff. But all these cadres were thin on the ground, and hence they could provide – with the best will in the world and even with the best transport which often was not available – only a small fraction of the advice which was desirable. Also in some instances[17], project selection proved flawed – often for understandable reasons, such as inappropriate advice or flawed professional views at an early stage of assessing sectoral prospects.

The Sales Augmentation Grant or SAG also deserves a mention in this context. It was designed to encourage output and sales from as early a stage as possible, in

---

[15] Phaleng Consultants, 1995 (op cit.), Chapter 6.

[16] And by Council Planning Officers and their counterparts in the towns.

[17] For example, fishing in Ngamiland where a number of projects failed, apparently because preparations were inadequate.

order to generate revenue and progress towards unaided viability. The SAG rates declined over time – so the more sold in the early years the more grant received.

Evidence from follow up studies is at best partial. Monitoring on the lines originally proposed was not feasible in many instances, and simply not undertaken in others. Following up in the evaluation studies was extremely difficult, particularly at the small-scale level. Overall, the above assessment does suggest that those setting up the scheme did anticipate at least the large majority of the key issues so far as maximising cost-effectiveness was concerned; they did set up methodologies and systems in many instances which can be seen in retrospect as having been on the correct lines. Mistakes were inevitably made; and perhaps the major mistake was to over-estimate the extent of resources realistically likely to be available for FAP appraisal, implementation, implementation support and (particularly) monitoring.

4. SOME CONCLUSIONS

This is not the place to set out detailed conclusions upon the 'success' of the Financial Assistance Policy. As a member of the latest evaluation team I had the opportunity to provide comments which were taken into account in their report.[18] However, a few points emerge from the above discussion.

I would suggest that the *objectives were clear at the outset* of the policy. That in itself is a major plus.

In particular, *the distinction between 'efficiency' and 'equity' objectives* (or economic and socio-political) *was reasonably clear* at the design stage.

I would further argue that the *FAP design* (i.e., the different grants and the system of time-limiting) *has proved to be reasonably in line with those objectives* and founded upon reasonable economic foundations.

Finally, the *design stands up fairly well* to consideration of its merits *when key cost-effectiveness criteria are assessed.*

Thus the FAP was aimed at an explicit set of objectives; its content and grant structure was designed with that set of objectives in mind; and due account was taken of the desirability of maximising benefits (in relation to objectives) and minimising costs (consistent with achieving those objectives). This is a more positive conclusion than has resulted from evaluations which I have been involved with for assistance schemes within the UK.

---

[18] Phaleng Consultants, 1995

APPENDIX. A BRIEF SUMMARY OF FINANCIAL ASSISTANCE POLICY GRANTS

This is a statement of FAP grants as per the original design.[19]

Small-scale

Under small-scale FAP the only assistance available was a one-off grant, based upon a maximum percentage of the total estimated investment cost.

The maximum percentage varied by location, being larger for rural than urban areas. There was also variation by gender, with females receiving a higher percentage than males. Owner-operators received a markedly higher percentage grant than those who were investors and not one hundred percent committed to (i.e., employed upon) involvement with the project's operation.

In addition to the formula approach, used to assess the maximum percentage grant available, there was also a limit on the size of grant available per full time job to be created.

Assistance was limited to citizens.

Medium and large-scale

The types of assistance available were broadly the same for each of these two categories. However, applicants for medium-scale assistance could choose between Automatic Financial Assistance (AFA) and Case-by-Case Financial Assistance (CFA).

There was again a maximum limit for CFA, which varied by location as with small-scale. Whilst some of the limits varied according to citizenship, assistance for neither medium nor large-scale (CFA or AFA) was limited to citizens.

Under CFA the forms of assistance included the items below.

A capital grant, in the form of a lump sum payment, based upon a multiple of the jobs to be created, subject to an overall limit of the percentage of total capital costs, varying by geographical locality.

An unskilled employment grant, based upon a (declining) percentage of the unskilled labour bill for the first five years of the project's implementation.

A training grant, reimbursing an agreed share of approved training costs throughout the same five year period.

A Sales Augmentation Grant (SAG), based upon percentages of sales revenue in each of the first five years, with these percentages again declining through this period. The SAG could be adjusted downwards to ensure that the total expected sum of all grants did not exceed the maximum permitted level.

Under AFA the capital and sales augmentation grants were replaced by a tax holiday. This consisted of a reimbursement of a share of tax paid. The shares varied by locality and again declined over time.

REFERENCES

Government of Botswana. 1982. *Financial Assistance Policy. Government Paper No.1 of 1982.* Government Printer, Gaborone.

Phaleng Consultancies. 1995. *The Third Evaluation of the Financial Assistance Policy (FAP).* Prepared for the Government of Botswana, Ministry of Finance and Development Planning. Government Printer. Gaborone.

Lipton, M. 1978. *Employment and Labour Use in Botswana.* Government Printer, Gaborone.

---

[19] Further details are available from various sources, e.g., Phaleng Consultants, 1995 *(op cit.)*, Appendix D.

Development of Botswana's Mineral Sector

Baledzi Gaolathe

1. INTRODUCTION

At the time that Botswana attained Independence in 1966 there was virtually no mining activity. The small mining works for iron, gold and asbestos which had been undertaken in the past had ceased. Quarrying on a small scale and limited extraction of manganese, as well as some prospecting, was all that was happening in the mineral sector. Botswana was one of the twenty-five poorest countries in the world with agriculture, dominated by the cattle industry, being her economic mainstay. Since Independence, the mineral sector has grown significantly to become a dominant economic factor in Botswana, which has helped her graduate from the list of poorest and least developed countries of the world. Copper-nickel mines have been opened at Selebi-Phikwe, Selkirk and Phoenix; diamond mines are in production at Orapa, Letlhakane and Jwaneng; a coal mine is producing at Morupule; and at Sua Pan, a soda ash and common salt processing plant has been established. Several mining leases[1] for small-scale mining of various minerals and industrial minerals are also in force. Mineral exploration activity, which was minimal at Independence, has been increasing over the years.

This paper briefly examines the growth of the mineral sector in Botswana and the extent to which the sector has been, will be or can be made more beneficial to the continued socio-economic development of the country. The space allocated to this paper does not permit a detailed discussion, but only an overview of this important industry. The policy, administrative and legal framework will be commented upon first in Section 2. The next four sections will respectively discuss the contribution of mineral development to Botswana's economy in terms of gross domestic product, revenue generation for Government, export earnings and employment creation.

Section 7 comments on retained values for copper-nickel, diamonds, coal and soda ash projects for selected years to obtain an appreciation of the net benefits for Botswana of those projects. Section 8 discusses Botswana's prospects for discovery of additional viable mineral deposits and potential development of the mineral sector in the future.

Section 9 examines the measures the mining companies have been taking to minimise the adverse impact of their operations on the environment. The last section is devoted to concluding remarks.

---

[1] There were 21 small mines' mining leases for various minerals and industrial minerals as of 30 April 1996.

2. POLICY, ADMINISTRATIVE AND LEGAL FRAMEWORK

The rapid development of the mineral sector over the years following Independence was to a large extent facilitated by formulation and implementation of improved mineral development policies, administrative machinery and legal framework. Botswana's mineral development policy objectives enunciated in successive National Development Plans (NDPs)[2] have been intended to achieve the general goal of maximising the sector's benefits to the country. These objectives encompass the promotion or acceleration of mineral prospecting and new mine development, maximization of economic and financial benefits resulting from mining operations, encouragement of activities that generate real value-added and linkages with the rest of the economy, creation of employment and training opportunities for citizens, and minimisation of environmental damage by mining operations.

The Botswana Government realised at the outset that it had neither the financial resources nor the expertise to embark on a successful programme of mineral development on its own. A decision was, therefore, taken to attract companies with the financial and technical know-how from the international private sector to take the lead in the exploration, development and operation of mines. The Botswana authorities generally approached mining from a developmental and commercial perspective, rather than from a dogmatic nationalist viewpoint, even at a time when many developing countries were nationalising major mining operations. A conducive environment for private sector investment was offered, consisting of a number of elements. Mineral rights, which at Independence were held by various entities including the state, tribal territories and private farmers, were vested in or brought under the ambit of the state through a process of negotiations with the affected parties. Furthermore, private mineral rights owners could keep their rights and carry out acceptable exploration programmes, or could pay a newly introduced mineral rights tax as penalty for lack of exploration, or surrender the rights. Over time they opted to surrender the rights to the state. The vesting of mineral rights in one entity, the state, considerably simplified procedures for obtaining prospecting licenses and mining leases. Mining companies were, therefore, saved from frustrations which often arise from negotiating with several authorities in the same country.

The Government has allowed a mixed economy to flourish and has followed a pragmatic policy on the question of state versus private ownership of assets of businesses. Botswana has evolved a very liberal foreign exchange control regime which permitted relatively free repatriation of dividends and profits, and virtually unrestricted freedom to import goods and services. This policy has been aided by maintenance of foreign exchange reserves at high levels. On the political front, the country has enjoyed internal peace, rule of law and a successful multi-party democracy, all of which have contributed to internal stability, which is one of the major prerequisites for significant investments by multinational mining corporations.

Furthermore, during these several years, the legislation governing mineral development in Botswana has been considerably improved and streamlined to provide a framework that strikes a reasonable balance between providing incentives to mining companies and achieving the national development objectives stated above. Mining

---

[2] A summary of mineral development policy is contained in National Development Plan 7, 1991–1997, Chapter 8, Section III.

companies take the risk of investing their money in mineral exploration and exploitation with the ultimate goal of realising a satisfactory return on their investment. Therefore, the nature of government policy on equity participation and taxation is a major element in the promotion of mining investment. The Botswana Government addressed this, and adopted and maintained a fiscal policy towards mineral development consisting of three major elements, namely, equity, taxation and royalties.

Equity participation was seen both as an instrument for obtaining an additional share of profits through dividends and as a mechanism that afforded Government direct representation on the boards of mining companies to provide a means for Government to have first hand information and direct say in the management of the nation's mineral resources. The arrangement ensures that Government policies and aspirations are understood by the private sector, while on the other hand authorities obtain a greater appreciation of the problems faced by the private sector mining companies' management. The first hand information obtained by Government representatives enables the Government to provide timely support services where required. Generally the role of the Government has been to ensure that mineral development was in line with the national objectives, influence being exercised through administration of exploration licenses and mining leases, as well as through equity participation and control of infrastructure.

The level of participation is a function of the specific nature of a project, though as a general rule the Government, at exploitation stage, expects to be granted, free of consideration, shares in the region of 15% and to have an option to purchase additional shares. The actual level of shareholding allotted to Government has been a function of negotiation between the parties. In pursuance of this policy the Botswana Government is a shareholder in all major mining projects except in Morupule Colliery where the option remains open for exercising in the future, possibly, when an expansion project is embarked upon. The Government holds 50%, 33% and 50% of the shares in companies operating diamond mines, the copper-nickel mine at Selebi-Phikwe and the soda ash/sodium chloride project at Sua Pan, respectively. In small mines, shareholding has been restricted to 15%. The 50/50 partnership between the Botswana Government and De Beers in Debswana reflects the dominant role of diamond mining in the economy of Botswana, the special arrangements for marketing Botswana diamonds through the Central Selling Organisation and the mature relationship developed between Government and De Beers over many years of negotiations and cooperation. On the Sua Pan project, Government had earlier planned to reduce its shareholding by selling some of its shares to Zimbabwean and Zambian interests, and to the International Finance Corporation and the Commonwealth Development Corporation. However, the weakening of soda ash markets, coupled with technical problems, during and after project implementation, discouraged participation of these parties resulting in the 50/50 partnership between the Government on one hand and Anglo American Corporation, De Beers, AECI[3] and some creditor banks on the other after the recent restructuring of the operating company which is now called Botswana Ash (Proprietary) Limited.

With regards to tax, mineral projects, especially small ones, are taxed at the tax rates applicable to other commercial enterprises. The present rate is 25%. For capital

---

[3] AECI stands for African Explosives and Chemical Industries, a big public corporation in which Anglo American Corporation of South Africa is a major shareholder.

expenditure, including exploration expenditure, the Income Tax Act provides a write-off schedule of ten years or the life of the mine whichever is shorter. The Act provides machinery for counteracting transfer payment practices. The Government has long recognised that major mineral projects normally do not easily fit into the prescribed tax set-up, and consequently the tax legislation makes provision for special tax agreements, which, after they have been concluded between the negotiating parties, have to be ratified by Parliament. These agreements have tended to provide some tax dispensations, such as rapid write-offs, and for additional profits taxes to be applied if the mineral projects performed better than anticipated.

Royalties are payable on all exploited minerals in terms of the Mines and Minerals Act. They are an allowable tax deduction, but are not fixed for all time. They may be adjusted upwards and downwards generally, or in respect of specific projects by regulations promulgated by the minister in terms of the Act. The Act also empowers the minister to enter into a special royalty agreement with a mining company, which may entail fixing royalties for a period of time, where circumstances dictate. The royalty rates on the gross market value of various minerals and mineral products presently in force are summarised in Table 1. Gross market value is defined as being the gross marketable value of the mineral or mineral product, less any costs incurred for transport of output prior to sale or disposal, for insurance and such other costs as the Minister may allow.

In the past, private sector companies have tended to be worried by this power to change the royalty, though they have appreciated the flexibility if exercised downwards, forgetting that while the Government is eager not to sell the national birthright, it is also desirous of not killing the goose that lays the golden egg. The Government fully recognises the role of the private sector and accepts its entitlement to a reasonable rate of return; therefore, in practice, the minister's powers have been reasonably exercised. It is believed Botswana has established a track record of negotiating fair agreements with the multinational mining corporations. Botswana is also aware of the school of thought advocating for a legislative framework that spells out all the terms in advance. While the approach may reduce uncertainty on the part of the investor, in the main it is doubtful whether it would result in fair deals where major projects are involved. The debate continues.

TABLE 1. CURRENT MINERAL ROYALTY RATES FOR BOTSWANA

MINERAL OR MINERAL PRODUCT	ROYALTY
Precious Stones, Petroleum and Natural Gas	10%
Coal, Precious Metals, Semi-Precious Stones, Radio-Active Minerals	5%
Building and Industrial Minerals, Oil Shale, Other Minerals or Mineral Products	3%

Efforts were made to build efficient institutional arrangements for the administration of mineral exploration and development. These institutions consist of the Department of Geological Survey, which services the mining industry at exploration or prospecting stage, the Department of Mines, which provides services at the exploitation or mining stage, and the Ministry of Mineral Resources and Water Affairs

Headquarters assisted by the inter-ministerial Mineral Policy Committee[4,] which provide the necessary policy guidance and take the lead in negotiations. Among the main functions of the Department of Geological Survey are to gather, assess and disseminate all data related to rocks, mineral deposits, general geology and groundwater resources of Botswana. The efficiency with which the Department carries out its duties has been a major determinant in the promotion of mineral exploration.

Mineral exploration in Botswana is governed by four Acts: the Mines and Minerals Act, which deals with the exploration and mining of minerals; the Mineral Rights in Tribal Territories Acts, which deals with the exploitation of industrial minerals by various districts for domestic purposes; the Precious and Semi-Precious Stones (Protection) Act, which provides for the protection of the precious stones industry and regulation of dealings in precious stones and semi-precious stones; and finally the Petroleum (Exploration and Production) Act, which deals with the exploration and production of petroleum. The Department of Geological Survey undertakes grass-roots type exploration in those areas where the private sector is not active, such as basic geological mapping and industrial minerals assessment. The policy is that the Department should undertake exploration work and gather information to a level where the private sector would be encouraged to apply for licences and carry out more detailed prospecting. The Department monitors prospecting by the private sector to ensure that they abide by the agreed work programmes and expenditure commitments.

Botswana has also received significant donor assistance in the gathering of valuable geological and mineral exploration information crucial for encouraging prospecting by the private sector. These aid projects undertake work directed to areas where the geology is not well known. Since the late 1970s several aid-funded projects have been undertaken in Botswana. The first was a CIDA[5] sponsored aeromagnetic survey which covered 80% of the country. The remaining 20% has now been covered by a European Union (EU) funded aeromagnetic survey. As a spin-off from the aeromagnetic surveys, follow-up drilling projects have been undertaken with the help of the Japanese, Germans, Swedes and the British. Work done with the assistance of these aid agencies has proved beneficial in that some of the project areas were subsequently taken up for prospecting by the private sector.

The Department of Mines has the prime responsibility of ensuring that the Government mineral development policies are effectively implemented and mineral legislation respected. It constitutes a major contact point with mining companies at exploitation stage and is therefore organised to make a major contribution to promotion of mineral investment in Botswana. The Department takes the lead in the evaluation of mining lease applications, and monitors and inspects ongoing operations both from the technical and safety related perspectives. Its staff also provide technical and professional support to Government directors serving in mining companies and negotiating teams.

---

4   The Mineral Policy Committee is advisory to Cabinet through the Minister of Mineral Resources and Water Affairs. Membership consists of Permanent Secretary in the Ministry of Mineral Resources and Water Affairs, Permanent Secretary to the President, Permanent Secretary in the Ministry of Finance and Development Planning, and the Attorney General. The Committee is serviced by various professionals including the Director of Mines, the Ministry's Economic Consultant and Chief Minerals Officer.

5   CIDA is an abbreviation for Canadian International Development Agency.

The statutory powers of the Department are derived mainly from the mineral legislation listed earlier, and also the Mines, Quarries, Works and Machinery Act and the Atmospheric Pollution Prevention Act. The major mining multinational corporations are not interested in the development of small mines. Consequently, the Department of Mines has been assigned the prime responsibility of promoting the growth of this sub-sector which has the potential to contribute to job creation and diversification of the economy. The various wings of the Mines Department have had to be strengthened commensurate with the growth of mining in Botswana. The development and operations wing has been particularly active on the promotion side, and in the servicing of the Mineral Policy Committee and negotiating teams.

It has already been stated that Botswana, being a mixed economy, has welcomed the involvement of the private sector in the exploitation of its mineral wealth. Such cooperation has largely been with multinational mining corporations, and for major projects it has been governed by special agreements negotiated at exploitation stage. The potential benefits these corporations can offer to a host developing country, such as Botswana, are the technical, managerial and financial services at all stages of a mining project, from prospecting through mining and processing to marketing of the end product. A major task of the host government is to ensure that these services are offered at least cost in terms of both financial and overall socio-economic benefits. A few comments on the subject of funding of some projects in Botswana are considered in order.

The initial capital cost of building the Selebi-Phikwe copper-nickel mine, which was commissioned in 1974, amounted to P4389 million in 1995 prices, of which P409 million was equity. The major sponsoring shareholders were Amax and the Anglo American Corporation. The Government was allocated 15% of equity free of consideration. The requisite infrastructure, mainly power, water, roads, railways and township was built from funds raised by Government from donors and external funding agencies including the World Bank, USAID[6] and CIDA. The total cost was P620 million in 1995 prices. As most of the financing for both the mine and infrastructure came from outside sources, the project was not a drain on local resources. The arrangements governing the project were extremely complex and took a long time to negotiate, and were enshrined in some forty interlocking agreements. In terms of the various completion guarantees, the major shareholders committed themselves to building the mine complex and ensuring that the plants performed to design specifications. When technical problems arose later, the shareholders met their commitments by injecting additional funds and expertise. The shareholders were also ultimate guarantors of some of the infrastructure loans.

Following a prolonged series of negotiations the Orapa, Letlhakane and Jwaneng diamond mines were built at a total original establishment cost of P1584 million in 1995 prices. They were commissioned in 1971, 1977 and 1982, respectively. Orapa and Letlhakane mines were financed 100% by De Beers by way of equity subscription. Jwaneng was also financed by equity subscriptions in the ratio 80% De Beers and 20% Government of Botswana. The Government's contribution was optional and was exercised to increase its share of the profits. Subsequent expansions of these mines, which cost a total of P957 million with completion of Jwaneng Fourth Stream in 1995, have been financed from internal savings, the ultimate sharing of the bur-

---

6   USAID is an abbreviation for United States Agency for International Development.

dens being functions of special agreements entered into between the parties. Most of the original infrastructure cost was included in the project funding. It is therefore evident that the original funding of diamond mines was also not a drain on national savings.

The soda ash project at Sua Pan, which became operational in 1991, presents a different picture in that the Government and other local sources made a major contribution to the capital cost of the project. The project was initiated as a joint venture between AECI and Government of Botswana with 52% and 48% shareholding, respectively. The cooperation agreement empowered each partner to invite participants of its choice to acquire part of its share of the equity. In the event, AECI allocated part of its holding to Anglo American Corporation and De Beers Holdings. The Government of Botswana has so far not been successful in disposing of some of its equity. By June 1992, the total capital cost of the project was P1391 million in 1995 prices of which P684 million came from shareholders as equity, P96 million as loan from Botswana banks and the rest as export credit and loans from external sources. In addition, the Government and some of its parastatals provided supporting infrastructure at a total cost of P339 million. In 1995, the project experienced financial and operational difficulties and was restructured with the Government becoming a 50% shareholder, Anglo American Corporation and associates becoming a 42% shareholder, and banks acquiring an 8% stake. The restructuring involved liquidation of the company, writing-off of P1.1 billion shareholders' and banks' investments, and refinancing of P131.5 million.

The coal mining project, namely Morupule Colliery, which was commissioned in 1973, was financed in its entirety by Anglo American Corporation. Hitherto, the Government has not taken an equity stake in the project.

In general, the experience in Botswana has been that, provided the particular project is feasible, technically sound and economically and financially viable, finance has always been packaged from one or more of the project sponsors, donor agencies, commercial banks, export credit institutions, end users of minerals to be mined and local sources. A substantial part of the finance invested in mineral development to date has come from outside sources, and therefore has spared local savings for other investments.

3. CONTRIBUTION OF MINERAL SECTOR TO GROSS DOMESTIC PRODUCT

Mineral development, though not yet fully diversified, has made a major contribution to the growth of the Botswana economy. Indeed, the mining industry was largely responsible for the graduation of Botswana from recurrent budget aid from the British Government and entitlement to International Development Association resources in the early 1970s, and from the world's least developed countries in the late 1980s. Table 2 depicts mineral sector contribution to Botswana's economy in terms of Gross Domestic Product (GDP) for selected years from 1972 to 1995.

At Independence, in 1966, the mineral industry contributed almost nothing to GDP. By 1972, diamond production at Orapa had started and, as Table 1 shows, the sector's contribution to GDP had jumped to 11% of the total which was then only P103.6

TABLE 2. MINERAL SECTOR CONTRIBUTION TO BOTSWANA GROSS DOMESTIC PRODUCT.

YEAR/ INDICATOR	1972	1976	1980	1981	1983	1985	1987	1989	1991	1993	1995
GROSS DOMESTIC PRODUCT (PULA MILLION)	103.6	300.4	875.5	899.9	1 153.1	1 828.6	2 809.8	5 836.8	7 475.2	9 126.0	12 530.3
MINING GDP (PULA MILLION)	11.2	42.0	201.6	201.6	366.6	753.1	1 229.8	2 969.3	3 012.0	3 042.3	4 086.3
MINERAL SHARE OF TOTAL GDP (%)	11	14	23	22	32	41	44	51	40	33	33

Source: Central Statistics Office.

million. By 1983, with production at Orapa doubled from 1978, Letlhakane and Jwaneng mines commissioned, and BCL copper-nickel project on stream, the industry was contributing 32% of GDP, which itself had grown more than ten times to over P1153 million. The mineral sector's share reached a peak in 1989, when it accounted for more than 50% of the GDP, which was then P5837 million or 182 times what it was in nominal prices at Independence. The industry's share has since decreased to 33% in 1995, but will again increase when the Orapa expansion project is commissioned in the year 2000. It must be appreciated that the GDP growth in other sectors has, to a significant extent, been induced by the mineral sector. Furthermore, the mineral sector GDP is dominated by diamonds, which account for more than 90% of the total. Overall, by the beginning of the 1990s the mineral-led Botswana economy had recorded an average annual rate of growth of 13% in real terms since Independence. The per capita GDP has grown from under P2000 in 1972 to nearly P9800 in 1995 prices.

These growth rates will be difficult to achieve and sustain in the future unless efforts are intensified to diversify the productive base of the economy. However, the mining industry has considerable potential to continue making contributions to the growth and sustenance of the Botswana economy in the long term. This aspect is commented upon in Section 8 which discusses the country's future mineral discovery prospects and development potential.

4. THE MINERAL SECTOR AS GENERATOR OF GOVERNMENT REVENUES

This section assesses the role of the mineral industry as a generator of revenue for Government. The Government uses these revenues to meet the costs of providing serviccs to the nation, such as social and physical infrastructure. It can also use such revenues to meet other development objectives, such as economic diversification and promotion of job creation, an objective which the modern mining industry cannot directly or effectively fulfil owing to its capital intensity. Table 3 gives some idea of the contribution of the mineral industry to Government revenues for various years from 1972, six years after Independence, to 1995.

It will be seen that the mineral sector contribution significantly increased over the period both in absolute terms and in relation to to-tal revenue. The mineral revenues to Government in-creased a hundred fold from P1 million in 1972, the first full year of Orapa Mine pro-duction, to nearly P100 million by 1981, reflecting the doubling of Orapa Mine production, the commission-ing of Letlhakane Mine and renegotiated fiscal regime during the late 1970s. After a moderate lull occasioned by the depressed diamond market, the revenues rapidly grew from P376 million in 1985 to P2005 million by 1991, reflecting the major contribution of the Jwaneng

TABLE 3. THE MINERAL SECTOR CONTRIBUTION TO BOTSWANA GOVERNMENT REVENUE

INDICATOR/ YEAR	GOVERNMENT MINERAL REVENUES (PULA MILLION)	TOTAL GOVERNMENT REVENUES (PULA MILLION)	MINERAL SHARE OF TOTAL REVENUES (%)
1972	1.0	19.3	5
1976	23.3	87.8	27
1980	76.6	249.1	31
1981	101.1	306.6	33
1983	99.5	393.7	25
1985	376.5	802.9	47
1987	845.0	1 547.5	55
1989	1 508.1	2 556.0	59
1991	2 005.3	3 740.7	54
1993	1 866.1	4 652.2	40
1995	2 278.7	4 492.5	51

Source: Ministry of Finance and Development Planning.

diamond mine, which was commissioned in 1982, and the improved market condi-tions. The revenues from minerals have since then continued to grow to reach over P2278 million by 1995, partly as a result of the commissioning of the recrush plant and the Fourth Stream expansion project at Jwaneng, which increased caratage pro-duction of that mine by over 40%. In percentage terms the mineral share of total Government revenues grew from 5% in 1972 to 33% in 1981, and reached a peak of nearly 60% in 1989. It has since been oscillating around 50% of the total.

A disturbing aspect of this development is that the Government has become over-whelmingly dependent on mineral revenues, especially from diamonds. Throughout this period other mineral projects yielded negligible revenues. The BCL copper-nickel project, which commenced operation in 1973, suffered from technical, financial and depressed mineral prices problems and ran losses during most of this period. The other big mineral project, soda ash, which became operational in 1991, has been suffering the same fate; in fact it has been a drain on Government revenues. These figures on mineral revenues underestimate the overall contribution of mining to Gov-ernment revenues. The greater portion of the remainder of the revenues comes from customs and excise under the SACU agreement, and returns from foreign exchange reserves managed by the Bank of Botswana. Mineral projects are major importers of capital goods and therefore indirectly contribute additional revenues through customs duties payable on these goods. The foreign exchange reserves and, therefore, the returns therefrom, have largely arisen from the export sales surpluses of the diamond industry.

This dependence on diamond revenues will undoubtedly increase during NDP 8 and probably beyond unless efforts are intensified to diversify the economy and broaden sources of revenue. During NDP 8, the diamond revenues will be boosted by the introduction of continuous operations at all Debswana mines effective from 1997 and the Orapa expansion project, which will double the caratage production of that mine to 12 million carats from the year 2000 onwards. From the above it can be concluded that the mining industry, especially diamond mining, has been and will continue to be an effective revenue generator for Government, giving it the ability to implement NDP 8 with minimal revenue constraints. However, while no major risks on the production front are foreseen, there is less certainty regarding sustenance of the diamond market whose buoyancy depends on affluence arising from good economic performance of major consuming countries, such as the United States, Japan and EU members.

It is encouraging to note that the Government has accumulated revenue surpluses over time which are part of the nation's accumulated foreign exchange reserves managed by the Bank of Botswana, which are now a major source of additional revenue to Government. Time has now come to deliberately set aside a portion of the diamond revenues for future generations as countries like Kuwait have done in the case of oil. Such a fund, which to start off could be set at ten percent of the said revenues, would be invested long term to generate a growing stream of income in the future when diamond production declines or markets soften.

5. THE MINERAL INDUSTRY AS A GENERATOR OF EXPORT EARNINGS

The mineral industry has been an overwhelming foreign exchange earner for the country. Table 4 illustrates the contribution of diamonds and copper-nickel to export earnings during alternate years from 1980 to 1995. Though Morupule Colliery was in production throughout the period its sales revenues, as can be seen in Table 7, were relatively small and it supplied only the local market, thereby saving foreign exchange which would have been spent on imported coal.

Table 4 shows that by 1980 the mining industry contributed 81% of export earnings, of which 60% and 21% were attributable to diamonds and copper-nickel, respectively. The value of total exports in current prices increased fifteenfold from P390.4 million in 1980 to P5 760.7 million by 1995. Throughout this period, except around 1981, when the diamond market was depressed, the contribution of diamonds and copper-nickel to total exports varied between 75% and nearly 90%, with the former accounting for between 60% and 84% of the total and the latter less than 10% in most years.

These figures demonstrate the high dependence of the Botswana economy on minerals, especially diamonds, for its export earnings. In fact, these figures slightly underestimate the shares of the industry as the contribution of small mines and the

TABLE 4. MINERAL SECTOR CONTRIBUTION TO BOTSWANA EXPORT EARNINGS

INDICATOR/ YEAR	TOTAL EXPORTS (PULA MILLION)	...OF WHICH DIAMONDS (PULA MILLION)	...OF WHICH COPPER/ NICKEL (PULA MILLION)	DIAMONDS SHARE (%)	COPPER-NICKEL SHARE (%)	DIAMONDS AND COPPER-NICKEL SHARE (%)
1972	30.3					
1976	153.2					
1980	390.4	235.7	80.8	60	21	81
1981	332.3	136.5	79.7	41	24	65
1983	696.7	459.2	65.8	66	9	75
1985	1 384.3	1 048.1	119.9	78	9	87
1987	2 664.7	2 251.4	118.2	84	4	88
1989	3 742.6	2 860.9	471.9	76	13	89
1991	3 738.0	2 941.5	296.4	79	8	87
1993	4 312.1	3 340.2	219.8	77	5	82
1995	5 760.7	4 090.0	287.2	71	5	76

Source: Central Statistics Office.

soda ash project is included in the remainder of the exports. Soda ash and common salt exports have been varying between P53 million and P114 million per annum since 1992.

These high levels of export earnings from diamonds throughout the post-Independence period coupled with the inflow of generous aid and private capital, protected Botswana from balance of payments problems and foreign exchange constraints. Moreover, they contributed significantly to the accumulation of foreign exchange reserves, the size of which is the envy of many developing countries. Table 5.9 of the Bank of Botswana 1995 Annual Report shows the build-up of the reserves from P293 million in 1982 to P13 251 million in 1995. The latter figure equates to 25 months of Botswana imports cover. In US Dollar terms, the reserves grew fifteen times from US$311 million to US$4696 million over the same period. The healthy balance of payments, coupled with this growing level of foreign exchange reserves, enabled Botswana to liberalise exchange controls, avoid import restrictions and the imposition of International Monetary Fund conditionalities as reason for financial support.

6. THE MINERAL INDUSTRY AS A GENERATOR OF EMPLOYMENT

In this section we examine the extent to which the mining industry has been contributing to the achievement of the job creation objective. Table 5 shows the number of people employed in the mining industry for selected years over the period 1972 to 1995.

In 1972 the industry employed some 3500 workers, a figure representing 9% of formal sector employment of 37 500 at the time. Thereafter employment gradually increased from 3500 to 7800 workers by 1980 and then stabilised at between 8000 and 9700 during the period 1980 to 1988. By 1989 the industry employed 11 050 workers and, since then to 1995, the figures have stabilised around 13 000 employees, whereas by 1995 total formal sector employment had reached the 233 000 mark. In percentage terms the mining industry contributed 9% of formal sector jobs from 1972 to 1980, thereafter, as formal employment grew rapidly, in other sectors, the figure decreased to 8% by 1981, to 6% by 1987; and lately the percentage has declined to 5%.

Clearly the mining industry in Botswana has not been an effective

TABLE 5. MINERAL SECTOR CONTRIBUTION TO BOTSWANA'S ECONOMY IN TERMS OF EMPLOYMENT

INDICATOR/ YEAR	TOTAL FORMAL EMPLOYMENT (x1000)	MINERAL SECTOR EMPLOYMENT (x1000)	MINERAL SECTOR EMPLOYMENT SHARE OF TOTAL (%)
1972	37.5	3.47	9
1976	59.6	5.45	9
1980	83.4	7.8	9
1981	97.4	8.1	8
1983	100.6	8.1	8
1985	116.0	9.28	8
1987	150.2	9.69	6
1989	189.5	11.05	6
1991	228.9	13.23	6
1993	227.6	13.08	6
1995	233.4	12.48	5

Source: Central stistics Office, Department of Mines.

means of direct large-scale job creation. Today's major mineral projects are characterised by capital intensity and automation. The industry is competitive, and must sustain high productivity for long-term survival. An example of the capital intensity of modern mineral projects is the Orapa expansion project, which is estimated to cost nearly P1.5 billion to produce an extra six million carats per annum, but will provide only 300 additional permanent jobs. On the other hand, subject to market behaviour, the project will generate significant net revenues. These revenues can be used by Government to promote other industries more suited to job creation in which Botswana might have a long-term competitive advantage.

The above characteristics of the mining industry mainly apply to bigger projects, not necessarily to small mines, which tend to be less capital intensive and, therefore, have greater potential for creating jobs. The full potential of this subsector is still to be realised in Botswana. Hopefully, during NDP 8 and beyond there will be tangible results arising from the assumption by the Mines Department of the responsibility to promote the growth of the small mines sub-sector. The Department has begun offering the sub-sector a variety of services including laboratory scale metallurgical test work, advice on mineral extraction technology and safe mine designs. Small mines qualify for the resources of the Financial Assistance Policy (FAP). The qualifying small mines have been defined to refer to labour intensive mining projects with investment capital typically ranging from P50 000 to P2 million.

It must be pointed out that the mining industry has made a major contribution to skill acquisition by its labour force. The mining labour force consists of semi-skilled, skilled, technical and professional employees who had to be trained at great expense by the mines. In fact, some have been leaving the mines to increase the pool of skilled manpower in other sectors of the economy. For example, Debswana has lost nearly 25% of all the skilled, technical and professional manpower it trained between 1969 and 1996. The entire work force of 13 000 is more than 90% localised. Furthermore, the ripple effects of the mine employees' incomes, which are above the national average, should not be underestimated. These workers are concentrated near the mines in localities where modern townships have emerged and are largely dependent on them for their continued existence. The Orapa and Letlhakane mines' 2600 workers sustain Orapa township with 10 000 inhabitants and have contributed to the rapid growth of Letlhakane village which now boasts of 19 000 people and has become both the capital and commercial centre of the Boteti sub-district. The 5000 employees of BCL help sustain Selebi-Phikwe township of 44 600 inhabitants. The Jwaneng mine with 2320 employees supports Jwaneng township of 14 000 people, while Morupule Colliery with 320 employees is the second biggest employer at Palapye with a population of over 19 000. The 550 employees of Botswana Ash occupy the new Sowa township with a population of 3000. The challenge to Botswana is to take advantage of the infrastructure of these towns and promote development of other productive activities to cater for their growing populations and to ensure continued viability of the settlements in the future when mining operations may reduce or cease.

7. RETAINED VALUES OF MINERAL PROJECTS

In a developing country such as Botswana, which still has to supplement its skilled manpower resources with expatriate labour and is heavily dependent on imported industrial and consumer goods, the gross estimation of foreign exchange benefits very often exaggerates the real benefits to the country. In the following pages an attempt, using Mikesell's[7] approach, will be made to estimate the retained values of mineral revenues to Botswana in selected years for the ongoing copper-nickel, diamond, coal and soda ash projects. The retained value is that portion of the value of the exports of a project that is retained in the domestic economy. It constitutes an approximate measure of the financial contribution made by the project to the economy as a whole by treating the local component of project costs as a benefit. Care should be exercised in interpreting the results of retained value analysis. For example, the income received by government and residents or citizens is all deemed as a benefit irrespective of the fact that some of it may be spent on imports. On the other hand, the project revenue spent on genuine local items or services may generate domestic multiplier effects. A further simplification is that the indirect revenues accruing to Government from project imports in terms of the SACU arrangements have been estimated by applying a factor of 16% to imports. Notwithstanding these qualifications, the method does provide another broad estimation of the benefits of a project beyond direct Government revenues.

Using Mikesell's terminology, the retained value (RV) of a project for a given period can be represented by the equation:

$$RV = W - SE + DP - Md + RO + L + DD + CT + WT + CU + OT$$

Where,
W = total wages, salaries, and salary supplements
SE = salaries of expatriates accruing abroad

DP = domestic purchases of goods and services

Md = import content of DP

RO = royalty payments to Botswana

L = payments to landowners

DD = dividends paid to Botswana Government and to Botswana resident equity shareholders.

CT = corporate income tax

WT = withholding tax on dividends to non-residents

CU = customs duties

OT = other taxes

The above equation may be shortened to:

$$RV = W - SE + DP - Md + T, \text{ where, } T = RO + L + DD + CT + WT + CU + OT$$

We shall first consider the Selebi-Phikwe copper-nickel project (BCL) for the years 1980, 1985, 1990 and 1995. The results of the above equation with figures obtained from BCL substituted for the four years are summarised in the Table 6.

TABLE 6. BCL COPPER-NICKEL PROJECT RETAINED VALUE (PULA '000) IN SELECTED YEARS

	1980	1985	1990	1995
W	17 610	28 973	65 264	106 143
-SE	1 127	1 557	4 229	4 759
DP	24 118	32 489	52 434	153 751
-MD	9 647	1 299	20 974	61 501
T	8 625	9 793	32 109	51 835
RETAINED VALUE	39 579	56 702	124 611	245 469
EXPORT VALUE	107 854	120 134	255 917	317 902
RV AS % OF EV	37%	47%	49%	77%

Source: Computed from information obtained from BCL Limited.

The figures obtained from BCL indicate that the company paid no taxes or dividends during the years considered and paid royalty in only two years. However despite continued losses and inability to pay taxes and dividends the company realised substantial retained values to the Botswana economy as shown in Table 6. In 1980, the retained value was 37% of export value, whereas for 1985 and 1990, the percentages were 47% and 49%, respectively. In 1995, the figure had increased to 77% reflecting a decreased expatriate wage bill in relation to the total wage bill. The retained value figures given in Table 6 are also an estimate of the net foreign exchange contribution of the copper-nickel project during the years in question. Had the indirect SACU revenues to Government arising from BCL imports been excluded, these figures would have been lower by five to ten percentage points. It is worth noting that the Ministry of

Mineral Resources and Water Affairs carried out a similar retained value exercise on BCL for the period 1994 to 2008 and arrived at a comparable average figure of 60% for the period.

Table 7 gives the results of the retained value analysis for Debswana diamond projects in respect of the years 1980, 1985, 1990 and 1995.

TABLE 7. DEBSWANA DIAMOND PROJECTS RETAINED VALUE (PULA '000) IN SELECTED YEARS

	1980	1985	1990	1995
W	10 309	40 650	103 253	198 049
−SE	1 612	5 632	12 432	17 326
DP	17 471	57 175	130 813	205 062
−MD	10 483	34 305	78 488	123 037
T	91 028	625 785	1 581 890	2 309 516
RETAINED VALUE	106 713	683 673	1 725 036	2 572 264
EXPORT VALUE	215 729	948 874	2 352 256	3 547 465
RV AS % OF EV	49%	72%	73%	73%

Source: Compiled from information obtained from Debswana Diamond Company (Pty) Limited.

The following results emerge from Table 7. In 1980, diamond exports realised nearly P216 million, of which P107 million or 49% was the retained value. In 1985, the export value had grown to some P949 million, and correspondingly the retained value had increased to P684 million or 72% of the export value. Between 1990 and 1995, the export value increased from P2352 million to P3547 million, while the retained value stabilised at 73% of export value. These are extremely high retained values in Botswana's circumstances and demonstrate the high profitability of the diamond industry and its significant contribution to Botswana economy through taxes, royalties, dividends, customs revenues and other payments to Government and through wages to citizens and purchases from local suppliers. The figures show significant improvement in the diamond projects' retained values when compared to the situation in the mid-1970s when a similar analysis produced retained values equivalent to 38%, 39% and 56% of export values for the years 1973, 1974 and 1975, respectively.

The retained values for Morupule Colliery for the same selected years 1980, 1985, 1990 and 1995 are summarised in Table 8. It should be noted that Morupule Colliery supplies only local consumers, hence the reference to value of production. It will be seen that the colliery's retained values for the period under consideration varied from 62% to as high as 85%. The figures reflect a major improvement compared to what the situation was in the 1970s when a similar exercise[8] yielded retained values ranging from as low as 30% of the value of production.

---

[8] See Harvey, C. (ed.) 1981. *Papers on the Economy of Botswana*, Chapter 6. Heinemann Educational Books, London

TABLE 8. MORUPULE COLLIERY RETAINED VALUE IN PULA FOR SELECTED YEARS

	1980	1985	1990	1995
W	853 570	1 505 822	4 568 217	7 830 712
−SE	156 417	244 136	543 454	753 542
DP	2 265 279	5 614 481	12 782 485	13 410 533
−MD	1 585 695	3 930 137	8 947 740	9 387 373
T	1 246 211	1 337 690	4 782 391	4 880 514
RETAINED VALUE	2 622 948	5 283 720	12 641 899	15 980 844
VALUE OF PRODUCTION	3 631 303	6 222 016	19 128 313	25 786 596
RV AS % OF VP	72%	85%	66%	62%

Source: Computed from data provided by Morupule Colliery (Pty) Limited.

Table 9 gives the results of the retained value analysis for the Botswana Ash soda ash and salt project for the years 1993 to 1995.

TABLE 9. BOTSWANA ASH RETAINED VALUE (PULA '000) IN 1992 – 1995

	1993	1994	1995
W	22 800	25 300	26 500
-SE	4 856	5 451	5 292
DP	49 200	58 300	53 800
-MD	11 316	11 077	18 830
T	5 960	6 012	5 706
RETAINED VALUE	61 788	73 084	61 884
EXPORT VALUE	70 800	99 200	117 400
RV AS % OF EV	87%	74%	53%

Source: Computed from data provided by Botswana Ash (Pty) Limited and Department of Customs and Excise.

From Table 9, it will be seen that, in 1993, the third production year of the project, the retained value was P62 million or 87% of the export value, a relatively high figure which partly reflected a low export value and injection of outside funds into the project to meet the losses it was incurring then. The project also benefited from significant local purchases with low import content such as water, power, coal and railway services. During the following years the retained value decreased to 74% and 53% in 1994 and 1995, respectively. The decrease occurred partly, as a result of growing export sales, from P70.8 million in 1993 to P117.4 million in 1995, with no corresponding increase in payment of taxes, customs duties etc. to Government. In fact, the project continued to run at losses during the period and only survived because of financial support from the sponsors, including Government. Nonetheless, the figures do show that meaningful value was retained in the national economy despite operational losses. Following restructuring in 1995, with ongoing aggressive cost cutting and product marketing, Botswana Ash now expects to reach profitability in the not too distant future.

In general, Botswana has still to fully exploit opportunities for increasing retained value and valued added from the mineral sector. It should be clear from the retained value analysis tables that the greater portion of the mine material inputs are imported from outside Botswana. These inputs ought to be identified and their local manufacture encouraged. A substantial portion, estimated to be 40% to 50%, of the remuneration of expatriate workers is directly remitted outside Botswana, and a portion of the balance spent on imported goods. In this regard part of the solution lies in continued training of local manpower to localise expatriate held jobs.

On the forward linkage front, progress has been slow in Botswana. Until the establishment of Botswana Diamond Valuing Company (Pty) Limited (BDVC) in 1974, the sorting and valuing of Botswana's diamond production was carried out in London by the Diamond Trading Company at a fee. Since then, all the sorting and valuation has been undertaken in Botswana by BDVC, and a labour force of more than 500 Batswana has been trained to take over from expatriates, only 19 of whom remain. Existing agreements with the Central Selling Organisation contain special arrangements to supply diamond polishing and cutting factories that may be established in Botswana and, to date, three diamond cutting and polishing factories have been established. These are Lazare Kaplan Botswana in Molepolole, Teemane Manufacturing Company in Serowe and Diamond Manufacturing Company in Gaborone. The first two factories have capacity to employ 500 people each, and the latter can employ 120 people. These factories are still at a development stage in terms of manpower training, and their long-term profitability is still to be proven against fierce competition from established low-cost cutting centres, such as India. Should these projects succeed, scope for replication would be enhanced. The BCL copper-nickel ore is processed through several stages to reach copper-nickel matte stage. The matte is then transported to refineries abroad for refining into copper, nickel and other end products. Hitherto, the marginal nature of the Selebi-Phikwe project and the large capital outlay required for a refinery to process the volume of matte produced have militated against the establishment of such a refinery in Botswana. The locally produced coal is used mainly by the Morupule power station, the copper-nickel smelter at Selebi-Phikwe, and by the soda ash salt works at Sua, all of which provide efficient ways of converting coal to different forms of energy and heat. Low prices and cost effective technology continue to hinder processing of Botswana coal to other hydrocarbons. The Sua project produces refined soda ash and sodium chloride. The challenge is to investigate the possibility of establishing a chemical complex that will use the refined products as feedstock.

8. Botswana's Future Mineral Development Potential

Although a lot has been done to collect and collate data on the geology of Botswana and promote development of Botswana's mineral sector, its potential has not yet been fully realised. The biggest barrier to mineral discovery has been the geographical setting of the country. More than 75% of Botswana is covered by the Kalahari sands, which conceal most of the rock outcrops. The sands are very thick and, therefore, the applicability of conventional exploration methods is limited. However, in recent years, progress has been made in developing various remote sensing exploration techniques that go a long way in overcoming the barrier created by the deep Kalahari sands. More work has also been done in studying mineral provinces of the relatively more explored neighbouring countries of South Africa, Zimbabwe, Zambia and Namibia with a view to extrapolating their extensions into Botswana.

Most of the bilateral and multilateral technical aid projects referred to in Section 2 used remote sensing techniques, and have been directed mainly to areas covered by Kalahari sands, where the geology was not well known. The first was a CIDA sponsored aeromagnetic survey, which covered 80% of the country, followed by a EU funded aeromagnetic survey, which covered the remaining 20%. As spin-offs from these aeromagnetic surveys, follow-up drilling projects were undertaken with the help of the Japanese, Germans, Swedes and the British. Work done with the assistance of these aid agencies has proved beneficial in that some of the project areas were subsequently taken up for prospecting by the private sector. For example, prospecting licenses for base and precious metals, were awarded to three companies – Goldfields, Ampal, and Molopo Botswana – over the Molopo farms complex which was the subject of the British aid programme.

Other aid projects included the Petro Canada sponsored seismic survey, and a follow up drilling project in the deep Nossop–Ncojane and Passarge basins in western Botswana to evaluate their hydrocarbon potential. An integrated geophysical survey over these basins was also sponsored by the EU. In addition, the EU sponsored an airborne electro-magnetic survey in parts of eastern Botswana where the target was base and precious metals, as well as ground water.

As already stated, detailed geological survey and mineral exploration in neighbouring countries led to identification of mineral provinces in those countries which lately have been extrapolated into Botswana. Four mineral provinces of Archaean age are known in Southern Africa. The first two are the Zimbabwe and Kaapvaal Cratons comprising geological structures with known occurrences of gold deposits within the green stone belt, chromite, copper and nickel. The Tati and Matsitama green stone belts are found on the western edge of the Zimbabwe Craton, with the former being popular for gold around Francistown and copper-nickel deposits at Phoenix and Selkirk. The third province is the Limpopo Mobile Belt, which is associated with copper-nickel deposits at Selebi-Phikwe. The fourth province is the Witwatersrand Sedimentary Basin, whose correlates are being investigated in the central southern part of the Kalahari basin.

Among the Proterozoic age mineral provinces in neighbouring countries, the Bushveld, Kalahari, Damara and Nama extend into Botswana; and their possible mineral deposits are concealed by the Kalahari sands. The Bushveld province which extends into Molopo Farms complex is associated with platinum group minerals. There are also two relatively well explored and defined phanerozoic mineral sub-provinces in Botswana. There are the Kalahari Kimberlite and the Limpopo Basin sub-provinces associated with significant diamond and coal deposits, respectively. Figure 1, depicts the geological framework of Botswana based on the information gathered through use of the various methods explained above.

FIGURE 1. BOTSWANA GEOLOGY

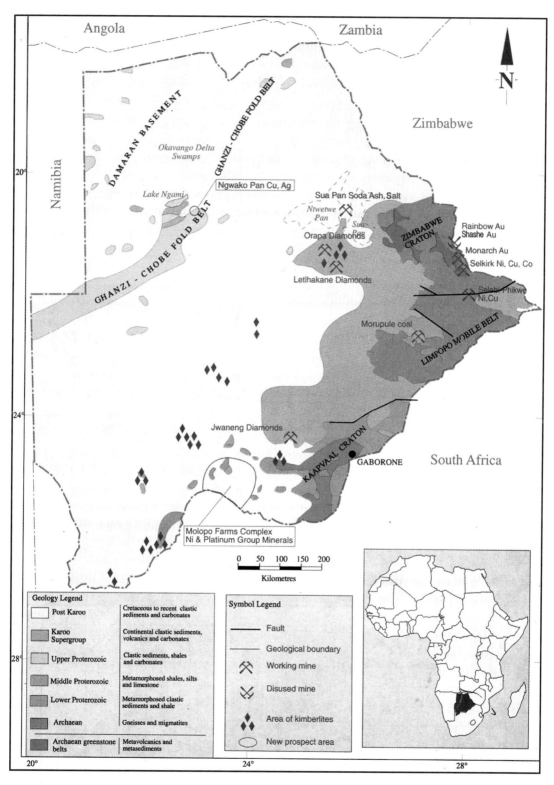

Source: Department of Geological Survey

From the information gathered so far, it is clear that Botswana has considerable potential for additional economic mineral discoveries. The geological information gathered hitherto has lead to increased prospecting in various parts of Botswana for various minerals in recent years. Figure 2 shows that the number of diamond prospecting licenses increased from 24 in 1980 to nearly 350 in 1995, while those of base and precious metals increased from 19 to 240. Total exploration expenditure also increased significantly from 10.7 million in 1985 to P85.9 million in 1995. In 1995 prices, the figure of P10.7 million converts to P32 million, and P78 million spent in 1991 converts to P125 million, to become the highest annual expenditure figure for the period. As depicted by the bar chart at Figure 3, throughout the period under consideration expenditure on diamond prospecting exceeded that on base and precious metal prospecting.

FIGURE 2. TOTAL NUMBER OFPROSPECTING LICENSES ISSUED TO COMPANIES

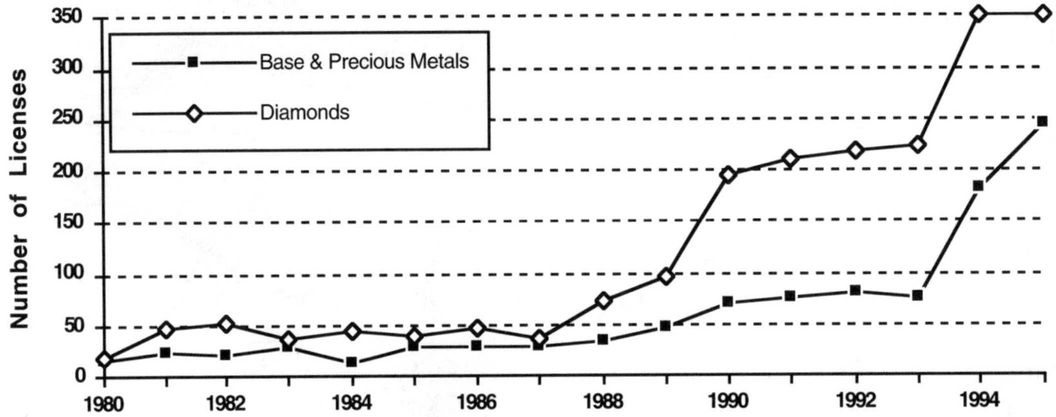

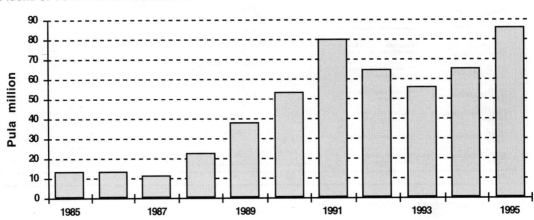

These levels of expenditure on mineral exploration, which are large by developing countries' standards, indicate that Botswana has increasingly become a relatively attractive environment for private sector mineral investment. The foregoing geological survey and exploration effort has shown that there are prospects for future development of several minerals.

FIGURE 3. TOTAL PROSPECTING EXPENDITURES

Brines

The brines of Sua Pan and adjacent areas in the Makgadikgadi depression in north eastern Botswana contain huge resources of common salt, soda ash, potash and other associated minerals as summarised in Table 10. The volume of the brine aquifer measures 32 billion cubic metres and is estimated to contain 8 billion cubic metres of brine reserves (assuming 25% porosity). A further 5.5 billion cubic metres of brine reserves are stored in the overlying sand and clay sequence, and would be expected to drain downwards into the aquifer, and, therefore, recoverable as the brine in it was depleted by pumping.

TABLE 10. TONNAGES OF PRINCIPAL SALTS IN THE BRINE AQUIFER OF SUA PAN AND ADJACENT AREAS

PRINCIPAL SALT	WEIGHT IN MILLIONS OF TONNES
Common Salt (NaCl)	1 026
Soda Ash (Na$_2$CO$_3$)	233
Salt Cake (NaSO$_4$)	10
Muriate of Potash (KCl)	34
Lithium Chloride (LiCl)	1

Source: Department of Geological Survey.

TABLE 11. SODA ASH/BOTSWANA ASH PRODUCTION OF SODA ASH AND COMMON SALT SINCE COMMISSIONING

YEAR	SODA	COMMON SALT
1991	[a]59 750	2 685
1992	116 431	41 889
1993	115 324	73 659
1994	161 903	141 563
1995	205 247	167 120
1996	110 000	120 000
ACTUAL PRODUCTION	768 655	546 916
PLANNED PRODUCTION	1 675 000	3 729 166
SHORTFALL	54%	85%

Note: [a] 7 months only.

Source: Computed from information provided by Botswana Ash (Pty) Limited.

Commercial development of these vast brines was hindered for a long time by lack of appropriate technology, high transport costs and by oversupplied markets. It was not until 1991 that a soda ash and common salt plant was commissioned at Sua Pan with capacity to produce 650 000 tonnes of salt and 300 000 tonnes of soda ash mainly to supply Southern African markets. By 1996, the plant had not achieved design production capacity owing to technical, financial and market problems encountered since commissioning. Table 11 illustrates the extent to which the soda ash and salt plant has fallen short of planned production.

The important point to appreciate is that these brines[9] are a major resource which constitute a feedstock for potential production of various salts and the establishment of chemical industries in the future. At planned production by Botswana Ash there is enough brine to sustain soda ash production for more than 700 years, and common salt for more than 1500 years. The scope for expanding production is therefore considerable.

---

[9]   A detailed description of Sua Pan brines is contained in the Department of Geological Survey's Report No.DG X/17/80 prepared by Dr D. Gould.

Coal and other hydrocarbons

Exploration to date has shown that extensive deposits of low BTU[10] and high ash steaming coal exist. Total resources of measured, indicated and inferred reserves are estimated at over 48 billion tonnes, and those of speculative or hypothetical[11] reserves add to around 164 billion. Table 12 indicates the geographic distribution and the broad classifications of Botswana's coal resources.

TABLE 12. COAL RESOURCES OF BOTSWANA

COALFIELD NAME	RESERVES X MILLION TONNES (MEASURED + INDICATED + INFERRED)	RESOURCES X MILLION TONNES (HYPOTHETICAL + SPECULATIVE)	TOTAL X MILLION TONNES
Morupule	9 824	8 248	18 072
Moijabana	2 406	1 133	3 539
Mmamabula	23 213	-	23 213
Letlhakeng	7 213	63 140	70 353
Ncojane	-	4 725	4 725
Dukwi	1 604	-	1 604
Mmamantswe	598	2 300	2 898
Serule	1 648	8 036	9 684
Dutlwe	2 070	69 670	71 740
Foley	-	6 860	6 860
Bobonong	-	179	179
ALL COALFIELDS TOTAL	48 576	164 291	212 867

Source: Computed from information provided by Department of Geological Survey.

The high transportation, especially overland, costs and the relatively low grade nature of the deposits have hitherto made large-scale mining of Botswana coal uneconomic. More exploration would be needed to determine mineability and other characteristics of these coalfields before large-scale mining could be undertaken. However, the improved regional geopolitical situation has revived interest in Botswana coal as possible feedstock for a large export power station. There has also been talk of mining and processing these vast coal deposits into syncrude and associated chemicals in the course of time.

At present, as already stated, there is only one coal mine, Morupule Colliery, in Botswana, with capacity to produce one million tonnes per annum. This mainly

---

[10] BTU refers to British Thermal Unit, a heat energy measure, equivalent to 1055×10^3 joules.

[11] Hypothetical coal resources refer to undiscovered resources that are reasonably expected to exist in these coalfields in light of known analogous geological conditions. Speculative coal resources also refer to undiscovered resources that are believed to exist but the occurrence probability being slightly lower than that of hypothetical resources.

supplies Morupule power station, BCL and Botswana Ash. The colliery, a subsidiary of Anglo American Corporation, was commissioned in 1973. In 1989, a dry screening plant was installed at the mine to grade coal for sale to other local consumers including textile companies, breweries, food processing plants, brick works and the BMC abattoirs at Lobatse, Francistown and Maun, as well as to Government institutions, such as health facilities and schools. Morupule Colliery sits on a massive coal deposit with thick seams, consistent qualities and few geological problems. The mine has considerable scope for expansion in the future as it is located in the Morupule coal field whose total reserves add up to an estimated 18 billion tonnes.

In the early 1980s, Botswana nearly embarked upon a major coal project[12] with potential socio-economic ramifications that, in conjunction with diamond mining, could have propelled Botswana to a higher orbit of development. In 1982, Shell, which by then had defined a large coal deposit at Kgaswe near Serowe containing 261 million tonnes of saleable coal, signed a joint venture agreement with Government containing terms under which that deposit could be developed for supplying export markets. The project envisaged establishing the mine in two phases of five million tonnes each to produce ten million tonnes per annum when complete. There was even talk of a third phase in the long term. The project, inclusive of requisite infrastructure, would cost over P9700 million in 1995 prices. It was expected to generate a revenue stream of P1464 million per annum and nearly 5000 permanent jobs, as well as substantial additional employment during construction. Shell would provide or guarantee most of the requisite finance. Other expected benefits included direct and indirect taxes to Government and infrastructure, such as a new township and the Trans-Kalahari Railway from the mine to Walvis Bay. The latter would open Southern Africa to the Atlantic, thereby reducing transport costs of trading with the western world. The project's implementation programme had ambitious plans for training locals and promoting local manufacturing to supply some needs of the project. The project was conceived following the findings of the *World Coal Report* which predicted that the price of oil would continue to increase as the supply of oil failed to cope with world demand. The Report, therefore, concluded that there was need for an alternative source of energy for the world. Given the controversies surrounding the development of nuclear energy at the time, coal was seen as a viable alternative.

By the mid-1980s the unexpected happened. The price of coal, especially steaming coal, had begun to decline and oil producers had increased supplies. Other coal producers with excess capacity and ready infrastructure had increased their production. The Kgaswe project ceased to be potentially viable, and had to be dropped. The sponsors accepted the reality with great disappointment. During the planning of the project a lot was learnt and extensive information documented and preserved for future use when circumstances become favourable. Hopefully, luck will be on the side of Botswana next time.

Copper-nickel

Copper mineralization exists at Ngwako Pan near Lake Ngami and over a length of

---

12   See B. Gaolathe, 'Kgaswe Project', paper presented to, and contained in, the proceedings of an International Seminar on Mineral Policy in Botswana organised by the Botswana Geoscientists Association, Gaborone 22–23 February 1988.

160 kilometres in the north west of the country although so far no location has indicated an economically exploitable grade. There is also copper in the Matsitama area, in the north-eastern part of the country, which is being evaluated. Estimated reserves amount to eight to ten million tonnes containing about two percent copper. Another deposit with potential to support a small mine is being evaluated at Bushman copper mine, which has long ceased to operate. The Selebi-Phikwe area has several million tonnes of proven and indicated ore reserves, some of which are being mined, containing about two percent copper-nickel. BCL currently produces over forty thousand tonnes of copper, nickel and other trace minerals from these deposits, while continuing to explore for more reserves. There are seven million tonnes of known copper-nickel reserves at Selkirk and Phoenix in the Francistown area, which are also being mined for toll processing at the BCL smelter. It is expected the increased copper-nickel exploration activity by BCL, which is partly funded by the EU Sysmin facility, will result in definition of additional ore reserves to extend the company's mine life beyond 2010.

Diamonds

As shown in Figure 2, a number of companies are actively prospecting for diamonds; and a number of diamondiferous pipes are being investigated in addition to those over which mining is already taking place. At Orapa and Jwaneng, reserves are large enough to sustain production from open cast operations well into the next century at currently planned annual production levels of nearly 12 million carats each. The Letlhakane mine deposits are also sufficient to sustain open cast mining operations there for nearly twenty years at current production capacity of 900 000 carats per annum. Feasibility studies are being finalised on the Gope diamond pipe in the Central Kalahari Game Reserve and BK pipes near Orapa. First indications are that any mines developed on these deposits will be marginal. The Government has granted De Beers Prospecting a five year mining lease to firm up potential viability of small pipes near Martins Drift. There is every indication that continued diamond exploration will result in additional viable discoveries in Botswana. To date more than one hundred kimberlites of various sizes, some containing diamonds, have been discovered in Botswana. Prospects for continued long-term mining of existing pipes and for discovery of additional viable pipes are good. The main risks lie in the area of marketing this essentially luxury commodity. However, with the cooperation of major producers, such as Botswana and the Russian Federation, there is every reason to expect that the Central Selling Organisation will continue to succeed in promoting the long-term stability of the diamond market. Being dependent on diamonds and having become the biggest gem diamond producer in the world, Botswana has special responsibility in promoting cooperation and orderly behaviour in the marketing of this commodity.

Other minerals

Agate, Botswana pink agate, moss agate, carnelian, chalcedony, crystal quartz and other semi-precious stones are found in the Bobonong area. The stones are gathered by residents, and their cutting and polishing has been in progress since 1975. Further exploration may prove the existence, in economic quantities, of other minerals, such as antimony, chromite, platinum, gold, silver, kyanite, iron, limestone, uranium, glass sand, asbestos, talc, gypsum, lead, zinc, platinum, feldspar, kaolin, graphite and serpentimite. Small quantities of antimony have been traced north of Francistown. Rocks known to be associated with chromite and platinum have been identified in the southern part of the country, and will be investigated in the coming years. Gold mining in Botswana, which started as long ago as 1868 near Francistown, ceased in 1964 partly as a result of depressed prices. The increase in the price of gold in recent years has stimulated interest in the more than 60 abandoned old gold workings in the area and other parts of the country; and limited production has since commenced. Low grade iron ore has been encountered in several places, and limestone occurs as calcrete and marble forms and in cement grade in scattered localities in the country. Uranium traces are also known to exist in Botswana.

More exploratory work is planned during NDP 8 and beyond by the Department of Geological Survey to undertake further assessment of the country's mineral resources potential. It is anticipated that the planned field work by the Department, in collaboration with technical assistance agencies, will throw better light on the potential, and thus encourage further private investment in the mineral sector. Future work will include acquisition of regional geochemical data and conducting of crustal studies to facilitate mineral deposit modelling, undertaking regional aeromagnetic and gravity surveys as well as high resolution airborne geophysics. All this work should result in greater understanding of the geology and potential mineralization of the areas covered by the deep Kalahari sands.

Policy review

The Government, with the assistance of the Economic and Legal Advisory Services Division of the Commonwealth Secretariat and in consultation with the mining industry representatives, has been reviewing certain aspects of mineral legislation and policy with a view to attracting further local and international investment in the exploration and exploitation of Botswana's mineral resources. The review was prompted by the need, in particular, to promote diversified activity in the prospecting for, and exploitation of, non-diamond minerals. It is also aimed at investors who are not aware of Botswana's good track record and who may base their decisions on the written legislation and policies. A number of areas in existing mineral development policy and legislation have been identified for possible improvement to enhance Botswana's competitiveness for mineral investment capital in relation to other countries, such as Chile and Peru, whose highly liberal legal and fiscal regimes have recently been attracting the lion's share of involvement of multi-national corporations in the exploration and exploitation of mineral resources.

The main areas identified for improvement, during these consultations, are summarised hereunder.

(i)   The mineral industry considers the wide ranging powers of ministerial discretion, contained in Botswana's mineral legislation, rather sweeping and therefore a disincentive to investment. To meet this concern, consideration is being given to reducing the unfettered aspects of ministerial discretion by amending the legislation to incorporate more of the principles of administrative law, namely, transparency, consistency, fairness and reasonableness.

(ii)   Botswana's mineral legislation does not give the prospector, who discovers a viable mineral deposit, the automatic right to be issued a mining lease. He has to fulfil certain prescribed conditions, but the ultimate decision to issue the lease rests with the Minister who may add other preconditions. This is a cause for concern to the private sector investors. The idea here is to improve automaticity from prospecting to mining while at the same time ensuring that the Government does not surrender ownership of mineral rights and, with it, the leverage to influence orderly development of the mineral industry.

(iii)   In terms of the existing laws, a prospector who discovers a sub-economic deposit with potential for future viability when, for example, prices improve or cost effective technology is found, loses his tenure over the deposit. What is at stake here is to find ways of entrenching rights but also ensuring that the discoverer does not sit on a deposit he considers uneconomic when other people have ideas of exploiting it profitably.

(iv)   The industry has proposed elimination of uncertainties relating to levels, variability and predictability of the fiscal regime applicable to mining; that is, royalty, income tax and equity participation. In terms of current legislation, royalties may be varied by the Minister upwards or downwards, generally or in relation to a particular mineral project. Applicable taxes have tended to be special with additional profit sharing formulas for very profitable projects. The present policy entitles Government to a 15% free participation in all mineral projects. This is regarded by the industry as additional tax. The authorities are in the process of reviewing the fiscal regime with a view to finding equitable ways of reducing the perceived uncertainties.

(v)   As additional incentives, the authorities are also considering the proposal to amend tax legislation to incorporate more liberal capital write-off and loss carry-forward provisions.

The writer takes the view that the existing mineral policies and legislation have served Botswana relatively well and that the discretions contained therein have been exercised reasonably and fairly to the mutual advantage of the investors and the nation. Therefore, in amending these policies and legislation, cognisance should be taken of Botswana's track record, and care should be exercised to strike an equitable balance between the needs of the investor and the nation.

From the foregoing discussion in this section, it can be concluded that Botswana has relatively great potential for developing her mineral resources in order to realise, in particular, her rapid economic growth objective. However, since minerals are non-renewable assets and mineral projects are not effective instruments of directly meeting other objectives, such as job creation, the other sectors of the economy ought to be vigorously promoted, and a portion of mineral revenues ploughed into viable sustainable investments.

9. ENVIRONMENTAL PROTECTION

The environmental media which assimilate the gaseous, liquid and solid wastes are no longer regarded as free goods, but are viewed as natural resources of great value, requiring attention by public authorities and the private sector. It was in recognition of environmental degradation problems posing a threat to the continued civilised existence of human beings on this planet, that a United Nations Conference on Human Environment was held in Sweden in 1972, and a second one in Brazil in 1992. The outcome of these conferences, together with other national and international consultations, have emphasised the need for a coordinated approach, at international, national and project levels, in devising and implementing measures for the protection of the environment. A coordinated approach is essential since the main transporters of waste, namely water and air, move freely across even international borders.

Botswana has been paying considerable attention to environmental protection in the planning and implementation of mineral projects. Guidelines and control measures have been codified in several acts of Parliament. The acts have been supplemented by further commitments to environmental protection contained in the concession agreements that have been entered into with mining companies. Timely action is necessary, since environmental rehabilitation measures taken too late are likely to be more costly, moreover the costs would unfairly fall on future generations. Generally, a policy of controlling pollution at source, using the best available technology and fully internalising all the environmental protection costs is preferable for a number of reasons. Apart from encouraging project promoters to earnestly seek and adopt less damaging processes, it facilitates measurement of costs and benefits prior to project implementation. In any event, it is easier to monitor and control pollution at sources than to identify, monitor and control or remedy its effects.

Apart from Government policy pronouncements on the environment, including the National Conservation Strategy adopted by Parliament in 1990, there is a body of legislation which provides the legal framework for controlling the impact of mining operations on the environment. The Mines, Quarries, Works and Machinery Act (1973), in addition to providing for matters affecting safety, health and welfare of persons employed in mining operations, empowers the Minister to make regulations, *inter alia*, for the 'protection and preservation of mines and for the protection and rehabilitation of the environment' where it is affected or likely to be affected by mining operations. The Mines and Mineral Act (1976) restricts prospecting within national parks and enforces rehabilitation of sites of mining operations on expiry of mining leases or termination of operations. The Atmospheric Pollution Prevention Act (1971) makes provision for the prevention of pollution of the atmosphere resulting from the carrying out of mining and other industrial operations. All mining leases issued or agreements entered into since Independence contain clauses on the environment which supplement or elaborate the provisions of the law. For example, the Master Agreement entered into, in 1972, between sponsors of the Selebi-Phikwe BCL copper-nickel project and the Government stated that 'the Company shall conduct its operations in such a manner as to prevent, or where prevention is not reasonably practicable, to mitigate consequences adverse to the environment and/or to the health of people affected by such operations'.

The Selebi-Phikwe copper-nickel mining, smelting and power station complex constituted a serious threat to the environment arising from sulphur dioxide gases that were to be emitted and from other wastes. To forestall the problem, the smelter complex incorporated a sulphur reduction plant to reduce the amount of sulphur dioxide emittable into the atmosphere, and, in the process, to produce elemental sulphur as by-product. This technology was chosen in preference to the alternative of manufacturing sulphuric acid because of the distance to potential markets for the acid. The smelter and power station stacks were to attain heights of 525 feet and 250 feet, respectively. These heights were considered enough to afford dilution and dispersion of toxic gases to acceptable concentration levels before reaching tree-line and ground levels. In the event, the sulphur reduction plant did not work and other measures of controlling sulphur dioxide emissions had to be adopted. Since then continuous monitoring has shown that sufficient dilution takes place to reduce ground level sulphur dioxide concentration in residential areas to internationally acceptable standards under most meteorological conditions. In general, through continuous improvement of extraction systems in the plant, the ground level sulphur dioxide concentration has continued to improve over the years. In the meantime, the technology for elemental sulphur production has been proven and BCL is reported to be re-evaluating the project for possible implementation in the future. On the effluent front, a series of sampling points have been established and water quality is monitored with respect to dissolved solids, metal content, acidity and other parameters. Over the years, the quality of the effluent is reported to have improved significantly due to measures taken to recycle poor quality effluent back to the plant for reuse. Plans are also underway to purify small seepage, containing some sulphides and metal sulphates, which still finds its way into the natural drainage.

The diamond mines, which are all open cast operations, pose no serious environmental hazards from emissions to the atmosphere and toxic effluent as the processing plants are electrically driven and the extraction processes are largely mechanical or physical and not chemical in nature. Various measures were, however, taken to ensure that diamond mining in Botswana remained as environmentally friendly as possible. The mining lease areas at Orapa, Letlhakane and Jwaneng cover a combined area of some 27 900 hectares, of which just under 3100 hectares have been disturbed by mining activity. The remaining area of nearly 25 000 hectares is either fallow land or is being managed as game parks. In line with the philosophy and values embodied in Debswana's corporate strategic plan adopted in 1995, detailed environmental situation analyses were recently carried out at all three of the Debswana operating mines. These showed that while the environmental impact was noticeable on the 11.5% of the lease area disturbed by mining activity, the rest of the area was either unaffected, or had been enhanced through the establishment of game parks populated by a variety of wildlife species. Formal comprehensive environmental management programmes have been adopted, with special attention being paid to the management of water, which is a scarce resource in Botswana, and the disposal of industrial waste. It is Debswana's objective to have the environmental management programmes on all its mines certified for compliance with the ISO 14001 standard by 1999.

The Sua Pan soda ash pr   ct was alive to environmental concerns throughout the developmental stage in the 1980s to commissioning in 1991, and even now the operating company, Botswana Ash, has a full time environmental officer. The company operates under a mining lease agreement which, among other things, calls for recognition of Sua Pan as an area of environmental importance. Consequently, the environmental measures adopted by the company have always recognised this uniqueness. For example, a large sum of money was spent on installing power lines underground in order to save the flamingo population that seasonally frequents the area of operations. Even some tree species had to be replanted in safer locations to give way to operations. The company also sponsored the establishment of the Nata Sanctuary and its management structure. The effluent from the refinery, which contains other salts for potential extraction in the future, is returned to the pan. Botswana Ash's future environmental management plans include: a review of its Environmental Conservation Policy to align it with AGENDA 21, UNCED Declaration on Environment and Development and the ICC Business Charter on Sustainable Development; adoption of the ISO 14000 Environmental Management Systems and UNEP Code of Ethics in International Trade in Chemicals; preparation of an Environmental Manual and State of the Environment Report on the company's leaseland.

The only coal mine in Botswana, Morupule Colliery, is an environmental friendly mine with no surface mining and no external pollution of consequence, other than very localised dust from the small live stockpile. The mine, with capacity to produce up to one million tonnes per annum, and very little treatment on site, is a relatively small mining operation. In the mining process, the coal dust is suppressed by the conventional wetting system.

The preceding discussion gives some indication of the progress Botswana has been making in meeting the objective of promoting environmental friendly mineral development. As far as can be ascertained, Botswana is among the countries which have made considerable headway in codifying environmental control legislation. A major aspect of the policy is one of ensuring that environmental protection measures are paid for by operations themselves, i.e., they are internalised. On the control side, the country still faces a shortage of local manpower with requisite expertise in environmental matters. Whereas in the past multinational mining corporations were uncooperative, nowadays they have become positively sensitive to environmental conservation concerns. Indeed, the adoption of ISO 14000 Environmental Management Systems by some of them is an indication of their commitment to meet, and even exceed the minimum national requirements. It must be added that Botswana is among the countries which are in the forefront in preserving pristine environments. Nearly 17% of the country's area comprises national parks or game reserves teeming with wildlife.

These efforts should not be interpreted to mean that Botswana is succeeding in solving all its environmental problems. This is not the case; there are still many environmental conservation problems arising from, for instance, overgrazing, deforestation, soil erosion, sanitation and water pollution.

10. CONCLUDING REMARKS

The above discussion attempted to give a brief explanation of the role of the mineral sector in the economic development of Botswana since Independence some thirty years ago. The sector, which was virtually non-existent then, rapidly increased its influence on the economy of the country, starting with the commissioning of the Orapa diamond mine in 1972 followed by the establishment of the Selebi-Phikwe copper-nickel mine in 1973, Letlhakane diamond mine in 1977 and Morupule Colliery in 1973. The Jwaneng diamond mine came into production in 1982, and by 1995 it had increased production twice, first by installation of the recrush plant (1990) and second by addition of a fourth stream (1995), which increased ore treatment capacity by a third. The medium size copper-nickel mines at Selkirk and Phoenix, whose ore is toll-treated at the BCL smelter, have recently been added to the list of producing mines, as has the soda ash and common salt works at Sua Pan.

The mineral industry in Botswana has largely been responsible for propelling the country's economy, whose average growth has exceeded ten percent per annum in real terms since Independence. Per capita GDP has grown from under P2000 to P9800 in 1995 prices, which is the equivalent of nearly US$3000. The industry, mainly diamond mining, has been the biggest contributor to Botswana's GDP, Government revenues and export earnings. But owing to its capital intensity and automation, it has not been a major provider of direct employment, though it has contributed to acquisition of skills by many Batswana.

The surpluses from diamond mining have helped the country to finance improvement of social and physical infrastructure, built foreign exchange reserves, enabled the progressive liberalization of exchange controls, and allowed Botswana to graduate from the category of least developed countries, and generally improved the welfare of its citizens.

The mineral sector itself is not sufficiently diversified. It is dominated by diamond mining. Worse still, the other two major mineral projects – the copper-nickel and soda ash projects – encountered technical, market and financial problems, which resulted in their failure to achieve anticipated profitability, and have led to calls for the Government to assist them financially.

The foregoing showed that Botswana possesses large reserves of diamondiferous ore bodies in the existing mines to sustain production at high levels for a very long time. Ongoing prospecting for diamonds holds promise for future viable discovery. However, the main risk rests with future market uncertainties; hence, the need to diversify the economy and reduce the country's dependence on this mineral. It was explained that the geology of Botswana holds promise for discovery of other minerals as a result of the growing attractiveness of Botswana for investment in mineral exploration and development.

There is, therefore, every reason to believe that the mineral industry has the potential to grow and diversify if prudently managed and promoted. Nevertheless, it must not be forgotten that minerals are wasting assets which are eventually, even if only after centuries, depleted. The challenge to Botswana is to use the mineral wealth wisely to promote a robust, sustainable and diversified economy. While the country's absorptive capacity remains limited, a percentage of mineral revenues must be set aside in a fund or similar instrument and invested for the future generations.

REFERENCES

Bank of Botswana. *Annual Report*, 1995.

Botswana Geoscientists Association, Seminar on Mineral Policy in Botswana, Proceedings, 22–23 February 1988.

Carney, J.N., Aldiss, D.T. and Lock, N.P. 1994. 'The Geology of Botswana', *Botswana Geological Survey Bulletin*, 37.

Debswana Diamond Company. *Annual Report, 1994*.

Gaolathe, B. 1980. 'The Costs and Benefits of Mineral Development'. MSc Thesis, University of Bradford.

Ministry of Finance and Development Planning. 1991. *National Development Plan 7, 1991–1997*, Chapter 8. Government Printer, Gaborone.

Ministry of Mineral Resources and Water Affairs. 1996. 'Mineral Development'. Draft Chapter for NDP 8.

Mikesell, R.F. 1983. *Foreign Investment in Mining Projects, Case Studies of Recent Experiences*, Chapter 3, BCL's Selebi-Phikwe Nickel/Copper Mine in Botswana. Oelgeschlager, Gun and Hain Inc., Cambridge, Mass.

Sohnge, A.P.G. 1986. *Mineral Provinces of Southern Africa, Mineral Deposits of Southern Africa*. Geological Society of South Africa. pp1–23.

Acknowledgements

I am indebted to the following for responding to my requests for certain unpublished information: BCL Limited, Botswana Ash (Pty) Ltd, Debswana Diamond Company (Pty) Ltd, Morupule Colliery (Pty) Limited, Ministry of Mineral Resources and Water Affairs, Department of Mines, Department of Geological Survey, Central Statistics Office and Department of Customs and Excise. I am also grateful to my personal secretary, Mercy Morapedi, for reducing my manuscript to a readable form.

Chapter 5

Employment and Living Standards

Trends in Real Wages and Labour Productivity in Botswana

W. Mandlebe

1. INTRODUCTION

With recent developments in international trade – especially the conclusion of the Uruguay Round agreement and the establishment of the World Trade Organization (WTO) – the coming decades look as if they will be characterised by strong competition among the economies of the world. As a consequence, it will be critical for producers in Botswana to become more competitive if they are to maintain, and hopefully expand their share of the market in the regional and global economies. While the principle of comparative advantage will continue to dictate world trading patterns, achieving competitive advantage through appropriate policies will be critical.

In Botswana, the need to increase productivity has become paramount as the country moves away from traditional to non-traditional exports. While Botswana has been fortunate to have high quality diamonds as its major export, this is a non-renewable commodity with very limited economic linkages, which will eventually be depleted, hence the need to diversify the economy in order to achieve another source of strong economic growth. The key to this is the expansion of non-traditional exports, which will, hopefully, provide adequate employment opportunities, which, in turn, will help reduce poverty. But non-traditional exports, such as tourism, adding greater value to goods produced in the livestock sector, expanding manufacturing and business service exports, must compete with similar industries in other countries, all of which are also trying to expand their markets. To have a competitive edge in these markets, domestic producers will have to produce high quality goods at low enough prices, such that they can compete with other similar goods produced in other countries. Some studies have shown that labour costs are among the most potent determinants of competitiveness (Porter, 1990).[1] Other determinants of competitiveness include a stable macroeconomic environment, innovation and economies of scale.

This paper discusses the impact of changes in real wages in relation to changes in labour productivity and the subsequent impact such changes have on the competitiveness of the Botswana economy. The plan of the paper is as follows. Section 2 reviews the historical trends in real wages and labour productivity in the country. Analysis of the trends is undertaken on a sectoral basis. There are many factors that may contribute to a divergence in the trends of real wages and labour productivity,

---

[1]   The idea of competitive advantage as put forward by Porter is still a subject of debate. Some recent work on the same topic, by among others, Paul Krugman have raised doubts about its validity.

including the small size of some sectors, the dominance of a few firms in some sectors, institutional rigidities or Government policies. Section 3 discusses the Government diversification strategy in the light of the levels of productivity in the sectors targeted as potential engines of growth. In recognition of the limited domestic market, the success of the diversification strategy will depend on how successfully the domestic producers can penetrate the world market, which is characterised by fierce competition among producers. Some policy options are discussed in Section 4 of the paper. Both short and long-term options are considered. Section 5 contains summary conclusions.

2. THE EVOLUTION OF REAL WAGES AND LABOUR PRODUCTIVITY

The evolution of real wages over the past two decades is shown in Table 1.[2] The average national real wage fell by 0.3% per annum between 1974/75 and 1993/94. Sectors which contributed to the decline were manufacturing falling by 4.9% per annum, construction by 4.1% per annum and services by 3.4% per annum. At the same time, sectors which recorded positive growth in real wages over the period included agriculture, with 2.6% growth, water and electricity with 3.3%, and transport and communications with 3.8%. In Government, real wages grew marginally, by 0.1% per annum over the period.

The decline in real wages in the three sectors of manufacturing, services and trade, which are targeted for economic diversification is, at first glance, a welcome development, since labour cost is one of the major costs of production. However, this development will need to be viewed against changes in labour productivity before conclusions can be drawn. This comparison is important because a fall in real compensation per worker will mean a fall in real labour cost per unit output, only if it is *not* accompanied by a similar, or greater, fall in the average productivity of labour.

Table 2 contains trends in labour productivity in Botswana over the two decades. Average labour productivity is defined simply as GDP at constant prices divided by employment. The trend in average labour productivity in many sectors over the period is a cause for concern. National labour productivity grew by 1.4% per annum over the period, mainly due to strong productivity growth in the mining sector reflecting the capital intensity of the mining operations. The water and electricity, transport and communications and Government sectors also registered positive growth in productivity over this time. However, the other sectors showed either no improvement in average labour productivity, or a decline in productivity.

The disappointing productivity performance in the manufacturing, trade and services sectors are of major concern since they are among those sectors that Government is currently encouraging as additional engines of economic growth. Over the period 1974/75 through 1993/94, labour productivity in manufacturing fell, on average, by 3.5% per annum. One possible cause of this decline is a gradual change in the composition of output in this sector towards more labour intensive products and techniques.

---

2   The real wage is defined as the average annual compensation of employees in a sector, deflated by implicit GDP deflator for the sector, or simply the real product wage.

Some of it may also be explained by the impact of the Financial Assistance Policy (FAP), which subsidises labour input. The capital grant under FAP is calculated on the basis of the number of employees – currently at P1200 person employed. While this grant could be justified as a correction to the market distortions caused by minimum wage regulations to the wage rate, it is evident that in the short run, this grant has provided some incentive for companies to over-employ labour, at least during the period of the support. This has a negative impact on productivity. Average labour productivity grew marginally by 0.4% per annum in the trade sector during the review period, while it actually fell in the services sector by 0.3% per annum.

TABLE 1. Trends in Real Wage Indices, (1974/75 = 100)

	AG	MN	MA	E & W	CO	TR	TPT	FI	SE	GVT	T
74/75	100.0	100.0	100.0	100.0	100.0	100.0	100.0	100.0	100.0	100.0	100.0
75/76	124.4	103.8	75.7	91.4	97.1	88.4	67.7	83.3	107.9	105.4	101.0
76/77	135.7	98.2	73.7	107.4	116.5	101.5	66.3	64.1	96.5	106.0	105.2
77/78	141.3	137.0	102.0	72.5	93.5	116.3	67.3	85.6	89.9	94.9	115.0
78/79	104.0	85.4	64.8	84.1	96.1	124.3	72.8	110.2	103.4	96.2	103.0
79/80	133.1	60.7	71.6	96.3	89.9	136.9	106.9	100.4	98.2	87.8	96.0
80/81	125.1	101.0	69.4	85.9	88.7	123.1	92.3	87.4	104.1	98.0	111.0
81/82	130.1	211.2	66.4	71.0	57.1	94.9	102.2	91.6	77.4	70.6	113.2
82/83	176.6	206.8	58.4	54.0	63.8	93.2	99.2	106.1	92.0	74.7	118.5
83/84	148.6	206.9	46.4	67.9	76.6	128.1	114.2	102.0	95.4	75.7	128.0
84/85	137.8	128.6	35.9	61.9	94.7	111.2	96.7	120.0	110.2	83.1	114.6
85/86	162.0	114.4	38.1	78.7	78.5	106.5	96.4	135.2	130.0	70.7	102.8
86/87	122.4	138.7	32.7	91.9	63.5	89.0	111.2	138.5	106.5	76.3	104.6
87/88	106.8	112.3	38.7	133.1	46.4	119.9	129.9	140.8	74.9	83.3	96.5
88/89	118.4	82.4	42.3	143.1	52.5	138.1	203.5	127.7	83.2	113.0	95.8
89/90	132.9	93.7	31.4	160.3	40.7	98.8	204.7	129.1	76.3	107.5	92.9
90/91	147.0	119.2	30.5	153.3	37.1	85.0	179.8	106.9	62.7	95.4	90.3
91/92	142.2	123.0	43.7	78.3	56.0	108.6	133.4	106.8	114.2	80.6	89.8
92/93	145.3	189.2	50.3	118.3	59.8	111.5	142.8	96.7	113.8	77.8	100.0
93/94	164.2	111.6	38.2	184.0	44.9	83.0	203.2	91.6	51.9	102.8	95.1
AAGR	2.6	0.6	-4.9	3.3	-4.1	-1.0	3.8	-0.5	-3.4	0.1	-0.3

Key: AG = Agriculture. MN = Mining. MA = Manufacturing. E&W = Electricity & Water. CO = Construction. TR = Trade. TPT = Transport. FI = Finance. SE = Services. GVT = Government. T = Total. AAGR = Average annual growth rates.

Source: Central Statistics Office, MFDP.

Table 2. Trends in Labour Productivity Indices, (1974/75 = 100)

	Ag	Mn	Ma	E & W	Co	Tr	Tpt	Fi	Se	Gvt	T
74/75	100.0	100.0	100.0	100.0	100.0	100.0	100.0	100.0	100.0	100.0	100.0
75/76	106.0	149.0	109.9	121.7	90.7	102.1	97.4	92.2	126.4	110.6	106.4
76/77	116.7	130.2	109.0	88.1	114.8	110.1	93.3	71.3	99.9	108.0	105.6
77/78	110.0	240.1	105.2	76.4	107.7	129.5	108.9	82.1	90.6	98.3	119.4
78/79	83.9	277.2	114.2	71.5	95.7	159.3	97.9	104.4	104.6	99.6	119.3
79/80	103.5	293.2	69.3	68.8	86.2	214.0	136.1	121.3	104.6	93.5	125.6
80/81	93.5	343.9	85.2	60.7	72.7	189.2	94.7	76.2	106.7	103.9	123.3
81/82	85.4	402.0	93.0	59.1	46.1	121.7	89.9	76.5	76.8	76.2	112.8
82/83	85.4	604.9	76.0	42.6	59.5	104.1	106.1	69.3	89.7	84.5	126.1
83/84	69.0	691.1	59.2	61.1	79.2	116.1	116.4	72.3	99.7	85.9	140.4
84/85	56.2	684.7	47.7	70.0	78.7	117.6	105.3	81.0	109.9	92.7	138.2
85/86	68.6	706.0	55.6	93.5	66.9	116.1	132.8	91.9	128.4	80.9	140.3
86/87	55.7	794.9	53.8	98.6	63.8	103.0	116.8	76.4	110.8	92.1	136.8
87/88	79.4	806.0	58.9	107.7	53.2	111.1	165.7	71.2	110.8	105.8	136.5
88/89	85.7	905.8	52.5	121.4	60.0	117.5	169.6	68.7	100.1	108.0	136.9
89/90	83.2	853.4	42.7	129.9	53.7	106.5	165.6	67.7	103.5	127.4	129.4
90/91	81.7	910.6	40.8	118.3	50.0	100.7	170.5	60.2	94.0	134.3	127.5
91/92	91.5	952.4	44.3	125.1	52.3	116.3	167.5	57.2	100.2	141.4	123.8
92/93	93.7	821.7	50.6	139.7	53.1	116.9	190.0	69.6	107.6	130.8	125.9
93/94	103.2	917.4	50.9	158.3	56.8	108.8	203.8	72.7	95.1	135.2	129.3
AAGR	0.2	12.4	-3.5	2.4	-2.9	0.4	3.8	-1.7	-0.3	1.6	1.4

Key: Ag = Agriculture. Mn = Mining. Ma = Manufacturing. E&W = Electricity & Water. Co = Construction. Tr = Trade. Tpt = Transport. Fi = Finance. Se = Services. Gvt = Government. T = Total. AAGR = Average annual growth rates.

Source: Central Statistics Office, MFDP.

According to neoclassical economic theory, labour should be paid the value of its marginal product. The relationship between the average product of labour and the real product wage can be established by using a simple production function, such as the Cobb-Douglas, given by equation (1):

$$X = AL^{\alpha}K^{\beta} \qquad\qquad (1)$$

$$\frac{\partial X}{\partial L} = \alpha AL^{\alpha-1}K^{\beta} = \alpha \frac{X}{L} \qquad\qquad (2)$$

Where:

X = value added
L = employment
K = capital stock
A = scaling factor
α = elasticity of output with respect to labour
β = elasticity of output with respect to capital

Assuming competition in product and labour markets, profit maximizing behaviour on the part of firms implies that the marginal product of labour is equal to the real product wage.

$$\frac{\partial X}{\partial L} = \frac{w}{P} \qquad (3)$$

Where:

w = nominal wage per employee
P = implicit output deflator

Combining equations (3) and (2) gives the following relationship:

$$\alpha \frac{X}{L} = \frac{w}{P} \qquad (4)$$

In theory, movements in the real product wage should display the same trend as that of the average labour productivity in a sector, which would keep the share of labour in the value of output stable. In Tables 1 and 2, this trend is observed. That is, those sectors whose real wages were declining also had their labour productivity declining at the same time. However, national average labour productivity grew by 1.4% per annum, while national real wage declined by 0.3% per annum over the period. Large divergences in the growth rates between labour productivity and real wage among certain sectors were also observed during the period. For instance, labour productivity in the mining sector grew by an average of 12.4% per annum during the period due to the capital intensiveness of the mining operations, and the high and increasing returns to mineral exploitation, while real wages in that sector grew marginally by 0.6% per annum. Similarly, sectors such as manufacturing and construction experienced large declines in their real wages of 4.9% per annum and 4.1% per annum, while their labour productivity declined by 3.5% per annum and 2.9% per annum, respectively.

The foregoing analysis indicates that, in general, real wages tended to move in tandem with productivity. However, the fall in labour productivity was not as great as that in real wages in the manufacturing sector, indicating some marginal improvement in productivity. In the trade sector, productivity rose marginally by 0.4% per annum while real wages declined, also marginally, by 1.0% per annum. The two indices declined in the financial sector over the period.

3. ECONOMIC DIVERSIFICATION AND COMPETITIVENESS

For the past two decades, Botswana has enjoyed impressive economic growth, mainly due to the mining sector. The mining projects not only provided direct employment and output, but also had widespread effects on the whole economy through Customs Union payments and mineral revenues, which enabled Government to finance development expenditures and expand the infrastructure, economic and social services.

Despite this performance, the need for economic diversification has always been in the forefront of the Government's development policy, as indicated by the successive themes of the past National Development Plans (NDPs). The themes for both NDP 7 and 8 emphasised the need for economic diversification as the basis for long-term economic development for the country. This is in recognition of the fact that diamonds are non-renewable commodities; and one day the supply will be exhausted. As a small country, Botswana has to focus its diversification strategy on expanding in regional and international markets through increased competitiveness.

One of the potential sectors for economic diversification is the tourism sub-sector. Botswana's natural beauty, found in the Okavango Delta, national parks and game reserves, offers a basis for more rapid tourism growth. However, the development of this sector would require certain policies and programmes to be put in place in order for it to compete successfully with other regional destinations. Some of the elements of such policies or strategies would be the need to create a conducive environment in terms of macroeconomic policies, creation of tourism infrastructure and publicity. There is presently a perception that Botswana is a high cost destination in terms of tourism. This is blamed on the strong currency in the region, high entrance fees as well as high labour costs. It would be critical that while the exchange rate policy is managed such that it promotes this sector, the growth in the unit labour cost is also contained in order to promote competitiveness. The regional approach towards tourism development is the promotion of 'regional tour packages'. The only way Botswana can compete in this regional market is to ensure that the growth in real wages is in line with increases in labour productivity. Furthermore, the unit labour costs should be competitive with those prevailing in other countries offering the same service.

A review of real wage trends and productivity in trade, a proxy sector for tourism, and two other sectors of manufacturing and finance, which are targeted by Government as possible additional engines of growth reveals some interesting insights. The movements in the real product wage and average labour productivity in these sectors, as given in Tables 1 and 2 above, indicates that the ratio of these two measures, which gives the share of labour in the value of output, has fallen by as little as one percent per annum in manufacturing and trade, and has risen by a little over one percent in finance. The share of the operating surplus in production has, therefore, gone up marginally in the former two sectors and gone down in the latter. Whether or not production has become correspondingly more or less profitable depends, however, on what has happened to the capital intensity of production in these sectors. Also, conclusions cannot be drawn on changes in relative competitiveness without making comparisons of movements in the above indicators across countries.

An alternative way to look at the issue of competitiveness would be to concentrate on unit labour cost of output, which is defined as the average real wage earnings divided by the average productivity of labour. Trends in the unit labour costs in the three sectors identified by Government as possible engines of growth can then be

FIGURE 1. TOTAL UNIT LABOUR COST

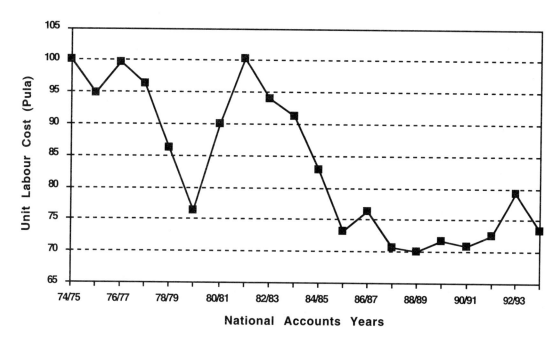

identified. Figure 1 shows trends in unit labour costs for the whole economy. In the period between 1974/75 and 1993/94, total unit labour costs declined, on average, by 1.4% per annum. To what extent this movement in unit labour costs has affected the competitiveness of Botswana producers in the international market depends on a number of factors, such as the extent to which international prices of traded goods have changed over the period; what has happened to the capital-labour ratio and to interest rates; and how labour costs have changed in the other trading partner countries. However, other things remaining equal, the implication of the decrease in unit labour costs over the period taken by itself is that Botswana has not been losing its competitiveness in the international market against other competitors over the period.

Trends in the movements of unit labour costs in sectors targeted by Government for economic diversification reveal the same picture as that of the overall economy, that is, the indices have been falling during the period. In general, the unit labour costs in all the three sectors were declining in line with falling real wages and labour productivity levels over the period. Manufacturing unit labour costs fell by an average of 1.4% per annum over the period while at the same time, real wages and labour productivity levels declined by 4.9% and 3.5% per annum, respectively. Figure 2 shows developments in unit labour costs in the manufacturing sector over the past two decades. Average labour productivity in the manufacturing sector declined from 114.2 in 1978/79 to a low of 40.8 in 1990/91, before recovering to 50.9 in 1993/94. A similar trend was observed in the real wage index when it declined from 102.0 in 1977/78 to 38.2. The fall in labour productivity in the manufacturing sector, which started around 1981/82 coincided with the introduction of the FAP in 1982. This programme has two objectives, viz. employment creation and economic diversification. The recent review of the programme in 1995 indicated that it had succeeded in meeting the first objective of employment creation for unskilled Batswana in a cost effective way. With regard to the second objective of sustainable economic diversifica-

FIGURE 2. UNIT LABOUR COST – MANUFACTURING

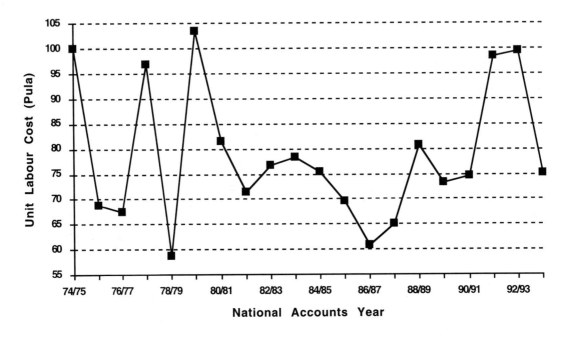

tion, the conclusion of the study was somewhat unclear. One thing that clearly emerges from the report is that jobs created under the programme remain vulnerable as many firms tend to fold up as soon as the FAP support elapses. The other effect of the programme was on labour productivity. While the fall in labour productivity in manufacturing sector cannot be totally ascribed to the introduction of the FAP, which subsidises the employment of labour, the coincidence of the fall in the labour productivity in this sector with the introduction of the programme in 1981/82 gives strong reason to suspect that the programme may have had a negative impact on labour productivity. However, the decline in the average unit labour cost in the sector is a desirable trend since it would ensure that domestic manufacturing enterprises are able to compete with others producing the same commodities in regional and international markets.

With regard to the finance sector, unit labour costs rose by an average of 1.2% per annum over the review period while real wages and labour productivity declined by 0.5% and 1.7% per annum, respectively. During the period 1980/81 and 1992/93, real wages rose faster than average labour productivity, resulting in a marginal increase in the unit labour costs. The period from 1980/81 to 1991/92 was characterised by an economic boom, as well as relatively low competition in the domestic financial market. Consequently, financial institutions could have been generally accommodative of wage increases in excess of the growth in labour productivity. The period starting 1992/93 marked the beginning of a mild downturn for the financial sector as the economy began to slow down, at a time when more financial institutions were entering the domestic market, thus increasing competition. The response of the major players in the sector to these challenges was to consolidate and restructure, resulting in retrenchments and adopting performance-based rewards to labour. As Botswana

FIGURE 3. UNIT LABOUR COST – FINANCE

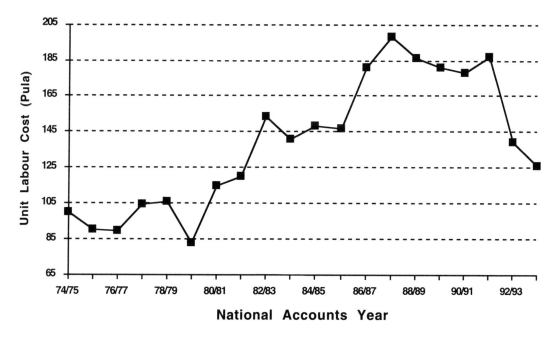

National Accounts Year

embarks on the road to establish itself as a financial services centre in the region, it will be developments in unit labour costs that will determine whether there is success or even survival. Services produced in such centres are supposed to be highly competitive. Botswana would have to establish itself as a highly competitive jurisdiction in order to compete with others. Relatively high unit labour costs due to either low average labour productivity growth or high real wages, *ceteris paribus*, will render the country uncompetitive *vis-à-vis* other jurisdictions offering the same services.

The third sector targeted by Government as a possible additional engine for growth

FIGURE 4. UNIT LABOUR COST –TRADE

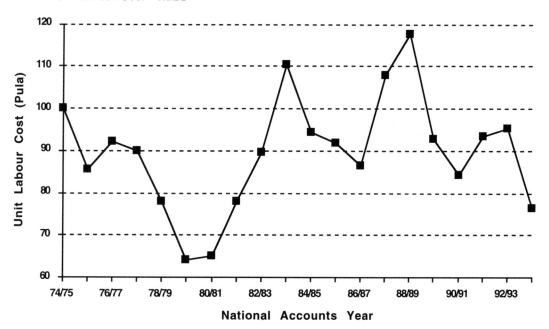

National Accounts Year

is tourism. In the absence of separate data on tourism, the trade sector data are used as a proxy for the tourism sector. However, some caveats are in order. One important point is that the trade sector is dominated by wholesale and retail trade, rather than tourism. In fact, the current contribution of the sub-sector to output, revenues and employment remain small. Nonetheless, the trade sector remains the closest proxy that can be used for tourism. There are indications that the tourism sub-sector has the potential to contribute more if developed in a sustainable and competitive way. The unit labour costs in the trade sector were decreasing, on average, by 1.4% per annum while real wages declined marginally by 1% per annum. Thus, labour productivity increased marginally by 0.4% over the period. Figure 4 shows developments in unit labour costs in the trade sector. The fall in unit labour costs by 1.4% per annum, indicates a marginal gain in competitiveness in this sector. The real wage index moved from 136.9 in 1979/80 to 83.0 in 1993/94 while that of average labour productivity fell from 214.0 to 108.8 over the same period. For most part of the period, the movements in the two indices displayed a close trend, save for 1979/80, when the average labour productivity index was way above 200, while that of real wages was around 130.

In general, the trends in the movements of unit labour costs in the three sectors targeted by Government for economic diversification revealed that the indices have been falling, on average, during the period under review. The general decline in unit labour costs, reflecting either the slow growth in real wages or some improvement in labour productivity in the economy implies increased competitiveness for domestic exporters in the international markets. The success of the Government's strategy of economic diversification in the future will therefore depend on the country's ability to maintain the strategy of real wage restraint and improved productivity, assuming other policies such as the exchange rate remains the same.

4. SOME POLICY OPTIONS

The above analysis reveals a number of issues that should be given serious consideration by Government if the objective of economic diversification through manufacturing, tourism and financial services is to be achieved. A concerted effort is required to control the growth in unit labour costs, in addition to maintaining a close alignment between movements in real wages and average labour productivity in the economy in general, and the targeted sectors in particular. Given that productivity improvement is a long-term goal, there will be a need to ensure that, in the short run, the growth in real wages in the economy is maintained around that of productivity. This can be achieved through a further liberalization of the labour market by simplifying the wage system and leaving employers and employees free to bargain. The recent liberalization of collective bargaining is a welcome development, but there may be need to revisit the issue of minimum wages as they do not seem to serve any economic purpose in an environment of surplus unskilled labour. Their immediate effect is to undermine employment creation. The emerging scarcity of jobs and the introduction of performance related schemes in some private sector enterprises should drive productivity improvements in the country. However, Government, as one of the major employers in the economy, can contribute significantly to the improvement in productivity in the country through down-sizing its work-force and the introduction of performance related pay schemes in the public sector.

In the medium to long term, improved labour productivity and lower unit labour costs will be the key to Botswana's competitiveness. Lower unit labour costs would help to ensure that domestically produced goods and services are competitive in the regional and international markets. To this end, the establishment of the Botswana National Productivity Centre and other related programmes aimed at increasing labour productivity and reducing unit costs of output should help in improving the country's competitiveness in the long run.

With regard to the FAP programme, there is a need to reconsider the incentives offered to ensure that the wage subsidy only compensates for the market distortion caused by the minimum wage regulations and nothing more. The present formulation is such that companies' entitlement to the capital grant is based on the number of people employed. That means, a highly productive company which meets its production targets with a lesser number of workers will be forced to engage more workers to meet its contractual obligations with the Government or else it would be required to pay back part of the capital grant advanced to it. The result is that when the programme expires after five years, these companies are usually compelled to restructure their operations. In some cases, companies close down because they cannot compete in the international markets at current levels of wages and labour productivity. The capital grant of the FAP should be tied to productivity improvements rather than to the absolute number of people employed.

5. SUMMARY AND CONCLUSIONS

The paper has reviewed trends in real wages, labour productivity and unit labour costs in the country over the past two decades. Unit labour costs have been declining in line with falling real wages and labour productivity. The country was able to maintain some competitiveness mainly due to the policy of wage restraint, which over compensated for the decline in labour productivity during the period.

To improve the competitiveness of these sectors, some policy actions will be required, which include, among others, continued restraining of real wage growth, improving labour productivity, relaxing constraints on the wage bargaining system, with the possible removal of minimum wages, and reviewing some components of the FAP scheme, such as the capital grant to make the system supportive of improvements in labour productivity. These are some of the hard policy options facing policy-makers as the country enters the 21st Century.

REFERENCES

Mazu, J. 1995. 'The Minimum Wage Revisited',*The Challenge*, July–August, 1995.

Gills, M. and Perkins, D.H., (eds.). 1987. *Economics of Development*. Norton and Company, New York.

Government of Botswana. 1991. *National Development Plan 7, 1991–1997*. Gaborone.

Ministry of Finance and Development Planning. *Budget Speeches 1992–96*. Gaborone.

Ministry of Finance and Development Planning. 1994. *Mid-Term Review of NDP 7*. Gaborone.

Ministry of Finance and Development Planning. 1996. *NDP 8 Macroeconomic Outline*. Gaborone.

Ministry of Finance and Development Planning. 1995. 'Draft FAP Annual Report'. Gaborone.

Ministry of Finance and Development Planning. 1994. *FAP Evaluation Report*. Gaborone.

Porter, M. E. 1990. 'The Competitive Advantage of Nations', *Harvard Business Review* (March–April, 1990), No.2.

Income Inequality in Botswana – Trends Since Independence[1]

D. J. Hudson and M. Wright[2]

1. INTRODUCTION

It has long been recognised that Botswana has an unequal distribution of income, whether incomes are measured on a household or individual basis. The unequal distribution of income in Botswana is not unusual among developing countries. Of those in Sub-Saharan Africa, it might be considered to be fairly typical (Bank of Botswana, 1996). But, at the same time, there are other developing countries where income is more equally distributed, and this equality has not necessarily been at the expense of lower overall living standards and rates of economic growth. Most notable in this regard are several of the so-called 'miracle' economies in East Asia.

Income inequality in Botswana has been a matter of official concern since Independence in 1966. The founding official policy document, the *Transitional Plan for Social and Economic Development,* stated that:

> 'A more equitable distribution of income is a long range objective of Government policy.' (Government of Botswana 1966, para. 49).

A more equal income distribution is widely seen as a key component of social justice, a basic objective of Government's development policy since the time of the second National Development Plan (NDP 2) (Government of Botswana, 1970).

The two key questions to be addressed in this paper are, first, what can be said about trends in income inequality in Botswana since Independence, and, second, to what extent have real income levels increased?[3]

Discussion of income distribution in many countries is hampered by the lack of reliable data. For example, in the UNDP Human Development Report for 1996, of 127 developing countries that are covered, the Report includes no information on income distribution for 79 more (UNDP, 1996, pp170–171).

A comparative study will conclude fairly quickly that Botswana is a relatively good performer in producing such information. Official commitment to the goal of greater income equality has been accompanied by substantial efforts to acquire relevant

---

[1] This paper was originally prepared for the symposium *The Quality of Life in Botswana* held in October 1996 in Gaborone, organised by the Botswana Society. An abbreviated version of the paper appears in *Poverty and Plenty: The Botswana Experience.* Botswana Society, Gaborone.

[2] The authors wish to thank those who have provided information, comments and other inputs for the preparation of this paper. In particular, colleagues at the Bank of Botswana, the Botswana Institute for Development Policy Analysis (BIDPA), and the Central Statistics Office (CSO).

[3] The closely related questions of the incidence and depth of poverty in Botswana are covered in the paper by Jefferis in this volume.

statistical information. Following early partial survey work conducted by the Central Statistics Office (CSO), Botswana was among the first countries in the world to take advantage of the World Bank programme initiated in 1973 to provide assistance in collecting data on income distribution. This resulted in the Rural Income Distribution Survey (RIDS) for 1974/75, which covered some ninety percent of Botswana's population, and included the first definition of a poverty datum line in Botswana. The RIDS was followed by two national Household Income and Expenditure Surveys (HIES 1 and HIES 2), for 1985/86 and 1993/94, (CSO, 1996a).

This said, availability and use of relevant data in Botswana is not unproblematic. Comparability between the surveys must be handled carefully, due to differences in both methodology and prevailing climatic conditions in the survey years which influence significantly incomes in the agriculture-dependent rural areas. While the RIDS coincided with rainfall that was about the best that Botswana has experienced in modern times, both of the later surveys were conducted during periods of extensive drought.

A major conclusion of this analysis is that there is no real evidence to support the suggestion that inequalities in Botswana have been widening. While this may have occurred in the decade immediately following Independence, the available evidence from the three surveys suggests, if anything, that inequalities have been reduced, if only slightly, since 1974/75. Also, while the comparison between the RIDS and the later surveys is clouded by the very different rainfall in the survey periods, the data from the two HIES show a very clear trend towards higher household incomes at all percentiles of the income distribution.

This goes some way to answering critics of Government's record who have alleged that income inequalities in Botswana are widening, and that much of the population has missed out on any substantial benefit from the overall growth in the economy. The facts, objectively measured and interpreted, point in the opposite direction. This does not, however, imply that poverty has been eliminated in Botswana. The assertion that people in Botswana, including the poor, are *on average* better off than previously, is not contradicted by the self-evident continued existence of pockets of extreme poverty in parts of the country.

This paper is organised as follows. Section 2 looks briefly at the history of early post-Independence concerns about income distribution in Botswana. This is in the context of illustrating certain important points and is not intended as a comprehensive historical account. Section 3 reviews the basic data sources, with particular attention to their compatibility for comparative purposes. Section 4 discusses some basic issues on methodology, while information on income distribution trends in Botswana from Independence to the most recent HIES is presented in Section 5. Important influences on the distribution of income are reviewed in Section 6. Concluding comments follow, which include some observations on Botswana's position in the international context.

2. INCOME DISTRIBUTION IN BOTSWANA: EARLY CONCERNS

While substantial economic development was yet to get underway in the pre-Independence economy, it should not be assumed that inequalities in incomes were absent at that time. The existence of significant inequalities in the Bechuanaland Protectorate is well attested to. There is a cogent case that such inequalities have not only long been a feature of Tswana society but were also an accepted and reinforced social norm, possibly with consequences continuing to the present day (Good, 1993).

In the run up to Independence, inequalities were a source of social pressures that were coalescing around the emerging modern political groupings. These included, *inter alia*: the demands from aspirant cattle farmers for better access to grazing lands; and the dissatisfaction concerning inequalities in conditions of work in the small urban-modern sectors – the wide disparities in civil service wages between the highest and the lowest ranks being an obvious example (Parsons *et al.*, 1995, p167 and p199).[4]

Nevertheless, in the years immediately prior to Independence there is little evidence that income distribution was a matter of concern to the Protectorate Administration. *The Bechuanaland Protectorate Development Plan, 1963–1968*, makes no reference to the issue (Bechuanaland Protectorate Administration, 1963). This lack of concern is not surprising. In the early 1960s income distribution issues had yet to emerge as a subject of serious concern worldwide (Fishlow, 1996). Moreover, in the absence of data to the contrary, enshrined in colonial development planning was the comforting belief that nearly all adult male Batswana were cattle owners (Parsons *et al.*, 1995, p204). This notion was, however, entirely without empirical support, as subsequently became clear.

As already noted, the issue of income distribution was from the start an explicit concern of the post-Independence Government, although at that stage it was not articulated beyond a general statement of long-term intent. The Transitional Plan noted, sensibly, that it was 'not meaningful', in the absence of relevant data, to discuss development objectives in terms of income levels (Government of Botswana, 1966, p42). However, the need for improved data was clearly recognised: the CSO had been formed and the Plan included provision in the capital budget for an agricultural census.

It was clear at an early stage that the development path being followed by Botswana would have significant distributional implications. Even before rapid levels of growth were achieved, only a small minority of Batswana were benefiting directly from the opportunities of a modern economy. The acceleration in economic development that followed Independence made this dilemma more acute. At the same time, the emergence of economic statistics began to quantify these inequalities. Notably, the 1967/68 Labour Census provided estimates of average wages in the various productive sectors, while the 1968/69 Agricultural Survey revealed the extent of rural inequalities, particularly in terms of cattle and land ownership (see Section 5).

As a consequence, a much more precise diagnosis could be made which both included and demanded the support of more accurate and wide-ranging statistics. This is seen clearly, for example, in NDP 2, which featured distributional concerns. In particular, while the extent of rural inequality indicated in the Agricultural Survey was noted as a matter needing attention '...as development proceeds...' (Government

---

[4]   The disparities in civil service wages were particularly severe because of the pressures of apartheid which impacted on the Bechuanaland administration because of its heavy reliance on South African personnel and the geographical anomaly of its headquarters being located in Mafeking (Colclough and McCarthy, 1980, Chapter 7). The legacy of this structure continued to be a problem for the Government of independent Botswana.

of Botswana, 1970, para.1.23), the most pressing concern was the emergence of a rural/urban divide. The consequences of planned mineral developments were likely to reinforce this trend:

'If Botswana is to avoid the social unrest caused by gross inequalities of wealth between the rural and urban sectors experienced in other African countries, wages [sic] levels on the mines and in Government ... must be restrained, and the surplus resources thus liberated used to promote social development.' (ibid., para.2.19)

During the period of NDP 2, policies based firmly on the objective of redistribution came into being. A principal example is the set of measures which followed the 1972 White Paper on the National Policy on Incomes, Employment, Prices and Profit, commonly referred to as the Incomes Policy.

This emphasis on the rural/urban'divide as the major source of inequalities is one that has persisted. But, while understandable given the development context, it can divert attention from other crucial distributional issues. By seeming to relegate inequalities within the rural sector to second order importance, it can risk ignoring a source of inequality which is both significant (especially given the dominance of the rural population at that time and for many years afterwards) and well-entrenched, having strong roots in traditional society. This point is taken up again in Section 5.

The heightened concern with distributional issues in Botswana coincided with an increased interest in such matters worldwide. The landmark year in this context is 1973, when the World Bank promoted poverty issues to the top of its agenda, including a reorientation of research to address distributional issues (Ahluwalia, 1996). Botswana was able to benefit from this, securing external assistance for the preparation of the RIDS.[5] The country was also an early beneficiary of the recommendations prepared by the United Nations Statistical Office (UNSO) on the measurement of household incomes in developing countries (UNSO, 1974).

Globally, questions of distribution held centre stage only briefly. The series of macroeconomic shocks, beginning with the oil price rises of the 1970s, meant that adjustment issues – how to restart the growth process on a sustainable basis – became dominant (Fishlow, 1996).[6] In Botswana, however, where growth continued to be delivered, the distribution of its fruits remained a central question.

3. THE MAIN DATA SOURCES

The backbone of this analysis comprises the three published surveys on income distribution in Botswana undertaken by the CSO. It is a basic premise of this paper that the 1974/75 RIDS, and the two HIES of 1985/85 and 1993/94 are reputable studies which allow well-based analysis of income distribution issues in Botswana.[7] They provide information on income levels and sources of rural incomes for a period cover-

---

5   One of the authors recalls the enthusiastic response from the floor by the Botswana delegation to the offer of financial assistance for household income surveys by Robert McNamara, then President of the World Bank, at the 1972 World Bank meeting in Nairobi.

6   Although ithas become increasingly recognised that, even in the context of macroeconomic stabilisation, the distributional impact of policies cannot be ignored (IMF, 1995).

ing nearly twenty years, and of urban incomes for nearly a decade. The published HIES tables include data on further breakdowns according to whether the head of household was male or female, and citizen or non-citizen.

This is not to say, however, that use of these surveys is unproblematic, especially in terms of their comparability, or that the data base is sufficient to shed light on all questions.

Comparing the surveys

Problems of comparability arise from two distinct sources. First, there are unplanned differences in exogenous conditions in the reference periods: most importantly, the amount of rainfall during the survey periods which can vary widely and influences the lives of so many people in Botswana. While the RIDS was conducted at a time of high rainfall and, consequently, a relatively buoyant agricultural sector, both HIES 1 and HIES 2 came during periods of severe drought. It is of course interesting to see how climate affects household incomes, both their level and distribution. But it is important to allow for these effects when trying to isolate underlying trends.

Second, there are methodological differences. The effect of these can be significant, and not allowing for this is a frequent weakness in making comparisons between the surveys. Both HIES 1 and HIES 2 followed basically the same methodology, although the breakdown by strata is somewhat different and must be handled carefully (see Section 4). However, the differences between the RIDS and the later surveys are significant. The most significant points to note are as follows.

a) Definition of household income
The RIDS used a more comprehensive definition of income, based on UNSO recommendations. This allowed for changes in asset values and the imputed rental income from home ownership. Importantly, this included measurement of the change in value of stocks of cattle as a basis for measuring the accrued income from cattle farming. In contrast, the HIES used a definition based on actual receipts; income from cattle, for example, was recorded only when a beast was sold or consumed domestically during the reference period, and imputed rental income was omitted altogether.

b) Coverage
(i)   In the RIDS, each household was surveyed for a few days each month over a period of one year, which allowed for variations in income and expenditure patterns to be picked up on a household basis. In contrast, the HIES are based on staggered enumeration periods of one month per household, and rely on the

---

7   On the same criterion, other possible sources have not been used. One such is the *Rural Economic Survey* conducted by the Bank of Botswana (Bank of Botswana, 1986). While this may have contributed some insights – notably concerning the financial arrangements of rural households – it is the view of the authors that this survey was flawed both in coverage and methodology, and as such, has little to add to a discussion of income distribution in Botswana. Another example is the 1978/79 HIES which the CSO conducted but did not release the results because they were considered unsatisfactory (CSO, 1996, p8).

size of the total sample, spread out over a longer period, to even out overall the effects of such variations.[8]

(ii) The RIDS was more comprehensive in identifying items used by households for home production: harvested crops, the gathering of edible wild food, collection of firewood, and own capital formation such as hut building. However, the valuation of these items involved a simple model based on a single price nationwide, while, in contrast, the HIES attempted to account for local variations in price.

(iii) The use of other data sources to verify the results. The RIDS matched the value of remittances from mineworkers as reported by households to the national average of such remittances, which was known from other sources.[9] The HIES have used commodity balances to verify reported consumption patterns and, where necessary, make adjustments to the survey data. Most notably, perhaps, this has been done for the consumption of alcoholic beverages.

c) Sampling unit

All three major surveys used the household as the unit that received income. Thereafter, for some purposes including, crucially, the summary measures of income distribution, the HIES published figures based on imputed individual incomes.

In general terms, the overall effect of these differences is to make income levels in the RIDS higher, but less equally distributed, than they would have been if the HIES methodology had been employed. Households across the population gain from points a) and b) (ii). For more wealthy rural households, the value of accrued income due to weight gains to cattle were important; while, for poorer households, imputed rent, consumption of own produce and gathering of wild food were significant income sources. Looking at the worked example in Appendix 14 of the RIDS (pp206–209), the largest individual income item was weight gains to cattle. This comprised 7.7% of 'gross available income', the measure used to map the income distribution. Adding own capital formation and imputed housing rentals, this rises to 13%; and to 16% if the gathering of wild food is also included.

The distribution of income was more unequal in the household measure since higher household incomes were positively correlated with household size. Hence, per capita incomes were more equally spread (Hudson, 1986). This feature has been reported for all three surveys. However, this is not an immutable law, but an empirical observation based on household composition. The most recent evidence also suggests that while overall household sizes have been falling and hence average per capita incomes have been rising more quickly than average household incomes, a significant proportion of poor households are also large households, suggesting that their members are very poor indeed.

---

8   Though the sample size for Botswana – 3600 households in 1993/94 – only allows for limited disaggregation. A larger sample size would be needed to achieve, with any reliability, a more detailed breakdown beyond the basic rural–urban and male–female divisions; as in, for example, the annual South African household survey, which is based on a sample of 30 000 households. Note that while it is usually easier for a more populated country to survey a larger sample, the population size itself has only a minimal effect on the size of the sample required for meaningful statistical analysis.

9   This involved the simplification of assuming equal monthly installments. Not realising this, some years later a World Bank research paper was written commenting on the astonishing regularity of the remittances sent home by Batswana mineworkers!

In making these points, there is no judgement being cast on which of the two survey methodologies is better. Both follow reputable guidelines: the RIDS used those provided at the time by the United Nations Statistical Office (UNSO); while the HIES cites recommendations of the International Labour Organization (ILO).[10] It might seem obvious that the more comprehensive approach to income measurement in the RIDS, together with the per capita measures of the HIES, would be the best combination. However, in practice the choice is not so simple.

The income measure in the RIDS is more pure in its relationship to classic theoretical definitions.[11] But the fuller coverage requires more resources, an important practical consideration when conducting a large-scale survey. This is especially the case given the many other surveys which the modern day CSO is committed to undertake, which both stretch the Office's resources and create a very real risk of 'survey fatigue' among the population. Also, some of this increased coverage was based on simple formulae, the appropriateness of which needs to be reviewed continually.[12]

The per capita income adjustment, based on a simple household head count is very rough and ready. It takes no account of either any economies of scale derived from larger households or the age composition of the household. Since one of the main objectives is to go beyond crude aggregate measures such as GDP per capita, it would seem desirable that the same crudeness does not infect the basic units in the analysis; although, on the other hand, an adjustment based on a simple head count does have the virtue of transparent simplicity. The choice of an equivalence scale, in particular the statistical weight given to children, can make a considerable difference when measuring inequality (Johnson, 1996). The use of such scales is a feature of the work that has been undertaken on poverty in Botswana where poverty datum lines have been calculated on the basis of household composition, (see the RIDS, CSO, 1984, and Government of Botswana, 1997). However, this work has yet to be extended systematically to cover the whole population.

Areas not covered

These surveys, while rich in information, are also strictly limited in what they can tell us, providing only periodic snapshots of household incomes. Two areas of major interest which are not covered are income mobility and intra-household distribution.

The data from the three main surveys are impersonal. That is, the progress of individual households – their income mobility – cannot be monitored. This is crucial. Looking at the overall level of incomes it may be possible to conclude that for every

---

[10] These different methodologies are not necessarily inconsistent. A wide variety of possible income measures exist, and the UNSO has helped to ensure that the approaches of themselves, the ILO and the World Bank are reconciled, at least in principle.

[11] The economic definition of income is usually taken to be the level of consumption that can be sustained without reducing the value of assets. While the gross available income' used in the RIDS is not fully in line with this, since it does not deduct depreciation on the value of household assets, clearly a receipts based approach diverges even further.

[12] Valuation of own produce is particularly problematic, as readily admitted by those responsible for compiling the surveys. While attempting to measure these values more accurately than the simple model used in the RIDS, CSO currently believes that there is a tendency to overvalue (CSO, 1996, p51). Also, the formulae used to estimate the value of the weight changes in cattle would have to be amended during drought years.

portion of the population, ranked according to income, incomes have increased. But this is not to say that every individual household has higher incomes; this would only be the case if the ranking remained unchanged between surveys. However, in conditions where mobility in the ranking is high, the overall higher income levels may hide a wide variety of winners and losers.

Of particular interest is the income mobility of the poor. Other things being equal, an economic structure which gives poor households a good chance of improving their lot – rising from rags to riches – may be considered more socially just.

There are no direct measures of income mobility in Botswana. This lack of data is not surprising. Proper survey work in this area is complex and frequently not available even in more developed countries. Also its collection may take some time with important aspects of income mobility emerging only between generations.

However, some insight into income mobility may be gained from structural analyses that examine the range of economic opportunities that face different sections of the population. This has been used frequently in Botswana, typically focusing on the distribution of cattle ownership, and associated issues, such as land rights, as indicators of opportunity. These analyses are examined further in Section 6.

Similarly there are no survey data on how household income is distributed among household members. Without some assumption that this matches the breakdown implied by the chosen 'equivalence scales', the use of these scales, whether crude per capita incomes or something more sophisticated, can be highly misleading in indicating the extent to which household income satisfies the needs of each household member. This will occur in situations where the household head has concerns other than equity; an obvious example is the contention that male heads may benefit from a disproportionate share of household income.

This paper does not get involved in a detailed discussion of this issue. This is not to deny its importance but, on the contrary, it is recognition that the topic cannot be given proper treatment here.

4. Some Issues of Methodology

The definition of income

The basis for comparison used here is *total household disposable income*, including cash income, income in kind, and imputed income. The cash income measure is also used, but primarily to indicate the importance of non-cash sources. These measures are drawn from the cross-sectional data in the RIDS, HIES 1 and HIES 2.

Cross-sectional snapshots provide only limited information, even if well-being is determined mainly by private incomes. For example, consumption patterns may be more informative, since some people will borrow and others will save from income. This is both to allow for short-term cyclical fluctuations and to optimise consumption over lifetimes, taking into account past and expected future income levels.

However, focusing on current disposable income has its advantages. It is consistent with mainstream, international analyses of income distribution, which is important for comparative purposes, and differences in income at a point in time are probably the most common notion of inequality (Johnson, 1996). As a practical matter, consumption typically involves more transactions than income with consequently a greater possibility of errors through under-reporting.[13] Finally, while it is easy to point to the limitations of the cross-sectional data, it is another matter altogether to account for all these difficulties in a well-based model of cyclical and life-cycle behaviour. While the recent study by BIDPA of poverty in Botswana chose to use consumption rather than income measures, (Government of Botswana, 1997) this has the more specific target of measuring whether in practice households are able to meet certain living standards. For this, data on actual consumption is clearly relevant.

Measuring inequality

The most widely used summary measure of income inequality is the Gini coefficient, and this forms the starting point of the analysis here. This is an *inclusive measure* of distribution – that is it uses information on the whole population[14] – which has the advantage of being directly related to the cumulative distribution of income as shown graphically by the Lorenz curve.[15] Other measures can also be used, such as the Theil indices, or the coefficient of variation. These may produce somewhat differing results, but the degree of correlation with the Gini coefficient tends to be high (Clarke, 1995). The main problem with the Gini coefficient is where the Lorenz curves from different distributions cross. In such cases a value judgement is needed to determine which distribution is more equal. Fortunately, this situation has not occurred in the case of Botswana.

In order to compare income levels, it is essential to convert the nominal incomes from the three survey periods into 'real' incomes. This is to take into account the differences in general price levels due to price inflation between the surveys. All incomes used in this analysis are expressed in June 1994 prices. Published consumer price indices (CPI) were used to make this adjustment. Between HIES 1 and HIES 2 this allows for a breakdown between rural and urban areas, but no further division is attempted, either geographically or by income group. Between the RIDS and HIES 1 the national CPI is used since a rural sub-index was not produced for that period.

Appropriate divisions of the population are a further consideration. Three basic divisions are considered here; rural/urban, male/female headed, and citizen/non-citizen headed. Of these, the last two are fairly straightforward, the household being

---

[13] Both income and expenditure measures are plagued by under-reporting, with people being reluctant to divulge details of what they regard as essentially a private matter. A good example is the adjustments that are often made to compensate for under-reporting expenditure on 'sin' goods such as alcohol and tobacco, as well as income from illicit activities.

[14] This is contrasted with *exclusive* measures which focus on only part of the population either because that is the subject of investigation (e.g., how many are below the poverty line), or for ease of exposition (the commonly used income shares measure, for example).

[15] The Lorenz curve is the cumulative income distribution measured in percentages. The Gini coefficient is the ratio of the area between Lorenz curve and the line of complete equality (where all the population have equal shares), and that between the lines of perfect equality and complete inequality (where all income is held by one unit). The Gini coefficient varies between zero (equality) and one (complete inequality). As a rule of thumb a value greater than 0.5 indicates a very unequal income distribution.

classified according to the status of the *de facto* household head, that is, the most senior household member present during the survey.[16]

The rural/urban classification presents more serious problems. This is because the CSO has, since the 1991 Census, introduced a new classification of 'urban villages'. This recognises that many of the characteristics of the urban economy – large population groupings and little reliance on agriculture for income – are no longer confined to areas that are designated as urban on an administrative basis. This transformation is, of course, an on-going process. For this study two definitions of rural are used for the HIES 2 data: *rural 1* includes urban villages, while *rural 2* is the new definition. Which is relevant depends on the context.[17]

5. Trends in Income Distribution since Independence

Before the RIDS

Prior to the RIDS, information on income distribution was gathered on a piecemeal basis, from a variety of sources. As already noted, these revealed two particular concerns.

First, was the disparity between rural and urban wages. NDP 2 reported that the average wage in full time agriculture was under R80 per annum, while that in other activities was R509 per annum, a differential of more than five hundred percent. Such income differentials were monitored through the Employment Surveys conducted by the CSO (see, for example, Government of Botswana, 1977, Table 2.3). It was further recognised that remuneration varied greatly within the formal sectors, with non-citizens typically benefiting from much higher incomes; as already noted, the discriminatory structure of civil service salaries was a particular source of friction. In 1974 the CSO conducted a study of household incomes in the poor 'peri-urban' areas that were developing alongside the urban centres (Central Statistics Office, 1974),

---

[16] Note, however, that the emphasis on the de facto household head is of some importance. This definition does not count the actual – *de jure* – head if they were absent during the reference period. This may be significant in cases where the household head is away for substantial periods in search of employment income. Other countries, Lesotho for example, have used the *de jure* approach.

[17] This change in classification raises problems of comparison, both practical and conceptual. At the practical level, allowing for this change is made more complicated because the new category is not in fact a pure subset of the previous rural sector. In practice, some of the urban villages, such as Palapye and Tlokweng were included in the urban sector in HIES 1. Therefore, the assumption that rural and urban villages in HIES 2 can be combined to make the equivalent of rural in HIES 1 (as used for example in Bank of Botswana, 1996) is in fact a simplifying approximation, rather than a fully accurate mapping. However, with this qualification, this assumption continues to be used here.

The conceptual question is whether the most appropriate comparison is on a geographical basis or one of economic structure. The former is being followed if urban villages are recombined with HIES 2 rural, and shows developments in income for people living in a particular *area*. However, for charting the development of incomes of people living in rural *conditions*, then comparing the rural categories in the surveys without adjustment would seem to be more appropriate. Clearly both comparisons can be relevant, depending on circumstances.

and in 1975 the Ministry of Local Government and Lands made a crude estimate of the distribution of cash income in Gaborone, primarily to help with planning urban housing requirements (Government of Botswana, 1977, Figure 2.8). However, all formal sector employees were in general classed among the 'fortunate few' (Parsons *et al.*, 1995, p321).

Second, there were the inequalities in agriculture in terms of ownership of the means of production. The 1968 Agricultural Survey indicated that 4% of the rural population owned 30% of the cattle, while 21% owned no cattle at all; and a further 13% were completely dependent on transfers for income, e.g., in the form of remittances from migrant mineworkers. With cattle the main source of power for ploughing, the first group also controlled the majority of large arable lands; and an estimated 90% of those owning no cattle failed to cultivate any land in the reference period.

On the basis of such considerations, tentative analyses of trends in income distribution started to be provided. For example, the Bank of Botswana, in one of its earliest annual reports, felt able to assert that the distribution of income in the years since Independence had '...almost certainly...' worsened (Bank of Botswana, 1977, p20). It chose to emphasise, in particular, the effects of rising real prices for cattle exports impacting on a highly skewed distribution of cattle ownership, thus making the important point that distribution of income among the citizen population was a principal factor in any trend toward greater inequality. This conclusion was supported, for similar reasons, in Colclough and McCarthy (1980).

A first official, published estimate of a Gini coefficient for Botswana followed from a World Bank study mission in 1974. This was based on very rough data for 1971/72. The estimated value was 0.57, suggesting a significant degree of inequality (see footnote 15). But in comparative terms this was assessed as being '...well within the range typically found among developing countries...' (Government of Botswana, 1977, para. 2.84). Following shortly after this report there was the much more comprehensive study in the RIDS. The rest of this section concentrates on comparing the information contained in the RIDS and HIES 1 and 2.

Post RIDS

Gini coefficients have been calculated for Botswana for all the three major surveys. A range of these are shown in Table 1. These are mainly drawn from the published surveys, but also included are figures, calculated for this paper by the CSO, which estimate Gini coefficients for HIES 1 and HIES 2 on a household, rather than a per capita basis.

Previous studies have concluded that the period between the RIDS and HIES 1 saw a reduction, albeit modest, in inequality, among rural incomes (Valentine, 1993, Bank of Botswana, 1996). This is based on the decline in the published rural Gini coefficient from 0.52 to 0.48. However, this is not a proper comparison since the RIDS figure was a household measure while that for HIES 1 was calculated on a per capita basis. On a household basis the rural Gini coefficient in HIES 1 is 0.51, a change from the RIDS that is too small to be statistically significant.

However, the measures do point to some reduction in inequality of income distribution between HIES 1 and HIES 2. At the national level and for urban areas this change has been very small. But for rural areas, on either definition, and especially for the cash income measure, the difference is more significant.

TABLE 1. GINI COEFFICIENTS IN BOTSWANA

		RIDS		HIES 1		HIES 2	
		HOUSE-HOLD	PER CAPITA	HOUSE-HOLD	PER CAPITA	HOUSE-HOLD	PER CAPITA
TOTAL	Cash				0.70		0.64
	Total			0.58	0.56	0.57	0.54
URBAN	Cash				0.56		0.55
	Total				0.54	0.60	0.54
URBAN VILLAGE	Cash						0.55
	Total					0.50	0.45
RURAL 1	Cash				0.67		0.60
	Total	0.52		0.51	0.48	0.50	0.43
RURAL 2*	Cash						0.59
	Total					0.49	0.41

Note: * Rural 2 excludes the newly defined category of urban villages.
Source: Central Statistics Office.

The importance of non-cash income in the rural areas is readily apparent. The much greater inequality of the cash income distribution reflects the prevalence of non-cash income sources for poorer rural families. It may be that this has become less important between HIES 1 and HIES 2. In the later survey, the gap between the cash and total income Gini coefficients declined somewhat, reflecting a greater degree of monetization in the economy.[18] But it remains an important distinction, and one which, unfortunately, is often not recognised in discussions of this issue.

While the rural economy appears to be characterised by slowly increasing equality, this conclusion means little in the absence of information on income levels. For example, migration away from rural areas by those with higher earning potential could have this effect, but in this context greater equality among those remaining would surely not be seen as progress.

However, this does not seem to be the explanation. Table 2 compares mean real household incomes. The figures from the RIDS are adjusted figures to make some allowance for the greater coverage of different sources of income used in that survey. To do this, all RIDS income levels have been deflated by a factor of 14%, an adjustment factor derived on the basis of the worked example in Appendix 14 in the RIDS (see Section 3 above). This is self-evidently very crude, which should be borne in mind when interpreting the results.

---

[18] This is slightly more so using the Rural 1 comparison, which is plausible since the inclusion of urban villages would suggest a greater importance of cash income, although again the difference is probably too small to be statistically significant.

TABLE 2. MEAN REAL INCOMES (PULA PER MONTH)

	RIDS	HIES 1 (1)	HIES 2 (2)	(2)/(1)
NATIONAL		777.4	1015.9	1.31
URBAN		1444.8	1710.1	1.18
URBAN VILLAGES			876.4	
RURAL 1	632	526.2	718.6	1.36
RURAL 2*			641.2	1.22

Note: * The ratio in the last column is measured as a proportion of Rural 1 in HIES 1.
Source: Central Statistics Office.

Between RIDS and HIES 1 mean rural incomes fell by nearly 18%. To the extent that the deflation adjustment to the RIDS is accurate, this can be taken as an indication of the impact of the drought in 1985/86. Since HIES 1, however, it seems clear that average household incomes have risen substantially by 31% for the country as a whole. The largest gains have been made in the rural areas; 36% on the Rural 1 definition, more than regaining the losses between the RIDS and HIES 1. Even the narrower, structural, definition of rural shows a marginally higher mean income than at the time of the RIDS. Conversely, the mean household income in urban areas grew by less than the national average. In all cases per capita real income will have increased somewhat more as average household sizes have declined; the median household size in 1985/86 was 4.05 compared to 3.51 in 1993/94, with the fall being about the same magnitude in both the rural and urban areas.

With inequalities not increasing and mean household income levels rising, it might be inferred that real income levels have been increasing for all sections of the population. For the country as a whole, this is confirmed by Figure 1 which compares the national income distributions for HIES 1 and HIES 2. Household real income levels in June 1994 prices, and measured on a logarithmic scale to help visual comparison, are plotted against the cumulative population. It is clearly a positive sign that the HIES 2 income distribution dominates that of HIES 1 in that income levels are higher for all sections of the population. But this conclusion should be qualified. First, as noted in Section 3, this type of snapshot says nothing about income mobility. This distribution may be – is likely to be – a combination of winners and losers. Second, more detailed snapshots point to a varying performance between groups. Table 2 already points to differences between the rural and urban categories. This is confirmed in Figures 2 to 5.

Figure 2 makes a visual comparison of the distribution of rural incomes for all three surveys, Rural 2 being used for HIES 2. The fall in real income levels between the RIDS and HIES 1 is shown clearly, with the HIES 1 distribution being dominated by that of the RIDS. Similarly, real income levels are higher across the distribution comparing HIES 2 and HIES 1. Comparing RIDS and HIES 2 is, however, more complex. Overall, the mean rural incomes in HIES 2 are higher, but this does not apply to the bottom quartile of the distribution. It seems that for this group the impact of Government policies such as drought relief and the development of other economic

FIGURE 1. INCOME DISTRIBUTION IN BOTSWANA, **1985/86** AND **1993/94**

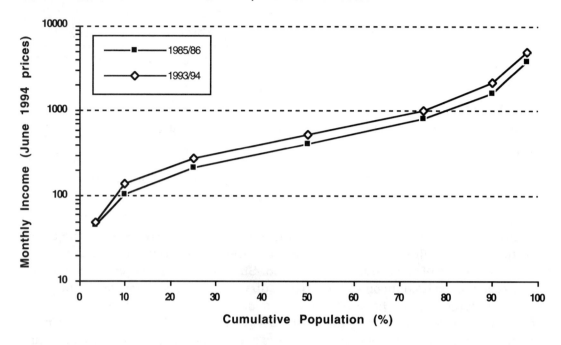

opportunities has yet to make good the gap in income opportunities as compared with those available at the time of the RIDS. While it is likely that the adverse weather conditions in 1993/94 played a large part in this, other factors are also likely to have been involved over a period of this duration. Finally, it should be noted that all three distributions converge at the top end of the distribution. While the small sample sizes make the accurate depiction of this 'tail' problematic, this is consistent with the view that the rich are still rich in all circumstances.

FIGURE 2. RURAL INCOME DISTRIBUTION, **1974/75** TO **1993/94**

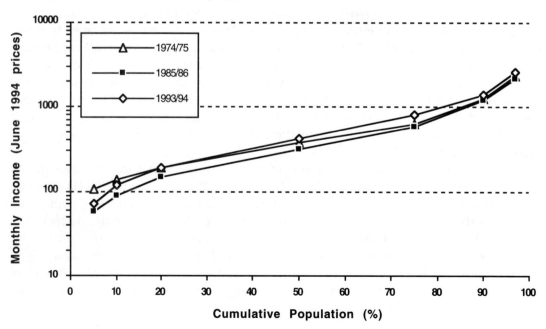

Figure 3 shows urban incomes. It seems clear that urban areas have not done so well in relative terms, since the vertical distance between the two lines is much less than for the rural households shown in Figure 2. This is especially striking for the poorest half of the urban population. A further breakdown suggests male-headed households were worst affected; some groups in this category may have lower real household incomes in 1993/94 compared to 1985/86.

FIGURE 3. URBAN INCOME DISTRIBUTION, 1985/86 AND 1993/94

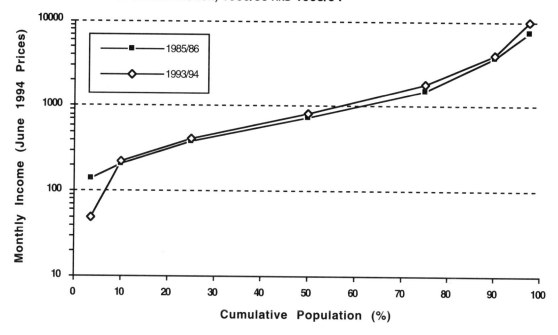

This conclusion may not seem very surprising. While drought conditions prevailed during both HIES 1 and HIES 2, the latter survey was conducted at a time of economic slowdown in the non-agricultural sectors, in which the urban areas were hard hit. In particular, the construction industry, which is overwhelmingly male in terms of employment, saw large numbers of job losses. Sectors, with predominantly female worforces – for example, the trade sector – while characterised by low wage rates, continued to maintain good employment levels. But factors other than the economic downturn should not be disregarded. Continued rapid migration and urban population growth, with consequent pressures upwards on unemployment levels and downwards on wages, may also have played a significant role.

Nevertheless, there remains a clearly positive gap between urban and rural income levels. The extent of this gap is suggested by Table 2, which shows that mean urban household incomes in 1993/94 exceeded those in urban villages and rural areas by 138% and 167%, respectively. However, it would be wrong to conclude immediately from these differences that the rural–urban divide is the major cause of overall inequality in incomes in Botswana or, importantly, that simply targeting support at the rural sector is the optimal way to help the poor.

Looking at mean incomes alone ignores the inequality within the sub-distributions. This exists to the extent that there is much overlap between rural and urban income levels. This is seen in Figure 4, which shows the urban and rural income distributions for 1993/94 together with the associated urban–rural income ratios. It appears that more than half the rural households are richer than the poorest 25% of urban households.[19] Looked at another way, if it were decided that the bottom 50% of rural dwellers were poor, a policy that targeted further assistance at these households only would lead to missing out 25% of urban and 47% of urban village households, or 44% of the total poor measured on this basis.

FIGURE 4. URBAN AND RURAL INCOME DISTRIBUTION, 1993/94

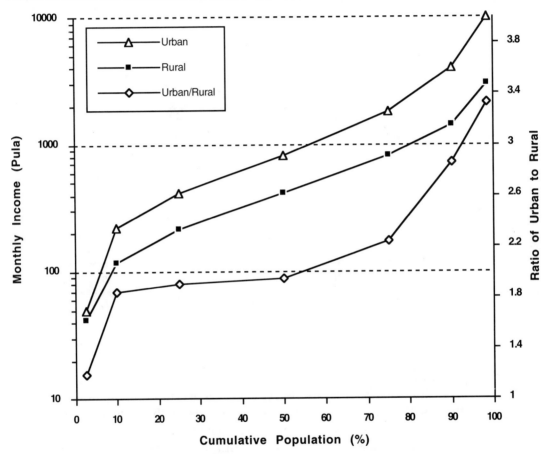

While the gap between the urban and rural rich widens considerably at higher income levels, it is equally true – and more important for policy purposes – that the gap between the poorest in both areas is very narrow. This is clear from Figure 4 and is measured directly in Figure 5, which plots the horizontal distance between the income distributions.[20] Similar 'income gap' lines are also included for the urban and rural areas in 1985/86 and for male and female-headed households during both periods.

---

19 This comparison assumes Purchasing Power Parity (PPP) between rural and urban incomes.

20 Thus, for example, the income of the fiftieth percentile in the rural population equals that of the twenty-fourth percentile in the urban population. This is shown in Figure 5 as a positive gap of 26% in favour of the urban population.

FIGURE 5. INCOME GAPS, 1985/86 AND 1993/94

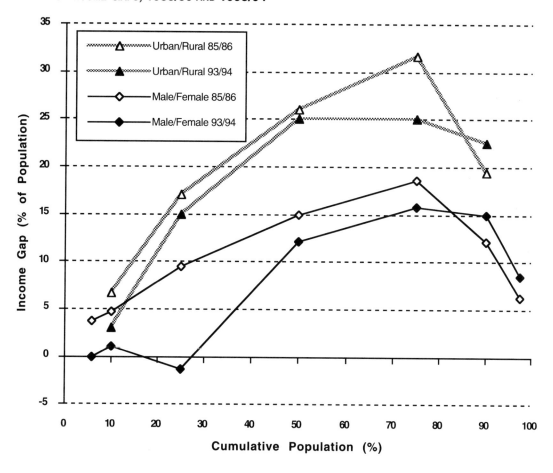

From Figure 5 it seems that the conclusion that the 'poor are equally poor' can be made more general, and also, to a lesser degree, that the 'rich are equally rich' with all the lines showing an inverted U shape. The degree of inequality between male and female headed households is consistently less than the rural/urban divide. Finally, the gaps appear to have been narrowing between the survey periods. This is most clear for the male/female division especially in the first three deciles, where the gap may have been eliminated if not reversed in HIES 2. Again this may be seen to reflect the relatively more severe negative impact of the recent economic downturn on male workers.

This analysis does not cover the differences in incomes of citizen and non-citizen headed households. The detailed data needed for inclusion in Figure 5 was not provided in the published HIES 2. Nevertheless, some indication can be given of the overall significance of non-citizen incomes. According to HIES 2, the mean income of the latter is about six times that of the former group, and the 3.5% of non-citizen households received 18.8% of total disposable income (HIES 2, p6). The assertion that the poor are equally poor in any group does not apply here, at least when excluding the illegal expatriate population. But this is hardly surprising given that expatriates are allowed to work in Botswana on the basis of skills which are scarce locally.

Excluding non-citizens' incomes increases equality, with the national Gini coefficient on a per capita basis falling from 0.537 to 0.467.[21] This is a significant difference which should be included in any profile of income distribution in Botswana. A further breakdown into rural and urban areas has not been attempted at this time, partly because of the small sample sizes for the non-urban strata (HIES 2, p6).

6. FACTORS AFFECTING INCOME DISTRIBUTION

The various factors that combine to produce the observed income distribution are highly complex. Attempting a full explanation is beyond the scope of this paper; yet, at the same time, the discussion remains incomplete without reference to causal factors. This section reviews some that might be considered of particular relevance to Botswana.

The drought cycle and the developing rural economy

As has been made clear, comparison of the income surveys conducted in Botswana is made difficult by the differences in rainfall during the reference periods. However, this problem is most acute when comparing income *levels*; it is less clear that the distribution will be affected unless it can be shown that the impact of climatic conditions, whether favourable or unfavourable, affects certain groups more than others.

We can be certain that there have indeed been such effects. Most obviously, the urban population and, increasingly, rural areas with decreased reliance on farming activities, are less affected by climatic factors. The economic cycle of booms and recessions is more important here than the drought cycle. To the extent that the process of urbanization continues, we can anticipate a diminishing importance of climatic effects on the income distribution as a whole.[22] With the population almost equally divided between rural and non-rural settlements, the effect of the rural/urban divide may now be at its zenith.

What about the effects of climate within the agriculture dependent population? Certainly all suffer from drought, whether it is through the weight losses and higher mortality of cattle or the low yields of harvested or gathered produce. But what more can be said?

Some authors have characterised the undoubtedly pernicious effects of drought as cumulative rather than cyclical; that is, drought results in a permanent, or at least long lasting, increase in inequalities. While the accumulation of livestock wealth by already rich owners suffers a significant but recoverable set back, the effect on the small farmer is to keep him small (Roe, 1980, p45 and Good, 1993, p224).

There may well be some truth in this. There is clear evidence that inequalities in cattle ownership in Botswana have been positively correlated with drought conditions (Valentine, 1993), and several analyses have used trends in cattle ownership as a proxy to hypothesise trends in income distribution in the absence of direct data (Colclough and McCarthy, 1980). The practice of *mafisa*, under which cattle owners

---

[21] This was not included in HIES 2 but was calculated specially for this paper by the CSO.

[22] This also raises the very relevant policy question of whether the current design of welfare safety nets, which have been based mainly on the premise that drought is the primary source of income loss in Botswana, continues to be relevant in the modern economy.

can allow their beasts to be looked after by other households who may in return take advantage of some of the benefits of cattle holding such as use for ploughing, may have ameliorated some of the worst effects of these inequalities. But the very context of this system is one of inequalities and patronage, both within the livestock sector and between arable and livestock farming (Roe, 1980, p45).

However, while cattle ownership may remain the central aspiration of many Batswana, as an index of rural incomes and economic opportunities it is an imperfect measure, and increasingly so.[23] Within agriculture, the rapid expansion of small-stock herds (i.e., sheep and goats) over much of the period since Independence represents a rational decision by small farmers to move to less drought-prone activities (Valentine, 1993, p112); and wider availability of tractor power, whether owned or hired, will have weakened the once binding relationship between arable and cattle farming. More generally, the importance of non-farm rural activities has increased, the introduction by CSO of the urban villages category being a clear recognition of this. This reflects both the increased scope of private sector activities and the continued extension of public services throughout the country.

This effect is important when comparing the two HIES. Valentine (1993) characterises the 1985/86 survey as demonstrating the role of transfers, both official and private, in preventing a collapse in rural incomes during the drought. The 1993/94 HIES points to the increasing role of employment incomes. The importance of earned income in rural areas (including urban villages) is estimated to have increased from 48% in 1985/86 to 62% in 1993/94, while that of transfers fell from 29% to 24% (Bank of Botswana, 1996). Since at the same time real rural income levels rose, this implies an even larger proportionate increase in the real value of earned incomes.

An important component of this increase in rural employment incomes may have been the increased value of payments being made under the drought relief programmes. The two major drought relief components, payments for ploughing and Labour Based Drought Relief (LBDR), increased by about 280% in real terms between the two surveys, which is about three times the growth in total rural disposable income. However, as a proportion, the contribution of drought relief to rural incomes is not high, so, overall, the impact of this very rapid growth has been muted. As a rough estimate it appears that it has contributed only about 15% of the reported increase in earned income between the two surveys.[24]

With the good rains in 1995/96, harvest conditions improved and most of the country was declared drought free.[25] In these circumstances it is important to consider the extent to which years of drought relief payments may have made sections of

---

[23] This is not only in Botswana. As a general point rural income and employment studies may have underrated the importance of off-farming employment opportunities in rural areas (see Fields, 1995, p501).

[24] This very approximate calculation is based on a comparison between the figures in the Government's Annual Statement of Accounts for 1993/94 and the analysis contained in the 1990 evaluation of the Drought Relief Programme (Government of Botswana, 1990).

[25] The President announced in August 1996 that drought relief would continue only in southern Kgalagadi, Charles Hill and Okavango. Some relief programmes would also be continued in Ngamiland but this was due to the special problems arising from the slaughter of cattle there to contain the outbreak of Contagious Bovine Pleuro-Pneumonia (CBPP). For the country as a whole the expected cereals harvest in 1996 was projected at 96 000 tonnes compared to 50 000 tonnes in 1995. If achieved this would be the largest harvest since 1988 (108 000 tonnes).

the rural communities overly dependent on these programmes. This is especially relevant since the large real increase in the value of drought relief payments is mainly attributable to the increased number of recipients.

It certainly appears that Government is concerned that such dependency may be a problem. For example, the *Botswana Daily News* in May 1996 carried a series of reports of, on the one hand, rural communities urging that LBDR be continued and, on the other, Government representatives emphasising that it was only a temporary measure.[26] A related problem is that elements of drought relief – notably ploughing subsidies – have been treated simply as a cash payment, rather than an incentive to continue with high risk farming activities. It would be ironic – and tragic – if the move away from drought conditions and any consequent reduction of drought relief programmes were to lead to greater impoverishment among sections of the population.

Economic growth and inequality

Until recently, it was widely believed that acceptance of greater inequalities was a necessary pre-condition for rapid economic growth. Theoretical growth models supported this. So, also, did empirical work, especially for developing countries. Under this paradigm, while it was hoped that all would benefit in absolute terms, the price of prosperity included an acceptance that the gap between rich and poor would grow wider, at least in the initial stages of development.

In the context of Botswana this has been a common view, given recent expression in Valentine (1993). Certainly, characteristics of Botswana's development, concentrated first in cattle and then in diamonds, may have tended to promote such a pattern, in that the direct benefits were restricted to a fortunate minority. The recognition of this by the Botswana Government and the consequent efforts to mitigate such tendencies towards inequality – especially the emergence of rural/urban divides – has, as already described, been both a central objective of the stated development policy, and a key yardstick for judging its success.

More recently, however, both theory and empirical research have emphasised the possibility that growth and equality can be – or, even more strongly, are likely to be – positively correlated; and, importantly, that Government policy may be able to promote both goals at the same time. This work is usefully reviewed in Clarke (1995) and Fishlow (1996), and is a major theme of the UNDP's recently published 1996 Human Development Report (UNDP, 1996).

While such a view seems to have achieved the status of a new conventional wisdom in some quarters[27], the statistical evidence is not unambiguous. For instance, it seems that the growth-equity relationship may be heavily affected by the inclusion in the data of certain cases, whether virtuous (high growth, high equality East Asia) or less so (low growth, low equality Latin America). However, it points to a richer mixture of relationships in the growth process rather than the rather 'dry' confines of traditional economic theory had been able to encompass.

---

[26] See for example the issues of 9 and 10 May.

[27] For example, at the time of the publication of its survey of the South African labour market in June 1996, a spokesman for the International Labour Organisation (ILO) was quoted as saying that, '...international evidence shows very, very clearly that economies with high degrees of inequality have lower levels of growth...' (*The Sunday Independent*, 23 June 1996).

Even if such a correlation could be established, it should be interpreted with extreme caution. Causal factors remain highly uncertain, and it should not be seen as implying that policies that aim at redistributing income are not harmful to growth prospects. Indeed, one reason why underlying equality may be conducive to growth is precisely because governments face less pressure to interfere directly with the distribution of income.

As an example of policy that may promote both growth and equality, it is likely that well chosen investment in education can have important positive effects in both areas: in the former by boosting the stock of human capital, in the latter by equipping individuals with skills to take advantage of opportunities and, more generally, to manage their lives more effectively. Research has pointed to strong returns from primary education in areas such as farming and micro enterprises (Turnham, 1993, Chapter 3); and greater equality seems to have a strong association with educational indicators, especially secondary education (Fishlow, 1996).

This is clearly of relevance for Botswana, appearing to be consistent with the current emphasis on expanding the coverage of secondary education, including calls for this process to be taken still further.[28] However, several important qualifications need to be made to the general statement that education is good for growth and equality.

First, the returns on such investments are not made overnight. Immediate growth prospects are unlikely to be affected, and, as such, might make these and other social expenditures prime candidates for cutbacks in the face of calls for greater fiscal stringency. In Botswana, this longer-term perspective needs to be properly allowed for by those who worry that the rate of return on recent Government investments has been falling (Bank of Botswana, 1994 and 1996).

On the other hand, while many may subscribe to the general proposition that education is good for both growth and distribution, the specifics of what components of education are important continues to be unresolved (Kremer, 1995). The context of time and place is likely to be very important. This is crucial for Botswana. Nobody doubts that in aggregate financial terms the commitment to invest in education is high in Botswana, but it is less clear that a policy underpinned by increasing the 'quantity' of education available will simply deliver the goods (see, for example, Hanushek, 1995). In recent years, rates of unemployment in Botswana have been high and rising, with the national unemployment rate increasing from an estimated 13.9% in 1991 to 21.2% in 1994 (CSO, 1996b). This unemployment has been particularly noticeable among the rapidly increasing numbers of secondary school leavers. In this context, it is not immediately clear that further educating the population will in itself provide the income generating opportunities that ultimately are the real source of growth and equality, and the types of worry referred to in the previous paragraph are indeed relevant.

Government Policies

From the evidence presented so far, with rising real income levels and no substantive evidence of greater inequality in its distribution it might be concluded that

---

[28] For example, the 1996 Private Sector Conference, organised by BOCCIM, recommended that Botswana should become an 'educated society' with everyone having education up to Form V or a vocational equivalent. The current target for Form V under the Revised National Policy on Education is 50%; the actual enrolment rate is about 30%.

Government policies have been broadly beneficial in these areas. Moreover, this has ignored the value of public services to households. This is likely to be substantial, especially for poor families (Jefferis, 1996).

This is, in general, a conclusion which this paper is inclined to support. But in saying this it should be recognised that the record of Government here has been mixed.

Most obviously perhaps, Government has a central role as the country's largest employer. The salary structure of the civil service has not only affected the lives of many households directly, but also more widely as it has set the tone for wages throughout the formal sector. The sharp changes in direction in Government's policy – here wage compression followed by decompression; large increases followed by wage restraint – are eloquent testimony both to the power of various groups of Government workers as interest groups, and to the genuine difficulties that can occur in reconciling the objectives of equity and efficiency. However, despite its prominence, it is easy to overemphasise the importance of Government wages on the national income distribution taken as a whole.

It is clear that Government has invested considerable resources in developing, reviewing and fine-tuning policies with a view to their distributional impact. The evolution of the incomes policy is a major example of this. Others include, *inter alia*, the various aspects of drought relief programmes, labour intensive rural road construction, nominal or free pricing for health and education, the Financial Assistance Policy (FAP), and so forth. The BIDPA poverty study is a further instance (Government of Botswana, 1997).

Conversely, it is not difficult to point to Government policies that have not been supportive of greater equality, in terms of either the distribution of income or equality of opportunity. Glaring examples include those which have favoured the rural elite; the various subsidies and tax concessions to cattle farmers, or the lax credit policies of the financial parastatals such as the Small Borrowers Fund of the National Development Bank. These have, unsurprisingly perhaps, been examined less closely. But where they have been scrutinised, the results have often been critical of the policies.[29] In saying this, however, the Botswana Government is hardly unique in currying favour with powerful interest groups.

There are also areas where, while the distributional consequences are difficult to evaluate, there is potential for harmful effects, especially if the policies are extended further. One example that has already been referred to is the long-run consequences of drought relief programmes which, if persistent and over-generous, can create a dangerous culture of dependency on Government.

Another important case is that of minimum wages. There is no doubt that such minima are well-intentioned. But the risk to job losses cannot be ignored in the face of highly competitive market conditions and/or potential for substituting capital for unskilled labour. The difference between low pay and no pay can have a major negative impact on the distribution of incomes. While it is of course desirable to have employment incomes that raise households above conditions of mere survival, to simply legislate for this can do more harm than good if, at the same time, the more basic

---

[29] For example, the 1990 evaluation of the Accelerated Rainfed Arable Programme (ARAP) concluded that while the per capita value of the programme was high, this was '...completely undermine(d)...'by the distributional effects which were heavily in favour of the few large beneficiaries of the ploughing subsidies (Government of Botswana, 1990).

causes of low pay – most notably low productivity – are left unaddressed. The indications that industry in Botswana has been benefiting recently from negative perceptions of labour market conditions in South Africa is a practical example of this.[30]

7. Concluding Observations

This paper has asked what can sensibly be said about trends in income distribution in Botswana since 1966. Based on mainstream statistical data sources, supplemented by other relevant information, it has been argued that while inequalities in Botswana remain extensive and, possibly, well-entrenched, the more extreme depictions of the situation have little to support them. In particular, there is no evidence that inequalities have widened in the last twenty years. There is even less reason to support the contention that the real income levels of most of the population have not risen as the country has developed. During the period over which information is available for the country as a whole, the most significant progress in terms of raising real household incomes and reducing inequalities has been made in the rural areas.

These conclusions are contrary to many popular perceptions and, in this context, it is worth repeating, again, that this in no way contradicts the evidence that points to incidences, probably widespread and severe, of poverty and inequality in Botswana. However, it should also be pointed out that much of this evidence is based on anecdotal reports and non-random case studies, which, while valuable, must be viewed in the context of national survey work conducted on a statistically valid basis. Examination of this work points clearly to the conclusions that we have drawn.

Nor should these conclusions be taken as a blanket endorsement for Government policies as they have affected income distribution. While the results may have, overall, been positive, this is not to say that in some instances, sometimes very important, this has not been the case.

How does Botswana fare internationally in terms of income distribution? The introduction to this paper asserted that Botswana is not atypical of many developing countries. In Sub-Saharan Africa, among the countries for which comparative data is readily available, only Ghana appears to have a substantially more equal distribution of income than Botswana. But, because of lower avarage income, this translates in to lower incomes for the poorer households compared to those in Botswana, despite their higher overall share of the national cake (Bank of Botswana, 1996).

Outside of Africa, almost any conclusion can be drawn depending on the basis for comparison. Botswana has performed better than some and worse than others. Latin American countries typically have had more unequal income distributions. There is widely supported evidence that income distribution in many industrial countries has been becoming more unequal in recent years (Johnson, 1996 and OECD, 1996), while rapidly growing Asian economies have often combined greater equality with rapid economic growth.

---

[30] It is also one that is not lost on the South African Government. In launching the new macroeconomic blueprint in June 1996, the Finance Minister explicitly suggested that the trade unions, through aggressive collective bargaining, may have been responsible for some of that country's unemployment.

Also, any international comparison is quickly clouded by problems of comparability. This paper has emphasised that, even within Botswana, proper comparisons are difficult, affected by issues of methodology, scope and quality of coverage, and exogenous circumstances. For international comparisons, these issues are magnified manyfold.

In this context, the continuing efforts of international organizations, such as the UNSO, to support the collection of improved and standardised data on incomes are welcomed. These may receive a further boost as issues of income distribution are once more returning to the fore internationally. The 1996 UNDP Human Development Report launches a fierce attack on the extent and the extremity of inequalities existing in the world economy today (UNDP, 1996).

This is a process which is continuing within the Southern African region. In mid-1996, Statistics Sweden combined forces with the SADC Secretariat to sponsor a workshop in Windhoek, Namibia, on a comparison of methodologies for the measurement of living standards and household incomes among the SADC countries. The ideas coming out of that workshop are being followed up by the SADC Secretariat and by the heads of statistical departments in the SADC governments.

REFERENCES

Ahluwalia, M.S. 1996. 'Comment on "Inequality Poverty and Growth: Where Do We Stand?"' In: Bruno, M. and Pleskovic. B, (eds.). *Annual World Bank Conference on Development Economics 1995.* World Bank, Washington.

Bechuanaland Protectorate Administration. 1963. *Development Plan 1963/68.*

Bank of Botswana. 1977. *Annual Report 1976.* Bank of Botswana, Gaborone.

Bank of Botswana. 1986. *Rural Income Survey.* Bank of Botswana, Gaborone.

Bank of Botswana. 1994. *Annual Report 1993.* Bank of Botswana, Gaborone.

Bank of Botswana. 1996. *Annual Report 1995.* Bank of Botswana, Gaborone.

Central Statistics Office. 1974. *A Social and Economic Survey of Three Peri-Urban Areas in Botswana.* Central Statistics Office, Gaborone.

Central Statistics Office. 1976. *Rural Income Distribution Survey in Botswana 1975/76.* Central Statistics Office, Gaborone.

Central Statistics Office. 1988. *Household Income and Expenditure Survey 1985/86.* Central Statistics Office, Gaborone.

Central Statistics Office. 1989. *A Poverty Datum Line for Botswana.* Central Statistics Office, Gaborone.

Central Statistics Office. 1996a. *Household Income and Expenditure Survey 1993/94.* Central Statistics Office, Gaborone.

Central Statistics Office. 1996b. 'Unemployment 1991–1994'. *Stats Brief 96/5.* Central Statistics Office, Gaborone.

Clarke G.R.G. 1995. 'More evidence on Income Distribution and Growth', *Journal of Development Economics,* Vol.47, pp403–427.

Colclough, C. and McCarthy, S. 1980. *The Political Economy of Botswana: A Study of Growth and Distribution,* Oxford University Press, Oxford.

Fields, G.S. 1995. 'Review of "Employment and Development: A New Review of Evidence" by David Turnham', *Journal of Development Economics,* Vol.47, pp497–502.

Fishlow, M. 1996. 'Inequality, Poverty, and Growth: Where Do We Stand?' In: Bruno, M. and Pleskovic. B, (eds.). *Annual World Bank Conference on Development Economics 1995.* World Bank, Washington.

Good, K. 1993. 'At the Ends of the Ladder: Radical Inequalities in Botswana', *Journal of Modern African Studies,* Vol.31, No.2, pp203–230.

Government of Botswana. 1966. *Transitional Plan for Social and Economic Development.* Government of Botswana, Gaborone.

Government of Botswana. 1970. *National Development Plan 2, 1970–75.* Government of Botswana, Gaborone.

Government of Botswana. 1977. *National Development Plan 4, 1976–81.* Government of Botswana, Gaborone.

Government of Botswana. 1990. 'Financial Efficiencies in Drought Relief', *Report on the Evaluation of the Drought Relief and Recovery Programme,* Volume 4.

Government of Botswana. 1997. *Poverty and Poverty Alleviation in Botswana.* Prepared by the Botswana Institute for Development Policy Analysis. (forthcoming).

Hanushek, A. 1995. 'Interpreting Recent Research on Schooling in Developing Countries'. *The World Bank Research Observer,* Vol.10, No.2, pp227–246.

Hudson, D. 1976. 'Rural Per Capita Income as Opposed to Rural Household Income', *Botswana Notes and Records,* Vol.17, pp192–193.

IMF. 1995. *Social Dimensions of the IMF's Policy Dialogue,* Pamphlet Series No.47. IMF, Washington.

Jefferis, K. 1997. 'The Quality of Life: Concepts, Definitions and Measurement'. In: Botswana Society, *Poverty and Plenty: The Botswana Experience.* Botswana Society, Gaborone.

Johnson, P. 1996. 'The Assessment: Inequality'. *Oxford Review of Economic Policy,* Vol.12. No.1.

Kremer, M.R. 1995. 'Research on Schooling: What We Know and What We Don't.' *The World Bank Research Observer,* Vol.10, No.2, pp247–254.

OECD. 1996. *Employment Outlook.*

Parsons, N., Henderson, W. and Tlou, T. 1995. *Seretse Khama 1921–1980.* The Botswana Society, Gaborone, and Macmillan Boleswa, Braamfontein.

Roe, E. 1980. *Development of Livestock, Agriculture and Water Supplies in Botswana Before Independence: A Short History and Policy Analysis.* Cornell University, Rural Development Committee Occasional paper No.10.

Turnham, D. 1993. *Employment and Development: A New Review of Evidence.* OECD, Paris.

UNDP. 1996. *Human Development Report 1996.* Oxford University Press, New York

UNSO. 1974. *Statistics of the Distribution of Income, Consumption and Accumulation: Draft Guidelines for the Developing Countries,* UN sales No.E/CN.3/462.

Valentine T.R. 1993. 'Drought, Transfer Entitlements, and Income Distribution: The Botswana Experience', *World Development,* Vol.21, No.1, pp109–126.

Poverty in Botswana[1]

Keith Jefferis

1. INTRODUCTION

The degree of poverty is an important defining characteristic of any society. If poverty is widespread, there will almost certainly be social tensions and problems, either because a large number of people are living a wretched life, or because there is a high degree of inequality between the haves and the have-nots. It is a multifaceted issue, with complex moral, social, political and economic dimensions. It is also at the forefront of notions of 'development', as any development strategy, which has as its intention the betterment of the lives of the population as a whole, must very early on address the task of reducing poverty. It is, therefore, an important policy issue. However, the complexity of poverty, in both its manifestations and causes, means that the choice of policies to alleviate poverty is not an easy one; those who claim that it is easy are usually dealing with the problem in a very superficial manner.

This paper attempts to deal with various aspects of the poverty issue as it affects Botswana. The complexity of the problem in this country is soon revealed: despite having experienced rapidly rising levels of national income over the post-Independence period, the incomes of many households and individuals remain very low. Yet at the same time, even people with low incomes have benefited from substantial improvements in the level of publicly provided goods and services (such as water, education, health care, roads) which are important determinants of the quality of life, and which, over time, have the potential to make significant contributions to preventing poverty from being perpetuated.

The paper is structured as follows. Section 2 discusses a conceptual framework for poverty, while Section 3 discusses its manifestations and causes. Section 4 covers some attempts to measure poverty in Botswana, and Section 5 uses these results to make some international comparisons of poverty. Section 6 concludes.

2. POVERTY: A CONCEPTUAL FRAMEWORK

Conventional 'economistic' definitions of poverty rest heavily upon income or consumption levels, an approach which dates back to work carried out in Victorian England by Booth and Rowntree. According to this definition, poverty is experienced by those

---

[1] This paper draws heavily upon work carried out during 1996 for the BIDPA (Botswana Institute for Development Policy Analysis) Poverty Study, and many of the ideas are derived from discussions and research carried out by the study team, of which the author was a member. Particular thanks are due to Tyrrell Duncan, Per Granberg, and Samuel Ndegwa, whose work contributed directly or indirectly to the contents of this paper. An earlier version of the paper was presented to the Botswana Society Symposium, *The Quality of Life in Botswana*, in Gaborone during October 1996. Revisions to the paper have benefited from comments made by participants at the Symposium, and from Jacob Atta and Charles Harvey.

whose incomes fall below some poverty datum line (PDL).[2] Although this has much practical merit, it is inadequate on its own as a means of conceptualising poverty. It is now widely accepted that poverty (or perhaps 'ill-being', a lack of 'well-being') needs a broader conceptualization, which can encompass some other components, besides income, of the quality of life. A second problem with income/consumption approaches is that typically the income definition is quite narrow, and pays insufficient attention to the value of common property resources (such as access to communal grazing land) and to state-provided commodities (such as free education). Such an approach has been used in Botswana, with the calculation of PDLs by the Central Statistics Office (CSO, 1991).

In the most recent investigation of poverty in Botswana, in 1996, the BIDPA Poverty Study team used 'an inability to meet basic needs' as a working definition of poverty. These basic needs encompass a variety of components, both physical and social. The physical needs include *nutrition* (enough food to maintain a minimum physiological standard), and access to adequate *shelter* and *clothing*. Social needs include the ability to meet essential *social commitments*, and basic *recreation*. While some of these basic needs can be defined quite precisely – nutritional needs can be related to the calorie intake that the body needs to survive and grow – others are more subjective. Social commitments, recreational needs, and, to a certain extent, clothing, will vary over time, and from one society to another. While it is quite right that basic needs, and poverty, should be defined with reference to a particular society, this does make international comparisons problematic.

It is also useful to conceptualise poverty and non-poverty in terms of *choices* (see Figure 1) Poverty can be seen as a situation of lack of choice, arising from low income or low human capacities. If a person has a low income, most or all of that income will be spent in meeting basic needs, and that person will have little or no choice in spending patterns. Nor will he or she have the ability to save. Similarly, a lack of education (leading to illiteracy or innumeracy), or poor health, may preclude that person from taking advantage of employment or other income-generating opportunities.

By contrast, income higher than the level required to meet basic needs enables a person to undertake discretionary spending on non-necessities. He or she may also save, thus building up a source of capital which further widens the range of available choices. Similarly, education and good health increase the range of available income-generation options and, more generally, the ways in which a person may choose to live his or her life. Non-poverty is therefore synonymous with having a range of choices.

It is important to note that within the framework outlined here, income includes, but is not restricted to, earned cash incomes. It may also include non-cash earned income, or income in kind, such as agricultural produce, which in some circumstances may be enough to support a comfortable lifestyle. Such incomes may be derived from employment or self-employment, or from assets (land, capital); they result directly from the economic system and may be termed *primary incomes* (Stewart, 1995).

Yet, in evaluating the relationship between incomes and poverty we must go beyond primary incomes to consider *secondary incomes*, which are the incomes people receive after taxation and benefits. Primary incomes may be supplemented by private

---

2   The proportion of a population below the poverty line is conventionally known as the 'headcount ratio'.

transfers (e.g., remittances from relatives), or public transfers (e.g., social security or welfare support measures, or the provision of free or subsidised public goods). Although primary incomes may in many cases be low, the extent of poverty ultimately depends upon secondary incomes. Some benefits or transfers which supplement primary incomes, especially those from public sources, may therefore be viewed as a *safety net* for the poor.[3]

FIGURE 1. CONCEPTUAL MODEL OF POVERTY AND NON-POVERTY AT THE HOUSEHOLD LEVEL

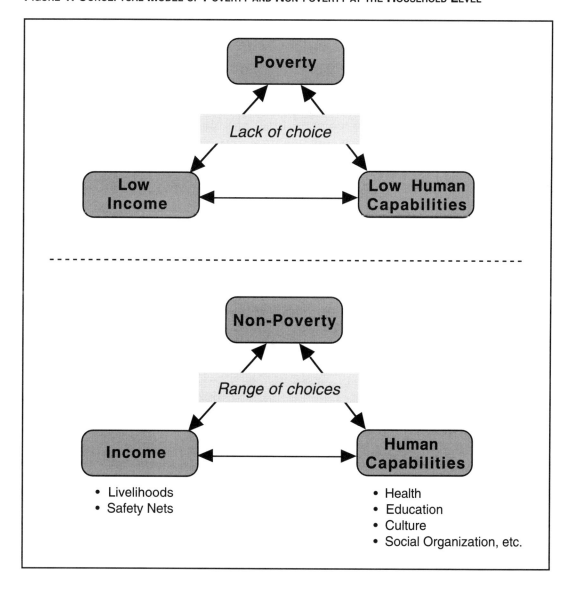

---

[3]   For such a safety net to be effective, benefits must be correctly targeted, and must reach the targeted beneficiaries. In practice, many such schemes are ineffective because the benefits are captured by middle or even high income earners.

3. Manifestations and Causes of Poverty

Manifestations of poverty

What form does poverty take in Botswana? In general it is a situation where the quality of life is very low, but beyond this we can identify a number of more specific manifestations:

- lack of adequate shelter and clothing;
- high mortality and morbidity;
- malnutrition;
- dependency (on relatives, neighbours, or the state);
- child vulnerability; and
- lack of economic and social mobility.

We should also distinguish between poverty, which affects a person, household, or group of people, at a particular point in time, and that which is entrenched and perpetuated over time. The latter is much more serious. While no poverty is good, it is less serious if those so affected have a realistic chance of getting out of poverty, or at least if their children have such a chance. Poverty is most serious when the conditions which give rise to it are reproduced from one generation to the next; one important aspect of poverty alleviation is to ensure that those who are born into poverty have a chance of economic and social mobility out of poverty.[4]

Causes of poverty in Botswana

The causes of poverty are many and complex. Any attempt to identify them is bound to be controversial, and may miss out factors which some consider to be important, and give undue emphasis to factors which others consider unimportant. The following is, however, an attempt to identify the causes of poverty, in terms of both *immediate causes* and *underlying causes*.

The *immediate causes* of poverty may be seen as due to a combination of failures on three levels.

1. Failure of economic opportunities

- A lack of jobs and opportunities for income generating activities, leading to high unemployment.
- Low wages for those in work, or low incomes from self-employment.

---

[4] Conventional cross-section household surveys provide a snapshot of poverty at a point in time. Even if a series of such surveys are carried out, they cannot show whether particular, individual households have remained in poverty, or moved in or out of poverty, because different households enter into the samples surveyed at different times. To trace the dynamics of poverty requires a continuous or repeated survey of the same households – a panel survey. Evidence from such surveys in the UK and the USA shows that in those countries at least, many of those in poverty at any point in time are only temporarily so. A UK survey found that although 17% of the population were in poverty in 1991 and 1992, only 10% were in poverty in both years. A survey of children in the USA over a 15 year period found that 40% experienced poverty at some point during the 15 years, but only 4% experienced more or less permanent poverty (Johnson, 1996).

2. Failure of (state) social provision

- Failure of social safety nets (inadequate coverage, low level of provision, inadequate targeting, or poor implementation).
- Inadequate provision of health care, education and so forth.

3. Failure of individual/family decisions

- An unequal distribution of income within the household, whereby some members of the household may end up in poverty even if overall household income is adequate; this may be manifested in low levels of child care, or inappropriate expenditure decisions (such as expenditure on alcohol rather than food).
- A dependency syndrome, whereby individuals expect Government to provide everything, and show a lack of initiative in helping themselves.
- Large family size, which increases the burden of dependency upon household income without contributing additional income.

There are of course many *underlying causes* leading to these immediate causes of poverty. The 'traditional' view is that the causes of poverty in Botswana are essentially drought and destitution. This view can be summarised as follows: in years of average to good rainfall, agriculture can provide sufficient incomes to keep households out of poverty. Furthermore, the extended family system should provide a mechanism for redistributing income between individuals, households and generations which ensures that the temporarily disadvantaged are provided for. Poverty only arises when agricultural incomes fail on a large scale (due to drought), or for those 'destitutes' without income or assets, who are unable to work, and who lack extended family support. Botswana's current policies to directly support low income households – drought relief and destitutes allowance – are based upon this approach.

However, there are several reasons to believe that the causes of poverty go beyond this, and hence that several categories of the poor are excluded from relief measures (see Food Studies Group, 1995). In particular, it is inadequate to see poverty primarily as a drought issue, and there is reason to believe that instead it has structural causes. In particular, the belief that agriculture can provide adequate (non-poverty level) incomes for large numbers of Batswana in years of normal rainfall must be challenged, for the reasons outlined below.

(i)   Many people are (or claim to be) better off in drought years (when drought relief schemes are in operation, providing income and food support) than in non-drought years, when they have to rely on agriculture; for many people agricultural incomes are below even the very low incomes received under drought relief schemes.

(ii) Although it is popularly held that this is because of worse rainfall now than 'long ago', it is more likely that increasing population pressure has meant that more and more arable farmers are being forced on to ever more marginal lands, where there is little prospect of making an adequate living.

(iii) The failure to achieve any significant productivity improvements in agriculture, despite high levels of Government subsidies and expenditure on agricultural development projects, extension services and so on, over a long period of time.

(iv) High rates of rural-urban migration, and the decline in the absolute numbers

(v) of those practising traditional agriculture, despite rapid population growth, reflecting a rational decision by many Batswana to give up on an activity which is highly risky, and has little prospect of offering adequate incomes (see Jefferis, 1995).

(v) As urbanization takes place (prompted by limited rural economic potential, and the perception of more favourable economic prospects in the towns), many of the young increasingly lack the knowledge, experience, ability and interest to try and scrape a living from agriculture, despite some such training taking place in schools.

(vi) Nearly half of rural households are female-headed, and many of them suffer from shortages of labour, draft power and other agricultural resources; they would face problems making a living from agriculture, even if climatic and soil conditions were better.

(vii) For inhabitants of western parts of the country, arable agriculture was never a viable option. Now, due to land alienation and other reasons, they cannot re-turn to other traditional lifestyles.

Rather than seeing poverty as resulting from drought, destitution and other 'excep-tional' circumstances, it is more accurate to see poverty as a result of highly adverse climatic and soil conditions, which means that agriculture, in general, does not have the potential to provide adequate (non-poverty) incomes for large numbers of Batswana. Poverty is, therefore, a structural characteristic of Botswana's rural areas. This is one of the main factors that distinguishes Botswana from other countries, especially in Sub-Saharan Africa, where one of the most effective potential means of poverty alle-viation is to 'sort out' agriculture, by reforms to pricing policies and the provision of extension services, so as to enable the underlying potential of agriculture to be real-ised. Botswana does not have that potential.

Moving away from this traditional view has quite serious implications for the con-ception of the nature of poverty, and policies to alleviate it. Under the 'drought and destitution view', only destitutes are in chronic (more or less permanent) poverty; those afflicted by drought are in transient (non-permanent) poverty. But if we ascribe poverty to structural factors rather than drought, then the chronic component of poverty becomes much larger, and transient factors less important. This obviously has important implications for poverty alleviation policies.

The weakness of agriculture in Botswana contributes to poverty beyond simply the inability of the rural population to earn reasonable incomes; it also contributes more generally to unemployment. In a more typical Sub-Saharan African society, where traditional agriculture might gainfully occupy 50% to 80% of the labour force, Botswana's level of formal sector jobs (50% of the labour force) and rapid employment growth would be more than sufficient to provide full employment. However, with tra-ditional agriculture occupying only an estimated 15% to 20% of the labour force, the actual unemployment rate is, in the mid-1990s, around 20% to 25%.[3] The increas-ingly serious unemployment problem in Botswana can be seen, therefore, as resulting from a combination of very limited opportunities in agriculture, combined with a failure of the economy to generate sufficient jobs (in both the formal and informal

---

[5] CSO (1996).

FIGURE 2. CAUSES OF POVERTY IN BOTSWANA

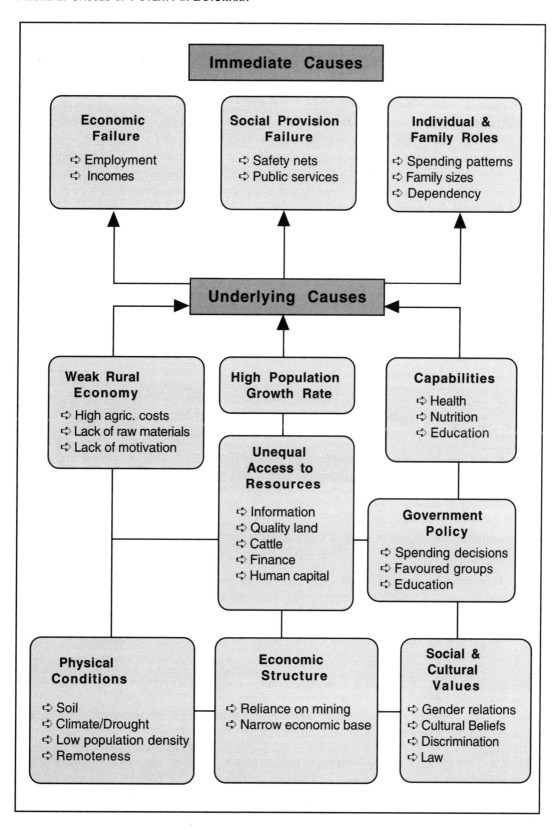

sectors) to absorb both new entrants to the labour force and those leaving the agricultural sector.[6]

Although agriculture (or lack of it) is perhaps the most important factor in explaining poverty in Botswana, there are other important features of the economy and society which also contribute to poverty (see Figure 2). These are outlined below.

(i) **Unequal distribution of access to and control over assets**, including human capital[7], land, cattle, finance, and other physical capital. It is worth noting that although in theory all Batswana have access to land for agricultural purposes, in many cases the available land is insufficient in quantity or quality to provide an adequate income. Other types of capital are also unequally distributed, and this reduces the ability of many households to generate incomes, especially when combined with imperfections in the financial system which restrict the ability of the poor to borrow.

(ii) **Inadequate capabilities** (both a cause and a consequence of poverty), including health, nutrition, and education.

(iii) **A high population growth rate** which makes it more difficult to provide social and public services to the entire population.

(iv) **The physical size of the country, low population density and remoteness of many communities**, which makes it difficult and expensive to ensure that the whole population has access to public services, such as education, health care, water, roads, electricity, and so on. It also further undermines the viability of agriculture, through the large distances to markets.

(v) **Government policies and spending decisions**, which may favour certain groups in society (such as cattle farmers) over others.

(vi) **Social organization, beliefs and practices,** which also have an impact on poverty, through such factors as:

gender relations, whereby women are in a subordinate position and may lose out on access to household income, and at the same time have greater responsibilities for financing child care. They may also have inferior access to bank credit;

fatalistic cultural beliefs (such as witchcraft), which may undermine the effectiveness of health care and reduce the incentive to take personal responsibility and initiative; and

negative or discriminatory attitudes towards particular groups in society (such as the Basarwa).

Several of these social factors are manifested in, and reinforced by the *legal framework* of the country.

---

6   It should also be noted that the rate of female participation in the labour force has risen, and this means that more jobs have to be provided in order to reach full employment.

7   Although human capital is unequally distributed, it should be noted that thirty years ago almost nobody in Botswana had any education, so human capital was quite equally distributed. The present situation is surely preferable.

There is a question over whether the structure of the economy, dominated by the mineral sector, has contributed in any way towards poverty. Many other *mineral-dominated economies* have suffered from a 'resource curse', which has undoubtedly contributed to more severe poverty than would have existed without minerals. This has generally been through wasteful use of mineral rents, which have not been invested in the efficient provision of public services, accompanied by 'Dutch Disease' effects whereby the strength of the minerals sector has squeezed out the production of other tradeable commodities, notably agricultural and manufactured products.

There is little evidence of this process happening in Botswana. Agriculture is weak and has declined, but for other reasons. Manufacturing has been through periods of varying fortunes, but has overall experienced quite impressive rates of growth and has not shown any tendency to decline through the mineral boom period. Non-mineral GDP has become more employment intensive, rather than less, as has happened in other mineral-boom economies. Furthermore, there is extensive evidence from human development indicators (such as life expectancy and literacy) that Botswana has wisely invested a substantial proportion of its mineral revenues in human development enhancing activities. It may well be that mineral revenues have contributed to *inequality* – which is common in mineral economies – but this is only one aspect of poverty. It may be more appropriate to note that Botswana's *narrow economic base* has contributed to poverty. Mining is relatively capital intensive, and the remaining sectors have proved unable to generate sufficient employment in a country with rapid population growth and large numbers of people migrating from the low-productivity agricultural sector.

Just as there are many causes of poverty in Botswana, poverty can be alleviated by a wide range of different policies: to improve health and education (and thus human capabilities); to improve income-generation capacity (and thus incomes); and to provide a safety net to those whose incomes fall below a certain level. These safety net policies are the most direct intervention against poverty and should provide the last line of defence against poverty; yet they are difficult to design and implement effectively, and are often very expensive.

4. MEASUREMENT OF POVERTY

Measurement of incomes and capabilities

Measurement of poverty is closely related to debates over measuring the quality of life (QOL) (see Jefferis, 1996). The conceptual approach used in the BIDPA study suggests that measurement should not just be of incomes, but should include factors relating to human capacities/capabilities. Indeed, many of the recent advances in measuring the QOL (such as Morris's Physical Quality of Life Index, or the UNDP's Human Development Index, HDI), reflect conceptual developments in this direction. Low QOL measurements may be interpreted as a reflection of poverty.

The numerous problems surrounding these measures of QOL are present in broad poverty measurements. It is widely agreed that health and education are the key contributors to building capacities, but how should they be measured? Do we use access (to primary health care, primary education, and so on,) or attainment (e.g., life expectancy, infant mortality, adult literacy)? What are the cut-off points defining adequacy? If we wish to use a composite measure (such as HDI), how do we weight the various components?

Poverty measurement still relies heavily on income based measures, despite recent conceptual advances. This reflects a number of factors, including both feasibility in terms of data availability and the arbitrary nature of answers to many of the questions posed above. Income based measures are used here, but supplemented with information on other dimensions of poverty.

Income poverty: the Poverty Datum Line (PDL)

The poverty line represents a real income level below which a person (or household) can be said to be poor. The standard approach is to start by estimating the income needed to buy sufficient food to meet specified calorie requirements. This may then be supplemented by the income required to buy other 'necessities'.[8] The cost of the basic necessities (food and non-food) then represents the PDL; the PDL may then be adjusted for inflation (to give comparability at different points in time), for regional differences in the costs of commodities (e.g., between urban and rural areas) and for household size (which affects the income required to keep all family members above the PDL).

The Botswana PDL is based on six categories of items which are considered to constitute the basic needs of a family in Botswana (CSO, 1991): food ('the minimum necessary to maintain physical health'); clothing (to meet minimum standards of

TABLE 1. EXAMPLES OF POVERTY DATUM LINES, 1993/94 (PULA PER MONTH)

TYPE OF HOUSEHOLD		URBAN	RURAL
Size	Composition (ages in brackets)	(Gaborone)	(Area C)
1	Male (20–54)	171	114
2	Male (20–54); Female (20–54)	260	216
3	Female (20–54); girl (2); girl (0)	269	235
4	Male (20–54); Female (20–54); boy (6); girl (2)	441	374
6	Female (65+); male (20–54); female (20–54); boy (16); girl (10); girl (2)	597	560
7	Female (65+); female (20–54); boy (16); girl (10); boy (6); girl (2); girl (0)	617	584
10	Male (65+); female (65+); male (20–54); female (20–54); boy (16); girl (10); boy (6); boy (4); girl (2); girl (0)	836	854

Source: CSO, 1991; BIDPA estimates.

---

8 While the calorific and nutritional requirements for basic food consumption do not vary a great deal between countries (although their cost may), the other components are more socially determined, and hence more variable.

legality, decency, practicality and warmth); personal items; household goods; shelter; and miscellaneous items. Detailed PDLs were calculated for ten different family types in two urban and four rural areas.[9] Sample PDLs are shown in Table 1.

When applied to data on household incomes and/or expenditures, PDLs can tell us which households are in poverty, i.e., with incomes below their relevant PDL.[10] However, the necessary data gathering exercise is relatively time-consuming and expensive, and is rarely done regularly in developing countries. It has only been done twice (for the whole country) in Botswana – the Household Income and Expenditure Surveys (HIES 1985/86 and 1993/94[11]). Nevertheless, these two HIES do enable us to gain a picture of the nature of poverty in Botswana, and of the changes which have taken place between the mid-1980s and the mid-1990s.

The conventional poverty line approach classifies those whose incomes fall below the poverty line as 'the poor'. The BIDPA team developed this further, following an approach suggested by Lipton (1983), with a division of the poor into 'moderately poor' and 'very poor'. As noted above, food costs make up a substantial proportion of the PDL basket in most countries (typically fifty percent or more). The cost of the food required to meet basic nutritional needs may be referred to as the 'food poverty line': those whose incomes fall below the food line are the very poor, while those whose incomes are above the food line but below the overall poverty line are the moderately poor.

Extent of Poverty

Preliminary analysis of the 1985/86 and 1993/94 HIES reveals a considerable amount of information about changes in the level of poverty in Botswana between the two surveys. It also gives indications of the characteristics of those in poverty, which in turn starts to throw some light on the causes of poverty.

How much poverty? The HIES data show that in 1993/94, 38% of Botswana households had incomes below the relevant poverty line[12] (see Table 2). Although this may be considered to be a rather high figure, the positive side of it is that poverty had declined significantly from 49% of households in 1985/86. Considering individuals rather than households, the figures are higher, as the poor have larger than average households. Whereas in 1985/86, 59% of Batswana lived in households with incomes below their poverty line, this had fallen to 47% in 1993/94. Despite the drop, nearly half of Batswana were still below the poverty line.

Besides the decline in poverty rates, there is evidence that there has been some 'trickle down' from Botswana's rapid economic growth, even to those near to the

[9]   Rather than there being one single Poverty Datum Line, Botswana therefore has 60 different PDLs, applicable to different family sizes in different locations, at any point in time.

[10]   There are a number of ways of defining and measuring incomes, each of which faces various conceptual and/or technical problems. In the BIDPA study, incomes were proxied by household consumption expenditure, which is widely considered to be the most reliable measure. See Granberg (1996).

[11]   The Rural Income Distribution Survey (RIDS) was carried out in 1974/75, but excluded urban areas.

[12]   The relevant poverty line depends on the size and composition of the household (in terms of numbers and ages of adults and children), and its geographical location.

Table 2. Poverty Rates – Headcount Ratio, 1985/86 and 1993/94 (% of population group below PDL)

	Total poor		Poor		Very poor	
	85/86	93/94	85/86	93/94	85/86	93/94
A. Households						
Urban	23	23	15	16	7	7
Urban villages	49	36	17	14	31	22
Rural	60	48	16	16	44	33
Total	**49**	**38**	**16**	**15**	**33**	**23**
B. Individuals						
Urban	30	29	20	19	10	9
Urban villages	58	46	20	17	38	29
Rural	68	55	17	16	51	40
Total	**59**	**47**	**18**	**17**	**41**	**30**

Note: Some totals may not add exactly due to rounding of decimals.
Source: HIES 1985/86, 1993/94 (CSO 1987 and 1995) and calculations by the BIDPA Poverty Study Team.

bottom of the income scale. In 1985/86, a household on the 10th income percentile had an income of P41.66 a month (i.e., 10% of households had incomes below this figure). By 1993/94, income at the 10th percentile had increased to P139.60 per month. After allowing for inflation, this represents an increase of 37% in real terms – an average real rate of growth of 4% a year.

Where is poverty? Unfortunately the HIES data cannot provide information on the distribution of poverty in the different districts of Botswana. However, it can show the broad division of poverty between urban and rural areas. Perhaps not surprisingly, poverty in rural areas is more severe than in urban areas. Table 2 shows that 48% of rural households were in poverty in 1993/94, compared to 36% of urban village households[13] and 23% of urban households. On an individual level, 55% of rural Batswana were in poverty, 46% in urban villages, and 29% in urban areas. Tables 3 and 4 confirm that poverty remains predominantly (but not exclusively) a rural problem, in that approximately 60% of all poor households, and nearly 70% of very poor households, are in the rural areas.

Depth of Poverty. We can obtain more detail on the poverty picture when we con-

---

[13] The 1991 Population Census introduced the category of 'urban village'. This denotes a settlement which is relatively large (over 5 000 inhabitants), and where less than 25% of the population derive the majority of their income from agriculture (in contrast to the 'rural' definition), but which do not have the administrative structures of urban areas. This latter point means that they remain administered by District Councils, rather than town/city councils. The 1985/86 HIES used only the urban/rural distinction.

sider the 'moderately poor', and the 'very poor'. In the country as a whole, most of those who are below the poverty line are in the very poor category (23% of households in 1993/94, compared to 15% in the moderately poor category). But there is a very different picture in urban as compared to rural areas. In the towns, the majority of the poor are only moderately poor (16%), with only a relatively small proportion (7%) in the very poor category. By contrast, in the rural areas, the majority of the poor are very poor (30% of households), and far fewer are moderately poor (14%). This indicates that the 'depth of poverty' (how far incomes fall below the poverty line) in the rural areas is much more severe than in the towns.

We therefore have six categories of poor (urban, urban village, and rural, each broken down into moderately poor and very poor). Further examination of the HIES data shows that in four of these six categories (both urban categories, and the urban village and rural moderately poor), the proportions of households remained more or less constant, or declined only slightly, between 1985/86 and 1993/94. However, there has been a sharp reduction in the proportion of rural very poor households, from 44% to 33%, and a similar reduction in the number of poor individuals, from 51% to 40%. This is very encouraging, as this is the largest single category of poor. A similar reduction occurred in the urban villages. Virtually all of the poverty reduction seen in Botswana between the mid-1980s and the mid-1990s has been due to a reduction in the proportion of rural (as defined in 1985/86) very poor – which is exactly what should have happened, given that this was the group in most need of poverty alleviation. This evidence therefore suggests that the policies or other factors responsible for poverty alleviation have been relatively well-targeted, and focused on the most needy.

TABLE 3. HOUSEHOLDS IN POVERTY, 1993/94 (NUMBER OF HOUSEHOLDS)

	URBAN	URBAN VILLAGE	RURAL	TOTAL
MALE-HEADED HH				
Total MHH	56 297	30 271	71 600	15 8168
of which:				
Non-poor	45 060	20 550	38 189	103 799
Poor	8 284	3521	9 086	20 891
Very poor	2 953	6 200	24 325	33 478
TOTAL POOR MHH	**11237**	**9721**	**33 411**	**54369**
	20.7%	*17.9%*	*61.5%*	*100.0%*
FEMALE-HEADED HH				
Total FHH	31 120	36 947	65 372	13 3439
of which:				
Non-poor	22 542	22 567	33 199	78 308
Poor	5 582	5 555	11 325	22 462
Very poor	2 996	8 825	20 848	32 669
TOTAL POOR FHH	**8578**	**14380**	**32173**	**55131**
	15.6%	*26.1%*	*58.4%*	*100.0%*
ALL HOUSEHOLDS				
Total HH	87 417	67 218	136 972	291 607
of which:				
Non-poor	67 602	43 117	71 388	182 107
Poor	13 866	9 076	20 411	43 353
Very poor	5 949	15 025	45 173	66 147
TOTAL POOR HH	**19815**	**24101**	**65584**	**109500**
	18.1%	*22.0%*	*59.9%*	*100.0%*

Source: HIES 1985/86, 1993/94 (CSO 1987 and 1995) and calculations by the BIDPA Poverty Study Team.

To summarise, these results from the HIES have both positive and negative aspects. Botswana still has a high poverty rate, but has seen a significant reduction in the proportion of its households in poverty between the mid-1980s and the mid-1990s. This reduction has been almost entirely due to an improvement in the position of the largest single group of people in poverty, the rural very poor. There is no evidence to support the claims of those who suggest that poverty has got worse in Botswana during the past decade. But it does also show that poverty remains widespread,

TABLE 4. POVERTY RATES - HOUSEHOLDS, 1993/94
(% OF POPULATION GROUP)

	URBAN	URBAN VILLAGE	RURAL	TOTAL
MALE-HEADED HH				
Non-poor	80%	68%	53%	66%
Poor	15%	12%	13%	13%
Very poor	5%	20%	34%	21%
TOTAL POOR MHH	**20%**	**32%**	**47%**	**34%**
FEMALE-HEADED HH				
Non-poor	72%	61%	51%	59%
Poor	18%	15%	17%	17%
Very poor	10%	24%	32%	24%
TOTAL POOR FHH	**28%**	**39%**	**49%**	**41%**
ALL HOUSEHOLDS				
Non-poor	77%	64%	52%	62%
Poor	16%	14%	15%	15%
Very poor	7%	22%	33%	23%
TOTAL POOR HH	**23%**	**36%**	**48%**	**38%**

Source: HIES 1985/86, 1993/94 (CSO 1987 and 1995) and calculations by the BIDPA Poverty Study Team.

and it is disturbing that 23% of households in Botswana – who may be termed the 'core poor', unable to afford their basic food needs – remain in severe poverty. Nevertheless, it shows that the economic growth of the second half of the 1980s did benefit the majority of Batswana; even the numbers of core poor have fallen significantly since the mid-1980s. It is most likely that improvement was due to the higher incomes which resulted from extremely rapid employment growth. And although the economic situation has been less favourable in the 1990s, the results also show that the recession of 1992/93, and rising unemployment, had not reversed the poverty alleviation gains of the 1980s (at least, not by 1993/94).

Most poverty gains were in the rural areas, where few of the formal sector jobs were created; we also know that agriculture has remained weak (both HIES years were drought years). This suggests that many of the poverty alleviation gains resulting from employment growth were indirect, mainly through the mechanism of increased transfers/remittances of those in work to relatives in rural areas.[14] This suggests that the role of the extended family mechanism, even if declining, remains important.

Households and Individuals. The HIES data are collected on a household basis. Whether a given level of household income is sufficient to keep a household out of poverty depends on the household size. Although there are no data on intra-house-

---

14 Although the role of direct employment creation in the rural areas should not be dismissed in poverty alleviation – there are substantial numbers of Government jobs (e.g., in the District Councils, and in the education and health services), in the rural areas, and other formal sector jobs (e.g., in shops, personal services, etc.) have followed.

TABLE 5. POVERTY RATES — INDIVIDUALS, 1993/94
(% OF POPULATION GROUP)

	URBAN	URBAN VILLAGE	RURAL	TOTAL
MALE-HEADED HH				
Non-poor	75%	57%	46%	56%
Poor	18%	15%	13%	15%
Very poor	7%	28%	41%	29%
TOTAL POOR IN MHH	**25%**	**43%**	**54%**	**44%**
FEMALE HEADED HH				
Non-poor	66%	52%	43%	50%
Poor	21%	19%	19%	19%
Very poor	14%	29%	38%	31%
TOTAL POOR IN FHH	**35%**	**48%**	**57%**	**50%**
ALL HOUSEHOLDS				
Non-poor	71%	54%	45%	53%
Poor	19%	17%	16%	17%
Very poor	9%	29%	40%	30%
TOTAL POOR IN ALL HH	**28%**	**46%**	**55%**	**47%**

Source: HIES 1985/86, 1993/94 (CSO 1987 and 1995) and calculations by the BIDPA Poverty Study Team.

hold income distribution (how income varies between different family members), we can see that poor households are generally larger. Therefore, the 37% of households in poverty in 1993/94 comprised individuals making up 46% of the population. In rural areas over half the population (52%) were in poverty, compared to 30% in urban areas. In both cases, as with households, there have been significant reductions since 1985/86.

Poverty and Gender. It has been argued that female-headed households (FHH) are more vulnerable to poverty than male-headed households (MHH) (see World Bank, 1990). Partly as a result, some of Botswana's production-oriented development assistance programmes particularly target women; under both the Financial Assistance Policy (FAP) and the Arable Lands Development Programme (ALDEP), women receive more favourable financial assistance than men.

Tables 3, 4 and 5 show the poverty data disaggregated by the gender of household head. This confirms (Table 4) that a higher proportion of FHH are poor (41%) than of MHH (34%). Data from the two HIES surveys (not reported here) also shows that in 1985/86 there was little difference between the poverty rates of FHHs and MHHs. This indicates that FHHs have fallen behind between the two surveys, and have benefited less from the reductions in poverty that have occurred in Botswana.

Beyond this, however, the results show some surprises. Firstly, there does not appear to be a greater depth of poverty among FHH than MHH; 62% of poor MHHs are very poor, similar to the 59% of poor FHHs in this category. Secondly, while the majority of poor FHHs are in the rural areas, there is no great difference between FHHs and MHHs (Table 3). In other words, while poor FHHs are concentrated in the rural areas, so are poor MHHs. Thirdly, while FHHs in the urban areas and urban villages appear to experience a higher poverty rate than do MHHs in those areas (Tables 4 and 5), there is little difference in the poverty rates amongst FHHs and MHHs in the rural areas (54% and 57% of individuals, respectively).

Therefore, while these results confirm that FHHs are poorer than MHHs, they also indicate that this is mostly due to higher poverty amongst FHHs (relative to MHHs) in the towns and urban villages, rather than in the rural areas. This is a somewhat surprising result, as there has been much attention focused on poor rural FHHs, with research (see van Driel, 1994) showing that in Botswana this is at least partly due to females being abandoned by male partners (or fathers of their children) in the rural areas without adequate means of support, and to a general decline in extended family support. While there is evidence in the HIES data (discussed below) to support this, it is important not to lose sight of the fact that MHHs in the rural areas are almost as poor as FHHs, albeit probably for different reasons. The different processes which appear to push MHHs and FHHs into poverty are discussed below.

Demographic and economic characteristics of the poor

Tables 6 to 9 present information concerning the demographic characteristics of poor households, with regard to age, education, household size, and dependency ratios.

Age. Age appears to have a positive relationship with poverty (see tables). Comparing the urban non-poor with the rural very poor, the latter are much older – 20 years for MHHs, 17 years for FHHs. In general, the poor FHHs have a younger head than poor MHHs.

Education. Whereas only a small proportion of urban non-poor household heads have not attended school (10% for MHHs, 14% for FHHs), a majority of heads of rural very poor households have never attended school (67% for MHHs, 61% for FHHs) (see Table 7). Note that the heads of poor FHHs are generally better educated than those of poor MHHs.[15]

Household size. The average size of poor households is much larger than that of non-poor households (3.3 persons for the urban non-poor, 6.1 for the rural very poor), although there is little difference between the sizes of poor MHHs and FHHs (see

TABLE 6. AVERAGE AGE OF HOUSEHOLD HEAD, 1993/94 (YEARS)

	URBAN	URBAN VILLAGE	RURAL
MALE HEADED HOUSEHOLDS			
Non-poor	38	42	50
Poor	40	48	54
Very poor	47	53	58
FEMALE HEADED HOUSEHOLDS			
Non-poor	35	42	45
Poor	37	48	51
Very poor	43	48	52

Source: HIES 1985/86, 1993/94 (CSO 1987 and 1995) and calculations by the BIDPA Poverty Study Team.

TABLE 7. EDUCATION OF HOUSEHOLD HEAD, 1993/94 (% OF HH HEADS THAT NEVER ATTENDED SCHOOL)

	URBAN	URBAN VILLAGE	RURAL
MALE HEADED HOUSEHOLDS			
Non-poor	14%	27%	39%
Poor	29%	57%	66%
Very poor	41%	67%	67%
FEMALE HEADED HOUSEHOLDS			
Non-poor	10%	17%	33%
Poor	18%	35%	46%
Very poor	29%	35%	61%

Source: HIES 1985/86, 1993/94 (CSO 1987 and 1995) and calculations by the BIDPA Poverty Study Team.

---

[15] This may be because males tended cattle and went to the mines, while the females stayed in the villages and went to school.

Table 8). Larger household sizes for the poor translate to higher *dependency ratios* (of children under 15, and elderly over 65, to working age adults[16]). The dependency ratio of 0.49 for the urban non-poor compares with 1.29 for rural very poor MHHs; for FHHs, 0.64 for the urban non-poor compares to 1.59 for the rural very poor. Note that the rural very poor have more than twice the dependency ratio of the urban non-poor. Also, FHHs have higher dependency ratios than MHHs, despite similar average family sizes, presumably reflecting greater incidence of households with only one adult amongst FHHs as compared to MHHs.

Employment and Income Sources. Tables 10 and 11 present information on the economic circumstances of poor households. Table 10, on employment status, confirms two expected points. First, there is a very clear relationship between poverty and lack of paid employment. Whereas 24% of the members of non-poor households are in paid employment, only 14% of the members of moderately poor households, and 10% of the members of very poor households, are employed.

TABLE 8. HOUSEHOLD SIZE, 1993/94 (AVERAGE NO. OF HOUSEHOLD MEMBERS)

	URBAN	URBAN VILLAGE	RURAL	TOTAL
MALE HEADED HOUSEHOLDS				
Non-poor	3.3	4.1	4.4	3.8
Poor	4.4	6.4	5.1	5.0
Very poor	4.5	6.9	6.1	6.1
TOTAL MHHs	**3.5**	**5.0**	**5.1**	**4.5**
FEMALE HEADED HOUSEHOLDS				
Non-poor	3.4	4.0	4.3	3.9
Poor	4.2	6.1	5.5	5.4
Very poor	5.3	5.7	6.1	5.9
TOTAL FHHs	**3.7**	**4.8**	**5.1**	**4.7**

Source: HIES 1985/86, 1993/94 (CSO 1987 and 1995) and calculations by the BIDPA Poverty Study Team.

TABLE 9. DEPENDENCY RATIO, 1993/94 (DEPENDANTS 0–15, 65+, PER ADULT)

	URBAN	URBAN VILLAGE	RURAL
MALE-HEADED HOUSEHOLDS			
Non-poor	0.5	0.6	1.0
Poor	0.6	0.9	1.1
Very poor	0.5	1.0	1.3
FEMALE-HEADED HOUSEHOLDS			
Non-poor	0.6	1.0	1.4
Poor	0.9	1.2	1.6
Very poor	0.7	1.2	1.6

Source: HIES 1985/86, 1993/94 (CSO 1987 and 1995) and calculations by the BIDPA Poverty Study Team.

This supports findings from the experiences of many other countries, that access to employment is extremely important in alleviating poverty. Second, female-headed households have less access to paid employment than male-headed households, with only 12% of the members of moderately poor FHHs, and 9% of members of very poor FHHs, employed. Given the apparent relationship between access to employment and avoiding poverty, it appears that the lower access to employment of FHHs is one of the factors contributing to their greater poverty. This conclusion is reinforced by the

---

[16] Note that this dependency ratio does not capture the possibility that the working age adults may be unemployed and thus dependent upon someone else.

different results from urban and rural areas. As noted above, FHHs experience a higher poverty rate than MHHs in the urban areas and urban villages, but not in the rural areas. The employment data show that in the urban areas and urban villages, FHHs have a lower percentage of household members in employment than MHHs, but that in rural areas, amongst poor households, there is no difference in employment rates between FHHs and MHHs; in both cases, it is around 8%.

Table 11 and Figure 3, on income sources, show the proportions of income coming from cash earnings (from employment and from business profits) and from gifts (both cash and in-kind); the latter are likely to consist primarily of remittances from absent family members. Again, there are clear patterns. First, and following on from the results in the previous paragraph, the poor obtain a lower proportion of their income from cash earnings than the non-poor. Second, FHHs obtain a lower proportion of their income from cash earnings than MHHs. Third, the poor obtain a higher proportion of their income from gifts (remittances) than the non-poor, and fourth, FHHs are much more dependent upon remittances than are MHHs.

Overall, these results indicate that poverty seems to be positively correlated with age, a lack of education, a lack of

TABLE 10. EMPLOYMENT STATUS, 1993/94 (% OF HOUSEHOLD MEMBERS IN PAID EMPLOYMENT)

HOUSEHOLD HEAD	MALE	FEMALE	ALL
ALL AREAS			
Non-poor	29%	19%	24%
Poor	15%	12%	14%
Very poor	11%	9%	10%
TOTAL POOR	**12%**	**10%**	**11%**
Total Households	21%	15%	18%
URBAN			
Non-poor	45%	28%	36%
Poor	28%	19%	23%
Very poor	24%	14%	19%
TOTAL POOR	**27%**	**18%**	**22%**
Total Households	40%	25%	32%
URBAN VILLAGES			
Non-poor	26%	20%	22%
Poor	17%	12%	14%
Very poor	12%	9%	10%
TOTAL POOR	**14%**	**10%**	**12%**
Total Households	20%	15%	18%
RURAL			
Non-poor	19%	13%	16%
Poor	7%	8%	8%
Very poor	9%	8%	9%
TOTAL POOR	**9%**	**8%**	**8%**
Total Households	13%	10%	12%

Source: HIES 1985/86, 1993/94 (CSO 1987 and 1995) and calculations by the BIDPA Poverty Study Team.

employment, large families, and high dependency ratios. In urban areas there is a positive correlation between poverty and gender, with FHHs having a higher poverty rate, although this pattern is much less evident in rural areas.

It was noted in Section 3 that access to earned incomes, and especially to wage employment, is one of the main causal factors determining poverty levels. This is supported by the empirical results reported above. The results also indicate other factors associated with poverty, which are likely to inhibit some individuals from gaining access to wage employment. Because they reduce a person's chances of obtaining employment, and therefore of making use of the main route out of poverty, these factors can be said to constitute a *poverty trap*. However, it appears that the nature of this poverty trap differs between MHHs and FHHs. In the rural areas at least, poverty amongst MHHs is more strongly associated with age and lack of education, which reduce the chances of gaining employment. Poverty amongst FHHs

TABLE 11. SOURCES OF INCOME 1993/94 (PULA PER MONTH)

	SOURCES OF INCOME						AS % OF TOTAL INCOME			
	MONEY EARNINGS	OWN PRODUCE CONSUMED	EARNINGS IN KIND	SCHOOL MEALS	GIFTS (REMITTANCES) RECEIVED	TOTAL	MONEY	IN-KIND	OWN PRODUCE	GIFTS
MALE-HEADED HH										
Non-poor	1453	75	118	34	82	1763	84%	16%	4%	5%
Poor	408	70	4	42	83	607	72%	28%	12%	14%
Very poor	239	61	3	39	83	424	64%	36%	14%	20%
TOTAL MHH	**1058**	**71**	**78**	**36**	**82**	**1326**	**82%**	**18%**	**5%**	**6%**
FEMALE-HEADED HH										
Non-poor	614	82	15	45	203	959	77%	23%	9%	21%
Poor	206	72	5	61	168	512	56%	44%	14%	33%
Poor	148	42	2	52	128	372	57%	43%	11%	35%
TOTAL FHH	**431**	**70**	**10**	**49**	**179**	**740**	**72%**	**28%**	**9%**	**24%**
ALL HH										
Non-poor	1092	78	74	39	134	1417	82%	18%	6%	9%
Poor	303	71	4	52	127	558	64%	36%	13%	23%
Poor	194	51	2	45	105	398	61%	39%	13%	27%
TOTAL HH	**771**	**71**	**47**	**42**	**126**	**1057**	**79%**	**21%**	**7%**	**12%**

Note: All figures are net, e.g., remittances are gifts received less those given; money income is after tax, etc.

Source: HIES 1985/86, 1993/94 (CSO 1987 and 1995) and calculations by the BIDPA Poverty Study Team.

FIGURE 3. SOURCES OF INCOME (PER MONTH, ALL BOTSWANA HOUSEHOLDS)

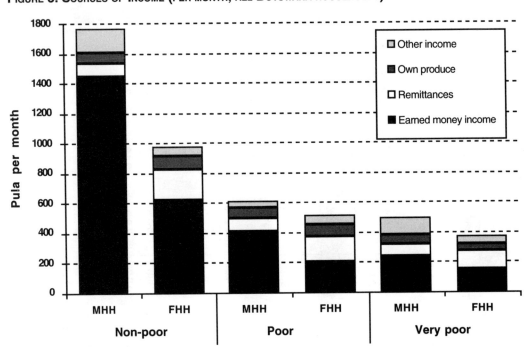

is also affected by these factors, but as the heads of poor FHHs tend to be better educated and younger than those of poor MHHs, poverty among FHHs is more strongly associated with large numbers of dependants. Due to the time which needs to be spent in the home looking after these dependants, poor FHHs are also constrained from gaining employment. However, what is surprising is that despite higher dependency ratios, FHHs in rural areas are no more likely to be in poverty than MHHs. Although left to look after children, FHHs are more likely to receive remittances than MHHs. While there are no doubt many poor rural FHHs left to look after large families without visible support, it would also appear that there are many poor MHHs where poverty is due to old age and lack of education. Furthermore, because FHHs (with fewer adults) are more likely to be labour-scarce than MHHs, the poverty of MHHs is more closely linked to the lack of opportunities in agriculture.

Capability poverty

The broad based approach to poverty used here proposes that poverty results from a lack of choices resulting from low income and/or low human capacities. We have discussed 'income poverty' above with reference to poverty lines. Ideally, this should be supplemented with consideration of 'capability poverty' – which may be viewed as factors which prevent or constrain the poor from climbing out of poverty. This is, however, a difficult concept to operationalise, partly because of the multiple dimensions of 'capabilities'. Nevertheless, it is important, because enhanced capabilities, such as good health and education, provide a route out of poverty, even if incomes are low. Conversely, low capabilities (or low access to capability – enhancing opportunities) contribute to the reproduction and entrenchment of poverty from one generation to the next.

It is also important to assess the capability dimensions of poverty because Botswana has been characterised by very high levels of public spending, financed by mineral revenues, on services such as health care, education, water supplies and so on.[17] While these have no immediate impact on incomes, and therefore do not show up in the poverty measures discussed earlier, they do have a major impact on the quality of life, and on peoples' longer term ability to raise their incomes. The widespread availability of these public services sharply distinguishes the position of an income-poor person in Botswana as compared with, for example, a similarly income-poor person in Brazil or Nigeria, where such services are simply not available.

An attempt to operationalise capability poverty has been made by UNDP in the 1996 Human Development Report (UNDP 1996), in the Capability Poverty Measure (CPM). This

> '...reflects the percentage of people who lack basic, or minimally essential, human capabilities. The CPM considers the lack of three basic capabilities. The first is the capability to be well-nourished and healthy – represented by the proportion of children under five who are underweight. The second is the capability for healthy reproduction – proxied by the proportion of births unattended by trained health personnel. The third is the capability to be educated and knowledgeable – represented by female illiteracy (UNDP 1996, p27).

In the same way as the headcount ratio measures the degree to which peoples' incomes fall below the poverty line, the CPM measures the extent to which capabilities fall below a certain level.

Botswana's score on UNDP's CPM IS 30.4, meaning that 30% of the population fall below this measure of capability poverty.[18] While there is an obvious need for improvement here, one important point is that fewer people suffer from capability poverty (30%) than suffer from income poverty (46%). This indicates that Botswana has done quite well in providing basic capability-enhancing services to the majority of the population (as reflected, on average for the whole population, by Botswana's high score on the HDI). For developing countries as a whole, the UNDP notes that capability poverty is in general *worse* than income poverty.

5. INTERNATIONAL COMPARISONS

Botswana has been widely criticised in the past for the perpetuation of a high degree of income inequality and poverty despite its rapid mineral-led economic growth. Al-

---

[17] Botswana's total of health and education spending is approximately US$250 per person per year. This compares with less than US$25 in Ghana, Kenya, Zambia and Malawi, $70 in Swaziland, US$170 in Mauritius, and is similar to levels in Malaysia and South Korea, which are both countries with much higher per capita national incomes (Source: IMF Government Finance Statistics, 1994).

[18] However, the UNDP's data on which this calculation is based appears to be partially incorrect. The UNDP quotes a child malnutrition rate for Botswana of 27%, whereas figures from Botswana's National Nutrition Surveillance Survey indicate that 14.7% of under five children were underweight in 1993, and that the proportion has been stable at around 15% for some years. Furthermore, the UNDP estimates female illiteracy at 42.2% in 1993, whereas detailed national estimates indicate that this was 29.7% in 1993. Using this data, a reworked CPM for Botswana (see BIDPA, 1996) shows a score of 22, rather than the UNDP's 30.4.

though much of this criticism has been ill-informed, paying scant attention to empirical data which does not fit in with preconceived notions, the scope for mis-interpretation is widened by the poor quality of much poverty and inequality data at an international level, especially when it comes to making comparisons between countries. Nevertheless, such international comparisons are important, and will continue to be made. Leaving inequality aside, below we briefly discuss Botswana's poverty record in an international context.

As noted above (and in Bank of Botswana, 1996, and Jefferis, 1996), international comparisons of poverty lines are complicated by a number of factors, in particular that the components of PDL baskets are in part socially determined and will therefore vary from one society to another. But for poor countries, where the concern of many people is with basic survival, some absolute measure of poverty is likely to be more relevant than for richer countries, where relative poverty is more appropriate. One attempt to quantify the level of absolute poverty in developing countries has been made by Ravallion et al., (1991) (RDV), who use 'upper' and 'lower' poverty lines of US$31 and US$23 per person per month respectively (the latter denoting extreme poverty, the former approximating the 'dollar a day' poverty line popularised by the World Bank).[19] They find that 33% of the population of developing countries are below the upper PDL, and 19% below the lower PDL; the corresponding figures for Sub-Saharan Africa are 47% and 31% (although with a wide margin of error). In Botswana, recall that some 47% of the population are below the PDL (Table 2 above), indicating a relatively high poverty rate for Botswana by developing country standards. However, such a comparison depends on whether an equivalent PDL is being used to calculate poverty rates in Botswana and in the Ravallion et al., (1991). If we convert Botswana's 1993/94 PDLs to US dollars, and deflate back to 1985 prices, we arrive at a figure for Botswana's poverty line of US$44 per person per month, about 40% higher than the figure used by Ravallion et al., (1991).[20]

The Botswana PDL figure therefore, appears to be relatively generous by international standards, which could partially account for the relatively high numbers of poor recorded in Botswana as compared with some other countries.[21] However, food costs in Botswana are higher than in many other developing countries (due to unfavourable agricultural conditions) and thus a higher monetary PDL value is required to provide the same standard of living (e.g., nutritional value).[22] Detailed analysis of PDLs for Botswana, Zimbabwe, and India carried out by BIDPA (1996) show that the physical components of Botswana's PDL basket are very similar to those of the other two countries, and indicates that the difference in monetary PDL values is almost entirely due to higher price in Botswana rather than more generous standards.

---

[19] Both figures are measured in 1985 prices, with national currency values converted to US dollars.

[20] This is calculated as follows. In 1993, Botswana's PDL for a household of three adult-equivalents (2 adults plus 2 children), was P441, giving a per adult PDL of P147. At the then (1993) Pula–US$ exchange rate of 0.4134, this converts to $60.76. Deflating this by the change in the US Consumer Price Index between 1985 and 1993 (37.6%), gives an equivalent of $44.15 (in 1985 prices) for the Botswana PDL.

[21] For example, the 1996 Human Development Report gives the proportion of the urban population below the PDL as 30% in Botswana and 25% in Uganda. The higher figure for Botswana is more likely to be the result of a higher PDL being applied (hence increasing the number of people with incomes below the PDL) than of a higher level of absolute poverty.

TABLE 12. CAPABILITY POVERTY AND INCOME POVERTY

	CAPABILITY POVERTY	INCOME POVERTY	GAP	GNP PER CAPITA
	CPM (%)	% below PDL	PDL-CPM	(US$, 1993)
Venezuela	15	31	16	2840
BOTSWANA	30	46	16	2790
Uganda	46	55	9	180
Peru	26	32	6	1490
Kenya	34	37	3	270
Zimbabwe	22	26	3	520
Sri Lanka	19	22	3	600
Thailand	21	22	1	2110
Ghana	39	36	-3	430
China	18	11	-7	490
Guinea-Bissau	57	49	-8	240
Tunisia	30	14	-16	1720
Indonesia	42	17	-26	740
Pakistan	61	34	-27	430
Bangladesh	77	48	-29	220
India	62	25	-36	300
Morocco	50	13	-37	1040

Source: UNDP (1996).

The Capability Poverty Measure (CPM) mentioned above can also be used to make international comparisons. This indicates that whereas Botswana has not done particularly well with regard to income poverty (the high proportion of the population which remain poor), it has done much better with regard to capability poverty. Table 12 shows income and capability poverty measures for 16 countries reported by UNDP (1996), plus Botswana. Whereas Botswana's income poverty measure is more than the average for this group of countries, its capability poverty measure is below the average. We can examine the relative performance across the two poverty measures by looking at the gap between the two (which shows if a country has done better on the capability measure than on the income measure). In Botswana's case the gap is 16%, loosely meaning that 16% of the population who are income-poor are not capability-poor. This is the second largest gap amongst the countries listed, and lends

22 Evidence from the PPP exchange rates used by UNDP (1996) indicates that the general price level in Botswana is approximately double that of developing countries as a whole, and therefore a higher PDL figure is justified. One of the few countries with higher prices than Botswana is Lesotho, which has even less favourable agricultural conditions.

support to the argument presented that Botswana has done much better at dealing with capability poverty than income poverty.[23]

6. SUMMARY AND CONCLUSIONS

Summary of results

A number of important conclusions can be drawn from this analysis, which provide some insights into the nature and extent of poverty in Botswana.

(i) There has been a significant decline in the poverty rate in Botswana, from 49% of households in 1985/96 to 38% in 1993/94.

(ii) The poverty rate for individuals is higher than that for households (as the poor tend to have larger households). In 1993/94, 47% of Batswana lived in households with incomes below the poverty line, down from 59% in 1985/86.

(iii) Poverty is more widespread in the rural areas (where it affects 48% of households and 55% of individuals) than in the urban villages (36% and 46%) or the towns (23% and 28%).

(iv) Most of the reduction in poverty has been amongst the rural very poor. As this is the largest single poverty group, this suggests that policies to alleviate poverty have had some beneficial effects and have been reasonably well-targeted.

(v) Despite this reduction in poverty, nearly a quarter of Botswana's households (23%) remain very poor (unable to afford basic food needs), and these households contain 30% of the country's population.

(vi) Within the overall poverty total, there is a higher rate of poverty amongst female-headed households (41%) than amongst male-headed households (34%). However, the difference is mainly due to a higher rate of poverty amongst FHHs in the urban areas and urban villages; in rural areas both male-headed and female-headed households experience similar poverty rates.

(vii) A number of factors are associated with high levels of poverty. These are age, gender, lack of education, large families, high dependency ratios, lack of employment, and living in rural areas.

(viii) These factors impact differently on male-headed and female-headed households. In MHHs, poverty is due primarily to old age and lack of education. In FHHs, it is due to higher dependency ratios and (in urban areas and urban villages) less access to employment.

Poverty and economic activity

The predominance of poverty in the rural areas is an indication of the weak economic base of rural areas, especially of agriculture. This is reflected in the low proportion of total income which is derived from own-produce consumed, even amongst the very poor. Indeed, one of the major causes of the widespread rural poverty, and the high

---

23 As noted in the section on capability poverty, the UNDP's measure understates Botswana's achievement on the CPM. If the corrected figure is used, the gap between the two poverty measures rises from 16% to 24%.

level of poverty generally in Botswana for a country of its income level, is adverse soil and climatic conditions, and the resulting limited agricultural potential. This contrasts sharply with the situation in most other African countries, where the basic physical conditions hold the potential for a substantial increase in rural incomes if other, complementary aspects of agricultural policy (such as price reform and appropriate technologies) are properly implemented.

However, the negative impact on poverty of Botswana's weak agricultural base has been offset by the impact of Botswana's rapid mineral-led economic growth. This has had two main benefits: first, providing the revenues which have financed the widespread provision of public services and social and economic infrastructure; and second, contributing to rapid employment growth during the 1970s and 1980s. The first has enabled Botswana to secure a comparatively low level of 'capability poverty'. The second, employment creation, has been the route through which income poverty has been reduced, through enabling people to move from low-income activities (such as traditional agriculture, piece jobs, informal sector activities) to higher-income employment in the formal sector. Most of these formal sector employment opportunities have been in the towns, and to a lesser extent in the urban villages. There has also been rapid growth in informal sector employment opportunities. Employment growth has prevented poverty from worsening in the urban areas, despite very rapid urban population growth. It has also contributed to reducing rural poverty through remittances sent from family members employed in the urban areas. There has been a dramatic shift in the ratio of those employed in the formal sector to those in traditional agriculture. Whereas in 1981, there were three people in traditional agriculture for every two people in the formal sector, by 1991 this had changed to three in the formal sector for every one in traditional agriculture. There is now much more scope for those receiving formal sector wages to send remittances to (the relatively small numbers) of those remaining in agriculture (Jefferis, 1995).

Poverty and gender

The HIES data indicate that poverty among FHHs often results from supporting a large number of dependants. Overall, FHHs have slightly larger household sizes than MHHs (although the pattern is not consistent across settlement types and poverty groups), but what is more striking is that FHHs have consistently fewer adults than MHHs. This indicates that there are more single adult households amongst FHHs, which is commensurate with other evidence that FHHs are often left with children by absent males. This in turn leaves FHHs relatively labour-scarce, which may in part account for their lower employment rates. However this is partially offset by higher levels of remittances received by FHHs, which suggests that at least some of the absent males, or other household members, such as mothers who are working in towns, are supporting their dependants in the rural areas. If it were not for remittances, FHHs would tend to have a much higher poverty rate than they actually do.

MHHs tend to have relatively more abundant labour, and a lower dependency ratio than FHHs. They therefore tend to have a higher proportion of their overall income derived from employment and other productive economic activities, such as self-employment and agriculture. Their poverty is more likely to be a result of age, lack of education, and, in the rural areas, lack of opportunities in agriculture.

Botswana in an international context

Comparative international data show that Botswana has a high level of income poverty relative to its GDP per capita – other countries with comparable levels of income have much lower income poverty levels. This is largely a reflection of poor agricultural potential – there is much less poverty in the towns where formal sector jobs are more abundant – as well as the high cost of living. However, the high levels of spending on public services have had a beneficial effect on building human capacities, and Botswana's level of capability poverty is relatively low by international standards. This is important in assessing the overall quality of life of the poor, particularly as capabilities are recognised as being crucial to avoiding perpetuation of poverty from one generation to the next. Its impact is already showing up in the reduction in poverty levels in Botswana between the mid-1980s and the mid-1990s, which contrasts with the experience of much of the rest of Sub-Saharan Africa, where poverty has worsened over the same period.

To further reduce poverty, Botswana faces two key tasks. First, to design poverty alleviation schemes that can effectively target the poor. These should not just operate in drought years, but must recognise that many households are locked into a poverty situation which does not depend on whether or not it rains. Such households fall into various categories. They include the labour-scarce poor, particularly FHHs with many dependants. There are also the labour-abundant poor, who may lack access to productive land, do not own cattle, and live in settlements which are too small and/or remote to provide economically viable jobs or opportunities for self-employment. There are also the destitute, disabled and elderly. Different types of interventions – some of which are already in operation – are required to alleviate poverty in these different groups. These include improving the coverage and quality of health and education services, providing income-support schemes for those who are unable to earn an income – targeted to those genuinely in need and designed so as not to encourage dependency – as well as efforts to change individual behaviour (smaller families). Although the urban poor are less numerous, they nonetheless form a significant group, and are likely to be disproportionately influential in political and social terms. Poverty alleviation policies must therefore also take them into account. In the longer term, however, the main way to deal with poverty is to ensure that there is sufficient job creation, in economically viable businesses, and that all households have access to adequate and sustainable incomes.

REFERENCES

Bank of Botswana. 1996. *Annual Report 1995*. Bank of Botswana, Gaborone.

BIDPA (Botswana Institute for Development Policy Analysis). 1996. *Study of Poverty and Poverty Alleviation in Botswana*. BIDPA, Gaborone.

Central Statistics Office. 1987. *1985/86 Household Income and Expenditure Survey*. Central Statistics Office, Gaborone.

Central Statistics Office. 1991. *A Poverty Datum Line for Botswana*. Central Statistics Office, Gaborone.

Central Statistics Office. 1995. *1993/94 Household Income and Expenditure Survey*. Central Statistics Office, Gaborone.

Food Studies Group. 1995. *Easing the Process of Transition: Towards a Revised National Food Strategy*. Rural Development Co-ordination Division, MFDP, Gaborone.

Granberg, P. 1996. 'Revised Poverty Datum Line Estimates for Botswana', *BIDPA Publication No.1*. Botswana Institute for Development Policy Analysis, Gaborone.

Jefferis, K. 1995. 'Is Agriculture Still an Important Source of Employment in Botswana?' *Barclays Botswana Economic Review*, Vol.6, No.1, pp13–14. Barclays Botswana, Gaborone.

Jefferis, K. 1997. *The Quality of Life: Concepts, Definitions and Measurement*. In: Botswana Society, *Poverty and Plenty: The Botswana Experience*. Botswana Society, Gaborone.

Johnson, P. 1996. 'The Assessment: Inequality', *Oxford Review of Economic Policy*, Vol.12, No.1, pp1–14.

Lipton, M. 1983. 'Poverty, Undernutrition and Hunger', *World Bank Staff Working Paper 597*. World Bank, Washington.

Ravallion, M., Datt, G. and van der Walle, D. 1991. 'Quantifying Absolute Poverty in the Developing World', *Review of Income and Wealth*, Vol.37 No.4, pp345–361.

Stewart, F. 1995. *Adjustment and Poverty: Options and Choices*. Routledge, London.

UNDP. 1996. *Human Development Report 1996*. Oxford University Press, New York.

van Driel, F. 1994. *Poor and Powerful: Female-headed Households and Unmarried Motherhood in Botswana*. Verlag für Entwicklungspolitik Breitenbach GmbH, Saarbrücken.

World Bank. 1990. *World Development Report: Poverty*. World Bank, Washington.

Chapter 6

International Trade and Botswana in the Regional Economy

Exchange Control Liberalization

Keith Jefferis

1. INTRODUCTION[1]

Exchange control regimes have been progressively liberalised in both developed and developing countries over the past two decades. Some countries have completely abolished both current and capital account controls, while others have taken major steps in that direction while retaining some restrictions. There are many reasons for this: the collapse of the Bretton Woods system of fixed exchange rates between major currencies; increased international trade and internationalization of production; improvements in technology and international communications; and the increased ability to evade controls. Many developing countries have of course implemented exchange control reform as part of broader economic liberalization programmes, often as part of IMF and World Bank sponsored policy packages which also include related liberalizations of foreign exchange markets and domestic financial systems.

Debate on this issue has been taking place in Botswana as elsewhere, but in somewhat different circumstances. The country has long had one of the most liberal exchange control regimes in Sub-Saharan Africa, and the debate over further reform is taking place from a position of economic strength rather than weakness. It is therefore a matter of internal policy choice rather than something being forced upon an unwilling Government by outsiders. Current account convertibility was achieved in 1995, and the issue now is to what extent, and how fast, should capital controls be relaxed, in the context of a small open economy where financial markets are relatively shallow, there are limited skills in the management of international capital flows, and there is limited control over some other economic policy variables.

2. ECONOMIC BACKGROUND

Botswana's record of economic development over the past twenty-five years bears a striking contrast to most of the rest of Sub-Saharan Africa. It has been one of the world's fastest growing economies, with an average annual economic growth rate of 12.8% between 1965 and 1990, has experienced persistent surpluses on both the Government budget and the balance of payments, has a relatively stable currency and has accumulated foreign exchange reserves equivalent to over two years of import cover. It is now classified as an upper-middle-income country with per capita GNP of US$2800 (World Bank, 1996). Much of this is due to the good fortune stem-

---

[1] For earlier work which this paper draws upon, see Jefferis and Harvey (1995), and Phaleng Consultancies (1994).

ming from very large diamond deposits which have made Botswana the world's second largest exporter of diamonds (by value) after Russia, but it has undoubtedly been enhanced by a record of pragmatic but cautious macroeconomic management which has enabled the country to avoid the mistakes of other African mineral exporters such as Zambia and Nigeria (Harvey and Lewis, 1990). Although growth has slowed over the past three years – due partly to the impact of global recession on the international diamond market – Botswana has avoided the economic crises faced by most other Sub-Saharan African economies, and is one of the few not to be undergoing structural adjustment therapy.

3. The Origins and Extent of Exchange Controls in Botswana

Prior to introducing its own currency (the Pula) in August 1976, Botswana operated South African exchange controls as part of its membership of the Rand Monetary Area. Following 'Pula Day', Botswana introduced its own system of controls. The main principles behind the exchange control regime adopted are outlined below.

- Foreign currency should be as freely available as possible for current account transactions, so that most imports of goods and services were allowed, as were dividend payments to foreign shareholders of businesses in Botswana and interest payments on foreign loans.
- Capital outflows were relatively tightly controlled, so that residents were not, in general, permitted to maintain foreign bank accounts and keep their savings overseas, or indeed to own any other kind of foreign financial asset.

The retention of strict capital controls reflected a number of factors. First, there was considerable uncertainty regarding the level of confidence that would be shown in the new currency and a concern that allowing permanent residents[2] to hold foreign currencies would undermine the Pula. Second, a large proportion of domestic assets was foreign owned. There was, therefore, a danger that if many of these foreign owners moved their capital out of the country over a short period of time, the capital outflow would cause Botswana's foreign reserves to fall sharply and lead to a shortage of local savings to finance local investment. Third, such an outflow of capital would reduce the tax base. Fourth, exchange controls were also used to ensure that foreign-owned companies brought in a certain amount of capital from external sources, by not allowing their local borrowing to exceed a proportion (which was increased over time from 100% to 400%) of capital brought into Botswana by the foreign investor.

There was one useful side effect of the new exchange control regime. Under the Southern African Customs Union (SACU) Agreement, the revenue due to Botswana is directly related to the value of its imports. In order to obtain foreign exchange, importers had to record details of all import transactions, which improved the accuracy of import data and therefore Botswana's share of SACU revenues. Unlike many other African countries, Botswana did not use exchange controls to maintain an overvalued exchange rate, nor to determine which imports would be permitted.

---

2   Temporary residents are subject to different exchange control regulations.

Since 1976, the exchange control regime has been progressively liberalised. The process included the delegation of most current account transactions to the commercial banks as Authorised Dealers, although the Bank of Botswana retained greater control over payments for services than for visible imports. Allowances on some service payments (such as remitted dividends) were made more generous, as were Residents' travel allowances, rules regarding the use of foreign credit cards, and the limits on borrowing by foreign companies. By the beginning of 1995, almost all current account exchange controls had been abolished, although considerable bureaucracy remained to verify that such transactions were not being used for capital purposes.[3] On 17 November 1995, Botswana accepted the obligations of Article VIII membership status at the IMF, under which a country pledges (amongst other things) not to introduce exchange control restrictions on current account transactions.[4]

In contrast to complete current account liberalization, capital account controls have remained more restrictive. However, there is evidence that in the past, capital account controls have been relatively leaky, thus undermining their effectiveness. This is partly a result of the openness of the economy – which facilitates the exploitation of leads and lags in international payments – and the ease of disguising capital account transactions as current account transactions. Capital may also be transferred through illegal means such as the over-invoicing of imports. Such a situation is regressive, in that larger economic agents (both companies and individuals) can more easily find ways around the controls, and the burden of the implicit taxation in exchange controls is shifted to those with less access to foreign exchange (Hansen, 1992 and Mathieson and Rojas-Suarez, 1993).

There has nevertheless been significant liberalization of capital controls. For instance, foreign portfolio investors are permitted to purchase shares on the Botswana Share Market, within fairly generous limits, and Botswana pension funds and life insurance companies can invest up to 70% of their assets abroad.[5] Since January

---

[3] This 'considerable bureaucracy' can, in practice, amount to the maintenance of continued restrictions on current account transactions. One practical problem has been that the financial institutions administering exchange controls have been very slow to demonstrate the change of attitudes that liberalisation entails; several banks have simply maintained their old forms and systems, despite liberalisation. Hopefully this problem will only be temporary.

[4] Countries can be members of the IMF under either Articles VIII or XIV of the IMF's Articles of Association. Under Article VIII, a country pledges not to use exchange controls over current account transactions nor to use multiple currency practices (such as dual exchange rates). However, many developing countries, which wished to join the IMF but maintain exchange controls, joined under Article XIV, which did not prohibit these practices. Moving to Article VIII indicates a country's commitment not to reintroduce exchange controls should it face balance of payments problems in the future. Until recently, only a few countries in Sub-Saharan Africa have been IMF members under Article VIII. Those which had accepted Article VIII by 1995 are: (with their date of acceptance given in brackets): South Africa (1973), Seychelles (1978), Swaziland (1989), The Gambia (1993), Mauritius (1993), Ghana (1994), Kenya (1994), Uganda (1994), Botswana (1995), Guinea (1995), Malawi (1995), Zimbabwe (1995), and Sierra Leone (1995).

[5] These restrictions are that (i) Non-residents may not beneficially own more than 5% of the issued share capital of any company that is listed on the Botswana share market; and (ii) as a group, Non-residents may not in total own more than 49% of the 'free' share capital in a listed company (where the 'free' shares are those not in the hands of controlling parent companies). Application for exchange control approval must be made to the Bank of Botswana for these limits to be exceeded. To date, however, these constraints have not been binding. There are no restrictions on repatriation of capital introduced under (i) and (ii) above.

1995, individual residents have been permitted to invest abroad up to P100 000 (approximately US$30 000) a year, and companies are allowed up to P1 million (US$300 000) for outward direct investments, without reference to the Bank of Botswana. The remaining restrictions are on capital outflows above the limits noted here, and on inward capital investments, such as the prohibition on purchases of Bank of Botswana Certificates (BoBCs) by non-residents, and limits on local borrowing by non-resident controlled companies.

4. THE COSTS OF EXCHANGE CONTROLS

The sum total of the above is that Botswana has historically had an exchange control regime that is more liberal than that of most other countries in Sub-Saharan Africa. Also in contrast to other countries, the system is in general quite efficiently administered. Nevertheless, exchange controls still have a significant impact, which involves costs to private sector businesses and to individuals. Moreover, Botswana's relative advantage has been reduced in the 1990s by rapid liberalization of foreign exchange transactions in some African countries as part of structural adjustment programmes (SAPs).[6] It will be further reduced if, as is widely anticipated, South Africa abolishes exchange controls.

Costs of Compliance. The direct costs of exchange controls include the salaries of the considerable number of staff engaged in administering exchange control in the Bank of Botswana and the commercial banks, the time which firms and individuals devote to dealing with exchange control matters, and in some cases the costs to firms of employing outside professionals in this regard. There are also the costs (in terms of bank charges and commissions) of extra foreign exchange transactions when firms engaged in foreign trade have to convert export receipts to Pula and then back to foreign currency to pay for imports. In a few cases, there are also lengthy delays while firms have to wait for exchange control decisions (such as those relating to complex share deals or payment for the import of services) to be made by the Bank of Botswana. Although current account restrictions are now unrestricted, the bureaucracy involved in ensuring that they are not disguised capital account transactions remains a burden. Given the shortage of skilled personnel in the business and financial sectors, it should be possible to utilise the people involved in complying with and administering exchange controls more effectively elsewhere.

Discouraging Inward Investment. Although Botswana's exchange controls have been designed so as not to discourage inward foreign direct investment – for instance by permitting the free repatriation of profits – it is still likely that foreign investment is discouraged. The number of such lost investments is inherently difficult to quantify, because it relates to 'what might have been', although it is probably quite small. An

---

6   Many countries with relatively weak economies moved to IMF Article VIII status before Botswana, even though Botswana could have easily consolidated its historically liberal position with regard to exchange controls by moving to Article VIII status much earlier. More recently, Zambia, Kenya and Mauritius have completely abolished exchange controls (including capital controls), and other countries (such as Uganda) are moving rapidly in this direction.

earlier study (Phaleng, 1994) found only two examples of inward investment which had not been implemented because of exchange controls. Moreover, severe shortages of matching resources (serviced land, skilled labour, executive housing and places in English-medium schools for expatriate children) in the 1980s meant that Botswana could not then have absorbed much, if any, additional foreign investment. With slower economic growth in the 1990s, however, these other constraints are less serious, and obstacles imposed by exchange control relatively more serious. Although approval for capital transactions may eventually be given, the time taken to obtain such approval, and the resources needed to satisfy regulators that transactions are legitimate, are themselves additional costs to investors. Even if exchange controls are in fact relatively liberal, their retention is often taken as a signal to outsiders of a highly restricted economy facing potential foreign exchange problems and a lack of confidence; conversely, their removal is a positive signal that the country does not over-regulate and has a well-run economy – it is a sign of confidence. Complete removal of exchange controls would clearly distinguish Botswana from most other Sub-Saharan African countries in the eyes of international investors

Restrictions on Savers. By restricting the ability of savers to invest their savings outside of the country, exchange controls have been the major reason for the build-up of excess liquidity in the financial system, and have given rise to negative real interest rates and a partial breakdown in the intermediation function of banks, which at times refused to accept large deposits (Bhuiyan, 1987; World Bank, 1989). They also restrict the ability of savers to engage in effective portfolio diversification, forcing them to concentrate their portfolios on a limited range of domestic assets, which may be subject to highly correlated risks, thereby reducing risk-adjusted average returns. More generally, savers are prevented from making the optimal allocation of their funds across all available currencies and instruments, in line with their individual choices and circumstances, and hence are penalised by being forced to make sub-optimal allocations and earning lower returns than would otherwise be possible. It has also led to the Bank of Botswana (and indirectly the Government) incurring substantial costs through the issue of BoBCs to mop up excess liquidity.

Essentially, exchange controls act as a tax on savers equal to the difference between domestic and international real interest rates.[7] As Figure 1 shows, real deposit rates in Botswana have been consistently below American levels, and mostly below those in South Africa. At present, it is very difficult to earn a positive real return on savings held in Pula (in fact this option is mainly available to those wealthy enough to invest in BoBCs). Internationally, however, there are a wide range of financial instruments available (including equities and bonds) which offer significant positive real returns. At present the Bank of Botswana, on behalf of the Government, benefits from this 'tax' through its near monopoly on the holding of foreign-currency denominated financial assets in the form of the foreign exchange reserves. Interest payments on BoBCs can be seen as a way of refunding this tax to savers, although not necessarily equitably, given that only larger savers have access to BoBC-linked returns.

Distortion of Market Forces. Low real interest rates and excess liquidity are

---

[7]   This tax was quite high during the 1980s but has been sharply reduced by increased interest rates in Botswana since 1991.

FIGURE 1. REAL DEPOSIT INTEREST RATES IN THE USA, BOTSWANA AND SOUTH AFRICA

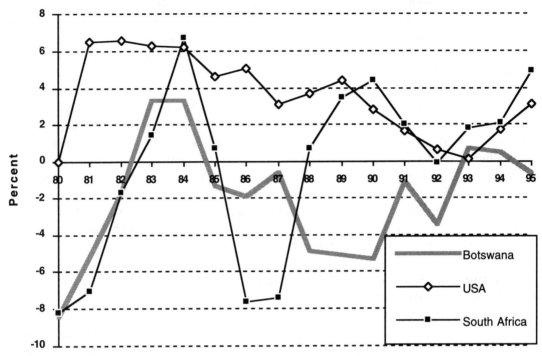

examples of a more general mis-pricing of domestic capital assets which result from exchange controls. Another example has been severe upward pressure on property prices, resulting in the over-pricing of housing; residential property has been one of the few assets offering attractive returns to savers, given low interest rates and no possibility of directly investing abroad. This mis-pricing, especially the over-pricing of domestic capital assets, may have itself deterred inward investment.[8]

Exchange controls represent an administrative restriction on the ability of the market mechanism to guide the allocation of financial and real resources in an economy. Unless there are clearly established market failure problems which need to be corrected (which does not appear to be the case here), such intervention is likely to reduce the overall level of economic efficiency, growth and incomes.

5. OTHER EFFECTS OF EXCHANGE CONTROLS

On a more positive note, there have been some benefits from exchange controls, most of which accrue to the Government.

- Tax revenues have been enhanced, by enabling the taxation of interest on local financial assets, whereas some of this would have been lost if, under capital account regulations, the acquisition of foreign financial assets by 'Residents' had been permitted (earnings from outside of Botswana are not taxable).

---

[8] It should be noted, however, that if exchange control abolition resulted in large capital inflows, then this could also lead to over-pricing of domestic capital assets, for instance through speculative bubbles in property and stock markets.

- The official foreign exchange reserves, held by the Bank of Botswana have been higher than they would have been without exchange controls, because (legal) capital outflows were prevented. This effect has been small, however, because a high proportion of domestic bank deposits are owned or controlled by Government (see Table 2) and hence there was limited potential for capital outflows (a point which is discussed in more detail below).

- The Government and the Bank of Botswana have benefited from their monopoly control of foreign financial assets, given that the real returns paid to holders of Pula savings have been much lower than those earned, on average, by the Bank of Botswana on the reserves, for most of the period since 1976. In other words, the 'tax' penalty on savers mentioned above contributed to Bank of Botswana profits and therefore to Government revenues. This contribution has now all but disappeared, given the recent increases in domestic real interest rates.

- Exchange controls have enabled greater independent control over interest rates, the money supply and exchange rates by Botswana's monetary authorities, at least to the extent that capital account controls are effective.

6. THE CURRENT ROLE OF EXCHANGE CONTROLS AND THE NEED TO DIVERSIFY

Although they probably played an important role in the early years after the introduction of the Pula in 1976, the original reasons for exchange controls have now fallen away. As a result of Botswana's diamond earnings and good economic management, the Pula is a strong currency, and the country has a very high level of foreign exchange reserves; by 1996, for instance, the reserves amounted to over three years of imports (see Table 1). Domestic savings have been very high, and even though they may in the very long run be insufficient to finance investment, Botswana is in a strong position to raise overseas loans or attract direct foreign investment. In view of the costs identified above, the present exchange control system is out of date and largely unnecessary. This suggests that exchange controls could be abolished at low (or zero) cost; meanwhile, some benefits might accrue.

Botswana's need to attract foreign investment cannot be overemphasized. Minerals in general, and diamonds in particular, will be unable to lead economic growth in Botswana as they have in the past – a point which has been emphasised by the reduction in economic growth rates since 1990. The task of economic diversification and the accompanying job creation lies at the centrepiece of the current and forthcoming National Development Plans (NDP 7, 1991–97, and NDP 8, 1997–2003). Given the small size of the domestic market, future leading sectors will need to be export oriented. Although Botswana does not particularly need financial resources (given the available stock of savings), it is the technical and managerial expertise that foreign investors bring, and their access to foreign markets, that are crucial at this stage of Botswana's development.

Although recent emphasis has been on developing an export-oriented manufacturing sector, such as in garments and textiles production, the record to date has been mixed (there has been no increase in the share of manufacturing in GDP over the past decade, although the share of manufactured goods in exports has risen). Botswana faces significant problems in achieving high rates of manufacturing growth of the order of those seen in, for instance, Mauritius, including factors such as high utility costs, shortages of serviced land, high labour costs in relation to productivity, distance from ports, and a lack of local raw materials. While there may be substantial potential for regionally competitive and successful exporting companies (mostly to South Africa), establishing a large-scale internationally competitive manufacturing sector will take much longer (Jefferis, 1996).

In view of this, Botswana cannot afford to rely upon any one source of future economic growth. The emphasis must be on wide diversification, including potential export service activities such as tourism, transport and a variety of financial and consultancy services. One advantage is Botswana's current financial strength, and yet the maintenance of exchange controls – specifically capital controls – may be preventing the country from exploiting this advantage to the full.

TABLE 1. FOREIGN EXCHANGE RESERVES

AS AT END OF	FOREIGN EXCHANGE RESERVES			IMPORTS (CIF)	IMPORT COVER
	Pula	US$ million	SDR	Pula million	months
1976	65	75	64	181	4
1977	83	100	83	232	4
1978	125	151	116	291	5
1979	211	267	203	425	6
1980	255	344	270	525	6
1981	223	253	218	663	4
1982	311	293	266	704	5
1983	457	396	378	806	7
1984	737	472	482	899	10
1985	1645	748	715	1096	18
1986	2201	1198	981	1331	20
1987	3152	2013	1421	1572	24
1988	4368	2257	1684	2173	24
1989	5248	2803	2127	3018	21
1990	6234	3331	2344	3619	21
1991	7707	3719	2599	3926	24
1992	8561	4031	2757	3969	26
1993	10 509	4097	2983	4270	30
1994	11 961	4402	3018	4408	33
1995	13 251	4696	3164	5302	30
1996	18 322	5028	3500	5723	38

Source: Bank of Botswana Annual Reports, various; IMF International Financial Statistics.

7. OTHER COUNTRIES' EXPERIENCES OF EXCHANGE CONTROL LIBERALIZATION

Before considering the likely impact of further exchange control liberalization on Botswana, we attempt to draw lessons from other countries' experiences. Over the past two decades a large number of developing countries have liberalised exchange controls, in many cases removing them completely. In some cases (especially in Africa) exchange control reforms have been part of reform packages implemented as Stabilization Programmes and SAPs under the auspices of the IMF and World Bank, but in others (notably in south and east Asia) they have simply been a natural economic progression, opening up strong and growing economies to greater integration with the international economy. In addition many developed countries have abolished exchange controls in recent years as part of a trend towards international economic integration, but also reflecting the difficulties (if not futility) of trying to implement exchange controls in an increasingly open and integrated international financial environment.

Our discussion will mostly concern capital controls, since it is only these that now remain in Botswana. It is worth noting that capital controls have historically been extremely widespread internationally. They are still common in developing countries, although the major industrial countries have now mostly removed capital controls completely – which has been a major component of global financial integration.

Despite being widely used, it is evident that capital controls can be circumvented and are often ineffective when there are strong incentives to avoid them. Many countries have experienced large-scale capital flight (or speculative capital outflows) when the expected returns on domestic investments are low relative to returns on investments abroad – a situation which has often arisen when interest rates are maintained at artificially low levels, leading to negative real returns on domestic financial assets. Measuring the extent of capital flight is difficult because of the illegal nature of some flows (such as smuggling and the over-invoicing of imports), but nevertheless it appears that capital flight is widespread. Argentina, Mexico and Venezuela, for instance, experienced massive capital outflows in the 1970s and early 1980s (Collins, 1988). More generally, Edwards (1989) examined the effectiveness of capital controls in 25 countries that experienced devaluations between 1962 and 1982, and concluded 'these data provide a very consistent picture of the ineffectiveness of capital controls' if an economy is subject to inconsistent macroeconomic – and in particular, fiscal, policies (pp192–193). Within Africa, Chuka (1992) considered that exchange controls in Malawi may well have actually induced capital flight, due to the adverse signals which controls gave to economic agents about the quality and consistency of macroeconomic management. Kahn (1991) examined capital flight from South Africa during the 1970s and 1980s, and concluded that it has been very high, on a par with levels found in Argentina and Mexico, amounting to US$30 billion between 1970 and 1985. South African capital flight mainly took place through the under-invoicing of exports, and to a lesser extent through the over-invoicing of imports, and in the peak year, 1978, it may have represented over 6% of GDP and 25% of gross domestic fixed investment. This is despite a relatively strict system of capital controls, and reflects South Africa's particular combination of both economic and political instability during the period. International evidence therefore suggests that exchange controls will be ineffective, and could do more harm than good, if they are used as a substitute for sound economic policies (Williamson and Lessard, 1987).

Turning now to exchange control liberalization, there have been a wide variety of international experiences. It is helpful to explore the reasons for successes and failures, to provide evidence of preconditions for successful liberalization and the appropriate sequencing of liberalization measures.

One factor which has been important in governing the appropriate timing for liberalization is the adequacy of foreign exchange reserves, although there is no explicitly stated minimum figure for reserves adequacy. When Singapore removed exchange controls its reserves were about US$1.5 billion (or about seven weeks of total imports). The South African authorities had informally set a reserves target of three months of import cover as one of the preconditions for abolishing its dual exchange rate system (the financial Rand), which was a major component of its exchange control system over the past two decades. It should be noted that these figures are far lower than Botswana's present level of import cover (see Tables 2 and 6).

Other important preconditions for successful capital account liberalization include (Hanson, 1992, Mathieson and Rojas-Suarez, 1993 and Williamson, 1991): maintaining a stable macro economy prior to and after liberalization; reducing fiscal deficits to levels which can be financed in a non-inflationary manner; minimising levels of inflation; increasing the flexibility of market driven changes in wages, prices and interest rates; liberalising the domestic financial system and encouraging competition; reducing differences between domestic and external financial market conditions (such as real interest rates); strengthening prudential supervision of the financial system to international levels; ensuring sufficient risk-management capability in the financial system; and a record of government that gives credibility to assurances that the policy regime will not be changed arbitrarily under adverse circumstances. Botswana would appear to meet most of these conditions, the main exceptions being a lack of wage flexibility in the labour market and a strong remaining official influence on interest rates.

Hanson (1992) highlights the stability of the macro economy, the size of the fiscal deficit, and domestic financial liberalization as key preconditions for a successful opening of the capital account. The degree to which these conditions were met is an important explanation for the contrast between the relatively successful liberalizations in East Asia (Malaysia, Indonesia, South Korea, Taiwan) as compared to the experiences of the southern cone countries (Argentina, Uruguay and Chile) where liberalization had to be reversed as the debt crisis intensified in the early 1980s.

Countries which fulfilled these preconditions and maintained them thereafter generally experienced substantial increases in gross capital flows with rising net capital inflows and higher reserves (in contrast to the concern in Botswana of capital outflows). Although some countries benefited from direct investment in response to improved macroeconomic fundamentals, much of these inflows consisted of short-term portfolio investment and a reversal of earlier capital flight, especially in Latin America. The potentially disruptive impact of such inflows is one reason for maintaining capital controls. In a flexible exchange rate regime, exchange rate appreciation often results. By appreciating the real exchange rate, this can cause problems for the competitiveness of exports. With fixed or managed exchange rates, capital inflows result in higher foreign exchange reserves, which can bring other problems. Unless they are sterilised through government bond sales, or there is some other form of tightening of monetary policy, the money supply will expand. This can in turn lead to inflationary pressures or asset price bubbles. Sterilization can also be expensive for the central bank and may require higher interest rates, thus attracting further capital inflows. Furthermore, portfolio capital can flow out as quickly as it flowed in, running down reserves, causing a liquidity crisis, raising the prospect of default on international debt payments, and depressing stock markets. Even Asian countries with sound macroeconomic management – such as Indonesia, Malaysia, Singapore and Hong Kong – have suffered from temporary capital outflows that threatened to be destabilising. More recently, the experience of Mexico in December 1994 has provided a salutary reminder of the vulnerability of countries to volatility in short-term capital flows. Capital account liberalization can therefore impose greater demands on domestic macroeconomic management capability, especially as capital flows tend to be much faster than current account (trade) flows in their response to underlying economic conditions. It is also a well-established theoretical and empirical result that small countries with open capital accounts will find it more difficult to control both interest rates and exchange rates.

On a more positive note, evidence suggests that capital account liberalization significantly improves the functioning of the domestic financial system, in terms of efficiency gains, and innovations in financial products and services, much of it under the influence of international competition. It also facilitates access to international financial markets, thus reducing borrowing costs for firms.

Varying approaches have been adopted towards the speed and sequencing of capital account liberalization. Several countries have dismantled controls quickly, including Argentina, Britain, Indonesia, Malaysia, New Zealand, Singapore, and Uruguay. Most countries have, however, followed the more gradual approach of first relaxing restraints on trade-related capital flows, followed by removal of restrictions on foreign direct investment; then by relaxation of restrictions on foreign portfolio investment; and finally removing constraints on other short-term financial flows. In South America, Chile liberalised the current account first, while Argentina and Uruguay started with the capital account. McKinnon (1982) argues that much of Chile's success, relative to Argentina, is due to this different sequencing of reform. In theoretical terms, early analysis (e.g., McKinnon, 1973 and Edwards, 1984) concluded that trade reform and current account liberalization should come before opening the capital account. Other authors (e.g., Krueger, 1984 and Michaely, 1986) have, however, questioned this process and argued for simultaneous liberalization of current and capital accounts because short-run adjustment costs and the political opposition to reforms which they generate are possibly more of a problem than the economic issues involved in liberalization. The evidence, however, suggests that success or failure with capital account liberalization has not depended on whether liberalization occurred quickly or slowly but on the credibility and consistency of other macroeconomic policies, especially anti-inflation policy and the achievement of an appropriate real exchange rate.

8. THE LIKELY BENEFITS OF EXCHANGE CONTROL LIBERALIZATION IN BOTSWANA

Despite Botswana's relatively liberal exchange control regime, it is currently more restrictive than (a) other small open economies in a relatively less advantaged position (e.g., Mauritius and Zambia) and (b) other countries which in previous decades opened up their current and capital accounts when they too were, at that time, comparatively not as well off (e.g., Malaysia and Singapore). On this basis of comparison, Botswana should already have liberalised much more extensively than it actually has. However, it is also necessary to consider the benefits and costs of liberalization in the specific context of the Botswana economy.

The first benefit would be a saving, to the private sector and to the economy as a whole, of the direct financial and time costs of exchange controls. The private sector would also benefit from greater freedom in its business affairs. Although the extent of such benefits are impossible to quantify, both would contribute to improved efficiency and economic growth.

Secondly, removal of exchange controls would clearly distinguish Botswana from most other Sub-Saharan African countries in the eyes of international investors. Whilst additional investment would probably not be very large in the manufacturing sector, it could have a greater impact on investment in services and finance. It would open up the possibility of Botswana developing as a regional headquarters for international companies, as a hub for regional transport operations, and also as a financial services centre, for instance by permitting inward portfolio investors to use Botswana as a base for outward investment in the region. Botswana may have missed part of the opportunity to be ahead of other countries, because of the exchange control liberalization taking place elsewhere. However, the confidence created by exchange control abolition should be greater in Botswana than in those countries liberalising as part of a World Bank Structural Adjustment Programme. For the latter, exchange control abolition appears to have been forced on governments, and is therefore likely to be seen as potentially reversible. Botswana, on the other hand, would be seen as abolishing exchange controls from a position of strength.

There should also be a positive net effect on job creation as a result of such inward investment. Some posts would disappear in the exchange control sections of the banking system, but given the general shortage of skilled personnel in Botswana, and the likelihood that new banking and financial activities would develop, it is likely that all of the individuals affected would be rapidly re-deployed.

There would also be benefits for a sustainable fiscal policy. It can be argued that an open capital account would have the benefit of imposing an external discipline on Government expenditure, which might assist the task of the Ministry of Finance and Development Planning (MFDP) in resisting calls from other ministries for unsustainable levels of spending. This is particularly relevant given the prospects of declining real mineral revenues over the next decade combined with domestic pressures for continued increases in public spending (Republic of Botswana, 1994); if internal discipline over public spending is less effective – as some commentators believe to be the case (Bank of Botswana, 1993 and Salkin, 1994) – then the external discipline of an open capital account could be an important benefit. Therefore removing exchange controls should contribute to greater macroeconomic stability in the future.

The experience of other countries suggests that any country which does not liberalise exchange controls will increasingly be left behind those that do, and runs the risk of being marginalised (or excluded) from international investment flows. This is perhaps the strongest argument for the further liberalization or abolition of exchange controls, if it is to maximise the benefits of its relatively liberal economic environment (by Southern African standards) and its financial strength, in attracting the foreign investment upon which much of the much-needed economic diversification depends.

9. BOTSWANA'S CONCERNS ABOUT EXCHANGE CONTROL LIBERALIZATION

A number of concerns about the likely effect of exchange control liberalization have been expressed by both the Government and some segments of the private sector. These primarily relate to the following possibilities:

A. that a substantial proportion of the foreign exchange reserves will flow out of the country;

B.   that the monetary authorities will be unable to react quickly enough to changes in international financial conditions or to large gross capital flows;

C.   that the Government will be less able to manage independently interest rates and exchange rates, two key macroeconomic policy variables, and that these will be forced to follow international levels rather than being set in accordance with Botswana's domestic economic priorities, and as a result that interest rates will rise, and that the exchange rate may be less stable in the future;

D.   that Botswana will suffer a loss of tax revenue and earnings on the foreign exchange reserves;

E.   that Botswana might be used as a conduit for capital flight from neighbouring states, or attract illegal 'money laundering' transactions.

We examine each of these concerns below.

A. Foreign exchange reserves.

With capital controls in place, the Government (through the Central Bank) retains a monopoly over the holding of foreign exchange and other foreign currency assets. If capital controls are abolished, this monopoly power is withdrawn, and anybody can hold foreign currency assets. Individuals and companies may therefore convert some of their Pula assets into foreign currency to invest overseas, which would result in a fall in the official foreign exchange reserves. However, it is necessary to analyse the likely size and impact of such a capital outflow, and this can be done by examining the composition of the assets which provide the domestic currency counterparts of the foreign exchange reserves. This can be done by considering the balance sheet of the Bank of Botswana (see Table 2).

The bulk of the Bank of Botswana's assets consist of the foreign exchange reserves, which amounted to over P18 billion, or approximately US$5 billion, at the end of 1996. The matching Bank of Botswana liabilities in turn represent assets of either the Government or the private sector. The potential outflow if capital controls are removed is restricted to the private sector-controlled elements of those Bank of Botswana liabilities (as the Government already has, through its ownership of the Central Bank, a foreign currency counterpart to its domestic currency assets, in the form of the existing official foreign exchange reserves).

The largest single element of the Bank of Botswana liabilities is Government deposits, which as at December 1996 represented around 40% of the total. Another 44% was made up of accumulated Bank of Botswana profits and reserves, and the liquid assets which the commercial banks are legally required to hold (and which are therefore indirectly under Government control). At December 1996, therefore, approximately 84% of Botswana's official foreign exchange reserves represented assets owned or controlled by the Government, and only 17% assets controlled by the private sector. If capital account controls were removed, the holders of the privately owned assets would be free to withdraw these deposits and place them directly overseas. But even if this applied to *all* of the private sector deposits, the official reserves would only fall by some 17%, leaving more than enough for the country's needs. In practice it is unlikely that the reserves would fall by anything like this amount, given that some part of private sector balances must be retained in Pula to meet transactions needs, and that some part of savings balances would continue to be held as Pula assets, to

TABLE 2. GOVERNMENT AND PRIVATE CONTROL OF FOREIGN EXCHANGE RESERVES (END-YEARS, 1990–95, PULA MILLION)

	1991	1992	1993	1994	1995	1996
FOREIGN EXCHANGE RESERVES	7 707	8 561	10 509	11 961	13 251	18 322
GOVERNMENT OWNED OR CONTROLLED:						
Government deposits	4 264	5 080	5 598	6 704	6 460	7 204
Bank of Botswana reserves	1 451	1 351	2 152	2 923	2 923	6 086
Other Bank of Botswana liabilities[a]	818	894	1 191	547	1 571	1 833
Required liquid assets	352	357	389	435	500	263
SUB-TOTAL	6 885	7 682	9 330	10 609	11 455	15 385
GOVT AS A % OF FOREIGN EXCHANGE RESERVES	89	90	89	89	8 6	8 4
PRIVATELY OWNED AND CONTROLLED:						
Notes and coin	222	233	275	303	319	356
Excess liquid assets[b]	102	141	217	275	525	1 150
Other deposits at Bank of Botswana	59	33	36	46	48	47
Bank of Botswana Certificates, and other[c]	565	682	842	958	1 132	1 641
SUB-TOTAL	948	1 089	1 369	1 582	2 023	3 194
PRIVATE AS % OF FOREIGN EXCHANGE RESERVES[d]	12	13	13	13	15	1 7

Notes:
[a] Mostly accrued profits owing to the Government, also including IMF Reserve Tranche and SDR allocation.
[b] Excess liquid assets less balances held abroad, because balances held abroad have already left the country.
[c] The private sector holders of BoBCs include Debswana and some parastatals, which could be regarded as being under Government control.
[d] Government plus private percentages add to slightly more than 100% of reserves, because of the presence of a small quantity of domestic assets on the assets side of the balance sheet of the Bank of Botswana.

Source: Bank of Botswana Annual Reports, various.

meet future Pula liabilities. Furthermore, since capital controls were partially liberalised in January 1995, there has been no significant capital outflow or reduction in the reserves. This is despite much higher real expected returns being available in South Africa than in Botswana, and indicates that there is substantial stickiness or imperfection with regard to capital movements by 'Residents', perhaps as a result of a strong aversion to exchange rate risk.

The same point can be illustrated in another way, by examining the causal components of the money supply. As Table 3 shows, Botswana's money supply has an unusual structure, in that net domestic credit is highly negative and that the gross reserves are nearly four times the level of the money supply. Clearly, the only way in which the reserves can be run down significantly is by a major expansion of Government spending – whatever the private sector does can have relatively little impact.

TABLE 3. Money Supply (December 1995, Pula million)

Credit to government	−7 242
Credit to private sector	1 787
Domestic credit	−5 445
External banking assets	18 624
Other items (net) [a]	−8 766
Money supply	4 413

Note: [a] This item mainly reflects revaluation gains and losses arising from the valuation of foreign exchange reserves in domestic currency.

Source: Bank of Botswana. Annual Report 1996.

The point is reinforced by the international comparison of the level of Botswana's reserves in relation to the money supply in Table 5.

It is important to note that even if private savers invest directly overseas, this simply means that some of the foreign reserves move from official (Government/Bank of Botswana) to private control; the *nation's* total stock of foreign reserves is unchanged. Private foreign deposits will earn a (tax exempt) income which will most likely be repatriated to Botswana, in which case the country will continue to benefit from earnings on the reserves. In fact it is quite plausible that total earnings on the reserves will increase. The official reserves have been invested conservatively in predominantly low risk, short and medium-term foreign assets, which tend to yield relatively low returns; if private savers were prepared to be more adventurous, expected earnings would increase but at the cost of higher risk.

Economic projections prepared for NDP 8 anticipate that there will be continued current and capital account surpluses for the period 1997–2003. As a result of balance of payments surpluses, the total level of the foreign exchange reserves are anticipated to rise. At the same time, the Government is projected to be running a continued budget surplus, due largely to rising mineral revenues which will cause its accumulated balances to continue rising. The share of the foreign exchange reserves over which Government has control is projected to fall during 1997 and 1998 (although whether this actually happens depends on Government spending out-turns during these two years), but then remain constant, at around 75%, during the remainder of NDP 8 (see Table 4). Government is therefore projected to retain control overt the bulk of the reserves, which are in turn projected to remain at more than adequate levels in terms of import cover during the forecast period. Only if there were attempts to keep domestic real interest rates significantly below international levels would much larger private capital outflows be expected, thus reflecting the obvious point that opening the capital account does effectively require that future real interest rates are competitive with those ruling internationally. It should be noted, however, that this would not necessarily require higher domestic nominal interest rates; it is preferable that higher real interest rates are achieved through lower inflation.

We therefore conclude that the size of Botswana's foreign exchange reserves is more than adequate to support the opening of the capital account, and any resulting reduction in the official reserves would be insignificant. It is also apparent that, on the basis of the best available forecasts, this finding will continue to apply for the next ten years, which provides plenty of time to adjust to any future changes in circumstances.

The above assumes that Government spending will be contained within the limits imposed by slower growing Government revenues over the next decade. If this does not apply, and there is continued rapid growth in spending, this would result in a large Government budget deficit, which would have to be financed either by drawing down the Government's own savings at the Bank of Botswana, or by Government

TABLE 4. PROJECTIONS OF GOVERNMENT SHARE OF RESERVES DURING NDP 8: BANK OF BOTSWANA
BALANCE SHEET (PULA MILLION)

	1995	1996	1997	1998	1999	2000	2001	2002
TOTAL BoB ASSETS	13 369	18 438	21 068	23 764	26 948	30 604	34 287	37 494
Foreign Exchange Reserves	13 249	18 322	20 936	23 625	26 802	30 451	341 26	37 325
Other assets	120	116	132	139	146	153	161	169
BoB LIABILITIES - GOVERNMENT	11 445	15 385	16 441	17 636	19 763	22 464	25 463	28 450
Government balances	6460	7204	14 105	14 862	16 486	18 614	20 975	23 267
BoB reserves	4492	7919	2041	2426	2870	3373	3934	4539
Required liquid assets	492	263	295	349	407	478	554	644
BoB LIABILITIES - NON-GOVERNMENT	1925	3052	4627	6128	7185	8140	8824	9044
TOTAL BoB LIABILITIES	13 369	18 438	21 068	23 764	26 948	30 604	34 287	37 494
Govt. as % of total reserves	86%	84%	79%	75%	74%	74%	75%	76%
Import cover (months)	28	38	32	32	31	30	29	28

Source: NDP 8.

borrowing (which runs the risk of 'crowding out' the private sector from financial markets). Both outcomes would lead to a reduction in the reserves. Whilst this could perhaps be prevented for a short time if capital controls were in place, this would simply be addressing the symptom of the problem, not its cause, which would lie in excessive Government spending and an unsustainable fiscal deficit. Regardless of whether exchange controls are in place, the level of Government spending remains the most important macroeconomic policy issue over the next decade.

It may be questioned as to whether the Government's own projections can be relied upon. In the past, economic projections from the MFDP have, if anything, been rather conservative and actual outcomes have been significantly more favourable than forecast.[9] There is of course the possibility of a major exogenous shock to the economy, a danger facing any country reliant upon export earnings from a single primary commodity. The worst-case scenario would be the collapse of the De Beers diamond cartel and a major drop in real diamond prices. This cannot be entirely ruled out given the current instability in Russia, but remains highly unlikely as it would not be in that country's long-term interest. Beyond this, it is worth noting that real diamond prices have probably been more stable than those of any other widely traded primary commodity, and forecasts based on current prices are more likely to be reliable than for other commodity exporters. Finally, and as noted above, should there be a major

---

[9] For instance, actual economic growth during the previous plan period (NDP 6, 1985–1991) was double the forecast rate of five percent a year.

Table 5. Foreign Exchange Reserves: International Comparisons, 1994

	Total [a] Reserves	Import Cover [b]	Reserves per head	Reserves/M2
	US$ million	months	US$ million	%
Argentina[c]	14 288	8.5	411	30
Bahrain	1 280	4.1	2 169	34
Botswana	**4 764**	**30.4**	**3 263**	**421**
Chile	14 140	10.7	996	57
Colombia	8 102	7.0	231	52
Indonesia[c]	13 708	4.0	71	19
Malaysia	23 774	3.7	1 149	30
Mauritius	863	5.5	764	29
Mexico	16 847	5.2	186	23
Philippines	6 372	2.7	91	17
Singapore	68 695	6.6	22 975	95
South Africa	2 820	1.1	68	4
Thailand	35 982	5.9	606	27
Turkey	12 442	4.2	202	30
Venezuela	6 283	6.3	290	53
Zimbabwe	596	3.6	52	34

Notes:
[a] Total reserves minus gold.
[b] Reserves/imports (cif).
[c] 1995 money supply data not available; 1994 figure used.

Source: IMF *International Financial Statistics.*

external shock the discipline imposed by an open capital account should help to enforce the necessary fiscal adjustment.

Although concern has mostly been expressed about capital outflows, the experience of other countries which have liberalised the capital account in a stable macroeconomic environment suggests that net capital inflows are more likely. Botswana's fledgling stock market has benefited from significant net inflows of foreign capital over the past two years, reflecting the increasing international interest in emerging markets as well as the spill-over effects (into the region) of renewed interest in South Africa. If the remaining controls on inward capital flows were relaxed or removed altogether, there is every prospect of further inflows as the process of global portfolio diversification continues, although the limitations imposed by the relatively limited range of financial assets available would soon be felt. This would go some way towards countering any capital outflow as a result of portfolio diversification by domestic investors.

The issue of whether the foreign reserves are large enough to support the removal of capital controls can also be considered in an international context. With regard to the adequate level of international reserves, most countries that have opened their capital account have done so with much lower levels of reserves than Botswana currently has, relative to the size of its import needs and of its domestic economy. Table 5 presents Botswana's foreign exchange reserves in international perspective, showing data on the levels of import cover provided by the reserves, and of foreign reserves *per capita*, for a range of developing countries which have been among the more progressive exchange control liberalisers in the past. On both counts, Botswana's gross reserves are extremely high by international levels. Import cover, at over thirty months, is nearly three times the level of the next highest country in the table (Chile). Reserves *per capita*, at US$3263, are second only to Singapore and compare with less than US$500 for most of the countries in the table. Given that Botswana has a very low level of international debt, the contrast would be even greater if net reserves were considered. These data support the conclusion that Botswana's reserves are more than adequate to cope with the abolition of capital controls.

B. Management of larger international capital movements

Regardless of the net capital flow position, it is likely that as a result of removing barriers to capital flows between Botswana and the international financial system, the size of gross capital flows will increase. Some of these are likely to represent short-term, potentially volatile, capital movements, and it will be necessary for the monetary authorities to be capable of responding much more quickly to such flows than they do at present. For instance, an inflow of foreign currency, converted to Pula, would lead to an increase in the money supply unless it was quickly sterilised through the issue of BoBCs. Although such a capital inflow has the beneficial impact of increasing the reserves, an increase in the money supply could lead to higher inflation or speculative asset price bubbles. If capital then flows out again, such bubbles can easily burst, unless the outflow is countered by the authorities buying back BoBCs from the public.

Capital flows tend to respond relatively quickly to differences in expected returns between markets, certainly when compared to changes in trade patterns. The monetary authorities would therefore have to respond in good time to increased gross capital flows, both inward and outward, in a manner which would maintain monetary stability. Such sterilization is quite difficult to do well, and can also be costly in terms of (say) increased interest rates which the central bank needs to pay to sell more bonds in response to a capital inflow. It would require some changes in the method of operation of the Bank of Botswana (for instance in maintaining a much more active tap-stock of BoBCs) and enhanced monetary management skills. These should not pose major problems in the long term. The current control by Government of the vast majority of the foreign exchange reserves limits the scope for outflows, and will continue to do so for a number of years. Substantial short-term inflows are already possible, *via* changes in short-term borrowing for trade purposes, and the authorities have managed this quite adequately in the past. Only if they greatly increased after exchange control abolition would there be an immediate management problem, but this is unlikely given the very limited range of marketable financial instruments available in Botswana. But if this is a concern, removal of controls on capital inflows can be the last element in a sequencing of capital account liberalization measures (see e.g., Galbis, 1996).

C. Interest rates, money supply and the exchange rate

An open capital account also changes the menu of options available for policy makers in the management of interest rates and exchange rates. In theory, in a small open economy with perfect capital mobility and fixed exchange rates, monetary policy becomes ineffective. That is, the money supply is affected by external factors (such as changes in trade or capital flows), and any attempts to change the money supply for domestic policy purposes is countered by capital inflows or outflows and hence changes in the reserves. Furthermore, capital mobility ensures that the domestic real interest rate cannot deviate from international rates for any sustained period. With fixed exchange rates, therefore, unrestricted capital flows render ineffective any attempts to control the money supply or domestic interest rates. For monetary policy to be effective, the exchange rate must be allowed to float – but the trade off is that control over the exchange rate is then lost.

In practice, however, the choice is not as stark as theory suggests. Capital mobility is not perfect (as domestic and foreign assets are not perfect substitutes), prices are not fully flexible, and exchange rates can be managed rather than fixed or freely floating. In Botswana's case the high level of the reserves adds further flexibility to policy choices, given that some capital outflows can be absorbed without running into reserve problems.

Indeed, the high level of the foreign exchange reserves forecast for the next decade should, assuming that the mechanisms are in place to absorb capital movements, enable the Government to manage both interest and exchange rates, within limits, in accordance with Botswana's domestic economic needs. On interest rates, these limits are that domestic rates could not deviate significantly from international rates (in real terms) for any prolonged period; very low interest rates (such as those experienced in the 1980s) might well lead to unsustainable capital outflows. However, it is now widely acknowledged that strongly negative real interest rates have adverse effects on the domestic economy (which is one reason why interest rates in Botswana have been raised recently, even with exchange controls still in place), and it seems unlikely that Government would wish to pursue a policy of negative real interest rates in the future. Another constraint is that long-term interest rates would have to rise relative to short-term rates, again reflecting more typical international interest rate structures (yield curves), but this is a desirable move in order to encourage the growth of long-term savings deposits and the eventual growth of a capital market. Even within these constraints, the Government would retain some flexibility, given the size of the reserves, to move interest rates upwards or downwards in accordance with domestic economic priorities; for instance, during a recession it would still be possible to reduce interest rates somewhat in order to boost investment and consumer spending. However, this flexibility would be more limited should Botswana attract large amounts of potentially volatile short-term/portfolio investments in Pula, and in this case a much closer tracking of international interest rates could be necessary if large inflows and outflows were to be avoided.

Botswana's real interest rates have increased steadily in recent years, and are broadly comparable with those in the major international economies (see Table 6). However, Botswana's interest rates remain significantly below those in neighbouring South Africa. In the medium term, Botswana's real interest rates may have to rise somewhat, if rates in South Africa remain high and capital becomes more mobile as a result of exchange control liberalization. In an international context, higher real in-

terest rates may also be required to provide a margin above rates in major developed economies sufficient to compensate for country (or regional) risk. The hope remains, however, that this can be achieved through lower inflation than through raising nominal interest rates. As a result there is no reason to believe that nominal interest rates would need to rise if exchange controls were removed. Nominal interest rates are far more dependent upon the inflation rate than on whether there are exchange controls in place.

Similarly, there would be

TABLE 6. INTERNATIONAL REAL INTEREST RATE COMPARISONS (END-1995)

	INFLATION (%) (CONSUMER PRICES)	3-MONTH MONEY MARKET RATES (%)	
		NOMINAL	REAL
Botswana	9.6	12.2	2.6
South Africa	9.4	17.7	8.3
USA	3.3	5.3	2.0
UK	2.4	5.9	3.5
Germany	2.8	3.3	0.5
France	1.7	3.3	1.6
Japan	0.5	0.5	0.0

Sources: IMF *International Financial Statistics*, Bank of Botswana *Annual Report 1996*.

flexibility to manage the exchange rate, but not to the extent of maintaining the value of the Pula at a level which was overvalued or undervalued with regard to long-term economic fundamentals. The target of exchange rate management in Botswana has been achieved to stabilise the real exchange rate of the Pula against the Rand over a long period, and this policy could continue[10]; there is unlikely to be any major impact on the exchange rate of the Pula as a result of removing capital controls. Relatively large fluctuations in the value of the Pula would only occur if Botswana moved to a floating exchange rate regime, but this is a separate policy decision (unlikely in the short to medium term) and certainly not a necessary consequence of exchange control liberalization. In the context of Botswana's economy, given the large size of some transactions (e.g., diamond sales) relative to the rest of the market, and the more general and well-established dangers of 'overshooting' in a floating exchange rate regime (where market-led exchange rate adjustments go too far and introduce excessive volatility), there would continue to be a strong case for exchange rate management for the foreseeable future. From a theoretical perspective, liberalising exchange controls mainly affects the exchange rates of those currencies which are overvalued. Although this applies to many countries in Africa, there is no evidence that the Pula is overvalued, given that there is no parallel market for the currency[11], that Botswana

---

10 Actually the policy has been to stabilise the trade-weighted real exchange rate, where trade weights are determined in relation to imports and non-traditional exports, of which Rand-denominated trade accounts for nearly 80%.

has experienced continuous current account surpluses since 1983 without any significant import restrictions, and has accumulated such high foreign exchange reserves.

If, at some time in the future, the reserves fell to an unsustainably low level this
would require changes in interest rates and/or the exchange rate. However, the current level of the reserves, and forecast levels for ten years are so high relative to any
conceivable net capital outflow that the monetary authorities will retain some flexibility in interest rate and exchange rate management for several years to come.

Some people have questioned whether, without exchange controls, the Pula would
be vulnerable to speculative attack. The answer to this is no. If currency traders
wished to speculate on a rise in the Pula, they would buy Pula in the hope that its
value would rise. However, with a managed exchange rate, the Bank of Botswana can
simply absorb the increased foreign currency inflows as higher reserves, leaving the
exchange rate unchanged and speculators unrewarded. Alternatively, traders may
wish to speculate on a fall in the Pula, by selling Pula for foreign currency. The extent
of such speculation is limited by the size of available Pula balances (the money supply, plus potential new borrowing from banks). As noted above, these balances are
relatively small and can easily be absorbed by the foreign exchange reserves. Even if
speculators wished to borrow from the banks in Pula to buy foreign currency, the
extent of such borrowing would be limited by the normal prudential banking regulations regarding primary reserve and liquidity requirements, as well as restrictions
relating to exposure to one borrower. It is important to note that currencies are vul
nerable to such speculative attacks *only* when they have relatively low foreign exchange
reserves and some fundamental policy misalignment, and this does not apply to
Botswana.

D. Losses of Government revenue

Earnings on foreign exchange reserves

Although it has been shown above that the potential outflow of foreign exchange
reserves is small relative to total reserves, there may be concern about the impact on
Government revenues, given that the Government's share of Bank of Botswana profits (which are derived from earnings on the reserves) is now its second largest source
of revenue.

For the purposes of illustration, consider what would happen if private savers, free
of all exchange controls, decided to convert the majority of their Pula financial assets
to foreign currency, leading to a ten percent fall in the foreign exchange reserves. At
the same time, this drawdown of Pula assets would lead to reduced private holdings
of BoBCs or lower deposits in the commercial banks (which would lead to reduced
bank holdings of BoBCs); the net result would be that holdings of BoBCs would fall by
approximately the same Pula amount as the foreign reserves, resulting in reduced
interest payments by the Bank of Botswana. Therefore, although Bank of Botswana
income would be reduced (because of lower forex reserves), Bank of Botswana expenses would also be reduced (because of lower BoBCs in issue).

---

[11] Until 1992 there was a small parallel market for the Pula *vis-à-vis* the Zimbabwe Dollar, but
the value of the Pula in this market was *higher* than the official rate.

Table 7 shows what the impact of this would have been on Bank of Botswana earnings and on Government revenues in 1994 and 1995. The situation is complicated by the fact that total Bank of Botswana 'earnings' are divided between direct income (such as interest received) on the reserves, and revaluation gains due to changes in the exchange rate between the Pula and the currencies in which the reserves are denominated.

TABLE 7. IMPACT ON GOVERNMENT SHARE OF BANK OF BOTSWANA PROFITS OF A 10% FALL IN THE FOREIGN RESERVES

PULA MILLION	1994		1995	
	ACTUAL	RESERVES 10% LOWER	ACTUAL	RESERVES 10% LOWER
Income from reserves	367	330	995	896
Interest on BoBCs	163	29	199	65
Other expenses	43	43	46	46
Net Income	161	259	750	785
Revaluation gains	1062	956	698	628
Revaluation reserve	2984	2878	3384	3314
Net income plus revaluation gains	1223	1214	1448	1413
BoBCs outstanding	1451	255	1964	639
Foreign reserves	11961	10765	13251	11926
Bank of Botswana payment to Government:	451	534	1051	1077
95% of net income	153	246	713	746
10% of revaluation reserve	298	288	338	331
Rate of return on reserves	11.9%	11.9%	12.8%	12.8%

Assumptions: 10% fall in reserves will reduce both income and revaluation gains by 10%. Reduction in forex reserves will be matched by equal reduction in BoBCs outstanding.

Source: Bank of Botswana Annual Reports and the author's calculations.

In both years, total Bank of Botswana earnings (including income from the reserves and revaluation gains) would have been slightly lower, because the savings from lower BoBC interest payments would not have been quite enough to compensate for the lower earnings on the reserves. However, net Bank of Botswana income (excluding revaluation gains) would have been *higher*, because savings in BoBC interest payments would entirely benefit the net income account, whereas lower earnings from the reserves are only partially applied to this account. As a result of the formula under which Government is paid (95% of net income and 10% of the balance on the revaluation reserve), Government revenues from the Bank of Botswana would have been higher each year even if the reserves had been 10% lower. The real danger to Government revenues, as with the level of the reserves, comes from the possibility of large Government budget deficits, which would cause the reserves to fall, and thus erode the revenue base.

Tax revenues

At present, under Botswana's source based taxation system, only income originating in Botswana is liable to taxation here; income originating elsewhere is not taxed. There has been some concern that with exchange control liberalization which permitted capital outflows, tax revenue would be reduced, if income earned on that capital were no longer to be taxed. In order to prevent this loss of tax revenue, recent liberalizations were accompanied by changes to the tax regulations, which deemed that income from investments outside of Botswana, if financed from Botswana-sourced funds, were liable to tax. This system can continue in the event of complete liberalization, so that income resulting from capital outflows by residents is still liable to Botswana taxation. Its effectiveness and enforceability would be enhanced by the negotiation of double taxation agreements with a wider range of countries, under which foreign tax authorities can report to Botswana on the relevant foreign earnings of Botswana residents. In the longer term, Botswana may wish to consider moving towards a global basis for taxation, although as this places much greater demands upon the tax authorities if the system is to be effectively enforced it is unlikely to be realistic to implement this in the foreseeable future. Much greater gains could come from proper implementation of the existing tax regulations.

At present the exchange control regulations are sometimes used to enforce other taxation regulations (i.e., some exchanges of Pula for foreign currency are only possible once tax clearance has been obtained). The question is whether such mechanisms should be retained for tax enforcement. With a large number of foreign-owned companies operating in the country, Botswana may be vulnerable to abuse of the taxation system (e.g., non-payment of withholding or capital gains taxes) which could be reduced through enforcing tax clearance for foreign exchange transactions. The disadvantage is that this would result in every single foreign exchange transaction having to be checked for tax, to determine whether or not it was actually liable for tax, resulting in the continuation of the very delays and bureaucracy which exchange control liberalization is intended to curtail. There would appear to be little merit in imposing an exchange control burden on the entire economy as a result of the inability of the taxation authorities to collect the revenues which are due to them by other means.

E. A conduit for capital flight

Without exchange controls Botswana might be used as a conduit for capital flight from South Africa, whereby funds which have been legally acquired in South Africa are exported in a way which contravenes that country's own exchange control regulations. Indications are that in the past capital flight from South Africa has been substantial (although not through Botswana); future levels will depend closely on the success of the political and economic reform process there. Although such funds are quite legal in terms of Botswana law, their acceptance could undermine relations with South Africa. Ultimately, however, it is South Africa's responsibility to enforce its own exchange control regulations, and this should not be used as an argument to delay desirable policy reforms in Botswana.

It is also possible that there might be attempts by outsiders to use a liberalised Botswana exchange control regime to 'launder' illegally acquired funds (such as from drug trafficking). The commercial banks already operate internal guidelines designed to exclude such transactions. Such guidelines might need to be strengthened, but there is no reason why effective practice cannot be developed jointly by the commercial banks and the Bank of Botswana, if necessary drawing upon the experience of other countries in similar situations.

10. Proposals for Reform

Removal of Botswana's remaining exchange controls, thereby achieving capital account liberalization and full convertibility of the Pula, would be a significant achievement which would mark out Botswana as distinctly different from other countries in Sub-Saharan Africa in general, and Southern Africa in particular. No other country could offer the same combination of a stable macro economy, a good past record of macroeconomic management, a high level of foreign exchange reserves, and no exchange controls. As such Botswana would be in a strong position to attract inward foreign investment into the region, especially in the area of international financial services and other related areas. There would also be significant savings in terms of reduced bureaucracy, and increased efficiency of business transactions.

At the same time, the potential disadvantages are few, and in particular the concern expressed about excessive capital flight from the country and reduction in foreign exchange reserves has been shown to be misplaced. If exchange controls are abolished, there could be a small loss of tax revenue in the short term, although in the longer term this should be compensated by the taxation of increased investment and economic growth. There would be some additional constraints imposed on the Government's ability to set interest rates and the exchange rate, but recent interest rate and exchange rate policy would appear to lie within these constraints, so that effectively there would be no change. Removing exchange controls would make it more difficult to engage in unsustainably high levels of Government spending in the future, and would impose a useful external discipline on any internal pressures to follow unsustainable fiscal policies. Although there should be no major movements in the exchange rate or interest rates as a result of removing exchange controls, management of the macro economy in the context of a liberalised relationship with the rest of the world will require the development of new skills and institutional capacity in the Ministry of Finance and Development Planning, the Bank of Botswana, and the commercial banks – not just to handle the technical issues, but also the policy dilemmas that would arise.

Should there be concern about the management of monetary policy in a liberalised environment, there are various measures which can be adopted to deal with the impact of larger gross capital flows on the money supply. One would be to retain restrictions on the purchase of BoBCs by foreigners (other countries which have liberalised the capital account do retain such restrictions, e.g., on the purchase of government paper by foreigners). An alternative is the use of carefully structured reserve requirements on certain types of deposits at commercial banks – for instance those held by non-residents – which can discourage capital inflows, especially those of a short-term or speculative nature (Helleiner, 1996).

On balance, therefore, Botswana has little to lose and much to gain by immediately removing remaining exchange controls, and achieving full convertibility of the Pula for both current and capital transactions. Such a 'big bang' approach would achieve the maximum favourable impact for Botswana, and once again serve to distinguish the country's relatively strong economic position in Sub-Saharan Africa. If the process is delayed too long, it is likely that Botswana will be left behind by the liberalization process taking place in other African countries, notably South Africa, which has already made clear its intention to remove all remaining exchange controls as soon as possible. If this should happen before Botswana completes liberalization, Botswana will face the choice of liberalising in a hurry to keep up with South Africa, thus possibly losing some control over its own liberalization process, or falling behind South Africa in the process and being disadvantaged from the point of view of attracting foreign investment.

References

Bank of Botswana. 1993. *Annual Report*. Bank of Botswana, Gaborone.

Bhuiyan, M.N. (ed.). 1986. *Selected Papers on the Botswana Economy*. Printing and Publishing Co. (Botswana), Gaborone.

Chuka, C.S. 1992. 'The Experience of Malawi'. In: African Centre for Monetary Studies, *Instruments of Economic Policy in Africa*. James Currey, London.

Collins, S. 1988. 'Multiple Exchange Rates, Capital Controls, and Commercial Policy'. In: Dornbusch, R. and Helmers, F.L.C.H. (eds.) *The Open Economy: Tools for Policymakers in Developing Countries*. World Bank, Washington.

Edwards, S. 1984. 'The Order of Liberalization of the External Sector in Developing Countries', *Princeton Essays in International Finance*, No.156.

Edwards, S. 1989. *Real Exchange Rates, Devaluation and Adjustment*. MIT Press, Cambridge, Mass.

Galbis, V. 1996. 'Currency Convertibility and the Fund: Review and Prognosis', *IMF Working Paper WP/96/39*, April. IMF, Washington.

Government of Botswana. 1990. *National Development Plan 7, 1991–97*. Ministry of Finance and Development Planning, Gaborone.

Government of Botswana. 1994. *Mid-Term Review of NDP 7*. Ministry of Finance and Development Planning, Gaborone.

Government of Botswana. 1996. *Macroeconomic Outline for National Development Plan 8*. Ministry of Finance and Development Planning, Gaborone.

Hanson, J. 1992. 'Opening the Capital Account: A Survey of Issues and Results', *World Bank Policy Research Working Paper, WPS 901*, May 1992.

Harvey, C. and Lewis, S.R. 1990. *Policy Choice and Development Performance in Botswana*. Macmillan Press, London.

Helleiner, G. 1996. 'Private Capital Flows and Development: The Role of National and International Policies', paper prepared for the Commonwealth Finance Ministers Meeting, Bermuda, September 1996.

Jefferis, K.R. 1997. 'The Characteristics of Successful Manufacturing Exports:

Botswana's Experience', *The Research Bulletin*, Vol.15, No.1. Bank of Botswana, Gaborone.

Jefferis, K. and Harvey, C. 1995. 'Botswana's Exchange Controls: Abolition or Liberalization', *Development Policy Review* Vol.13, No.3, pp277–305.

Kahn, B. 1991. 'Capital Flight and Exchange Controls in South Africa'. *Research Paper No.4.* LSE Centre for the Study of the South African Economy and International Finance, London.

Krueger, A. 1984. 'Problems of Liberalization'. In: Harberger, A. (ed.) *World Economic Growth.* ICS Press, San Francisco.

Mathieson, D. and Rojas-Suarez, L. 1993. 'Liberalization of the Capital Account: Experiences and Issues', *Occasional Paper No.103*, March 1993, IMF, Washington.

McKinnon, R.I. 1973. *Money and Capital in Economic Development.* Brookings Institution, Washington.

McKinnon, R.I. 1982. 'The Order of Economic Liberalization: Lessons from Chile and Argentina'. In: Brunner, K. and Meltzer, A. (eds.) *Economic Policy in a World of Change.* North Holland, Amsterdam.

Michaely, M. 1986. 'The Timing and Sequencing of a Trade Liberalization Policy', In: Choski, A. and Papageorgiou, D. (eds.) *Economic Liberalization in Developing Countries.* Basil Blackwell, London.

Phaleng Consultancies. 1994. *Report on Exchange Control Liberalization.* BOCCIM/BDC, Gaborone.

Salkin, J.S. 1994. 'The Economy in 1993', *Barclays Botswana Economic Review*, Vol.5, No.1.

Williamson, J. and Lessard, D.R. 1987. *Capital Flight: The Problem and Policy Responses.* Institute for International Economics, Washington.

Williamson, J. 1991. 'On Liberalising the Capital Account'. In: O'Brien, R. (ed.) *Finance and the International Economy: 5.* Oxford University Press, Oxford.

World Bank. 1989. *Botswana: Financial Policies for Diversified Growth.* World Bank, Washington.

World Bank. 1995. *World Development Report.* World Bank, Washington.

Botswana's International Trade Policies

J. Clark Leith[1]

1. INTRODUCTION

Every country in the world must settle on an international trade policy. The basic question is: to what extent does it pursue a set of policies which in some way restricts the free flow of international trade? Few countries, if any, choose either extreme – perfectly free international trade, or prohibition of all international trade. Thus, at least some intervention is commonly encountered. Botswana is no exception.

Botswana's policy interventions in the arena of international trade are, however, more varied and complex than most small countries. Botswana simultaneously is a member of a customs union with one group of neighbouring countries, has a free trade agreement with another, participates in a highly successful cartel governing its principal export, has preferential access to a large, highly protected market for another major export, and has pursued an exchange rate policy which has led to the accumulation of two years worth of current account payments. As if this were not enough, negotiations are currently underway to overhaul the customs union, and to add overlapping free trade agreements between the customs union and several more neighbours, and another one with the European Union (EU).

Overall then, it is clear that Botswana's trade patterns have been influenced significantly by a wide ranging set of trade policies. This mix of policies is in part the result of historical accident, and in part the outcome of deliberate choices made by the authorities over the years. The purpose of this paper is to describe the main features of the policies, and identify their principal effects. In the process, a number of important issues in negotiations and policy discussions currently underway are highlighted.

2. TRADE PATTERNS

By way of background it is important to note a key feature of Botswana's trade picture: high commodity concentration of exports and geographic concentration of imports. This concentration is both the cause and the result of the policy choices.

Diamonds account for 70% or more of Botswana's merchandise exports in recent years, which in turn represent over 40% of GDP. Because of this dominant position, changes in diamond exports have a significant impact on total exports and the entire

---

[1] The author is indebted to colleagues in the Botswana Ministries of Commerce and Industry, and Finance and Development Planning for extensive discussions on many of the issues taken up here. In addition, the paper has benefitted considerably from the comments of anonymous referees.

FIGURE 1. DIAMOND AND OTHER EXPORTS, 1990 TO 1995 (PULA MILLION)

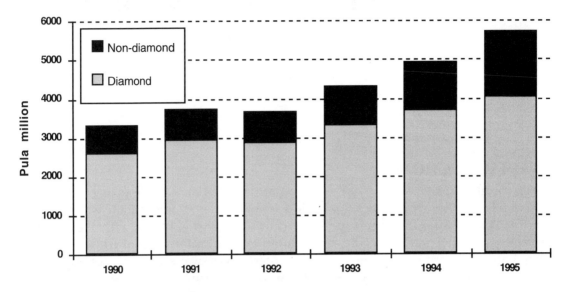

economy. Figure 1 shows diamonds versus all other exports in recent years. Of the other exports, copper-nickel is responsible for 5% to 8% of the total and beef about 4%, while textiles account for around 3%, with assembled vehicles growing rapidly to over 15% in 1995. The major non-diamond exports are depicted in Figure 2.

FIGURE 2. NON-DIAMOND EXPORTS, 1991 TO 1995 (PULA MILLION)

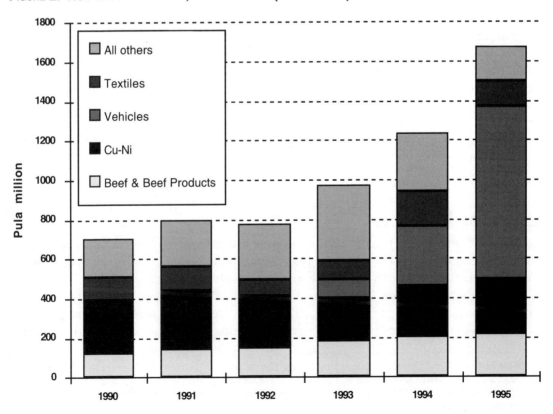

On the import side, the vast majority of Botswana's imports come from the Southern African Customs Union (SACU) consisting of Botswana, Lesotho, Namibia, South Africa and Swaziland, with relatively small shares coming from other sources (see Figure 3).

Figure 3. Sources of Imports, 1990 to 1995 (Pula million)

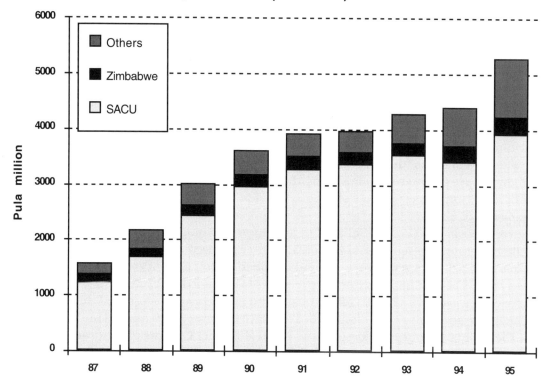

3. Participation in Diamond Central Selling Organisation

Diamond exploration was commenced by De Beers of South Africa before Botswana's Independence, but it was not until shortly after Independence that diamonds were discovered. At a very early stage a decision was made to participate in the diamond Central Selling Organisation, under the auspices of De Beers, and an agreement was signed in 1969. At that point, it could be argued, Botswana had little choice. The country was surrounded by minority white regimes, and De Beers was in a very powerful position to extract a deal tilted to its interests.

Yet there are a number of important features of the diamond market which made it possible for a mutually profitable deal to be struck between Botswana and De Beers. The Central Selling Organisation had already been successfully managing the diamond market for several decades, in sharp contrast with repeated failures of many other international commodity agreements covering raw materials of various kinds. This was due, in large part, to inherent characteristics of the diamond market which made it a prime candidate for a successful cartel, but also to the skilful management of that market by the Central Selling Organisation over the decades. Demand for gem diamonds is inherently inelastic, as there are few substitutes. Both the level of demand and its inelasticity have been reinforced by the Central Selling Organisation advertising, emphasising the unique nature of the gem, its characteristic use for engagements, and the message, implicit in the slogan 'diamonds are forever', that they do not lose their value.

There are relatively few producers of gem quality diamonds in the world, making it more manageable to reach agreement among them, and to enforce marketing restrictions, in contrast with the situation of the Organization of Petroleum Exporting Countries. Such restrictions are essential when there is a significant gap between price and marginal costs, and this is especially serious in the short-run where production costs are largely sunk (as they are in diamonds). Stabilization is especially important when the problem is disturbances arising from the demand side. In the absence of intervention, this would tend to make both price and producer income unstable.

Successful market interventions of this type require that the buyers are unable or unwilling to organise countervailing actions. Partly because the buyers are individuals widely dispersed throughout the world, and because the existing holders of diamonds have an interest in ensuring that the price does not fall, there is unlikely to be any effort on the consumer side to break the market hold by the Central Selling Organisation.

Nevertheless, the Central Selling Organisation has had to enforce strict discipline on the buyers at the ten 'sights' it holds each year when it offers diamonds for sale. Further, according to reports, it has had to spend substantial sums buying up stocks which reach the market from non-participants. The internal situation in several such source countries, including Angola, Russia, and Zaire, have exacerbated this problem.

The Botswana deposits of diamonds are relatively low cost to mine. This has meant that the profits from the success of the Central Selling Organisation in maintaining diamond prices are potentially greater than for marginal producers, while the short-run gain from cheating would be very large. In light of these conflicting incentives, Botswana was able to negotiate a mutually beneficial deal with De Beers and thus with the Central Selling Organisation, such that the principal export has earned significantly more revenue, and that revenue has been substantially more stable, than would be the case in the absence of such an arrangement. Those agreements have been renewed from time to time over the years, indicating that this continues to be a central feature of Botswana's trade policy.

The Botswana Government has a major stake in the success of the diamond sector. As part of the arrangements made in granting mining rights, Government receives not less than 75% of the profits of the diamond mining business. In keeping with that stake, Government has substantial representation on the board of Debswana, the local subsidiary of De Beers, and in 1987 bought shares in De Beers itself, which gave the Botswana Government representation on the De Beers board.

Arising from the substantial Government interest in the profits of the diamond sector are two features of the Botswana strategy for its primary export which stand in contrast with the strategy adopted elsewhere. First, the Botswana Government has bought into the long-run optimization strategy of De Beers, rather than pursue short-term gains at the expense of the long-term success of the cartel.[2] Second, the Botswana

---

[2] Compare this with the approach of countries exporting other minerals, such as tin and petroleum.

Government has supported the use of a low-cost marketing channel to handle the sale of the diamonds from the producer to the Central Selling Organisation, rather than dissipate the rents through more costly marketing arrangements.[3]

4. OTHER EXPORTS

In recent years, diamonds have accounted for over 70% of exports. Three other exports (copper-nickel, meat and textiles) have each accounted for about 3% to 5% of the total. In addition, starting in 1993, assembled motor vehicles have grown to be the largest gross (but not net of imported kits) non-traditional export. While small relative to diamonds, each has particular features and different destinations (see Figure 2).

The copper-nickel mine, which opened in the 1974, sells its output effectively on the world market. Refining of copper-nickel matte is very intensive in electricity. Because Botswana is not endowed with cheap electricity, once the ore has been refined the matte is sent to countries with low cost hydro-electricity for further processing. The fully refined copper and nickel is then sold to the consuming countries, which provide no concessional markets for the Botswana-sourced metals. Consequently, Botswana faces the instability of the world market for these primary commodities. The mine has, nevertheless, enabled some Batswana mineworkers, who did not have their contracts renewed in South Africa, to be re-employed in Botswana.

In recent years Botswana has developed a textile export industry. A significant portion of the textile exports are the result of special trade arrangements. The industry began largely as the result of Government assistance provided under an industrialization incentive programme known as the Financial Assistance Policy (FAP). FAP commenced in the early 1980s, shortly after the time of Zimbabwe's independence, and for a variety of reasons attracted a number of firms from that neighbour. Not only was there uncertainty about the future in Zimbabwe, but Botswana and Zimbabwe continued the 1956 free trade agreement between the Bechuanaland Protectorate and the Federation of Rhodesia and Nyasaland, so that firms moving to Botswana continued to maintain access to the Zimbabwe market. The arrangement also, crucially, included favoured access by Zimbabwe importers to foreign exchange to purchase imports from Botswana. For its part, Botswana, had no foreign exchange rationing. The overvalued Zimbabwe Dollar made it profitable for the textile producers to locate in Botswana to serve the Zimbabwe market.

Following Zimbabwe's independence in 1980, negotiations were carried on sporadically to replace the colonial free trade arrangement with an agreement between the two sovereign nations. Finally, in 1988 an agreement was signed which updated the arrangement.

Botswana's trade with Zimbabwe grew rapidly in the second half of the 1980s. However, when Zimbabwe eventually realigned its currency in 1991, producers located in Botswana were considerably less competitive, and exports to that destination, especially textiles, tailed off.

---

[3] Compare this with the patronage-ridden marketing arrangements for Ghana's cocoa and Zambia's copper, which absorbed substantial portions of the value of the product.

Since under a free trade arrangement each party is free to set its own external tariff, thus potentially allowing low-cost imported inputs to be used in exports to the free trade partner, a central concern of both parties has been the issue of rules of origin. Under the 1988 renewal, rules of origin based on material content, rather than an economic concept of value added were adopted. Further, the decision over whether or not a particular establishment would satisfy the domestic content requirement was lodged ultimately in the customs service of the *importing* nation. Since customs services almost invariably respond to domestic producer rather than consumer interests, this feature has seriously limited the potential growth of trade between the two countries.

Meanwhile, Botswana's membership in the SACU provided textile producers with potential access to the large South African market. Initially that access was not utilized substantially. Somewhat fortuitously, as local producers found it difficult to compete in the Zimbabwe market due to Zimbabwe's major real depreciation, Botswana's competitive position *vis-à-vis* South Africa improved, and several new producers were able to penetrate that market.

In the late 1980s, some Asian textile producers were unable to fulfil their export quotas under the Multi-Fibre Agreement, thus making the markets available to producers from other sources. At the same time, in an effort to provide a more stable employment base for the region around the copper-nickel mine, the Botswana Government established an additional incentive programme[4] for firms to locate in that region, but only for exports destined outside the Southern African Customs Union. However, the 1995 Budget announced a country-wide company tax rate of 15% for firms qualifying as 'manufacturing', and thus a major element of the location specific incentive disappeared.

Motor vehicle assembly has become a rapidly growing source of Botswana exports to SACU. Semi-knocked down kits are imported from outside SACU at low duty and excise tax rates under a special provision of the common external tariff, and the assembled vehicles are sold within SACU at highly protected prices. The largest operation is that of Hyundai automobiles from South Korea, while kits from Scania and Volvo come from Sweden. Exports of motor vehicles, which began to grow rapidly in 1993, exceeded the value of each of meat, copper-nickel, and textile exports (but not domestic value added) by 1994. South Africa took exception to the use by Hyundai of what they regarded as a 'loophole' in the duty and excise tax rates, and after considerable discussion it was agreed to allow Hyundai to continue only if it switched to using completely knocked down kits. At the time of writing this had been agreed to, with a grace period allowed for the switch over to occur.

A further special trade arrangement applies to beef exports. Botswana's vast grazing lands accommodate a cattle herd that on average exceeds two million head. The cattle destined for the export market are slaughtered locally, producing a high quality cold dressed beef. Part of the beef is shipped to the region, especially South Africa under the protection of the common SACU external tariff.[5] The majority of beef exports, however, are destined for the EU under the special provisions of the Lomé

---

[4] The principal incentives were a reduction of the company tax rate to 15%, efforts to provide appropriate infrastructure including adequate and affordable factory space, and a vigorous promotional programme. This was in addition to the incentives available under FAP. As a consequence the total incentive packages available were quite substantial.

Convention. This arrangement provides for a rebate to Botswana of ninety percent of the EU import levy, which is sufficiently lucrative that the Botswana Government spends substantial sums to ensure that the beef meets EU standards, and especially that it is free of foot and mouth disease. Despite this, Botswana has not been able to fulfil the EU quota in recent years, due largely to the slow spread of fully commercialised cattle ranching. The remaining beef exports go to South Africa, and some to the Indian Ocean island of Réunion.

The next Lomé Convention is to come into effect early next decade. It is expected that there will be a phasing out of these special concessions. This will require a major increase in efficiency by Botswana beef producers if they are to remain competitive in world markets.

The combination of rapidly growing exports of assembled vehicles and textiles, together with the continued traditional beef exports, have made South Africa the largest destination for Botswana's non-diamond exports.

5. IMPORTS

The vast majority of imports are also subject to preferential arrangements. As a member of SACU, Botswana provides duty free access to imports from the other partners, while imports from other sources face the SACU common external tariff. In addition, the free trade agreement with Zimbabwe provides goods which meet local content requirements with duty free access to the Botswana market.

The benefits and costs of Botswana's SACU membership as of 1987 have been quantified.[6] The three principal effects are summarised in Table 1. The common external tariff, which under the current arrangement is set unilaterally by South Africa, means that purchasers of importables who reside inside the common external tariff, must pay the world price plus the tariff for importable goods, regardless of whether the goods are manufactured in the domestic economy, in a SACU partner (effectively South Africa) or are imported from outside SACU. The principal impact of this on Botswana consumers is the escalated cost of imports from *all* sources, both SACU and non-SACU, amounting to over ten percent of GDP in 1987. In other words, this is equivalent

TABLE 1. EFFECTS OF SACU, 1987 (% OF GDP)

EFFECT	% OF GDP
PRICE-RAISING ON:	
imports from all sources	−10.13
exports to SACU	+0.81
COMPENSATION	+8.08
NET GAIN (+) OR LOSS(−)	−1.24

Source: Leith, *op. cit.*

to an excise tax on imports from all sources, paid not to the Government of Botswana, but paid to the Government and/or the manufacturers of South Africa. Offsetting this slightly is the effect of the SACU tariff raising the prices on Botswana's exports to SACU, amounting to less than one percent of GDP.

---

[5] It should be noted, however, that SACU permits the use of certain non-tariff barriers for agricultural products, which have been used from time to time by South Africa to limit the competition from Botswana in top grade beef.

[6] See Leith (1992).

An important feature of SACU is the compensation arrangement, whereby South Africa compensates the other members for the costs of membership. The formula, provides for a sharing of total SACU customs revenue, based on recent import shares. It takes no *direct* account of the height of the common external tariff, especially when the common external tariff is in excess of the maximum revenue[7] level, as it has been for some time. It does include a factor which amplifies the share of the customs revenue which is intended to compensate the smaller members (Botswana, Lesotho, Namibia, and Swaziland, or BLNS) for certain negative effects of the SACU, including the fact that the BLNS pay higher than world prices for South African goods, the polarization of industry in South Africa and away from the smaller members, and the lack of fiscal discretion for the BLNS due to the fact that the common external tariff and the excise taxes are determined unilaterally by South Africa. The formula does not deduct anything for the exports by BLNS to other SACU partners at prices above world prices. All of this is over-ridden by a provision which yields the BLNS a minimum of 17% of the value of imports, paid with a two year lag. The compensation paid to Botswana for 1987 amounted to just over 8% of GDP.

Overall, adding these effects together, the net *cost* to Botswana in 1987 was 1.24% of GDP. In other words, as the numbers in Table 1 indicate, Botswana consumers have paid the equivalent of an excise tax to a combination of the South African Government and the South African producers, which has *not* been fully offset by countervailing payments to the Botswana Government or Botswana producers: some of the 'tax equivalent' collected from Batswana effectively remains in South Africa, and never returns to Botswana. This net negative position has been the source of dissatisfaction with the SACU terms for some time, and discussions among the members about reforming the customs union have been undertaken sporadically since about 1980. It was not until the new Government in South Africa took power in 1994 that renegotiations began in earnest. At the time of writing those negotiations are still underway. The following issues are under discussion.

First and foremost, the compensation formula is in contention. As the common external tariff comes down in the next few years, in keeping with the South African commitment to WTO, the price-raising effect on imports will fall, but the current formula would continue to compensate the BLNS members on the basis of their imports from all sources. When the tariff reductions have been completed, and if import composition remains roughly as it is at present, the BLNS members will end up being overcompensated for the price-raising effect on their imports. This is because the price-raising effect on imports will fall (as will the much smaller price-raising effect on BLNS exports to SACU), while the compensation will not fall. For example, if the tariff level drops by one quarter, and the volume and composition of trade remained constant relative to GDP, then the numbers in Table 1 would be (as a percent of GDP):

- price-raising effect on imports = −7.6%;
- price-raising effect on exports to partners = +0.6%;
- for a net −7.0%, while compensation would still exceed 8%.

Further, since the current formula takes no account of the price-raising effect of the

---

7   Thus, as the tariff rate increases from a low level, the total revenue collected increases to a maximum, but if the rate continues to increase, the revenue collected falls, and eventually reaches zero if the tariff becomes prohibitive.

common external tariff on BLNS exports to partners, as those exports grow (e.g., Botswana's exports of textiles and motor vehicles), there is no reduction in the compensation which South Africa pays to the BLNS.

In addition to this concern, South Africa would like to try to cap the entitlements to compensation at the value of the customs duty collections on imports from outside the SACU. The grounds for this approach are based on the logic of bureaucratic compartmentalization – that funds in one pot could be redistributed within that category, but not between pots – rather than economic analysis of South Africa's extra benefits from its preferred access to the BLNS markets. Given past experience with South Africa's unilateral actions changing the common external tariff, such as the 1988 imposition of surcharges which more than doubled the net loss to Botswana, the BLNS members have been wary of agreeing to any arrangement which would leave the funds available for compensation determined by South Africa independently of the price-raising effects.

A new agreement is hoped to contain changes in a second major area: decision-making, including the setting of the common external tariff. The existing agreement states simply that the South African external tariff shall be the common external tariff for the SACU. A South African body, listening largely to South African specific interests, has administered the tariff, making frequent changes as it saw fit, which then had to be immediately implemented by the BLNS. It is hoped that the new agreement will contain new provisions for making decisions, including procedures for making changes to the common external tariff. The approach is hoped to include a voting scheme for major issues which would not allow either South Africa, or BLNS as a group, to achieve a majority alone.

One consequence of the old procedures for setting the tariff is that the common external tariff is both very high and very complex.[8] Table 2 reports the nominal and effective rates of protection corresponding to the major tradeable producing sectors in Botswana for 1995 (see Appendix for details of the calculations). Particularly noteworthy are the very high rates for the dairy, and the textile and clothing sectors. Also notable is the negative value added at world prices found in the meat sector. This reflects the extent to which the combination of the common external tariff and the preferred access to the EU market has permitted costs in Botswana to escalate.

Establishing a new voting procedure, and a new tariff-making arrangement within that framework, will only be the beginning. Sorting out the details of the new common external tariff will not be easy. Botswana has signalled that it would prefer a common external tariff which is *low, simple, uniform, and stable*.[9] Such a tariff would lower the costs to the purchasers of imports from the very high common external tariff, and thus permit a reduction in the compensation claims by the BLNS. It would also provide a basis for the development of internationally competitive industry within the SACU, and would minimise the manipulation of the tariff by specific interests. A low tariff might also reduce the revenue, but for the Botswana Government, in contrast with other SACU members, this would be manageable because of the other robust revenue sources.

---

[8] For example, the average nominal tariff rate on dutiable imports (weighted by imports) into the US in the early 1990s was less than 5%, while the average for Botswana was well in excess of 20%.

[9] Ministry of Finance and Development Planning (1994).

Another area of likely change concerns industrial promotion arrangements. The existing agreement contains two provisions which allow the BLNS to promote industrial development within their territories. The first is an 'infant industry' clause which allows the smaller members to protect industries within their territories against imports from all sources, including elsewhere in the SACU. The protection must be for a limited period of time, up to a maximum of eight years.

Only two industries in Botswana have been accorded this protection: beer and soap. The duties paid on imports of such goods to Botswana go to the customs revenue pool, and not to the Government of Botswana.[10] To minimise this, the infant industries have typically been granted very high protection, with the intention of making the duty paid cost of competing imports prohibitive. To protect the Botswana consumer, price controls were employed linking the price to that of the former imports from South Africa.[11]

The device of infant industry protection has not proved effective in creating new industries in the BLNS. In most cases, because the market was so small, there would only be one domestic producer licensed to produce behind the protective wall. Despite the monopoly position (or perhaps because of it), the initial interests frequently faced serious quality problems and loyalty to traditional brands, resulting in consumer rejection. The protected industries found that cost reduction during the period of protection proved extremely difficult to achieve, and when the period of protection ran out, they faced serious adjustment problems. But for Botswana, in both the beer and soap cases, that adjustment has been successfully made.

TABLE 2. NOMINAL AND EFFECTIVE RATES OF PROTECTION, 1995 (PERCENTAGE)

SECTOR	NOMINAL[a]	EFFECTIVE[b]
FARMING	22.5	29.3
MINERALS	1.1	0.8
MEAT AND PRODUCTS	19.3	∞[c]
DAIRY AND OTHER AGRICULTURAL PRODUCTS	49.9	239.7
BEVERAGES	30.4	24.2
TEXTILES, CLOTHING, ETC.	46.9	150.7
PETROLEUM, CHEMICALS, AND PLASTICS	10.7	−0.7
METAL PRODUCTS	12.4	14.3
OTHER MANUFACTURES	15.8	19.3

Notes:

a   The 'nominal rate of protection' or 'nominal tariff' refers to the tariffs or other import duties which must be paid on an imported good, as a proportion of the foreign price. Since this raises the price of foreign goods by that proportion, it provides domestic producers of competing goods with the opportunity to raise their prices by that same proportion.

b   The 'effective rate of protection' refers to the extent to which the tariffs permit the prices of the final goods to increase, net of the increases in tradeable input costs due to tariffs on those inputs, expressed as a proportion of value added in that industry, calculated at world prices.

c   The ∞ rate indicates that the value added, when inputs and outputs are deflated to world prices, is negative, and hence the denominator of the effective rate of protection is less than zero.

Source: Appendix.

---

10   However, through the working of the compensation formula, whereby Botswana receives the minimum 17% of the value of imports, the net effect is that 83% of the duties paid on such goods by the consumers of Botswana go to the customs revenue pool (effectively the Government of South Africa), and not to the Government of Botswana.

11   As is common with price controls the world over, these were not wholly effective.

A second type of infant industry protection permitted under the existing agreement is one which allows one of the BLNS members to seek a change in the common external tariff in order to permit an industry to be established in its territory to serve the entire SACU market. Such protection would only be granted by the common external tariff if the industry could be expected to supply a substantial portion of the SACU market. This arrangement has been little used, but was employed by Botswana to launch the soda ash project at Sua Pan, to serve the South African market for this industrial chemical.

Alternatives to these types of protection arrangements have been proposed. In particular, the use of reduced duties on material inputs as a means of increasing the effective rate of protection, would be less costly to the consumer, and would maintain a competitive environment.

The experience with the soda ash project has revealed another weakness in the current agreement; that is, inadequate anti-dumping procedures. The processing plant at Sua Pan came on stream just as a major world recession hit, and the world supply of soda ash moved to surplus, leading many offshore producers to cut prices in international markets substantially below the cost of production. The response of the SACU to this dumping was largely ineffective, leaving the Botswana producer with a much smaller share of the market than had been anticipated, eventually forcing the original firm into bankruptcy. Consequently, Botswana wishes to see more effective anti-dumping procedures, designed to deal both with dumping from outside and within the SACU.

Botswana's imports from Zimbabwe began to grow following the 1988 revision to the 1956 agreement, but it took the major real exchange rate depreciation by Zimbabwe in 1991 to improve their competitive position in Botswana. Since then, those imports have fluctuated in nominal terms, largely due to Zimbabwe's erratic real exchange rate.

6. EXCHANGE RATE POLICY

In addition to policies acting directly to affect commodity trade, another policy instrument, the exchange rate, has been used effectively over the years to further Botswana's interests. The principal thrust of policy has involved pegging of the currency at a level which accumulated and then maintained substantial foreign exchange reserves. The Pula is pegged in value against a basket consisting of regional and major international currencies. This is a genuine peg in that the Bank of Botswana buys and sells foreign exchange at the posted rates without any rationing of foreign exchange. While there are some modest exchange controls still present, these effectively do not restrict current account payments. Over the years the Bank has built up substantial exchange reserves, to the point that the reserves currently represent about two years' worth of current account payments (see Figure 4). The level of the exchange rate, in the face of the substantial foreign exchange reserves, reveals the deliberate decision to avoid the well-know 'Dutch Disease' effect of a strong currency crowding out all but the most robust export activities.

A sub-theme of policy has been to place considerably greater emphasis on the exchange rate with the South African Rand. This reflects the greater importance of

FIGURE 4. FOREIGN EXCHANGE RESERVES AND CURRENT ACCOUNT PAYMENTS, 1982–95 (US$ MILLION)

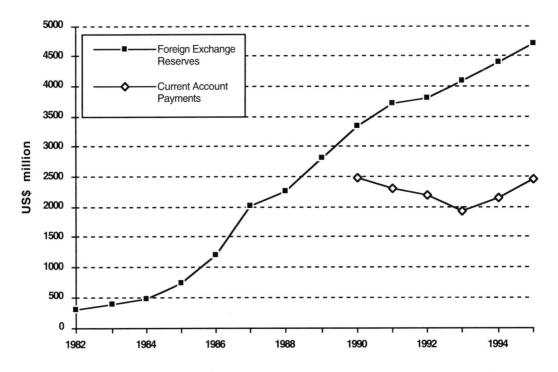

the Rand relative to the other regional and major international currencies for imports and non-traditional exports. It emerges in two related ways: in the selection of the weights in the basket; and the choice of focus for real exchange rate monitoring.

The Rand now has a very heavy weight in the basket; and over the past few years, the policy has emphasised the maintenance of a stable *real* exchange rate against the Rand (see Figure 5).[12] This was not always the case, for in the early years after the Pula was established as a separate currency from the Rand (1976) the Pula was initially pegged against the US Dollar. This was changed to a peg against a basket consisting of 50% Rand and 50% SDR in 1980. In addition, there have been various revaluations and devaluations from time to time, when the choice of weights did not yield the desired outcome in the face of fluctuations of cross exchange rates. For example, from late 1980 the Rand began a long period of depreciation against the US Dollar, initially due to a sharp fall in the price of gold, but later due to the capital outflow from South Africa associated with divestiture. With the 50% Rand weight in the basket, this meant an appreciation of the Pula against the Rand. This led to modest devaluations of the Pula in late 1984, twice in 1985, and again in 1986.

The period of the early 1980s reveals an interesting terms of trade effect arising from exchange rate changes. Since the vast majority of Botswana's exports are denominated in hard currencies, and the vast majority of imports are denominated in Rands, the rapid depreciation of the Rand and hence the Pula against the Dollar and other hard currencies meant that Botswana obtained a terms of trade windfall during the period from 1981 through 1986. However, between mid-1986 and 1990, the real

[12] The real exchange rate calculations use the relevant national consumer price indexes as this is the only series available in Botswana on a timely basis.

FIGURE 5. REAL EXCHANGE RATE INDICES RAND/PULA AND US DOLLAR/PULA, 1976–96

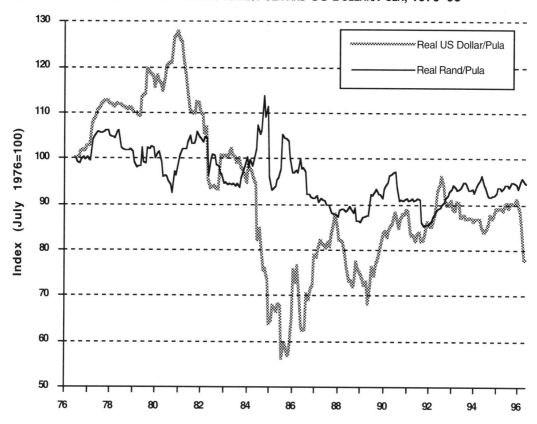

appreciation of the Pula against the Dollar while the real exchange rate against the Rand remained roughly constant, effectively meant that most of that gain was wiped out.

7. FURTHER PREFERENTIAL ARRANGEMENTS ON THE HORIZON

As if the foregoing tangle of overlapping special arrangements governing Botswana's trade were not enough, two further major changes are on the horizon at the time of writing. While it is too early to tell precisely what the likely outcomes will be, the nature of the issues is clear. The proposed new arrangements are:

- a free trade agreement between the members of the Southern African Development Community (SADC), consisting of the five SACU members plus seven other countries of the region (Angola, Mozambique, Malawi, Mauritius, Tanzania, Zambia and Zimbabwe); and
- a free trade agreement between South Africa, and hence SACU, and the EU.

These proposed arrangements are under discussion while the SACU renegotiation process is still underway. Since some of the features of the new SACU treaty are still to be decided, it is virtually impossible to identify with certainty how a SADC free trade agreement or an EU–SACU free trade agreement would interact with the new SACU. Nevertheless, certain key effects can be identified.

SADC Free Trade

In mid-1996, at a ministerial meeting of the SADC members, a trade protocol commit-ting the members to move towards free trade among themselves was signed. The intention appears to be to transform SADC into a free trade area, and perhaps more, by early in the next decade. Given Botswana's major role in SADC, as the seat of the secretariat, and simultaneous with membership in SACU, the potential interaction between the two arrangements is significant.

There are three effects of a simultaneous SADC free trade agreement and an ongo-ing SACU which are worth noting. Needless to say, these effects will depend on the precise arrangements made, but the potential effects can be identified.

First, since a SADC free trade arrangement would presumably include the current SACU members, South Africa would continue to have duty free access to the SACU markets, which collectively make up South Africa's largest market for its non-gold exports. Unless South Africa agreed to continue to pay the BLNS compensation in some form for the price-raising effect of the SACU tariff on the BLNS imports, the latter could lose a significant source of Government revenue. In recent years this has run at 15% of Botswana's Government revenues, and about 6% of GDP. Not only is this Government revenue, but it is a real income transfer which is, as noted above, only partial compensation for the loss of real income to Botswana arising from the price-raising effect of the SACU tariff on imports. For the other BLNS members, the loss of the compensation would be an even larger share of Government revenues and of GDP.

Second, even if South Africa agreed to continue to compensate the BLNS, but not the rest of SADC, there could be a significant impact on BLNS revenues. This could occur in the following way. If imports into South Africa from the rest of SADC were to displace imports which currently come from outside the common external tariff, the customs revenue pool could be reduced significantly. South Africa, for its part, as noted above, has sought to limit its compensation payments to the BLNS to the size of the common customs revenue pool. If such a limit were part of a renegotiated SACU, and a SADC free trade agreement were implemented, then the compensation to the BLNS would be reduced significantly.

Third, the status of the SACU common external tariff would have to be sorted out if a SADC free trade agreement were implemented. If the common external tariff of SACU remains in place for the BLNS, the other SADC members could use their own tariff schedules to affect their input costs to gain a competitive advantage over firms located in the BLNS producing for any of the BLNS, SACU or SADC markets.

In brief, there is the possibility that a SADC free trade agreement, while keeping SACU in place, could put Botswana at a serious disadvantage with high-priced im-ports, low compensation, and no freedom to reduce tariffs to maintain its competitive position *vis-à-vis* the other non-SACU members of SADC.

SACU free trade with EU

Following South Africa's 1994 election, the possibility of the EU including South Africa in some form of preferential arrangement was broached. South Africa wanted to be granted access on the same basis as members of the so-called Lomé Convention governing trade between the EU and its former colonial territories. South Africa wanted an arrangement which would not require it to make reciprocal concessions. At the time of writing the matter had not been settled, although the EU position was that South Africa did not merit non-reciprocal concessions. Thus, preferential entry to the EU market would require South Africa to grant similar concessions to European goods entering South Africa. This would inevitably have a dramatic effect on the implicit SACU common external tariff and hence affect the entire BLNS–South African trading and compensation relationship.

There would be two significant, but offsetting, effects of preferential SACU tariff rates for EU goods. First, concessional entry to SACU of imports from the EU could significantly reduce the price-raising effect of the common external tariff on BLNS imports, both from the EU and from South Africa. The size of this effect clearly depends on the magnitude of whatever concessions are agreed and the extent to which EU-sourced goods are substitutes for the current sources, but this could be a means whereby the SACU common external tariff is reduced at a rate much faster than South Africa is currently committed to under the World Trade Organisation.

While reducing the cost of imports to the BLNS, the concessional imports from the EU could readily erode the common customs pool. As noted earlier, this could affect the compensation payments to the BLNS.

The likely net impact of these two effects together is inherently uncertain, for it depends on which goods and the magnitude of the concessions which are adopted. As so often happens with overlapping layers of trade distortions, the possibility that the outcome might be inferior to the starting point is serious.

8. CONCLUSION

For thirty years Botswana has been able to take advantage of its unique position to employ trade policy to enhance the usual gains from trade. The great bulk of exports are sold at prices above competitive world prices. Imports are purchased at above world prices as well, but much of this effect is offset via compensation payments. This outcome is in contrast with the usual presumption that a small open economy has no effect on its terms of trade. Botswana has effectively improved its terms of trade by the use of trade policy.

Looking to the future, however, there are some clouds on the horizon. The renegotiation of SACU, the potential of a SADC free trade area, a SACU–EU free trade area, future changes in the Lomé Convention, and the potential emergence of major non-Central Selling Organisation diamond sources, all raise the distinct possibility that many of these gains might evaporate. Whether or not this occurs, will depend crucially on the details of what is negotiated in the various special arrangements which affect Botswana's interests.

APPENDIX: CALCULATION OF NOMINAL AND EFFECTIVE RATES OF PROTECTION[13]

This appendix reports on the methodology employed in calculating the nominal and effective rates of protection reported in Table 2 of the text.

Formula

The formula for the effective rate of protection is:

$$ERP_j = \left(t_j - \sum_i a_{ij} t_i \right) / v_j$$

where:

ERP_j	=	effective rate of protection of sector j;
t_j	=	nominal tariff rate on imports of good j;
a_{ij}	=	tradeable inputs of good i per unit of output of good j, at world prices;
t_i	=	nominal tariff rate on imports of good i;
v_j	=	value added per unit of output in production of good j, at world prices.

Data

The underlying nominal tariff rates were calculated by the Industrial Development Commission of South Africa, inclusive of estimated agricultural tariff equivalents, for the year 1995.

The input-output information is from the Botswana Social Accounting Matrix (SAM) for 1992/93, constructed by the Botswana Central Statistics Office. This provides data on 29 producing activities and 54 commodities.

Nineteen output sectors were constructed from the 29 producing activities. This was necessary because in a number of cases the production classification and commodity classification overlapped, and the only way to achieve a correspondence between production activity and commodities was to aggregate more than one production activity.[14] For each output sector, a nominal rate of protection was calculated. Where a sector included more than one commodity, the commodity nominal tariff rates were weighted by total commodity use within the sector. The correspondence between production activities, commodities, and sectors is recorded in Table A1.

The nominal tariff rates were aggregated into the 54 commodities using a software package developed by the World Bank, called SINTIA-T. Since, at the time of the work, trade data for 1993 were the latest available, the weights were on the basis of 1993 imports. The nominal tariff rates for tradeable commodities are recorded in Table A2.

---

[13] The participation of S. Chakrabarti and K. Ndobano of the Botswana Ministry of Finance and Development Planning in the calculation of the nominal rates of protection is gratefully acknowledged.

[14] For example, the commodity classification distinguishes between cattle and other livestock, while the production classification includes cattle produced by traditional agriculture as one activity and all livestock produced on freehold farms as part of another activity. The only solution was to aggregate all agricultural production activity into one producing sector.

Methodological Issues

If there are non-traded input sectors in an economy, it is possible for some of the effective protection to be shared with these non-traded inputs. The solution normally adopted is to treat such input sectors as part of domestic value added when calculating the effective rate of protection, which has been followed in this case. The non-traded commodity inputs were defined as those for which there were no imports from the rest of the world.

Another methodological choice concerns the treatment of depreciation. In these calculations it has been treated as part of value added.

The SAM is constructed using domestic prices. Hence the value added and input coefficients are calculated in terms of domestic prices. These had to be deflated to world prices.

TABLE A1. CORRESPONDENCE BETWEEN SECTORS, PRODUCTION ACTIVITIES, AND COMMODITIES

Sector	Production	Commodities
S 1	P1 TA Cattle P2 TA – Other P3 Freehold Farms P4 Hunting, Fishing and Gathering	C1 Cattle C2 Other Livestock C3 Fruits, Vegetables, Nuts C4 Cereals C5 Other Agricultural
S 2	P5–10 Mining	C6–8 Mining Minerals C54 Soda Ash C9 Sand and Gravel C10 Cement
S 3	P11 Meat Processing	C11 Meat and Products
S 4	P12 Dairy and Other Agricultural Products	C12 Dairy Products C13 Oils and Fats C14 Flour C15 Prepared Foods
S 5	P13 Beverages	C16 Beer and Soft Drinks C17 Other Beverages C18 Tobacco
S 6	P14 Textiles	C19 Textiles C20 Clothing and Footwear C21 Hides and Skins
S 7	P15 Chemicals	C22 Petroleum C23 Chemicals C24 Plastics

S 8	P16 Metal Products	C28 Metals
		C29 Metal Goods
S 9	P17 Other Manufacturing	C25 Wood Products
		C26 Paper Products
		C27 Bricks, Glass and Ceramic
		C30 Mechanical Engineering
		C31 Electrical Engineering
		C32 Vehicles
		C33 Other Manufacturing
S10	P18 Water	C34 Water
S11	P19 Electricity	C35 Electricity
S12	P20 Construction	C36 Construction
S13	P21 Wholesale and Retail Trade, Hotel and Restaurants	C37* Wholesale and Retail Margins
		C38 Hotel and Restaurant
S14	P22 Rail Transport	C39 Rail Transport
	P23 Road Transport	C40 Road Transport
	P24 Air Transport	C41 Air Transport
	P25 Other Transportation	
S15	P26 Communications	C42 Communications
S16	P27 Banking Insurance	C43* Financial Institutions
S17	P28 Business Services	C44 Business Services
S18	P29 Ownership of Dwelling	C45* Rent
		C46* Ownership of Dwelling
S19	P30 Central Government	C47* Central Government
	P31 Local Government	C48* Local Government
	P32 Domestic Services and Traditional Doctors	C49 Education
		C50 Health – Private
	P33 Other Private Services	C51* Health – Subsidised
	P34 Private Non-profit	C52* Domestic Services
	Institutions serving households	C53 Personal Services

Note: * indicates a non-traded commodity.

Source: Central Statistics Office, *1992/93 Social Accounting Matrix.*

TABLE A2. COMMODITY NOMINAL TARIFF RATES

COMMODITY	NOMINAL TARIFF RATE (%)
C1	0.0
C2	0.0
C3	11.1
C4	51.5
C5	14.2
C6–8	1.1
C9	3.8
C10	0.0
C11	19.3
C12	53.7
C13	35.9
C14	60.5
C15	43.5
C16	16.4
C17	75.8
C18	44.7
C19	32.4
C20	55.7
C21	24.3
C22	7.6
C23	13.1
C24	12.5
C25	13.4
C26	10.4
C27	12.9
C28	10.6
C29	15.4
C30	6.0
C31	11.9
C32	27.5
C33	17.6
C34–C54	0.0

Source: Author's calculations.

REFERENCES

Central Statistics Office. 1996, *Social Accounting Matrix 1992/93.* Central Statistics Office, Gaborone.

Leith, J.C. 1992. 'The Static Welfare Effects of a Small Developing Country's Membership in a Customs Union: Botswana in the Southern African Customs Union', *World Development,* Vol.20, No.7, pp1021–1028.

Ministry of Finance and Development Planning, 1994. 'An Overview of the SACU from the Botswana Perspective: Implications of the Historical Record and Contemporary Situation for Re-negotiation of the Agreement', *The Research Bulletin,* Vol.12, No.1, pp13–32. Bank of Botswana, Gaborone.

The Selebi-Phikwe Regional Development Project

A Case Study of the Costs and Benefits of Foreign Direct Investment

D. Cowan

1. INTRODUCTION

The 1990s have witnessed rapid growth in private capital flows to developing countries in the form of both portfolio flows and foreign direct investment (FDI). For developing countries, many of which were often relatively hostile to foreign investors in the 1960s and 1970s, attracting these funds, especially FDI, is now widely seen as very important to promote both job creation and industrialization. However, in the rush to attract foreign investors, many countries seem to have forgotten that economic theory shows that there are costs and benefits associated with foreign investment; and that these costs and benefits should be weighed up before extending the red carpet to investors.

In the case of Botswana, the country has always remained open to, and had a positive attitude towards private foreign investors. Moreover, in order to obtain investment incentives available to firms locating in Botswana (namely Financial Assistance Policy (FAP) grants), proposed projects have to undergo a rigorous cost-benefit analysis before any monies are disbursed. Under this incentive programme, investors have to demonstrate that their proposed project can generate an economic rate of return of over six percent over a ten year period with the provision of FAP. However, while individual investment projects are subject to this test, there has been some tentative evidence presented in the Maendeleo consultancy report *Review of the Selebi-Phikwe Regional Promotion Programme* (Duncan et al., 1992)[26], the World Bank (1993) report *Opportunities for Industrial Development in Botswana*, the Bank of Botswana 1994 Annual Report and the Phaleng consultancy report, 'ICR Mission for the Selebi-Phikwe Technical Assistance Project' (Hudson, 1995), that the Selebi-Phikwe Regional Development Project (SPRDP) may be a case where the costs of attracting investors outweigh the benefits. With the effective winding-up of the project during 1996, this study looks at this issue, and tries to draw a number of lessons from it for Botswana's future strategy to attract FDI.

---

[1]   Although the authors also noted that it was too early to be able to really judge the sustainability of the Programme, and recommended a further review in 1995.

2. A BRIEF BACKGROUND TO THE DEVELOPMENT OF SELEBI-PHIKWE AND THE RATIONALE FOR THE SELEBI-PHIKWE REGIONAL DEVELOPMENT PROJECT (SPRDP)

The development of Selebi-Phikwe from a cattle post to the third largest town in Botswana can best be dated from 1956. In this year, discussions between Kgosi Tshekedi Khama and Sir Ronald Prian of the Roan Selection Trust led to an agreement to start prospecting for minerals in north-east Botswana. Bamangwato Concessions Limited (later to be restructured as BCL Limited) was in turn formed in 1959 to carry out any mining operations. Although the initial search was for precious minerals and metals, namely gold and diamonds, in 1965 the main mineral discovered in Selebi was copper. However, by itself, the copper ore was considered of insufficient quality to justify commercial mining. As a result, prospecting attention was shifted ten kilometres to the north, to Phikwe, where the copper deposits are combined with nickel.

The initial shafts were sunk in 1967, and work on the open pit began in March 1973. Because of the low ore content and remote location of the mine, from the early stages of the project it was envisaged that some processing would have to be conducted on site in order to add value to the ore and reduce transport costs associated with exporting the finished product. Unfortunately, some major technical problems were associated with the installation and operation of the chosen smelter, and it was only in March 1974 that the first copper-nickel matte was produced for overseas sale.

Since its opening in 1973, BCL has easily been the single most important source of employment for the town and surrounding region, and by 1992 employed around 5000 persons directly. In fact, the growth of the mine and the town have been inextricably linked. According to the 1971 Population Census, Selebi-Phikwe was the fourth largest town in Botswana, with 9% of the country's urban population.[2] However, in a special population census conducted for Selebi-Phikwe in 1975, the population had grown to a staggering 20 522 making it the third largest town. By the 1981 Census, Selebi-Phikwe remained the third largest town in the country with 18% of the urban population. Although since

TABLE 1. POPULATION OF SELEBI-PHIKWE

	1971	1975	1981	1991
TOTAL POPULATION	5 259	20 522	29 469	39 772
MINE/QUARRY EMPLOYEES	3 058	3 144	4 308	5 451
PAID EMPLOYEES	N/A	6 683	10 113	15 568

Source: Population Censuses, 1971, 1975, 1981 and 1991.

1981 the growth of Selebi-Phikwe has slowed down compared to the growth of other urban areas (according to the 1991 Census it now contains only 12% of Botswana's total urban population), it has remained the third largest urban centre in Botswana

Another important feature of the development of the copper-nickel mine in Selebi-Phikwe is that the vast majority of the jobs created are both skilled, and well paid in relation to Botswana's minimum wages. In 1992, the average citizen wage paid at the

---

2   However, it should be noted that the several problems with the 1971 Census indicate that the figures could have substantially underestimated the size of the town.

mine was around P1000 a month, compared to a minimum wage in manufacturing of P184 a month.[3]

However, since its establishment in the mid-1970s, the long-term commercial viability of the Mine has been questioned a number of times.[4] As a result, the potentially disastrous impact of its closure has always hung over the town. Not surprisingly, the Government has been willing to entertain plans to encourage diversification of the town's economic base.

The first step taken by the Government in this direction was the establishment of a Selebi-Phikwe Continuation Study Group (SPCSG) in 1982. This had the broad remit of examining various approaches to improve the economic diversification policy in Selebi-Phikwe. In addition, as an interim measure to encourage investment in the town compared to other urban locations in Botswana, after the 1984 evaluation of the Government's Financial Assistance Policy Selebi-Phikwe was classified as a rural area when considering applications for FAP.[5] This entitled investors to a marginally superior range of financial benefits compared to FAP.

The SPCSG gave its recommendations to Government in 1985. The centrepiece of these was the idea that Government should establish a comprehensive 'Regional Development Strategy' for Selebi-Phikwe. This would involve efforts to develop both industrial and agricultural projects in the town and wider region, coordinated by a promotion unit which was to be located in Selebi-Phikwe, but under the direct control of the Ministry of Finance and Development Planning (MFDP).

To help finance this economic diversification strategy, the Government secured a US$7.6 million loan from the World Bank in August 1987. This was to support five projects which were to make up the overall regional development strategy.

(i)   Support to help establish light manufacturing industry in Selebi-Phikwe.
(ii)   Support for the establishment of an irrigated agricultural programme in the vicinity of Selebi-Phikwe.
(iii) Support to explore the best approach to road building and infrastructural development in the region.
(iv)   Support for the training of local government officials.
(v)   A housing development programme.[6]

---

3   The minimum wage in manufacturing in May 1992 was P1.15 an hour. Based on a 40 hour week and a 4 week month, the average per month is P184. The BCL wage is based on the total citizen wage bill in 1992 divided by the number of citizen employees.

4   The main problem facing the mine since its inception has been the low copper ore content. At 0.7%, this has always meant that the mine was a marginal project (despite Government claims to the contrary), and has meant that the financial viability of the project is heavily dependent on the associated nickel output. This problem has been compounded by initial technical difficulties with the smelter, which meant that a large debt was accumulated in the early years of the project, and although rescheduled at various times, this has been a heavy, and ongoing, financial burden. In addition, given the marginal nature of the ore body, variations in the world price of the ore and the high operating costs associated with the remoteness of the mine have additionally impacted on its profitability. Finally, a series of labour disputes in the early days of the Mine's operation further eroded the project's financial health.

5   Selebi-Phikwe was classified as a 'Rural Area East'. This meant that investors who located there, and receive FAP, are entitled to slightly improved terms such as greater capital grants for small-scale projects, and more generous tax reimbursement rates for automatic (now abolished), medium and large-scale FAP.

Of the US$7.6 million available to the Government, a total of US$6.7 million had been drawn down by the end of 1995. This underspending was largely because the fifth element of the loan, the housing development programme, was never implemented. In addition to the World Bank loan, the Government also contributed P3.7 million directly to the programme during the eight years of its life (see Table 2).

The data in Table 2 also show that approximately fifty percent of the expenditure on the programme was used to run the regional industrial, infrastructural and agricultural development programme. Moreover, the majority of this money was spent on the establishment and operating costs of running the Selebi-Phikwe Regional Development Promotion Unit (hereafter called 'the Unit').

When the Project was initially conceived, the aim was that the agricultural and industrial components of the Regional Development Programme would be treated as equally important. Then, after an initial five year period, the relative merits of each would be assessed. However, it was apparent before the end of this five year period that the prospects for sustained diversification of the economy into agricultural activities were very limited, and this aspect of the project was slowly wound down before being abandoned in 1993. Consequently, more effort has been focused on the industrial component of the Project from a relatively early stage of its operation.

TABLE 2. SELEBI-PHIKWE TECHNICAL ASSISTANCE PROJECT: ACTUAL PROJECT COSTS, 1987–1995 (US$ MILLION)

	LOCAL FINANCING	WORLD BANK FINANCING	TOTAL FINANCING
REGIONAL DEVELOPMENT	0.9	4.1	5.0
LOCAL GOVERNMENT TRAINING	2.8	2.6	5.4
TOTAL	3.7	6.7	10.4

Source: World Bank (1995).

From almost the start of the Project, the Unit also argued that in order to attract foreign investors to Selebi-Phikwe the Government would have to re-assess its overall investment incentive policy. In 1989, the Unit helped draw up a Special Incentive Package (SIP) that was to apply to firms locating in Selebi-Phikwe. As well as the constraint on their physical location, firms applying for the package also had to meet other eligibility criteria for the SIP including exporting 100% of their output outside the Southern African Customs Union (SACU) and a target of employing a minimum of 400 Batswana within two years of their establishment. In addition, and very importantly, in order to qualify, the investment must also be promoted by an internationally established company that has been in existence for at least ten years and is willing to invest at least 25% of the project's fixed and working capital. The main benefits of the package are outlined below.

---

6   According to the World Bank (1995), this was never implemented because of 'unclear implementation policies within the Ministry of Local Government, Lands and Housing, and lack of Bank supervision. This component was not critical, and its lack of completion did not impact severely on the project's objectives'.

(i)   A capital grant towards the establishment of the project up to a maximum of 65% of the total capital invested in the project or P1000 per citizen job, whichever is smaller.

(ii)   A step down reimbursement of unskilled labour costs over the five years, starting with 80% in the first two years, 60% in the third, 40% in the fourth and 20% in the fifth.

(iii) A training grant covering 50% of any off-the-job training and approved in-house training programmes undertaken in the first five years of the project.

(iv)   A sales augmentation grant equivalent to 8% of invoiced sales in the first two years of the project, and 6%, 4% and 2% in the subsequent three years.

(v)   A 15% rate of company income tax for the first twenty years of the life of the project, and exemption from payment of withholding tax on dividends paid from after tax profits during the first ten years of the project's life.

Another important aspect of the Project was that the Government, the Selebi-Phikwe Town Council and the Unit also took steps to ensure that certain industrial plots in Selebi-Phikwe were reserved solely for the use of foreign investors into Botswana. This was considered particularly important given past difficulties experienced by foreign investors in obtaining suitable industrial premises within Botswana in appropriate time frames. The Unit and the Government also agreed with the Botswana Development Corporation (BDC) to build 6000 square metres of factory shells by the end of 1989. However, this programme experienced a number of delays, with BDC eventually building 10 000 square metres of factory space by the middle of 1992.[7]

Although the overall package offered to foreign investors seems very similar to those available in export processing zones (EPZs) found in other developing countries, the SPRDP was not really such a zone. First, while firms locating in Selebi-Phikwe had to be within the town's boundaries, they were not required to be physically separated from the rest of the country by a fence as in many EPZs; in other words, they were not a special enclave. The reason for this was that they did not have any special privileges in being able to import goods duty free for processing and re-export as in most EPZs. Moreover, although the facilities provided at Selebi-Phikwe were good, they were not significantly superior to those found in other major urban areas in the country. Finally, although there was some streamlined administration for firms locating in Selebi-Phikwe due to the efforts of the Unit, companies locating there still had to deal with the Government through the normal bureaucratic procedures unlike under many EPZ arrangement[8], for example, in order to obtain manufacturing licenses or work permits.

While the SIP package was heralded as an important feature in attracting firms to Selebi-Phikwe, several points should be noted. First, of the seventeen companies that had located in Selebi-Phikwe by 1995, only one, SportsLine, actually obtained SIP

---

[7]   At the time of writing (September 1996), BDC are currently building a further 10 000 square metres which should be completed at the end of 1996.

[8]   Firms locating in Selebi-Phikwe could apply for a rebate of duties paid on imports of materials used in goods that were exported. While this amounts to the same thing as being able to import materials duty free, it is both more time consuming and cumbersome than the procedures in a typical EPZ. For more details on features of a typical EPZ, and the difference with Selebi-Phikwe, it is possible to obtain a background paper for this article by Cowan and Phetwe (1997).

incentives. Second, apart from the tax concession, the actual terms offered were nearly identical to those available to medium and large-scale firms applying for FAP on a 'case by case' basis.[9] Moreover, from 1994 the concessional tax benefit was gradually eroded with the reduction of corporation tax to 35%, and then 25% in the 1995 Budget, along with the announcement that the Government would introduce company tax at a rate of 15% for 'manufacturing firms'.[10] This means that the additional tax benefits for locating in Selebi-Phikwe have effectively been eliminated.

In conclusion, the SPRDP was established by the Government of Botswana in 1988 in order to diversify the economy of Selebi-Phikwe away from its heavy dependence on the BCL mine. Initially, it offered several important inducements to locate in the town over and above those available in the rest of Botswana, and this made it similar to, although not exactly, an export processing zone. Since 1994, those specific advantages have been eroded by measures which mean that the incentives to locate in Selebi-Phikwe are broadly similar to those available to locate anywhere in the country. As well as the erosion in value of these special incentives, at the end of 1995, the component of the World Bank loan that was used to fund the Regional Development Unit was also drawn down, and during 1996 the Unit had been absorbed into the Trade and Investment Promotion Agency (TIPA). This effectively marks the end of the Government's attempt to attract investment to one specific area of Botswana, and coupled with the concerns already raised over the economic costs of the Project, make it an opportune moment to embark on a detailed cost-benefit study of it.

3. THE WELFARE IMPLICATIONS OF FOREIGN INVESTMENT: EVIDENCE FROM EXISTING EMPIRICAL STUDIES AND SOME IMPLICATIONS FOR BOTSWANA

Concern over the welfare implications of foreign investment has been an important area of concern for governments and academics since the 1960s. The work conducted to date has looked at both the theoretical issues involved, and attempted to empirically estimate the impact of foreign investment on a country's welfare.

Of the theoretical work, the seminal article on the welfare implications of foreign investment was by McDougall (1960). Using a simple two country model as in Figure 1, countries A and B have a combined capital stock of Oa-Ob.

Before liberalization of capital flows, Oa-Q amount of capital is held in country A, with a rate of return Oa-Ra; and Ob-Q capital is held in country B earning a rate of return Ob-Rb. However, if capital controls are lifted, capital will flow to projects where it earns a higher rate of return, or will move from country A to country B to the point where the rate of return on capital in the two countries is equalised at Q*.

The welfare implications of this are that country A loses income from investment Q*QDG, but this is replaced by earnings from capital invested in country B of Q*QKG

---

9   The main benefit was the 15% company income tax rate, which compared to a national rate of 40% at the time of introduction.

10   At the time of writing, this tax concession is still in the process of being implemented. The main factor causing delay has been the difficulty in defining what economic activities constitute manufacturing.

(at the interest rate R*). The increased income to country A is the triangle GKD; country B, as a result of the additional capital QQ*, sees total income rise by QQ*GF which after paying Q*QKG to investors from country A leaves a net gain of GKF, or the increased real output of the increased investment; while the overall gain to the two countries is represented by the triangle GDF.

FIGURE 1. THE WELFARE IMPLICATIONS OF FOREIGN INVESTMENT: A SIMPLE TWO COUNTRY MODEL

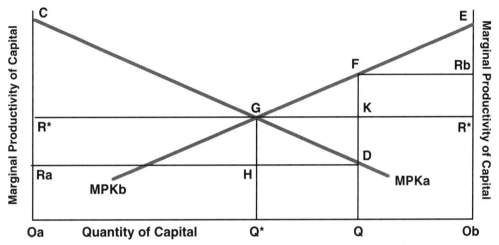

Under this simple model with free capital flows and no distortions, both countries improve their economic welfare as a result of the liberalization of capital flows. However, it is simple to add a number of distortions that can influence the distribution of these gains.[11] For example, the introduction of a fifty percent tax on the profits earned from the investment in country B means that additional benefits deriving to the host country would be half of the area Q*QHD.[12] One can also see that in a multi-country situation where investment incentives are on offer to attract capital inflows, the net gain to the country would be a combination of this tax revenue plus the real output gains *minus* any subsidies, investment inducements or free or subsidised services provided by the host government.

Although McDougall's model is simple to understand, the identification of all the costs and benefits of a foreign investment project coupled with placing the correct monetary values on them remains very difficult. Nevertheless, several general attempts have been made. Probably the most important of these are by Reuber (1973), Grubel (1974), Lall and Streeton (1977) and Encarnation and Wells (1986). Of these four studies, the one by Grubel concentrates primarily on the welfare aspects of taxing foreign investment. This concludes that taxation of US investment overseas is the most significant welfare gain to the host country.

In contrast, the other three studies are more comprehensive and try and take into

---

[11] MacDougall does in fact do this, by examining the impact of taxation, external economies, economies of scale and imperfect competition on the welfare implications of the flow of capital.

[12] Introducing a tax would, of course, also influence the flows of capital, and the example given here is purely illustrative. For a more detailed discussion on this, and optimal tax rates, see Parry (1990).

account all the possible costs and benefits of foreign investment on a host country. Despite substantially different methodologies used in these three studies, as Encarnation and Wells (1986, p61) note, they all reach very similar conclusions: 'that in countries with limited domestic markets, barriers to trade, and subsidised inputs, the incidence of economically harmful proposals submitted by prospective investors is high – comprising a substantial minority of import substituting projects'. These three general studies on the economic costs and benefits of foreign investment also conclude that, by and large, foreign investment projects aimed at production for export are much less likely to provide a negative rate of return for their host country. This is largely attributed to the general observation that these projects are provided with less subsidies compared to tariff protected import substituting industries (in whatever form).

However, the potential for economic losses to occur, even with export oriented projects, is illustrated by a recent study by Warr (1990) on the economic costs and benefits of a number of East Asian EPZs. In examining four EPZs in Indonesia, Korea, Malaysia and the Philippines, Warr showed that the main benefit to the host countries was the employment of labour and the purchase of non-subsidised domestic inputs, such as the payment of rent or electricity. The main costs to the country were the provision of the zones infrastructure, any subsidies associated with providing utilities, especially electricity, and the administrative costs of running the zone. While he concludes that the zones examined in Indonesia, Korea and Malaysia were of benefit to the host country, the one in the Philippines was not, due to the high cost of its construction and overgenerous subsidies.

Do these general observations extend to Botswana? In contrast to many developing countries, Botswana has, in the main, deliberately chosen not to provide either tariff protection or monopoly privileges to foreign investors locating in the country. However, because of its membership in the SACU, some firms locating in Botswana do receive a considerable degree of protection from international competition because of SACU's high common external tariffs. This is especially the case for firms locating in heavily protected sectors, such as textiles and vehicles production, and selling either domestically or exporting to the SACU market.

In the case of a cost-benefit analysis, the best approach would be to accept that membership in SACU does impose a substantial cost on Botswana, as shown by Leith (1992) and others. However, the Government of Botswana has decided to accept this cost in return for other perceived benefits. Therefore, as long as a foreign investor is not given tariff protection in excess of those provided under SACU, it imposes no additional costs on Botswana. This is certainly the case with all investors who have located in Selebi-Phikwe.[13]

In contrast, a very different situation exists in the provision of subsidised inputs. While foreign investors in Botswana have not received subsidised raw material inputs, especially utilities, the majority have benefited from generous levels of Government assistance, mainly through the Financial Assistance Policy: just as in the case of the SIP package, if awarded, this can provide both a contribution towards the capital of many projects, and a subsidy to labour costs over a five year period. As has been clearly pointed out by Lewis et al. (1991), 'the Financial Assistance Policy is to some

---

[13] There have only been a limited number of exception to this general rule. According to Lewis et al. (1991), these have been Kgalagadi Breweries and Kgalagadi Soap Industries.

extent a substitute for protection via tariffs or quantitative restrictions', although perhaps more accurately, it should be seen as a labour subsidy.[14] As already noted, in the case of the SPRDP, in addition to FAP grants, the Government also offered an extra incentive, the Special Incentive Package, to firms that export all of their products outside the SACU region.[15] As shown in the general theoretical work on the issue of foreign investment, this has the potential to further reduce the benefits of a foreign investment project in Selebi-Phikwe to Botswana, although it should improve the profitability of the project to the investor.

In conclusion, economic theory and completed studies show that it is possible to give away the potential benefits to the host country of foreign investment projects. This usually occurs due to high levels of protection offered to the investor, subsidies for various inputs used by the investor, or large tax holidays. In the case of Botswana, the key problem would not seem to be that of protection. Instead, the main loss to the country in the case of the SPRDP is likely to be associated with the provision of FAP and the infrastructure and administrative costs.

4. PAST EFFORT TO EVALUATE THE COSTS AND BENEFITS OF THE SELEBI-PHIKWE REGIONAL DEVELOPMENT PROJECT, AND A NEW APPROACH

A number of studies have attempted to evaluate the performance of the Selebi-Phikwe Regional Development Project. Probably the two most important are the Maendeleo consultancy report (Duncan *et al.*, 1992), and the recent end of project evaluation by Phaleng Consultants for the World Bank (Hudson 1995). Although limited by a combination of time and data deficiencies, both reports have attempted to provide a relatively rigorous critique of either the Project's job creation record, and/or the cost-effectiveness of creating jobs. They have concluded that:

(i) the SPRDP has had a reasonably good record in creating jobs, at around 500 a year between 1989 and 1994[16]; and

(ii) the jobs created cost approximately the same, or at worse, only marginally more, than those created solely using the grants provided under FAP.[17]

Looking at each of these points in more detail raises some important issues. First,

---

[14] One of the main rationales behind the FAP labour subsidy, is that given Botswana's relatively high wages in relation to productivity, the subsidy should allow firms locating in Botswana to employ labour which can then be trained to increase its productivity. Hence, it is gradually phased out over five years. Unfortunately, one problem with the FAP has been that some firms close down when the subsidy runs out.

[15] Although SportsLine did sell some of their products in the local market with Government approval.

[16] The figures in this study show that an average of 332 jobs a year were created from 1989 to 1994, but this figure increases to 578 if jobs created in the first half of 1995 are also included. The differences are due to a variety of factors including data inconsistencies, the time of year when the number of jobs created were counted, etc.

[17] The difference in the two conclusions depends on the number of jobs created at the time of the study in relation to the committed financial outlay.

the record of job creation is very difficult to assess on objective criteria. Initially, a target of 10 000 jobs was proposed by the Government on the basis that this would provide something close to the equivalent purchasing power of the 4000 jobs that would be lost if the BCL mine closed. However, soon after the establishment of the Unit this goal was reduced to 2000 jobs within a five year period of its establishment. By 1995, the Unit claims to have created 1993 jobs, so on this fairly straightforward criteria it could be concluded that the job creation record was good.

However, by standards in other countries the job creation record is relatively poor: the record of EPZs in various Asian countries and Mauritius shows that well designed projects aimed at attracting foreign investors and offering similar facilities to the SPRDP can create 10 000 jobs within a five year time span.[18] However, it would also be unfair to assume that investment promoters, even if well-funded, could compete with East Asian countries when attempting to promote Selebi-Phikwe as a location for inward investment when few foreign investors have even heard of Botswana, much less such a remote location within the country.

There is also the problem of sustaining jobs beyond the FAP payout period. Evidence from other EPZs (such as that provided by Warr, 1990), and other studies of foreign investment in the textile industry (such as those reported by Cable and Persuad, 1987) show that the type of firms attracted to a project such as Selebi-Phikwe are highly likely to be footloose in nature. Therefore, as noted in all the major reviews of the Selebi-Phikwe project, creating jobs is like pouring water into a bucket with holes in it. While some of the water will be lost out of the bottom, you have to keep pouring in sufficient water to raise the overall water level and then maintain it. In the case of job creation, this will be achieved if approximately one in every ten firms attracted by the financial incentives will stay beyond the life of the incentive package.

Unfortunately, the evidence shows that this has not yet happened in Selebi-Phikwe. To date, of the seventeen firms attracted to Selebi-Phikwe only four, Seemac, Feseco, Polycraft/Marble Products and SportsLine have stayed longer than the life of their five-year FAP packages (see Table 3).

Moreover, of these , SportsLine was restructured in order to obtain additional FAP support, but still closed down in early 1996; while Seemac and Feseco only survived one year beyond the FAP support period. Of the existing firms, interviews held during recent site visits[19] gave the impression that while some of the projects are doing satisfactorily, and look like they will stay beyond the life span of their FAP grants, others are actively considering closing down when their FAP packages come to an end.

This lack of sustainability becomes particularly important when assessing the cost implications of job creation. Take, for example, the conclusions of the report by Duncan et al. (1992, p49). This concluded that it cost approximately P16 000 to create a job under the SPRDP, consisting mainly of the annual costs of running the Promotion Unit and FAP grants. However, such a subsidy is 'justified economically only if jobs established last for a period of twelve years and company tax is paid at the standard

---

[18] See Warr (1990) or Cowan and Phetwe (1997).

[19] Physical interviews and subsequent telephone conversations were conducted by the author between July 1995 and August 1996. The general intentions of factory managers interviewed seem to be similar to those reported to other groups who have also visited industrialists in Selebi-Phikwe in the last couple of years, for example, the World Bank project review committee.

TABLE 3. MANUFACTURING JOBS CREATED BY THE SPRDP, 1989–1995[a]

COMPANY	1989	1990	1991	1992	1993	1994	1995	OP[b]
SEEMAC	70	173	302	325	292	270		6
GANTRON	3	63	182	219				4
FESECO	15	16	18	20	22	15		6
BARKATI	50	55	56					3
POLYCRAFT/ MARBLE PRODUCTS	12	101	136	95	41	75	39	7
FASHION ENTERPRISES	20	132	167					3
MDT MANUFACTURING		7	12	18				3
TEXTILE (SPORTSLINE)		216	728	737	558	786	1182	6
BULK TRADE/ PLASTICS					8	8	6	3
TEX						900	1084	2
COMBINED FEED STUFFS[c]						5	4	2
BACKPACKER						53	121	2
KIWI						7	10	2
BEACH CLUB						9	775	2
FOSROC							37	1
ORO-BOT							440	1
CAPITAL GARMENTS							350	1
TOTAL	**170**	**763**	**1601**	**1405**	**921**	**1993**	**4048**	

Notes:

[a] Jobs created are an average for the year, from the figures published in the SPRDP quarterly reports up to June 1995.

[b] Years in operation.

[c] Actually closed down in the third quarter of 1994, re-opened in the first half of 1995, and currently temporarily closed down again.

Source: SRDP Quarterly Reports.

rate of 40%, or thirteen to fourteen years if tax is paid at the SIP rate of 15%'. Yet, as the data in Table 3 clearly illustrates, no firm created by the Project has looked like it will survive for even a decade in Selebi-Phikwe, and of those that have been established in Selebi-Phikwe so far, many, including the largest employer to date, SportsLine, have barely made any profit. As a result, very few have paid any corporation tax, never mind for the prolonged period required to economically justify the cost of job creation in the town.

Similarly, the value of job creation in Hudson (1995) is based on a survival rate of 54% of firms operating beyond five years. On this basis, the report concludes a 'very tentative preliminary finding' that, in purely economic terms, the SPRDP represented a net loss to the country.[20] However, Hudson also notes that if the social benefits of the jobs created were included, then this overall loss to Botswana may be transformed into a small gain, although no effort is made to actually quantify this statement. This automatically raises the question: would this conclusion hold if the actual survival rate of firms in Selebi-Phikwe is included in the equation?

Given that the evaluations of the SPRDP conducted so far have strongly pointed to the fact that the SPRDP has not been a cost effective way of creating jobs, there would seem to be a pressing need to provide a more detailed analysis of the costs and benefits of the project to the country. A relatively simple way to approach the above problem is to adapt the methodology used by Warr (1990) in his World Bank sponsored study of the costs and benefits of EPZs, with some minor modifications to take into account specific features of the SPRDP[21] and the Botswana economy. Warr's approach uses the following equation to highlight the main costs and benefits of an EPZ.

$$N_t = \left(L_t w + M_r P_M + E_r P_e + R_t + T_t\right)S*_F$$
$$- \left(L_t w* + M_t P*_M + E_t * P*_e + B_t S*_k\right) - A_t - K_t$$
(1)

where:

N_t is the net cost or benefit in year t ;

L_t is total employment in year t ;

w is the wages paid to employees;

M_t represents the domestically supplied raw materials used in year t ;

P_m is the price paid for the raw materials;

E_t is the amount of output from utilities consumed during year t ;

P_E is the price paid for the utility usage;

R_t is the repayment of domestic borrowing in year t , both interest and capital;

T_t denotes taxes paid in year t ;

$S*_F$ denotes the ratio of the shadow and actual exchange rates;

$w*$ is the shadow price of labour;

$P*_M$ is the shadow price of raw materials;

$P*_E$ is the shadow price of utilities;

B_t is the domestic borrowing in year t ;

$S*_k$ is the shadow price of capital compared to its market price;

A_t represents the administrative cost of running the zone in year t ;

K_t denotes the capital cost, (including maintenance) of the physical infrastructure of the zone to the Government in year t .

Looking at each of these points in greater detail helps to highlight many of the issues that have to be considered in a study of this type. In this analysis, the easiest approach has been to consider the offsetting costs and benefits of each component of the equation simultaneously in the light of the history of the Selebi-Phikwe project and overall Government economic policy.

---

[20] Unfortunately, by borrowing this figure from their previous review of FAP, Hudson (1995) does not take into account the much higher failure rate of firms attracted to Selebi-Phikwe by the Unit. If this was included, the economic loss to Botswana would be much greater as the cost of FAP provision is spread over far less job years created.

[21] Which, as mentioned, is not strictly an EPZ.

One of the most commonly cited benefits of establishing an EPZ, or a project such as the SPRDP, are the foreign exchange earnings generated. However, this assumes that the exchange earnings of a company locating in Selebi-Phikwe accrue directly to Botswana, whereas in practice they actually accrue to the companies that have located there. They are then used to purchase goods and services from the domestic market, various imported inputs, or repatriated as profits. As a result, any cost-benefit analysis is only interested in the proportion of foreign exchange that is converted into local currency and is subsequently spent in the host economy, in other words expenditure in Pula on domestically produced goods and services.

Another problem that arises when valuing foreign exchange earnings, is determining the correct exchange rate at which they are converted into domestic currency values. As noted in many studies, this is because the official exchange rate of some countries does not represent the rate that would be determined by the market. As a result, the net benefits of a project are calculated not at the official rate, but at the shadow exchange rate (in the equation this is shown as S^*_F). This more accurately represents the opportunity cost of the project.

In the past, given its high level of dependence on mineral resources and the fact that the country has been subject to some symptoms of the so-called 'Dutch Disease'[22], it has been assumed in official studies that Botswana has an overvalued exchange rate in the order of ten percent. However, in the recent Third Evaluation of FAP (Phaleng Consultancies, 1995), a shadow exchange rate was not used on the grounds that it is far from clear whether the Pula is overvalued or not. This viewpoint is also supported in a recent article by Leith (1996). In the light of this, no shadow exchange rate was used in this study, although it should be noted that if the traditional assumption of a shadow rate of ten percent over the current exchange rate was used, it would mean that the net benefits of the project are greater than stated in these conclusions.

The second most commonly cited benefit of a project such as Selebi-Phikwe, is the increased employment it generates. This is represented in the equation by $L_t w$, or total employment in any given year multiplied by the wages paid to employees. However, a cost of the project is that the labour attracted to employment in Selebi-Phikwe by the Unit is then not available for employment in other projects throughout Botswana. As such, the use of labour in the SPRDP has an opportunity cost, represented by the shadow price for labour, or $L_t w^*$. In general, it is assumed that Botswana does not have a shortage of unskilled labour, and that the employment generated in Selebi-Phikwe is not depriving other employers of labour. However, it is still taking workers away from other tasks, even if only subsistence agricultural production or informal sector economic activities. Various studies have been conducted to estimate the value of the shadow wage in Botswana in the light of these assumptions, and these have concluded that the shadow price of labour is approximately half the minimum wage rate for manufacturing, a figure that will be used in this study.

Most foreign investors, such as those that have located in Selebi-Phikwe, tend to purchase the vast majority of their raw materials from abroad. However, they may also purchase some domestically. This represents a benefit for the local economy, as represented by $M_t P_m$. However, as in the case of labour, these raw materials could have been used for alternative projects. This represents a cost to the economy, espe-

---

[22] For example see Harvey, C., 1992, 'Botswana: Is the Economic Miracle Over?', *Journal of African Economies* Vol.1, No.3.

cially if it is operating near to full capacity. Having said that, in the case of Selebi-Phikwe, the domestically supplied raw materials are likely to be only extremely limited, and therefore unlikely to have led to shortages elsewhere in the economy. Therefore, their purchase represents a gross benefit to Botswana valued at market prices.

Another important form of expenditure in the domestic economy by foreign investors in Selebi-Phikwe is on utilities. While this is a benefit to Botswana, this benefit must be offset against the cost of providing the utility. Because utilities are theoretically provided on a cost recovery basis in Botswana, this effectively means that there is no net benefit to the economy as a whole resulting from expenditure on utilities[23] so it is excluded from the overall cost-benefit analysis.

If a company has borrowed money on the domestic market to finance a project, then the finance is no longer available for other projects. This represents a cost to Botswana, and the cost is magnified if the lending was at a subsidised rate of interest. In the case of Botswana, since 1990 there has been a concerted effort by the Bank of Botswana to push up interest rates towards internationally comparable levels. As a result, the cost of subsidising domestic borrowing by foreign companies has fallen considerably. This cost to Botswana is offset when a company repays the loan with interest. This is represented in the benefit side of the equation by the variable R_t.

As well as the profits from commercially-based domestic lending to foreign investors, other benefits to Botswana include expenditure by investors on financial and domestically supplied services such as banking and financial services, maintenance of factories, machinery and transport, offset by their relevant shadow prices. As in the case of domestic raw material purchases, these are taken from the firms FAP application forms and it is assumed that the provision of such services are not restricting their provision to other enterprises or individuals in Botswana (they have no shadow prices).[24]

In addition to borrowing from commercial banks, some foreign investors into Botswana have also secured loans from the Botswana Development Corporation (BDC). While borrowing from commercial banks does not represent a cost to Botswana if the loan is fully repaid at the market rate of interest, the lending from BDC, at a subsidised interest rate, represents a more significant cost to Botswana. This cost is compounded when the loans are not serviced on a regular basis, and the money invested may be lost forever when a company goes bankrupt. As Table 4 shows, BDC also has some equity investments in a number of the companies being considered in this study. Again, if this was a purely market oriented financing deal, and the returns from the investments offset the initial cost and the risks of failure, it would have no overall cost to Botswana. If, however, the return on equity does not reflect these costs, which seems to be effectively the case with BDC equity, then there is a cost to Botswana.

The most recent example of the costs of BDC lending to Botswana in the case of the SPRDP was SportsLine, and the debt write-off has been included as a cost within the FAP provision. Apart from SportsLine, because the rest of the debt has not yet been written off, it is not included as a cost to Botswana. However, it should be noted that

---

[23] While in general this is true, it may be that some of the costs charged in the case of Selebi-Phikwe do not reflect true cost recovery. However, the difference is likely to be so small as to be negligible.

[24] The main exception to this could be the provision of accountancy services, where there is a limited supply and shortages exist in Botswana.

the high level of provision against the debts indicates that BDC is not very optimistic about recovering the money, and that if these companies failed, this would represent a substantial cost to Botswana.

TABLE 4. BDC LENDING TO COMPANIES ATTRACTED BY THE SPRDP (PULA MILLION)

	POLYCRAFT/ MARBLE	TEXTILE (SPORTSLINE)	TEX	BACKPACKER	BEACH CLUB
EQUITY	0.24	2.01		0.44	
LOAN	1.07	14.49	1.4	0.32	3.84
PROVISION		17.99	1.4	0.32	3.84
WRITE OFF		3.50			

Source: BDC Annual Reports.

The final variable in the benefits component of the equation is total taxes received by the Government in any given year. However, as in the case of many EPZs, the main source of tax revenue (corporation tax) paid by firms that have located in Selebi-Phikwe has been very low. This is because very few of the firms that have located there have yet made sustained profits over a prolonged period. In addition, the majority of employees in Selebi-Phikwe pay no income tax as they are only earning marginally above the minimum wage. On the positive side, unlike a traditional EPZ, firms in Selebi-Phikwe do have to pay import duties on imported raw materials. This is a net benefit to Botswana and the value of it is included as part of the value of domestically purchased raw materials.

In addition, in the case of Selebi-Phikwe the Government also offers substantial financial inducements to firms to locate in Botswana. As already mentioned, this is in the form of both FAP grants and SIP concessions, and represents a considerable cost to Botswana which should be included in the overall equation to estimate the net cost or benefit of the Selebi-Phikwe project. In addition to the actual grants, an additional cost to Botswana is the alternative uses of Government funds spent on the investment inducements and the cost of administering these allowances. This latter point is more important than it may initially seem, because significant skilled labour is required to oversee the FAP/SIP grant allocation procedures in a Government system which is already suffering significant capacity constraints. Moreover, the National Development Bank (NDB) charges the Government to disburse the monies. While Phaleng Consultancies (1995) chose to exclude these costs in their overall evaluation, they did provide an estimate for the overhead costs involved in administering FAP: this was five percent of total disbursements for medium and large-scale projects. This administration cost, and the value of FAP disbursed, are also included in the modified equation as I_t (Equation 2).

As well as FAP grants, another important cost component of the project is the annual running costs, A_t. These are largely related to the operation of the Unit. In the main, this has been funded by the US$4.1 million loan from the World Bank, although the Government of Botswana has also contributed US$0.9 million to this.

As for K_t, the basic infrastructure of a 35.6 hectare industrial estate divided into 75 plots of varying size already existed in 1988 prior to the establishment of the SPRDP.[25] After an evaluation of the existing infrastructure, the Unit estimated that it would require 12 hectares of land. In June 1990, 15 plots covering these 12 hectares were reserved for investments attracted to Selebi-Phikwe by the Unit. While there is little doubt that some of the cost of providing this infrastructure should be included as a cost associated with the SPRDP, in practice it is extremely difficult to find details of how much the original estate cost and what percentage should be attributed to the Project. As a result, this cost has been overlooked, although if included it would raise the overall cost of infrastructure.

Another important infrastructure cost associated with the project has been the provision of factory shells. While some have been provided by the private sector, and the profits made on them therefore reflect a net gain to Botswana (if the money remains in the country[26]), the majority have been provided by BDC and these have more important cost implications. In general, factory provision does not represent a cost to Botswana if the rents charged effectively cover the costs of provision. Given rents of only P5.5 a square metre, compared to rents of up to P10 a square metre for similar factory shells in Gaborone, this does not seem to have been the case with BDC factory shells, and this element of subsidy should be included as part of the overall cost of provision of the SPRDP.[27]

In the light of the above analysis, the main modification required to the original equation is to include the costs of providing FAP and SIP. This is represented by I_t in the cost bracket of the equation below. In addition, the utilities expenditure component has been excluded, as have shadow prices which are not being used, and RT is modified to represent the benefit to Botswana of domestically purchased services. As such Equation 2 is as follows:

$$N_t = \left(L_t w + M_t P_m + R_t + T_t\right) - \left(L_t w^* + I_t\right) - A_t - K_t \quad (2)$$

Finally, although both the external and dynamic costs and benefits of foreign investment have been ignored in some studies, including Warr's work on EPZs, in the case of Selebi-Phikwe it would be hard to ignore them given the apparent impact that the project has had on the development of the town: this has been from both higher levels of consumption created by direct employment and the subsequent development of public and private sector infrastructure in the town and wider region.[28] All these factors have, in turn, created additional jobs either in the retail industry or in supplying goods and services to contractors and sub-contractors. In fact, there is an overwhelming consensus amongst those interviewed as part of this work, and who have seen Selebi-Phikwe grow in the last decade, that the current prosperity of the

---

25 According to the survey by IDI, there were 54 businesses occupying 61 plots and employing 1956 people. Of these, 17 were manufacturing companies employing 834 persons.

26 It could be assumed that the benefits associated with the private provision of some factories in Selebi-Phikwe are offset by the costs of providing the basic infrastructure of the industrial estate. Therefore, the main cost to Botswana is that incurred by BDC in providing factory shells.

27 Although it does not follow that even identical factory shells in Selebi-Phikwe should automatically have the same rental value as those in Gaborone.

28 The provision of Government funded infrastructure, such as the Sefophe–Martin's Drift and the Bobonong–Lekkerpoet roads, would require a separate cost-benefit study of its own.

town is, in the main, directly related to the expansion of its economic base beyond the copper-nickel mine. In addition to these benefits, it has also been argued that there are important, but less tangible benefits of the SPRDP to Botswana, such as the creation of a trained industrial workforce, and that even if not employed in Selebi-Phikwe, this labour can find work elsewhere. Given this, it would seem important to include estimates of some of the indirect and dynamic benefits associated with the SPRDP.

Unfortunately, placing a value on these external and dynamic benefits is nearly impossible. As a result, this study has excluded them from its main calculations, but does not deny that they exist, and that they may even be substantial.[29]

5. THE COSTS AND BENEFITS OF THE PROJECT – THE FINDINGS OF THIS STUDY

Any study of this nature is bound to suffer from lack of accurate data. This is because firms have gone bankrupt and the data have disappeared, or because existing firms either do not keep proper records or are unwilling to divulge information. Government records may also be weak in places. As a result, some assumptions have to be made. However, as with most investment projects of this type, when firms apply for financial grants, such as FAP and SIP, considerable information on proposed expenditure, profitability and tax revenue is available. Unfortunately, application forms for all companies do not seem to exist, so the next best step has been to average out the data for the companies from whom the information was available.[30] This gives an indication of what a 'typical' company in Selebi-Phikwe proposed to spend each year on various categories of expenditure over a ten year period (see Table 6). The FAP application forms also provide projected tax revenues. While these expenditures or payments may not have been the values which materialised, it is the best that is available given the circumstances.[31]

In addition, although the Unit is closing, and because many of the firms attracted by the Unit to Selebi-Phikwe are still in operation and generating income and employment to Batswana, this study has developed two possible scenarios for the Project.[32] Both cover the period when the Regional Development Unit was in actual operation (up until mid-1996) and both also assume that two of the projects currently in the pipeline will actually locate in Selebi-Phikwe. These will create 500 jobs each and receive FAP. However, in the first scenario the trend over the first six years of the project is maintained, and all firms close when the life of their FAP runs out. In the second, a more optimistic outcome is put in place. In this it is assumed that around

---

[29] As Encarnation and Wells (1986, p65) note, 'although we recognise the potential importance of these type of benefits, we suspect that it is the direct positive impact on the national product that is the contribution most sought by countries when they accept foreign investment'.

[30] Although not a perfect way to choose a sample, it is, at least, on the surface random.

[31] Similar application forms for government funding are also the main source of information used in the other cost-benefit studies on the impact of foreign investment cited in this paper.

[32] These are shown in Appendix 1.

fifty percent of projects currently operating in Selebi-Phikwe maintain operation beyond the life of their FAP grants.[33] In this second scenario, the costs and benefits are then extended over a longer time frame up to the year 2003, or a fifteen year period in total.

The easiest cost and benefit to evaluate in this study is that of labour. Figures on the total number of persons employed at the factories attracted to Selebi-Phikwe by the Regional Development Project are given in Table 3. The vast majority of these are domestic unskilled labour paid at only a minimal percentage, on average about ten percent, over the minimum wage.[34] Assuming that the shadow wage for labour is half the minimum wage in manufacturing, then the benefits that accrue to Botswana in any given year are the difference between the actual wage paid and the shadow wage. These have then been valued in constant 1989 prices.

The other set of data readily available are the value of FAP grants that have been disbursed to the firms currently established in Selebi-Phikwe. Figures from MFDP show that from the Project's establishment until the end of 1995, P26.6 million had been disbursed under the various components of FAP. This is likely to increase marginally, but not significantly as most firms have now received the bulk of FAP payments due to them. To take this into account, an additional ten percent of FAP already disbursed will be included in the total. In addition, during the life of both scenarios it is assumed that two additional firms are attracted. These are assumed to employ 500 people each, and the FAP disbursed is estimated at P3.7 million per firm. Finally, an additional five percent of this total has been added to represent the administrative costs of providing FAP.

TABLE 5. FAP GRANTS DISBURSED TO PROJECTS IN SELEBI-PHIKWE, END 1995 (PULA MILLION)

CAPITAL	LABOUR	SALES	TRAINING
4 608 475	16 996 888	4 429 8888	847 261

Source: MFDP.

Although in practice FAP grants have not been disbursed on a regular annual basis, in the case of this study it has been assumed that the total amount spent has been spread evenly over the life of the project and revalued to constant 1989 prices.[35]

In addition to FAP, the costs to BDC associated with the restructuring of SportsLine have been included for the year 1996. Moreover, 25% of the outstanding BDC loans to the other companies are also included in the two scenarios in the year that the company is assumed to go bankrupt.

---

[33] Although it is always difficult to ascertain the exact intentions of entrepreneurs, recent anecdotal evidence from factory operators in Selebi-Phikwe, including the author's own discussions with them, indicate that some are very confident that they will maintain operations beyond the life of their current FAP package, and are currently expanding operations. Others, meanwhile, are far more pessimistic about the future.

[34] Estimates made from interviews with factory operators in Selebi-Phikwe.

[35] This is primrily because, given the time constraints, it was not possible to obtain the annual disbursements. However, it is unlikely to have a significant impact on the overall costs of FAP provision.

Unfortunately, to date the tax received from companies attracted by the Unit has been extremely minimal at P574 243[36], although this should increase as some of the projects operating in Selebi-Phikwe start to generate significant taxable incomes. In the case of Scenario 1, income from tax is unlikely to increase. However, in Scenario 2 some firms should start to generate tax payments to the Government. In this case, the projections used here are the same as in the FAP application forms converted to 1989 constant prices.

Using the eight obtainable FAP application forms, the average level of expenditure on domestically supplied raw materials and services was calculated for all the companies. This was then converted into 1989 constant prices, and the total expenditure on these items for a given year was determined by multiplying the number of companies operating by the average (the average values are shown in Table 6).

As already noted, given the existing data deficiencies, the main infrastructure costs associated with the Project are assumed to

TABLE 6. YEARLY EXPENDITURE ON DOMESTICALLY SUPPLIED RAW MATERIALS AND SERVICES (EIGHT COMPANY AVERAGE IN 1989 PRICES)

EXPENDITURE CATEGORY	VALUE IN PULA
Domestically Purchased Raw Materials*	164 103
Resident Supplied Services	74 929

Note: * Using a combination of the recent Social Accounting Matrix and the External Trade Statistics, it is assumed that the expenditure on domestically supplied raw materials is 10% of the total raw materials purchased figure on the FAP forms. The rest is imported.

Source: Author's calculations.

be the cost of building the BDC factory shells offset by the rent paid on them. To date, BDC has been given two tranches of Government money to build factory shells: P13.5 million in 1990; and P6.9 million in 1996. These are counted as a one-off cost to Botswana. However, the benefit is the subsequent flow of rents from the factories. In the case of the first factory shells to be built, from BDC accounts, total rental paid to date is P777 605.[37] This sum has then been spread evenly over the years 1994 to 1996, when it was collected. Future rents in both scenarios are calculated at full occupancy of the first factory spaces at the current collection rate, 60%; and on a 50% occupancy of the second factory spaces from 1997 at the same collection rate (assuming there are enough firms operating to make this viable).[38] All these figures have then been converted into constant 1989 prices.

Finally, there is the administrative cost of running the project. This consists of a World Bank loan for the operation of the Unit (US$4.1 million) and an additional component provided by the Government (US$0.9 million). After a four-year grace period, the World Bank component has to be repaid over seventeen years at a variable interest rate, which for this study will be assumed to be the base rate on the loan of 8.5%. Essentially, the study works out the present value of the total of these repayments in 1989 prices and this is included under the administrative costs of the project in the first year of its operation. The Government's costs are based on its yearly

---

[36] Figure provided by MFDP for all firms in Table 3.

[37] Rent arrears from occupied BDC factories are currently P540 805.

[38] For example it has been assumed that no rent will be collected from 2000 to 2003 in Scenario 1.

financial disbursement to the project in constant 1989 Pula prices.

As shown in Appendix 2, the annual total of these costs and benefits in constant 1989 prices was then determined over the life span of the two scenarios. These annual totals were discounted at a rate of 6%[39], and summed to give the net present value of the Project in both scenarios. This is then expressed as a percentage of 1989 total GDP and manufacturing GDP to give an idea of the overall cost or benefit to Botswana.

6. CONCLUSIONS

Although there can be little doubt that some of the above calculations are crude, they cover the key direct costs and benefits of the project, and use the best estimates of the prices and quantities involved given the available data. Additional work involved in improving them is unlikely to yield substantial gains in the accuracy of the data used in this study, although it should be noted that given the relatively small sizes of the losses and gains involved, any significant changes in the values of the costs and benefits will have an important impact on the overall welfare implications for Botswana.

As highlighted in Appendix 2, this study concludes that under Scenario 1 the project will represent a net cost to Botswana. However, if employment levels of around 5000 persons can be maintained (by attracting a couple of new firms to Selebi-Phikwe who only receive FAP grants to induce them to locate there, and which offsets any of the current investors leaving), then the Selebi-Phikwe Regional Development Programme could yield a positive net benefit to Botswana. Under Scenario 1, the net present value in 1989 prices is estimated to be –P31.8 million, which compared to GDP of P6 187.1 million in 1989, represents a loss to Botswana in the region of 0.5% of GDP. In contrast, under Scenario 2 the net present value is approximately P20.0 million, or a gain to Botswana of 0.3% of GDP. Compared to manufacturing GDP of P306.7 million in 1989, Scenario 1 represents a loss of 10.4%, while Scenario 2 represents a gain of 6.5%.

As noted earlier, however, the loss to Botswana identified under Scenario 1 only includes the direct costs and benefits, and the loss can be partially offset by the positive net external benefits of the Project to the town of Selebi-Phikwe and the surrounding region of the Project. Whether these benefits represents 0.5% of GDP is beyond the scope of this study, but it would seem unlikely. Nevertheless, these benefits are still important and should not be overlooked.

The study also shows that in the case of Botswana, the key direct benefits of a project of this type are not the tax revenues generated, but the links into the domestic economy. In this case, the employment created and the spending on domestically produced raw materials and services. In fact, in Scenario 2, the positive overall benefit of the project largely arises because of the job creation record which is predicted for the period 1997 to 2003. In fact, the increase in the number of jobs created to over 4000 in the course of 1995 can be seen as a watershed when attempting to measure the Project's success or failure. Moreover, Scenario 2 shows that if the number of jobs

---

[39] The six percent discount rate used here is the one traditionally used to evaluate projects in Botswana. It reflects the rate of return earned on the country's foreign exchange reserves, or the opportunity cost of using the capital.

averages around 5000 for the next six to eight years, then the combined benefits of these jobs, the increased domestic spending and the tax which will materialise as the firms move into more sustained profitability, can generate a significant overall benefit for Botswana. In contrast, in Scenario 1 the poor job creation record of the Project means that the costs of establishing the SPRDP, and the FAP disbursed, are never fully recouped.

In many ways, this outcome fits in with the work by Warr (1990) on EPZs in Asia. In the cases he looked at, the overwhelming benefit of an EPZ to an economy derives from the value of wages paid to citizens above the shadow wage, and, as in the case of Selebi-Phikwe, only much later the tax revenue that arises as firms move into sustained profitability (although this only comes into play if tax holidays are not extended).[65] Only in the case of Indonesia, where some of the firms have strong linkages with the domestic textile industry has substantial benefit come from raw material purchases.

In conclusion, the verdict as to whether the SDRDP will generate a net benefit for Botswana is still unclear. If the project does not succeed in sustaining its current job levels for at least the next five years, it is likely to represent a direct overall cost to Botswana (ignoring the impact of externalities). However, if the Project can continue to maintain its current employment levels for at least five years, with only FAP grants paid out by the Government to attract new firms to locate there, then it seems that the Project could start to generate a net benefit to Botswana. In other words, the large increase in the number of jobs created since 1995 has meant that the project seems to have started generating significant benefits to Botswana, which could, in the next five years, start to offset the high start-up costs of the Project. This is an encouraging result.

Finally, the SPRDP shows that governments can walk a thin line in using fiscal incentives to attract foreign investment. While projects like Selebi-Phikwe can generate substantial benefits to a host country, they can also end up costing governments large sums of money that generate very few significant benefits.

---

[40] The conclusion by Warr (1990) that increased employment is the main benefit of an EPZ is not surprising given the high levels of employment created in the EPZs examined, often in the region of 10 000 jobs plus. If this number of jobs plus had been created by the SPRDP project, this study would have reached the same conclusion.

APPENDIX 1

PROJECTED JOBS CREATED BY SPRDP 1996–2000. SCENARIO 1[41]

	1996	1997	1998	1999	2000	2001	2002	2003
SAVANAH	23	25	30	30	30	0	0	0
TEX	1027	1100	1100	0	0	0	0	0
COMBINED FEED STUFFS+	4	4	4	0	0	0	0	0
BACKPACKER	152	152	160	0	0	0	0	0
KIWI	10	10	0	0	0	0	0	0
BEACH CLUB	1800	1900	2000	0	0	0	0	0
FOSROC	40	40	30	20	0	0	0	0
ORO–BOT	680	700	700	700	0	0	0	0
CAPITAL GARMENTS/ NORTHERN KNITWEAR	1435	1500	1600	1600	0	0	0	0
FIRM A	500	500	500	500	500	0	0	0
FIRM B	500	500	500	500	500	0	0	0
TOTAL (NO. OF COMPANIES OPERATING)	6171 (11)	6431 (11)	6624 (10)	3350 (6)	1030 (3)	0	0	0

PROJECTED JOBS CREATED BY SPRDP 1996–2003. SCENARIO 2[42]

	1996	1997	1998	1999	2000	2001	2002	2003
SAVANAH	23	25	30	30	30	30	0	0
TEX	1027	1100	1100	0	0	0	0	0
COMBINED FEED STUFFS+	4	4	4	0	0	0	0	0
BACKPACKER	152	152	160	160	160	160	160	160
KIWI	10	10	0	0	0	0	0	0
BEACH CLUB	1800	1900	2000	2000	2000	2000	2000	2000
FOSROC	40	40	30	20	0	0	0	0
ORO–BOT	680	700	700	700	700	700	700	700
CAPITAL GARMENTS/ NORTHERN KNITWEAR	1435	1500	1600	1600	1600	1000	500	0
FIRM A	500	500	500	500	500	500	500	500
FIRM B	500	500	500	500	500	0	0	0
TOTAL (NO. OF COMPANIES OPERATING)	6171 (11)	6431 (11)	6624 (10)	5510 (8)	5490 (7)	4390 (6)	3860 (5)	3360 (4)

---

[41] This scenario is fictitious and should not be taken to indicate the financial, or actual, prospects for any of the named companies.

[42] See footnote 41.

APPENDIX 2

SCENARIO 1 – PROJECT EFFECTIVELY CLOSED BY 2000

	1989	1990	1991	1992	1993	1994	1995	1996	1997	1998	1999	2000	Total
NET BENEFITS (ALL IN CONSTANT 1989 PRICES)													
Employment	175 032	712 316	1 644 979	1 444 118	868 658	1 814 033	3 372 933	4 674 865	4 427 850	4 147 200	2 118 649	592 005	
Domestically Purchased Raw Materials	984 618	1 312 824	1 312 824	984 618	820 515	1 641 030	1 805 133	1 805 133	1 805 133	1 641 030	984 618	492 309	
Domestically Purchased Services	449 574	599 432	599 432	449 574	374 645	749 290	824 219	824 219	824 219	749 290	449 574	224 787	
Tax Revenue	82 035	73 640	65 892	56 732	49 598	44 828	40 571	0	0	0	0	0	
NET COSTS (ALL IN CONSTANT 1989 PRICES)													
Factory Provision Minus Rent	0	0	10 831 435	0	0	–141 640	–128 191	2 985 970	–218 309	–198 514	–92 905	–84 434	
FAP	2 546 348	2 285 770	2 045 259	1 760 960	1 539 509	1 391 447	1 259 321	2 718 682	1 149 385	1 460 983	860 253	781 808	
Admin Costs	38 780 908	291 355	147 358	286 391	722 494	53 627	152 370	0	0	0	0	0	
Total Benefits	1 691 259	2 698 212	3 623 127	2 935 043	2 113 416	4 249 181	6 042 856	7 304 217	7 057 202	6 537 520	3 552 841	1 309 101	
Total Cost	41 327 256	2 577 125	13 024 053	2 047 351	2 262 003	1 303 434	1 233 501	5 704 652	931 076	1 262 469	767 347	697 374	
OVERALL COST OR BENEFIT	*–39 635 997*	*121 087*	*–9 400 926*	*887 692*	*–148 587*	*2 945 747*	*4 759 356*	*1 599 565*	*6 126 126*	*5 275 061*	*2 785 493*	*611 727*	*–24 073 666*
NET PRESENT VALUE (1989)	–39 635 997	114 233	–8 366 791	745 323	–117 695	2 201 234	3 355 158	1 063 802	3 843 607	3 122 295	1 555 405	322 250	–31 797 176

8 FIRM AVERAGE EXPENDITURE

Domestically Purchased Raw Materials	164 103
Domestically Purchased Services	74 929

TOTAL FAP DISBURSED (E/O 1995)	26 567 494
plus (new firms and undisbursed)	2 533 625
plus 5% admin costs	1 455 055
TOTAL	30 556 174
AVERAGE ANNUAL	2 546 348

SCENARIO 2 - FIRMS CURRENTLY OPERATING MAINTAIN PRODUCTION

	1989	1990	1991	1992	1993	1994	1995	1996	1997	1998	1999	2000	2001	2002	2003	Total
NET BENEFITS (ALL IN 1989 PRICES)																
Employment	175 032	712 316	1 644 979	1 444 118	868 658	1 814 033	3 372 933	48 018 371	4 427 850	4 147 200	3 484 703	3 155 444	2 522 994	2 016 877	1 757 276	
Domestically Purchased Raw Materials	984 618	1 312 824	1 312 824	984 618	820 515	1 641 030	1 805 133	1 805 133	1 805 133	1 641 030	1 312 824	1 148 721	984 618	820 515	656 412	
Domestically Purchased Services	449 574	599 432	599 432	449 574	374 645	749 290	824 219	824 219	824 219	749 290	599 432	524 503	449 574	374 645	299 716	
Tax Revenue	82 035	73 640	65 892	56 732	49 598	44 828	40 571	0	0	0	2 192 063	2 142 779	1 560 038	1 560 038	604 336	
NET COSTS (ALL IN 1989 PRICES)																
Factory Provision Minus Rent	0	0	1 606 426	0	-19 952	-30 055	-27 201	424 910	-33 715	-30 658	-22297	-20 264	-17 269	-13 607	-12 370	
FAP	2 037 078	1 828 616	1 636 207	1 408 768	1 231 607	1 113 157	1 007 457	2 489 693	941 264	885 281	688 202	625 446	568 540	516 894	469 914	
Admin Costs	38 780 908	291 355	147 358	286 391	722 494	53 627	152 370	0	0	0	0	0	0	0	0	
Total Benefits	1 691 259	2 698 212	3 623 127	2 935 043	2 113 416	4 249 181	6 042 856	50 647 723	7 057 202	6 537 520	7 589 022	6 971 447	5 517 224	4 772 075	3 317 740	
Total Costs	40 817 986	2 119 971	3 389 991	1 695 159	1 934 149	1 136 730	1 132 626	2 914 603	907 550	854 623	665 905	605 182	1 512 101	503 287	457 544	
OVERALL COST OR BENEFIT	-39 126 727	578 241	233 136	1 239 884	179 266	3 112 451	4 910 230	47 733 120	6 149 652	5 682 897	6 923 117	6 366 265	4 005 123	4 268 788	2 860 196	55 115 639
NET PRESENT VALUE (1989)	-39 126 727	545 511	207 490	1 041 031	141 996	2 325 804	3 461 518	31 745 251	3 858 368	3 363 698	3 865 832	3 353 669	1 990 423	2 001 374	1 265 068	20 040 306

8 FIRM AVERAGE EXPENDITURE

Domestically Purchased Raw Materials	164 103
Domestically Purchased Services	74 929

TOTAL FAP DISBURSED (E/O 1995)	26 567 494
plus (new firms and undisbursed)	2 533 625
plus 5% admin costs	1 455 055
TOTAL	30 556 174
AVERAGE ANNUAL	2 037 078

REFERENCES

Bank of Botswana. 1994. *Annual Report.* Bank of Botswana, Gaborone.

Cable, V. and Persuad, B. 1987. *Developing with Foreign Investment.* Croom Helm, London.

Central Statistics Office. 1996. *Social Accounting Matrix.* 1992/93. The Department of Printing and Publishing Services, Gaborone.

Central Statistics Office (various years) *External Trade Statistics.* Government Printer, Gaborone.

Chakravarty, S. 1987. 'Cost Benefit Analysis'. In: Eatwell, J., Milgate, M. and Newman, P. (eds.) *The New Palgrave : A Dictionary of Economics.* Macmillan Press, London.

Cowan, D. and Phetwe, M. 1997. 'Export Processing Zones: Does the Mauritian Experience Provide Lessons for Botswana's Efforts to Diversify Exports and Boost Employment?' *The Research Bulletin,* Vol.15, No.1. Bank of Botswana, Gaborone.

Duncan, T., Jefferis, K. and Smith, J. 1992. *Review of the Selebi-Phikwe Promotion Programme.* Maendeleo (Pty) Ltd, Gaborone.

Encarnation, D. and Wells, L. 1986. 'Evaluating Foreign Investment'. In: Moran, T. (ed.). *Investing in Development: New Roles For Private Capital.* Overseas Development Council, Washington.

Grubel, H. 1974. 'Taxation and Rates of Returns from Some US Assets Held Abroad', *Journal of Political Economy,* Vol.82, No.3.

Phaleng consultancies.1995. *The Third Evaluation of the Financial Assistance Policy (FAP).* Ministry of Finance and Development Planning, Gaborone.

Hudson, D. 1995. *ICR Mission for the Selebi-Phikwe Technical Assistance Project,* unpublished report by Phaleng Consultants.

Lall, S. and Streeton, P. 1977. *Foreign Investment, Transnationals and Developing Countries.* Westview Press, Boulder, Colorado.

Leith, J.C. 1992. 'The Static Welfare Economics of a Small Developing Country's Membership in a Customs Union: Botswana in the South African Customs Union'. *World Development,* Vol.20, No.7, pp1021–1028.

Leith, J.C. 1996. 'Botswana's Exchange Rate Policy', *The Research Bulletin,* Vol.14, No.2. Bank of Botswana, Gaborone.

Lewis, S., Sharpley. J. and Harvey, C. 1991. 'Botswana'. In: Riddell, R. (ed.) *Manufacturing Africa – Performance and Prospects in Seven Countries in Sub-Saharan Africa.* James Currey, London.

McDougall, G. 1960. 'The Benefits and Costs of Private Investment from Abroad: A Theoretical Approach', *Economic Record,* March Issue, Vol.36.

Parry, T. 1980. *The Multinational Enterprise: International Investment and Host-Country Impacts.* JAI Press Inc., Greenwich, Connecticut, USA.

Reuber, G. 1973. *Private Foreign Investment in Development.* Clarendon Press, Oxford.

Roemer, M. and Stern, J. 1975. *The Appraisal of Development Projects: A Practical Guide with Case Studies and Solutions.* Praeger Publishers, New York.

SPRDU, (Various). *Quarterly Reports Prepared for the Ministry of Finance and Development Planning,* 1988–1995.

Warr, P. 1990. 'Export Processing Zones'. In: Milner, C. (ed.) *Export Promotion Strategies: Theory and Evidence from Developing Countries.* Harvester Wheatsheaf, Hemel

Hempstead.

World Bank. 1993. *Opportunities for Industrial Development in Botswana: An Economy in Transition.* World Bank, Washington.

World Bank. 1995. *Implementation Completion Report – Selebi-Phikwe Technical Assistance Project Loan 2695-BT.* World Bank, Washington.

Epilogue

Policy Choices and Economic Prospects for Botswana

Preparing a book such as this one is a somewhat protracted affair, and by the end it is sometimes difficult to see the wood from the trees. This raises all sorts of questions, such as what was the point of the book and has it achieved its goals, whatever these were? Having had some time to reflect on the papers in the book, it is now apparent to us that preparing the book has been a useful exercise for a variety of reasons.

The book brings together many authors with diverse viewpoints and opinions, and should serve as a useful reference point for future researchers on the economy of Botswana. However, it does more than that. Taken either separately, or together, the papers in the book highlight several important lessons for policy makers in Botswana.

Botswana has progressed a long way since Independence. Indeed, a major motivation for this book was to mark the thirtieth anniversary of Independence with a critical review of the economy's development over those three decades.

This progress is clearly shown in the development of an institution such as the Bank of Botswana, or in the process of economic transformation. Moreover, much of this transformation has been achieved against the background of a relatively equitable distribution of income, where many different actors in the economy have benefited from the changes. Yet, the book reminds us that economic development is not a one-off exercise, and it is evident from nearly all the papers that the authors feel Botswana still has a long way to go in order to fulfil society's aspirations.

In addition, many of the papers in the book allude to the possibility that the next stage of economic development is likely to be harder than during the first thirty years. Again, we hope the papers in this book provide food for thought at a time when Botswana is entering the period of National Development Plan 8, and when Government has taken the initiative of asking the people of Botswana to prepare a national vision of how the country should have developed by 2016, when the nation will celebrate its fiftieth anniversary.

While the process of economic development is always a difficult and challenging one, the Government of Botswana rose to this challenge and devised a highly effective development strategy based upon the prudent management and investment of the country's diamond windfall. In contrast, the next stage is to move beyond diamond-led growth and chart a new course where there is no obvious route map. To do this will require some hard decisions to be made.

Having said that, the book identifies key areas where Government must make just such important policy decisions. First, several authors argue that savings are the key to investment and growth, and that creating an attractive environment to encourage high levels of private savings will be crucial for future development. Second, others clearly show that the development of internationally competitive manufacturing and financial sectors will be one of the keys to providing future income and employment opportunities. Moreover, an essential ingredient for the rapid development of these sectors is likely to be foreign investment, but in order to lure investors the Government needs to make important policy decisions to ensure that the country is an attractive location while avoiding giving away the potential benefits to Botswana from such investments. It is also clear that a sound macro economy and financial incentives alone are not the only components to attracting foreign investors. The third pillar of the strategy is to ensure that Batswana workers remain competitive in the global economy; and that there is a welcoming environment and a helping hand through the bureaucratic procedures that have to be completed. In other words, Government must play a facilitating and supporting role for the private sector in an increasingly efficient manner; as well as promote an environment where households are encouraged to become self-reliant through hard work and high levels of savings.

Another theme raised, is that Botswana has become highly integrated into the world economy, and this integration will increase further as the economy develops and exchange controls are abolished. This, too, will pose enormous policy challenges for Government, which must ensure that it maintains macroeconomic stability that will be conducive to private sector investment against the background of these changes.

In fact, the policy challenges that Government will face in the coming decades are another key theme raised in the book. In this respect, Government economic policy, both monetary and fiscal, must become more sophisticated in order to cope with a larger and more developed economy, and to take into account the cycles in economic activity that have started to emerge in Botswana (and are part and parcel of a healthy, dynamic capitalist economy). An important lesson from the book is that steady rates of economic growth and stable inflation are preferable to large year-to-year fluctuations. Large annual fluctuations in growth or prices often lead to unsound and unsustainable economic activities, which, when they collapse, cause more harm than good and can erode confidence in the economy. Related to this lesson is the need to avoid creating unsound and unsustainable expectations such as happened in the late 1980s and early 1990s, when people behaved as if asset prices in Botswana would rise forever, and certainly to much higher levels than could be justified by economic fundamentals.

Naturally, the book also highlights the key role that the Central Bank can play, and will continue to play in the country's on-going economic development. As mentioned, the book contains a detailed history of the Bank of Botswana, but it also looks at how the Bank has helped promote and regulate a healthy financial sector, which is a key aspect of a successful developing economy. Finally, several papers in the book emphasise that rather than squandering diamond windfalls on unproductive investments, a key element of the Bank of Botswana's role in the country's development strategy to date has been, and will remain, the prudent management of the country's foreign exchange reserves.

Finally, there are two key broad, yet important, issues that are continually raised throughout the papers. First, economic development does not occur overnight. It is the steady accumulation of wealth in terms of physical and human capital. This includes the development of infrastructure, of the natural resource base, and of human skills, namely human relations and knowledge. This latter resource, knowledge, is particularly important in the development process, as it tells people how to do things, how to avoid repeating past mistakes, and how to cope with problems when they arise. It will also help people cope more successfully with the information-driven society of the future.

In addition, in order that knowledge is used by Batswana to its best effect, there is a need to ensure that an open and transparent environment for policy debate is maintained. In such an environment, issues can be openly discussed and analysed, and the costs and benefits of alternative policies laid out clearly and objectively for every-one to see; and even if decisions are made on the basis of non-economic criteria, at least society is aware of the trade-offs involved. Moreover, in such an environment it is more likely than not that better decisions, and ones that contribute more to achiev-ing national development goals, will be made.

We hope the reader found the papers as interesting to read, as we found them when helping to guide their preparation.

The Editors.
Gaborone
April 1997